EVOLVE

TEACHER'S EDITION
WITH TEST GENERATOR

Chris Speck, Wayne Rimmer, Aida Sahutoglu,
Katy Simpson, and Raquel Ribeiro dos Santos

1

with teacher development by Amanda French,
Craig Thaine, and Alex Tilbury

CAMBRIDGE UNIVERSITY PRESS

CAMBRIDGE
UNIVERSITY PRESS & ASSESSMENT

Shaftesbury Road, Cambridge CB2 8EA, United Kingdom

One Liberty Plaza, 20th Floor, New York, NY 10006, USA

477 Williamstown Road, Port Melbourne, VIC 3207, Australia

314–321, 3rd Floor, Plot 3, Splendor Forum, Jasola District Centre, New Delhi – 110025, India

103 Penang Road, #05–06/07, Visioncrest Commercial, Singapore 238467

Cambridge University Press & Assessment is a department of the University of Cambridge.

It furthers the University's mission by disseminating knowledge in the pursuit of
education, learning and research at the highest international levels of excellence.

www.cambridge.org
Information on this title: www.cambridge.org/9781108405126

© Cambridge University Press & Assessment 2019, 2022

It is normally necessary for written permission for copying to be obtained in advance from a publisher.
The worksheets, role play cards, tests, and tapescripts at the back of this book are designed to be copied and
distributed in class. The normal requirements are waived here and it is not necessary to write to Cambridge
University Press for permission for an individual teacher to make copies for use within his or her own classroom.
Only those pages that carry the wording '© Cambridge University Press & Assessment' may be copied.

First published 2019

20 19 18 17 16 15 14 13 12 11 10 9

Printed in Great Britain by CPI Group (UK) Ltd, Croydon CR0 4YY

A catalogue record for this publication is available from the British Library

ISBN 978-1-009-23167-1 Student's Book with eBook
ISBN 978-1-009-23176-3 Student's Book with Digital Pack
ISBN 978-1-009-23177-0 Student's Book with Digital Pack A
ISBN 978-1-009-23178-7 Student's Book with Digital Pack B
ISBN 978-1-108-40894-3 Workbook with Audio
ISBN 978-1-108-40859-2 Workbook with Audio A
ISBN 978-1-108-41191-2 Workbook with Audio B
ISBN 978-1-108-40512-6 Teacher's Edition with Test Generator
ISBN 978-1-108-41062-5 Presentation Plus
ISBN 978-1-108-41201-8 Class Audio CDs
ISBN 978-1-108-40791-5 Video Resource Book with DVD
ISBN 978-1-009-23149-7 Full Contact with Digital Pack

Additional resources for this publication at www.cambridge.org/evolve

Cambridge University Press & Assessment has no responsibility for the persistence or accuracy
of URLs for external or third-party internet websites referred to in this publication,
and does not guarantee that any content on such websites is, or will remain,
accurate or appropriate. Information regarding prices, travel timetables, and other
factual information given in this work is correct at the time of first printing but
Cambridge University Press & Assessment does not guarantee the accuracy of such information
thereafter.

ACKNOWLEDGMENTS

To our student contributors, who have given us their ideas and their time, and who appear throughout this book:

Anderson Batista, Brazil; Carolina Nascimento Negrão, Brazil; Felipe Martinez Lopez, Mexico; Jee-Hyo Moon, South Korea ; Jinny Lara, Honduras; Josue Lozano, Honduras; Julieth C. Moreno Delgado, Colombia; Larissa Castro, Honduras.

And special thanks to Katy Simpson, teacher and writer at myenglishvoice.com; and Raquel Ribeiro dos Santos, EFL teacher, EdTech researcher, blogger, and lecturer.

Authors' Acknowledgments:

The authors and publishers acknowledge the following sources of copyright material and are grateful for the permissions granted. While every effort has been made, it has not always been possible to identify the sources of all the material used, or to trace all copyright holders. If any omissions are brought to our notice, we will be happy to include the appropriate acknowledgements on reprinting and in the next update to the digital edition, as applicable.

Photo:

Key: B = Below, BG = Background, BL = Below Left, BR = Below Right, C = Centre, CL = Centre Left, CR = Centre Right, L = Left, R = Right, TC = Top Centre, TL = Top Left, TR = Top Right.

The following photographs are sourced from Getty Images.

Student's Book: p. 1, p. 2 (Gabi), p. 8 (CR), p. 14 (L), p. 36 (email), p. 106 (C): Hero Images; p. 2 (Karina): oscarhdez/iStock/Getty Images Plus; p. 2 (Antonio): Vladimir Godnik; p. 2 (Max): DMEPhotography/iStock/Getty Images Plus; p. 2 (map): Colormos/The Image Bank; p. 2 (network): OktalStudio/DigitalVision Vectors; p. 2 (globe): Image by Catherine MacBride/Moment; p. 4: Tara Moore/Taxi; p. 4, p. 6, p. 22 (living room), p. 24 (lamp), p. 52 (CR), p. 66 (photo 5), p. 68 (2d, 2f, 2i), p. 82 (TC), p. 88, p. 117, p. 120 (fish), p. xvi (read): Westend61; p. 7: ATGImages/iStock Editorial/Getty Images Plus; p. 8 (1.1a): . shock/iStock/Getty Images Plus; p. 8 (1.1b): Carl Olsson/Folio Images; p. 8 (1.1c): Phil Boorman/Cultura; p. 8 (1.1d), p. 54 (college), p. 62 (photo h), p. 74: Caiaimage/Sam Edwards; p. 8 (1.1e): Mark Edward Atkinson/Blend Images; p. 8 (1.1f): Thomas Northcut/DigitalVision; p. 8 (1.1g), p. 36 (man), p. 37, p. 49 (CR): Sam Edwards/Caiaimage; p. 8 (1.1h): Glow Images, Inc/Glow; p. 8 (BR), p. 98 (walk): Alistair Berg/DigitalVision; p. 9 (L): ajr_images/iStock/Getty Images Plus; p. 9 (R): Ivan Evgenyev/Blend Images; pp. 10, 20, 30, 42, 52, 62, 74, 84, 94, 106, 116, 126: Tom Merton/Caiaimage; p. 10 (photo a): Georges De Keerle/Hulton Archive; p. 10 (photo b): Monica Schipper/FilmMagic; p. 10 (photo c): DEA/D. DAGLI ORTI/De Agostini; p. 10 (photo d): Scott Gries/Getty Images Entertainment; p. 10 (photo e, i): Bettmann; p. 10 (photo f): Sgranitz/WireImage; p. 10 (photo g): Christopher Furlong/Getty Images News; p. 10 (photo h): Dan Kitwood/Getty Images Entertainment; p. 10 (photo j): ALFREDO ESTRELLA/AFP; p. 11: Thomas Barwick/Stone; p. 13: Paco Navarro/Blend Images; p. 14 (couple), p. 20: Ronnie Kaufman/Larry Hirshowitz/Blend Images; p. 14 (Erika): Tony Anderson/DigitalVision; p. 14 (boy): Flashpop/Stone; p. 14 (woman): aldomurillo/E+; p. 16: Alyson Aliano/Image Source; p. 17: Richard Jung/Photodisc; p. 18: powerofforever/E+; p. 19: Steve Prezant/Image Source; p. 21, p. 30 (chair): Johner Images; p. 22 (bedroom): svetikd/E+; p. 22 (bathroom): JohnnyGreig/E+; p. 24 (bed): Diane Auckland/ArcaidImages; p. 24 (chair): Daniel Grill; p. 24 (table): Steve Gorton/Dorling Kindersley; p. 24 (desk): pbombaert/Moment; p. 24 (bookcase): Andreas von Einsiedel/Corbis Documentary; p. 24 (couch): Fotosearch; p. 24 (shower): RollingEarth/E+; p. 24 (refrigerator): Karen Moskowitz/The Image Bank; p. 24 (TV), p. 80, p. 114 (woman): Tetra Images; p. 24 (sink): Mark Griffin/EyeEm; p. 24 (rug): Art-Y/E+; p. 25: Hinterhaus Productions/Taxi;p. 26 (coffee): Dobroslav Hadzhiev/iStock/Getty Images Plus; p. 26 (tea): a-poselenov/iStock/Getty Images Plus; p. 26 (sugar): Maximilian Stock Ltd./Photographer's Choice; p. 26 (milk): YelenaYemchuk/iStock/Getty Images Plus; p. 26 (cookie): SvetlanaKoryakova/iStock/Getty Images Plus; p. 27: Shestock/Blend Images; p. 28 (TL), p. 84 (soccer): Hinterhaus Productions/DigitalVision; p. 29 (TR): Lilly Bloom/Cultura; p. 30 (TL), p. 108 (book): PeopleImages/DigitalVision; p. 30 (sofa): jakkapan21/iStock/Getty Images Plus; p. 30 (bookcase): Hany Rizk/EyeEm; p. 30 (couch): Nicholas Eveleigh/Photodisc; p. 30 (bed): Artem Perevozchikov/iStock/Getty Images Plus; p. 30 (desk): tifonimages/iStock/Getty Images Plus; p. 30 (chair): SKrow/iStock/Getty Images Plus; p. 30 (refrigerator): Customdesigner/iStock/Getty Images Plus; p. 30 (TV1): Dovapi/iStock/Getty Images Plus; p.30 (TV2): Jorg Greuel/Photographer's Choice RF; p. 30 (dinning), p. 34 (CR): s-cphoto/E+; p. 30 (frame): Matthias Clamer/Stone; p.30 (rug): Chaloner Woods/Hulton Archive; p. 30 (lamp): xxmmxx/E+; p. 30 (plant), p. 61 (BG), p.66 (photo 2), p. 72 (cat), p. 118 (bread): Dorling Kindersley; p. 33: VCG/Getty Images News; p. 34 (tablet): daboost/iStock/Getty Images Plus; p. 34 (earphone), p. 72 (cat), p. 118 (tomato): Dave King/Dorling Kindersleyl; p. 34 (phone): Lonely_/iStock/Getty Images Plus; p. 34 (laptop): scanrail/iStock/Getty Images Plus; p. 34 (smartwatch): Nerthuz/iStock/Getty Images Plus; p. 35: Images By Tang Ming Tung/DigitalVision; p. 36 (cellphone): hocus-focus/iStock/Getty Images Plus; p. 36 (chat): David Malan/The Image Bank; p. 36 (tab, text): ymgerman/iStock Editorial/Getty Images Plus; p. 36 (game): Keith Bell/Hemera/Getty Images Plus; p. 36 (phone): Bloomberg; p. 36 (symbol): jaroszpilewski/iStock/Getty Images Plus; p. 38: ferrantraite/E+; p. 39: John Fedele/Blend Images; p. 41 (C): Adrin Gmez/EyeEm; p. 41 (CR): Tim Hawley/Photographer's Choice RF; p. 42 (TR): Lilly Roadstones/Taxi; p. 42 (BR): Caiaimage/Tom Merton; p. 43: Digital Vision./Photodisc; p. 44 (walk): Inti St Clair/Blend Images; p. 44 (run): JGI/Tom Grill/Blend Images; p. 44 (work): Squaredpixels/E+; p. 44 (study): Geber86/E+; p. 44 (soccer): Thomas Barwick/Taxi; p. 47: David Stuart/Stockbyte; p. 48: Christopher Malcolm/The Image Bank; p. 49 (B): Wavebreakmedia/iStock/Getty Images Plus; p. 51: Juanmonino/E+; p. 52 (man): Jacqueline Veissid/Blend Images; p. 52 (commuters): Ovidio Ferreira/EyeEm; p. 53: David Nunuk/All Canada Photos; p. 54 (mall), p. 62 (photo c): Henglein And Steets/Photolibrary; p. 54 (store): m-imagephotography/iStock/Getty Images Plus; p. 54 (hotel): John Warburton-Lee/AWL Images; p. 54 (school): Robert Daly/Caiaimage; p. 54 (restaurant): Tom Merton/OJO Images; p. 54 (supermarket): David Nevala/Aurora; p. 54 (museum): Eric VANDEVILLE/Gamma-Rapho; p. 54 (hospital), p. 62 (photo g): Steven Frame/Hemera/Getty Images Plus; p. 54 (café): Klaus Vedfelt/Taxi; p. 54 (bookstore): M_a_y_a/E+; p. 54 (thetre), p. 62 (photo e): Clara Li/EyeEm; p. 54 (park), p. 62 (photo a): Eric You/EyeEm; p. 54 (zoo): John Hart/EyeEm; p.55: fotoVoyager/E+; p. 56 (1a): Aimin Tang/Photographer's Choice; p. 56 (1b): Barry Kusuma/Stockbyte; p. 56 (1c): Alan_Lagadu/iStock/Getty Images Plus; p. 56 (1d): swedewah/E+; p. 56 (1e): Witold Skrypczak/Lonely Planet Images; p. 56 (statue): Jeremy Walker/Photographer's Choice; p. 57: cinoby/E+; p. 58: JGI/Jamie Grill/Blend Images; p. 59: Julia Davila-Lampe/Moment Open; p. 60 (BG): Macduff Everton/Iconica; p. 60 (CR): Cesar Okada/E+; p. 60 (TL): Neil Beckerman/The Image Bank; p. 61 (waterfall): Kimie Shimabukuro/Moment Open; p. 61 (Christ): joSon/The Image Bank; p. 61 (flower): SambaPhoto/Cristiano Burmester/SambaPhotol; p. 61 (monkey): Kryssia Campos/Moment; p. 62 (BG): Planet Observer/UIG/Universal Images Group; p. 62 (photo b): Bernard Jaubert/Canopy; p. 62 (photo d): Caiaimage/Robert Daly/OJO+; p. 62 (photo f): Gary Yeowell/The Image Bank; p. 65: jameslee999/Vetta; p. 66 (photo 1): Phil Boorman/The Image Bank; p. 66 (photo 3): Vincent Besnault/The Image Bank; p. 66 (photo 4): David Zach/Stone; p. 66 (photo 6): LM Productions/Photodisc; p. 67: Jonathan Knowles/The Image Bank; p. 68 (2a, 2b): alvarez/E+; p. 68 (2c): Samuelsson, Kristofer; p. 68 (2e): Plume Creative/DigitalVision; p. 68 (2g): Jordan Siemens/Taxi; p. 68 (2h): Ezra Bailey/Taxi; p. 69: Lorentz Gullachsen/The Image Bank; p. 70 (BL): Robert Kneschke/EyeEm; p. 70 (BG), p. 108 (beautiful): Dougal Waters/DigitalVision; p. 71: Flavio Edreira/EyeEm; p. 72: Lane Oatey/Blue Jean Images; p. 73: Dave Nagel/Taxi; p. 75: Mint Images RF; p. 76 (surf): Christian Kober/AWL Images; p. 76 (skateboard): yanik88/iStock/Getty Images Plus; p. 76 (snowboarding): Maximilian Groß/EyeEm; p. 76 (draw): Ruth Jenkinson/Dorling Kindersley; p. 76 (boys): Resolution Productions/Blend Images; p. 76 (paint): Glowimages; p. 76 (sing): Kyle Monk/Blend Images; p. 76 9(dance): catalinere/iStock/Getty Images Plus; p. 76 (guitar): Justin Case/Taxi; p. 76 (swim): pixdeluxe/E+; p. 76 (wheel): Philip Gatward/Dorling Kindersley; p. 76 (CR), p. 121: Jose Luis Pelaez Inc/Blend Images; p. 77: Lilly Roadstones/The Image Bank; p. 78: Reza Estakhrian/Iconica; p. 79: PeopleImages/E+; p. 81: Allison Michael Orenstein/The Image Bank; p. 82 (TL): Kristy-Anne Glubish; p. 82 (TR): PhonlamaiPhoto/iStock/Getty Images Plus; p. 84 (photo 1): ibrahimaslann/iStock Editorial/Getty Images Plus; p. 84 (photo 2), p. xvi (teacher): Marc Romanelli/Blend Images; p. 84 (photo 3): Yew! Images/Image Source; p. 84 (photo 4): PaulBiryukov/iStock/Getty Images Plus; p. 85: Johannes Spahn/EyeEm; p. 86 (airplane): Jan Stromme/The Image Bank; p. 86 (woman): Caroline Schiff/Taxi; p. 86 (girl): Peathegee Inc/Blend Images; p. 86 (country): Instants/E+; p. 86 (parrot): Busakorn Pongparnit/Moment; p. 86 (boat): Richard Cummins/Lonely Planet Images; p. 86 (park): Lidija Kamansky/Moment Open; p. 87 (C): Waring Abbott/Michael Ochs Archives; p. 87 (hikers): Debra Brash/Perspectives; p. 87 (Lake): Jeff Greenberg/Universal Images Group; p. 89: Cláudio Policarpo/EyeEm; p. 90: Image Source; p. 92: Anna Gorin/Moment; p. 93: hadynyah/E+; p. 94 (Jim): John Lund/Marc Romanelli/Blend Images; p. 93 (Flo): Blend Images – Erik Isakson/Brand X Pictures; p. 94 (Carter): Alexander Robinson/Blend Images; p. 97: Darryl Leniuk/DigitalVision; p. 98 (TL): Chan Srithaweeporn/Moment; p. 98 (art): Randy Faris/Corbis/VCG; p. 98 (dinner, shopping): Cultura RM Exclusive/Frank and Helena; p. 98 (airport): Maskot; p. 98 (picnic): Uwe Krejci/DigitalVision; p. 99: Billy Hustace/Corbis Documentary; p. 100 (fall): Shobeir Ansari/Moment; p. 100 (summer): AL Hedderly/Moment; p. 100 (spring): Lelia Valduga; p. 100 (rainy): Chalabala/iStock/Getty Images Plus; p. 100 (dry): skodonnell/E+; p. 101: Julia Davila-Lampe/Moment; p. 102: Caiaimage/Chris Ryan; p. 103: filadendron/E+; p. 104: Rudimencial/iStock/Getty Images Plus; p. 105: ©Leonardo Muniz/Moment; 106 (TL): Toshi Sasaki/Photodisc; p. 106 (TC): skynesher/iStock/Getty Images Plus; p. 106 (TR): AJ_Watt/E+; p. 106 (CL): Luke Stettner/Photonica; p. 106 (CR): Mike Kemp/Blend Images; p. 107: Shanina/iStock/Getty Images Plus; p. 107 (TR): Simon Winnall/Taxi; p. 108 (kart): Images Of Our Lives/Archive Photos; p.108 (awful): PM Images/Stone; p. 108 (dog): Kevin Kozicki/Image Source; p. 108 (baby, quiet baby): Emma Kim/Cultura; p. 108 (fast car): Martin Barraud/Caiaimage; p. 108 (slow car): Michael Mrozek/EyeEm; p. 108 (shoe): Jeffrey Coolidge/The Image Bank; p. 108 (vacation): swissmediavision/E+; p. 109: Satoshi Yamada/EyeEm; p. 110: NexTser/iStock/Getty Images Plus; p. 111: real444/E+; p. 112: Mark Cuthbert/UK Press; p. 113: Mike Powell/Stone; p. 114 (toy car): Peter Zander/Photolibrary; p. 114 (shoe): Willer Amorim/EyeEm; 114 (comic): Bernd Vogel/Corbis; p. 115: George Steinmetz/Corbis Documentary; p. 116: Shan Shui/DigitalVision; p. 118 (chicken): Floortje/E+; p. 118 (coconut): RedHelga/E+; p. 118 (pineapple): Moodboard Stock Photography Ltd./Canopy; p. 118 (apple): t_kimura/E+; p. 118 (soup): David Marsden/Photolibrary; p. 118 (butter): SvetlanaK/iStock/Getty Images Plus; p. 118 (banana): Andy Crawford/Dorling Kindersley; p. 118 (cheese): Steven Mark Needham/Corbis Documentary; p. 118 (potato): jerryhat/E+; p. 114 (beef): Frank Bean/UpperCut Images; p. 118 (sandwich), p. 125: LauriPatterson/E+; p. 118 (orange): julichka/E+; p. 118 (lamb): pmphoto/iStock/Getty Images Plus; p. 118 (crackers): Bernard Prost/StockFood Creative; p. 118 (CR): Stephanie Leong/EyeEm; p. 119: Lumina Images/Blend Images; p. 120 (steak): Joy Skipper/Photolibrary; p. 120 (pizza): Nomadsoul1/iStock/Getty Images Plus; p. 120 (beans): Angela Bragato/EyeEm; p. 120 (chocolate): Angela Bragato/EyeEm; p. 120 (cookies): DigiPub/Moment; p. 120 (water): Retno Ayu Adiati/EyeEm; p. 122: Justin Case/The Image Bank; p. 123: Maarten De Beer/EyeEm; p. 124 (couple): Klaus Vedfelt/DigitalVision; p.124 (Chinese): Naltik/iStock/Getty Images Plus; p. 124 (Mexican): rez-art/iStock/Getty Images Plus; p. 124 (Italian): Jon Spaull/Perspectives; p. 126: andresr/E+; p. 143 (livingroom): imagenavi; p. 143 (kitchen): Glasshouse Images/Corbis. **Teacher's Book:** p. T-194: Gearstd/iStock/Getty Images Plus; p. T-199, p. T-227 (photo 3), p. T-235 (Lucas): Wavebreakmedia/iStock/Getty Images Plus; p. T-205 (photo 1): Tara Moore/Taxi; p. T-205 (photo 2): Yellow Dog Productions/The Image Bank; p. T-205 (photo 3): Hero Images; p. T-205 (photo 4): Hill Street Studios/Blend Images; p. T-205 (photo 5): Elenathewise/iStock/Getty Images Plus; p. T-205 (photo 6): HBSS/Corbis; p. T-205 (photo 7): Chris Ryan/Caiaimage; p. T-205 (photo 8): Jon Feingersh/Blend Images; p. T-206 (bag): mawielobob/iStock/Getty Images Plus; p. T-206 (tag): Poh Kim Yeoh/EyeEm; p. T-206 (man): drbimages/E+; p. T-206 (cats): Dixi_/iStock/Getty Images Plus; p. T-206 (men): Highwaystarz-Photography/iStock/Getty Images Plus; p. T-206 (tickets): Francesco Scatena/iStock/Getty Images Plus; p. T-206 (ticket): France68/iStock/Getty Images Plus; p. T-206 (old woman): JohnnyGreig/iStock/Getty Images Plus; p. T-206 (handbag): myasinirik/iStock/Getty Images Plus; p. T-206 (woman): Compassionate Eye Foundation/Ezra Bailey/DigitalVision; p. T-206 (friends): Caiaimage/Martin Baurraud; pp. T-207, T-208: Richard Cummins/Lonely Planet Images; p. T-212: Simon Winnall/Taxi; p. T-227 (photo 1): Siri Stafford/DigitalVision; p. T-227 (photo 2): Leland Bobbe/The Image Bank; p. T-227 (photo 4):Tomwang112/iStock/Getty Images Plus; p. T-227 (photo 5): Caiaimage/Sam Edwards; p. T-227 (photo 6): Bounce/Cultura; p. T-227 (photo 7): Emma Kim/Cultura; p. T-227 (photo 8): Jamie Garbutt/DigitalVision; p. T-227 (photo 9): Compassionate Eye Foundation/Natasha Alipour Faridani/DigitalVision; p. T-228 (photo A): svetikd/E+; p. T-228 (photo B): JohnnyGreig/E+; p. T-228 (photo C): Westend61; pp. T-230, T-231 (laptop): scanrail/iStock/Getty Images Plus; pp. T-230, T-231 (smartwatch): Nerthuz/iStock/Getty Images Plus; pp. T-230, T-231 (tab): daboost/iStock/Getty Images Plus; pp. T-230, T-231 (mobile): Lonely__/iStock/Getty Images Plus; pp. T-230, T-231 (earphone), p. T-247 (tomato): Dave King/Dorling Kindersley; p. T-233 (family): Inti St Clair/Blend Images; p. T-235 (Steve): Maica/iStock/Getty Images Plus; p. T-235 (Haruka): Hero Images; p. T-235 (Fabio): Tetra Images/Brand X Pictures; p. T-235 (Santiago): Inti St Clair/Digital vision; p. T-235 (Ana): Tetra Images/Brand X Pictures; p. T-235 (Felipe): Compassionate Eye Foundation/Steven Errico/Digital vision; p. T-235 (Richard): andresr/E+; p. T-235 (Ming): XiXinXing; p. T-235 (Marina): Bobex-73/iStock/Getty Images Plus; p. T-235 (Rosa): Tatiana Kolesnikova/moment; p. T-235 (Amanda): Ariadne Van Zandbergen/Lonely Planet Images; p. T-235 (Yejoon): Image Source/Photodisc; p. T-235 (Antonia): Caiaimage/Paul Bradbury; p. T-236 (snow): Aimin Tang/Photographer's Choice; p. T-236 (winter): borchee/E+; p. T-236 (plants): swedewah/E+; p. T-236 (mountain): Johannes Spahn/EyeEm; p. T-236 (lake): Alan_Lagadu/iStock/Getty Images Plus; p. T-236 (hill): Witold Skrypczak/Lonely Planet Images; p. T-236 (beach): cinoby/E+; p. T-236 (forest): Macduff Everton/Iconica; p. T-236 (island): Barry Kusuma/Stockbyte; p. T-236 (flower): Lorentz Gullachsen/The Image Bank; p. T-236 (desert): George Steinmetz/Corbis Documentary; p. T-236 (river): Neil Beckerman/The Image Bank; p. T-239 (draw): Ruth Jenkinson/Dorling Kindersley; p. T-239 (dance): catalinere/iStock/Getty Images Plus; p. T-239 (fix): Philip Gatward/Dorling Kindersley; p. T-239 (paint): Glowimages; p. T-239 (guitar): Justin Case/Taxi; p. T-239 (sing): Kyle Monk/Blend Images; p. T-239 (skateboard): yanik88/iStock/Getty Images Plus; p. T-239 (snowboard): Maximilian Groß/EyeEm; p. T-239 (languages): Resolution Productions/Blend Images; p. T-239 (surf): Christian Kober/AWL Images; p. T-239 (swim): pixdeluxe/E+; p. T-240: Reza Estakhrian/Iconica; p. T-241 (TR): NanoStockk/iStock/Getty Images Plus; p. T-241 (CR): Martin Child/Photolibrary; p. T-241 (BR): John Coletti/Photolibrary; p. T-243: Ronnie Kaufman/Larry Hirshowitz/Blend Images; p. T-247 (chicken): Floortje/E+; p. T-247 (coconut): RedHelga/E+; p. T-247 (bread): Dorling Kindersley; p. T-247 (pineapple): Moodboard Stock Photography Ltd./Canopy; p. T-247 (apple): t_kimura/E+; p. T-247 (soup): David Marsden/Photolibrary; p. T-247 (butter): SvetlanaK/iStock/Getty Images Plus; p. T-247 (banana): Andy Crawford/Dorling Kindersley; p. T-247 (cheese): Steven Mark Needham/Corbis Documentary; p. T-247 (potato): jerryhat/E+; p. T-247 (steak): Frank Bean/UpperCut Images; p. T-247 (sandwich): LauriPatterson/E+; p. T-247 (orange): julichka/E+; p. T-247 (lamb): pmphoto/iStock/Getty Images Plus; p. T-247 (cracker): Bernard Prost/StockFood Creative.

The following photographs are sourced from other libraries.

Student's Book: p. 76 (music): otnaydur/Shutterstock; p. 84 (CR): AlanHaynes.com/Alamy Stock Photo. **Teacher's Book:** p. T-237 (music): otnaydur/Shutterstock.

Illustrations **Student's Book:** by Ana Djordevic (Astound US) p. 5; Alejandro Mila (Sylvie Poggio Artists Agency) pp. 23, 30; Joanna Kerr (New Division) pp. 44, 50, 100; Dusan Lakicevic (Beehive Illustration) pp. 24, 46, 88, 90, 91. **Teacher's Book:** by Martin Sanders (Beehive Illustration) p. T-200; Lyn Dylan (Sylvie Poggio Artists) pp. T-202, T-244; Denis Cristo (Sylvie Poggio Artists) pp. T-214, T-229, T-248, T-263; Ana Djordevic (Astound US) p. 225.

Front cover photography by Arctic-Images/The Image Bank/Getty Images.

Audio production by CityVox, New York.

CONTENTS

Introduction

Introduction	T-vi
Course components	T-xi
Student's Book contents	T-xii
Unit structure and tour	T-xvi
Safe speaking environments	T-xxii
Teacher development introduction	T-xxiv
Pronunciation support	T-xxviii

Teacher's notes

Unit 1	I am …	T-1
Unit 2	Great people	T-11
Unit 3	Come in	T-21
Review 1	(Units 1–3)	T-31
Unit 4	I love it	T-33
Unit 5	Mondays and fun days	T-43
Unit 6	Zoom in, zoom out	T-53
Review 2	(Units 4–6)	T-63
Unit 7	Now is good	T-65
Unit 8	You're good!	T-75
Unit 9	Places to go	T-85
Review 3	(Units 7–9)	T-95
Unit 10	Get ready	T-97
Unit 11	Colorful memories	T-107
Unit 12	Outdoors	T-117
Review 4	(Units 10–12)	T-127

Grammar and vocabulary practice

Grammar practice teacher tips	T-129
Grammar practice with answer key	129
Vocabulary practice teacher tips	T-141
Vocabulary practice with answer key	141

Other Student's Book pages

Progress check introduction	T-152
Progress check Units 1–3	152
Progress check Units 4–6	153
Progress check Units 7–9	154
Progress check Units 10–12	155
Student A / Student B communicative activities	156
Language summaries	T-161
Student's Book audio scripts	T-173

Photocopiable activities

Contents	T-176
Teacher's notes – Grammar	T-177
Photocopiable activities – Grammar	T-186
Teacher's notes – Vocabulary	T-215
Photocopiable activities – Vocabulary	T-224
Teacher's notes – Speaking	T-249
Photocopiable activities – Speaking	T-254
Workbook answer key	T-266
Workbook audio scripts	T-282

EVOLVE

SPEAKING MATTERS

EVOLVE is a six-level American English course for adults and young adults, taking students from beginner to advanced levels (CEFR A1 to C1).

Drawing on insights from language teaching experts and real students, EVOLVE is a general English course that gets students speaking with confidence.

This student-centered course covers all skills and focuses on the most effective and efficient ways to make progress in English.

Confidence in teaching.
Joy in learning.

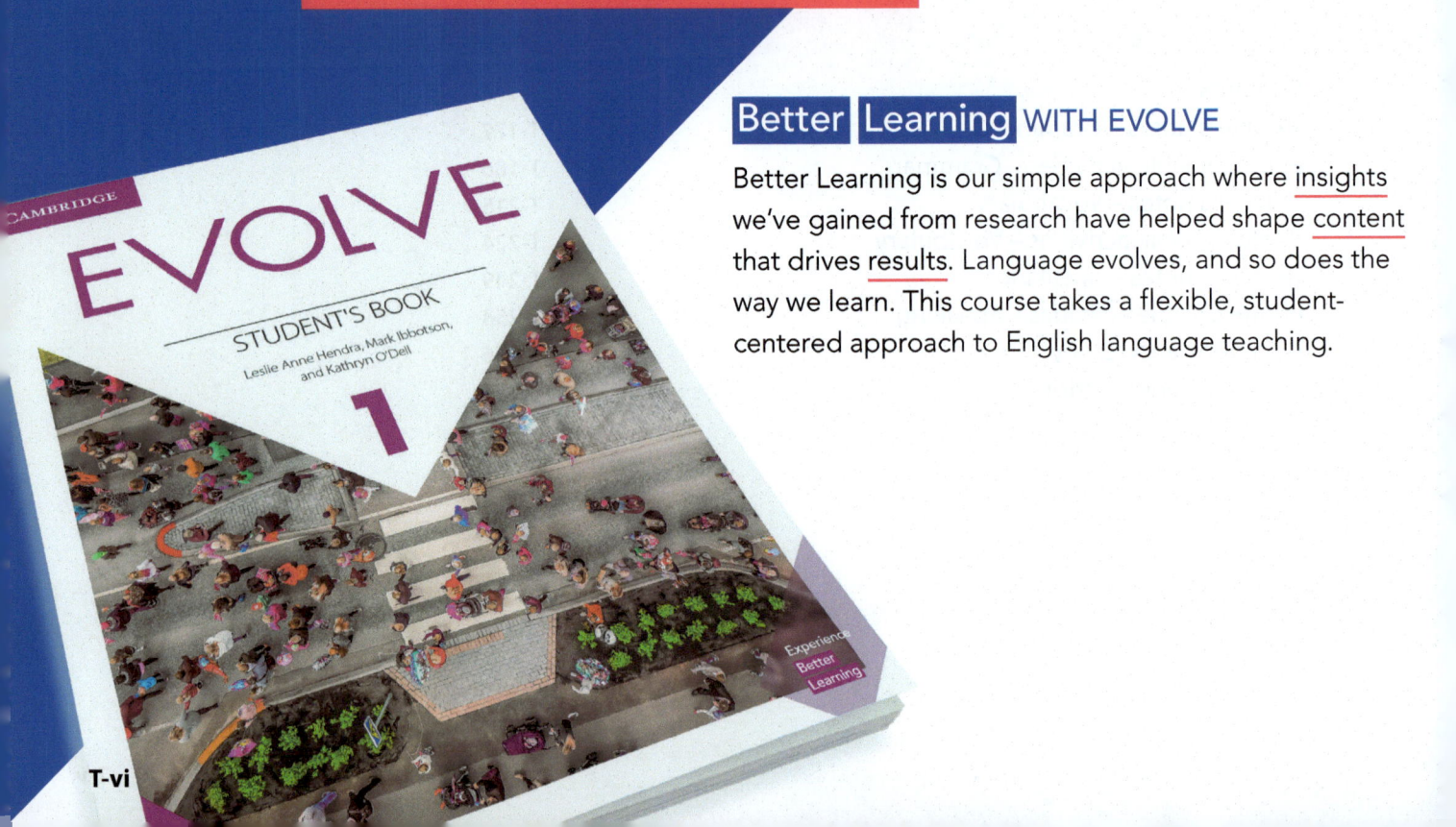

Better Learning WITH EVOLVE

Better Learning is our simple approach where insights we've gained from research have helped shape content that drives results. Language evolves, and so does the way we learn. This course takes a flexible, student-centered approach to English language teaching.

Meet our student contributors ▶

Videos and ideas from real students feature throughout the Student's Book.

Our student contributors describe themselves in three words.

LARISSA CASTRO
Friendly, honest, happy
Centro Universitario Tecnológico, Honduras

JINNY LARA
Free your mind
Centro Universitario Tecnológico, Honduras

CAROLINA NASCIMENTO NEGRÃO
Nice, determined, hard-working
Universidade Anhembi Morumbi, Brazil

JOSUE LOZANO
Enthusiastic, cheerful, decisive
Centro Universitario Tecnológico, Honduras

JULIETH C. MORENO DELGADO
Decisive, reliable, creative
Fundación Universitaria Monserrate, Colombia

ANDERSON BATISTA
Resilient, happy, dreamer
Universidade Anhembi Morumbi, Brazil

FELIPE MARTINEZ LOPEZ
Reliable, intrepid, sensitive
Universidad del Valle de México, Mexico

JEE-HYO MOON (JUNE)
Organized, passionate, diligent
Mission College, USA

Student-generated content

EVOLVE is the first course of its kind to feature real student-generated content. We spoke to over 2,000 students from all over the world about the topics they would like to discuss in English and in what situations they would like to be able to speak more confidently.

The ideas are included throughout the Student's Book and the students appear in short videos responding to discussion questions.

INSIGHT
Research shows that achievable speaking role models can be a powerful motivator.

CONTENT
Bite-sized videos feature students talking about topics in the Student's Book.

RESULT
Students are motivated to speak and share their ideas.

You spoke. We listened.

Students told us that speaking is the most important skill for them to master, while teachers told us that finding speaking activities which engage their students and work in the classroom can be challenging.

That's why EVOLVE has a whole lesson dedicated to speaking: Lesson 5, *Time to speak*.

Time to speak

INSIGHT

Speaking ability is how students most commonly measure their own progress, but is also the area where they feel most insecure. To be able to fully exploit speaking opportunities in the classroom, students need a safe speaking environment where they can feel confident, supported, and able to experiment with language.

CONTENT

Time to speak is a unique lesson dedicated to developing speaking skills and is based around immersive tasks which involve information sharing and decision making.

RESULT

Time to speak lessons create a buzz in the classroom where speaking can really thrive, evolve, and take off, resulting in more confident speakers of English.

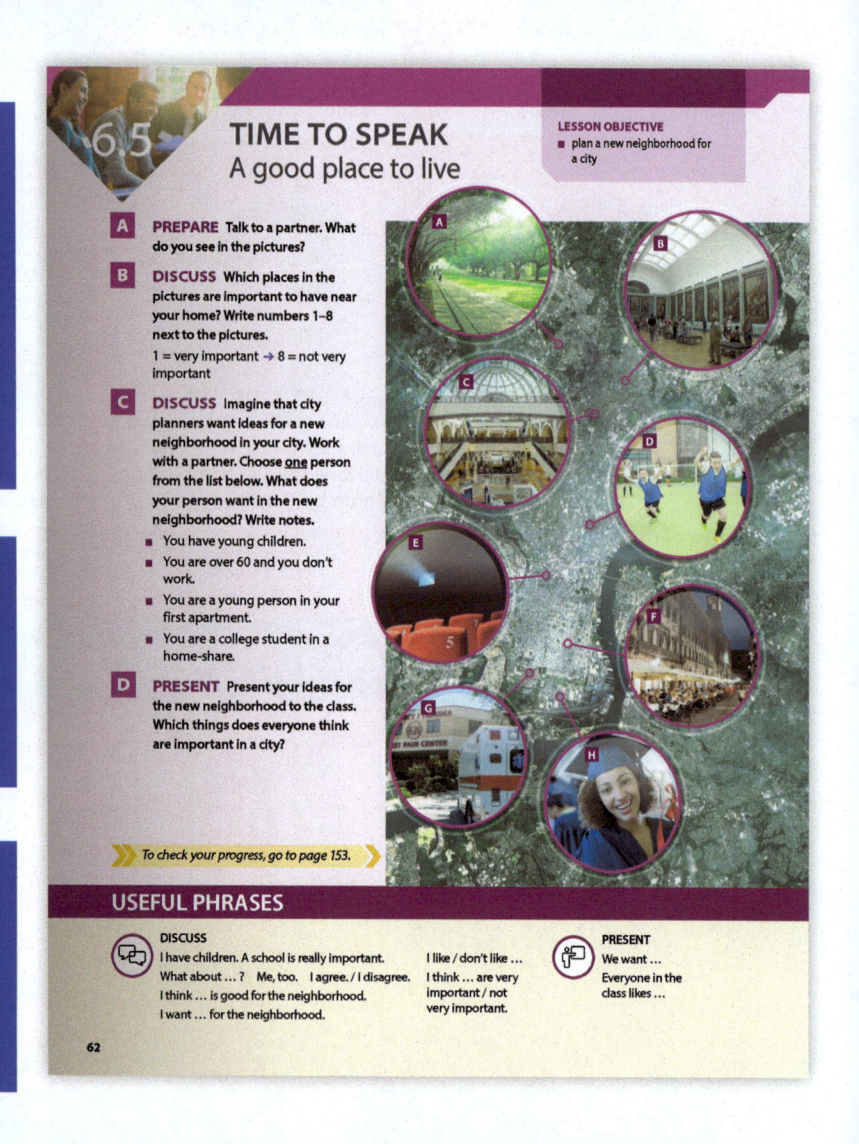

Experience Better Learning with EVOLVE: a course that helps both teachers and students on every step of the language learning journey.

Speaking matters. Find out more about creating safe speaking environments in the classroom.

T-viii

Designed for success

A safe speaking environment is one that helps to relieve the anxiety that many students feel about speaking. It's an environment where producing the language is not an end in itself, but more a "tool" in which they can practice speaking English while achieving a collaborative goal.
EVOLVE's Time to speak lessons offer teachers the opportunity to create a safe speaking environment, and the teacher's notes provide the support to help them do this.

Time to speak teacher's notes

The teacher's notes offer a step-by-step guide for the teacher to all elements of the lesson, including classroom and time management.

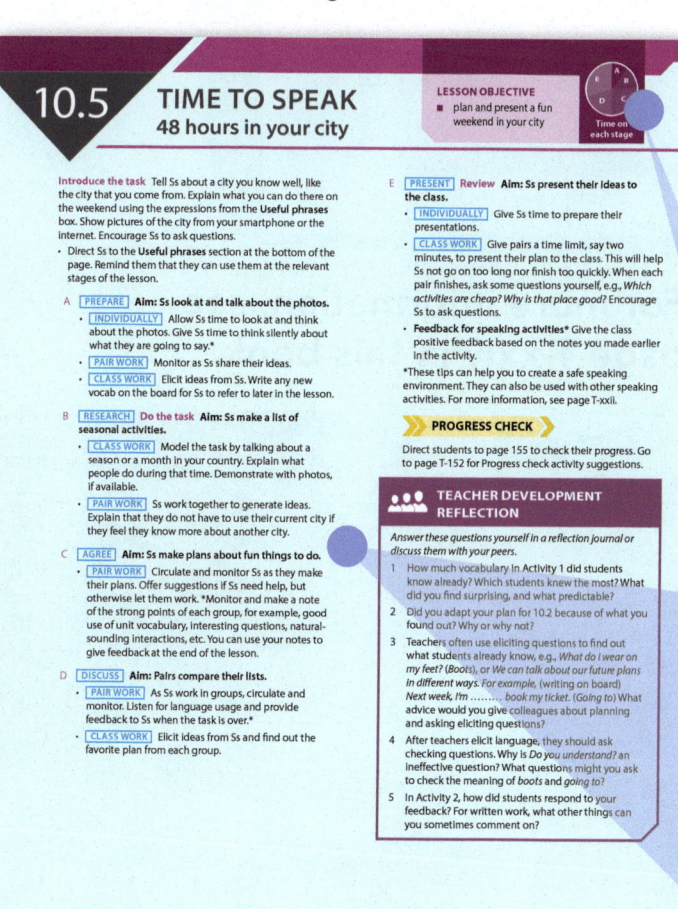

"With the teacher's notes, it was like baking a cake; it was so easy to follow the steps."

Salvador Coyotecatl Sánchez, Teacher, Mexico

- An illustrated indicator shows the recommended portion of class time for each activity in the lesson.

- The notes provide tips on:
  - giving students preparation time before they speak
  - monitoring
  - how and when to give feedback
  - giving positive feedback
  - error correction

"Students who are usually shy now speak naturally because they have more time to develop their speaking."

María Azucena Rivera, Teacher, Mexico

Integrated teacher development

The integrated development program in EVOLVE offers practice activities that teachers can integrate into their EVOLVE lessons, opportunities for reflection on the activities, and follow-up reading material and videos to consolidate the theory behind the activities.

There are three development themes integrated into each EVOLVE level.
- **Teaching and developing speaking skills**
- **Support in the classroom and learner management**
- **Language acquisition**

Each theme is divided into manageable strategies, which are explored individually in separate units. The structure of the program in each unit is as follows:
- Each strategy is introduced at the beginning of the unit, with a reading text or video suggested as an extra development resource.
- There are two suggested activities based around practicing the strategy within the teacher's notes for each unit.
- A reflection box at the end of the unit offers questions to think about individually or to discuss with other colleagues

For more information, see page T-xxiv in this book.

Cambridge Dictionary

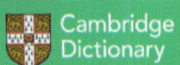

Make your words meaningful

Free, high quality, corpus-informed dictionaries and language learning resources are available online at **dictionary.cambridge.org.** The dictionary definitions are written especially for learners of English, the site is optimized for smartphones, and you can also join our Cambridge Dictionary communities on Facebook, Twitter, Instagram and YouTube. The only dictionary site you need to recommend to your learners!

For students

Student's Book
- Focus on speaking in *Time to speak*
- Corpus-informed grammar and language features
- Language presented in context
- Relevant functional and real-world strategies
- Optional videos of real students as language models accessible via QR code
- Optional phone activities in each unit

Also available:
Student's Book, A and B versions
with Digital Pack
with Digital Pack, A and B versions

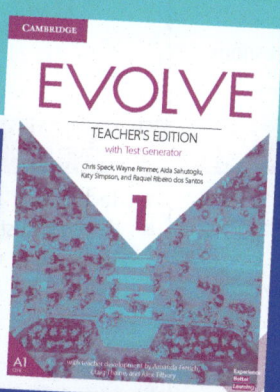

Workbook
- Comprehensive practice and consolidation of new language in every unit
- Downloadable Workbook audio

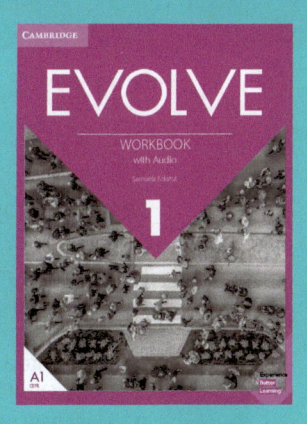

Also available:
Workbook with Audio, A and B versions

Digital Workbook
- Bite-sized homework activities for study at home or on the go
- Mobile-friendly and also accessible on tablet and desktop
- Allows teachers to easily track students' performance

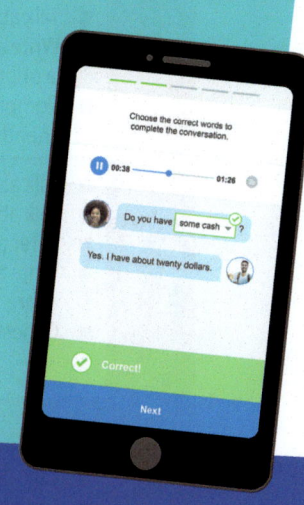

For teachers

Teacher's Edition with Test Generator

Supports teachers in facilitating student-centered lessons
- Includes homework ideas, mixed-ability activities, extra activities, and grammar and vocabulary support
- Integrates a Teacher Development Program into the teacher's notes
- Offers photocopiable worksheets, answer keys, audio scripts, and much more
- Offers ready-made tests as well as question bank for the creation of custom tests

Presentation Plus
- Contains the Student's Book and Workbook for whiteboard presentation, with integrated mark-up tools, answer keys, audio, and video
- Quick access to the full class audio program, video program, and games

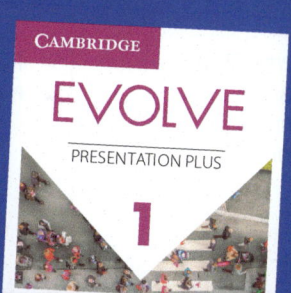

Video Resource Book
- Videos complement, consolidate, and extend language and themes in the Student's Book.
- Videos include a drama series and short documentaries.
- Worksheets exploit the videos in class.
- Teacher development opportunities and teacher tips for using video in the classroom

Class Audio CDs
- Contain all Student's Book audio tracks

T-xi

CONTENTS

	Learning objectives	Grammar	Vocabulary	Pronunciation
Unit 1 I am …	■ Say where you're from ■ Ask for and give personal information ■ Check into a hotel ■ Write a profile ■ Meet new people	■ I am, you are ■ What's … ?; It's …	■ Countries and nationalities ■ The alphabet ■ Personal information ■ Numbers (1–10) ■ Jobs ■ Greetings, introductions, and goodbyes	■ /ɪ/ and /i/ vowel sounds
Unit 2 Great people	■ Talk about your family ■ Describe friends and family ■ Talk about ages and birthdays ■ Write a post about friends in a photo ■ Compare information about friends and family	■ is / are in statements and yes/no questions ■ is not / are not ■ Prepositions of place	■ Family ■ Numbers (11–100) ■ Adjectives to describe people ■ really / very ■ Dates	■ Saying numbers ■ Listening for short forms
Unit 3 Come in	■ Talk about your home ■ Talk about furniture ■ Offer and accept a drink and snack ■ Write an email about a home-share ■ Choose things for a home	■ Possessive adjectives; possessive 's and s' ■ It is (statements and questions with short answers) ■ Information questions with be	■ Rooms in a home ■ Furniture ■ Drinks and snacks	■ /k/ at the start of a word
Review 1 (Review of Units 1–3)				
Unit 4 I love it	■ Talk about your favorite things ■ Say how you use technology ■ Talk about how you communicate ■ Write product reviews ■ Talk about your favorite music	■ Simple present statements with I, you, we ■ Simple present yes/no questions with I, you, we ■ a/an; adjectives before nouns	■ Technology ■ Words for using technology ■ Music	■ Stressed words ■ Listening for the end of a sentence
Unit 5 Mondays and fun days	■ Talk about weekday and weekend activities ■ Tell the time and talk about your routines ■ Show you agree and have things in common ■ Write a report about your activities ■ Compare different work weeks	■ Simple present statements with he, she, they ■ Questions in the simple present	■ Days and times of day ■ Everyday activities ■ Telling the time	■ Syllables in words
Unit 6 Zoom in, zoom out	■ Talk about places in the city ■ Talk about nature in your area ■ Ask for and give directions ■ Write a fact sheet about a place in nature ■ Plan a new neighborhood for a city	■ There's, There are; a lot of, some, no ■ Count and non-count nouns	■ Places in cities ■ Nature	■ /ɪr/ and /er/ sounds ■ Listening for important words
Review 2 (Review of Units 4–6)				

Functional language	Listening	Reading	Writing	Speaking
- Check in to a hotel **Real-world strategy** - Check spelling		**Meet the artists** - Profiles of two artists	**A profile** - A personal or work profile - Capital letters and periods	- Introduce yourself - Say where you're from - Say and spell personal information - Arrive at a hotel and check in **Time to speak** - Talk to people at a party
- Ask about and say people's ages and birthdays; give birthday wishes **Real-world strategy** - Correct yourself	**Here's my band** - A conversation between friends		**A post** - A post about friends in a photo - *and* to join words and sentences	- Describe the people in a picture - Talk about your family - Describe your friends and family - Talk about ages and birthdays **Time to speak** - Talk about things in common
- Make and reply to offers **Real-world strategy** - Ask about words you don't understand		**A home-share in Burnaby** - Emails about a home-share	**An email** - An email about a home-share - Question marks	- Describe a house in a picture - Talk about rooms in your home - Talk about unusual furniture - Offer a drink or snack **Time to speak** - Discuss what furniture to buy for a new home
- Ask about a new topic; ask for a response **Real-world strategy** - Show you are listening	**Product reviews** - A radio program about product reviews		**A review** - A product review - *but* and *because*	- Talk about things that you love or like - Talk about your favorite technology - Discuss what phone plan is good for you - Talk about how you communicate with people **Time to speak** - Talk about your favorite music
- Show you agree or have things in common **Real-world strategy** - Short answers with adverbs of frequency		**Work, rest and play** - An article about work-life balance	**A report** - A report about your activities - Headings and numbered lists	- Talk about your fun days - Say when and how often you do things - Talk about your daily routine - Compare information about your activities **Time to speak** - Talk about the best week for your body clock
- Ask for and give directions **Real-world strategy** - Check information	**Walk with Yasmin** - A podcast about a place in nature		**A fact sheet** - A fact sheet - Order size and opinion adjectives	- Describe a picture of a city - Talk about good places in your neighborhood - Talk about nature in your area - Give directions to a visitor **Time to speak** - Talk about a good place to live

T-xiii

	Learning objectives	**Grammar**	**Vocabulary**	**Pronunciation**
Unit 7 **Now is good**	- Talk about activities around the house - Ask and answer questions about travel - Share news on the phone - Write a blog about things happening now - Ask what people are doing these days	- Present continuous statements - Present continuous questions	- Activities around the house - Transportation	- *-ing* at the end of the word
Unit 8 **You're good!**	- Talk about your skills and abilities - Say what you can and can't do at work or school - Say why you're the right person for a job - Write an online comment with your opinion - Talk about what people in your country are good at	- *can* and *can't* for ability; *well* - *can* and *can't* for possibility	- Verbs to describe skills - Work	- Saying groups of words - Listening for *can* and *can't*
Unit 9 **Places to go**	- Talk about travel and vacations - Make travel plans - Ask for information in a store - Write a description of a place - Plan a vacation for someone	- *this* and *these* - *like to, want to, need to, have to*	- Travel - Travel arrangements	- Saying prices
Review 3 (Review of Units 7–9)				
Unit 10 **Get ready**	- Make outdoor plans for the weekend - Discuss what clothes to wear for different trips - Suggest plans for evening activities - Write an online invitation - Plan and present a fun weekend in your city	- Statements with *be going to* - Questions with *be going to*	- Going out - Clothes - Seasons	- The letter *s* - Listening for *going to*
Unit 11 **Colorful memories**	- Describe people, places, and things in the past - Talk about colors and memories - Talk about movies and actors - Write an email about things you keep from your past - Talk about TV shows from your childhood	- Statements with *was* and *were* - Questions with *was* and *were*	- Adjectives to describe people, places, and things - Colors	- /oʊ/ and /ɑː/ vowel sounds
Unit 12 **Stop, eat, go**	- Talk about snacks and small meals - Talk about meals in restaurants - Offer and accept food and drink - Write a restaurant review - Create a menu for a restaurant	- Simple past statements - Simple past questions; *any*	- Snacks and small meals - Food, drinks, and desserts	- /h/ and /r/ sounds - Listening for *Do you want to…?*
Review 4 (Review of Units 10–12)				

Grammar charts and practice, pages 129–140   Vocabulary exercises, pages 141–152

Functional language	Listening	Reading	Writing	Speaking
- Answer the phone and greet people; ask how things are going **Real-world strategy** - React to news		**Jamie's blog** - A blog about a difficult place	**A blog post** - A blog about a busy place - *and*, *also*, and *too*	- Talk about the lives of people in a picture - Talk about good and bad times to call someone - Tell a friend what you are doing right now - Talk about your news **Time to speak** - Talk about your life these days
- Ask for and give for opinions **Real-world strategy** - Explain and say more about an idea	**Technology Talks** - A podcast about computers		**A comment** - Comments about an online post - Quotations	- Discuss activities you do - Talk about skills you have - Talk about what you can and can't do at work - Ask and answer questions in a job interview **Time to speak** - Discuss national skills
- Ask for and give information **Real-world strategy** - Ask someone to repeat something		**Places to go near Puno** - A travel guide	**A description** - A description of a place - Imperatives to give advice	- Talk about a place you like - Describe people and places in a picture - Talk about organizing a trip - Ask for information at an airport store **Time to speak** - Talk about planning a vacation
- Make, accept, and refuse suggestions **Real-world strategy** - Say why you can't do something	**Montevideo** - A TV travel show		**An invitation** - An event invitation - Contractions	- Talk about your plans for the future - Talk about outdoor activities in your city - Talk about clothes to take for a trip - Talk about where to go out for dinner **Time to speak** - Plan a fun weekend in your home city
- Express uncertainty **Real-world strategy** - Take time to think		**Picturing memories** - An article about things people keep	**An email** - An email to a friend - Paragraphs and topic sentences	- Describe a happy time in your life - Talk about things you remember - Talk about colors you remember from when you were a child - Talk about people in a movie **Time to speak** - Present your memories of a TV show from your past
- Offer, request and accept food and drink **Real-world strategy** - Use *so* and *really* to make words stronger	**Where do you want to eat?** - A conversation about restaurants on a food app		**A review** - A restaurant review - Commas in lists	- Describe a good meal you had - Talk about snacks and small meals you like - Talk about a meal you had in a restaurant - Ask for food in a restaurant or at a friend's house **Time to speak** - Design a menu for a new restaurant

T-xv

EVOLVE unit structure

Unit opening page
Each unit opening page activates prior knowledge and vocabulary and immediately gets students speaking.

Lessons 1 and 2
These lessons present and practice the unit vocabulary and grammar in context, helping students discover language rules for themselves. Students then have the opportunity to use this language in well-scaffolded, personalized speaking tasks.

Lesson 3
This lesson is built around a functional language dialogue that models and contextualizes useful fixed expressions for managing a particular situation. This is a real-world strategy to help students handle unexpected conversational turns.

Lesson 4
This is a combined skills lesson based around an engaging reading or listening text. Each lesson asks students to think critically and ends with a practical writing task.

Lesson 5
Time to speak is an entire lesson dedicated to developing speaking skills. Students work on collaborative, immersive tasks that involve information sharing and decision-making.

UNIT OPENING PAGE

Unit objectives
- show communicative learning objectives
- focus on the real-life applications of the language

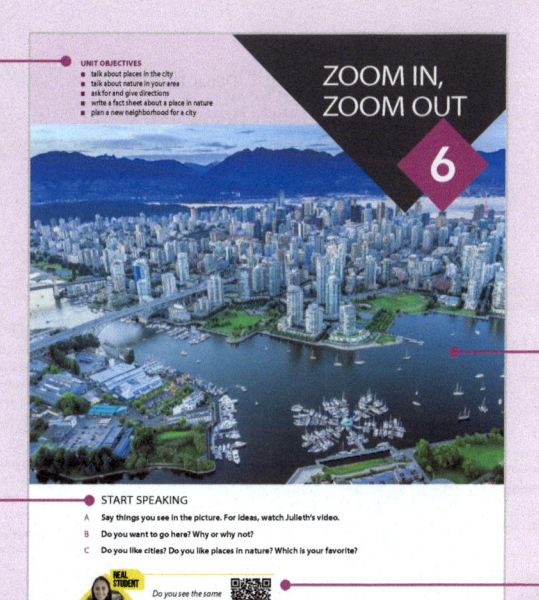

Striking images
- get students talking

Start speaking questions
- engage students in the unit topic
- provide speaking practice
- recycle language from previous lessons

Real Student videos
- provide students with achievable speaking models
- motivate students

LESSON 1

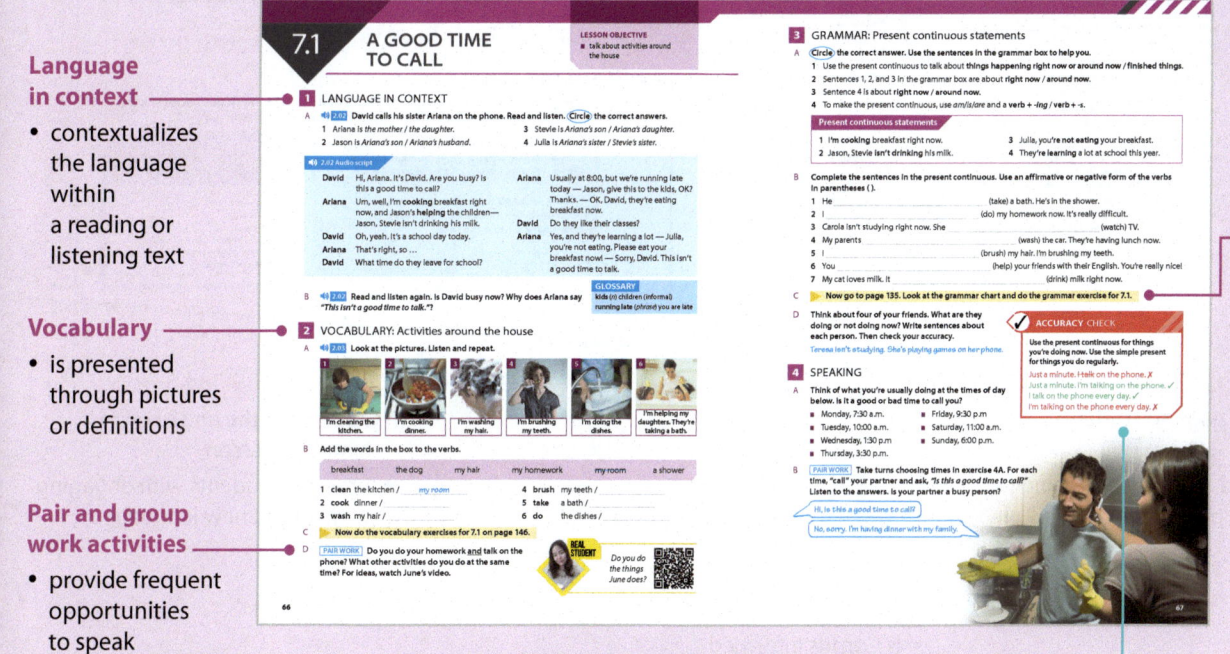

Language in context
- contextualizes the language within a reading or listening text

Vocabulary
- is presented through pictures or definitions

Pair and group work activities
- provide frequent opportunities to speak
- encourage students to practice new language

Grammar reference and practice
- is an essential part of the lesson
- contains more detailed grammar charts
- provides meaningful controlled grammar practice

Accuracy checks
- are Corpus informed
- help students avoid common errors
- encourage learner autonomy by giving them the opportunity to self-edit

Accuracy check

INSIGHT
Some common errors can become fossilized if not addressed early on in the learning process.

CONTENT
Accuracy check highlights common learner errors (based on unique research into the Cambridge Learner Corpus) and can be used for self-editing.

RESULT
Students avoid common errors in their written and spoken English.

T-xvii

LESSON 2

Vocabulary practice
- is an essential part of the lesson
- provides meaningful controlled practice

Grammar
- is taught inductively
- is clearly presented using examples from the reading or listening text

Notice features
- contain important language information

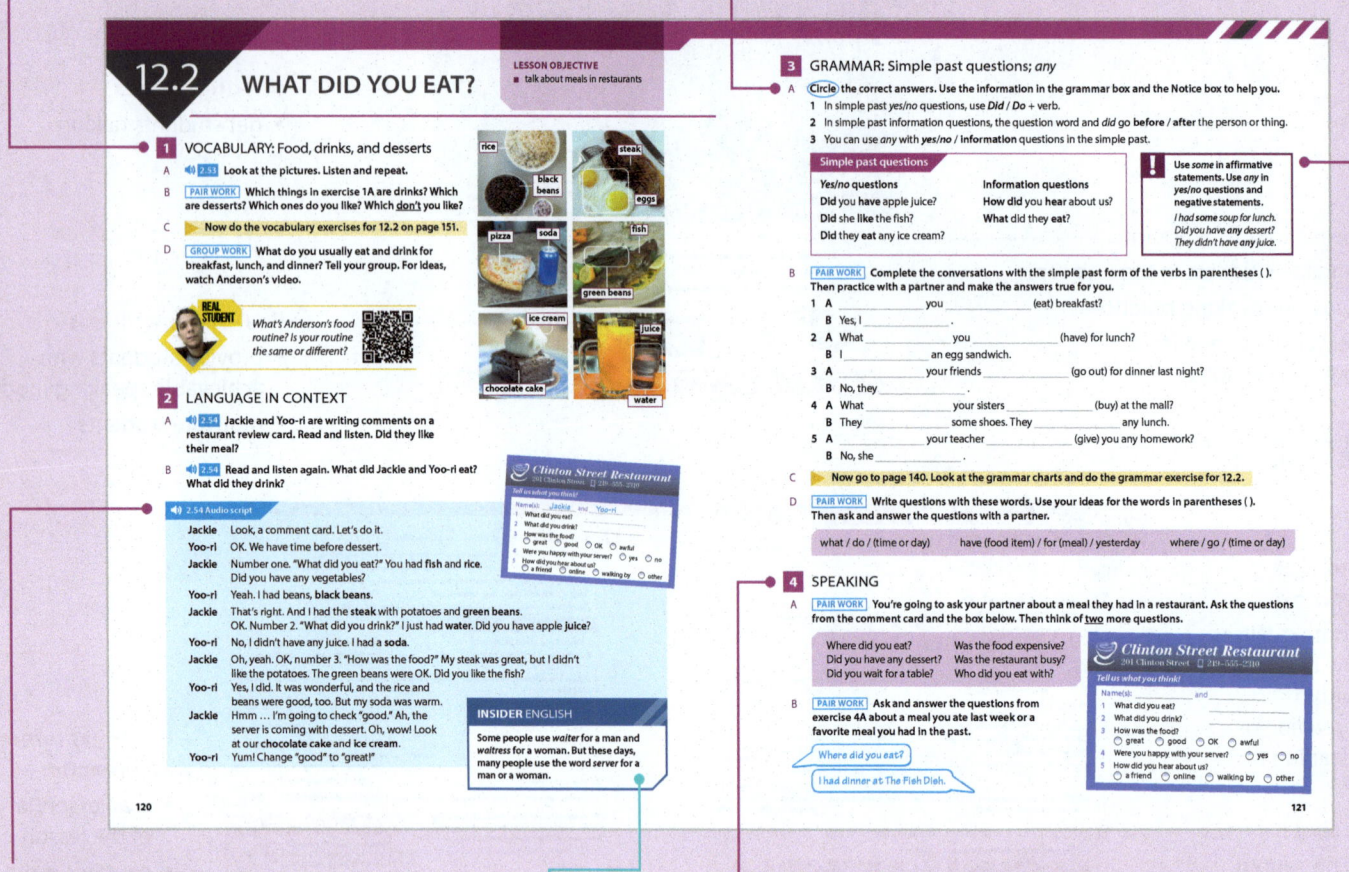

Audio scripts
- appear on the page so students can focus on language
- can be covered in the first listening to provide extra listening practice

Insider English
- is Corpus informed
- shows how words are used in real-life contexts

Extended speaking practice
- appears at the end of every language lesson
- provides students with engaging ways to use new language

Insider English

INSIGHT
Even in a short exchange, idiomatic language can inhibit understanding.

CONTENT
Insider English focuses on the informal language and colloquial expressions frequently found in everyday situations.

RESULT
Students are confident in the real world.

T-xviii

LESSON 3

Functional language conversations
- present phrases for everyday situations
- support students who need to travel to communicate with English speakers in their own country

Real world strategy
- provides students with strategies to manage communication successfully

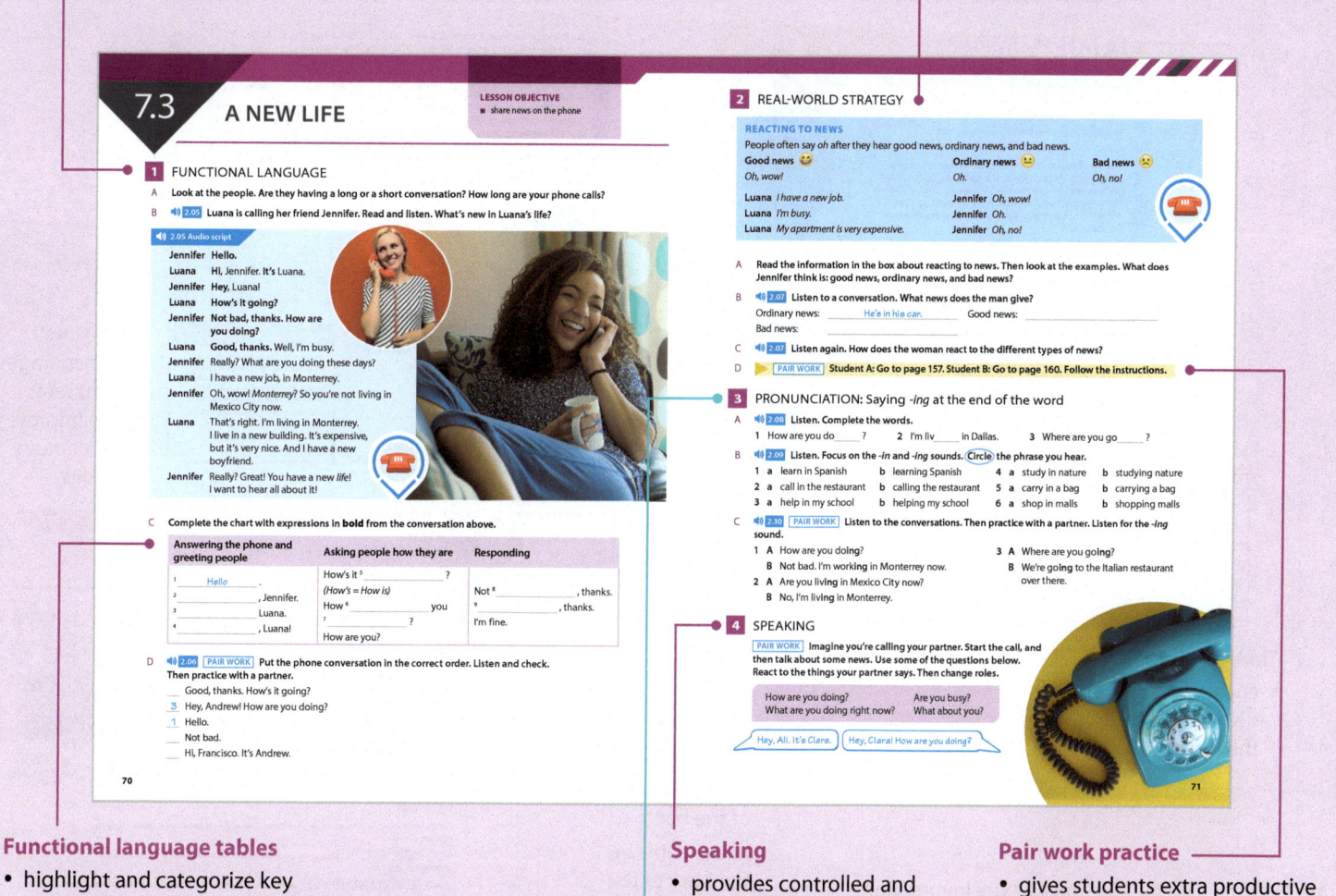

7.3 A NEW LIFE

LESSON OBJECTIVE
- share news on the phone

1 FUNCTIONAL LANGUAGE

A Look at the people. Are they having a long or a short conversation? How long are your phone calls?

B 🔊 2.05 Luana is calling her friend Jennifer. Read and listen. What's new in Luana's life?

2.05 Audio script

Jennifer Hello.
Luana Hi, Jennifer. It's Luana.
Jennifer Hey, Luana!
Luana How's it going?
Jennifer Not bad, thanks. How are you doing?
Luana Good, thanks. Well, I'm busy.
Jennifer Really? What are you doing these days?
Luana I have a new job, in Monterrey.
Jennifer Oh, wow! *Monterrey?* So you're not living in Mexico City now.
Luana That's right. I'm living in Monterrey. I live in a new building. It's expensive, but it's very nice. And I have a new boyfriend.
Jennifer Really? Great! You have a new *life*! I want to hear all about it!

C Complete the chart with expressions in **bold** from the conversation above.

Answering the phone and greeting people	Asking people how they are	Responding
¹ _Hello_ .	How's it ⁵ _____ ?	Not ⁸ _____ , thanks.
² _____ , Jennifer.	(How's = How is)	⁹ _____ , thanks.
³ _____ , Luana.	How ⁶ _____ you ⁷ _____ ?	I'm fine.
⁴ _____ , Luana!	How are you?	

D 🔊 2.06 PAIR WORK Put the phone conversation in the correct order. Listen and check. Then practice with a partner.
___ Good, thanks. How's it going?
_3_ Hey, Andrew! How are you doing?
_1_ Hello.
___ Not bad.
___ Hi, Francisco. It's Andrew.

2 REAL-WORLD STRATEGY

REACTING TO NEWS
People often say *oh* after they hear good news, ordinary news, and bad news.
Good news 😊 Ordinary news 😐 Bad news 😟
Oh, wow! Oh. Oh, no!
Luana I have a new job. Jennifer Oh, wow!
Luana I'm busy. Jennifer Oh.
Luana My apartment is very expensive. Jennifer Oh, no!

A Read the information in the box about reacting to news. Then look at the examples. What does Jennifer think is: good news, ordinary news, and bad news?

B 🔊 2.07 Listen to a conversation. What news does the man give?
Ordinary news: ___He's in his car.___ Good news: _____
Bad news: _____

C 🔊 2.07 Listen again. How does the woman react to the different types of news?

D ▶ PAIR WORK Student A: Go to page 157. Student B: Go to page 160. Follow the instructions.

3 PRONUNCIATION: Saying -ing at the end of the word

A 🔊 2.08 Listen. Complete the words.
1 How are you do___? 2 I'm liv___ in Dallas. 3 Where are you go___?

B 🔊 2.09 Listen. Focus on the *-in* and *-ing* sounds. (Circle) the phrase you hear.
1 a learn in Spanish b learning Spanish 4 a study in nature b studying nature
2 a call in the restaurant b calling the restaurant 5 a carry in a bag b carrying a bag
3 a help in my school b helping my school 6 a shop in malls b shopping malls

C 🔊 2.10 PAIR WORK Listen to the conversations. Then practice with a partner. Listen for the *-ing* sound.
1 A How are you doing? 3 A Where are you going?
   B Not bad. I'm working in Monterrey now. B We're going to the Italian restaurant over there.
2 A Are you living in Mexico City now?
   B No, I'm living in Monterrey.

4 SPEAKING

PAIR WORK Imagine you're calling your partner. Start the call, and then talk about some news. Use some of the questions below. React to the things your partner says. Then change roles.

How are you doing? Are you busy?
What are you doing right now? What about you?

Hey, Ali. It's Clara. Hey, Clara! How are you doing?

70   71

Functional language tables
- highlight and categorize key phrases for students to practice

Speaking
- provides controlled and freer practice of functional language

Pair work practice
- gives students extra productive practice of new language

Productive pronunciation activities
- focus on areas that commonly prevent effective communication
- help scaffold the final speaking activity

Pronunciation

INSIGHT
Research shows that only certain aspects of pronunciation actually affect comprehensibility and inhibit communication.

CONTENT
EVOLVE focuses on the aspects of pronunciation that most affect communication.

RESULT
Students understand more when listening and can be clearly understood when they speak.

T-xix

LESSON 4

Authentic reading texts
- appear in six units of the book

Model writing texts
- provide a model for students to analyze

Writing skills
- focus on subskills that students need to write their texts

Think critically
- encourages students to discuss and engage with the topic

Register check
- gives extra information about how to communicate in different situations

Authentic listening texts
- appear in six units of the book
- have scripts in the back of the Teacher's Edition

Receptive pronunciation activities
- focus on pronunciation features that commonly cause difficulty for learners

Glossary
- encourages students to improve dictionary skills

Register check

INSIGHT
Teachers report that their students often struggle to master the differences between written and spoken English.

CONTENT
Register check draws on research into the Cambridge English Corpus and highlights potential problem areas for learners.

RESULT
Students transition confidently between written and spoken English and recognize different levels of formality as well as when to use them appropriately.

T-xx

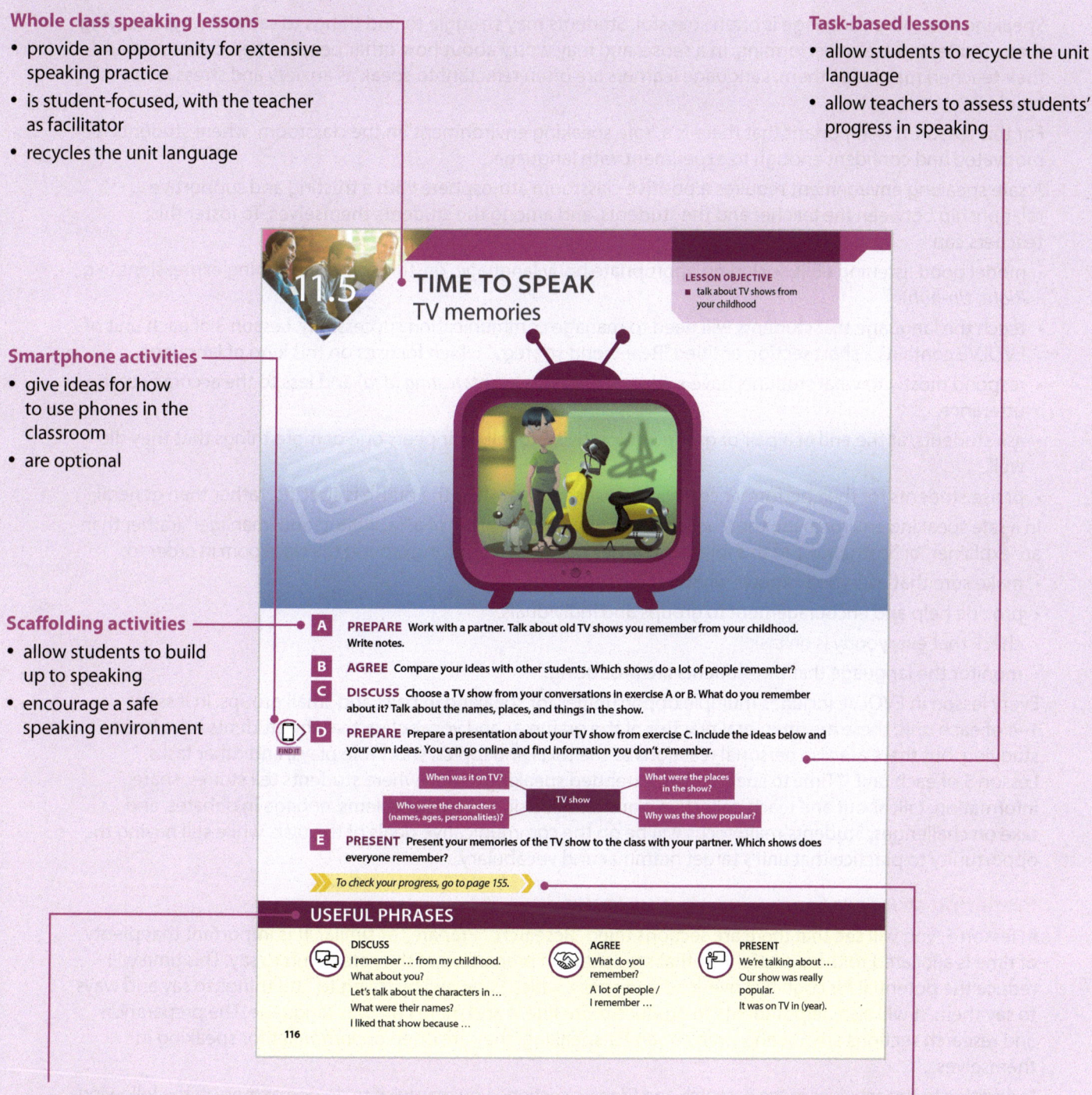

LESSON 5

Whole class speaking lessons
- provide an opportunity for extensive speaking practice
- is student-focused, with the teacher as facilitator
- recycles the unit language

Task-based lessons
- allow students to recycle the unit language
- allow teachers to assess students' progress in speaking

Smartphone activities
- give ideas for how to use phones in the classroom
- are optional

Scaffolding activities
- allow students to build up to speaking
- encourage a safe speaking environment

11.5 TIME TO SPEAK
TV memories

LESSON OBJECTIVE
- talk about TV shows from your childhood

A PREPARE Work with a partner. Talk about old TV shows you remember from your childhood. Write notes.

B AGREE Compare your ideas with other students. Which shows do a lot of people remember?

C DISCUSS Choose a TV show from your conversations in exercise A or B. What do you remember about it? Talk about the names, places, and things in the show.

D PREPARE Prepare a presentation about your TV show from exercise C. Include the ideas below and your own ideas. You can go online and find information you don't remember.

- When was it on TV?
- Who were the characters (names, ages, personalities)?
- TV show
- What were the places in the show?
- Why was the show popular?

E PRESENT Present your memories of the TV show to the class with your partner. Which shows does everyone remember?

To check your progress, go to page 155.

USEFUL PHRASES

DISCUSS
I remember … from my childhood.
What about you?
Let's talk about the characters in …
What were their names?
I liked that show because …

AGREE
What do you remember?
A lot of people / I remember …

PRESENT
We're talking about …
Our show was really popular.
It was on TV in (year).

116

Useful phrases
- provide language for different stages of the lesson
- help students communicate their ideas fluently

Progress checks
- appear in the back of the book
- help students evaluate their progress from the unit and prove what they have learned
- can be used in class or for homework

T-xxi

SAFE SPEAKING ENVIRONMENTS

Speaking in another language is often stressful. Students may struggle to find things to say and ways of saying them. Students are also performing, in a sense, and may worry about how other people (their colleagues and their teacher) may judge them. Language learners are often reluctant to speak as anxiety and stress levels build up.

For this reason, it is important that there is a "safe speaking environment" in the classroom, where students feel motivated and confident enough to experiment with language.

A safe speaking environment requires a positive classroom atmosphere with a trusting and supportive relationship between the teacher and the students, and among the students themselves. To foster this, teachers can:

- model good listening skills, including appropriate body language, gestures, and confirming expressions (e.g., *Right, Uh-huh*).
- teach the language that students will need to manage communication successfully. Lesson 3 of each unit of EVOLVE contains a short section entitled "Real-world strategy" which focuses on this kind of language.
- respond mostly to what students have said (e.g., *That was an interesting idea*) and less to the accuracy of the utterance.
- ask students, at the end of a pair or group work activity, to tell their peers one or more things that they did well.
- praise students for their performance. This is most effective when the praise is specific, rather than general.

In a safe speaking environment, the teacher's main role becomes that of a "facilitator" and "manager" (rather than an "explainer" or "instructor"). In this role, the teacher will often be moving around the classroom in order to:

- make sure that everybody knows what they should be doing.
- provide help and encouragement to groups and individuals.
- check that everybody is on task.
- monitor the language that the students are producing.

Every lesson in EVOLVE includes multiple opportunities for speaking in pairs and small groups. In lessons 1–4 of each unit, these are often oral practice of the grammar and vocabulary that the students have been studying, but there are also personal reactions to the texts and topics, short role plays, and other tasks. Lesson 5 of each unit ("Time to speak") is an extended speaking lesson where students tell stories, share information, talk about and reach collective plans and decisions, solve problems, engage in debates, and take on challenges. Students' main focus will be on the communicative goals of the task, while still having the opportunity to practice that unit's target grammar and vocabulary.

Preparing students for communicative tasks

In lesson 5, you will see that there are sections titled "Research," "Prepare," or similar. It is important that plenty of time is allocated to these sections so that students can prepare what they are going to say. This time will reduce the potential for cognitive overload and stress, which is caused by trying to find things to say and ways to say them. It will also help students to produce more fluent and more complex language. The preparation and research sections are not only *preparation* for speaking: they are often *opportunities* for speaking in themselves.

In addition to the activities in the Research and Prepare sections, you may wish to do one or more of the following:

- give students time to think silently about the task they are going to perform.
- give students time to take notes about what they are going to say.
- allow students to brainstorm ideas with another student.
- give students time to research (e.g., online) the topic they are going to talk about.
- encourage students to rehearse mentally what they are going to say.
- give students time to review relevant vocabulary notes or look up useful vocabulary in a dictionary.
- extend the list of phrases that are provided at the bottom of each lesson 5.

These techniques may also be used before other pair and group work activities in the book (e.g., the first page of each unit).

Giving feedback on speaking tasks

Until students feel confident in speaking tasks, it is probably best to leave error correction until the end of the activity. While the students are speaking, take notes on anything you want to focus on in a later correction slot. Here are some ideas for building a safe speaking environment in the context of correction:

- decide, in advance of the activity, that for some groups you will focus on the content and for others you will focus on examples of accurate or appropriate language use.
- draw attention to examples of accurate and appropriate language (e.g., avoiding a very common mistake).
- write (anonymized) examples of things you have heard on the board, but mix up examples of errors and good language use. The students' first task is to identify the examples of good language use.
- invite all students to suggest corrections or improvements to the language that is being focused on. One way of doing this is by putting students into groups to talk about the improvements or changes before conducting feedback with the whole class.

Maximizing the amount of speaking

For students to gain full benefit from pair and group work activities, they must speak a lot and push themselves to use the full extent of their language resources. This does not always take place when students do a speaking task, so it is sometimes a good idea to repeat the activity. The second time around, students are usually more fluent and more accurate. In order to maintain motivation, however, students will need a reason to repeat something they have just done. It is often possible for students to work with a different partner the second time, but here are some other ways of managing task repetition:

Different roles

In some tasks, one member of a pair may be more of a listener than a speaker. When the task is repeated, the roles are reversed. In some tasks, individual students may be allocated specific roles, such as note-taker, language monitor, chair, or timekeeper. When the task is repeated, the allocation of these roles is changed.

Time limits

Students repeat the task with a different partner, but are given less time for the repetition.

No notes

When students have made notes in preparation for a task, they may be asked to repeat it without referring to their notes.

Additional planning time

Give students extra planning time before they repeat the task with a new partner.

Record and repeat

Students record their speaking with audio or video. After spending time analyzing their language and perhaps transcribing some sections of it, they repeat the task.

Many factors, some outside the control of the teacher, can impact the development and maintenance of a safe speaking environment. There is not one single correct way of promoting such an environment, or of building positive relationships in a classroom. However, these suggestions should help you to realize these goals. They are intended to be options for you to experiment with and modify to suit your own classes.

EFFECTIVE TEACHER DEVELOPMENT

It is widely agreed that the main goal of teacher development is to effect positive change in teaching practice and, as a result, to enhance students' learning. Cambridge University Press has analyzed research on teacher development worldwide in order to determine the key factors that make a teacher development program successful. We have identified seven principles that lie at the heart of effective teacher development programs. The Cambridge Teacher Development approach states that successful development programs should be:

IMPACTFUL
To be impactful, a program needs to help teachers set objectives in effecting this change and track their progress against those objectives.

NEEDS-BASED
An effective program should address the daily challenges faced by teachers and learners.

SUSTAINED
In order for a program to be effective, it needs to be continuous. In the same way that students need time and frequent practice to use new language confidently, teachers need time to apply new strategies confidently in the classroom.

PEER-COLLABORATIVE
Peer collaboration is one of the greatest motivating factors for teachers in their development. Teachers are more likely to succeed in their development when they share their ideas and experiences with their peers.

IN-PRACTICE
Teacher development programs are more successful when they focus on practice rather than on theory alone.

REFLECTIVE
For teachers to make positive changes in teaching practice, it is essential for them to reflect on their current practices and any new strategies they learn.

EVALUATED
In order for teachers to make a real impact, it is essential for them to track and measure progress in their own and their students' performance.

TEACHER DEVELOPMENT IN EVOLVE

How does EVOLVE Teacher Development meet INSPIRE principles?

EVOLVE Teacher Development is **impactful**. It sets out clear objectives for every unit, as well as for the level as a whole.

The program takes a **needs-based** approach by integrating activities within the teacher's notes, fitting development strategies into everyday teaching. Elements of the program also offer extra support to those wishing to gain Cambridge qualifications, such as TKT or ICELT. You can choose to focus on one, two, or all three strategies in each level, depending on your needs and interests.

Our program has a strong focus on **practice**. Each unit offers two practice opportunities to develop an aspect of your teaching skills. Our **sustained** approach means that you will build on your skills throughout the course.

Reflection questions at the end of each unit help you to track and **evaluate** your progress.

These questions help you develop greater awareness of what you do in the classroom and why you do it. This, in turn, enables you to make positive changes to your teaching.

If possible, make this reflection stage a **collaborative** activity by sharing your answers to reflection questions with your peers at the end of every unit.

A1 SYLLABUS

Strategy 1: Classroom management	Strategy 2: Teaching vocabulary	Strategy 3: Building learners' confidence to speak
Unit 1: Collaboration • Playing games to learn names • Working together to recreate a simple text	**Unit 2: Presenting new vocabulary*** • Conveying and eliciting vocabulary • Using word puzzles to make language memorable	**Unit 3: Meaningful drilling** • Using meaningful drilling of sentences • Using meaningful drilling of dialogues
Unit 4: Opening and closing lessons • Starting lessons with conversations • Ending lessons with review	**Unit 5: Recording and memorizing vocabulary** • Recording vocabulary using spidergrams • Memorizing vocabulary using disappearing drills	**Unit 6: Planning** • Planning what language to use in speaking activities • Planning what to say in speaking activities
Unit 7: Pair and group work • Maximizing practice opportunities • Encouraging quieter students to speak	**Unit 8: Practicing vocabulary*** • Personalizing vocabulary practice • Peer testing vocabulary	**Unit 9: Listening to learner language** • Listening for target language • Recording students' speaking
Unit 10: Teacher roles* • Finding out what students already know • Giving supportive feedback	**Unit 11: Language awareness*** • Using guided questions to raise awareness • Helping students to use language accurately	**Unit 12: Providing feedback on spoken language** • Providing immediate feedback • Providing delayed feedback

*These items are linked to ICELT and TKT objectives.

HOW TO FOLLOW THE TEACHER DEVELOPMENT PROGRAM

- Read the syllabus on page T-xxv and think about which of the three themes you feel would benefit you the most. You might want to follow one, two, or all three of the themes.

- Before teaching a new unit, read the Teacher Development introduction. If you have time, you can also read the suggested text to learn more about the unit's development focus.

- Try out the activities in class.

- It's a good idea to keep a Teacher Development journal to keep track of your progress.

- You can also use your journal to make note of any Teacher Development activities you particularly enjoyed, as many of the activities can be adapted to use in different contexts. If possible, share your experiences and ideas with other teachers, either in person or in an online forum.

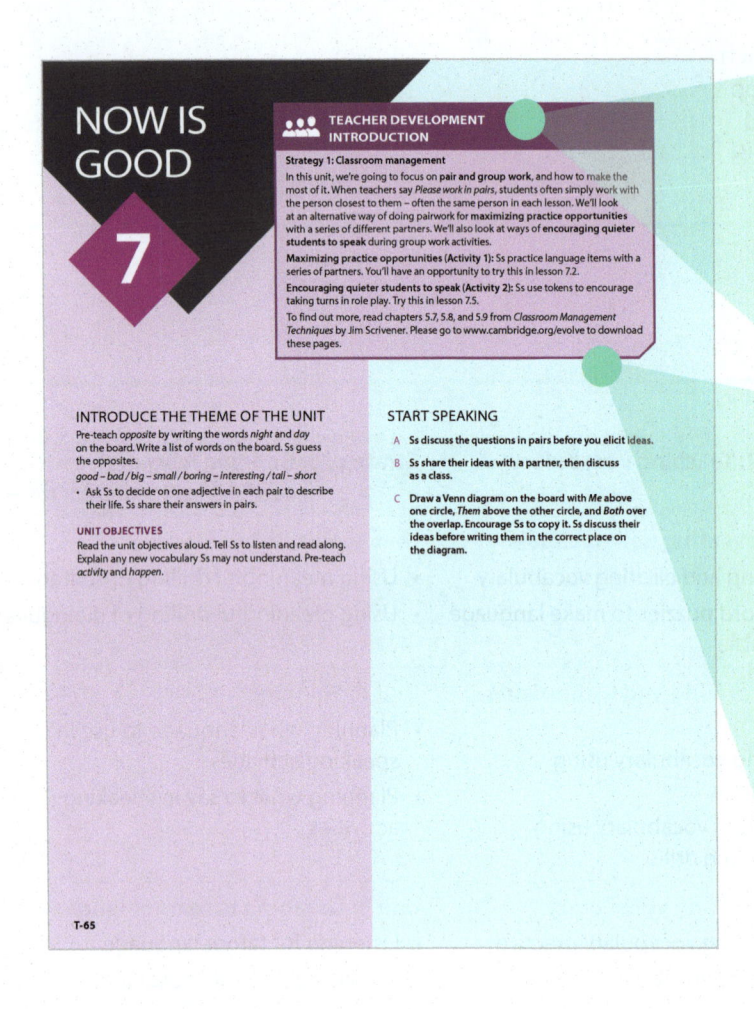

The **introduction** appears at the beginning of every unit. Here you can read a brief description of the Teacher Development focus and learn about the two Teacher Development activities that will be included in the unit. You can also find out about optional extra reading on the unit's teacher development focus here.

The **extra reading** texts, such as the one referred to in the introduction above, can be found at **www.cambridge.org/evolve**. We suggest additional reading texts to supplement your development throughout the program. These reading texts aim to give you a deeper understanding of the theory behind the unit's Teacher Development focus. You don't need to read the texts in order to complete the Teacher Development activities, but you might find it useful to do so.

Two **Teacher Development activities** appear in every unit. They can be alternative instructions for Student's Book activities, or extra activities that can be used during the lesson.

These activities offer a practical way to make positive changes in the classroom.

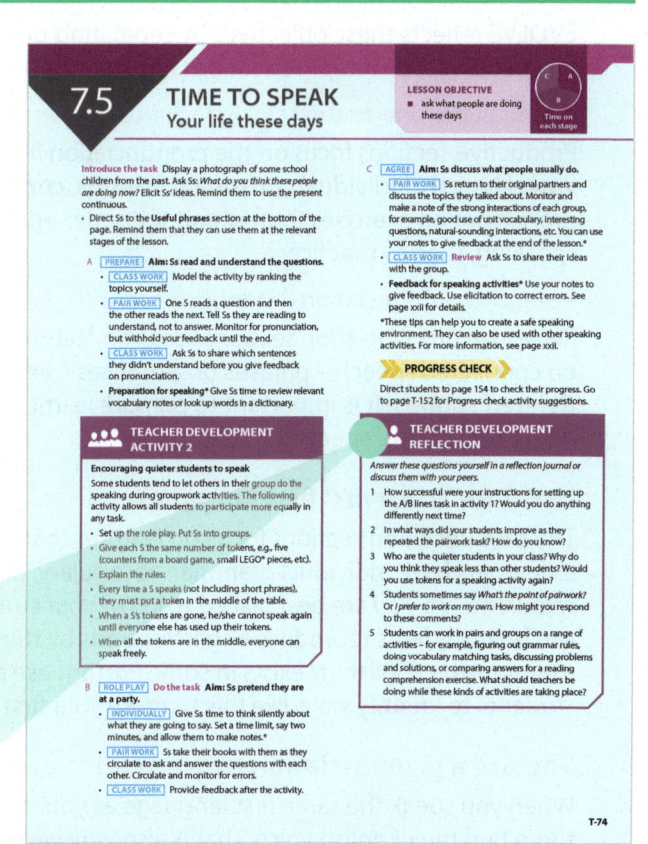

Reflection questions appear at the end of each unit. They help you to keep track of your progress. You can write the answers to these in a journal or share them with your colleagues.

PRONUNCIATION SUPPORT

Overview of Pronunciation sections

Most students learn English today to communicate with speakers of many different first languages. They often don't need, or want, to sound like so-called "native speakers;" their objective is to speak clearly and be understood, and to understand other speakers of English.

EVOLVE reflects these objectives by separating pronunciation activities into *productive* sections (pronunciation for speaking) and *receptive* sections (pronunciation for listening).

Productive pronunciation (saying sounds)

Productive sections focus on the pronunciation features that are most important in *clear communication*: **vowel length**, individual **consonant sounds**, **consonant clusters**, and **word stress**. The productive pronunciation exercises throughout the series encourage students to listen, to notice, to compare to their own speaking, then to practice.

Receptive pronunciation (listening for sounds)

Receptive pronunciation sections focus on features that are usually *less clear* to listeners. These primarily focus on connected speech – phrases or sentences – and include features like **linking sounds**, **weak forms**, and **deleted sounds**. It is important to prepare learners to hear connected speech but less important that students adopt this style of speaking.

Use your students' first language

The pronunciation sections focus on features that are likely to be most useful for your students. However, just as learners have individual grammar, vocabulary, or skills needs, so will they have individual pronunciation requirements. *You* are best placed to know *your* students' needs because you speak their language, and you can help students reproduce English sounds by thinking about similar sounds in your own language. For example, the English /r/ exists in some Portuguese accents at the end of words like *valor*. Work with your students to identify ways like this to make your first language a useful resource.

You are a pronunciation role model

When you speak the same first language as your students, you can be a role model for their speaking and help them find their English voice. That is also why we use other role models in the form of real student speakers from around the world throughout the series.

Tips for teaching pronunciation

To help students with their pronunciation in the productive sections:

Repeat (drill) the word or phrase. These drills provide important practice and give students confidence:
- Model the word or phrase.
- Ask students to repeat the word or phrase as a group.
- Students repeat the word or phrase with a partner.
- Individual students say the word or phrase to the class.

Use role models. Consider using clear speakers in the class as models, and model words yourself. This can be very motivating, and it reinforces the message that all accents are valid.

Find alternatives for phonemic symbols. We use phonemic symbols throughout the series for ease of reference, but you can use words as examples of sounds when you teach individual sounds. For example, to work on the /eɪ/ vowel sound, write *play* on the board and ask students for words with the same vowel sound.

Use a dictionary and draw symbols. Use a dictionary to check which syllable is stressed in a word. The stress is usually marked by ' before the stressed syllable, e.g., /sək'ses fəl/. On the board, however, it is clearer to write the word with a dot above the stressed syllable, e.g., *successful*. Encourage students to use stress bubbles when recording new words in their vocabulary notebooks.

Use gestures. You and your students can clap the rhythm of a word together. For example, *successful* = quiet clap, loud clap, quiet clap. You could also show this rhythm by holding up three fingers and using a clenched fist on the other hand to "bounce" from finger to finger, bouncing higher on the middle finger to show that this is stressed.

Demonstrate sounds. Pronunciation work in the classroom can be physical (and fun!), particularly when showing how sounds are articulated in the mouth. For example:
- Show students how to round their lips to make /w/.
- Show students how your top teeth touch your bottom lip to make /v/.
- Tell students to touch their throats to feel the vibration of **voiced sounds**, e.g., /d/ should vibrate because it is voiced, whereas /t/ should not vibrate because it is unvoiced.

Give good feedback. It is important to give your students feedback on their pronunciation. However, we recommend waiting until after the initial notice stage because students might adapt their pronunciation on their own.

Students want to understand spoken English and be understood, but they often don't want to sound like a native English speaker. Therefore, it's important not to compare your students' pronunciation to mother-tongue English speakers. Avoid language such as *good*, *bad*, *mistake*, *natural*, and *perfect* when you comment on your students' pronunciation. Instead, use more neutral terms such as *clear* and *unclear*.

GLOSSARY

Consonant sounds sounds made by the tongue, teeth, or lips. For example, the /tʃ/ in *watch*.
Consonant clusters a group of consonant sounds with no vowel sounds. For example, /str/ at the beginning of *street*.
Deleted sounds the syllables we don't pronounce.
Linking sounds the way two or more words flow together and sound like one word
Voiced sounds the sounds that are produced with a vibration. For example, /v/.
Word stress the syllables we say a bit longer and louder than the other syllables in a word
Weak forms the syllables we don't stress in a word.

I AM …

1

TEACHER DEVELOPMENT INTRODUCTION

Strategy 1: Classroom Management – Collaboration
In this unit, we're going to focus on **collaboration** – that is, helping students work together and feel comfortable with classmates. By encouraging collaboration, teachers can create positive learning environments for students. This is just as important for students who only attend part-time, or for a few weeks, as it is for students attending longer, full-time courses. **Learning names** is an important first step – both for teachers and for classmates. **Creating synergy**, or providing activities which show students how they can achieve more by working together, is another thing teachers can do right from the beginning of a course.

Learning names (Activity 1): Ss mingle and learn each other's names. Try this after **Start Speaking**.

Creating synergy (Activity 2): Ss work together to recreate a simple text. Try this in lesson 1.3.

To find out more, read pages 76–87 from *Classroom Management Techniques* by Jim Scrivener. Please go to www.cambridge.org/evolve to download these pages.

INTRODUCE THE THEME OF THE UNIT
- Write *Where are you from?* and *I'm from [your country].* on the board. Model the question and answer.
- Crush up a piece of paper to use as a ball, gently throw the paper to a S, and ask: *Where are you from?* Elicit: *I'm from ____.*
- Have the S toss the ball back to you and repeat your question. Repeat. Have Ss pass the ball of paper between each other, asking and answering.

UNIT OBJECTIVES
Read the unit objectives aloud. Tell Ss to listen and read along. Explain any new vocabulary Ss may not understand.

START SPEAKING
OPTIONAL ACTIVITY Ss watch the video to find out where Josue is from.

> **REAL STUDENT**
> Hello, my name is Josue Lozano. I am from Tegucigalpa in Honduras.

TEACHER DEVELOPMENT ACTIVITY 1

Learning Names
Teachers can create good rapport between students by ensuring they know each other's names. This helps them ask each other for help with tasks, refer to others during feedback, and interact more naturally.

- Ss complete the **START SPEAKING** task.
- Ask Ss to call out their names, one by one. Write them on the board.
- Draw a 3x3 grid on the board. Ask Ss to copy it.

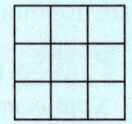

- Ss choose nine names from the board and write one name in each square. The teacher does the same with the grid on the board.
- Demonstrate the next stage with two students.
  T Hello. I'm (*your name*).
  S I'm Simone.
  T Nice to meet you. (*T crosses out "Simone" from grid.*)
  T Hi. I'm (*your name*).
  S Hi. I'm Roberto.
  T Nice to meet you.
- Ss move around the classroom, using model dialogue, trying to find people on their grid.

T-1

UNIT OBJECTIVES
- say where you're from
- ask for and give personal information
- check into a hotel
- write a profile
- meet new people

I AM ...

1

START SPEAKING

CLASS WORK Say your name. Watch Josue for an example.

I am Marco.

I am Anya.

REAL STUDENT

Where is Josue from?

1.1 I'M BRAZILIAN. AND YOU?

LESSON OBJECTIVE
- say where you're from

1 VOCABULARY: Countries and nationalities

A 🔊 1.03 Complete the chart. Then listen and check.

Capital city	Country	Nationality
Brasília	Brazil	¹ _____
Santiago	Chile	Chilean
Beijing	China	Chinese
Bogotá	² _____	Colombian
Quito	Ecuador	Ecuadorian
Paris	France	French
Tegucigalpa	Honduras	Honduran
Tokyo	Japan	Japanese
Mexico City	³ _____	Mexican
Lima	Peru	Peruvian
Moscow	Russia	⁴ _____
Seoul	South Korea	South Korean
Madrid	Spain	Spanish
Washington, D.C.	the United States	American

B ▶ Now do the vocabulary exercises for 1.1 on page 141.

C **PAIR WORK** Talk to a partner. Say your name, nationality, and city.

> Hi! I'm Yessica. I'm Peruvian, and I'm from Callao.

> Hello! I'm Daniel. I'm from Madrid, in Spain.

2 LANGUAGE IN CONTEXT

A Read the messages from students and teachers. What cities are they from? Who is a teacher?

International school project

- Hi!
- Hi, I'm Gabi. I'm **Brazilian**. I'm from **São Paulo**.
- You're from **Brazil**! Wow! My name is Karina, and I'm from **Colombia**.
- Are you from **Bogotá**?
- No, I'm not. I'm from **Medellín**.

Write a message …

International school project

- My name is Antonio. I'm from **Mexico City** – in **Mexico**!
- Hi, I'm Max. I'm **Russian**. I'm from **Moscow**.
- Hi, Max. Are you a teacher?
- Yes, I am. And you?
- No, I'm not a teacher! I'm a student.

Write a message …

1.1 I'M BRAZILIAN. AND YOU?

LESSON OBJECTIVE
- say where you're from

- **Introduce the task** Display a map of the world from the internet or write a list of countries on the board.
- Point to different countries and ask Ss to identify them in English. Ask: *What's this country? What is the capital city?*
- Say or write on the board true and false sentences, e.g.,
  The capital city of Brazil is São Paulo.
  Quito is the capital city of Ecuador.
  New York City is the capital city of the United States.

Use countries from the chart in the lesson. Ask Ss if the sentences are true or false, and to correct the false statements.

> **VOCABULARY SUPPORT** Remind Ss that countries are nouns and nationalities are adjectives. Help Ss understand what *nouns* and *adjectives* are.

1 VOCABULARY: Countries and nationalities

A 🔊 **1.03** Before Ss fill in the chart, remind them of the map you displayed to start the lesson.
- Ss complete the chart individually as best they can.
- When Ss have finished, play the audio and ask them to check their chart.
- Play the audio while Ss read and pause after each line. Ss repeat. Listen for any pronunciation errors.

> **Answers**
> 1 Brazilian 2 Colombia 3 Mexico 4 Russian

> **VOCABULARY SUPPORT** Make it clear to Ss that *I am* is the same as *I'm*. The form with the apostrophe is the contracted, or shortened, form.
> *I am = I'm*
> *you are = you're*
> Using the contracted form makes the language less formal and is common in spoken English.

> 📎 **EXTRA ACTIVITY**
> Give Ss up to ten nationalities to learn for the next class. In the next session, dictate the ten nationalities for Ss to spell on pieces of paper with their books closed. Ask Ss to exchange papers and correct their partner's work before you elicit answers and write them on the board.

B Direct Ss to page 141 to complete the vocabulary exercises. Teacher tips for vocabulary exercises are on page T-141.

C **PAIR WORK** Review If possible, put Ss in different pairs to give them a chance to listen to different people talk. Circulate and monitor.

2 LANGUAGE IN CONTEXT

A Ask Ss to do this individually and then share with a partner. Elicit answers. Then ask Ss to read again aloud in pairs with each S taking a role.

> **Answers**
> Gabi: São Paulo   Max: Moscow
> Karina: Medellín   Max is a teacher.
> Antonio: Mexico City

> 📎 **EXTRA ACTIVITY**
> Ask Ss to choose a capital city and a country from the chart in exercise 1, then ask them to stand up and walk around the classroom. They should ask: *Where are you from?* and respond: *I'm from [a country].* using the city and country they have chosen. They should talk with as many members of the class as possible. Monitor and correct pronunciation.

T-2

3 GRAMMAR: *I am, you are*

A **Present the grammar** Before Ss circle the answers, explain that they can refer to the examples in the grammar box.

- Use concept questions to check that Ss understand. Ask: *Are you from Bogotá?* to elicit *Yes, I am / No, I'm not.*
- To practice negatives, tell Ss you will give them a positive sentence and they must make it negative. Say: *I'm from Madrid* to elicit *I'm not from Madrid.* Repeat with other questions.
- Answer any questions Ss may have about the grammar.

> **Answers**
> 1 Are you … ? 2 Yes, I am. 3 No, I'm not.

> **GRAMMAR SUPPORT** It can be impolite to answer a question with simply *Yes* or *No*. Remind Ss that they should use short answers: *Yes, I am.* or *No, I'm not.* to avoid sounding rude.

B Ss complete the sentences individually before sharing their answers with their partner.

> **Answers**
> 1 I 2 You 3 Are 4 am

> **EXTRA ACTIVITY**
> Ask Ss questions individually. Ask *Are you from Quito?* and Ss respond *Yes, I am* or *No, I'm not.* Ask other questions: *Are you in room 3A? / Are you Mexican? / Are you a teacher?*

C Direct Ss to page 129 to complete the grammar exercise. Teacher's tips for grammar exercises are on page T-129.

- Remind Ss that in English we need pronouns to accompany verbs, in either long or short forms.
- *Am Spanish* should be *I am Spanish* or *I'm Spanish* as in the sentences in the **Accuracy check**. *Is English* should be *He is English* or *He's English*.
- Write the following sentences on the board and ask Ss to write the correct versions before they check with a partner.
    1 *Am from Honduras.*
    2 *Yes, am Peruvian.*
    3 *No, am not American.*

> **Answers**
> 1 I am / I'm from Honduras.
> 2 Yes, I am / I'm Peruvian.
> 3 No, I am / I'm not American.

D After Ss have written their sentences, they share them with their partner. Elicit answers from confident speakers in the class. If you have a small class, mark Ss' sentences individually.

> **Answers**
> 1 I'm Alex.
> 2 I'm from Orlando.
> 3 I'm American.
> 4 I'm from the United States.

E **PAIR WORK** **Do the task** Model a sample dialogue with a volunteer. As Ss do the role play, circulate to listen for errors and good use of language.

4 SPEAKING

A **GROUP WORK** Ask Ss to imagine a new identity. Completing this task will help Ss in the next section. If Ss can't think of a place, they can use a town and city from the list on page 2 to help them.

- **OPTIONAL ACTIVITY** Before you play the video, make sure Ss know that they should listen for Anderson's city, nationality, and country. Ask Ss to watch the video then share their answers with a partner. Play multiple times if necessary.

> **REAL STUDENT**
> Hello. My name is Anderson. I am from São Paulo in Brazil. I am Brazilian.

> **VOCABULARY SUPPORT** Don't worry about repeating audio or reading text again. Repetition is a good way for Ss to learn.

- **Review** Encourage Ss to circulate around the classroom, sharing their information with other members of the class. Get involved yourself and interact with the Ss. Monitor for examples of language usage, such as pronunciation and grammar, and provide feedback at the end.

3 GRAMMAR: *I am, you are*

A Circle the correct answers. Use the sentences in the grammar box to help you.
1. For questions (?), say **Are you … ? / You are … ?**
2. For affirmative (+) answers, say **Yes, I am. / Yes, I'm.**
3. For negative (-) answers, say **No, I am not. / No, I'm not.**

I am (= I'm), you are (= you're)

I'm Brazilian.
You're from Mexico City.

I'm not from Lima.
You're not from Bogotá.

Am I in room 6B?
 Yes, **you are.** / No, **you're not.**
Are you from Tokyo?
 Yes, **I am.** / No, **I'm not.**

B Complete the sentences.
1. _____ 'm Ecuadorian.
2. Wow! _____ 're from Rio!
3. _____ you from Quito?
4. **A** Are you American?
    B Yes, I _____ .

C ▶ Now go to page 129. Look at the grammar chart and do the grammar exercise for 1.1.

D Look at the chart. You are Alex. Write four sentences. Then read the information in the Accuracy check box and check your work.

Name	City	Nationality	Country
Alex	Orlando	American	the United States

1. _____
2. _____
3. _____
4. _____

✓ **ACCURACY CHECK**

Use *I* with *am*.
~~Am~~ Spanish. ✗
I'm Spanish. ✓

E PAIR WORK Choose a name. Don't tell your partner. Ask and answer questions to find the person.

- **Harry**, student, New York, American
- **Barbara**, student, New York, Brazilian
- **Mike**, student, Chicago, American
- **Victor**, student, Chicago, Brazilian
- **Kristy**, teacher, New York, American
- **Nayara**, teacher, New York, Brazilian
- **Robert**, teacher, Chicago, American
- **Juliano**, teacher, Chicago, Brazilian

Are you a student?
Yes, I am.
Are you from New York?
No, I'm not. I'm from … .

4 SPEAKING

GROUP WORK Imagine you're a different person. Choose a new name, city, nationality, and country. Talk to other people. Ask questions. For ideas, watch Anderson.

REAL STUDENT — What's Anderson's city, nationality, and country?

3

1.2 WHAT'S YOUR LAST NAME?

LESSON OBJECTIVE
- ask for and give personal information

1 LANGUAGE IN CONTEXT

A 🔊 **1.04** Rudy and Juana are at a conference. Listen to the conversation. Check (✓) the information they say.

- ☐ college name
- ☐ company name
- ☐ email address
- ☐ first name
- ☐ last name (= family name)

INSIDER ENGLISH

Say *Uh-huh* to show you are listening.
My last name is Garcia. G-A-R-C-I-A.
Uh-huh. What's your email address?

B 🔊 **1.04** Read and listen again. What information do they spell?

🔊 **1.04 Audio script**

Rudy	So, your **first name** is Juana. H-U- …
Juana	No. J-U-A-N-A. My **last name** is Garcia. G-A-R-C-I-A.
Rudy	Uh-huh. What's your **email address**?
Juana	It's juanagarcia@bestmail.com.
Rudy	And what's the name of your **college**?
Juana	It's Garcia College. I'm Juana Garcia from Garcia College!
Rudy	Great! OK, my last name is Jones.
Juana	OK. What's your email address?
Rudy	It's rudythejones@kmail.com.
Juana	Rudy*the*jones! The? T-H-E?
Rudy	Yes. R-U-D-Y-T-H-E-J-O-N-E-S.
Juana	From Jones College?
Rudy	No! From Miami Dade College.

4

1.2 WHAT'S YOUR LAST NAME?

LESSON OBJECTIVE
- ask for and give personal information

- **Introduce the task** Write *name what's your?* on the board and ask Ss to unscramble the sentence.
- Scramble only one or two of the following sentences on the board for Ss to write and unscramble:
  Where are you from? / What's your email address? / What's the name of your college? / What's your address? / Are you Brazilian?
- Ss now ask each other the questions in pairs. Check their ideas by asking individual Ss.

1 LANGUAGE IN CONTEXT

Warmer Ask Ss to close their books. Explain *conference* and the context of the audio. Ask them to listen and write any people's names they hear.
- Play the audio and elicit answers.

A 🔊 **1.04** **Open books and read the instructions together.**
- Play the audio and ask Ss to complete the activity as they listen.

> **Answers**
> college name, email address, first name, last name

B 🔊 **1.04** Before Ss read and listen, point out the capital letters separated by hyphens. Direct them to listen for the letters in the audio.

> **Answers**
> email address, first name, last name

📎 EXTRA ACTIVITY

Ask Ss to read the dialogue again in pairs as a role play. Monitor and listen for any errors in pronunciation. Refer Ss to the **Notice** box on page 5 to help them say the characters in the email addresses.

T-4

2 VOCABULARY: The alphabet; personal information

A 🔊 **1.05 Present the vocabulary** Say the letters individually and ask Ss to repeat aloud.
- Play the audio while Ss follow along.
- Play audio again, pausing after each letter for Ss to repeat.

> **VOCABULARY SUPPORT** The English vowels *a*, *e*, and *i* are often an area of confusion, especially in spelling. Write the vowel sounds on the board and have Ss repeat after you.

> 📎 **EXTRA ACTIVITY**
> Spell your own name as a model. Then tell Ss to spell their first and middle names to each other in pairs. Monitor and check vowel sounds. Ask volunteers to spell their names to the class.

B 🔊 **1.06 Review** Play the audio as many times as necessary for most Ss to arrive at the answers.

> **Answers**
> 1 c 2 a 3 b 4 c 5 b

> 🔊 **1.06 Audio script**
> 1 My first name is Raymond: R-A-Y-M-O-N-D
> 2 My last name is Cummings: C-U-M-M-I-N-G-S
> 3 My email address is cg_smith@kmail.com C-G-underscore-S-M-I-T-H
> 4 The name of my college is Wallace College: W-A-L-L-A-C-E
> 5 My company is Jefferson Sales: J-E-F-F-E-R-S-O-N

C Direct Ss to page 141 to complete the vocabulary exercises. Teacher's tips for vocabulary exercises are on page T-141.

D PAIR WORK **Review** Direct Ss to read the **Notice** box again. Model the activity by spelling some of your own personal information. As Ss work, circulate and listen for any errors to provide feedback at the end.

3 GRAMMAR: *What's … ? It's …*

A **Introduce the grammar** Before Ss circle the answers, explain that they can refer to the examples in the grammar box.

> **Answers**
> 1 What's 2 It's

- **Present the grammar** Read the grammar chart aloud and make sure Ss are aware that the apostrophe *s* is a contracted or short form of *is*. Read the **Accuracy check** box to reinforce understanding.
- Ask individual Ss the questions and have them respond with their own information.

> 📎 **EXTRA ACTIVITY**
> Dictate these sentences and ask Ss to put the apostrophe in the correct place:
> *What's your name? / It's Monday. / What's the name of your college? / It's Main Street. / I'm from the United States.*
> Write answers on the board and ask individual Ss to spell some of the words.

B **Do the task** Ss complete the sentences individually before checking their answers with the class.

> **Answers**
> 1 What's the name of your company? c It's Warton Homes.
> 2 What's your last name? b It's Mendes.
> 3 What's your email address? a It's luzmendes@xyz.com.

C Direct Ss to page 129 to complete the grammar exercise. Teacher's tips for grammar exercises are on page T-129.

4 SPEAKING

A **Review** Ask individual Ss to read the words in the word box aloud.
- Ask Ss to write down their own information on a piece of paper to carry around the class in the next task.

B CLASS WORK **Monitor** as Ss circulate and share their information with other Ss. Monitor, listening for errors in grammar and pronunciation.

> 📎 **EXTRA ACTIVITY**
> Draw a chart on the board and ask Ss to copy it.
>
> | First name | | |
> | Last name | | |
> | Nationality | | |
> | Email address | | |
> | College name | | |
>
> - Ss write fake information in the first column. They should NOT use their own information.
> - Ss share the new information with a partner, asking questions from this unit and recording their partner's answers in the second column.

2 VOCABULARY: The alphabet; personal information

A 🔊 1.05 Read and listen. Then listen again and repeat.

Aa Bb Cc Dd Ee Ff Gg Hh Ii Jj Kk Ll Mm
Nn Oo Pp Qq Rr Ss Tt Uu Vv Ww Xx Yy Zz

B 🔊 1.06 Listen and (circle) the spelling you hear.

1 **first name:** a Raymund   b Raimund   c Raymond
2 **last name:** a Cummings   b Cummins   c Comyns
3 **email address:** a cb_smith@kmail.com   b cg_smith@kmail.com   c cd_smith@kmail.com
4 **college:** a Wallice   b Wallis   c Wallace
5 **company:** a Jeferson   b Jefferson   c Jeffersen

C ▶ Now do the vocabulary exercises for 1.2 on page 141.

D PAIR WORK Talk to a partner. Say your first name, last name, email address, and college or company name.

> ❗ In email addresses:
> - "." is "dot"
> - "@" is "at"
> - "_" is "underscore"

3 GRAMMAR: *What's … ?, It's …*

A (Circle) the correct answers. Use the sentences in the grammar box to help you.

1 For questions, say *What's … ? / It's …*
2 For answers, say *What's … ? / It's …*

> *What's …? (= What is), It's … (= It is)*
>
> **What's** your first name?   **It's** Juana.
> **What's** the name of your college?   **It's** Garcia College.

✓ **ACCURACY CHECK**

Use the apostrophe (').

~~Whats~~ your first name? ✗
What's your first name? ✓
~~Its~~ Juana. ✗
It's Juana. ✓

B Write *What's* or *It's* in the spaces. Match the questions (1–3) with the answers (a–c). Then check your accuracy.

1 _____ the name of your company? ___
2 _____ your last name? ___
3 _____ your email address? ___

a _____ luzmendes@xyz.com.
b _____ Mendes.
c _____ Warton Homes.

C ▶ Now go to page 129. Look at the grammar chart and do the grammar exercise for 1.2.

Luz Mendes
SALES
✉ luzmendes@xyz.com
📞 (467) 555-2932
WARTON HOMES

4 SPEAKING

A Look at the information in the box. (Circle) three things to talk about.

| college name | company name | email address | first name | last name |

B CLASS WORK Talk to other people. Ask questions about the information in the box.

💬 *What's the name of your college?*   💬 *It's Wallace College.*

5

1.3 THIS IS THE KEY

LESSON OBJECTIVE
- check in to a hotel

1 VOCABULARY: Numbers

A 🔊 1.07 Listen and repeat the numbers.

0 zero	3 three	6 six	9 nine
1 one	4 four	7 seven	10 ten
2 two	5 five	8 eight	

INSIDER ENGLISH

For **0**, say *zero* or *oh*.
Your room number is two-**zero**-one.
My address is seven-**oh**-nine …

B PAIR WORK Say a number from exercise 1A. Your partner points to the number. Then change roles.

2 FUNCTIONAL LANGUAGE

A 🔊 1.08 Paulo is at a hotel. Read and listen. Check (✓) the information the hotel clerk asks for.

- ☐ cell phone number
- ☐ company
- ☐ name
- ☐ city
- ☐ email address
- ☐ room number

🔊 **1.08 Audio script**

Clerk	Welcome to New York! What's your name?	**Paulo**	OK.
Paulo	I'm Paulo Vasques. **I'm here for three nights.**	**Clerk**	Thank you. **This is the key.** It's room 6B.
Clerk	Ah, yes. **What's your cell phone number?**	**Paulo**	6D. Thanks.
Paulo	It's (593) 555-2192.	**Clerk**	No, you're not in 6D. **You're in room 6B.**
Clerk	Thanks. And what's your email address?	**Paulo**	Oh, OK. Thank you.
Paulo	It's pvasques89@travelmail.org.	**Clerk**	You're welcome.
Clerk	Thanks. One moment. **Please sign here.** Here's a pen.		

B Complete the chart with expressions in **bold** from the conversation above.

Checking in (clerk)

What's your [1]_____ number?
Please [2]_____ here.
Here's a [3]_____.
This is the [4]_____.
It's room 6B.
[5]_____ room 6B.

Checking in (Paulo)

[6]_____ (593) 555-2192.
I'm here for three [7]_____.

C 🔊 1.09 Complete the conversations. Then listen and check. Practice with a partner.

1 **A** What's your *email / cell phone number*? **B** *I'm / It's* (593) 555-3194.
2 **A** Please *sign / write* here. **B** OK.
3 **A** Hello. Welcome to the Garden Hotel. **B** Thanks. I'm here for two *mornings / nights*.
4 **A** *This is / It's* the key. You're in room 4D. **B** OK. Thanks.
5 **A** *Here's a / You're* pen. **B** Thank you.

6

1.3 THIS IS THE KEY

LESSON OBJECTIVE
- check into a hotel

TEACHER DEVELOPMENT ACTIVITY 2

Creating Synergy

Teachers can encourage students to work together by demonstrating how a teamwork approach can lead to better results.

- Ss look at photo of Paulo. Tell Ss he is talking to a clerk. Ask Ss to suggest what they are talking about.
- Ss close their books.
- Write the first part of the audioscript on the board
  Clerk   Welcome _____
  Paulo
  Clerk
  Paulo
  Clerk   _____ address?
- Tell Ss they will hear this part *only once*, and after they must write the missing text. Tell them not to worry!
- Ss listen.* As soon as the teacher stops the audio, each S writes as much as possible from memory – even if it's just a couple of words.
- Ss pair up, compare, and add.
- Ss work in groups, and continue comparing and adding.
- Complete the text on the board by asking Ss to suggest the missing text.

*If you prefer, read the audioscript aloud, but do this at normal speed.

Introduce the lesson Write each number 0–10 on individual sheets of paper so they are easily visible. Hold up a number and ask Ss to say the correct word. Continue until Ss recognize all the numbers.

- Ask Ss to write 0–10 on small pieces of paper. In pairs, one S shows a number while the other names it.

1 VOCABULARY: Numbers

A 🔊 **1.07** Play the audio and have Ss repeat. Read the Insider English box with the class.

B **PAIR WORK** Read the instructions aloud. Model the activity by saying a number and getting Ss to point to the number. Monitor.

> **VOCABULARY SUPPORT** Telephone numbers are said as separate numbers in English and often separated by dashes, e.g., 345-6318. Hotel rooms can be said as separate numbers as well as large numbers, e.g.,
> 212 – *two twelve*   915 – *nine fifteen*

📎 EXTRA ACTIVITY

Dictate an individual six-digit phone number to each student. Keep a record of each S's number. Draw a telephone keypad on the board. Pretend to push each button and say the number to "dial" one of the phone numbers.
- Repeat. Ss listen to the numbers carefully to determine if it is their number. Ss can also come to the front of class and "dial" other Ss.

2 FUNCTIONAL LANGUAGE

A 🔊 **1.08** Before you play the audio, read the list of items with Ss to make sure they are familiar with the terms.

- Ask questions to check understanding: *What's your name? What city are you from? What's your cell phone number? What is the room number?* (perhaps the number of your classroom) *What is your email address?*
- Play the audio once or twice and let Ss check the answers.
- Play the audio a third time and pause after each item is mentioned.

> **Answers**
> The hotel clerk asks for Paulo's name, cell phone number, and email address.

B Ss work individually before sharing their answers with a partner. Elicit answers by asking individual Ss to read the phrases.

- For more practice, ask Ss to read and role play the dialogue in pairs before switching roles. Monitor and listen for pronunciation errors.

> **Answers**
> 1 cell phone   2 sign   3 pen   4 key   5 You're in   6 It's
> 7 nights

C 🔊 **1.09** **Review** Ss complete the activity individually. Then play the audio as Ss check their answers.

- Ask Ss to practice with a partner.

> **Answers**
> 1 cell phone number, It's   2 sign   3 nights   4 This is
> 5 Here's a

T-6

3 REAL-WORLD STRATEGY

A 🔊 **1.10** **Introduce the task** Before you play the audio, make sure Ss read and understand the sentences. Play the audio. Repeat if necessary. Elicit answers.

> **Answers**
> 1 a hotel   2 cell phone number

> 🔊 **1.10 Audio script**
>
> A Hello. Welcome to the Westside Hotel. What's your name?
> B My name is Lisa Carlton. I'm here for two nights.
> A How do you spell your last name?
> B C-A-R-L-T-O-N.
> A Ah, yes. Here you are. What's your cell phone number?
> B It's (555) 889-3245.
> A OK. Thank you. And what's your email address?
> B It's lcarlton01@bestmail.com.

B 🔊 **1.10** After reading the **Checking Spelling** box, play the audio as many times as Ss need.

> **Answer**
> her last name

> 📎 **EXTRA ACTIVITY**
>
> Write *My name is Sam Moore. I come from Canada.* Invite Ss to make questions with *How do you spell …?* to elicit *How do you spell your first name / your last name / Canada?* Ask Ss to write a similar sentence. In pairs, they ask the same questions.

C 🔊 **1.11** Play the audio as Ss just listen.
- Repeat and Ss answer.
- Ss share their answers in pairs. Monitor.
- Ss circulate around the class, sharing their answers with many different partners.

4 PRONUNCIATION: Saying /ɪ/ and /i/ vowel sounds

A 🔊 **1.12** Play the audio. Ask Ss to repeat, paying attention to the short and long vowel sounds.

B 🔊 **1.13** As an example, elicit the answer for *email*.
- Ss guess the answers. Play the audio and tell Ss to check their ideas. Check answers as a whole class.

> **Answers**
> 1 B   2 A   3 A   4 B   5 B   6 B

C 🔊 **1.14** **PAIR WORK** Ask students to read the conversations and identify the /ɪ/ and /i/ sounds.
- Play the audio. Tell Ss to check their ideas. Then play the audio again for the class to repeat.
- Ss practice the conversations in pairs. Monitor and provide feedback as necessary.

5 SPEAKING

A **PAIR WORK** Ss work in pairs to order the conversation. Allow them some time to do this.
- Circulate and offer to help when needed.
- When finished, elicit the answers from volunteers.

> **Answers**
> (left column) 7, 5, 2, 8, 6 (right column) 3, 4, 9, 1

- In pairs, ask Ss to role play the conversation. Monitor and listen for any errors.

B **PAIR WORK** **Do the task** Elicit the names of hotels in the city where Ss live. Write the names on the board. Choose one you like.
- Model the role play with a volunteer.
- Monitor pronunciation as Ss complete the role play. Listen for language usage, such as pronunciation and grammar, and give feedback at the end.

C **PAIR WORK** **Review** Put Ss into pairs and assign each one to be either Student A or Student B. Ask Student As to turn to page 156 and Student Bs to turn to page 158.
- Read through the instructions aloud for Ss and make sure they understand all the information on their cards. Elicit and write sample questions that Ss will use to get the information from their partner, e.g., *What's your first name? What is your email address?*
- Model a sample dialogue with a volunteer.
- Ss do the task. As Ss complete the task, circulate and monitor. Ss check their answers with each other when they finish.
- Ask for volunteers to demonstrate their dialogues to the rest of the class.

> 📎 **EXTRA ACTIVITY**
>
> Play tic-tac-toe with the words from this lesson. Use words like *his, he's, it's, am, are*. Also, use question words like *how, what,* and *where*. Draw a tic-tac-toe grid with 3x3 squares on the board. Write one word in each square. Put Ss into two teams (X and O). Ask Ss from the X team to choose a square and make a sentence or a question with the word, e.g., *His name is Paulo.* or *What's your name?* If the sentence is correct, write *X* in the square. Repeat with the O team. Ss continue to take turns. The first team which connects three *X*s or *O*s in a row (vertically, horizontally, or diagonally) wins. For full details on how to play tic-tac-toe, see page T-251.

3 REAL-WORLD STRATEGY

A 🔊 **1.10** Listen to a conversation. Circle the correct answers.

1 The woman is at *a hotel / home*.　　2 She says her *room number / cell phone number*.

B 🔊 **1.10** Read about checking spelling in the box below. Listen to the conversation again. What does the man ask the woman to spell?

> **CHECKING SPELLING**
>
> To check spelling, ask *How do you spell your first name / your last name / it?*
> *My name is Paulo Vasques.*
> *How do you spell your last name?*
> *V-A-S-Q-U-E-S.*

C 🔊 **1.11** Listen to the questions. Answer the questions and spell words.

1 How do you spell your last name?　　*R-I-V-E-R-A.*

4 PRONUNCIATION: Saying /ɪ/ and /i/ vowel sounds

A 🔊 **1.12** Listen and repeat the two different vowel sounds.

/ɪ/ s**i**x You're in room **6**A.　　/i/ thr**ee** You're in room **3**A.

B 🔊 **1.13** Look at the underlined letters below. Then listen and repeat. What vowel sounds do you hear? Write A for words with /ɪ/, for example *six*. Write B for words with /i/, for example *three*.

1 ___ **e**mail　　3 ___ **i**nformation　　5 ___ k**ey**
2 ___ **i**s　　4 ___ pl**ea**se　　6 ___ compan**y**

C 🔊 **1.14** **PAIR WORK** Listen to the conversations. Underline words with the vowel sounds /ɪ/ and /i/. Then practice with a partner.

1 **A** Is this your key?　　**B** No, it's the key for room three.
2 **A** What's your company email address?　　**B** It's c.b.smith@wallis.com.
3 **A** What's your Instagram name?　　**B** It's SusieSix.

5 SPEAKING

A **PAIR WORK** Put the conversation in the correct order. Then practice with a partner.

[7] **A** Thanks. One moment. Please sign here.
[5] **A** Great. Thank you. And what's your email address?
[ ] **B** I'm Marie Bernard. I'm here for two nights.
[ ] **B** OK.
[ ] **B** It's mbernard87@mymail.org.
[ ] **A** Ah, yes, two nights. What's your cell phone number?
[ ] **B** It's (298) 555-1257.
[ ] **A** Thank you. This is the key. It's for room 7C.
[1] **A** Hi. Welcome to the Tree House Hotel! What's your name?

B **PAIR WORK** Choose a hotel in your city. One person is a hotel clerk, and the other person is a visitor. Then change roles.

> Hi. Welcome to the International Hotel. What's your name?

> I'm Jae-hoon Park. I'm here for two nights ....

C ▶ **PAIR WORK** Student A: Go to page 156. Student B: Go to page 158. Follow the instructions.

Welcome to the Tree House Hotel!

7

1.4 MY PROFILE

LESSON OBJECTIVE
- write a profile

1 VOCABULARY: Jobs

A 🔊 1.15 Listen and repeat.

- salesperson
- artist
- teacher
- student
- hotel clerk
- doctor
- chef
- server

2 READING

A SCAN Read the profiles. Circle three job words from exercise 1A.

B READ FOR DETAILS Read the profiles again. Complete the chart.

First name	Akemi	
Last name		Silva
City		
Nationality		
Company		
School		

C PAIR WORK One person is Akemi. One person is Frank. How are you different?

> I'm Akemi. I'm a student.

> I'm Frank. I'm not a student. I live in Texas …

! Use *but* to connect two different ideas.
I'm Peruvian, **but** my home is in the United States.

! People say, *I'm from Paris*. People also say, *I* **live** *in Paris*. (= Paris is my home now.)

STUDIO 10
STORE PROFILES
Meet the artists

ABOUT AKEMI

I'm Akemi Tanaka. I live in San Diego, but I'm not American. I'm Japanese. My company is Tanaka Paints. My phone number is (324) 555-6053, and my email is akemit2000@tanakapaints.com. I'm an artist, and I'm a student, too. The name of my school is The Art Institute. It's in California.

ABOUT FRANK

My name is Frank Silva. I live in Austin, Texas, in the United States. I'm American and Brazilian. The name of my company is Designs by Frank. It's in my home in Austin. I'm an art teacher, too. The classes are in my home. My phone number is (780) 555-5230, and my email is designsbyfrank@blinknet.com.

1.4 MY PROFILE

LESSON OBJECTIVE
- write a profile

Introduce the vocabulary Write the word *Jobs* on the board. Underneath this, write *server*. Then, without speaking, act the role of a server, pretending to take an order, carry a tray, put plates in front of Ss, etc. Then point to the board and elicit *server*. Repeat with several other jobs taught in 1A.

- If appropriate for your class, write on the board *What's your job? I'm a teacher.* Ask individual Ss the same question.

1 VOCABULARY: Jobs

A 🔊 **1.15 Do the task** In pairs, Ss look at the pictures and take turns saying the jobs.

- Play the audio, pausing after each word for Ss to repeat as a group.
- Play the audio again. Pause after each word and ask a volunteer to respond. Check for pronunciation of *chef:* /ʃef/.

EXTRA ACTIVITY

Scramble the letters of the names for jobs on page 8 and write them on the board. Give Ss time to unscramble the words before checking with their partner and the rest of the class.

e.g., *recateh – teacher*

2 READING

A **Review** Allow Ss time to read the text individually before you check the answers.

- Direct Ss to read the two **Notice** boxes, then ask Ss to read the profiles again. They can ask their partner or check a dictionary to find any other unfamiliar vocabulary.

Answers
artist, student, teacher

B Ss complete the chart individually before sharing their answers with a partner. To review the answers, draw or display the box on the board and write in each answer as you elicit it from Ss.

Answers

First name	Akemi	Frank
Last name	Tanaka	Silva
City	San Diego	Austin, Texas
Nationality	Japanese	American and Brazilian
Company	Tanaka Paints	Designs by Frank
School	The Art Institute	

HOMEWORK IDEAS

Ask Ss to record themselves on their smartphones reading one of the profiles. Encourage Ss to play back the recording and check their own pronunciation.

C **PAIR WORK** Pre-teach the word *different* before you begin this activity.

- As Ss work in pairs, circulate and listen for errors to offer feedback later.
- Ss write down their differences for you to check.

Suggested answers

Akemi	I'm a student / not a teacher.
Frank	I'm not a student / a teacher.
Akemi	I'm not American.
Frank	I'm American.
Akemi	I'm Japanese.
Frank	I'm American and Brazilian.
Akemi	I'm from San Diego.
Frank	I'm from Austin.
Akemi	My company is Tanaka Paints.
Frank	The name of my company is Designs by Frank.
Akemi	My phone number is (324) 555-6053.
Frank	My phone number is (780) 555-5230.
Akemi	My email is akemit2000@tanakapaints.com.
Frank	My email is designsbyfrank@blinknet.com.

EXTRA ACTIVITY

Ask Ss to work in pairs to think about ways they are different from each other. Ask: *How are you different?* Ss discuss and write down three differences. Monitor Ss while they complete the activity. When Ss finish, ask them to share their differences with the class.

T-8

3 WRITING

A **Introduce the task** Read the instructions aloud with Ss. Allow them time to read the profiles individually. Elicit answers to the questions.

> **Answers**
> Juan Carlos Fernandez is from Peru. Katya Ivanova is from Russia. Katya is a student.

B PAIR WORK While Ss discuss, circulate and monitor. If your class is less confident, you may want to do this activity as a whole group.

> **Suggested answers**
> The profile of Juan Carlos is a work profile. The profile of Katya is a personal profile.

C Read the rules for using capital letters aloud with Ss. Give examples for each one, e.g., for names of people – Juan Carlos Fernandez.

- Encourage Ss to work together to find two additional rules.
- Read through the **Register check** as a class. Ss look for examples of *Hello, Hi,* and *Hey* in the profiles. Ask: *Which profile is informal?*

> **Answers**
> For *I*: *I am Peruvian, I am from Trujillo, I am a salesperson, I'm Katya Ivanova, I'm Russian, I'm an English student*
> For names of people: *Juan Carlos Fernandez, Katya Ivanova*
> For names of places, companies, schools: *Trujillo, Lima, Omega Sales, St. Petersburg, Popov College of English*
> For nationalities and languages: *Peruvian, Russian*
> At the beginning of sentences: *Hello, My, I, The, Hi!, I'm, It's*

> **VOCABULARY SUPPORT** A **work profile** contains job details, work email, and place of work.
> A **personal profile** contains where you come from, your address, and email.

D Ask Ss to spend a few minutes choosing a profile and thinking of the information they will include in it. This is a good opportunity to recycle some of the questions from earlier in this unit.

- Ask Ss questions individually: *Where are you from? / How old are you?* This will give Ss more to write about in the next part of the lesson.
- **Do the task** As Ss write, circulate and monitor. Ss can use the profiles in 3A to help them. Look at Ss' work and offer feedback. Assist Ss with spelling by writing challenging words on the board. This will allow all Ss to see the word and use it if they wish. If you can, correct Ss' work as you go. Allow them as much time as they need.

> 🚶 **FAST FINISHERS**
> Ss can write another work or personal profile based on one of the job pictures in 1A. They can make up information for the profile, including name, email address, and cell number.

E GROUP WORK **Review** Ss will review and practice the questions they have learned in this unit.

- Ss read each other's profiles and decide if they are personal or work profiles.

> 📎 **EXTRA ACTIVITY**
> Encourage Ss to use questions from activities 3A and 3B on page 5 to ask a partner about their written profile. Model a few sample questions, e.g., *What's your last name? What's your email address?* Monitor as Ss discuss, listening for pronunciation and grammar. Praise students for good usage of language when the activity is finished.

T-9

3 WRITING

A Read the profiles of two people. Where are they from? Who is a student?

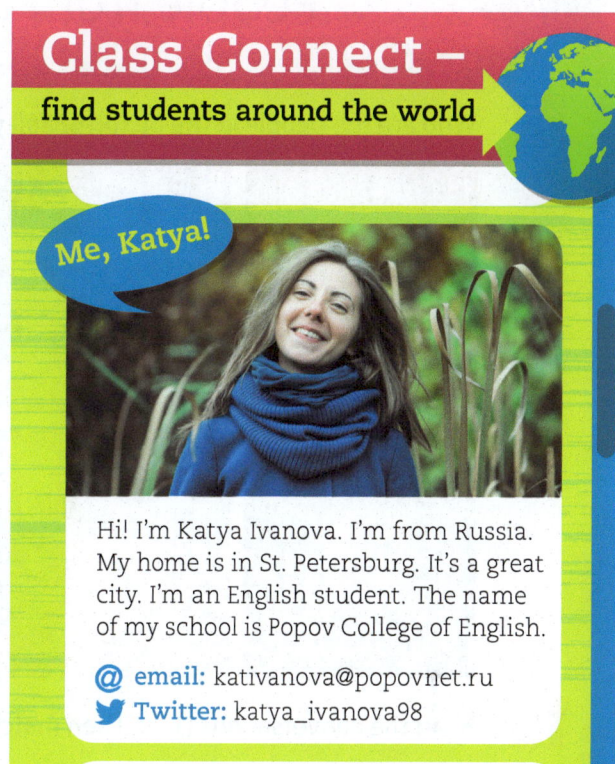

Business Weekly
Meet the sales team

Lima, Peru

Hello. My name is Juan Carlos Fernandez. I am Peruvian. I am from Trujillo, but I live in Lima now. I am a salesperson. The name of my company is Omega Sales. My email is jcfernandez_511@omsmail.com, and my cell phone number is (962) 555-3198.

Class Connect –
find students around the world

Me, Katya!

Hi! I'm Katya Ivanova. I'm from Russia. My home is in St. Petersburg. It's a great city. I'm an English student. The name of my school is Popov College of English.

@ **email:** kativanova@popovnet.ru
Twitter: katya_ivanova98

B PAIR WORK   THINK CRITICALLY   The two profiles are different. Why? Discuss with a partner.

C WRITING SKILLS   Read the rules. Then find <u>two</u> or more examples for the rules in the profiles.

ABC

Use capital letters (A, B, C …):
- for *I* (*I'm*)
- for names of people
- for names of places, companies, schools
- for nationalities and languages
- at the beginning of sentences

Use a period (.) at the end of statements.

REGISTER CHECK

Hello, *Hi*, and *Hey*

Use *hello* in formal writing or speaking, for example at work.
Hello. My name is Juan Carlos Fernandez.

Use *hi* in informal writing or speaking, with friends and family. Use *hey* when you speak to friends and family.
Hi! I'm Katya Ivanova.

WRITE IT

D Choose a work profile or a personal profile. Then write your profile. Use the profiles in exercise 3A for an example.

E GROUP WORK   Work in groups. Read other profiles. Are they work profiles or personal profiles? Say why.

9

1.5 TIME TO SPEAK
People from history

LESSON OBJECTIVE
- meet new people

A Who are the people in the pictures? Tell your partner.

B Read the conversations (1–3). Then match them to a–c. Which conversation is with three people?

- **a** an introduction ___
- **b** a greeting ___
- **c** a goodbye ___

1. **A** Good evening.
   B Hello. How are you?
   A I'm fine, thanks. And you?
   B I'm fine.

2. **A** Gabi, this is Caio.
   B Hi, Gabi. Nice to meet you.
   C Nice to meet you, Caio.

3. **A** See you later.
   B Bye.

C **PREPARE** Practice the conversations from exercise B. Then change roles.

D **RESEARCH** Imagine you're at a party for people from history. Choose a person. You can go online and find the nationality and home city for your person. Create and write down a cell phone number.

E **ROLE PLAY** Imagine you're the person from exercise D. Meet other people at the party. Write notes.

F **AGREE** Say the nationality, city or phone number of a person from the party. Other students say the person.

G **DISCUSS** Who is your favorite person from the party?

To check your progress, go to page 152.

USEFUL PHRASES

ROLE PLAY
Are you (American)?
Yes, I am. / No, I'm not. I'm …
I'm from (city).
How do you spell it?
A What's your cell phone number? B It's …

AGREE
The person is from (city). / The phone number is …
It's (name of person).

DISCUSS
My favorite person is …
Me, too.

1.5 TIME TO SPEAK
People from history

LESSON OBJECTIVE
- meet new people

Time on each stage

Introduce the task **Aim:** Introduce the concept of famous people. Write *famous* on the board. Say: *Tell me the name of a famous person.*
- **CLASS WORK** Make a list on the board of Ss' top ten suggestions. Search for *famous people in the world* online and check if Ss' ideas are correct.

A **Aim:** Identify famous people.
- **GROUP WORK** Ss discuss the photos before you elicit answers.

> **Answers**
> A Nelson Mandela B Michelle Obama C Leonardo da Vinci D Rain E Frida Kahlo F Steve Jobs G Malala Yousafzai H J. K. Rowling I Marilyn Monroe J Pelé

B 🔊 1.16 **Aim:** Introduce the language.
- **INDIVIDUALLY** Ss read, listen, and match.
- **PAIR WORK** Elicit answers. Encourage Ss to role play the conversations together.

> **Answers**
> a 2 b 1 c 3

C **PREPARE** **Do the task** **Aim:** Practice using the language.
- **GROUP WORK** Model the conversations with one or more confident Ss to demonstrate pronunciation and intonation.
- **PAIR WORK** Monitor for pronunciation as Ss read the conversations.
- **CLASS WORK** Ask volunteers to perform the conversations for the class.

D **RESEARCH** **Aim:** Prepare to talk about a famous person.
- **GROUP WORK** Encourage Ss to choose an interesting person. Refer them to the list of famous people from the start of the lesson. Ss can use their phones to find information they need. Encourage Ss to rehearse what they are going to say in their heads.

E **ROLE PLAY** **Aim:** Ss share their information. Ask individual Ss to read the expressions in the **Useful phrases** box aloud. Spend time drilling these and making sure Ss understand them.
- **GROUP WORK** Ss make a list of the name, city, and fake cell phone number of the other Ss in class.
- Ss circulate carrying their numbered lists. They role play their famous person and collect the names and cell phone numbers of the other "famous" people.
- Monitor and listen for errors that you can correct later.

F **AGREE** **Aim:** Consolidate language.
- Ask Ss to return to their seats.
- **GROUP WORK** Elicit a cell phone number from a S. The rest of the class refers to their notes and guesses whose number it is. Continue with other nationalities, numbers, or cities.

G **DISCUSS** **Aim:** Ss share their opinions.
- **GROUP WORK** Elicit which "famous person" Ss liked the most and why.

Review **Feedback for speaking activities*** Give the class positive feedback based on the notes you made earlier in the activity.

*These tips can help you to create a safe speaking environment. They can also be used with other speaking activities. For more information, see page xxii.

▶▶ PROGRESS CHECK ▶▶

Direct students to page 152 to check their progress. Go to page T-152 for Progress check activity suggestions.

👥 TEACHER DEVELOPMENT REFLECTION

Either answer these questions yourself in a reflection journal or discuss them with your peers.

1. What strategies have you used for learning students' names?
2. In some teaching situations, it may not be appropriate for students to use each other's first names. What is your experience?
3. How can you make sure that new students who join an existing class feel comfortable with their classmates?
4. Teacher Development Activity 2 is known as a dictogloss. How well did Ss do this activity? Would you use a dictogloss again, and if so, would you do anything differently?
5. Jim Scrivener says, "The term *synergy* refers to the energy and achievement that comes when people combine their abilities and efforts to work together, seemingly achieving more than the sum of what all the individuals could achieve on their own." What kind of activities could you do to create synergy in a class of students with very different levels of ability?

T-10

GREAT PEOPLE

2

TEACHER DEVELOPMENT INTRODUCTION

Strategy 2: Teaching vocabulary – Presenting new vocabulary
In this unit, we look at techniques for presenting vocabulary which actively involve Ss and give them the chance to show what they already know.

Conveying and eliciting (Activity 1): This fundamental technique is based on the principles of "meaning first" and "ask, don't tell." You will have the opportunity to try this in lesson 2.1.

Word puzzles (Activity 2): These are three techniques for lifting vocabulary off the page to make simple but engaging puzzle activities. You can try one of these in lesson 2.3.

To find out more about different ways of presenting vocabulary, read Chapter 5 of Ruth Gairns and Stuart Redman, *Working with Words*, pp. 73–85. Please go to www.cambridge.org/evolve to download these pages.

INTRODUCE THE THEME OF THE UNIT

Books closed. Draw your family tree on the board. Include yourself and several relatives, such as *father, sister, son, etc.* Draw blank lines for other family relationships.
- Ask Ss to brainstorm other family members. See how many relatives Ss can name. Allow Ss to use a dictionary.

UNIT OBJECTIVES
Read the unit objectives aloud. Tell Ss to listen and read along. Explain any new vocabulary that Ss may not understand.

START SPEAKING

Ask Ss to look at the picture in pairs and say words about the people. They can talk about relationships, nationalities, ages, etc.
- In mixed ability classes, stronger Ss could be paired with weaker Ss.

EXTRA ACTIVITY

Ss draw a box with six squares and choose six words for family members (*mother, father, sister, brother*, etc.), which they write in the squares. Play bingo by reading out the names of family members. Vary this by asking a S to act as the bingo caller in the next game. For details of how to play bingo, see page T-216.

UNIT OBJECTIVES

- talk about your family
- describe friends and family
- talk about ages and birthdays
- write a post about friends in a photo
- compare information about friends and family

GREAT PEOPLE

2

START SPEAKING

Look at the picture. Say words about the people.

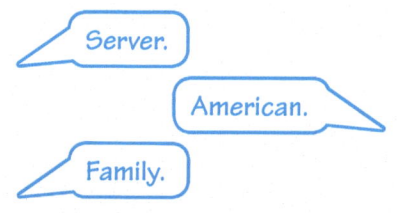

- Server.
- American.
- Family.

2.1 A FAMILY PARTY

LESSON OBJECTIVE
- talk about your family

1 LANGUAGE IN CONTEXT

A 🔊 **1.16** Sara and Liz are at a party. Read and listen to the conversation. How old are David and Emily? Who are Elizabeth One and Elizabeth Two?

🔊 **1.16 Audio script**

Sara What a great party, Liz! Are your **children** here?
Liz Yes, they are. David … He's my **son**. He's eight. And the girl with him is my daughter Emily. She's ten.
Sara And the man … Is he your **husband**?
Liz No, he's my **brother** Marcus. My husband isn't here.
Sara Oh, OK. Are your **parents** here?
Liz No, they're not. Oh, look. Here's my **grandmother**. She's 86. Grandma, this is my friend Sara.
Grandma Nice to meet you, Sara. I'm Elizabeth.
Sara Nice to meet you. Hey, are you both Elizabeth?
Liz Yes, we are! With friends, I'm Liz. But in my family, she's Elizabeth One, and I'm Elizabeth Two!

REGISTER CHECK

Some words for family are formal and informal. Use formal words at work. Use informal words with friends and family.

Formal	Informal
grandfather	grandpa
grandmother	grandma
father	dad
mother	mom

GLOSSARY
both (*det*) two people/things

2 VOCABULARY: Family; numbers

A 🔊 **1.17** Listen and repeat the words in the family tree.

B Read the sentences below about Liz and her family. Then complete the family tree with the names in **bold**.

- Liz = sister of **Marcus**.
- **Kyle** = uncle of Liz.
- **Tim** = cousin of Liz.
- **John** = grandfather of Liz.
- Anna = wife of **Paul**.

C 🔊 **1.18** Complete the table with words from the family tree. Then listen and check.

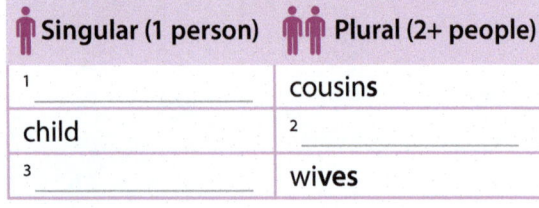

👤 Singular (1 person)	👥 Plural (2+ people)
1 _____	cousins
child	2 _____
3 _____	wi**ves**

D [PAIR WORK] Make three more sentences about the people in the family tree. Then compare with a partner.

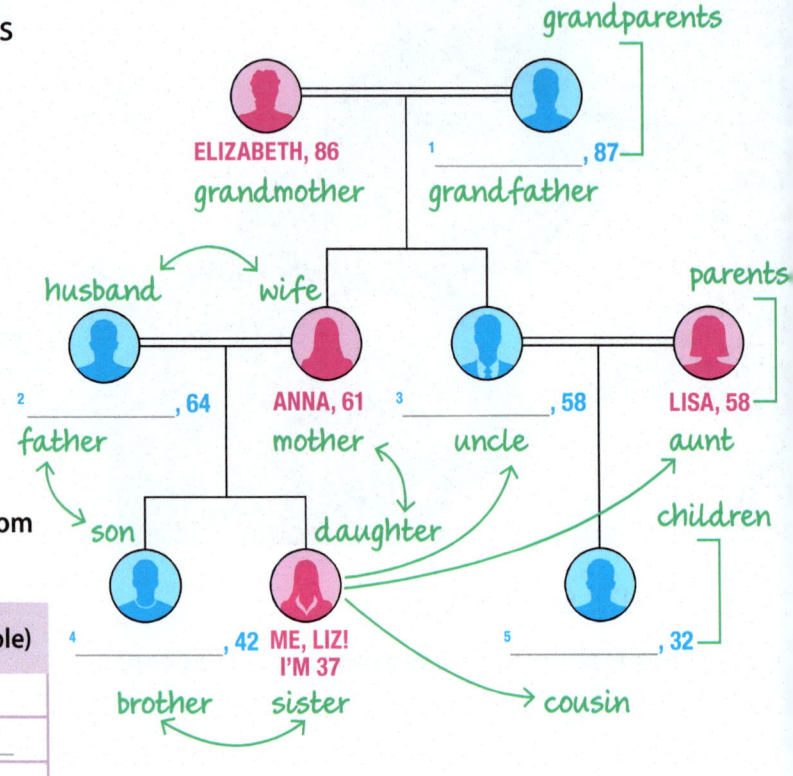

Family tree:
- ELIZABETH, 86 — grandmother
- 1 _____, 87 — grandfather
- grandparents
- husband / wife
- 2 _____, 64 — father
- ANNA, 61 — mother
- 3 _____, 58 — uncle
- LISA, 58 — aunt
- parents
- son / daughter
- 4 _____, 42 — brother
- ME, LIZ! I'M 37 — sister
- 5 _____, 32 — cousin
- children

12

2.1 A FAMILY PARTY

LESSON OBJECTIVE
- talk about your family

TEACHER DEVELOPMENT ACTIVITY 1

Conveying and eliciting

This basic presentation technique is based on two principles: first, we should communicate the meaning of a word to Ss <u>before</u> we focus on the word itself, and second, we should give Ss the chance to show us if they know a word <u>before</u> telling them.

- After exercise 1A, tell Ss to close their books. On the board, draw a simple stick figure and say: *This is Liz*. Write *Liz* under the figure.
- Draw a second figure labeled *Marcus* with a line to show that he's Liz's brother. Elicit *brother* from Ss with a gapped sentence: *Marcus is the … of Liz*. Write *brother* next to Marcus. Ss repeat the word.
- Build up the rest of the family tree in the same way, step by step: draw a part of the tree to show Ss the meaning (conveying), ask Ss if they can give you the word (eliciting), write the word, and ask Ss to repeat.
- When the family tree is complete, Ss compare with the tree on page 12. They should be the same!

Introduce the lesson Show Ss some pictures of your family and introduce them, e.g., *This is my sister. He's my son. Here's my uncle.* Write these sentences on the board.

1 LANGUAGE IN CONTEXT

🔊 **1.16 Introduce the task** Books closed. Play the audio. Ss write down as many family members as they hear.

Answers
son, daughter, husband, brother, grandmother

A 🔊 **1.16 Do the task** Read the instructions aloud for Ss. Make sure they understand the questions.

- Play the audio as Ss read and answer the questions. Watch Ss' faces to see if they are keeping up with the speed of the dialogue. Pause and repeat the audio if necessary.
- Ask Ss to role play the dialogue in pairs as a follow up. Monitor for pronunciation as Ss talk.
- **Review** Read the **Register check** as a class. Concept check by saying words from the box and asking Ss if the words are formal (to use at work) or informal (to use with friends and family.)

Answers
1 David is eight. Emily is ten.
2 Liz and her grandmother/grandma.

2 VOCABULARY: Family; numbers

A 🔊 **1.17 Present the vocabulary** Play the audio. Pause after each word and ask the class to repeat. Ask individual Ss to repeat again.

🔊 **1.17 Audio script**
grandmother, grandfather, grandparents, husband, wife, father, mother, uncle, aunt, parents, son, daughter, children, brother, sister, cousin

B Individually, Ss complete the descriptions, then share their answers with the class. Help Ss read aloud the equations as complete sentences when you elicit answers.

Answers
1 John 2 Paul 3 Kyle 4 Marcus 5 Tim

VOCABULARY SUPPORT Many languages distinguish between the father's or mother's side of the family for uncles, aunts, and cousins. Explain that English has just one name that covers both.

VOCABULARY SUPPORT Point out the silent letters in *aunt, cousin,* and *daughter*. Encourage Ss to be aware that we don't always say all the letters in English.

C 🔊 **1.18** Before Ss start, make them aware of plural forms in English. On the board, write: *brother = 1* and *brothers = 2+*. Write more examples and ask Ss to make the plurals, e.g., *mother – mothers, husband – husbands*.

- With a partner, Ss complete the chart.
- Play the audio as Ss check their answers.
- Play the audio again and ask Ss to repeat the words.

Answers
1 cousin 2 children 3 wife

VOCABULARY SUPPORT Many English irregular plurals are common words.
wife – wives   child – children   man – men

D **PAIR WORK** For an added challenge, encourage Ss to invent personal details about the people in the family, such as what they do for work. For example, *Lisa is the aunt of Liz. She is a teacher.* For lower level Ss, provide sentence frames, e.g., *Marcus and Tim are _____*.

T-12

E 🔊 **1.19** **Introduce the task** Books closed. Write or display a selection of numbers from 11–100.
- Point to each number. Ss say the numbers together.
- Monitor as Ss write the numbers. Ss then check their answers with each other.
- Play the audio. Pause to write the numbers on the board, allowing Ss to correct their own work.

> **Answers**
> 11, 12, 13, 14, 15, 16, 17, 18, 19, 20, 21, 22, 30, 40, 50, 60, 70, 80, 90, 100

F Direct Ss to pages 141–142 to complete the vocabulary exercises. Teacher's tips for vocabulary exercises are on page T-141.

> **MIXED ABILITY**
> By pronouncing words together as a group and not individually, weaker Ss feel supported and more able Ss can take a lead. Individual SS do need to be asked to produce answers, but not every time.

3 GRAMMAR: *is / are* in statements and *yes/no* questions

Introduce the lesson Show Ss a picture of a family. Say who the people are, e.g., *This is my brother. He's 22.* Write: *Yes, he is.* and *No, he isn't.* Ask questions to elicit short answers, e.g., *Is he my sister?* to elicit *No, he isn't.*

A **Introduce the task** Before Ss circle the answers, explain that they can refer to the examples in the grammar box.
- Go back to the picture from the **Introduce the lesson** section. Review the questions. Add *we* questions like *Are we American?* or *Are we English?* to elicit short answers.
- **Do the task** Ss circle the answers. Review the answers as a class.

> **Answers**
> 1 is 2 are

B Ss complete the sentences individually before sharing their answers with their partner.

> **Answers**
> 1 is, She's   2A Are, 2B they are   3 is, He's
> 4A Is, 4B she is   5 are

C Model the sample answer with a volunteer. Ask Ss to match the sentences and the answers individually before they check with a partner. As you elicit answers, make sure Ss read the complete sentences and answer.

> **Answers**
> 1 b 2 d 3 c 4 a

D Direct Ss to page 130 to complete the grammar exercise. Teacher's tips for grammar exercises are on page T-129.

> 📎 **EXTRA ACTIVITY**
> Dictate the following sentences. Change them if necessary to make them more relevant to your Ss.
> *Are you [Argentinian]?*
> *Is your [sister] English?*
> *Are we Spanish?*
> Elicit answers and write or display the correct sentences on the board. Ask Ss to discuss the questions with a partner. Elicit answers asking many Ss the same question.

4 SPEAKING

A **PAIR WORK** Before Ss begin, draw a simple example of your own family tree on the board. Identify the members and say *This is [my father]*, etc.
- **OPTIONAL ACTIVITY** Watch Julieth's video. Answer any questions Ss may have about the vocabulary. Elicit the answer to *Who does Julieth talk about?* Then ask: *Is your family the same or different?* Have Ss discuss in pairs.

> **REAL STUDENT**
> Here's my family tree. So here are my sisters, Camila and Jessica. She is 23 and she is 21. Here are my mom and my dad. She is Yamile and he is Luis. And here are my grandparents. So she is Bertha, here is José Antonio, and here is Lucila and here is [inaudible]. And that's my basic family tree.

> **Answers**
> Answers may vary.

- Ask Ss to draw their own family tree and allow them time to do this.
- When most Ss have finished, ask Ss to come back together as a class. Model the sample dialogue. Now Ss share their family tree with a partner. They can use their OBJs to display any pictures of their family they may be happy to share.

B **GROUP WORK** Ask Ss to work in groups of three or four. Explain they are going to share pictures and ask and answer questions about their families. You could model this by telling Ss about your own family again.
- As Ss work, circulate while listening for examples of pronunciation or grammar. Give feedback at the end of the activity.

T-13

E 🔊 1.19 Write the numbers. Then listen and repeat.

11 eleven ___ sixteen 21 twenty-one ___ sixty
12 twelve ___ seventeen 22 twenty-two ___ seventy
13 thirteen ___ eighteen 30 thirty ___ eighty
___ fourteen ___ nineteen ___ forty ___ ninety
___ fifteen 20 twenty ___ fifty 100 one hundred

F ▸ Now do the vocabulary exercises for 2.1 on page 141.

3 GRAMMAR: *is / are* in statements and *yes/no* questions

A **Circle** the correct answers. Use the sentences in the grammar box to help you.
1 Use *is / are* with *he* and *she*.
2 Use *is / are* with *we*, *you*, and *they*.

> **is / are in statements and yes/no questions**
>
> **Are** your children here?
>   Yes, they **are**.
> He**'s** my son (*'s = is*). He**'s** eight.
> She**'s** my daughter. She**'s ten**.
>
> **Is** he your husband?
>   No, he**'s** my brother Marcus.
> **Are** you both Elizabeth?
>   Yes, we **are**.

B **Complete the sentences.**
1 This _____ my sister. _____ 23.
2 A _____ your parents Colombian? B Yes, _____ _____.
3 This _____ my grandfather. _____ 88.
4 A _____ your mother at home? B Yes, _____ _____.
5 We _____ Russian. We live in Moscow.

C **Match the questions with the answers. Then answer the questions so they're true for you.**
1 Are your parents American? _b_
2 Are you 21? ___
3 Is your best friend in class? ___
4 Is your teacher Canadian? ___

a Yes. She's from Toronto.
b No. They're Colombian.
c No, he's at work.
d Yes, I am.

D ▸ Now go to page 129. Look at the grammar chart and do the grammar exercise for 2.1.

4 SPEAKING

A **PAIR WORK** Draw a simple family tree. Then talk to a partner about people in your family. Ask and answer questions. For ideas, watch Julieth.

> This is Marcos. He's from Mexico City. He's 25.

> Is he your brother?

REAL STUDENT
Who does Julieth talk about? Is your family tree the same or different?

B **GROUP WORK** Tell your group about three people from your family tree. You can show pictures of the people on your phone.

FIND IT

13

2.2 THEY'RE REALLY FUNNY!

LESSON OBJECTIVE
- describe friends and family

1 LANGUAGE IN CONTEXT

A Read the messages. Where is Lara from? Where is she now? Who are the other people in the pictures?

B Read the messages again. Find the numbers in the messages. What are they?

> four   12   19   24   85

Four days with my family

Hi! I'm Lara. I'm 24. I live with my family in Texas, but we're not in Texas now. We're with Grandma Vera at her home in Miami ☀ Here's a picture of me … and here are pictures of my family 😍

Look at my mom and dad. My parents are both 50 – not **old**, and not **young**! My mom is **short** and my dad is **tall**. They're not **boring**! They're both really **funny**.

This is Erika. She's my sister – and she's my best friend! ❤ She's 19. She's a student, and she's very **smart**. She's **shy**, but she's **friendly**, too.

This is Justin. He's my brother. He's funny. 😂 He's young (12), but he's not short – he's really tall.

This is my grandmother, Grandma Vera. She's old (85!), and she's very **interesting**. She's a good grandma! ❤

2 VOCABULARY: Describing people; really / very

A 🔊 **1.20** Listen and repeat the adjectives below. Then find them in the messages. Match the adjectives to the people.

Age	Appearance	Personality		
old	short	boring	funny	shy
young	tall	friendly	interesting	smart

B (Circle) *really* and *very* in the messages. Do they make the adjectives stronger (++) or weaker (--)?

14

2.2 THEY'RE REALLY FUNNY!

LESSON OBJECTIVE
- describe friends and family

Introduce the lesson Display or draw a picture (or find one from the internet) of one of your friends, real or imaginary. Tell your Ss about him or her: *This is my friend [Ramon]. He's [44]. He's [a salesperson].* Elicit more questions from Ss, e.g., *Is he American?* Answer using short answers.

1 LANGUAGE IN CONTEXT

A Do the task Ss read the texts individually, then share their answers with a partner. Elicit answers from the class.

> **Answers**
> Lara is from Texas. She's in Miami now. The pictures show her mom and dad, her sister and brother, and her grandmother/grandma.

B As Ss read again, ask them to circle the numbers. Ss share with a partner what the numbers represent. Then elicit answers.

> **Answers**
> four: The family is in Miami for four days.
> 19: Her sister Erika is 19.
> 24: Lara is 24.
> 12: Her brother Justin is 12.
> 85: Her grandmother Vera is 85.

- Ask Ss to read the messages aloud in pairs. Monitor and listen for any errors in pronunciation. Give feedback.

2 VOCABULARY: Describing people; *really / very*

Introduce the task Refer to the picture you displayed at the beginning of the session. Tell your Ss about the person again. Write the lesson adjectives on the board. If necessary, explain adjectives, e.g., *He's [interesting]. He's not [short].*

A 🔊 1.20 Present the vocabulary Say the adjectives and ask Ss to repeat them aloud after you. Ss find the adjectives individually before you check as a class. Play the audio while Ss read. Play audio again, pausing after each word for Ss to repeat.

> **Answers**
> Mom: short
> Dad: tall
> Mom and dad: really funny, not boring
> Erika: very smart, shy, friendly
> Justin: funny, young, tall
> Vera: old, interesting

B Review Ss circle the words in the messages. Elicit answers.

> **Answers**
> *Really* and *very* make the adjectives stronger.

T-14

C Ss circle the correct words individually before sharing their answers with a partner. Elicit answers from the class.

> **Answers**
> 1 tall   2 interesting   3 old   4 smart   5 funny   6 friendly

D Direct Ss to page 142 to complete the vocabulary exercises. Teacher's tips for vocabulary exercises are on page T-141.

3 GRAMMAR: *is not / are not*

Introduce the grammar Say: *I'm [American]. I'm not [Mexican]*. Point to a S and ask them to repeat using their information. Say: *We're [funny], we're not [old]*. and ask Ss to repeat. Repeat with other words like *short, rich, Spanish*, etc.

A **Present the grammar** Before Ss circle the answers, explain that they can refer to the examples in the grammar box.
- Remind Ss that contracted forms have the same meaning as long forms and are common in spoken English.
- Ss circle the correct answers individually, then check answers as a class.

> **Answers**
> 1 's not   2 're not

- Read the **Notice** box with Ss. Check understanding by writing gapped sentences on the board. In pairs, Ss fill in the negative form.
  Simon ____ interesting.
  She ____ boring.
  Maria and Jose ___ from Argentina.
  We ____ old.

> ### 📎 EXTRA ACTIVITY
> Say long forms in sentences and ask Ss to repeat the sentences using the short form, e.g.,
>   He is not from the United States. = <u>He's</u> not from the United States.
>   She is Mexican.
>   He is not from London.
>   They are not boring.
>   We are interesting.

B Ss complete the sentences individually before checking their answers with a partner and then with the class.

> **Answers**
> 1 He's not   2 She's not   3 We're   4 She's not   5 They're   6 You're not

C Direct Ss to page 130 to complete the grammar exercise. Teacher's tips for grammar exercises are on page T-129.

D **PAIR WORK** **Do the task** Before Ss begin, show a picture of a friend and write or display two true and two false sentences on the board about them, e.g., *She's funny. / She's not boring. / She's a teacher. / She's not from London*. Ask Ss to decide which sentences are not true.
- Role play the model conversation with a volunteer.
- Ss now write sentences about their own friend. As Ss write, circulate around the classroom. Check that Ss are on task and offer corrections.
- Ss share their information with a partner before you elicit examples from volunteers. Listen for language usage that you can review with Ss at the end of the activity. Give feedback.

4 SPEAKING

A **Review** Model the task by writing the name of a member of your family on the board. Add some adjectives under the name, e.g., *happy, beautiful, funny*. Allow Ss some time to write their lists.

> **Answers**
> Answers may vary.

- **OPTIONAL ACTIVITY** Ss watch the video. Ask Ss: *Are your family or friends the same as Larissa's?* Have Ss compare notes in pairs. You may want to explain the meaning of *best friend* and *a little bit* [adj].

> **REAL STUDENT**
> Hello, my name is Larissa. I have two best friends. My first best friend: She is very friendly, she is interesting to meet, and she is very smart. My second best friend: He is a little bit shy and he is funny.

B **GROUP WORK** Ask a volunteer to share their information with you and write it on the board. Ask them for more information and write these sentences on the board as you say them.
  How old is [she]?
  Where is [she] from?
  Which city is [she] from?
- Put Ss in groups. Monitor as they talk. Listen for errors in grammar and pronunciation that you can correct with Ss when the activity is over.

C Circle the correct word to complete the sentences.

1 A Is he short?
   B No, he's not. He's *tall / shy*.
2 A Is she boring?
   B No! She's really *short / interesting*.
3 A How old is your grandmother?
   B She's 90. She's very *young / old*.
4 A Is Mi-jin a college student?
   B Yes. She's really *smart / short*.
5 A Is your cousin interesting?
   B Yes, and he's *boring / funny*.
6 A Are your children shy?
   B No, they're very *friendly / interesting*.

D ▶ Now do the vocabulary exercises for 2.2 on page 142.

3 GRAMMAR: *is not / are not*

A Circle the correct answers. Use the sentences in the grammar box and the Notice box to help you.
   1 For negative (–) statements with *he* and *she*, use *'s not / 're not*.
   2 For negative statements with *we*, *you*, and *they*, use *'s not / 're not*.

is not (= 's not) / are not (= 're not)	
He**'s not** short.	They**'re not** boring!
She**'s not** from Miami.	We**'re not** in Texas.
Erika **isn't** old.	My parents **aren't** from Miami.

! After pronouns (*he, she, we, you, they*), use *'s not* and *'re not*.
   She**'s not** tall.
   You**'re not** from South Korea.
   After nouns (people, places, and things), use *isn't* and *aren't*.
   Filip **isn't** American.
   My friends **aren't** boring.

B Complete the sentences with a subject (*he, she, you, we, they*) and an affirmative (+) or negative (–) verb.
   1 ___He's not___ old. He's young.
   2 She's friendly and really funny. _____ shy.
   3 _____ from Brazil. We're not from Argentina.
   4 _____ Juliana. She's Camila.
   5 _____ my cousins. They're not my brothers.
   6 _____ American. You're Canadian.

C ▶ Now go to page 130. Look at the grammar charts and do the grammar exercise for 2.2.

D [PAIR WORK] Write two true sentences and two false sentences about a friend or a person in your class. Then exchange sentences with a partner. Correct the false sentences.

   My friend Carina is not tall. She's very funny. She's from Japan. She's smart.

   She is very funny, and she's smart. She's tall, and she's not from Japan.

   Correct!

4 SPEAKING

A Choose four people, for example, family or friends. Write adjectives to describe them. For ideas, watch Larissa.

B [GROUP WORK] Talk about your people. You can show pictures on your phone. Ask for more information about people, for example, age, nationality, and city.

REAL STUDENT
Are your family or friends the same as Larissa's?

15

2.3 WHEN IS YOUR BIRTHDAY?

LESSON OBJECTIVE
- talk about ages and birthdays

1 FUNCTIONAL LANGUAGE

A 🔊 1.21 Read and listen. How many parties does Vivian talk about?

1.21 Audio script

Lucas	This is a really great picture!
Vivian	Oh, thanks.
Lucas	Are they your children?
Vivian	Yes. This is Miranda. **She's eight.**
Lucas	Miranda. Nice name.
Vivian	And this is Carlos.
Lucas	How old is he?
Vivian	He's three years old.
Lucas	When's his birthday?
Vivian	It's March 28. **His party is on March 29.**
Lucas	Oh, right. He's four this month!
Vivian	Yeah. And **Miranda's birthday is April 2.**
Lucas	So two birthday parties in five days.
Vivian	Yeah, two parties. No, sorry, three parties! One party for Carlos, one party for Miranda, and then one party with the family.
Lucas	Well, say "**Happy birthday!**" from me!

B Complete the chart with expressions in **bold** from the conversation above.

Asking about ages and birthdays	Saying ages and birthdays	Giving birthday wishes
1 _____ old is he?	She 3 ___ eight.	6 _____ birthday!
When's your birthday?	He's three 4 _____ old.	
2 _____ 's his birthday? 🚹	His party is 5 _____ March 29.	
When's her birthday? 🚺	Miranda's birthday is April 2.	

2 VOCABULARY: Saying dates

A 🔊 1.22 Look at the chart. Listen and repeat the months. What month is your birthday month?

Months					
January	February	March	April	May	June
July	August	September	October	November	December

Dates			
1 first	7 seventh	13 thirteenth	19 nineteenth
2 second	8 eighth	14 fourteenth	20 twentieth
3 third	9 ninth	15 fifteenth	21 twenty-first
4 fourth	10 tenth	16 sixteenth	22 twenty-second
5 fifth	11 eleventh	17 seventeenth	30 thirtieth
6 sixth	12 twelfth	18 eighteenth	31 thirty-first

B 🔊 1.23 PAIR WORK Now listen and repeat the dates. Then say the date of your birthday.

> My birthday is February eighth.

2.3 WHEN IS YOUR BIRTHDAY?

LESSON OBJECTIVE
- talk about ages and birthdays

TEACHER DEVELOPMENT ACTIVITY 2

Word puzzles

When presenting new vocabulary to Ss, we can use simple puzzles to engage Ss' interest, give them a chance to show what they already know, and help make language more memorable.

- After exercise 1B, Ss close their books.
- Option 1: Ordering. Put the names of the twelve months on the board, but in random order. Ss try to put the months in the correct order.
- Option 2: Gapped words. Put the months on the board in order, but with letters missing, e.g., just the first letter (J…), just the first and last letters (J…y), or just the consonants (Jnry). Ss add the missing letters to complete the words.
- Option 3: Anagrams. Put the months on the board in order, but with the letters scrambled, e.g., AAJNRUY. Ss put the letters in the right order to spell the words.
- To check their answers, Ss look at the table on page 16. Then they listen to the months and repeat.

Introduce the lesson Display a picture of a family; it could be your own. Point to the people and say: *This is [my dad]. [He's 56]. [His] birthday is [June 21]*. Repeat for the other people in the photo.

1 FUNCTIONAL LANGUAGE

A 🔊 **1.21** **Play the audio as Ss read and listen. Elicit the answer, and play the audio again if needed.**

> **Answer**
> Vivian talks about three parties.

B **Ask Ss to complete the chart in pairs before you elicit the answers.**

- Ask Ss to practice saying the expressions with their partner. Monitor for pronunciation.
- Drill Ss by asking individuals to read the expressions. Monitor and check for pronunciation.

> **Answers**
> **Asking about ages and birthdays**
> 1 <u>How</u> old is he?
> 2 <u>When</u>'s his birthday?
> **Saying ages and birthdays**
> 3 She<u>'s</u> eight.
> 4 He's three <u>years</u> old.
> 5 His party is <u>on</u> March 29.
> **Giving birthday wishes**
> 6 <u>Happy</u> birthday!

2 VOCABULARY: Saying dates

A 🔊 **1.22** **Present the vocabulary** **Play the audio while Ss read. Play the audio again, pause after each word, and ask Ss to repeat as a group. Check pronunciation by asking individual Ss to say each word again.**

> **VOCABULARY SUPPORT** English uses ordinals to say the date. Ss often forget to add the *th*, *st*, and *nd*. Here's the format for saying dates in English:
> *January first / March twenty-second*
> Point out that ordinals are not used in writing. Write on the board:
>
> | Read/Write | > | Say |
> |---|---|---|
> | January 1 | > | January first |
> | March 22 | > | March twenty-second |

B 🔊 **1.23** **PAIR WORK** **Play the audio up to *sixth*. Ask Ss to repeat the items they hear.**

- Continue playing to *twelfth* and ask Ss to repeat. Do the same to *eighteenth* and then to *thirty-first*. Demonstrating the words in chunks makes it easier for Ss to remember them.
- Ss now exchange birthdays in pairs.

T-16

C **PAIR WORK** Write or display your own birthday on the board and model how to say it.
- Ss complete the activity individually, then practice with a partner. Monitor for pronunciation of ordinals and months. Give feedback at the end.

> **EXTRA ACTIVITY**
>
> **Play calendar games.** Print out or ask Ss to draw a calendar.
>
> **Play traditional bingo.** Ss cross off the days as you or a volunteer says them. For details on how to play bingo, see page 219.
>
> **Ask Ss to write the numbers 1–10** on paper. Call out *Number 1: the 27th is a Monday,* and Ss use the calendar to decide if this is true or false. Continue with questions 2–10.

3 REAL-WORLD STRATEGY

A 🔊 **1.24 Introduce the task** Before you play the audio, ask Ss to read and check that they understand the sentences. Play the audio. Repeat if necessary. Elicit answers.

> **Answers**
> 1 The conversation is about a <u>child</u>.
> 2 The man says an <u>age</u>.

> 🔊 **1.24 Audio script**
>
> A How old is your daughter?
> B She's thirty. No, sorry, thirteen!
> A Thirteen. OK!

B 🔊 **1.24** Play the audio as many times as Ss need. Elicit answers.

> **Answers**
> First he says "30." Then he says "13."

C **Do the task** Read the **Correcting Yourself** box with Ss. Elicit answers as a class.

> **Answer**
> He says "No, sorry, thirteen."

- Model correcting yourself by saying your birthday wrong and using *No, sorry …* or *I mean …* Ask Ss to work in pairs. They give the wrong information and then correct themselves using the phrases.

D **PAIR WORK** **Review** Put Ss into pairs and assign each one to be either Student A or Student B. Ask Student As to turn to page 156 and Student Bs to turn to page 159.
- Read through the instructions aloud. Ask a volunteer Student A to read the sentences in the speech bubbles.

Say more example sentences with the wrong date and then correct yourself, e.g., *Pedro. His birthday is May 16. No, sorry, it's May 6.*
- Monitor as Ss complete the task.

4 PRONUNCIATION: Saying numbers

A 🔊 **1.25** Ask Ss to look at the underlining in the example. Tell them that here, stress shows the difference between similar-sounding words.
- Play the audio and have the class repeat, paying attention to the different stress patterns.
- Play the audio again. Ss underline the stress in each word. Check answers as a whole class.

> **Answers**
> 13 thir<u>teen</u> / 30 <u>thir</u>ty   14 four<u>teen</u> / 40 <u>for</u>ty
> 15 fif<u>teen</u> / 50 <u>fif</u>ty   16 six<u>teen</u> / 60 <u>six</u>ty
> 17 seven<u>teen</u> / 70 <u>sev</u>enty 18 eigh<u>teen</u> / 80 <u>eigh</u>ty
> 19 nine<u>teen</u> / 90 <u>nine</u>ty

B **PAIR WORK** Model the activity. Say a number from the chart and ask a student to point to it. Then change roles.
- Ss work in pairs to complete the activity. Monitor and provide help when needed.

5 SPEAKING

A **PAIR WORK** **Introduce the task** Allow time for Ss to work individually to match the conversations. Circulate and offer to help as needed.
- When finished, elicit the answers from volunteers. Then, ask Ss to practice the exchanges with a partner. Check for meaning by asking individual Ss to answer the same question.

> **Answers**
> 1 d   2 c   3 b   4 a

B **PAIR WORK** **Do the task** Ss complete the task in pairs. Circulate and monitor to keep Ss on task. Listen for errors you can discuss at the end of the activity.

> **EXTRA ACTIVITY**
>
> **Play bingo** after doing exercise 4. For details on how to do this, see page 219. Ask S volunteers to act as the bingo callers for variation.
>
> **Play true or false** after exercise 5. Ss stand up and say their date of birth, e.g., *August seventh.* Other Ss decide if the birthday is true or false.
>
> Alternatively, write the names of famous people on the board (with a picture, if possible) and their birth dates. Students guess which are true and false.

T-17

C **PAIR WORK** Imagine the dates below are your birthday. Work with a partner. Ask questions and say the birthdays.

1 May 8
2 November 23
3 August 31
4 April 19
5 January 25
6 June 4

> When's your birthday?
>
> It's May eighth.

3 REAL-WORLD STRATEGY

A 🔊 1.24 Listen to a conversation. Circle the correct answers.
1 The conversation is about a *wife / child*.
2 The man says an *age / birthday*.

B 🔊 1.24 Listen again. What number does the man say first? Then what correct number does he say?

CORRECTING YOURSELF
To correct yourself, say *No, sorry* or *Sorry, I mean …* and say the correct word.
He's twenty. No, sorry, twenty-one.
It's March twenty-first. Sorry, I mean May twenty-first.

C Read the information in the box above about correcting yourself. What does the man say?

D **PAIR WORK** Student A: Go to page 156. Student B: Go to page 159. Follow the instructions.

4 PRONUNCIATION: Saying numbers

A 🔊 1.25 Listen and repeat the numbers. Then listen again and underline the stress.

13 thir**teen** / 30 **thir**ty
14 fourteen / 40 forty
15 fifteen / 50 fifty
16 sixteen / 60 sixty
17 seventeen / 70 seventy
18 eighteen / 80 eighty
19 nineteen / 90 ninety

B **PAIR WORK** Look at the numbers in the chart. Student A says a number. Student B points to the number. Then change roles.

| 13 | 80 | 40 | 18 | 30 | 60 | 19 |
| 70 | 15 | 17 | 50 | 90 | 14 | 16 |

5 SPEAKING

A **PAIR WORK** Match sentences 1–4 to sentences a–d. Then practice with a partner.
1 How old is your brother? ___
2 When's your birthday? ___
3 My brother is 30 today. ___
4 It's my birthday today. ___

a Happy birthday!
b Say "Happy birthday!" from me.
c It's June 18.
d He's 23.

B **PAIR WORK** Say the name of a friend, then say his/her birthday. Make underline{one} mistake. Then correct yourself.

> My friend Julia. Her birthday is June fifth. No, sorry, June sixth.

2.4 HERE'S MY BAND

LESSON OBJECTIVE
- write a post about friends in a photo

1 LISTENING

A **PAIR WORK** Talk to a partner. Say what you see in the picture on page 19.

B 🔊 1.26 **LISTEN FOR GIST** Listen to Isabel talk to a friend, Linda. What do they talk about?

C 🔊 1.26 **LISTEN FOR DETAILS** Listen again. (Circle) the words that Isabel uses to describe the people.

> boring   cool   friendly   funny   interesting   shy   smart

2 GRAMMAR: Prepositions of place

A Look at the picture on page 19 and complete the sentences with the words in the box.

> between   in   ~~in~~   next to   on the left

1 We're not ____in____ Las Vegas! We're _____ Seattle, at college.
2 This is Joshua, on the right. And this is Nuwa, _____.
3 I'm Isabel. Guy is _____ me.
4 Guy is _____ Nuwa and me.

3 PRONUNCIATION: Listening for short forms

A 🔊 1.27 Listen. Write the words you hear. Then write the full forms.

1 ____Here's____ my band. = ____Here is____   3 _____ really funny. = _____
2 _____ in Seattle. = _____   4 _____ great! = _____

B 🔊 1.28 Complete the conversation with the words in the box. Listen and check.

> I'm   It's   She's   What's   When's

1 Nice to meet you, Sara. _____ Elizabeth.
2 A _____ your birthday?
   B _____ March 14.
3 This is Nuwa. _____ really smart.
4 _____ your name?

18

2.4 HERE'S MY BAND

LESSON OBJECTIVE
- write a post about friends in a photo

Introduce the lesson Display or draw a picture of your own friends or use a picture of a famous family from the internet that your Ss will know. Explain to Ss who they are. Use some of the target adjectives in this unit to describe them. *This is [Jo]. She's [funny].*

1 LISTENING

A PAIR WORK Ss discuss what they see with several partners. What more do they see?

> **Suggested answers**
> Two women, two men, four friends, a band, young people

B 🔊 1.26 Review by explaining to Ss to listen for gist and what that means. (Gist means the general topic of the conversation.) Ask Ss to close their books. Play the audio.

> **Answer**
> They talk about Isabel's college band.

> 🔊 **1.26 Audio script**
>
> **Isabel** So, Linda – here's my band!
> **Linda**   Wow! Are you good?
> **Isabel** No! Well, we're not *bad*.
> **Linda**   And where are you in this photo?
> **Isabel** We're not in Las Vegas! We're in Seattle, at college.
> **Linda**   Are they your friends from college?
> **Isabel** Yeah. This is Joshua, on the right.
> **Linda**   Yeah?
> **Isabel** He's really funny.
> **Linda**   Great! And this is … ?
> **Isabel** This is Nuwa, on the left.
> **Linda**   OK.
> **Isabel** She's really smart. And I'm here, and Guy is next to me. He's between Nuwa and me.
> **Linda**   Sorry, what's his name?
> **Isabel** Guy. He's really cool … but he's shy.
> **Linda**   He's a shy Guy!
> **Isabel** Yeah!

C 🔊 1.26 Review by explaining to Ss what details are (here: descriptions of a person, where they're standing). Play the audio again while Ss circle the answers. Play again if necessary. Elicit answers.

> **Answers**
> cool, funny, shy, smart, shy

VOCABULARY SUPPORT Check Ss' understanding of prepositions by drawing (or displaying) simple balls on the board. Shade one to illustrate the preposition, e.g.,

For *in*, put the shaded ball inside another.

2 GRAMMAR: Prepositions of place

A **Introduce the grammar** Ss do the task individually before sharing their answers with a partner.

> **Answers**
> 1 *in*, in   2 on the left   3 next to   4 between

3 PRONUNCIATION: Listening for short forms

A 🔊 1.27 Demonstrate by writing *I'__* on the board. Say *I'm* and elicit the word that's contracted: *am*. Tell Ss that this is a short form and they are common in English.
- Play the audio and ask Ss to write the words.

> **Answers**
> 1 Here's, Here is   2 We're, We are   3 He's, He is
> 4 You're, You are

B 🔊 1.28 Ss look at the words in the box and guess the answers.
- Play the audio and tell Ss to check their ideas.

> **Answers**
> 1 I'm   2A When's   2B It's   3 She's   4 What's

> 📱 **SMARTPHONE ACTIVITY**
>
> After exercise 1, ask Ss to share a picture of their friends on their smartphone with a partner and describe them. Circulate as Ss explain. Monitor and check for errors.

T-18

4 WRITING

A **Introduce the task** Allow Ss time to read the post individually. Encourage them to ask you or their partner about any words they don't know. Elicit answers.

> **Answers**
> Joshua – 22, Isabel – 20, Nuwa – 21, Guy – 20

B **PAIR WORK** Ss answer the questions in pairs. While they discuss, circulate and monitor. If your class is less confident, you may want to do this activity as a whole group.

> **Suggested answers**
> The band's name is the first letter of each member's names. It's an interesting name. It's easy to remember.

C Read the rules for Ss. Tell Ss to underline *and* in the example sentences and identify what it connects. Then elicit answers.

> **Answers**
> 1 b 2 a

D To model the activity, work as a class to underline *and* in the first sentence of the text. Ask: *Does and connect words or sentences?* Elicit answer. Then allow Ss time to read and underline other examples in the text.

> **Answers**
> **To connect words**
> He's really friendly <u>and</u> funny.
> She's very interesting <u>and</u> smart.
> Guy is between Nuwa <u>and</u> me.
> **To connect sentences**
> We're four students at college in Seattle, <u>and</u> we're in a band.
> He's 22, <u>and</u> he's from Chicago.
> I'm 20, <u>and</u> I'm the "I" in the band name.
> She's Chinese, <u>and</u> she's here for school.
> He's 20, <u>and</u> he's the "G."

> ### 📎 EXTRA ACTIVITY
> Write or display the following sentences on the board. Ask Ss to work in pairs to add the word *and* to each one.
> *I live with my brother [and] my sister.*
> *I like soccer [and] I like basketball.*
> *They are interesting [and] smart.*
> Alternatively, use other example sentences with *and* from the book.

E **FIND IT** Ask Ss who don't have photos on their phones to bring in a photo ahead of time. Alternatively, bring in magazine photos or print pictures from the internet for Ss to use. You could also ask Ss to draw a very basic sketch of themselves with three of four friends.

- Tell Ss not to write. They spend a few minutes thinking of the information they will put in their description.
- Ask Ss questions individually: *Who is in the picture? Where are you?* This will give Ss more to write about in the next part of the lesson. Ask: *Who is next to him?* to encourage them to practice using prepositions.
- Allow Ss time to write their descriptions. Circulate and answer questions. Assist Ss with spelling by writing challenging words on the board. This will allow all Ss to see the word and use it if they wish.
- If possible, correct Ss' work individually when they finish. Ask Ss to share their photo and description with a partner.
- Next, encourage Ss to circulate around the room and share their work with other members of the class. Monitor as students look at and read each other's work.
- Ask a volunteer to display their photo and read their description to the whole class. Encourage any questions the class might have about the photo or post.
- Read the **Accuracy check** box as a class. Write the following sentences on the board.
  1 Cindy is between John and I.
  2 Peter is on the left, next to I.
- Ss correct in pairs before you elicit answers as a class.

T-19

4 WRITING

A   Read the post. How old are the students?

SOCIALHUB

JING
September 12 at 2:24pm

We're four college students in Seattle, and we're in a band. The name of the band is *JING*. Joshua is on the right. He's 22, and he's from Chicago. He's really friendly and funny. The first letter in *JING* is for Joshua. I'm Isabel. I'm 20, and I'm the "I" in the band name. I'm next to Joshua. Nuwa is on the left. She's 21. She's Chinese, and she's here for school. She's very interesting and smart. She's the "N." Guy is between Nuwa and me. He's 20, and he's the "G." He's shy, so he's the last letter in the name!

Nuwa Guy Isabel Joshua

👍 Like   💬 Comment   ➤ Share

👍 35   ❤ 35

B   **PAIR WORK** **THINK CRITICALLY** Why is the name of the band "JING"? Is it a good name?

C   **WRITING SKILLS** Read about two ways to use *and*. Match them (1–2) to the correct example sentence (a–b).
1   Use *and* to connect words. ___
2   Use *and* to connect two sentences and make one long sentence. ___

a   We're four college students in Seattle, and we're in a band.
b   She's very interesting and smart.

D   Read the post again and underline examples of *and*. Does *and* connect words or sentences?

WRITE IT

E   Choose a picture of you with three or four people. Write a post about the picture. Say where you are (*in* + city/country). Say where people are in the picture (*next to, on the left/right, between*). Give information about the people. Use *and* to connect words and sentences. Then check your accuracy.

ACCURACY CHECK

After prepositions, use *me*, not *I*.
Guy is next to I. ✗
Guy is next to me. ✓
He's between Nuwa and I. ✗
He's between Nuwa and me. ✓

Seattle

19

2.5 TIME TO SPEAK
True for me

LESSON OBJECTIVE
- compare information about friends and family

A Which family members are in the picture? Compare your ideas with a partner.

B **PREPARE** Complete the sentences so they're true for you.
1. My mom is _____ (nationality).
2. My dad is _____ (age).
3. My grandmother is _____ (name).
4. My grandfather is from _____ (city).
5. My best friend is _____ (personality).
6. My birthday is in _____ (month).

C **DISCUSS** Say your answers from exercise B. Your partner says "True for me" or "Not true for me." Then change roles.

> My mom is Brazilian.
> Not true for me.
> My dad is 50.
> True for me.

D Read the instructions. Then talk to people in your class.

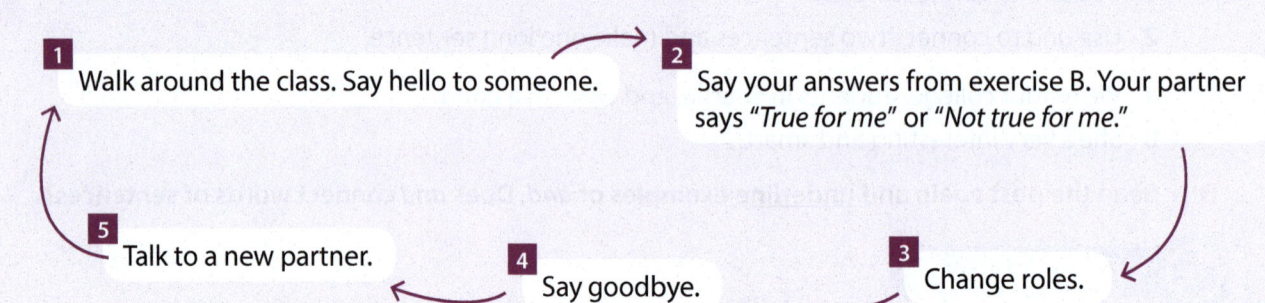

1. Walk around the class. Say hello to someone.
2. Say your answers from exercise B. Your partner says "True for me" or "Not true for me."
3. Change roles.
4. Say goodbye.
5. Talk to a new partner.

E **PRESENT** Who has the same answers? Who has different answers? Tell the class.

To check your progress, go to page 152.

USEFUL PHRASES

DISCUSS
Hello./Hi.
True for me.
Really? (for surprise)
My name is …
Not true for me.
Goodbye.

PRESENT
(Name) is the same.
(Name) is different.

2.5 TIME TO SPEAK
True for me

LESSON OBJECTIVE
- compare information about friends and family

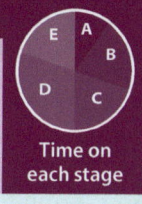

Time on each stage

Introduce the lesson Write on the board *My dad is [American]. My brother is [23]. My birthday is in [June]* or something similar. Ask Ss to write three sentences that are true about their family. Circulate and offer help. Ask Ss to share their sentences when they finish.

Direct Ss to the **Useful phrases** section at the bottom of the page. Remind them that they can use the phrases at the relevant stages of the lesson.

A **Aim: Review the vocabulary.**

- GROUP WORK   Allow Ss time to discuss the photo together in groups before you elicit answers.

> **Suggested answers**
> mother, daughter, daughter, father, grandmother, daughter, grandfather, son

B PREPARE   **Do the task** **Aim: Provide personal information.**

- INDIVIDUALLY   Ss complete the sentences.
- CLASS WORK   Ask for a volunteer to read each sentence. Monitor for pronunciation.

C DISCUSS   **Aim: Share answers.**

- PAIR WORK   Remind Ss to answer only the questions they can (e.g., some might not have grandparents). Alternatively, they could replace family members for some questions.
- **Extra speaking practice*** Ss complete the task with one partner, then repeat with another.

D **Aim: Practice using the language.**

Tell Ss to memorize their answers to exercise B so they do not have to carry their books when they mingle with various partners. You can write or display the prompts on the board.

- GROUP WORK   Ss circulate. Monitor their pronunciation. Listen for examples of language usage that you can share with Ss when they finish the activity. Give positive feedback when Ss produce accurate and appropriate language.*

E PRESENT   **Aim: Ss find out what they have in common.**

- CLASS WORK   Ss take turns reading aloud their sentences from exercise B.

- GROUP WORK   Review   Ss work in small groups and see what they remembered about each other. They ask each other *yes/no* questions to see if they are correct, e.g., *Luisa, is your father from California? Yes, he is. / No, he isn't.*

As a class, ask Ss:

> Which nationalities are the same?
> What ages are the same?
> What names are the same?
> Which cities are the same?
> What personalities are the same?
> Which months are the same?

Elicit answers as you go.

*These tips can help you to create a safe speaking environment. They can also be used with other speaking activities. For more information, see page xxii.

PROGRESS CHECK

Direct students to page 152 to check their progress. Go to page T-152 for Progress check activity suggestions.

TEACHER DEVELOPMENT REFLECTION

You can answer these questions in a reflection journal or discuss them with your peers.

1. Development Activity 1 is based on the idea that we should first convey the meaning of a word and then try to elicit the word itself from Ss. What do you see as the advantages of this approach? Why not just show Ss the completed family tree from the beginning?

2. As you went through the presentation, were the meanings clear to Ss? How many of the family words were known to Ss, and how many were new? How easy was it to create the family tree on the board? Overall, what advice would you give to a colleague who wants to use this kind of presentation?

3. Development Activity 2 offers three different puzzle activities. Which did you choose? Why? Do you think the other options would have been more, equally, or less effective?

4. In what ways did the activity benefit Ss? Why not just give Ss a list of the twelve months?

COME IN

3

TEACHER DEVELOPMENT INTRODUCTION

Strategy 3: Building learners' confidence to speak – Meaningful drilling

There are many reasons why drilling new grammar structures and expressions with students can help develop their speaking skills. It helps students to focus on the pronunciation and to remember the form. Sometimes teachers write the complete sentence or question on the board and ask students to repeat it. One problem with this is it doesn't make students think about the language the teacher drills. One way to make drilling more meaningful is by only writing word prompts on the board and drilling from these. The teacher gives an oral model and the students repeat with the prompts as support. This gets students working a little harder and it may help them remember chunks of language. You can read more about helping students remember new language on pages 91–92 of *Dialogue Activities* by Nick Bilbrough (Cambridge University Press 2007). Please go to www.cambridge.org/evolve to download these pages.

INTRODUCE THE THEME OF THE UNIT

Books closed. Show, display, or draw a picture of your house; it could be real or imaginary. Tell Ss about the house. *This is my house. It is in [Brazil]. I live here with [my family].*

UNIT OBJECTIVES

Read the unit objectives aloud. Tell Ss to read along. Explain any new vocabulary that Ss may not understand.

START SPEAKING

Read the questions as a class before Ss begin discussing with a partner. Elicit some of their ideas.

EXTRA ACTIVITY

Ask the following questions:
Where is your house?
What isn't in your house?

T-21

UNIT OBJECTIVES
- talk about your home
- talk about furniture
- offer and accept a drink and snack
- write an email about a home-share
- choose things for a home

COME IN

3

START SPEAKING

A Look at the picture. Where is this house?

B Who is in the house?

C What is in the house?

3.1 WELCOME TO MY HOME

LESSON OBJECTIVE
- talk about your home

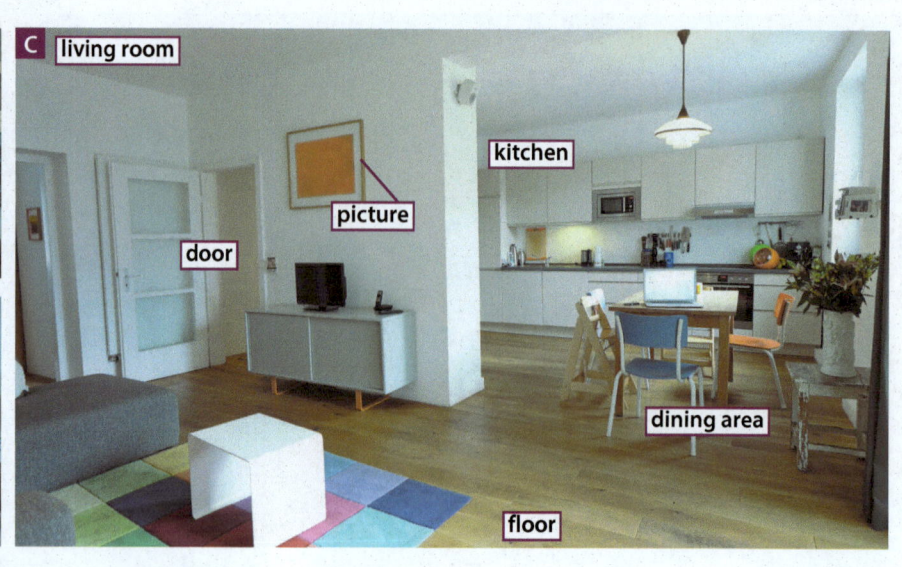

A — bedroom, wall
B — bathroom, window
C — living room, picture, door, kitchen, dining area, floor

1 VOCABULARY: Rooms in a home

A 🔊 **1.29** Listen and repeat the words in the pictures. Which words are rooms? Which words are things in rooms?

B **PAIR WORK** Talk to a partner. What's your favorite room in the pictures?

C ▶ Now do the vocabulary exercises for 3.1 on page 142.

2 LANGUAGE IN CONTEXT

A 🔊 **1.30** Alina gives a video tour of her family's home. Listen and read. How many rooms does she talk about?

a six b seven c eight

B 🔊 **1.30** Listen again. Answer the questions.
1 What is on the wall?
2 Who is in the kitchen?
3 How many bathrooms are in the apartment?
4 What are the names of the cat and the dog?

C **PAIR WORK** What are your favorite rooms? Talk to a partner. For ideas, watch Felipe's video.

Hi! Welcome to my new home. I mean, my *family's* new home. We live in an apartment, not a house. OK. First, this is the **living room**, with my mom's favorite **picture** on the **wall**. And this is the **dining area**. It's good for family dinners, or pizza with my friends. And this is the **kitchen**, through the **door**! My mom and her friend are in there now. OK, and this is the **bathroom**, the family bathroom. And here, this is my parents' **bedroom**, with a second bathroom. And this is my bedroom, with two **windows**. Oh! This is Milka. She's our cat. And this is Sergei's room. He's my brother. Hey! T-Rex is on Sergei's bed! Bad dog! On the floor! Now! T-Rex is Sergei's dog. OK, now say "hi" to the camera, T-Rex. Welcome to our apartment!

REAL STUDENT — *What are Felipe's favorite rooms? Are your favorite rooms the same?*

✓ ACCURACY CHECK

Use *the* when you talk about a specific thing in your home: *the* floor in *the* kitchen, *the* window (in my room), or *the* picture on *the* wall.

22

3.1 WELCOME TO MY HOME

LESSON OBJECTIVE
- talk about your home

Introduce the lesson Show or display famous houses from around the world or the town / city / area you are in. You can type *famous houses* into a search engine to find some pictures.
- Ask *Where is it? / What is it?*
- Suggested buildings: Palacio de la Moneda (Chile) / Palacio de Narino (Bogotá) / Imperial Palace (Beijing) / The White House (Washington DC) / Buckingham Palace (London) / St. Basil's Cathedral (Moscow)

1 VOCABULARY: Rooms in a home

A 🔊 **1.29 Introduce the task** Books open. Play the audio as Ss read. Play audio again, pausing after each word so Ss can repeat. Monitor pronunciation. Elicit answers as a class.

> **Answers**
> Rooms: bedroom, bathroom, living room, kitchen, dining area
> Things in rooms: wall, door, window, floor, picture

B **PAIR WORK** Pre-teach the word *favorite*. Ss share their answers in pairs. Elicit ideas as a class.

> **Answers**
> Answers may vary.

C Direct Ss to page 142 to complete the vocabulary exercises. Teacher's tips for vocabulary exercises are on page T-141.

2 LANGUAGE IN CONTEXT

A 🔊 **1.30** Books closed. Play the audio, then ask *What rooms do you hear?*
- **Do the task** Books open. Play the audio as Ss read. Play audio again if necessary. Ss share their answers to 2A in pairs before you elicit.

> **Answers**
> c eight

B 🔊 **1.30** Individual Ss read the questions aloud to the class. Play audio. In pairs, Ss discuss answers. Elicit Ss' responses.

> **Answers**
> 1 A picture / My mom's favorite picture
> 2 My mom and her friend / Alina's mom and her friend
> 3 Two
> 4 The cat is Milka. The dog is T-Rex.

- Prepare Ss to read the **Accuracy check**. Draw or display a picture of a room or ask Ss to look at a picture on page 22. Point to the window and say *the window*. Exaggerate *the*. Repeat with other items in the room.
- Read the **Accuracy check** as a class. Point to the same items and ask Ss what they are. Elicit *the window*, *the door*. Repeat. Write or display the following sentences and ask Ss to correct them.
  1 *Are you in the kitchen or a dining room?*
  2 *A window in my bedroom is big.*

> **Answers**
> 1 Are you in the kitchen or the dining room?
> 2 The window in my bedroom is big.

C **PAIR WORK** **Review** Model a discussion with a volunteer. Ask: *What is your favorite room?* Elicit *The [kitchen]*. Ss now ask and answer in pairs. Monitor. Listen for use of language you can share as examples later. Give feedback.
- **OPTIONAL ACTIVITY** Ss watch the video and say whether their favorite rooms are the same as Felipe.

REAL STUDENT
Hi my name is Felipe. My favorite room is the kitchen. My second favorite room is the kitchen. No, it's my living room.

FEEDBACK SUPPORT Positive feedback will greatly help Ss' motivation. Be specific about positive feedback. Say: *Good pronunciation of [room]*, or *Good – you used* the *in your sentences*.

T-22

3 GRAMMAR: Possessive adjectives; possessive 's and s'

Introduce the task Draw or display a picture of a room in a house. It could be your living room. Point to the furniture and say: *This is my [chair]. This my [son's] [TV]. These are my grandparents' [books].* Exaggerate possessive adjectives and the possessive *s*. Show or draw a picture of a different room. Ss exchange similar information about the room. Monitor.

A Introduce the grammar Before Ss circle the answers, explain that they can refer to the examples in the grammar box.

> **Answers**
> 1 possession   2 before   3 singular   4 plural

B Do the task Model the example. Ss complete the sentences individually before sharing their answers with their partner. Make sure Ss read the complete sentence to the class.

> **Answers**
> 1 your   2 their   3 John's   4 his   5 Our   6 cat's
> 7 Their   8 her

C Direct Ss to page 130 to complete the grammar exercise. Teacher's tips for grammar exercises are on page T-129.

D PAIR WORK **Review** Allow Ss time to complete the questions before sharing their answers. Elicit answers; ask Ss the same question to get a range of answers. Make sure all Ss get a chance to speak.

> **Answers**
> Answers may vary.

4 SPEAKING

A Before Ss begin, draw or display a simple, hand-drawn floor plan of your house on the board.

- Point to the rooms and say: *This is my [apartment]. This is my [living room]. This is my [brother's room].*
- Allow Ss time to draw a plan of their house or apartment.

EXTRA ACTIVITY

Don't hesitate to draw on the board. Ss do not expect your pictures to be good. Pictures are powerful ways of communicating information and activating concepts in Ss' minds.

B GROUP WORK Ss work in groups of three or four. Explain they are going to share their plans by asking each other questions. Monitor as Ss share their information.

- Circulate as Ss work. Listen for examples of pronunciation or grammar to discuss at the end of the activity. Give feedback.

TEACHER DEVELOPMENT ACTIVITY 1

Meaningful Drilling: Sentences

Before getting students to do the pair work, you can drill example sentences from prompts to give them confidence.

- Show the plan of the home on the board.
- Write the following prompts on the board: *this / apartment / is / door / this / living room / two windows*
- Tell Ss not to look at their book and elicit the following sentences from them: *This is my apartment. This is the door. And this is the living room with two windows.* (The main stresses are underlined.)
- Give a clear oral model of the sentences and ask Ss to repeat together.
- Drill individual Ss and correct any language problems.
- Put Ss in pairs to practice. Monitor and correct.
- Ask Ss to do the Pair Work activity and say more example sentences.

T-23

3 GRAMMAR: Possessive adjectives; possessive 's and s'

A Circle the correct answers. Use the sentences in the grammar box and the Notice box below to help you.
1. The 's in *Sergei's room* = **possession** / **is**.
2. Possessive adjectives (for example, *my, our, his* …) go **before** / **after** a noun.
3. Add 's to **singular** / **plural** nouns.
4. Add an apostrophe (') after *s* of a **singular** / **plural** noun.

> **Possessive adjectives; possessive 's and s'**
>
> Welcome to **my** home.   This is **your** bedroom.
> This is **her** bedroom.   This is **his** bedroom.
> This is **their** bedroom.   This is my parents' bedroom.
> Milka is **our** cat.   T-Rex is Sergei**'s** dog.
> This is my apartment. **Its** windows are old, but **its** doors are new.

> **!** a **noun** = a person or thing, for example, *Katya* or *room*.
> Singular nouns are **1 thing**.
> Plural nouns are **2+ things**.

B Complete the sentences. Use the possessive form of the word in parentheses ( ).
1. Is ____your____ (you) apartment in the city?
2. It's not _____ (my parents) bedroom.
3. What's _____ (John) last name?
4. Maria is _____ (he) wife.
5. _____ (We) home is in Santiago.
6. The _____ (cat) name is Milka.
7. _____ (They) daughter is a college student.
8. What's _____ (she) email address?

C ▶ Now go to page 130. Look at the grammar charts and do the grammar exercise for 3.1.

D [PAIR WORK] Complete the sentences with information about you. Then compare with a partner.

> My *dog's* name is Friday.

1. _____ name is _____ .
2. _____ last name is _____ .
3. _____ is my best friend. _____ home is in _____ .
4. My _____ home is great. _____ living room is really interesting.
5. _____ is my cousin. The name of _____ company is _____ .

4 SPEAKING

A Draw a plan of your home, with all the rooms.

B [GROUP WORK] Talk about the rooms in your homes.

> This is my apartment. This is the door. And this is the living room, with two windows. This is my bedroom.

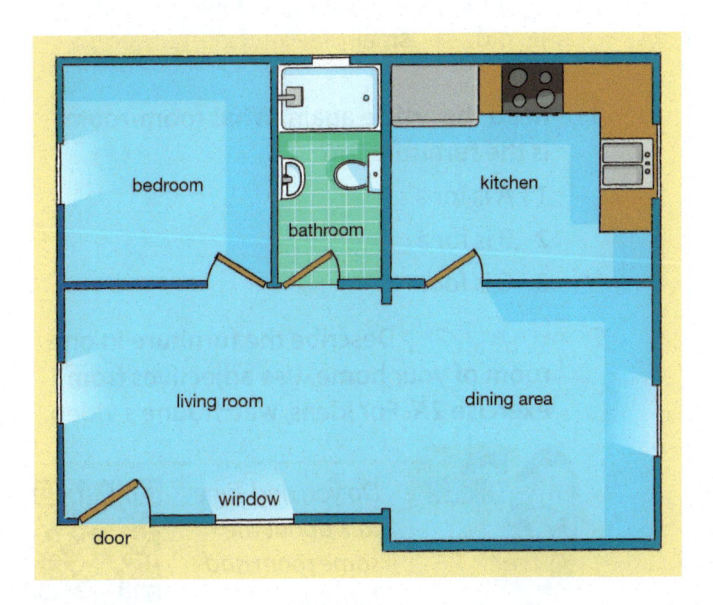

23

3.2 IS IT REALLY A CHAIR?

LESSON OBJECTIVE
- talk about furniture

1 VOCABULARY: Furniture

A 🔊 1.31 Listen and repeat the words. Then complete the chart below. Some furniture is in more than one room.

bed, chair, table, desk, bookcase, couch
shower, refrigerator, television/TV, sink, rug, lamp

Bedroom	Living room	Dining area	Kitchen	Bathroom
bed				

B **PAIR WORK** Work with a partner. Say furniture from exercise 1A. Your partner says where it is in his/her home.

A table.

In the kitchen. And in the living room.

C ▶ Now do the vocabulary exercises for 3.2 on page 143.

2 LANGUAGE IN CONTEXT

A **PAIR WORK** Choose words to describe the picture in the article.

big	boring	cool	funny
great	interesting	new	nice
old	small		

B Read the article again. What room/rooms is the furniture for?

1. A is for a _____.
2. B is for a _____.
3. C is for a _____.

C **PAIR WORK** Describe the furniture in one room of your home. Use adjectives from exercise 2A. For ideas, watch June's video.

REAL STUDENT *Do you and June talk about the same room and furniture?*

NO SPACE? NO PROBLEM!

Is your house or apartment small? Is it *really* small? No space for big furniture? No problem!
It's time for smart furniture …

A This **desk** isn't just a desk. It's a desk and a **bed**. It's great for college students.

B Is this one **chair**? Or two chairs? It's both! It's one big chair for you, or it's two small chairs for you and a friend.

C Is your living room small? No dining area in your home? This **couch** and **table** are good for a small space. First, it's a nice table for dinner. Then it's a couch!

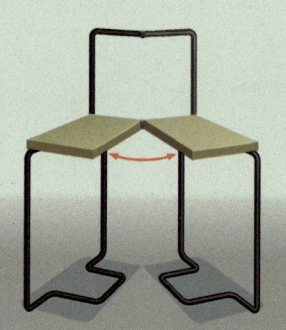

24

3.2 IS IT REALLY A CHAIR?

LESSON OBJECTIVE
- talk about furniture

Introduce the lesson Display a picture of a living room from your house or from the internet. Point to the furniture and ask Ss: *What is this?* See how many words they know. Repeat with a kitchen, bedroom, and bathroom.

1 VOCABULARY: Furniture

A 🔊 1.31 **Present the vocabulary** Play the audio, pausing after each word so Ss can repeat.

- **Do the task.** Ss complete the chart. Review the answers as a whole class.

> **Answers**
> Bedroom: bed, desk, bookcase, television/TV, rug, lamp
> Living room: chair, table, desk, bookcase, couch, television/TV, rug, lamp
> Dining area: chair, table, rug
> Kitchen: chair, table, refrigerator, rug, sink
> Bathroom: shower, rug, sink

B **PAIR WORK** As Ss share information, circulate and monitor for pronunciation. Listen for the use of *the* in sentences.

> **Answers**
> Answers may vary.

C Direct Ss to page 143 to complete the vocabulary exercises. Teacher's tips for vocabulary exercises are on page T-141.

2 LANGUAGE IN CONTEXT

A As a class, ask Ss to identify the furniture in the picture. Explain that the illustration is one part of an advertisement for "smart" furniture; the desk / bed couch / table are not shown.

- Ask volunteers to read the adjectives. Check Ss' understanding.
- Point to the pictures in 1A above. Ask Ss to say what adjectives they think describe the furniture.

> **Suggested answers**
> cool, funny, great, interesting, new

B Ss complete the task individually before sharing their answers with the class.

> **Answers**
> 1 bedroom 2 living room / dining area
> 3 living room / dining area

C **PAIR WORK** Review Ss use the words from exercises 1A and 2A to describe furniture in a room of their home. Allow Ss a few minutes to prepare before they start speaking. Monitor and provide feedback at the end of the activity.

- **OPTIONAL ACTIVITY** Ss watch the video. Ask: *Do you and June talk about the same room and furniture?*

> **REAL STUDENT**
> Hello, I'm June. This is my living room and dining room. This is my dining room. This is my dining table, with five dining chairs.

📱 SMARTPHONE ACTIVITY

Go back to the pictures you showed or drew at the beginning of this lesson. Point to some of the furniture and say the names.

- Ask Ss to draw or show a picture on their smartphone of a room in their house and share similar information. Circulate and monitor as they talk. Listen for pronunciation.

🎲 EXTRA ACTIVITY

Play furniture bingo. For details of how to play this game, go to page T-216.

Make furniture anagrams. Ss scramble words and test other Ss.

Give simple spelling tests on paper; for variation, Ss read the words aloud.

Search online for a word search maker to create a furniture vocabulary search game.

T-24

3 GRAMMAR: *It is*

Introduce the lesson Write these sentences on the board.
It's new. / It isn't new. / Is it new?

- Explain the terms *positive*, *negative*, and *question*, and ask Ss to identify which sentence is which. Use symbols (+) (–) (?) to identify them.
- Ask Ss to write two negative and positive sentences and two questions in pairs.
- Elicit some answers and write them on the board.

A **Present the grammar** Read the grammar box as a class. Explain that in questions, the verb and pronoun change places. Answer questions.

- Display one of the rooms from the previous lesson. Check understanding of short answers by pointing to an item and asking *Is it [a chair]?* Elicit the answers, *Yes, it is.* or *No, it isn't.* Repeat. Then point to an item and prompt Ss to make a question, e.g., *Is it a couch?*
- Before Ss circle the answers, explain that they can refer to the examples in the box on the right.

> **Answers**
> 1 thing   2 Is it …?

B **Do the task** Ss complete the sentences individually before checking their answers with a partner and then the class.

> **Answers**
> 1 It's, d   2 Is it, b   3 It's, a   4 Is it, c
> a It's   b it's not, It's   c it's not, It's   d Is it

🏃 FAST FINISHERS

Ask Ss who finish quickly to check their work for mistakes or write two more sentences.

C Direct Ss to page 131 to complete the grammar exercise. Teacher's tips for grammar exercises are on page T-129.

D **PAIR WORK** Before Ss begin, display a picture you have used of a room. Model sample sentences for Ss. *The chair is boring. The chair isn't old.*

- Try to pair weaker Ss with stronger Ss.
- Allow Ss time to write their sentences.
- Ask Ss to check their sentences with their partner.
- Elicit some examples sentences from Ss and write them on the board, correcting as you go.

> **Answers**
> Answers may vary.

4 SPEAKING

FIND IT

A **Review** Before Ss start, show your own design for a piece of furniture on the board. Draw a table. Say: *This is a table.* Elicit the question: *Is it a table?* Respond with *Yes, it is.* Review the prompts to be sure Ss understand them.

- Ss work alone. They think of design ideas based on the prompts or their own ideas. They can either draw them or search for pictures on their smartphone. Monitor as Ss work to offer ideas or help.

B **PAIR WORK** Monitor as Ss discuss their pictures. Listen for errors in grammar and pronunciation.

- When Ss have finished, ask volunteers to show their ideas to the class. Encourage other Ss to ask questions. Give feedback.

> 📎 **EXTRA** ACTIVITY
>
> Play grammar tic-tac-toe. Fill the squares with grammar words *is*, *isn't*, *are*, *aren't* and pronouns *he*, *she*, *it*, *we*, *they*. For full details on how to play this game, see page T-251.

T-25

3 GRAMMAR: *It is*

A (Circle) the correct answers. Use the sentences in the grammar box to help you.
1. Use *It's* and *It's not* for a **man or woman / thing**.
2. To make a question with *It is*, say **Is it … ? / It's … ?**

> **It is in statements and yes/no questions**
>
> It's a desk and a bed.   Is it *really* small?
> It's not one chair, it's   Yes, **it is**.
> two chairs!   No, it **isn't**.

B Complete the sentences. Then match 1–4 with a–d.

1. **A** Their house isn't old. _____ new. ___
2. **A** Where's Toronto? _____ in the United States? ___
3. **A** We're in your kitchen. _____ really cool. ___
4. **A** Where's your desk? _____ in your living room? ___

a. **B** Thanks. _____ small, but it's really nice.
b. **B** No, _____ _____ in Canada.
c. **B** No, _____ _____ in my bedroom.
d. **B** Oh. _____ a big or small house?

C ▶ Now go to page 131. Look at the grammar chart and do the grammar exercise for 3.2.

D [PAIR WORK] Write an affirmative (+) and negative (−) sentence for the rooms and furniture below. Then compare with a partner.

My TV is in my bedroom. It's not new, but it's OK.

1. my TV _____
2. my desk _____
3. my refrigerator _____
4. my bedroom _____
5. my kitchen _____

4 SPEAKING

A Design something for the home. Use the ideas below or your ideas. Draw a picture or find a picture online.

> an interesting lamp   a big rug   a great shower   a cool desk   a TV for the wall

B [PAIR WORK] Look at your partner's picture. Guess what it is. Is it cool? Is it interesting?

— Is it a lamp?
— Yes, it is.

3.3 COFFEE OR TEA?

LESSON OBJECTIVE
- offer and accept a drink and snack

1 VOCABULARY: Drinks and snacks

A 🔊 1.32 Listen and repeat the words. Which things are drinks? Which thing is a snack?

coffee

a cookie

milk

sugar

tea

2 FUNCTIONAL LANGUAGE

A 🔊 1.33 Adam offers a drink and snack to his friend James. Read and listen. Which drink and snack from exercise 1A does James choose?

INSIDER ENGLISH

Use *sure* in informal speech to say *yes*.
Sure. A cookie, please.
Don't say *Sure, please*.

🔊 1.33 Audio script

Adam	Coffee or tea?		James	In that cup? Six! No. Two, please.
James	Coffee, please.		Adam	Just two. And …
Adam	With milk?		James	Ah! Cookies! Hmm …
James	No, thanks.		Adam	They *are* small!
Adam	OK … Here you are.		James	Next to the big cup, yeah – they're really small! But sure. **A cookie, please.**
James	Thanks. Wow, this is a big cup!			
Adam	It is! **Sugar?**		Adam	Here you are!
James	Yes, please.		James	Thank you.
Adam	One? Two?			

B Complete the chart with expressions in **bold** from the conversation above.

Making offers	Replying to offers
Coffee ¹_____ tea?	Coffee, ³_____ .
²_____ milk?	⁴_____ , thanks.
Sugar?	⁵_____ , please.

26

3.3 COFFEE OR TEA?

LESSON OBJECTIVE
- offer and accept a drink and snack

Introduce the lesson Write or display *coffee*, *tea*, and *milk* on the board. Ask: *Coffee, tea, or milk?* Ss respond with the one they want. Ask Ss what other drinks they know and write them on the board. To help Ss, display labeled photos of a few different drinks or allow them to use a dictionary. Once you have a range of drinks on the board, Ss ask their partner what they want by choosing three of the words from the board, e.g., *coffee, tea, or milk?*

1 VOCABULARY: Drinks and snacks

A 🔊 **1.32 Introduce the task** Ask Ss to look at the picture and identify the items. Play the audio, pausing after each word for Ss to repeat. Elicit answers from the class.

> **Answers**
> Drinks: coffee, milk, tea
> Snack: a cookie

2 FUNCTIONAL LANGUAGE

A 🔊 **1.33** Books closed. Play the audio. Ask: *What does James choose?* Elicit answers.

> **Answer**
> He wants coffee with milk and sugar and a cookie.

- Open books. Play the audio again while Ss read and listen.
- Read the **Insider English** box as a class. To check understanding ask individual Ss, *Coffee?* They respond with *Sure* or *No, thanks.* Try other drinks like milk or tea.

B Individually, Ss complete the chart before sharing answers with a partner. Elicit answers and make sure Ss read the whole phrase, not just the word.

> **Answers**
> 1 or   2 With   3 please   4 No   5 Yes

> ### 📎 EXTRA ACTIVITY
> Ask Ss to role play the activity with a partner, then change roles. Circulate and listen as Ss read. Next, ask Ss to try the role play in pairs without reading and their books closed. Finally, ask volunteer Ss to model the role play as a demonstration for the class.

T-26

3 REAL-WORLD STRATEGY

A 🔊 **1.34** **Introduce the task** Read vocabulary items aloud with Ss. Play the audio. Repeat as necessary.

> **Answers**
> tea, sugar, a cookie

> 🔊 **1.34 Audio script**
>
> A Coffee or tea?
> B Tea, please.
> A Sugar?
> B Yes, please.
> A Milk?
> B No, thanks.
> A OK. And a biscuit?
> B Sorry, I don't understand. What's a … biscuit?
> A This is a biscuit.
> B Oh, a cookie.
> A Yes. In the United States, it's a cookie. Here in Australia, it's a biscuit.
> B OK! So, yes, please.
> A Here you are.

B 🔊 **1.34** Play the audio again. Repeat as necessary. Elicit answers.

> **Answers**
> biscuit; It means "cookie."

C **Do the task** Read **Asking About Words You Don't Understand** with Ss. Check understanding. Write more food words that Ss might not know. If they have trouble understanding, show a picture from the internet either on the board or on your smartphone, or draw a picture. Point to each word and ask Ss to repeat the sentence *Sorry, I don't understand. What's a [word]?* Drill Ss on the sentence chorally.

- Then ask Ss to answer the questions in pairs before you elicit the answers.

> **Answers**
> 1 He says, "Sorry, I don't understand."
> 2 He says, "What's a biscuit?"

4 PRONUNCIATION: Saying /k/ at the start of a word

A 🔊 **1.35** Play the audio. Ask Ss to repeat the words beginning with /k/. Focus on producing the /k/ clearly.

B 🔊 **1.36** Ss work in pairs to say the words.
- Play the audio. Ss compare ideas in pairs. Check answers.

> **Answers**
> 1 B 2 A 3 A 4 B 5 A 6 B

C **PAIR WORK** Ask the class to repeat the words.
- Put Ss into pairs to speak. Monitor for Ss who do not say the /k/ clearly and provide support.

5 SPEAKING

A **PAIR WORK** Model a sample dialogue with a volunteer. Monitor as Ss role play, checking for pronunciation and assisting where necessary.
- Give positive feedback where appropriate or wait until the end of the activity.
- Ask volunteer Ss to perform their dialogue for the class.

> 📱 **SMARTPHONE ACTIVITY**
>
> Ask Ss to record their conversation on their smartphone. Encourage them to listen to their conversation and think about their own pronunciation and notice any grammar errors they made.

> 👥 **TEACHER DEVELOPMENT ACTIVITY 2**
>
> **Meaningful Drilling: Mini dialogue**
>
> Before students create their own dialogues, you can build one with them as a class. Write the words in parentheses on the board. Then work with the class to build the following dialogue. Main stresses are underlined.
>
> A A <u>cook</u>ie? (*cookie?*)
> B <u>Sor</u>ry, I don't under<u>stand</u>. What's a <u>cook</u>ie? (*not understand / what's ?*)
> A <u>This</u> is a <u>cook</u>ie. (*this*)
> B <u>Yes</u>, please. (*yes*)
>
> - Elicit the first question and answer. Give a clear oral model and drill all Ss.
> - In open class, tell pairs of Ss they are A and B. Pairs say the exchange. Do this with different pairs and correct them if necessary.
> - Ss practice the exchange in closed pairs.
> - Repeat the procedure with the second exchange.
> - Ss practice all four lines of the dialogue in closed pairs.
> - Ss make up their own mini conversations.

T-27

3 REAL-WORLD STRATEGY

A 🔊 **1.34** Listen to a conversation. What does the man want?

coffee ☐   tea ☐   milk ☐   sugar ☐   a cookie ☐

B 🔊 **1.34** Listen again. Circle the word the man doesn't understand. What does it mean?

> biscuit   coffee   cookie   tea

> **ASKING ABOUT WORDS YOU DON'T UNDERSTAND**
> To ask about a word, say *Sorry, I don't understand. What's a (word)?*
> *Sorry, I don't understand. What's a biscuit?*

C Read the information on asking about words you don't understand in the box above. Answer the questions.
1. What does the man say when he doesn't understand?
2. How does he ask about the word?

4 PRONUNCIATION: Saying /k/ at the start of a word

A 🔊 **1.35** Listen and repeat. Focus on the /k/ sound.
1. **C**offee or tea?
2. This is a big **c**up!
3. A **c**ookie, please.

B 🔊 **1.36** Listen. Which speaker (A or B) says the /k/ sound? Write A or B.
1. coffee ___
2. cookie ___
3. kitchen ___
4. cup ___
5. couch ___
6. cool ___

C **PAIR WORK** Work with a partner. Say the words in exercise 4B. Does your partner say the English /k/ sound?

5 SPEAKING

PAIR WORK Work with a partner. One person is A. The other person is B. Then change roles.

A Offer your partner a drink/snack from exercise 1A.
B Ask about a word: "Sorry, I don't understand. What's (a) … ?"
A Point to a picture of the word on page 26: "This is (a) … ."
B Say "Yes, please." or "No, thanks."

27

3.4 HOME-SHARE

LESSON OBJECTIVE
- write an email about a home-share

1 READING

A SCAN Francisco is a student. He's in Burnaby in Canada for a year. He wants a room in a home-share. Scan the ad. Who is the owner of the house?

B READ FOR MAIN IDEAS Read the emails. What does Francisco ask questions about?

Home-share in Burnaby « Back to results

One bedroom, with furniture, in a five-bedroom house. Great for a student. Fifteen minutes from Morden College. No pets. From March 1. $650 a month. Contact: John Redmond at jredmond@bestmail.com

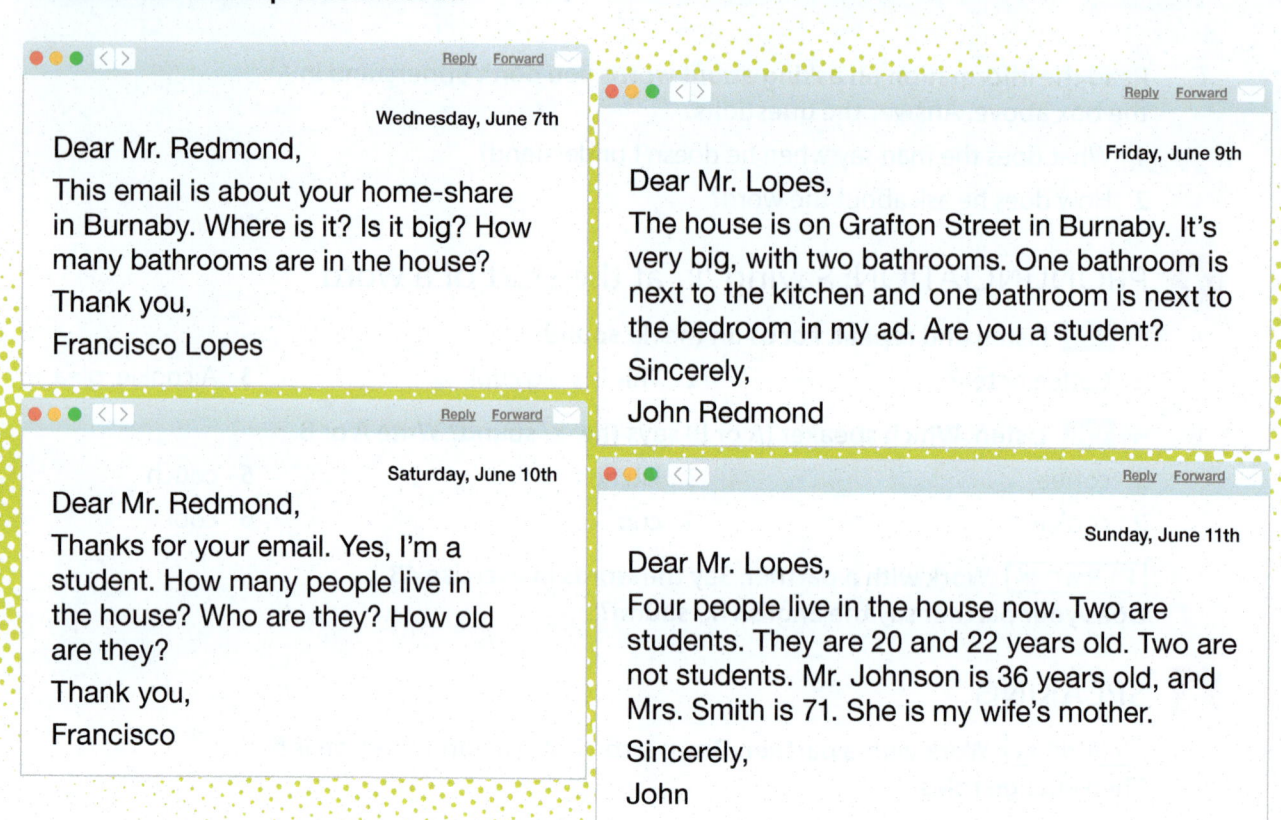

Wednesday, June 7th

Dear Mr. Redmond,
This email is about your home-share in Burnaby. Where is it? Is it big? How many bathrooms are in the house?
Thank you,
Francisco Lopes

Friday, June 9th

Dear Mr. Lopes,
The house is on Grafton Street in Burnaby. It's very big, with two bathrooms. One bathroom is next to the kitchen and one bathroom is next to the bedroom in my ad. Are you a student?
Sincerely,
John Redmond

Saturday, June 10th

Dear Mr. Redmond,
Thanks for your email. Yes, I'm a student. How many people live in the house? Who are they? How old are they?
Thank you,
Francisco

Sunday, June 11th

Dear Mr. Lopes,
Four people live in the house now. Two are students. They are 20 and 22 years old. Two are not students. Mr. Johnson is 36 years old, and Mrs. Smith is 71. She is my wife's mother.
Sincerely,
John

2 GRAMMAR: Information questions with *be*

A PAIR WORK Complete the questions with question words from the emails in exercise 1B. Then find John's answers to the questions. Use the questions and answers to have a conversation with a partner.

1. _____ is it?
2. _____ _____ bathrooms are in the house?
3. _____ _____ people live in the house?
4. _____ are they?
5. _____ _____ are they?

B ▶ Now go to page 131. Look at the grammar chart and do the grammar exercise for 3.4.

C PAIR WORK THINK CRITICALLY Is this a good place for Francisco to live? Why or why not?

28

3.4 HOME-SHARE

LESSON OBJECTIVE
- write an email about a home-share

Introduce the lesson Explain the idea of sharing your home with other people. Ask Ss: *Do you live with friends or family? Is it good?* Elicit ideas.

1 READING

A Read the instructions aloud for the class. Make sure they understand the task. Tell Ss that when we look for specific information in a text we *scan* it to find that information. Ask Ss to scan the ad for the name of the owner of the house. Ss share their answers with a partner.

> **Answer**
> John Redmond

B Allow time for Ss to read individually. Remind them to identify questions by their punctuation. Encourage them to underline the questions in the emails.

> **Answers**
> where it is, if it is big, how many bathrooms are in the house, how many people live there, who they are, how old they are

- Ask one S at a time to read each sentence of the emails. Monitor for pronunciation and check that Ss understand the meaning.

2 GRAMMAR: Information questions with *be*

A **PAIR WORK** In pairs, Ss complete the questions before you elicit the answers as a class. Then Ss find the answers to the questions in the emails.

> **Answers**
> 1 Where: Grafton Street in Burnaby
> 2 How many: two bathrooms
> 3 How many: four people
> 4 Who: two students, Mr. Johnson, and Mrs. Smith
> 5 How old: 20, 22, 36, 71

B Direct Ss to page 131 to complete the grammar exercise. Teacher's tips for grammar exercises are on page T-129.

C **PAIR WORK** Ss discuss and change the answers in pairs. Elicit ideas and generate class discussion.

EXTRA ACTIVITY

Run a grammar auction. Put Ss into two teams. Give Ss some fake money in the form of playing cards, paper or tokens. Run an auction. Write some sentences on the board (or dictate the sentences). Half are correct and half have a grammar mistake. Don't tell Ss which ones are which. Ss must bid for and buy the good sentences and reject the bad sentences. When Ss finish, the team with the most correct sentences and the most money wins. Vary the game by getting a S volunteer to run the auction. You can use the following sentences.

Incorrect	Correct
My house very big.	How many bedrooms are in the house?
Is you a student?	The bathroom is next to the bedroom.
I'm isn't a student.	How old is he?

SMARTPHONE ACTIVITY

Ss use their smartphones to find a picture of a house or apartment they like. They share the picture with a partner. Ss ask and answer questions about the home, e.g., *Where is it? How many bathrooms are in it?* As Ss discuss, circulate and monitor.

T-28

3 WRITING

Introduce the task Show three or more pictures of bedrooms or living rooms from the internet, a magazine, or a newspaper. You could also draw top-down room plans with names on the furniture. Ask Ss *Which room is good for you?*

A **Read the instructions aloud with Ss, then allow them time to read the emails individually. Ss share their answers with a partner before you elicit them. If desired, ask Ss to read the emails aloud to practice pronunciation.**

> **Answers**
> 1 The owner is a woman.
> 2 Two questions are about the house. Two questions are about the people.
> 3 A kitchen and a bedroom. The bathroom is in the email, but not in the pictures.
> 4 Yes, it is. The house is big. There's a bedroom for Francisco. Three college students live there. They go to the same college.

B **Ss circle their answers individually before you check as a class.**

> **Answers**
> 1 one question mark   2 the end

- Direct Ss to the **Register check** box. Make sure Ss understand the difference between *formal* and *informal*. Check concepts by asking *What words do you use with your teacher?* to elicit *Dear, Thank you,* and *Sincerely*. Ask: *What words do you use with your friends?* Elicit: *Hello, Hi, Thanks,* and *Love*.

C **Write it** Before Ss start, ask, *Which house is good for you?* Elicit the things they want in a house, such as the number of bedrooms, a lawn, a big kitchen, etc. This will give Ss some ideas for what to write about.

- Ss write their emails. Encourage them to use the emails on page 29 to help them. Support Ss by circulating and monitoring their work. Assist Ss with spelling by writing challenging words on the board.

> **🏃 FAST FINISHERS**
> If some Ss finish quickly, tell them to check their work for mistakes. Circulate and help them identify errors. If possible, Ss should correct emails before they pass them on.

D **PAIR WORK** **Read the instructions as a class so that all Ss are clear on the task.**

- Continue to circulate to make sure that Ss understand their classmates' emails. Monitor and offer suggestions and spelling advice. If possible, Ss should correct their emails before giving them back.

E **PAIR WORK** **After Ss read their replies, direct them to tell their partner if the house would be good for them. Read Ss' work yourself or ask for volunteers to read aloud both their email and the reply to the class.**

- Allow other Ss to say if the house would be a good place to live.
- These emails might be good to share on your class social media page or on your institution's website. Photograph good examples with your smartphone.

> **✏ HOMEWORK IDEAS**
> Ss write an email about their house or apartment. They say what rooms are in their homes and the people who live there. Ss should write 50 words, either as an actual email that they send to you or on paper that they turn in. Correct Ss' emails and give feedback. In the next class session, present one or two emails that have strong use of language covered in this lesson.

Home-share on BOND STREET

✉ Contact owner

3 WRITING

A Francisco writes to the owner of a second home-share. Read the emails. Answer the questions.

1. Is the owner a woman or a man?
2. How many questions are about the house? the people?
3. Look at the pictures above. Which rooms do you see? Which room is in the email but isn't in the pictures?
4. Is it a good place for Francisco? Why or why not?

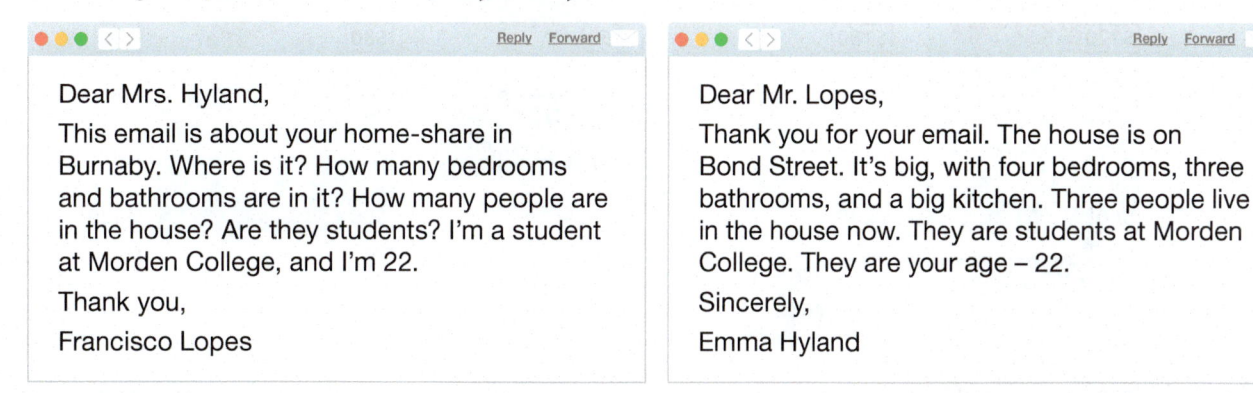

Dear Mrs. Hyland,

This email is about your home-share in Burnaby. Where is it? How many bedrooms and bathrooms are in it? How many people are in the house? Are they students? I'm a student at Morden College, and I'm 22.

Thank you,
Francisco Lopes

Dear Mr. Lopes,

Thank you for your email. The house is on Bond Street. It's big, with four bedrooms, three bathrooms, and a big kitchen. Three people live in the house now. They are students at Morden College. They are your age – 22.

Sincerely,
Emma Hyland

B **WRITING SKILLS** (Circle) the question marks (?) in Francisco's email, above. Then (circle) the correct answer in the rules, below.

1. Use **one question mark / two question marks** for each question.
2. The question mark is at **the end / the beginning** of each question.

⌖ WRITE IT

C Write an email to the owner of a home-share. Start with:
This email is about … Ask questions about the house and the people.

D **PAIR WORK** Exchange emails with a partner. Write a reply to your partner. Write about a bad place or a good place.

E **PAIR WORK** Read your partner's reply. Is it a good place or a bad place?

REGISTER CHECK

Formal, polite emails and informal, friendly emails use different words.

Formal	Informal
Dear	*Hello / Hi*
Thank you	*Thanks*
Sincerely	*Love*

3.5 TIME TO SPEAK
A new home

LESSON OBJECTIVE
- choose things for a home

Hi, I'm Jason. I'm 25 years old. I'm single, and I'm a student. I ♥ soccer and parties. This is my new apartment!

A DISCUSS Talk about Jason's new home with a partner. Say the rooms you see. Is it a good home for him?

B PREPARE Talk about the things in the pictures. Which rooms are good places for them?

A $120
B $180
C $150
D $80
E $30
F $60
G $280
H $330
I $80
J $120
K $20
L $60
M $10
N $10
O $10

C DECIDE With a partner, make a list of things to buy for Jason's new home. You have $1,000.

D PRESENT Compare your lists. Which list is the class' favorite?

To check your progress, go to page 152.

USEFUL PHRASES

DISCUSS
This is the (kitchen/…)
It's good for him. / It's not good for him.

PREPARE
Where's a good place for a (couch/…)?
In the living room?

DECIDE
What's important for Jason?
This is a big/small (TV).
It's $180 ($ = dollars).
It's expensive. ($$$)
It's cheap. ($)

What about this (TV/…)?
This TV is good for Jason.
I agree. / I don't agree.
Good idea!

3.5 TIME TO SPEAK
A new home

LESSON OBJECTIVE
- choose things for a home

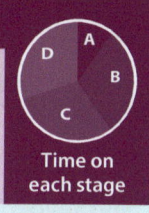

Introduce the task Tell Ss about you and your family. (You can invent the details.) Say: *I have five children and two dogs.* Draw or show a picture of a house that would not be suitable for you. For this example, show a very small house. Ask Ss: *Is this house good for me?* Elicit answers. Ask: *What house is good for me?* Elicit suggestions.

- Direct Ss to the **Useful phrases** section at the bottom of the page. Remind them that they can use them at the relevant stages of the lesson.

A **DISCUSS** **Introduce the vocabulary** **Aim:** Discuss information about Jason.

- **CLASS WORK** Ask Ss to name the areas in Jason's home. Encourage them to compare it to their own homes and say what is similar and different.
- **PAIR WORK** Ss then work together to complete the activity.

> **Answers**
> bathroom, kitchen, bedroom, living room
> Yes, it is a good home for him, because it is small and he is single and a student.

B **PREPARE** **Do the task** **Aim:** Ss consolidate vocabulary.

- **PAIR WORK** As Ss discuss which rooms would be best for the items, circulate and monitor. Give Ss time to review relevant vocabulary notes or look up words in a dictionary.* Elicit answers.
- **CLASS WORK** Ask Ss: *How much is the couch?* Elicit the answer. Check that Ss understand the $ symbol and can say *dollars*.
- **PAIR WORK** In pairs, get Ss to ask and answer *How much is the [bed]?* Monitor.

C **DECIDE** **Aim:** Ss choose items for Jason's home.

- **PAIR WORK** Ss can use their smartphones to calculate the amount of money they will spend. Monitor and make a note of the strong aspects of Ss' speaking, for example good use of unit vocabulary, interesting questions, natural-sounding interactions, etc.* You can use your notes to give feedback at the end of the lesson.

D **PRESENT** **Review** **Aim:** Ss find out what they have in common.

- **PAIR WORK** Ask pairs of Ss to attach their lists to the classroom walls. Ss circulate and look at each one with their partner.
- **CLASS WORK** When they have finished, ask Ss to share their findings with the whole class. Ask: *What items are on everyone's list? What items are left out? Which list is your favorite?* Elicit answers.

*These tips can help you to create a safe speaking environment. They can also be used with other speaking activities. For more information, see page xxii.

>> **PROGRESS CHECK** >>

Direct students to page 152 to check their progress. Go to page T-152 for Progress check activity suggestions.

TEACHER DEVELOPMENT REFLECTION

Either answer these questions yourself in a reflection journal or discuss them with your peers.

1. How much more challenging was it for students to repeat from prompts?
2. How easy was the transition for students from this kind of drilling to the freer practice where they talked about their own ideas?
3. What aspects of the language did they find most difficult – the form, the pronunciation? Did you need to do much correction?
4. Which pronunciation features did you focus on most when drilling – sounds, stress, or intonation?
5. Drilling from prompts does make students think a bit harder. Why is this often a good thing?
6. Will you do this kind of drilling with all new language you teach? Why or why not?

T-30

REVIEW 1 (UNITS 1–3)

Introduce the review Before beginning the review, write *Grammar*, *Vocabulary*, and *Functional language* on the board.
- Set a time limit of two minutes. Ss close their books and work in small groups to remember as much as they can about the grammar, vocabulary, and functional language of Units 1–3. Groups write words, phrases, and example sentences in each category.
- Check answers as a class.

1 VOCABULARY

A **Write the following headings on the board: *Country, Nationality, Job, Family, Furniture*. Check that Ss understand each category.**
- In pairs, ask Ss to write two words under each heading before sharing with their partners. Elicit some suggestions from the class and write them under the headings.
- Ask Ss to do the task individually before they share with a partner. Elicit answers as a class.

Answers

Countries	Nationalities	Jobs	Family	Furniture
Brazil	French	artist	parents	bookcase
Colombia	Honduran	chef	cousin	table
Mexico	Peruvian	server	brother	desk
South Korea	Japanese	hotel clerk	wife	refrigerator

2 GRAMMAR

A **Write the following sentences on the board. Direct Ss to make each one negative.**

I am Chinese – [I'm not Chinese.]
She is happy – [She isn't happy.]
We are rich – [We aren't rich.]

- Ss do the exercise individually.
- Check answers as a class.

Answers
1 is 2A Are 2B I'm not 3 isn't 4 is 5 aren't
6 A Is 6B it is

B **Draw the following table on the board. Leave out the words in bold. Ask Ss to copy the chart and work in pairs to write the correct missing words. Elicit answers as a class.**

my	mine
you	yours
his	his
her	hers
we	our
they	their

- Ss do the exercise individually before checking with a partner.

Answers
1 My 2 our 3 Vic's 4 My 5 Our 6 her

C **Write three sentences about your own home and family on the board. For example:**

My sister is 29 years old.
There is a refrigerator in my kitchen.
My father is a teacher.
I have a big living room.

- Direct Ss to write three sentences about their own homes and families on a piece of paper. Circulate and monitor as they write. Offer help with spelling and vocabulary as needed.
- Ss share their sentences with a partner. Elicit examples from volunteers to read aloud.

3 SPEAKING

A **PAIR WORK** Read the task aloud to the class. Then think about a famous person the whole class will know. Describe the person using target language from Units 1–3. Ask Ss to guess who the person is.
- Allow Ss a few minutes to make notes. They may use their smartphones to research any information they need. If Ss struggle to guess the person, you could write a list of people for them to choose from.
- As Ss describe and guess, circulate and monitor for examples of language usage you can share with Ss at the end of the task.

B **Allow Ss time to write their sentences and help correct them. Ask Ss to share their corrected sentences with the class.**

REVIEW 1 (UNITS 1–3)

1 VOCABULARY

A Write the words in the correct place in the chart.

artist	chef	French	Mexico	server
bookcase	Colombia	Honduran	parents	South Korea
~~Brazil~~	cousin	hotel clerk	Peruvian	table
brother	desk	Japanese	refrigerator	wife

Countries	Nationalities	Jobs	Family	Furniture
Brazil				

B Write one more word for the categories in exercise 1A.

2 GRAMMAR

A Complete the sentences with the words in the box.

| 're not | 's | 's | Are | I'm not | Is | isn't | it is |

1 Loretta _____ friendly. She's nice, too.
2 A _____ you shy?   B No, _____.
3 Donna _____ 14. She's only 13.
4 What _____ your last name?
5 They _____ from Chicago. They're from Dallas.
6 A _____ your company in China?   B Yes, _____.

B Circle the correct answers.

¹ *My / I* name is Sam, and this is Vic. We're brothers. This is ² *their / our* apartment. ³ *Vic / Vic's* room is big. ⁴ *My / His* room is small, but it's OK. It's next to the kitchen! We're in apartment 22B. ⁵ *We / Our* sister and ⁶ *her / his* husband are in apartment 23B.

C Write five things about your home and family. Use possessive adjectives and possessive *'s/s'*.

3 SPEAKING

A **PAIR WORK** Think of a person you and your partner know. Think about the person's job, age, nationality, and other information. Describe the person. Your partner guesses the person. Then change roles.

> She's a student. She's 21. She's our friend. She's Peruvian. She's very funny.

> Is it Alessa?

B Write two sentences about your partner's person.

4 FUNCTIONAL LANGUAGE

A (Circle) the correct answers to complete the conversation.

Teacher Welcome to the college language center. What's your name?
Sabrina It's Sabrina Calvo.
Teacher How do you [1] *spell / mean* your last name?
Sabrina C-A-L-V-O.
Teacher Thank you. OK. [2] *How / When* old are you, and [3] *how's / when's* your birthday?
Sabrina I'm [4] *21 / 21st*. My birthday [5] *is / are* August 2.
Teacher OK. You're [6] *on / in* room 6C. Sorry, I [7] *spell / mean* room 6D. It's next to the library.
Sabrina Sorry, I don't [8] *understand / mean*. [9] *Where's / What's* a library?
Teacher It's a room with books.
Sabrina OK. Thank you.

B Complete the conversation with the words in the box. There is <u>one</u> extra word.

> milk   please   tea   thanks   yes

Server Coffee or [1] _____?
Ivan Tea, [2] _____.
Server OK. With [3] _____?
Ivan No, [4] _____.

5 SPEAKING

A **PAIR WORK** Choose <u>one</u> of the situations below. Talk to a partner. Have a conversation.

1 You are at a hotel. A clerk asks for your personal information. Answer the questions. Look at page 6 for useful language.

> Good evening. Welcome to Hotel 24. What's your name?

2 You ask a friend about his/her family's ages and birthdays. Your friend answers your questions. Look at page 16 for useful language.

> Is this your daughter? How old is she?

3 A friend is at your home. Offer him or her a drink and a snack. Look at page 26 for useful language.

> Coffee or tea?

B **PAIR WORK** Change roles and repeat the situation.

4 FUNCTIONAL LANGUAGE

A Ask individual Ss the questions from the conversation. *What's your name? How do you spell it? How old are you? When is your birthday?* Elicit answers.
- Ss do the exercise individually.
- Elicit answers from the class.
- Pairs read the conversation together.

> **Answers**
> 1 spell 2 how 3 when's 4 21 5 is 6 in 7 mean
> 8 understand 9 What's

B **Ss do the exercise individually.**
- Check answers as a class.

> **Answers**
> 1 tea 2 please 3 milk 4 thanks

5 SPEAKING

A PAIR WORK Read each situation aloud. Encourage volunteers to read the example sentences after the descriptions.
- Ss choose one of the three situations and prepare a conversation. They should make notes, but not write the full conversation. For extra support, refer Ss to the functional language lessons from units 1–3.
- Monitor as pairs have their conversations. Listen for examples of language usage and provide feedback to Ss.

B PAIR WORK **Pairs change roles and repeat their conversations.**
- Choose pairs to perform their conversations for the class. If possible, choose a pair for each of the three situations.

T-32

I LOVE IT

4

TEACHER DEVELOPMENT INTRODUCTION

Strategy 1: Classroom management – Opening and closing lessons

In this unit, we'll focus on **opening and closing lessons** and establishing good habits for these stages. Clearly, it's better both for teachers and students if classes start on time; one way to encourage this is by **starting with conversation** – chatting with the first few students to arrive. That conversation can help teachers naturally review language from previous lessons, or introduce the lesson topic or language point. It's also better if the end of lessons can be productive rather than rushed, so **ending with review** is something that teachers should do regularly.

Starting with conversation (Activity 1): Encourage Ss to arrive on time by using conversation to introduce new language items. Try this before **START SPEAKING**.

Ending with review (Activity 2): Ss are involved in preparing review activities. Try this after lesson 4.2.

To find out more, read chapters 7.1 and 7.9 from *Classroom Management Techniques* by Jim Scrivener. Please go to www.cambridge.org/evolve to download these pages.

INTRODUCE THE THEME OF THE UNIT

- Ask Ss: *What technology is in your bag?* Elicit their answers and write the items on the board, such as cell phone, laptop, tablet, etc.
- Write on the board *I like …* and *I love …* and draw emojis or pictures to illustrate these verbs.
- Encourage Ss to say what they like and love. This can be things, places, or people.

UNIT OBJECTIVES

Read the unit objectives aloud. Tell Ss to listen and read along. Explain any vocabulary that Ss might not understand, such as any technology vocabulary.

START SPEAKING

A Ss ask and answer the questions in pairs.

B Ask for volunteers to tell the class about things they like or love.
- **OPTIONAL ACTIVITY** Ss watch the video and identify the things that June and Felipe love. Then they say whether they like or love the same things.

REAL STUDENT

Hello, I'm June. I love my car. / Hi, my name is Felipe. I love my dog.

TEACHER DEVELOPMENT ACTIVITY 1

Starting with conversation

The way teachers start a lesson is very important. It's an opportunity to talk to students in a natural way, and find out more about them. During the conversation, the teacher can also either *review* vocabulary and grammar items from previous lessons, or *introduce* them. This approach discourages other students from being late, when they realize they are missing a useful stage of the lesson.

- Start chatting with the first Ss to arrive.
- Move the conversation on by showing Ss your phone; e.g.,

    T I like my* phone, but it's old.* And it's big. Can I see your phone?

    Ss (*showing phones*) Here.

    T Do you like your phone?

    S Yes, it's good/ it's small.

    T I want to buy one like that. Is it expensive?

    S Not expensive. Cheap.

- Write two or three sentences from the conversation on the board.
- Proceed with **START SPEAKING**.

*Review of *my* and *It's* + *adj* from Unit 3.

UNIT OBJECTIVES
- talk about your favorite things
- say how you use technology
- talk about how you communicate
- write product reviews
- talk about your favorite music

I LOVE IT

4

START SPEAKING

A Look at the people in the picture. Where are they? Why are they here?

B Talk about things you like 😊 or love ❤. For ideas, watch the video with June and Felipe.

REAL STUDENTS

What do June and Felipe like or love?

4.1 FAVORITE THINGS

LESSON OBJECTIVE
- talk about your favorite things

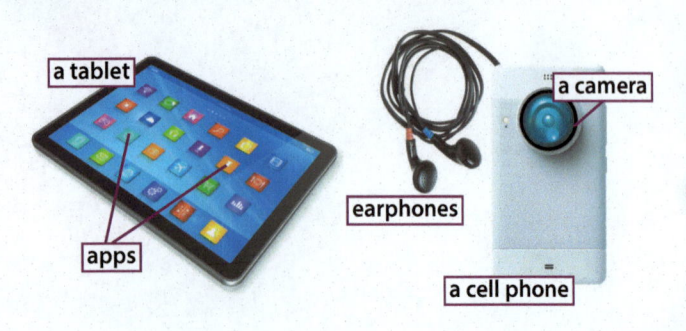

- a tablet
- apps
- earphones
- a camera
- a cell phone
- a game
- a laptop
- a smartwatch

! A **laptop** is a **computer**.

1 VOCABULARY: Technology

A 🔊 1.37 Look at the pictures above. Listen and repeat the words.

B **PAIR WORK** Look at the pictures again. Which things do you like? Which things <u>don't</u> you like? Tell a partner.

😊 I like this.   ☹ I don't like this.

C ▶ Now do the vocabulary exercises for 4.1 on page 143.

2 LANGUAGE IN CONTEXT

A Read the webpage. What things from exercise 1A do the people talk about? Which thing on the webpage isn't in the pictures above?

zozo — **I love my refrigerator. Am I OK?**

COMMENTS

JJ — You love a refrigerator! No, you're not OK! We love people – we don't love things.

erico-hello — I don't agree, JJ! I love my family … and I love my smartwatch. We love people, *and* we love things.

vera — True. I love my cell phone and the apps on it. I don't have a tablet, but I really want an iPad. Yes, it's OK to love things. But a *refrigerator*? I have a nice refrigerator. I *like* it, but I don't *love* it.

stee33 — I don't love my refrigerator, but I love the things in it! 😋

B Read the webpage again. Are sentences 1–6 true or false for the people? Circle the correct answer.

1 I have a refrigerator.   For zozo, this is *true / false*.
2 I love things.   For erico-hello, this is *true / false*.
3 I have a tablet.   For vera, this is *true / false*.
4 I want a tablet.   For vera, this is *true / false*.
5 I have a cell phone with apps.   For vera, this is *true / false*.
6 I love my refrigerator.   For stee33, this is *true / false*.

34

4.1 FAVORITE THINGS

LESSON OBJECTIVE
- talk about your favorite things

Introduce the lesson Books closed. Tell Ss the title of the lesson is "Favorite Things." Check understanding, and then ask Ss to discuss their favorite things with a partner. They can use the phrases *I like …* and *I love …* from the unit opener. Elicit some ideas and write on the board. Write words like *family* and *friends* on one side of the board, and other words like *house, cell phone, car,* and *money* on the other side. Check that Ss understand all the words, then elicit how the two groups are different.

1 VOCABULARY: Technology

A 🔊 **1.37 Introduce the vocabulary** Play the audio as Ss read. Play audio again. Pause after each word and Ss repeat together. Help Ss with any pronunciation difficulties.

B **PAIR WORK** Model examples of the sentences you want Ss to say, e.g., *I like my smartphone. I don't like my watch – it's old!* Ss work in pairs. Monitor and check for pronunciation.

> **VOCABULARY SUPPORT** Explain that we often use *love* to refer to things as well as people. This is an informal way of speaking. e.g., *I love Chinese food.* To make the distinction between *like* and *love* clearer, you can act this out by exaggerating the way you speak.

> **GRAMMAR SUPPORT** Many languages simply use *no* before a verb to form the negative. In English, use *don't* before verbs and *not* with the verb *to be*. Check and correct Ss who say *I no like …* or *I not like …*

C Direct Ss to page 143 to complete the vocabulary exercises. Teacher's tips for vocabulary exercises are on page T-141.

> 📎 **EXTRA ACTIVITY**
>
> **Play board scrabble** with technology words. For details of how to play, see page T-217.

2 LANGUAGE IN CONTEXT

A Read the instructions and comments aloud with the class. Explain words that Ss do not know, e.g., *want* and *have*. Then ask Ss to read the comments again with one S reading a sentence before you move to the next.
- Monitor for pronunciation and answer any questions about meaning.
- Ss discuss the questions in pairs before you elicit answers.

> **Answers**
> The people talk about a smartwatch, a cell phone, and a tablet.
> A refrigerator does not appear in the pictures in 1A.

B Ss complete the true / false task individually, then check their answers with a partner. Elicit answers.

> **Answers**
> 1 true   2 true   3 false   4 true   5 true   6 false

T-34

3 GRAMMAR: Simple present statements with *I, you, we*

Introduce the grammar Write on the board: *I love my phone.* Ask Ss to make it negative. Elicit: *I don't love my phone.* Say other sentences and ask them to form the negative. Make the sentences relevant to your Ss if possible. Use only *I, you,* and *we*. For example: *I like soccer. / You love your TV. / We have a desk. / I want a drink.*

A **Present the grammar** Before Ss circle the answers, explain that they can refer to the explanations in the grammar box.

- Ask volunteers to read the example sentences in the simple present aloud. Ss can now check with a partner before you elicit their answers.

> **Answers**
> 1 generally true   2 *I, you,* or *we*   3 negative   4 the same

B Ss complete the sentences individually before sharing their answers with their partner.

> **Answers**
> 1 love   2 don't like   3 have   4 don't have
> 5 don't want   6 want

C Direct Ss to pages 131–132 to complete the grammar exercise. Teacher's tips for grammar exercises are on page T-129.

D PAIR WORK Ss write their positive or negative sentences individually before sharing with a partner. Ask volunteers to tell you sentences about themselves.

> **Answers**
> Answers may vary.

4 SPEAKING

A PAIR WORK Read the directions aloud for Ss. Model the example conversation with a volunteer. Monitor as they talk, listening for language usage, such as pronunciation or grammar, that you can give feedback on at the end of the activity.

- When Ss have finished, elicit the things they both liked. See if there is something everyone in the class likes or loves. Write on the board: *We love …* and *We like …* and complete as a whole class.

- **OPTIONAL ACTIVITY** Ss watch the video and identify the things that Anderson has. Then they say whether they have the same things. You way want to explain the meaning of *many*.

> **REAL STUDENT**
> Hi. I am Anderson. I have a cell phone and many apps. I also have a computer to play.

T-35

3 GRAMMAR: Simple present statements with *I*, *you*, *we*

A **Circle** the correct answers. Use the sentences in the grammar box to help you.
1 Use the simple present for things that are **generally true** / **finished**.
2 Use *I, you,* or *we* / *I'm, you're,* or *we're* with present simple verbs.
3 Use *don't* in **affirmative** / **negative** simple present statements.
4 Simple present verbs have **the same** / **different** spelling after *I*, *you*, and *we*.

Simple present statements with *I, you, we*	
I **love** my watch.	I **don't love** my refrigerator.
I **have** a cell phone.	I **don't have** a tablet.
You **want** a tablet.	You **don't want** a watch.
We **love** our family.	We **don't love** things.

B Complete the sentences with the words in the box.

> don't have   don't like   don't want   have   love   want

1 My new smartwatch is cool.
  I _____ it!
2 I _____ my earphones. They aren't very good.
3 I _____ 85 apps on my cell phone.
4 We _____ games on our cell phones. We don't like them.
5 I don't like tablets. I don't have a tablet, and I _____ a tablet.
6 Your laptop is really old. You _____ a new laptop.

C ▶ Now go to page 131. Look at the grammar chart and do the grammar exercise for 4.1.

D PAIR WORK Complete the sentences. Make them true for you. Then compare with a partner.
1 I _____ a smartwatch.
2 I _____ my cell phone.
3 I _____ games on my cell phone.
4 I _____ tablets.
5 I _____ a new computer.

4 SPEAKING

PAIR WORK What technology do you have? What do you love? What don't you like? Tell your partner. For ideas, watch Anderson's video.

> I have a good app. It's KickMap. I love it.

> I like iPhones. I want a ...

REAL STUDENT

Do you have the same things?

4.2 MY PHONE IS MY WORLD

LESSON OBJECTIVE
- say how you use technology

1 LANGUAGE IN CONTEXT

A 🔊 1.38 Read and listen. Olivia is at a phone store, TechUBuy. (Circle) the things she talks about.

| family | friends | her laptop | her phone | school | work |

GLOSSARY
phone plan (n) a service you pay for to make calls, send messages, and use the internet on your cell phone

🔊 **1.38 Audio script**

Clerk Welcome to TechUBuy!
Olivia Hi! I want a new phone plan. I love my phone. It's my world! But my plan is expensive.
Clerk Do you know which plan you want?
Olivia No. I have no idea.
Clerk OK. First, I have some questions. What do you do on your phone? Do you **call** your friends?
Olivia No. I **chat** with my friends, but I don't *call* them. We **send messages**. And we **leave voice messages**.
Clerk Ah, yes. And do you **send emails**?
Olivia Yes. I **read emails** on my phone – from friends and for work.
Clerk And what else? Do you **listen to music** on your phone?
Olivia Yes, I do, and I **watch videos**. I also **use social media** – I **post photos**, **leave comments**, …
Clerk OK. Your phone really *is* your world! So, we have three phone plans …

2 VOCABULARY: Using technology

A Read the chart. Which verbs are <u>not</u> in the conversation in exercise 1A?

INSIDER ENGLISH
Say *What else?* to ask for more information about a topic.
And what else? Do you listen to music on your phone?

verbs + nouns		
buy apps / games / music / movies	**play** games	**leave** voice messages / comments
call friends / family	**post** photos / comments	**use** apps / social media / technology
chat with friends / family	**read** emails / messages	
listen to music	**send** emails / (text) messages	**watch** movies / videos / TV
… on the internet … on my computer / laptop … on my cell phone / tablet … on my smartwatch		

I call family on my cell phone.  | I listen to music on my phone.  | I chat with friends on the internet.  | I use apps on my cell phone and tablet.  | I play games on my computer.  | I read emails on my tablet.  | I send text messages on my phone.  | I post photos on the internet.

B 🔊 1.39 Look at the pictures. Listen and repeat. Then say <u>three</u> things you do.

C ▶ Now do the vocabulary exercises for 4.2 on page 144.

4.2 MY PHONE IS MY WORLD

LESSON OBJECTIVE
- say how you use technology

Introduce the lesson Explain the phrase *my phone is my world* means *my phone is very important to me*.
- Ask Ss to rank the following items in order of importance (1–5) with 1 = very important and 5 = not very important: *laptop / phone / tablet / TV / computer*
- Ask Ss to share their answers, then generate some discussion as a class around their ideas.

1 LANGUAGE IN CONTEXT

A 🔊 **1.38** **Introduce the task** Before you play the audio, explain the glossary. Tell Ss that the conversation has many new words. Tell them to listen only for the gist and the things / people Olivia talks about.
- Play the audio while Ss read. Ss circle the things / people, then check with a partner. Play the audio again as needed.

> **Answers**
> her phone, friends, work

> 🔗 **EXTRA ACTIVITY**
>
> Ask Ss to role play the dialogue with a partner. Monitor. Ss change roles. Get Ss to try to remember the dialogue with their books closed while they do the role play again.

2 VOCABULARY: Using technology

A Read the directions for the class. Ask a volunteer to read the first phrase. Ask: *Is this in the conversation?* to elicit *yes* or *no*. Ask Ss to work together, taking turns reading each sentence aloud and deciding if it is in the conversation or not.

> **Answers**
> **Play (games)** is not in the conversation in exercise 1A.

- Draw Ss' attention to the **Insider English** box and the phrase *what else?* Check for understanding.

B 🔊 **1.39** **Review** Play the audio as Ss read. Play again, pausing after each sentence so the class can repeat. Monitor for pronunciation. Ss tell their partner three things they do.

> **Answers**
> Answers may vary.

C Direct Ss to page 144 to complete the vocabulary exercises. Teacher's tips for vocabulary exercises are on page T-141.

> 🔗 **EXTRA ACTIVITY**
>
> Play tic-tac-toe with simple verbs such as *call, chat, use, play, read, send, post, watch*. In two teams, Ss make sentences. Demonstrate with one or two example sentences, e.g., *I play games on my phone.* For details of how to play this game, see page T-251.

T-36

3 GRAMMAR: Simple present yes/no questions with I, you, we

A Before Ss circle the answers, explain that they can refer to the explanations in the grammar box.

- **Present the grammar** Read the grammar box aloud. Check Ss' understanding by asking quick questions to elicit the answer *Yes, I do* or *No, I don't*. Ask: *Do you use social media?* Elicit answers. Ask questions with other verbs, e.g., *Do you like your phone? Do you live in [London]? Do you want a drink?* etc.

Answers
1 Do   2 don't

GRAMMAR SUPPORT In this section, you are looking for grammatical accuracy, so it's acceptable to correct Ss when they make mistakes. If Ss make mistakes, tell them in a supportive way and allow them time to correct themselves.
Do you like movies?
Yes, I like.
[repeat with questioning intonation: *I like?* Pause.]
Yes, I do.

B Read instructions aloud. To make sure Ss know what to do, ask a volunteer to complete the first question. Ss check their answers in pairs before you elicit them from the class.

Answers
1 Do you listen to music on your computer?
2 Do you play games on your phone?
3 Do you and your friends send text messages to your teachers?
4 Do you post comments on social media?
5 Do you watch videos on your laptop?

C PAIR WORK Monitor for pronunciation and any grammatical errors as Ss ask and answer the questions in exercise B. Provide feedback when they finish. Ask volunteers to share their answers with the class. Do all the Ss have the same answer to one of the questions?

D Direct Ss to page 132 to complete the grammar exercise. Teacher's tips for grammar exercises are on page T-129.

4 SPEAKING

A PAIR WORK Ss discuss the question in pairs before you elicit ideas.

B PAIR WORK Ask Ss to read the plans before you start. Make sure they understand all the words and expressions. Refer them to the questions in exercise 3B of the Grammar section, which will help them.

- As Ss discuss, circulate and monitor their progress. Listen for examples of language usage to give feedback at the end of the activity.
- When Ss finish, ask volunteers to demonstrate their conversation for the class.
- Give feedback.

EXTRA ACTIVITY

Do a class survey. In pairs, Ss draw up a list of technology questions using *Do you … ?* For example:
Do you have a laptop?
Do you buy music on the internet?
Do you play video games?
Do you use Instagram?

- Circulate and check the questions before Ss go around the classroom asking and answering the technology questions with their classmates. Monitor for grammar and pronunciation.

TEACHER DEVELOPMENT ACTIVITY 2

Ending with review

Make review a habit for most lessons, with students taking responsibility for it.

- Before the lesson, cut up 20 strips of paper and find a small box.
- At the end of the lesson, demonstrate a review task:

  T Tell me one new word or phrase from today.
  S *Voice message*.
  T What verb do I need?
  S *Leave*.
  T So on this strip of paper – I write *leave a voice message*. Another word or phrase?
  S *Refrigerator*.
  T How many syllables does refrigerator have?
  Ss Five.
  T Where's the stress?
  Ss re-FRIG-er-a-tor.
  T So, I write *a refrigerator* on the strip – and mark the stress.

- In groups, Ss choose and record words/phrases from the lesson on paper strips.
- Put the strips in the box. In future lessons, Ss use these to review or test each other.
- Repeat the procedure by recording new vocabulary on strips in future lessons.

T-37

3 GRAMMAR: Simple present yes/no questions with I, you, we

A Circle the correct answers. Use the sentences in the grammar box to help you.
1. To make simple present questions, use *Do* / *Are* + the subject (for example, *I* or *we*) + a verb.
2. To make negative short answers, use *do* / *don't*.

Simple present yes/no questions with I, you, we	
Do I **post** good photos?	Yes, you **do**. / No, you **don't**.
Do you **use** social media?	Yes, I **do**. / No, I **don't**.
Do you **know** which plan you want?	Yes, I **do**. / No, I **don't**.
Do you and your friends **send** emails?	Yes, we **do**. / No, we **don't**.

B Complete the *yes/no* questions. Use the words in parentheses ( ).
1. _____ on your computer? (*you, listen to music*)
2. _____ on your phone? (*you, play games*)
3. _____ to your teachers? (*you and your friends, send text messages*)
4. _____ on social media? (*you, post comments*)
5. _____ on your laptop? (*you, watch videos*)

C PAIR WORK Ask and answer the questions so they are true for you. Say *"Yes, I do."* or *"No, I don't."*

D Now go to page 132. Look at the grammar chart and do the grammar exercise for 4.2.

4 SPEAKING

A PAIR WORK What do you do on your phone and the internet? Compare with a partner.

B PAIR WORK Look at the cell phone plans. Which plan is good for you? Why? Ask and answer questions with a partner. Use the conversation on page 36 to help you.

> Do you play games on your phone?

> No, I don't. I call friends and family, and I send text messages. I don't use social media on my phone. Plan 1 is good for me.

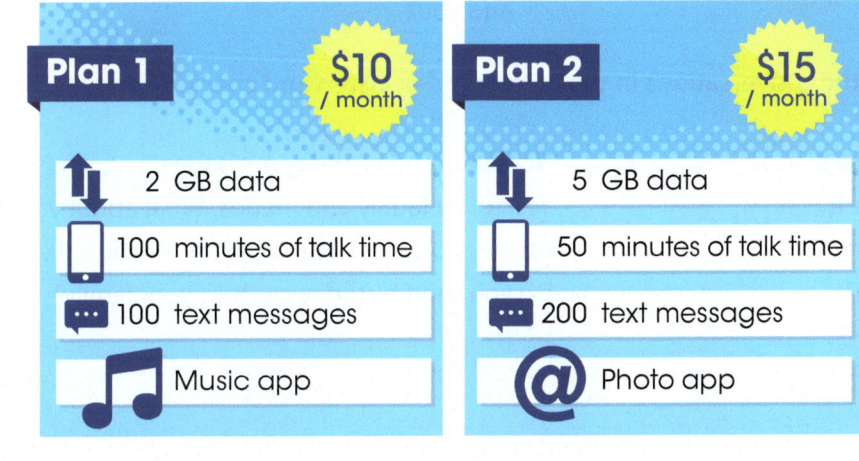

Plan 1 — $10 / month
- 2 GB data
- 100 minutes of talk time
- 100 text messages
- Music app

Plan 2 — $15 / month
- 5 GB data
- 50 minutes of talk time
- 200 text messages
- Photo app

Plan 3 — $20 / month
- 10 GB data
- 60 minutes of talk time
- 50 text messages
- 5 games

4.3 WHAT ABOUT YOU?

LESSON OBJECTIVE
- talk about how you communicate

1 FUNCTIONAL LANGUAGE

A **PAIR WORK** How do you communicate with family and friends? Check (✓) the things you use. Then compare with your partner.

- ☐ cards
- ☐ email
- ☐ letter
- ☐ phone
- ☐ social media
- ☐ video chat

B 🔊 1.40 Rocío, a college student in Los Angeles, talks to her new friend Jeff. Read and listen. How do they communicate with family and friends?

🔊 1.40 Audio script

Jeff	So, you're from Chile. Does your family live in Chile, too?
Rocío	Yes, but LA is my home now! I use technology to chat with my family. I call my parents on my phone, and I send messages to my brothers. It's really nice.
Jeff	Right. **What about email?**
Rocío	Yeah. I send emails to my friends in Chile. **How about you?**
Jeff	I like email, but I use Facebook, too.
Rocío	OK. I like Instagram.
Jeff	Oh, yeah? **Do you post photos?**
Rocío	Yes, photos of LA. My family and friends really like them. **Do you post photos, too?**
Jeff	No, but I post comments on other people's photos.
Rocío	Nice comments?
Jeff	Yes, of course!

C Complete the chart with expressions in **bold** from the conversation above.

Asking about a new topic	Asking for a response
1 _____ email?	3 _____ post photos,
2 _____ post photos?	4 _____ ?
Do you send cards? / use social media?	5 _____ about you?
	What about you?
	And you?

D 🔊 1.41 **PAIR WORK** Put the conversations in the correct order. Listen and check. Then practice with a partner.

1. ___ Yes, I do. Do you use it, too?
   ___ Yes, it is. I really like it.
   _1_ Do you use Instagram?
   ___ No. Is it interesting?

2. ___ No, but I send birthday messages.
   ___ Yes, to my family and friends. What about you?
   ___ Hmm … birthday messages are OK, but I like cards.
   _1_ Do you send birthday cards to your family?

4.3 WHAT ABOUT YOU?

LESSON OBJECTIVE
- talk about how you communicate

Introduce the lesson Dictate these sentences and ask one or two volunteers to write them on the board.

Who do you talk to?
How do you talk to them?

- Explain the meaning of *who* and *how*. Ss discuss the questions with each other.
- Monitor and listen to them speaking. You might like to answer these questions yourself before you elicit ideas from the class.

1 FUNCTIONAL LANGUAGE

A **PAIR WORK** Read the vocabulary words before Ss discuss the options to make sure they understand. Monitor as Ss discuss. Elicit answers.

> **Answers**
> Answers may vary.

B 🔊 1.40 **Do the task** Play the audio as Ss read and listen. Elicit the answer. Check for any words Ss would like explained.

- Play the audio again, pausing after each line. Ask Ss to repeat either individually or as a whole class. Monitor for pronunciation.

> **Answer**
> Rocío: phone, email, Instagram
> Jeff: email, Facebook

C Allow Ss some time to complete the activity in pairs. Elicit answers.

> **Answers**
> **What about** email?   **Do you** post photos, **too**?
> **Do you** post photos?   **How** about you?

D 🔊 1.41 **PAIR WORK** Review Model the first part of the conversation with a volunteer to make sure Ss know what to do. Ss complete the task individually before checking with a partner.

- Play the audio and ask Ss to check. Ss role play the conversation with their partner. Circulate and monitor for pronunciation.
- Ask volunteers to demonstrate for the class.
- Give feedback.

> **Answers**
> **Conversation 1**
> 2 Yes, I do. Do you use it, too?
> 4 Yes, it is. I really like it.
> 1 Do you use Instagram?
> 3 No. Is it interesting?
> **Conversation 2**
> 3 No, but I send birthday messages.
> 2 Yes, to my family and friends. What about you?
> 4 Hmm … birthday messages are OK, but I like cards.
> 1 Do you send birthday cards to your family?

📎 EXTRA ACTIVITY

Ask Ss to create similar dialogues about different websites or apps they use. These could be Facebook, Instagram, Snapchat, WhatsApp, or other applications they use. Ss can write these down or simply say them. Again, encourage Ss to use brand names so that any lack of vocabulary does not stop conversation. Monitor for grammar and pronunciation. To reinforce accuracy, Ss could record the dialogues on their smartphones and play them back to listen.

T-38

2 REAL-WORLD STRATEGY

A **Introduce the task** Read the dialogue with a volunteer. Elicit answers.

> **Answer**
> Rocío says, "OK."

> **VOCABULARY SUPPORT** Explain that body language is an important tool in communication. Nodding, smiling, and frowning are all important non-verbal forms of communication. Explain that *yeah* is informal, but totally acceptable. Also, tell Ss that all of the Real-World Strategy phrases have similar meanings and can be used in the same way.

B 🔊 **1.42** Play the audio. Play again if Ss require it. Elicit answer.

> **Answer**
> phone (parents), email (son and daughter)

> 🔊 **1.42 Audio script**
> A Do you talk to your family on the phone?
> B Well, I talk to my *parents* on the phone. They're 81 years old.
> A OK.
> B So they don't like computers. They like the phone.
> A Yeah.
> B But I send emails to my son and daughter.
> A Right.

C 🔊 **1.42** Play the audio again. Elicit answers.

> **Answers**
> She says: "OK," "Yeah," and "Right."

D **PAIR WORK** **Review** Put Ss into pairs and assign each one to be either Student A or Student B. Ask Student As to turn to page 156 and Student Bs to turn to page 159.

- Read the instructions aloud and then allow Ss time to read through the chart. Check understanding. Ask one of the Student As: *What topic will you ask about?* Elicit something like *Do you have a laptop?* Write this on the board. Elicit an answer, e.g., *Yes, of course.* Ask a Student B: *What will you ask about?* Elicit something like *Do you send emails?* Write this on the board and elicit an answer. Explain that Ss can use any of the questions or answers from page 39 to help them.
- Circulate and monitor as Ss do the task.
- When complete, ask volunteers to demonstrate their dialogue in front of the class. Give positive feedback.

3 PRONUNCIATION: Saying stressed words

A 🔊 **1.43** Play the audio. Ss discuss the questions in pairs. Check answers. It may be useful to remind Ss that they saw stress in Unit 2 to show how similar-sounding words are different. Here, stress shows the important words (often the nouns, verbs, and adjectives) in a question or sentence.

> **Answers**
> 1 What about **email**?
> 2 How about **you**?
> 3 Do you post **photos**?
> These words are stressed because they are the focus of the question.

B 🔊 **1.44** Ss guess the stressed words before comparing with a partner.

- Play the audio and have Ss check their answers. Then check as a class.

> **Answers**
> A Do you use **Facebook**?
> B Yeah. How about **you**?
> A Me, too. I post photos and comments.
> B Do you **post videos**?
> A No. But I send videos on WhatsApp.
> B Do you use **video chat**?
> A Yeah, video chat is great.

C **PAIR WORK** Play the audio again. Have the whole class repeat each line.

- Put Ss into pairs to speak.

4 SPEAKING

A **Review** Read the question aloud. Give Ss two or three minutes to write a list. Encourage Ss to use brand names so they can talk about what they actually like.

> **Answers**
> Answers may vary.

B **PAIR WORK** Practice the model conversation with a volunteer. Ask Ss to role play the conversation with a partner. Then tell Ss to talk to their partner about how they communicate. Encourage them to ask questions and to show they are listening.

- Circulate and monitor as they talk.

> 📎 **EXTRA ACTIVITY**
> After activity 4, Ss have a circle discussion on the various topics. For details on how to run a circle discussion, see page T-102.

2 REAL-WORLD STRATEGY

SHOWING YOU ARE LISTENING
To show you are listening, say *Right*, *Yeah*, or *OK*.
Jeff   I use Facebook, too.
Rocío   OK. I like Instagram.

A   Read about how to show you are listening in the box above. What does Rocío say?

B   🔊 1.42 Listen to a conversation. How does the man communicate with his family?

C   🔊 1.42 Listen again. What does the woman say to show she's listening?

D   PAIR WORK Student A: Go to page 156. Student B: Go to page 159. Follow the instructions.

3 PRONUNCIATION: Saying stressed words

A   🔊 1.43 Listen and repeat the questions. Which words are stressed? Why are they stressed?
   1 What about email?   2 How about you?   3 Do you post photos?

B   🔊 1.44 Listen and <u>underline</u> the stressed words in the questions.
   A Do you use Facebook? (1 word)
   B Yeah. How about you? (1 word)
   A Me, too. I post photos and comments.
   B Do you post videos? (2 words)
   A No, but I send videos on WhatsApp.
   B Do you use video chat? (2 words)
   A Yeah, video chat is great.

C   PAIR WORK Practice the conversation in exercise 3B. Does your partner use stressed words?

4 SPEAKING

A   Think about ways to communicate with people. Which ways do you use? Write a list.

B   PAIR WORK Talk to a partner about how you communicate. Ask questions to start a new topic. Show you are listening.

- I use Instagram. It's great.
- Yeah.
- Do you use Instagram, too?
- Yes, and I use Snapchat. What about you?
- I don't use Snapchat.

4.4 GREAT! FIVE STARS

LESSON OBJECTIVE
- write product reviews

1 LISTENING

A PAIR WORK Read the definition of "product review." Then answer the questions with a partner.

GLOSSARY
product review *(n)* people's opinions and comments about things they buy

1 Do you buy things on the internet?
2 Do you look at or write product reviews?

B 🔊 1.45 LISTEN FOR GIST Listen to product reviews from three vloggers. Match the reviews (1, 2, and 3) to the products below.

an app ___   a TV ___   a tablet ___

C 🔊 1.45 LISTEN FOR MAIN IDEAS Listen again. How many stars do you think the vloggers give? Circle your answer. Then compare with a partner.

Review one:
★☆☆☆☆ / ★★★★☆

Review two:
★★☆☆☆ / ★★★★★

Review three:
★☆☆☆☆ / ★★★☆☆

D PAIR WORK THINK CRITICALLY Talk to a partner. Which review is useful to you?

2 GRAMMAR: *a/an*; adjectives before nouns

A Circle the correct answers. Use the sentences in the grammar box to help you.

1 Use *a* or *an* with a **singular** / **plural** noun.
2 Use ***a*** / ***an*** before most vowel sounds (*a, e, i, o, u*).
3 Use ***a*** / ***an*** before a consonant sound (*b, c, d, …*).
4 **Use** / **Don't use** *a* or *an* with plural nouns.

a/an; adjectives before nouns

a/an	no *a/an*
You take **a photo**.	You take **photos**. (plural nouns)
A tablet is expensive.	**This tablet** is expensive. (*this* + noun)
I have **an uncle**.	I have **two uncles**. (number + noun)
We live in **a house**.	**Our house** is small. (possessive adjectives)
You have **a new phone**.	His phone **is new**. (*be* + adjective)

B Use the words to make sentences. Then check your accuracy.

1 a / cell phone. / I / new / want _____
2 two / We / in / TVs / our house. / have _____
3 app / really / This / interesting. / is _____
4 you / an / Do / iPad? / have _____
5 like / tablets? / Do / you _____

✓ **ACCURACY CHECK**

Don't use *a/an* with a plural noun.

We have computers at work. ✓
We have a computers at work. ✗

C ▶ Now go to page 132. Look at the grammar chart and do the grammar exercise for 4.4.

4.4 GREAT! FIVE STARS

LESSON OBJECTIVE
- write product reviews

Introduce the lesson If possible, show a product review on a website like Amazon or another online retailer. Explain *review*. Ask Ss: *How many stars?*

- If possible, show a product with a good rating. Ask: *Is this a good product?* to elicit *Yes, it is.* Show a picture of a badly rated product and ask: *Is this good?* to elicit *No, it isn't.*

1 LISTENING

A PAIR WORK **Introduce the task** Ask a volunteer to read the definition for the class. Ss discuss the questions in pairs before you elicit interesting answers.

Answers
Answers may vary.

B 🔊 1.45 **Do the task** Explain the task and read the items with Ss. Play all three parts of the audio before you elicit the answers. Here, Ss listen for the gist, in that they are looking for general topics, not details. Elicit the answers and ask Ss to explain clues that helped them identify the product.

Answers
an app: C, a TV: A, a tablet: B

🔊 1.45 Audio script

A I have two TVs. This one is in my bedroom, on my desk. I like it because it's small. I don't like big TVs. Also, it's not expensive. $119 is a good price. It's cheap, but it's nice.
B I love games, and this tablet is great for games. It's really fast, and it has a nice design. It's $415. Not cheap. But it's expensive because it's a great product. I love it.
C This is an app for photos. You take a photo. Then you change it with the app, but it's difficult, and the photos aren't good. A bad app? Yes! Sorry, but I don't like it.

C 🔊 1.45 Play the audio. Ask Ss to check their answers with a partner. Repeat the audio again, pausing after each section to elicit the answer from Ss.

Answers
Review one: four stars, Review two: five stars, Review three: one star

D PAIR WORK **Review** Circulate and monitor as Ss discuss the question. When eliciting answers, ask: *Why is the review useful?*

2 GRAMMAR: *a/an*; Adjectives before nouns

A **Introduce the grammar** Check that Ss understand *plural / singular, vowel / consonant*, and *noun / adjective / possessive*. Elicit examples and write them on the board.

- Before Ss circle the answers, explain that they can refer to the examples in the grammar box.
- **Present the grammar** Ask volunteers to read each pair of sentences in the chart. Ss circle the correct answers in pairs before you elicit answers.

Answers
1 singular   2 an   3 a   4 Don't use

B **Do the task** Ss complete the task individually before sharing their answers with a partner and then the class.

Answers
1 I want a new cell phone.
2 We have two TVs in our house.
3 This app is really interesting.
4 Do you have an iPad?
5 Do you like tablets?

- Read the **Accuracy check** box as a class together. Write or display the following sentences on the board.
  1 *I have a pets.*
  2 *There are a laptops in our school.*
  3 *Does your phone have an apps?*
- Ask Ss to correct the sentences in pairs before you elicit the answers as a class.

Answers
1 I have pets.
2 There are laptops in our school.
3 Does your phone have apps?

VOCABULARY SUPPORT Count nouns are nouns that can be made plural by adding an *s*, such as *games, tablets,* or *TVs*.

C Direct Ss to page 132 to complete the grammar exercise. Teacher's tips for grammar exercises are on page T-129.

T-40

3 PRONUNCIATION: Listening for the end of a sentence

A 🔊 **1.46** Encourage Ss to read the sentences and predict what they will hear.
- Play the audio and check answers as a whole class. Explain that we often know a sentence is finished when the speaker's voice goes down. When a sentence isn't finished, the speaker's voice is often high.

> **Answers**
> 1 A   2 B
> 2B is finished: This tablet is great for games.

B 🔊 **1.47** Encourage Ss to read the sentences and predict what they will hear.
- Play the audio and check answers as a whole class.

> **Answers**
> 1 I like it because it's small.
> 2 It's cheap, but it's nice.
> 3 It's really fast and it has a nice design.
> 4 It's expensive because it's a great product.

4 WRITING

Introduce the topic Write the last product you bought on the board giving a one- to five-star rating and explaining why. On paper, Ss write the name of the last thing they bought online and rate it. Collect papers. Choose a random paper. Search an online store (that allows reviews) and display the item. Compare ratings. Ask who bought the item and why they gave the rating they did.

A [PAIR WORK] **Introduce the task** Ss read the reviews first. Explain any unfamiliar words. Ss answer the questions in pairs. Elicit answers.

> **Answers**
> earphones, a chair; other answers will vary

B **Do the task** Ss scan for specific detail and complete the chart. When finished, Ss share their answers in pairs or groups. Elicit answers.

> **Answers**
>
> | | Earphones | Chair |
> |---|---|---|
> | Title | *Expensive, but nice* | *A cheap chair!* |
> | Number of stars | 4 | 2 |
> | Price ($) | $89.99 | $29.50 |
> | Good or bad product? | Good | Bad |

C Ss recall the item they wrote about in **Introduce the topic** or choose another item. They search for it on their smartphones and look at the reviews. Ss share the information with a partner. Ask a few Ss to share their answers.

D **Do the task** Allow Ss time to find the words in the text. Ask a volunteer to read them aloud. Ss complete the rules in pairs before you elicit the answers.

> **Answers**
> 1 different   2 give a reason

E **Introduce the task** Ss discuss the products they will review.
- Read the **Register check** aloud. Explain that exclamation points (!) are used in informal writing. Volunteers read the example sentences aloud. Monitor intonation.
- **Do the task** Give Ss time to write. Encourage them to refer to the reviews in exercise 4A to help. Correct Ss' work before the next section.

F [PAIR WORK] **Review** While Ss talk, circulate and monitor. Ask Ss to move around the class and share their reviews with other partners.
- When Ss finish, volunteers read their product reviews aloud. You can share these on your class's social media page.

3 PRONUNCIATION: Listening for the end of a sentence

A 🔊 **1.46** Listen. Which sentence do you hear: A or B? Which speaker is finished?

1. **A** I love games. ↗
   B I love games. ↘

2. **A** This tablet is great for games. ↗
   B This tablet is great for games. ↘

B 🔊 **1.47** Listen. Draw one ↗ and one ↘ for each sentence.

1. I like it because it's small.
2. It's cheap, but it's nice.
3. It's really fast, and it has a nice design.
4. It's expensive because it's a great product.

4 WRITING

A **PAIR WORK** Read the product reviews. What are the products? Do you like them? Do you want them?

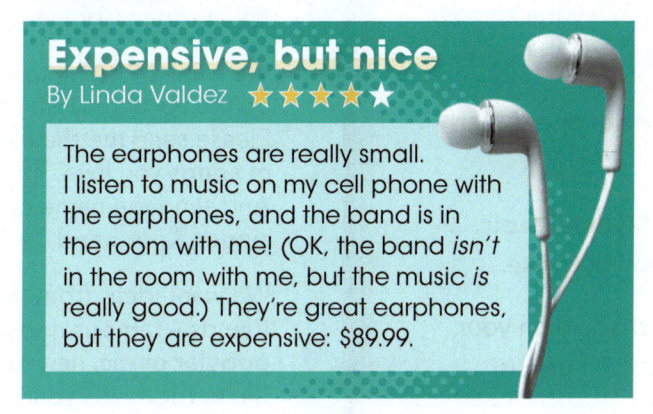

Expensive, but nice
By Linda Valdez ★★★★☆

The earphones are really small. I listen to music on my cell phone with the earphones, and the band is in the room with me! (OK, the band *isn't* in the room with me, but the music *is* really good.) They're great earphones, but they are expensive: $89.99.

A cheap chair!
By Carl Rogers ★★☆☆☆

This chair is cheap. It's $29.50. I have two chairs – one chair for me, and one chair for my wife. We sit in them and watch TV. I don't like it because it's small, and I'm a big man. I don't sit *in* the chair. I sit *on* it! Is it comfortable? NO!

GLOSSARY
comfortable (*adj*) good to sit on

B Read the reviews again. Complete the chart.

	Earphones	Chair
Title	Expensive, but nice	
Number of stars		
Price ($)		
Good or bad product?		

C Choose a product you know or find a product on the internet. Find the information in exercise 4B.

D **WRITING SKILLS** Circle the words *but* and *because* in the reviews above. Then circle the correct answer in the rules.

1. Use *but* to add an idea that is **the same / different**.
2. Use *because* to **give a reason / ask a question**.

REGISTER CHECK

In informal writing, use exclamation points (!) after funny sentences or after words and sentences with a strong feeling, for example, with *love*, *like*, or *don't like*.
I don't sit *in* the chair. I sit *on* it!
Is it comfortable? NO!

WRITE IT

E Write reviews for a good product <u>and</u> a bad product. Use the products below or your own ideas. Write a title, number of stars, and the price.

| an app | a camera | a desk | a game | a lamp | a tablet | a watch |

F **PAIR WORK** Read a partner's reviews. Do you like their products? Do you want them?

4.5 TIME TO SPEAK
Playlists

LESSON OBJECTIVE
- talk about your favorite music

A Read the text message. What is the message about?

B 🔊 1.48 Use words from the message to complete the definitions (1–5). Then listen and check.
1 A playlist is a list of your favorite s_____.
2 People in a b_____ play music or sing.
3 A s_____ is a person in a band. He or she sings the words in a song.
4 F_____ music is music that everyone knows.
5 P_____ music is music that everyone likes.

C **PREPARE** Talk to a partner. Say the name of one singer, one band, and one song you like.

D **DISCUSS** Tell your partner about your favorite music. Make a list of singers, bands, and songs you both like.

E **AGREE** Find singers, bands, and songs that are on your list and on other people's lists. Which music is famous? Which music is popular?

F **DECIDE** Imagine you're going to the party in the text message. Talk to people in your group. Find songs that everyone likes. Then choose ten songs for the party playlist.

Party music

Hi, friends! The big party is on Saturday night. Yes! 🎈

We want GREAT music on the party playlist. Please send me the names of **songs** you love. 💜 And send the name of the **singer** 🎤 or **band**. 🎸

We want ideas from our friends – **famous** music, **popular** music, new music, old music … It's *your* party! 🎵

To check your progress, go to page 153.

USEFUL PHRASES

DISCUSS
This song is my favorite.
Me, too!
I don't like this song.

AGREE
What music do you have on your list?
I have (song/singer/band) on my list.
Let's have this song on the list.
I don't want this song on the list.
What do you think?

DECIDE
Do we want (song/singer/band) or (song/singer/band)?
Here are our ten songs for the party playlist.

4.5 TIME TO SPEAK
Playlists

LESSON OBJECTIVE
- talk about your favorite music

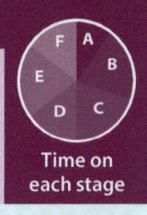

Time on each stage

Introduce the lesson Ask: *What's your favorite song?* and *What music do you like?* Ss share answers in pairs before you elicit ideas.

- Direct Ss to the **Useful phrases** section at the bottom of the page. Remind them that they can use them at the relevant stages of the lesson.

A **Do the task** Aim: Ss read a short message and discuss the meaning.

- INDIVIDUALLY Ss read to understand the main idea and answer the question.
- PAIR WORK Ss share ideas before you elicit answers as a class.

> **Answers**
> The message is about a party on Saturday night. It asks people to send the names of their favorite songs.

B 🔊 **1.48** Aim: Ss listen and complete the definitions.

- PAIR WORK Ss complete the task together.
- INDIVIDUALLY Ss listen and check their answers. Ask Ss to read the complete sentences when you elicit answers. Correct pronunciation.

> **Answers**
> 1 songs 2 band 3 singer 4 Famous 5 Popular

C PREPARE Aim: Ss share songs they like.

Give Ss some ideas by telling them about a singer or song you like.

- PAIR WORK Ask Ss to write the names of their partner's favorite singer, song, and band on a small piece of paper. Ss fold the paper and you collect them.
- CLASS WORK Open one piece of paper at random and play some of the music from YouTube or your smartphone.

D DISCUSS Aim: Ss share musical tastes.

- PAIR WORK Circulate and monitor as Ss discuss music.
- **Extra speaking practice*** Ss work in pairs before repeating the task in fours.

E AGREE Aim: Ss find out what they have in common.

- GROUP WORK Pairs now circulate and share their ideas with other pairs. When Ss speak, focus on their performance, rather than their accuracy.* Give them feedback based on how well they completed the task.

F DECIDE Review Aim: Ss decide on songs that they like best.

- GROUP WORK Ss share and choose their songs in small groups. Circulate and monitor, listening for language usage you can give feedback on at the end of the activity.* Ask Ss to write their list of songs on a piece of paper, which you collect.
- CLASS WORK Share Ss' lists on social media or display them on the classroom wall. If there is one song that everyone likes, consider playing the video online.

*These tips can help you to create a safe speaking environment. They can also be used with other speaking activities. For more information, see page xxii.

⪢ PROGRESS CHECK ⪢

Direct students to page 153 to check their progress. Go to page T-152 for Progress check activity suggestions.

Review Elicit Ss' favorite songs in English. Make sure most Ss like the song and that the lyrics are simple. For the next session, find the lyrics online and make a worksheet for Ss to use while they listen to the song. This could be a gap fill or just lyrics they can read. Play the song for Ss. As a variation, Ss make a lyrics worksheet for their classmates.

👥 TEACHER DEVELOPMENT REFLECTION

Answer these questions yourself in a reflection journal or discuss them with your peers.

1. What personal information did you learn about your students by chatting with them before the lesson? How can you use some of this information in future lessons?

2. What adjectives from Unit 3 did students use to describe their phones? When you wrote the sentences from your conversation on the board, did late students try to copy them down?

3. A colleague says, "My class is supposed to start at 9 a.m., but some students don't show up until 9:05. I just sit there and look at my notes. I feel so uncomfortable." What advice would you give your colleague?

4. What other things could students add to their strips of paper? For example, if they record a verb, they can also indicate any necessary preposition, e.g., listen *to* music or the radio.

5. Some teachers regularly close lessons by summarizing what they did. What are the advantages of doing this? How can you involve students in the summary process?

MONDAYS AND FUN DAYS

5

TEACHER DEVELOPMENT
INTRODUCTION

Strategy 2: Teaching vocabulary – Recording and memorizing vocabulary

After we've presented new vocabulary, we need to help our Ss to record and memorize it for future use.

Spidergrams (Activity 1): This is a way of recording vocabulary which Ss can continue to use independently beyond the classroom. You will have the opportunity to demonstrate this in lesson 5.1.

Disappearing drill (Activity 2): A repetition activity for the whole class with an added element of memory challenge keeps Ss engaged and entertained. You can try this in lesson 5.2.

To find out more about ways of helping Ss to record and memorize vocabulary, read Chapter 6 of Ruth Gairns and Stuart Redman, *Working with Words*, pp. 86–100. Please go to www.cambridge.org/evolve to download these pages.

INTRODUCE THE THEME OF THE UNIT

Elicit the days of the week from Ss and write them on the board in random order. Then ask: *What do you do on Monday? on Tuesday?*, etc. Briefly discuss routine activities and write these on the board. Allow Ss to use a dictionary if they wish.

In pairs ask Ss to copy the days and the activities on pieces of paper or index cards, then put the days in the correct order along with their related activities. When Ss have finished, draw a calendar on the board and ask a volunteer to write the days in the correct order. Have other volunteers fill in their routine activities and tell them to the class. Pairs should make any needed changes to their work.

UNIT OBJECTIVES

Read the unit objectives aloud. Tell Ss to listen and read along. Explain any vocabulary that Ss might not understand, such as *routine, weekend, agree, common*, and *report*.

> **VOCABULARY SUPPORT** In this unit, a **report** is information about a person's routine. It's not an academic or work-based report.

START SPEAKING

Ss answer the questions in pairs. Circulate and monitor, listening for good answers to the questions to share when the activity is over. Elicit answers.

UNIT OBJECTIVES
- talk about weekday and weekend activities
- tell the time and talk about your routines
- show you agree and have things in common
- write a report about your activities
- compare different work weeks

MONDAYS AND FUN DAYS

5

START SPEAKING

A Look at the picture and describe the people. Who are they? Where are they?

B Are they happy? Is it a fun day?

C For you, what is a fun day?

5.1 PLAY OR FAST-FORWARD?

LESSON OBJECTIVE
- talk about weekday and weekend activities

1 VOCABULARY: Days and times of day; everyday activities

A 🔊 1.49 Listen and repeat. What's your favorite day? What's your favorite time of day?

weekdays: Monday | Tuesday | Wednesday | Thursday | Friday
weekend: Saturday | Sunday

Times of day: morning, afternoon, evening, night

B 🔊 1.50 Listen and repeat the sentences.

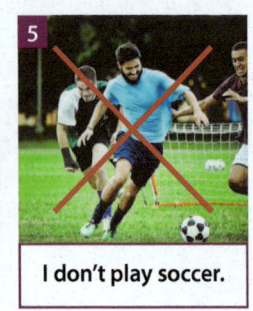

1. I go out in the evening.
2. I run on Monday and Friday.
3. I work on the weekend.
4. I study in the morning.
5. I don't play soccer.

C PAIR WORK Which sentences in exercise 1B are true for you? Tell your partner. Then say <u>two</u> more true sentences about your activities.

D ▶ Now do the vocabulary exercises for 5.1 on page 144.

2 LANGUAGE IN CONTEXT

A Read the article. Who are Sam and Justine? What activities does Sam do on weekdays?

GLOSSARY
after (*adv*) he works, then he plays soccer
before (*adv*) he runs, then he goes to work
every (*det*) 100% (of days / evenings)
way of life (*phrase*) how you live your life

PLAY ▶ or FAST-FORWARD? ⏩

By Matt Newman

Weekdays = **work** or **study**. **Weekends** = fun. Right? Not for my brother, Sam! For Sam, *every* day is a fun day! He works from **Monday morning** to **Friday afternoon**, but he usually **runs** in the morning before work. On Monday and **Thursday**, he **plays soccer** after work, and he **goes out** with friends on **Wednesday**. He doesn't go out *every* evening – on **Tuesdays** he stays home and watches TV. His way of life is ▶ "play now."

My sister, Justine, is very different. She has fun, but not every day. From Monday to Friday, she works. She doesn't have time for sports, and she hardly ever goes out! It's OK because Justine has free time on the weekend. She chats with family in the afternoon and then goes out with friends at night. Her way of life is work, work, work, and ⏩ "fast-forward to the weekend."

😊😊 Sam and Justine are both happy people, but their ways of life are *very* different. What about you? What's *your* way of life?

44

5.1 PLAY OR FAST-FORWARD?

LESSON OBJECTIVE
- talk about weekday and weekend activities

Introduce the lesson Write *morning, afternoon, evening, night* on the board. Ask Ss to tell their partner which part of the day is their favorite and why. Elicit answers.

1 VOCABULARY: Days and times of day; everyday activities

A 🔊 1.49 **Introduce the task** Play the audio through once. Play the audio again, pausing after each word so that Ss can repeat. Ask individual Ss to read the words aloud without the audio.

B 🔊 1.50 Have Ss look at the pictures. Play the audio once through as Ss read and listen. Play again, pausing so that Ss can repeat after each sentence. Correct pronunciation.

> **VOCABULARY SUPPORT** Remind Ss that there are three main prepositions for time.
> *on* = days
> *in* = morning, afternoon, evening
> *at* = night and tim*es (7 o'clock)*.

> 📎 **EXTRA ACTIVITY**
> Repeat the days of the week as a whole class. Then, ask individual Ss to say the days of the week in succession as each Ss says a different day. After Sunday, go back to Monday. Start again if a S says the wrong day. Try to go around the class without Ss making any mistakes.

C **PAIR WORK** Ask Ss to decide the sentences that are true for them before they share their ideas with a partner. Elicit answers.
- Review the sentences with Ss and check understanding of *go out*. Say: *When I go out, I meet a friend. We have coffee. What do you do?*
- Ask Ss to say two more sentences that are true for them. They share these with a partner before you elicit some examples and write them on the board.

D Direct Ss to page 144 to complete the vocabulary exercises. Teacher's tips for vocabulary exercises are on page T-141.

👥 TEACHER DEVELOPMENT ACTIVITY 1

Spidergrams

Making spidergrams helps Ss to make connections and remember new words – and provides a useful record for Ss to study at home.

- On the board, show Ss how they can make a spidergram of different kinds of information about an important word, e.g., spelling, pronunciation, word class, meaning, translation, and example sentence.

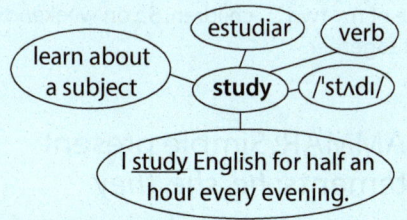

```
  learn about      estudiar    verb
   a subject  \      |         /
               \     |        /
                 study  /ˈstʌdi/
                    |
           I study English for half an
              hour every evening.
```

- Working alone, Ss choose a word from exercise 1 and make their own spidergram. Encourage Ss to improvise, e.g., they can show meaning with a picture or write a rough pronunciation in their own native language.
- Ss show one another their spidergrams in small groups.
- Encourage Ss to use spidergrams to record important vocabulary in the future. Discuss the benefits of recording vocabulary in this way.

2 LANGUAGE IN CONTEXT

Introduce the task Draw the following icons on the board in a line and elicit what they mean from Ss: *rewind, play, fast forward,* and *pause*. Ask Ss on which machines they see these icons.

⏪ ▶ ⏩ ⏸

A **Do the task** Ss read the article with the focus questions in mind: *Who is Sam?* and *Who is Justine?* Some Ss might find this quickly.
- Allow everyone time to finish reading the text before you elicit the answers. Ask Ss to tell you any unfamiliar words, and draw their attention to the **Glossary**.
- If Ss have difficulty, read the article with them. Interpret as you go and then elicit who Sam and Justine are.

> **Answers**
> Sam is Matt's brother and Justine is his sister.
> Sam usually runs in the morning before work. On Monday and Thursday he plays soccer after work, and he goes out with friends on Wednesday. On Tuesdays he stays home and watches TV.

T-44

B **Ask Ss to discuss the answers to the questions in pairs.** Encourage them to support their answers with examples from the reading.

> **Answers**
> Sam: Play now
> Justine: Fast-forward to the weekend

C PAIR WORK **Do the task** Ss discuss the question in pairs or small groups.

> **Answer**
> Answers may vary.

- **OPTIONAL ACTIVITY** Ss watch June's video and decide whether their way of life is the same or different.

> **REAL STUDENT**
> Hello, I'm June. For me, it's fast-forward to the weekend. On weekdays, uh … I mostly uh … take care of my two … children. So on weekends we go out together.

3 GRAMMAR: Simple present statements: *he, she, they*

Introduce the grammar Show a picture of a person – it could be a member of your family or a picture from the internet. Tell your Ss a few positive and negative things about him or her to model the grammar in this unit, e.g., *He works in Tokyo. He doesn't speak Spanish.*

Ask a volunteer to tell the class about a person.

A **Present the grammar** Before Ss circle the answers in pairs, explain that they can refer to the examples in the grammar box. Elicit answers as a class.

- Ask volunteers to read through the grammar box aloud.

> **Answers**
> 1 he and she
> 2 has
> 3 doesn't

> **GRAMMAR SUPPORT** Highlight the *s* used in most verbs with *he / she / it*. Explain that we don't use the *s* when the verb is negative.

> **EXTRA ACTIVITY**
> Verbally say positive sentences and ask Ss to reply back with the negative, e.g., *He drinks coffee.* to elicit *He doesn't drink coffee.* (Make sure Ss don't say *He doesn't drinks coffee.*!) Make sentences personal to Ss. Be sure Ss understand that in this context *drink* is a verb.
> - More sentences to try:
>   *He works in [London]. / She lives in [Mexico]. / We like [soccer]. / They speak [Spanish].*

B Ss complete the sentences independently before sharing their answers. Ss read the full sentence aloud when you elicit answers.

> **Answers**
> 1 play 2 doesn't 3 have 4 plays 5 has 6 don't

C Direct Ss to the adverbs of frequency chart. Go back to the picture you showed in the introduction section. Make some sentences about them to explain the adverbs, e.g., *He always goes to work.*

- Ss complete the sentences in pairs.
- Ss read the complete sentence when you elicit answers.

> **Answers**
> 1 often 2 always 3 always 4 sometimes 5 never
> 6 usually

D Direct Ss to page 133 to complete the grammar exercise. Teacher's tips for grammar exercises are on page T-129.

> **GRAMMAR SUPPORT** Adverbs of frequency usually come before the main verb in a sentence.
> *I never play soccer. / I always speak English.*
> - To practice this, write some sentences on the board and ask Ss to add an adverb of frequency in the right place to make a true sentence about themselves. Here are some sentences you could use.
>   *I go to work. / My classmates talk in class. / My family eats cookies.*

4 SPEAKING

A **Do the task** Ask Ss to think of three to five friends or family members. Ss write their lists.

B PAIR WORK **Review** Ss tell their partner about their chosen friends and family and their ways of life.

- Give feedback on the use of language you heard.

B What's Sam's way of life: "play now", or "fast-forward"? What's Justine's way of life?

C **PAIR WORK** What's your way of life: "play now" or "fast-forward to the weekend"? Tell your partner. For ideas, watch June's video.

REAL STUDENT Are you the same as June?

3 GRAMMAR: Simple present statements with *he*, *she*, *they*

A Circle the correct answers. Use the sentences in the grammar box to help you.
1 In affirmative statements with **he and she** / **they**, most simple present verbs end in *-s*.
2 The verb *have* is irregular. In affirmative statements with *he* and *she*, use **have** / **has**.
3 To make negative statements with *he* and *she*, use **don't** / **doesn't** + verb.

Simple present statements with *he*, *she*, *they*
He **works** Monday to Friday.   She **doesn't have** time for sports.
She **chats** with family in the afternoon.   They **don't go out** every evening.
She **has** fun, but not every day.   My dad **doesn't play** soccer.
They **have** fun on the weekend.

B **Complete the sentences with the words in the box.**

> doesn't   don't   has   have   play   plays

1 My friends _____ video games every weekday evening.
2 On weekdays, my sister _____ go out in the evening.
3 Every day, my sister and her husband _____ tea in the morning.
4 Pedro _____ soccer on his college team, but not in every game.
5 My mom _____ a tablet, but she doesn't use it.
6 My grandparents _____ work, so from Monday to Friday they're at home.

C **Look at the sentences in exercise 3B and the adverbs of frequency chart. Then circle the correct answers.**
1 My friends *often* / *hardly ever* / *never* play video games.
2 On weekdays, my sister is *always* / *sometimes* / *never* at home in the evening.
3 My sister and her husband *always* / *hardly ever* / *never* drink tea in the morning.
4 Pedro *always* / *sometimes* / *never* plays in his college soccer games.
5 My mom *always* / *often* / *never* uses her tablet.
6 My grandparents are *usually* / *hardly ever* / *never* at home on weekdays.

Adverbs of frequency
always   100%
usually
often
sometimes
hardly ever
never   0%

D ▸ Now go to page 133. Look at the grammar chart and do the grammar exercise for 5.1.

4 SPEAKING

A **Look at the activities in exercise 1B on page 44. What activities do your family or friends do? When do they do them? Write a list. Use adverbs of frequency.**

B **PAIR WORK** Talk to a partner about your family and friends' activities. Who is "play now"? Who is "fast-forward"?

> My sister is "play now." She often goes out in the evening…

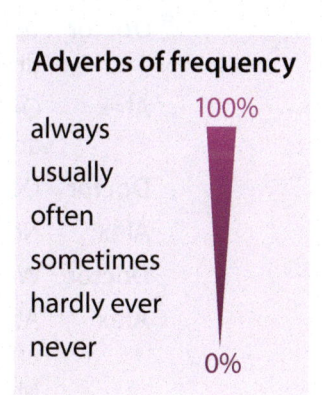

45

5.2 LISTEN TO YOUR BODY CLOCK

LESSON OBJECTIVE
- tell the time and talk about your routines

1 VOCABULARY: Telling the time

A 🔊 1.51 **PAIR WORK** Listen and repeat the times. Then point to a picture and ask *"What time is it?"* Your partner says the time.

It's eight **o'clock**.

It's five-fifteen.
It's **(a) quarter after** five.

It's three-thirty.

It's ten forty-five.
It's **(a) quarter to** eleven.

It's nine-oh-five.
It's five **after** nine.

It's six-fifty.
It's ten **to** seven.

It's **12:00 p.m.** / It's **noon**.
It's **12.00 a.m.** / It's **midnight**.

a.m. = before 12 noon
p.m. = after 12 noon
to = before

B ▶ Now do the first vocabulary exercise for 5.2 on page 145.

GLOSSARY
routine (*n*) the things you do every day at the same time
tired (*adj*) you are sleepy
late (*adj*) toward the end of the morning or evening

2 LANGUAGE IN CONTEXT

A 🔊 1.52 Read and listen. Alex talks to his doctor. What is Alex's problem? What is your "body clock"?

🔊 **1.52 Audio script**

Alex	I'm always so tired.
Doctor	Tell me about your routine, Alex. What time do you **get up**?
Alex	On weekdays, I usually get up at **7:45**, and I go to class at **8:30**.
Doctor	Do you **eat breakfast**?
Alex	No, I don't. But I **drink coffee**.
Doctor	When do you eat?
Alex	At noon. Then I **go to class** again in the afternoon. I usually **have dinner** at **9:00**. My parents don't like that.
Doctor	Well, it is very late. Do they have dinner before you?
Alex	Yes, they do. Usually at **6:00**.
Doctor	Does your mom make dinner for you?
Alex	No, she doesn't. I make it.
Doctor	OK. What do you do on weekends?
Alex	On Friday and Saturday, I go out with friends. I usually **go to bed** at **2:00** or **3:00 a.m.** And on Sunday, I get up really late and watch TV.
Doctor	Alex, it's time to listen to your body clock!

B 🔊 1.52 **PAIR WORK** Listen again. Write notes about Alex's routine. Compare with a partner.

He doesn't eat breakfast. He drinks coffee.

C ▶ Now do the second vocabulary exercise for 5.2 on page 145.

REAL STUDENT

Is your routine different from Josue's, or the same?

D **PAIR WORK** Is your routine the same as or different from Alex's? Tell your partner. For ideas, watch Josue's video.

5.2 LISTEN TO YOUR BODY CLOCK

LESSON OBJECTIVE
- tell the time and talk about your routines

Introduce the lesson Draw a big circular clock on the board. Ask Ss to copy. Write the words for each number around it. Write *o'clock* at the top. Draw hands on the clock so it is one o'clock. Elicit *one o'clock, two o'clock*, etc. as you point to different numbers.

- Explain that *noon* is 12 o'clock during the day and *midnight* is twelve o'clock at night.

1 VOCABULARY: Telling the time

A 🔊 **1.51** **PAIR WORK** **Do the task** Play the audio, pausing after each sentence so that Ss can repeat together. Play again, pausing after each sentence and having an individual S repeat.

- Remind Ss about *a.m.* and *p.m.*
- Check understanding of *quarter to X, noon,* and *midnight*.
- Model the speaking. Point to a picture and ask: *What time is it?* Have a volunteer tell you the time. Then ask Ss to work in pairs to continue the task.

B Direct Ss to page 145 to complete the first vocabulary exercise. Teacher's tips for vocabulary exercises are on page T-141.

TEACHER DEVELOPMENT ACTIVITY 2

Disappearing drill
A traditional drill asks Ss to repeat target vocabulary many times to help memorization, develop confidence, and improve pronunciation. This activity adds an element of memory challenge to the traditional drill, making it fun and helping maintain Ss' interest.

- Draw six to eight large circles on the board and write a time in each. Use a simple format, e.g., 8:30.
- Point randomly at different circles and have Ss say the times together. Make sure they use full sentences, e.g., "It's eight-thirty!" Continue pointing and drilling.
- After a while, erase one of the times so that only the empty circle is left. Continue the drill, including the empty circle. Now Ss have to remember what time was written there.
- Gradually erase more times as the drill proceeds. See if Ss can continue until all the times have disappeared and there are only empty circles on the board!

2 LANGUAGE IN CONTEXT

Present the vocabulary Write *routine* on the board. Elicit the meaning. Tell Ss your routine. Use *get up, eat breakfast, have dinner,* and *go to bed*.

Explain and discuss the meaning of *body clock*. Ask: *Do you always get up at the same time?* Elicit.

> **VOCABULARY SUPPORT** *Body clock* is the biological clock inside your body that wakes you up in the morning and makes you feel tired at night.

- Ask Ss to share the times that they do these things with the class. Ask: *When do you eat breakfast?* Elicit the time. Correct any errors you hear.

A 🔊 **1.52** Read the instructions aloud. Ask Ss to guess what a body clock is.

- Play the audio as Ss listen and read.
- Ask Ss to compare their answer about Alex with a partner. Elicit as a class.

> **Answers**
> Alex is always tired.
> Your body clock is your body's natural need to sleep, eat, etc. at particular times.

B 🔊 **1.52** **PAIR WORK** **Do the task** Model the example sentences so Ss get the idea of taking notes.

- Play the audio. Allow time for Ss to write their sentences before they compare them with a partner.
- Elicit answers from the class and write them on the board.

> **Answers**
> Alex gets up at 7:45. He doesn't eat breakfast. He drinks coffee. He goes to class at 8:30. He eats at noon. He goes to class in the afternoon. He usually has dinner at 9:00 p.m. On Friday and Saturday he goes out with friends. He usually goes to bed at 2:00 or 3:00 a.m. On Sunday he gets up really late and watches TV.

C Direct Ss to page 149 to complete the second vocabulary exercise. Teacher's tips for vocabulary exercises are on page T-141.

D **PAIR WORK** Ss compare their routines to Alex's. They say what is similar and what is different.

- **OPTIONAL ACTIVITY** Ss watch Josue's video and say whether their routine is the same or different.

> **REAL STUDENT**
> Hello, my name is Josue Lozano. I usually get up at 7:00. I go to class at 9:00 and eat lunch at 1 p.m.

T-46

3 GRAMMAR: Questions in the simple present

Introduce the task Write: *Do you get up early?* Elicit *Yes, I do.* or *No, I don't*. Write: *What time do you get up?* to elicit an answer. Ask Ss to explain the difference. Elicit that questions that start with *do/does* are *yes/no* questions, and questions that start with question words such as *what, why,* and *where* are questions that require more information in the answer.

A **Before Ss circle the answers, explain that they can refer to the examples in the grammar box.**

> **Answers**
> 1 Do   3 Do or Does + person or thing + verb
> 2 Does   4 before

- **Present the grammar** Ask volunteers to read the grammar chart. Check Ss' understanding using concept questions; ask individual Ss both *yes/no* questions and information questions. Make the questions relevant to Ss if possible, e.g., *Do you watch TV in the evening?* and *What do you watch?* Ask each S a question.

B **PAIR WORK** Ss complete the sentences individually before checking their answers with the class.

- Ss role play the conversations. Monitor and check for pronunciation.

> **Answers**
> **Conversation 1**
> A **What time** do you go to work?
> B I **go** to work at 7:00.
> A Wow! **When** do you go to bed? ("What time" is also acceptable.)
> B I usually go to bed after midnight. I'm always tired!
> **Conversation 2**
> A **Do** they play soccer?
> B **Yes**, they do. What about you?
> A No, I **don't**.
> **Conversation 3**
> A **Does** Martin have a new job?
> B Yes, he **does**.
> A **Where** does he work?
> B He **works** in an office.

C **Direct Ss to page 133 to complete the grammar exercise. Teacher's tips for grammar exercises are on page T-129.**

D **Allow Ss time to write the questions. Check for grammar and spelling before Ss ask and answer questions with their partner.**

> **Answers**
> Answers may vary.

- Read the **Accuracy check** aloud. Ask Ss to correct the following sentences individually before checking with a partner.
    1 When they study?
    2 Where Manuel work?
    3 What time you have dinner?

> **Answers**
> 1 When **do** they study?
> 2 Where **does** Manuel work?
> 3 What time **do** you have dinner?

E **PAIR WORK** Circulate and monitor as Ss ask each other questions and answer them. Listen for language usage and provide feedback at the end of the task.

- Ask volunteers to present their questions and answers to the class.

- Ask students what new information they learned about their classmates.

4 SPEAKING

A **Review** Before Ss discuss the question, read the examples and talk about your and your own family's routines. Monitor as Ss talk.

B **PAIR WORK** After Ss discuss this with a partner, ask them to circulate around the class discussing with three or four other Ss if they listen to their body clock.

- Monitor and listen to Ss as they talk. Listen for language usage that you can give feedback on when the activity is over.

- When finished, ask how many Ss listen to their body clock.

- Give feedback.

> **EXTRA ACTIVITY**
>
> Do a class survey. Ss write down four *yes/no* questions and four information questions. Check that their questions are grammatically correct. Ask them to go around the room asking three other Ss for their answers. Monitor and check for pronunciation.

3 GRAMMAR: Questions in the simple present

A Circle the correct answers. Use the sentences in the grammar box to help you.
1. With the pronouns *I*, *you*, *we*, and *they*, use **Do** / **Does**.
2. With the pronouns *he*, *she*, and *it*, use **Do** / **Does**.
3. In yes/no questions, the word order is **Do** or **Does** + person or thing + verb / **Do** or **Does** + verb + person or thing.
4. In information questions, put the question word(s) (for example, *Where* or *What time*) **before** / **after** *do* and *does*.

Questions in the simple present

Yes/no questions
Do I **have** class today?
Do you **go out** with friends?
Does he **go** to classes every day?
Does it **have** good apps?
Do they **have** dinner before you?

Information questions
How do I **get** to class?
What time do you **go out** with friends?
When does he **go** to classes?
What does it **have**?
Where do they **eat** dinner?

B PAIR WORK Complete the conversations. Use the audio script on page 46 to help you. Then practice them with a partner.

1. A _____ _____ do you go to work?
   B I _____ to work at 7:00.
   A Wow! _____ do you go to bed?
   B I usually go to bed after midnight. I'm always tired!
2. A _____ they play soccer?
   B _____ , they do. What about you?
   A No, I _____ .
3. A _____ Martin have a new job?
   B Yes, he _____ .
   A _____ does he work?
   B He _____ in an office.

C ▶ Now go to page 133. Look at the grammar charts and do the grammar exercise for 5.2.

D Write **three** questions about your partner's routine. Use the words in the box to start your questions. Then check your accuracy.

Do … ?   What … ?   What time … ?
When … ?   Where … ?

✓ **ACCURACY CHECK**

Use *do* or *does* with information questions in the simple present.
Where Margaret work? ✗
Where does Margaret work? ✓

E PAIR WORK Ask and answer the questions from exercise 3D with a partner.

4 SPEAKING

A Think about your routines and your family's routines. What do you do? When do you do it?

B PAIR WORK Ask your partner about their routines and their family's routines. Do they listen to their body clock?

When do you get up?

I usually get up at 7:30, but my sister gets up at 5:00!

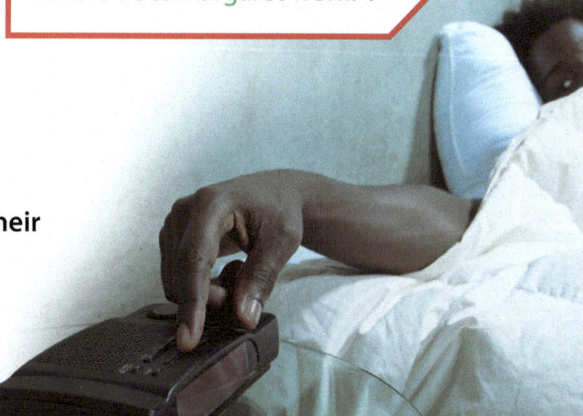

47

5.3 ME, TOO

LESSON OBJECTIVE
- show you agree and have things in common

1 FUNCTIONAL LANGUAGE

A 🔊 1.53 The men are at work. Read and listen to their conversation. What do both the men do?

> 🔊 1.53 Audio script
>
> A Do you always run at lunchtime?
> B Yeah, I usually run for about 30 minutes.
> A That's cool. It's good to go out.
> B **I agree.** And what about you? Do you run?
> A Hardly ever. Well, I play basketball.
> B So you run a lot!
> A **That's true.** But I don't have the ball a lot! I'm not very good.
> B **Me, neither.** But basketball is fun.
> A **Yeah, I know.**
> B I play with friends.
> A **Me, too.** Hey, we have a game on Thursday after work. Play with us!
> B Thursday. Um … yeah, OK.
> A Great! Now I'm not the only bad player.
> B Very funny!

B Complete the chart with expressions in **bold** from the conversations above.

Showing you agree	Showing you have things in common
I ¹ _____ .	⁴ _____ , neither. (-)
That's ² _____ . / That's right.	Me, ⁵ _____ . (+)
³ _____ , I know.	

C Choose the correct answers to complete the conversations. Then practice with a partner.

1. A I play basketball on the weekend.
   B *Me, too / Me, neither*. I play on Sunday.
2. A Soccer is great.
   B I *agree / right*. Do you play?
3. A This game is boring.
   B *Yeah, I know / Me, neither*. The team isn't very good.
4. A I don't get up late on Saturday.
   B *Me, too / Me, neither*. I get up at 8.

5.3 ME, TOO

LESSON OBJECTIVE
- show you agree and have things in common

Introduce the lesson Write or dictate the following activities or activities that might be relevant to your Ss:

work / watch TV / hang out with my friends / play sports / use the internet / go to a club / drive in the city, etc.

- Ask Ss to rank the activities 1–5 with 1 being their favorite activity. Ss then work together and ask if they like or don't like these things. They ask: *Do you like…?* and say: *Yes, I do.* or *No, I don't.*

1 FUNCTIONAL LANGUAGE

A 🔊 **1.53** Play the audio while Ss read. Play again if Ss wish until everyone has an answer.

- Play audio again. Pause after each sentence and Ss repeat together.

Answers
They both play basketball.

B Do the task Ss complete the chart in pairs before you check as a class. Check Ss' understanding of short concept questions by saying: *I think soccer is fun.* and point to a S. He or she responds: *Me, too.* Say: *I don't like coffee.* Elicit: *Me, neither.* Make the sentences relevant to Ss.

Answers
1 agree   2 true   3 Yeah   4 Me   5 too

C Review Ss complete the activity individually before checking their answers in pairs and then sharing with the class.

Answers
1 Me, too.
2 I agree.
3 Yeah, I know.
4 Me, neither.

📎 EXTRA ACTIVITY

Ask Ss to make two lists: *Things I like* and *Things I don't like*. Ss fill the lists with five items; they could be food, sports, music, activities, etc. Ss then share their list with a partner, talking about things they agree with and the things they have in common.

T-48

2 REAL-WORLD STRATEGY

Introduce the lesson Elicit a list of adverbs of frequency from Ss and write them on the board. Dictate two questions: *How often do you get up early? How often do you go to bed late?* Ask Ss to write their responses and check their own spelling before they share their answers with a partner. Monitor as they talk.

A **Introduce the task** After reading the box, elicit answers as a class.

> **Answers**
> B runs a lot. A doesn't run a lot.

B 🔊 **1.54** Play the audio as many times as Ss want. Ask Ss to check with a partner before you elicit answers as a class.

> **Answer**
> The woman

> 🔊 **1.54 Audio script**
> A You run, right?
> B Yeah, every morning.
> A So do you get up early?
> B Usually.
> A On weekends, too?
> B That's right.
> A No way!
> B Do *you* get up early on weekends?
> A Never!

C 🔊 **1.54** Play the audio again, pausing at sections if necessary so Ss can follow. Ss complete the task individually.

> **Answers**
> The man says *Never*. The woman says *Usually*.

> 📎 **EXTRA ACTIVITY**
> Check Ss' understanding by asking them individual, relevant questions like *Do you get up early?* to elicit *always, never,* etc. Make the questions relevant to your learners.

D PAIR WORK **Review** Put Ss into pairs and assign each one to be either Student A or Student B. Ask Student As to turn to page 157 and Student Bs to turn to page 159.

- Read through the instructions in part 1 aloud and check understanding.
- Allow Ss time to fill out the sentences alone using the adverbs. Circulate and monitor if needed.
- Bring the class together. Ask volunteers to read the speech bubbles aloud. Write *taxi driver* on the board and point to yourself to show this is your job. Ask Ss to ask you similar questions as a model for the activity. Answer using adverbs.
- Ss do the task. Monitor as Ss complete the task.

3 PRONUNCIATION: Saying syllables in words

A 🔊 **1.55 Introduce the task** Explain the meaning of *syllable*. Choose a S with a two- / three-syllable name. Write it on the board. Then say it aloud and show the syllables on your fingers.

- Play the audio. Ss check answers in pairs, then share as a whole class.

> **Answers**
> 1 1 2 3 3 2

B 🔊 **1.56** Ss guess the answers.

- Play the audio and have Ss repeat as a whole class. Check answers.

> **Answers**
> 1 2 2 2 3 3 4 1 5 1 6 2

C Refer Ss to page 48. Elicit an example, e.g., *lunchtime* = 2 syllables.

- Ss work alone before comparing with a partner. Check answers.

> **Suggested answers**
> 1 one syllable: lunch, cool, true, ball, good, play, friends
> 2 two syllables: lunchtime, ever, minute, neither, Thursday, player, very, funny, boring, early

4 SPEAKING

A Monitor and circulate as Ss make their lists. Spell any words Ss need on the board so everyone can see them.

> **Answers**
> Answers may vary.

B PAIR WORK Circulate and monitor as Ss discuss. Ask Ss to share their answers with other classmates.

- Listen for language usage, such as grammar and pronunciation, that you can give feedback on when the activity is over.
- When Ss finish, elicit what they have in common and write it on the board.
- Give feedback.

2 REAL-WORLD STRATEGY

SHORT ANSWERS WITH ADVERBS OF FREQUENCY
People sometimes answer questions with adverbs of frequency, not complete sentences.
A Do you always run at lunch?
B Usually. And what about you? Do you run?
A Hardly ever.

A Read about short answers with adverbs of frequency in the box above. Who runs a lot: A or B? Who doesn't run a lot?

B 🔊 1.54 Listen to a conversation. Who gets up early on the weekend: the man, the woman, or both of them?

C 🔊 1.54 Listen again. What one-word answer does the man say? What one-word answer does the woman say?

D ▶ PAIR WORK Student A: Go to page 157. Student B: Go to page 159. Follow the instructions.

3 PRONUNCIATION: Saying syllables in words

A 🔊 1.55 Listen. How many syllables do you hear? Write 1, 2, or 3.
1 run ___   2 basketball ___   3 soccer ___

B 🔊 1.56 Say the words. How many syllables are there? Write 1, 2, or 3. Listen and check.
1 weekend ___   3 usually ___   5 sport ___
2 Wednesday ___   4 chat ___   6 morning ___

C Look at the audio script on page 48. Find more examples of words with one or two syllables.

4 SPEAKING

A Write a list of things you do often. Write how you feel about the activities.

chat with friends online – fun
watch TV – interesting

B PAIR WORK Tell your partner what you do and how you feel about the activities. Your partner says when he/she agrees and when you have things in common. Then change roles and repeat.

On weekdays, I watch TV in the evening.

Me, too.

It's sometimes interesting.

Yeah, I know.

5.4 A HAPPY LIFE

LESSON OBJECTIVE
- write a report about your activities

1 READING

A **SKIM** Look at the picture and the title. What is the magazine article about?

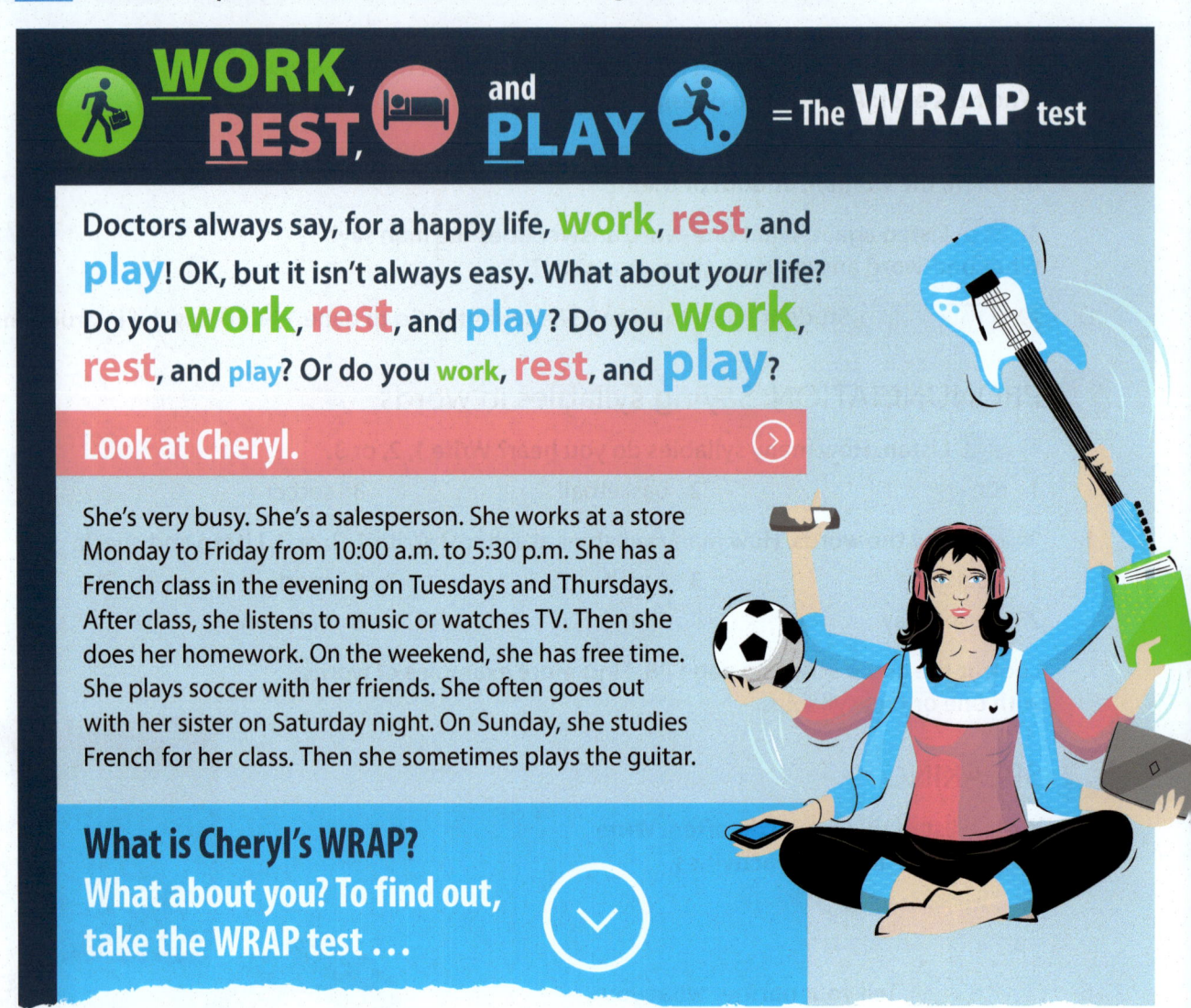

WORK, REST, and PLAY = The WRAP test

Doctors always say, for a happy life, **work**, **rest**, and **play**! OK, but it isn't always easy. What about *your* life? Do you **work**, rest, and play? Do you **work**, **rest**, and play? Or do you work, **rest**, and **play**?

Look at Cheryl.

She's very busy. She's a salesperson. She works at a store Monday to Friday from 10:00 a.m. to 5:30 p.m. She has a French class in the evening on Tuesdays and Thursdays. After class, she listens to music or watches TV. Then she does her homework. On the weekend, she has free time. She plays soccer with her friends. She often goes out with her sister on Saturday night. On Sunday, she studies French for her class. Then she sometimes plays the guitar.

What is Cheryl's WRAP?
What about you? To find out, take the WRAP test …

B **READ FOR DETAILS** Read the article again. Complete the chart with the correct verbs.

Work		Rest		Play	
works	at a store	_____	music	_____	soccer
_____	a French class	_____	TV	_____	with her sister
_____	her homework			_____	the guitar
_____	French				

C **PAIR WORK** **THINK CRITICALLY** Which WRAP result is true for Cheryl?

1 **work**, rest, and play   2 **work**, rest, and **play**   3 work, **rest**, and **play**

5.4 A HAPPY LIFE

LESSON OBJECTIVE
- write a report about your activities

Introduce the lesson Write *work*, *rest*, and *play* on the board. Tell Ss about the things you do in your own life to work, rest, and play. Show relevant pictures you might have on your smartphone. Now ask Ss to tell each other what they do to work, rest, and play. Monitor their conversations. Then elicit Ss' ideas.

1 READING

A **Introduce the task** Give Ss a short time to read the text. Elicit answers.
- Ask individual Ss to read a sentence of the text aloud. In this way, several Ss get reading practice and the class won't lose focus while listening to just one person.
- Check that Ss understand all words in the reading and allow them to translate if necessary.
- Direct Ss' attention to the picture of Cheryl. Call on a volunteer to describe what they see. Lead a class discussion about how the picture relates to the article.

> **Answer**
> The article is about work, rest, and play.

> **VOCABULARY SUPPORT** Reading a text quickly to get an overall idea of what it is about is called *skimming*. Reading and looking for a specific piece of information is called *reading for detail*. Explain to Ss that exercise A is a *skimming* task and exercise B is a *reading for detail* task.

B **Introduce the task** Review verbs as a part of speech in English. Ask: *How do we know if a word is a verb? (It describes action.)*
- Ss scan the text for information to complete the chart individually. Then they share their answers with a partner. Ask Ss to read the whole sentences when you elicit the answers. Monitor for pronunciation.

> **Answers**
> **Work: works** at a store, **has** a French class, **does** her homework, **studies** French
> **Rest: listens** to music, **watches** TV
> **Play: plays** soccer, **goes out** with her sister, **plays** the guitar

C **PAIR WORK** Monitor as Ss discuss the question. Encourage them to come to an agreement with their partner before you elicit answers from the whole class.

> **Answer**
> 2 **work**, rest, and play

> **📎 EXTRA ACTIVITY**
>
> Direct Ss to page 46 to review telling the time. Draw or show clocks displaying various times and elicit the correct times. Write: *What time do you … ?* on the board as a stem. Expand by asking *What time do you have English class?* Elicit answers from the class.
> - Ss work in pairs with one partner acting as Cheryl. They ask and answers questions about her day, e.g., *What time do you work at the store? I work at the store from 10:00 a.m. to 5:30 p.m.* Ss draw from the reading to ask and answer questions. When they have finished, encourage them to ask and answer personal questions about their own lives with each other using *What time do you … ?* Monitor as they talk. Elicit examples from the class when they finish.

T-50

2 WRITING

Introduce the task Tell Ss what you do every day. Use the sentences in the WRAP report as a model. Show or draw any pictures you might have to help explain your story. Ask Ss: *Are you the same as me?* Elicit their ideas.

A **Read the text together as a class. Ss answer the questions in pairs.**
- Direct Ss to the **Register check** box. Ask volunteers to read the text aloud. Monitor for pronunciation. Check Ss' understanding by asking them questions, which they answer with the time followed by *in the morning, in the afternoon,* or *at night*.

  What time do you [start work]?
  What time do you [have dinner]?

  > **Answers**
  > He teaches, watches TV, and plays basketball on weekdays. He studies English and reads books on the weekend.

B **Pre-teach the word *heading*** by showing an online or print newspaper and pointing to the headline. If Ss ask, note that headings are a kind of title, but that titles name things (e.g., books, movies, reports) and headings do not. Ss think about the answers alone before you elicit them aloud.

  > **Answers**
  > Students circle the headings: Rest, Play, My WRAP result
  > What do they show? c – the different topics in the report

C **Ss answer in pairs before checking back with the rest of the class.**

  > **Answers**
  > b Andre's activities

D **Ask Ss to talk to a partner**, explaining the things they do to work, rest, and play. Talking in pairs may give Ss more ideas to write about. They can use vocabulary from this unit to help them.
- Circulate as Ss write, discussing their ideas with them.

E **Do the task** As Ss write, circulate and monitor their work. Ss can use the WRAP report in exercise 2A to help them as well as the one on page 50.
- Write on the board any words Ss may need spelled so everyone can see them.

F PAIR WORK **Review** If possible, mark Ss' texts before they share them with a partner and discuss their WRAP results.

G GROUP WORK As groups talk, monitor for pronunciation and grammar. When Ss finish, bring them back together and discuss their ideas. Find out which WRAP result is the most common.

🚶 FAST FINISHERS

Write *always, usually, sometimes, never* on the board as column heads. Ask Ss to copy these in their notebooks and then write two sentences in each column using the appropriate adverb.

always	usually	sometimes	never
	I usually play soccer on Friday.		

Remind Ss that adverbs of frequency usually go before the main verb.

T-51

2 WRITING

A Read Andre's WRAP report. What does he do on weekdays? What does he do on the weekend?

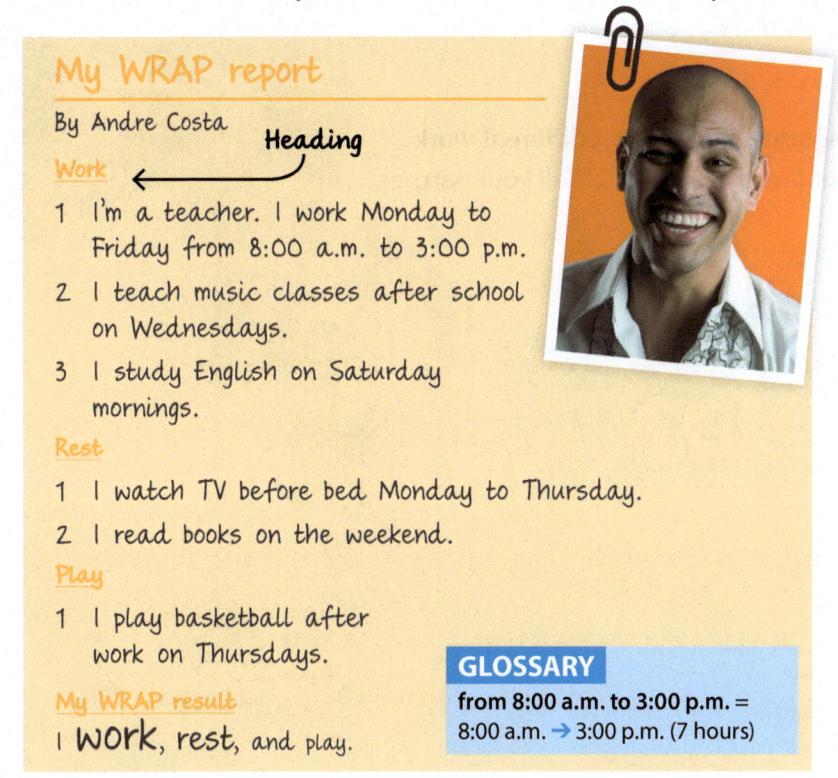

My WRAP report

By Andre Costa

Work ← Heading

1. I'm a teacher. I work Monday to Friday from 8:00 a.m. to 3:00 p.m.
2. I teach music classes after school on Wednesdays.
3. I study English on Saturday mornings.

Rest

1. I watch TV before bed Monday to Thursday.
2. I read books on the weekend.

Play

1. I play basketball after work on Thursdays.

My WRAP result

I **work**, **rest**, and **play**.

GLOSSARY
from 8:00 a.m. to 3:00 p.m. = 8:00 a.m. → 3:00 p.m. (7 hours)

REGISTER CHECK

Write *a.m.* and *p.m.* after times.
I work Monday to Friday from 8:00 a.m. to 3:00 p.m.

Say *in the morning*, *in the afternoon*, or *at night* after times.
Andre says, "I sometimes go to bed at 1:30 in the morning."

B **WRITING SKILLS** Look at the heading "Work." (Circle) the other headings in the report. What do they show?

  a days and times in the report
  b different sports in each part of the report
  c the different topics in the report

C Look at the numbered lists in the report above. What do the lists show?

  a Andre's test results (= answers)
  b Andre's activities
  c Andre's classes

D Write notes in the chart below with your information. Use the chart in exercise 1B for an example.

Work	Rest	Play

WRITE IT

E Write your WRAP report. Use headings and numbered lists. Include activities, times, and days.

F PAIR WORK Work with a partner. Read your partner's report. What's his/her WRAP result?

G GROUP WORK Compare reports in your group. Tell the group about your partner.

> Sora works at a restaurant on the weekend. She …

51

5.5 TIME TO SPEAK
Life = 5 + 2

LESSON OBJECTIVE
- compare different work weeks

A PREPARE Read the magazine article about different work weeks. Which week is your favorite: A, B, or C? Tell your partner.

END OF THE TWO-DAY WEEKEND?

For a lot of people, life = 5 + 2. They work 5 days and have 2 days for the weekend. But is this good? Imagine:

Week A	We work 4 long days (10 hours) and have 3 days for the weekend.
Week B	We work 6 short days (6½ hours) and have 1 day for the weekend.
Week C	We work 7 very short days (5½ hours) and don't have a weekend.

B DISCUSS Imagine you have a "week A" life. Talk to a partner. Describe your routine. What do you do, and when do you do it? Then talk about week B and week C.

C DECIDE Which week is good for your body clock: A, B, C, or "5 + 2"? Why?

D AGREE Tell the class which week is your favorite. Which week does everyone like? Which week does no one like?

To check your progress, go to page 153.

USEFUL PHRASES

PREPARE
Which week is your favorite?
Week … is my favorite.

DISCUSS
I have a week A/B/C life.
I get up / have breakfast at …
I work from … to …
Before/After work, I …
I have free time from … to …

DECIDE
Week … is good for me because …
I like / don't like week … because …
I want free time on the weekends / in the evenings.
I like long /short work days.

5.5 TIME TO SPEAK
Life = 5 + 2

LESSON OBJECTIVE
- compare different work weeks

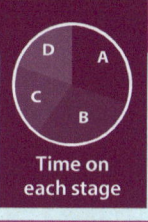

Time on each stage

Introduce the task Display a picture of a country village or farm. Ask Ss about what it's like to work there. Ask: *Do people work hard here? How often do they work?* Elicit answers. Now show Ss a picture of a busy city. Ask the same questions. Teach and write the word *compare* on the board. Ask Ss to compare the two pictures and places.

- Direct Ss to the **Useful phrases** section at the bottom of the page. Remind them that they can use them at the relevant stages of the lesson.

A **PREPARE** **Do the task** **Aim: Ss read about different types of weeks.**

Explain that = is a symbol that means *equals* and + is a symbol that means *plus*. Ask Ss where else they have seen these symbols.

- **CLASS WORK** Ask Ss: *What does the title mean?* Read the text together. Explain any words Ss may find difficult.
- **PAIR WORK** Monitor as Ss discuss the question before you elicit their ideas.

B **DISCUSS** **Aim: Ss discuss their routines.**

- **PAIR WORK** Allow Ss time to discuss all three types of week. Tell them to compare their routines for each week.
- **PAIR WORK** Ask Ss to consider if their discussion of the routines changes their answer in exercise A. Circulate and monitor Ss as they discuss.

C **DECIDE** **Aim: Ss choose the best week.**

- **PAIR WORK** Give Ss a time limit to make a decision, say two minutes.

D **AGREE** **Aim: Ss share their choices with the rest of the class.**

- **INDIVIDUALLY** Before Ss share their ideas, tell them to practice what they are going to say in their own language.* They should make notes and do the task again in English.
- **CLASS WORK** Ask individual Ss to explain to the rest of the class which kind of week they like and why. Have a class vote on which week Ss like best.

Review Use reformulation to correct errors. See page xxii for details.*

*These tips can help you to create a safe speaking environment. They can also be used with other speaking activities. For more information, see page xxii.

PROGRESS CHECK

Direct students to page 153 to check their progress. Go to page T-152 for Progress check activity suggestions.

TEACHER DEVELOPMENT REFLECTION

You can answer these questions in a reflection journal or discuss them with your peers.

1 Development Activity 1 shows Ss a new way of recording vocabulary. How do your Ss usually record vocabulary? What are the advantages of the spidergram format? Are there any disadvantages?

2 How did your Ss cope with these aspects of the spidergrams: showing meaning, showing pronunciation, identifying word class (noun, verb, etc.), translation and creating example sentences? What kind of help did you need to provide in each case?

3 Development Activity 2 is a traditional choral drill with an added element of a memory challenge. Did your Ss enjoy the activity? Did they manage to continue until all the circles were empty? Why or why not?

4 Aside from helping Ss with memorization, what are the advantages of drilling new words, expressions, or structures?

T-52

ZOOM IN, ZOOM OUT

6

TEACHER DEVELOPMENT INTRODUCTION

Strategy 3: Building learners' confidence to speak – Planning

When we speak in our first language, we typically think about what we want to say and how we want to say it. We can usually do this very quickly. However, when we speak in a second language, it takes more time to do this. Sometimes teachers forget that students need time to think about the content and the language they will need to speak, especially lower-level students. With many speaking activities, it helps students if you give them some time to plan their ideas and the language that is necessary. This means that speaking activities will often begin with a minute of silence while students do this and make notes if necessary. You can read more about planning speaking on pages 6 and 7 of Philip Kerr's article *How much time should we give to speaking practice?* You can find it here:

http://www.cambridge.org/elt/blog/wp-content/uploads/2017/12/CambridgePapersinELT_TimeForSpeaking_2017_ONLINE1.pdf

INTRODUCE THE THEME OF THE UNIT

Talk to Ss about where you come from or a place that you know well. Show photographs you might have of buildings or landmarks. Tell Ss about your favorite place in the town/city. Answer any questions Ss have about where you come from.

UNIT OBJECTIVES

Read the unit objectives aloud. Tell Ss to listen and read along. Explain any new vocabulary Ss may not understand, such as *nature*, *directions*, and *neighborhood*.

START SPEAKING

A **In pairs, Ss say what they see in the picture. Elicit ideas when they finish.**

- **OPTIONAL ACTIVITY** Ss watch Julieth's video and identify the things she mentions. They say if they see the same things in the picture.

> **REAL STUDENT**
>
> I can see a lot of buildings, uh … mountains, a lot of them. Uh … I can see a lake, a very big lake, some boats, a very big bridge, uh … houses, … uh, trees, grass, skies …

B **In pairs, Ss discuss why they would or would not like to go there.**

C **Ss answer in pairs. Elicit ideas.**

UNIT OBJECTIVES
- talk about places in the city
- talk about nature in your area
- ask for and give directions
- write a fact sheet about a place in nature
- plan a new neighborhood for a city

ZOOM IN, ZOOM OUT

6

START SPEAKING

A Say things you see in the picture. For ideas, watch Julieth's video.

B Do you want to go here? Why or why not?

C Do you like cities? Do you like places in nature? Which is your favorite?

REAL STUDENT

Do you see the same things as Julieth?

53

6.1 GOOD PLACES

LESSON OBJECTIVE
- talk about places in the city

1 LANGUAGE IN CONTEXT

A 🔊 1.57 Lucas and Robert are in New York City. Read and listen to their conversation. Where is Lucas from? Where is Robert from? What does Lucas want to do on Saturday?

B 🔊 1.57 Read and listen again. Are the sentences true or false?

1 Lucas has a lot of time in New York City.
2 There is no restaurant in the hotel.

🔊 1.57 Audio script

Lucas I'm here, in New York City, for a week. And then I go home to Paris on Sunday.

Robert So you don't have a lot of time to see my great city.

Lucas No, I don't. There's no free time this week – it's work, work, work! But I have some time on Saturday.

Robert OK. There are a lot of places to see and things to do on the weekend. Where is your **hotel**?

Lucas It's near Central Park.

Robert No way! Central Park is great. There are some interesting museums near the **park**. Oh, and there's a **zoo** in the park!

Lucas Cool! What about places to eat? There's no **restaurant** in my hotel.

Robert Hmm … for breakfast, there's a nice **café** near here. And there are a lot of great restaurants in this neighborhood, too.

Lucas Great. Do you know some good **stores**? I don't have a lot of free time, but …

Robert Oh, yeah. There are a lot of great stores in New York. So … no museum, no park, no zoo – just shopping?

Lucas Yes!

GLOSSARY
neighborhood (n) an area of a city

INSIDER ENGLISH
Use *No way!* to show surprise.
No way! Central Park is great.

2 VOCABULARY: Places in cities

A 🔊 1.58 Listen and repeat the words.

- bookstore
- hospital
- movie theater
- restaurant
- supermarket
- café
- hotel
- museum
- school
- zoo
- college
- mall
- park
- store

B ▶ Now do the vocabulary exercises for 6.1 on page 145.

C **PAIR WORK** Which three places in cities do you both like? Which three <u>don't</u> you like?

6.1 GOOD PLACES

LESSON OBJECTIVE
- talk about places in the city

Introduce the lesson Display pictures of well-known places from the town you are in. Elicit the names of these places from Ss. Ask: *What's your favorite place in this town? What place don't you like?* Ask Ss to suggest more pictures and show them to the class.

1 LANGUAGE IN CONTEXT

A 🔊 **1.57 Introduce the task** Play the audio while Ss read. Direct them to the **Glossary** box. Ask Ss to identify any more words they don't understand, then explain them.

- Ss discuss the questions in pairs before sharing their answers with the class.

> **Answers**
> Lucas is from Paris. Robert is from New York City.
> Lucas wants to go shopping on Saturday.

B 🔊 **1.57** Play the audio again. Ask Ss to answer the questions individually before sharing their answers with a partner. Elicit answers.

> **Answers**
> 1 False 2 True

- Read the **Insider English** box. Check understanding by telling individual Ss *I live on a boat.* to elicit *No way!* Ask Ss to write or say a sentence that can't be true and could elicit *No way!*

2 VOCABULARY: Places in cities

A 🔊 **1.58** Play the audio while Ss read. Pause after each word and ask individual Ss to repeat.

B Direct Ss to page 145 to complete the vocabulary exercises. Teacher's tips for vocabulary exercises are on page T-141.

C **PAIR WORK** Read the instructions aloud for Ss. Ask them to discuss the questions in pairs.

T-54

3 GRAMMAR: *There's, There are; a lot of, some, no*

Introduce the grammar Think about the city you and your Ss are most familiar with. Write sentences about the city using *there is …* and *there are …*, e.g., *There is a [museum]. There are some [parks]*. Underline the *is a* in the first sentence and the *are some* in the second sentences. Ask Ss: *Why do we use* is *and* are? to elicit *one thing = is / two or more things = are*. Also underline the *s* on the end of the noun in the second sentence and ask *Why do we use* s *here?* Elicit: S *makes a noun plural*.

A Before Ss circle the answers in pairs, explain that they can refer to the examples in the grammar box. Elicit answers from individual Ss.

> **Answers**
> 1 singular   2 plural   3 no
> 4 when you don't know how many things there are

- **Present the grammar** Ask different volunteers to read through the sentences in the grammar box aloud. Monitor pronunciation and explain any vocab Ss need.

> **GRAMMAR SUPPORT** To illustrate *no, a, some,* and *a lot of*, draw a box on the board and say *no*. Put a dot in the middle, say *a*. Now add five more dots, say *some*. Add many more dots and say *a lot of*.

B Ask Ss to circle the correct answers individually before they check with a partner. When eliciting answers, ask Ss to read the full sentence aloud.

> **Answers**
> 1 There are   2 There's   3 some   4 a   5 a lot of   6 no

C Direct Ss to page 134 to complete the grammar exercises. Teacher's tips for grammar exercises are on page T-129.

D Remind Ss of the introduction task. Allow them time to write their sentences. Spell any words that Ss need on the board so everyone can see and use them. Circulate around the class providing help.

- Ask volunteer Ss to read the **Accuracy check** box aloud. Write, dictate, or display the following sentences and ask Ss to correct them.
  1 There is some parks near my home.
  2 There are a lot of store in the city.
  3 There is a lot of cafés next to the park.

> **Answers**
> 1 There **are** some parks near my home.
> 2 There are a lot of store**s** in the city.
> 3 There **are** a lot of cafés next to the park.

- Ask Ss to check for mistakes in the sentences they wrote. Elicit some example sentences and write these on the board.

> **Answers**
> Answers may vary.

E **PAIR WORK** Ask Ss to share their sentences with a partner. Elicit some examples from volunteers and write them on the board.

4 SPEAKING

A **PAIR WORK** Model the sample sentences by asking a volunteer to read them aloud. Ask: *What is there in your neighborhood?* Elicit some answers.

- As Ss talk, circulate and monitor for grammar and pronunciation. Wait until the end of the activity before you give any feedback.
- Elicit ideas from the whole class when they finish.
- Give feedback.

3 GRAMMAR: *There's, There are; a lot of, some, no*

A Circle the correct answers. Use the sentences in the grammar box to help you.
1. Use *There's* with **singular** / **plural** nouns.
2. Use *There are* with **singular** / **plural** nouns.
3. Use *an* / *no* in negative sentences.
4. Use *some* for **exact numbers** / **when you don't know how many things there are**.

> *There's (= There is), There are; a lot of, some, no*
>
> **There's** no free time this week.
> **There's** a zoo in the park.
> **There's** a nice café near here.
>
> **There are** some interesting museums near the park.
> **There are** a lot of good places to see on the weekend.
>
> **no** = zero
> **a/an** = one
> **some** = a small number
> **a lot of** = a large number

B Circle the correct words to complete the sentences.
1. *There's / There are* a lot of stores in the mall.
2. *There's / There are* a supermarket near the college.
3. There are *a / some* good cafés on Boston Road.
4. There's *a / a lot of* big hospital in the city.
5. There are *a lot of / no* stores, so it's great for shopping.
6. In my city, there are *a / no* zoos.

C ▶ Now go to page 134. Look at the grammar chart and do the grammar exercise for 6.1.

D Write sentences about your city. Use *there is/there are, a/an, some, a lot of,* and *no*. Then check your accuracy.

There's _____.
There's _____.
There are _____.
There are _____.
There is/are no _____.

> ✓ **ACCURACY** CHECK
>
> Use *there are*, <u>not</u> *there is*, before *a lot of* and *some* + plural noun.
>
> There ~~is~~ some museums in this city. ✗
> There are some museums in this city. ✓

E PAIR WORK Compare your sentences with a partner.

4 SPEAKING

PAIR WORK Talk about the things in your neighborhood. Then compare with a partner. What's the same? What's different?

> There are some good restaurants near my home.

> Same! And there's a movie theater near my home.

6.2 CITY LIFE, WILD LIFE

LESSON OBJECTIVE
- talk about nature in your area

1 VOCABULARY: Nature

A 🔊 1.59 Listen and repeat the words. Which picture is your favorite? Which words describe water?

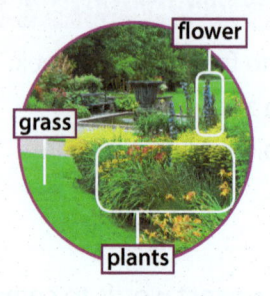

Labels on pictures: snow, mountains, river, island, beach, ocean, forest, lake, tree, flower, grass, plants, hill, desert

B Cross out the word that does not belong.
1 lake   ~~flower~~   ocean
2 plants   trees   snow
3 river   desert   lake
4 grass   beach   ocean
5 forest   ocean   trees
6 mountain   hill   island

C ▶ Now do the vocabulary exercises for 6.2 on page 146.

2 LANGUAGE IN CONTEXT

A Read the article. Choose a good title.
1 What's your favorite city?
2 Are you close to nature?
3 Do you like nature?

B PAIR WORK Take the test. Then compare your answers with a partner.

Do I like nature? Sure. We all love flowers and trees. But I live in a big city, so I don't live close to nature … Or do I? What about you? Take the test. For each sentence, (circle) all the answers that are true for you.

	In your neighborhood	In your city (e.g., in a park)	1–3 hours from your city	Not near your city
There's a lot of **grass**.	A	B	C	D
There are a lot of **flowers**.	A	B	C	D
There are some **trees**.	A	B	C	D
There's a **river**.	A	B	C	D
There's a **lake**.	A	B	C	D
There's a **forest**.	A	B	C	D
There are some **mountains and hills**.	A	B	C	D
There's a **beach**.	A	B	C	D
There's an **ocean**.	A	B	C	D
There are a lot of **plants**.	A	B	C	D

♡ 21   💬 25   🔄 14

A = 3 points,   **B** = 2 points,   **C** = 1 point,   **D** = 0 points

Are you close to nature?
45–60 points
Nature is everywhere!
30–44 points
There's a lot of nature near you.
15–29 points
There's some nature near you.
1–14 points
There isn't a lot of nature near you.
0 points
You only see nature on TV!

C PAIR WORK Give examples of nature in your city. For ideas, watch Larissa's video.

REAL STUDENT
Are your answers the same as Larissa's?

56

6.2 CITY LIFE, WILD LIFE

LESSON OBJECTIVE
- talk about nature in your area

Introduce the lesson Show or display a picture of a place in nature. This could even be a photograph that you've taken. Ask Ss to write down five things they can see in the picture to find out what vocabulary they already know. Write the items on the board. Look for words from the next exercise.

1 VOCABULARY: Nature

A 🔊 **1.59** **Present the vocabulary** Play the audio, pausing after each word so Ss can repeat.
- Play audio again. Ask individual Ss to say the words aloud. Monitor for pronunciation.
- Ss give their answers to the class.

> **Answers**
> Words that describe water: river, ocean, lake.

B Ss work in pairs to choose the word that does not belong. When you elicit the answers from the class, ask Ss to explain why the word does not belong.

> **Answers**
> 1 flower   2 snow   3 desert   4 grass   5 ocean
> 6 island

C Direct Ss to page 146 to complete the vocabulary exercises. Teacher's tips for vocabulary exercises are on page T-141.

2 LANGUAGE IN CONTEXT

A Ask volunteers to read the titles aloud. Monitor for pronunciation. Ss read the article individually before deciding on a title with a partner. Take a class vote to see which is the best.

> **VOCABULARY SUPPORT** *Close to nature* means being in close proximity to natural things such as mountains, forests, and animals.

B **PAIR WORK** Ss take the test individually, add up their scores, and read the results. Then ask Ss to compare their answers with a partner, noting which ones are the same and which are different.

C **PAIR WORK** **Review** Ss work together to list examples of nature in their city.
- **OPTIONAL ACTIVITY** Ss watch Larissa's video and identify the things she mentions. They say if they have the same things in their neighborhood. You may want to look up and/or explain what a *soccer court* is.

REAL STUDENT
Hello, my name is Larissa. In my neighborhood, there are trees. It's cool by the trees here, um … there isn't a park, but there is a soccer court.

📱 SMARTPHONE ACTIVITY
Ask Ss to share their own nature pictures with a partner. They look for places from exercise 1. Then Ss present their nature photos to the class.

📎 EXTRA ACTIVITY
Play nature vocabulary bingo with the words from exercise 1. For details of how to play, see page T-216.

T-56

3 GRAMMAR: Count and non-count nouns

Introduce the lesson Write or dictate eight to ten nouns and ask Ss to write them as plural. Use words that Ss have seen in the book so far, e.g., *book / car /* shop */ house / tea / coffee / sugar.*

- Elicit answers if possible. Explain that there are two types of nouns: count and noncount. This lesson presents one kind of noncount: mass or collective nouns that cannot be easily counted (e.g., *sugar* and *coffee*, which have too many grains to count).

A **Introduce the grammar** Before Ss circle the answers, explain that they can refer to the examples in the grammar box.

> **Answers**
> 1 singular and plural forms
> 2 singular
> 3 There are
> 4 There's

- **Present the grammar** Read the grammar box as a class. Individual Ss read each sentence aloud. Check for understanding by saying sentences with a *beep* sound in the middle. Ss replace the *beep* with a word. Do this orally. Use examples from the grammar chart, e.g., There are [beep] oceans near here. (Answer = no) There are [beep] plants (Answer = some) Use sentences that are relevant to your learners.

> **GRAMMAR SUPPORT** Count nouns are nouns we can count and become plural by adding *s*. For example, *a flower, five flowers,* etc. Non-count nouns are words that we can't count, and therefore don't ever become plural, e.g., *water, grass, tea.*

> **EXTRA ACTIVITY**
> Display or write a collection of words from exercise 1 on the board. Give Ss a time limit, about a minute, to identify and write target words. One minute for singular nouns, then elicit answers. One minute for plural nouns, elicit answers. One minute to identify and write down the non-count nouns, elicit answers.

B **Do the task** Ss complete the sentences individually before checking their answers with a partner, and then the class.

> **Answers**
> 1 trees 2 ocean 3 nature 4 restaurants 5 grass
> 6 hotels

C Direct Ss to page 134 to complete the grammar exercise. Teacher's tips for grammar exercises are on page T-129.

D PAIR WORK **Review** Model the first sentence by changing it on the board to make it true for you. Ss do the task individually before sharing their ideas with a partner.

4 SPEAKING

A Before Ss begin, display a picture of a place that you know well. To provide a model for Ss, use *there is* and *there are* to describe the scene. Answer any questions Ss may have.

- Ss choose a place and spend a few minutes thinking about the nature there. They can use their smartphone or the internet to look for a picture.
- Ask Ss to write down as many words as they can to describe the place before they share their ideas with a partner.

B PAIR WORK Ss now share their ideas (and pictures) with a partner. Ss should describe the place as best they can using the target language.

- Circulate and monitor, listening for good examples of English to share with Ss at the end of the activity.

> ### TEACHER DEVELOPMENT ACTIVITY 1
>
> **Planning language**
> When students plan language, it helps them recall language from the lesson and perhaps add one or two new words to their speaking activity.
>
> - With books closed, give instructions for 4A and ask Ss to think of a city.
> - Tell them to think about what this place looks like and make sure they know the words for most of the things in nature.
> - Ask Ss to write down all the words from 6.2 they can use to describe the city.
> - Give them about a minute to find the two or three new words on their phone. Monitor and help with pronunciation.
> - Also ask Ss to find pictures to show the meaning of the new words to their partner.
> - Tell Ss they have 30 seconds to study all the vocabulary they have planned.
> - Tell them to try to do the activity without looking too much at their vocabulary lists.

3 GRAMMAR: Count and non-count nouns

A (Circle) the correct answers. Use the sentences in the grammar box to help you.
1. Count nouns have **plural and singular forms** / **no singular or plural form**.
2. Use *a/an* with **singular** / **plural** count nouns.
3. Use ***There's*** / ***There are*** with plural count nouns.
4. Use ***There's*** / ***There are*** with singular count nouns and non-count nouns.

Count and non-count nouns		
Singular	**Plural**	**No singular or plural form**
There's a **river** in my city.	There are two **rivers**.	There's no / some / a lot of **grass**.
There's an **ocean** near here.	There are no **oceans** near here.	There's no / some / a lot of **water** in the ocean.
	There are some **plants**.	
	There are a lot of **flowers**.	

B Complete the sentences with the correct form of the nouns in parentheses ( ).
1. There are no ____trees____ (tree) in my neighborhood.
2. There's an _____ (ocean) three hours from my city.
3. There's a lot of _____ (nature) in this city.
4. There are some _____ (restaurant) on my street.
5. There is no _____ (grass) near my house.
6. There are a lot of _____ (hotel) in my city.

C ▶ Now go to page 134. Look at the grammar chart and do the grammar exercise for 6.2.

D [PAIR WORK] Change the sentences in exercise 3B so they're true for you and your city. Compare your sentences with a partner.

> There are some trees in my neighborhood.

4 SPEAKING

A Choose a city in your country or in a different country. Think about the nature there.

B [PAIR WORK] Work with a partner. Tell your partner about the place. Does your partner know the place?

> There's a beach in the city.
> There are no hills or mountains.
> There are a lot of trees …

> I know! It's Tampa, in the U.S.!

6.3 IS IT NEAR HERE?

LESSON OBJECTIVE
- ask for and give directions

1 FUNCTIONAL LANGUAGE

A Look at the pictures. The woman is in Quito, Ecuador. What places do you see on the map on her phone?

B 🔊 1.60 Read and listen. The woman asks two people for directions. What places does she ask about?

🔊 1.60 Audio script

1 A Excuse me. Do you speak English?
B Yes, I do.
A Oh, good! **Where's** Garcia Moreno Street? **Is it near here?**
B Yes, it is. Uh … turn left here. **Go one block**, and then **turn right**. **That's** Garcia Moreno Street.
A OK, great! Thanks.

2 A Excuse me. **Is this** Garcia Moreno Street?
B Yes, it is.
A Where's the City Museum?
B **It's that way. Go straight. It's on the left.** Or come with me! It's on my way to the supermarket.

C Complete the chart with expressions in **bold** from the conversations above.

Asking for directions	Giving directions
Where am I? / Where are we?	Turn left. / 4 _____ .
I don't understand the map.	5 _____ way.
1 _____ Garcia Moreno Street?	Go one 6 _____ . / Go 7 _____ .
Is it 2 _____ ?	It's on the right. / 8 _____ .
Excuse me. Is 3 _____ Garcia Moreno Street?	It's over there. / It's here!
	9 _____ Garcia Moreno Street.
	Look on your phone. Zoom in / zoom out. It's here.

D 🔊 1.61 [PAIR WORK] Complete the conversations. Then listen and check. Practice with a partner.

1 **A** Excuse me. *It's / Where's* Central Station?
   B Go one *way / block*. It's on the left.
2 **A** *Is this / Is it* San Gabriel Street?
   B No. *Turn / It's* right. That's San Gabriel Street.
3 **A** Is the language center *go straight / near here*?
   B Yes. It's over *there / go one block*.

6.3 IS IT NEAR HERE?

LESSON OBJECTIVE
- ask for and give directions

Introduce the lesson Display a map application on the board or on your smartphone. If possible, show your local area. Look for a landmark. Ask and write on the board: *Where is [landmark]?* Elicit and write *go left*, *go right*, and *go straight* on the board.

- Try again with a different landmark. Explain that we often use gestures to talk about directions, usually a finger pointing in the right direction.

1 FUNCTIONAL LANGUAGE

A Introduce the task Ss answer the question in pairs about the picture.

> **Sample Answers**
> café, mall, museum, supermarket, hotel, train station, restaurant

B 🔊 **1.60** Play the audio as Ss read. Pause after Conversation 1 for Ss to write the answer. Continue to play the audio. Ss share their answers after they have read and listened to Conversation 2.

> **Answers**
> She asks about Garcia Moreno Street and the City Museum.

- Play the audio again, pause after each line and Ss repeat either individually or as a group.
- Ss role play the conversations then repeat and switch roles. Monitor and check for pronunciation.

C Ss complete the chart individually before they share their answers with a partner. Elicit answers. Make sure Ss read the whole sentence.

> **Answers**
> 1 Where's 2 near here 3 this 4 Turn right 5 It's that
> 6 block 7 straight 8 It's on the left 9 That's

D 🔊 **1.61** **PAIR WORK** Ss work in pairs to complete the conversations. Play the audio when Ss have finished so they can check their answers.

- Ask Ss to practice the sentences with a partner. Monitor for pronunciation.

> **Answers**
> 1 A Excuse me. **Where's** Central Station?
>   B Go one **block**. It's on the left.
> 2 A **Is this** San Gabriel Street?
>   B No. **Turn** right. That's San Gabriel Street.
> 3 A Is the language center **near here**?
>   B Yes. It's over **there**.

📎 EXTRA ACTIVITY

With the help of Ss, list some local landmarks or places of interest near your class. Ss work in pairs and ask: *Where is [landmark]?* Their partner then uses the language from the chart to give directions.

- Vary this task by having Ss use a map application on their phone. They can give directions in any city in the world.

T-58

2 REAL-WORLD STRATEGY

A 🔊 **1.62** Books closed. Play audio. Ss listen and make note of any streets or places they hear. Books open. Ss listen again and share their answer with a partner.

> **Answers**
> He wants to go to the City Hotel.

> 🔊 **1.62 Audio script**
> A Excuse me. Is the City Hotel near here?
> B Yes. Turn left here. Go straight. It's on the right.
> A So, turn left here. Go straight. It's on the right.
> B Yes.

B 🔊 **1.62** Read the sentences with Ss to make sure they understand. Play the audio again. Ss share their answers with a partner.

> **Answers**
> 2 He repeats the woman's words.

C 🔊 **1.63** **Do the task** Direct Ss to **Checking Information**. Read the explanation and the conversation with a volunteer.

- Model the strategy by telling a volunteer: *It's on the left.* and having them say: *So, it's on the left.* Practice with other volunteers using different phrases for directions.
- Put Ss in pairs. Play the audio, pausing after each phrase so Ss can repeat the information back to their partner. Monitor for pronunciation.

> 🔊 **1.63 Audio script**
> 1 Turn right here. Then turn right again.
> 2 Go one block. Then turn left.
> 3 Go straight. Turn left. Then turn right.
> 4 Go three blocks. It's on the left.

D **PAIR WORK** **Review** Put Ss into pairs and assign each one to be either Student A or Student B. Ask Student As to turn to page 157 and Student Bs to turn to page 159.

- Before you begin, ask Ss to memorize some directions that you say aloud and then repeat them back to you, e.g., *Go straight. Turn right. It's over there.* Ask individual Ss to repeat the directions back to you.
- Read through the instructions aloud and check understanding. Explain that Ss should read their directions slowly for their partners.
- As Ss do the task, circulate and monitor.

3 PRONUNCIATION: Saying /ɪr/ and /er/ sounds

A 🔊 **1.64** Play the audio. Have Ss repeat, paying attention to the vowel sounds.

B 🔊 **1.65** Check that Ss understand the activity. Have Ss first read the words and guess the answers, then compare with a partner. Encourage Ss to try saying the words aloud.

- Play the audio. Check answers as a whole class.

> **Answers**
> 1 A 2 B 3 B 4 A 5 B 6 B 7 A 8 B

C 🔊 **1.66** **PAIR WORK** Play the audio. Pause it after each line and ask the class to repeat.

- Ss practice in pairs. Monitor and provide feedback.

4 SPEAKING

A **PAIR WORK** Ss put the conversation in order individually before sharing their answers with a partner. As Ss role play, monitor for pronunciation.

> **Answers**
> A Excuse me. Where's the Park Hotel?
> B It's that way. Go straight. Then turn left. It's on the left.
> A So, go straight. Then turn left. It's on the left.
> B Yes.

FIND IT

B Read both the situations as a class to check for meaning. Allow Ss time to think about the situation they have chosen and to prepare for the role play in the next activity.

C **PAIR WORK** Ss now work in pairs and role play the situation.

- Circulate and monitor for pronunciation.
- When finished, ask volunteers to perform their situation for the class. Give praise.

TEACHER DEVELOPMENT ACTIVITY 2

Planning content

For speaking activities where students have a role or a specific point of view, they need time to plan their ideas as much as the language. Note that in this activity, students get extra speaking practice planning what they will say.

- Put Ss in pairs, but ask them to work alone to think about and decide which two people are easy to talk about. Allow up to two minutes for this.
- Ask the two Ss to talk to compare their ideas, then they decide which person they will be.
- Ss make notes together on the things their person wants in the new neighborhood – just words, not sentences.
- Tell them they can look up only two or three new words.
- In pairs, Ss practice their presentation using the pronoun *we*.
- Ss present their ideas to the whole class.

2 REAL-WORLD STRATEGY

A 🔊 **1.62** Listen to a conversation. Where does the man want to go?

B 🔊 **1.62** Listen again. The man wants to check the information. What does he do?
1 He asks the woman to repeat her words.
2 He repeats the woman's words.

> **CHECKING INFORMATION**
> To check you understand, say *So, …* and repeat the information.
> It's that way. Turn left here. Go one block, and then turn right.
> So, turn left here. Go one block, and then turn right.

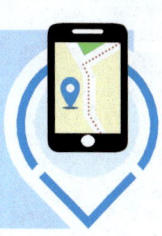

C 🔊 **1.63** Read about checking information in the box above. Then listen to the directions. Check the information.
1 Turn right here. Then turn right again.   *So, turn right here. Then turn right again.*

D ▶ PAIR WORK Student A: Go to page 157. Student B: Go to page 159. Follow the instructions.

3 PRONUNCIATION: Saying /ɪr/ and /er/ sounds

A 🔊 **1.64** Listen and repeat. Focus on the sound of the letters in **bold**.
/ɪr/ Is it n**ear** h**ere**?   /er/ Wh**ere** is th**eir** house?

B 🔊 **1.65** Listen. Write A for words with /ɪr/. Write B for words with /er/.
1 clear ___   3 chair ___   5 there ___   7 year ___
2 they're ___   4 earphones ___   6 parent ___   8 square ___

C 🔊 **1.66** PAIR WORK Listen to the conversations. Then practice with a partner.
1 A Wh**ere**'s Bl**air** Street?
   B It's n**ear** h**ere**. Go to the town sq**uare** and then turn right.
2 A Wh**ere** are your p**ar**ents?
   B Th**ey're** over th**ere**, on the ch**airs**.

4 SPEAKING

A PAIR WORK Put the conversation in order. Then practice it with a partner.
___ So, go straight. Then turn left. It's on the left.
___ Yes.
___ Excuse me. Where's the Park Hotel?
___ It's that way. Go straight. Then turn left. It's on the left.

B Work alone. Choose **one** of the situations below.
1 Imagine you are at the City Museum in Quito, Ecuador. Look at the map on the cell phone on page 58. Choose a place to go.
2 Imagine you are in another city. You can go online and find a map of the city. Choose where you are and a place to go.

C PAIR WORK Ask a partner for directions. You can use your phone to help you. Then change roles.

FIND IT

59

6.4 A FOREST IN THE CITY

LESSON OBJECTIVE
- write a fact sheet about a place in nature

1 LISTENING

A Look at the pictures. Where is the woman? What do you see?

B 🔊 1.67 **LISTEN FOR DETAILS** Listen to the podcast *Walk with Yasmin*. Where is the forest?

C 🔊 1.67 **LISTEN FOR EXAMPLES** Listen again. Check (✓) the words Yasmin says.

Forest	☐ animals	☐ grass	☐ an ocean	☐ a river
	☐ flowers	☐ a mountain	☐ plants	☐ trees
City	☐ hospitals	☐ museums	☐ restaurants	☐ stores
	☐ hotels	☐ people	☐ schools	☐ zoos

2 PRONUNCIATION: Listening for important words

A 🔊 1.68 Read the sentences below. Focus on the underlined words. Then listen. Which sentence do you hear, A or B?

　A   There <u>are</u> some tall trees <u>and</u> a lot <u>of</u> big plants here.
　B   There are some <u>tall trees</u> and a <u>lot</u> of <u>big plants</u> here.

B 🔊 1.69 <u>Underline</u> the important words in each sentence. Listen and check.
　1   There's a river near me.　　　　　　　　　(1 word)
　2   There are a lot of interesting animals here.　(3 words)
　3   I'm on a mountain in a forest.　　　　　　(2 words)
　4   There's an ocean and some beautiful beaches.　(3 words)

6.4 A FOREST IN THE CITY

LESSON OBJECTIVE
- write a fact sheet about a place in nature

Introduce the lesson Display a picture of a place you know well. It could be a city or a natural place you have visited. Use simple language to describe the place to Ss. Use the phrases *There is / are …* and *It has …* Write five simple sentences about the place on the board. One sentence is false and the other four are true. Ss guess which sentence is false.

1 LISTENING

A Ss discuss the questions together. Elicit answers when finished. Encourage students to guess where in the world these photos were taken.

> **Suggested answers**
> She is in a national park or forest. There are trees, rocks, mountains, a beach, and water.

B 🔊 **1.67 Do the task** Read the instructions with Ss to check for understanding. Play audio as Ss listen. Ss share their answers.

> **Answer**
> Rio de Janeiro

> 🔊 **1.67 Audio script**
>
> Welcome to "Walk with Yasmin." Where am I today? Well, there are some tall trees and a lot of big plants here. And do you hear the water? There's a river near me, too. And listen! There are a lot of interesting animals here. But I'm not in a zoo.
>
> I'm on a mountain in a forest. But trees and animals aren't the only things near me. There's an ocean and some beautiful beaches. And there are people, too. More than six million people! And a lot of buildings – hotels, stores, and restaurants.
>
> So where am I? This is Tijuca Forest, in the big, busy city of Rio de Janeiro.

C 🔊 **1.67 Review** Ss look over the word lists to check for understanding. Play audio again. Ss check answers in pairs.

> **Answers**
> Forest: animals, a mountain, an ocean, a river, plants, trees
> City: hotels, people, restaurants, stores

2 PRONUNCIATION: Listening for important words

A 🔊 **1.68** In pairs, Ss read the sentences and predict the answers.
- Play the audio and check answers.
- Explain that important words, for example nouns and verbs, are usually more stressed than other parts of speech.

> **Answer**
> Sentence B

B 🔊 **1.69** Ss read the sentences, check understanding, and predict which words will be stressed. Have them compare answers in pairs.
- Play the audio. Check answers.

> **Answers**
> 1 There's a <u>river</u> near me.
> 2 There are a <u>lot</u> of <u>interesting animals</u> here.
> 3 I'm on a <u>mountain</u> in a <u>forest</u>.
> 4 There's an <u>ocean</u> and some <u>beautiful beaches</u>.

T-60

3 WRITING

A **Introduce the task** Read the instructions aloud to Ss. Allow time for them to read the fact sheet individually. Ss share their answers with a partner before you elicit them and write them on the board. Make sure Ss understand what a fact is *(something that exists and can be proven as true)*.

> **Answers**
> plants, trees, rivers, waterfalls, interesting animals and birds, mountains, a statue

B **PAIR WORK** Ss answer the question in pairs before checking as a class.

> **Suggested answer**
> The language in the fact sheet is more formal, so the full forms are used.

> **EXTRA ACTIVITY**
> Write some contractions on the board and ask Ss to write out their long forms. Here are some contractions you could use.
> there's – there is / it's – it has or it is / I'm – I am / he's – he is / we're – we are / they're – they are

C **Introduce the task** Ss discuss with a partner what an *opinion* is. Then ask the whole class what is meant by an *opinion adjective* and elicit some examples, e.g., *funny, interesting*.

- Repeat with size adjectives and elicit examples, e.g., *large, short*, etc. Now direct Ss to do the task in pairs before you elicit the answers.

> **Answers**
> opinion adjectives: interesting, nice
> size adjective: big

D Ss work individually and circle the correct answers. Check as a class.

- Write or display more sentences on the board. Try to make them personal to your Ss or area. Ss put the expressions in parentheses at the end in the correct position, e.g., *There are [a lot of] great places in my country.* (a lot of) *I come from a [great] small village.* (great)

> **Answers**
> 1 before   2 before

- Draw Ss attention to the **Register check**. Ask a volunteer to read through the explanation.

E Discuss the places that Ss could write about. It could be a place they have been or a place they would like to go.

- Give Ss time to discuss their ideas with a partner. They can use their smartphone to find any information they may need.

F As Ss write, circulate and monitor. Offer to spell any challenging words on the board so that everyone can see them.

- If possible, correct Ss' factsheets individually. Ask Ss to share their factsheets with classmates.
- As a whole class, ask a volunteer to present their factsheet to the class. You or the volunteer can read their work aloud. Encourage questions from the rest of the class.

3 WRITING

A Read the fact sheet. What is in Tijuca Forest?

FACT SHEET: Tijuca Forest

Tijuca Forest is in Rio de Janeiro, Brazil.

It is a nice, big forest. It is 39 square kilometers.

There are a lot of plants and trees in the forest.

It has nice rivers and waterfalls.

It has a lot of interesting animals and birds.

There are some mountains in the forest. One famous mountain is Corcovado Mountain.

There is a tall statue on Corcovado Mountain. It is the Christ statue.

Brazilians love the forest, and people from many countries visit it.

Tijuca Forest is very important to Rio de Janeiro.

Taunay Waterfall
Capuchin monkey
Tropical flowers
Christ the Redeemer

B PAIR WORK THINK CRITICALLY There are no contractions in the fact sheet (for example, *It's, There's*). Why not?

C Read the sentences from the fact sheet. Underline two opinion adjectives and one size adjective.

It has a lot of interesting animals and birds.

It is a nice, big forest.

REGISTER CHECK

Really and *very* make adjectives stronger. Use *very* in writing. *Really* is common in speaking.

*Tijuca Forest is **very** important to Rio de Janeiro.*

D WRITING SKILLS Read the rules below. (Circle) *before* or *after*. Use the sentences in exercise 3C to help you.

1 *Some, a lot of,* and *no* go **before** / **after** opinion adjectives (for example, *good, nice, interesting*).

2 Opinion adjectives usually go **before** / **after** size adjectives (for example, *big, small, tall*).

E Choose a natural area to write about. You can go online to find facts about where it is, how big it is, what nature is there, and who goes to it. Use *very*. Do not use contractions. Remember to write adjectives in the correct order.

WRITE IT

F Write a fact sheet about a place in nature. Write five or six sentences. Use the fact sheet in exercise 3A for an example.

6.5 TIME TO SPEAK
A good place to live

LESSON OBJECTIVE
- plan a new neighborhood for a city

A PREPARE Talk to a partner. What do you see in the pictures?

B DISCUSS Which places in the pictures are important to have near your home? Write numbers 1–8 next to the pictures.

1 = very important → 8 = not very important

C DISCUSS Imagine that city planners want ideas for a new neighborhood in your city. Work with a partner. Choose <u>one</u> person from the list below. What does your person want in the new neighborhood? Write notes.

- You have young children.
- You are over 60 and you don't work.
- You are a young person in your first apartment.
- You are a college student in a home-share.

D PRESENT Present your ideas for the new neighborhood to the class. Which things does everyone think are important in a city?

≫ To check your progress, go to page 153.

USEFUL PHRASES

DISCUSS
I have children. A school is really important.
What about … ?   Me, too.   I agree. / I disagree.
I think … is good for the neighborhood.
I want … for the neighborhood.

I like / don't like …
I think … are very important / not very important.

PRESENT
We want …
Everyone in the class likes …

62

6.5 TIME TO SPEAK
A good place to live

LESSON OBJECTIVE
- plan a new neighborhood for a city

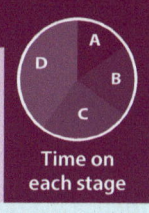

Time on each stage

Introduce the task Show a picture of a city or a town you all know on a map app. Ask, dictate, or write on the board *What is important in a city?* Elicit ideas and write them on the board, e.g., *school, hospitals,* etc.

- Direct Ss to the **Useful phrases** section at the bottom of the page. Remind them that they can use them at the relevant stages of the lesson.

A **PREPARE** **Aim: Introduce the vocabulary needed.**
- **PAIR WORK** Allow Ss time to discuss the photos together before they share their ideas with the class.

> **Suggested answers**
> A a park   B an art museum   C a mall   D a soccer field
> E a movie theater   F a restaurant   G a hospital
> H a student (university)

B **DISCUSS** **Aim: Ss decide what's most important for a city.**
- **INDIVIDUALLY** Set a time limit for Ss to rank the pictures alone, say two minutes.
- **PAIR WORK** Ss share their answers. Encourage Ss to give reasons.
- **CLASS WORK** Elicit some answers from individual Ss.

C **DISCUSS** **Aim: Ss write a wish list for a neighborhood.**
- **PAIR WORK** As Ss discuss, circulate and monitor. Keep Ss on task by offering suggestions or ideas. Monitor and make a note of the strong contributions of each pair, for example good use of unit vocabulary, interesting questions, natural-sounding interactions, etc.* You can use your notes to give feedback at the end of the lesson.

D **PRESENT** **Aim: Ss share their ideas with the whole class.**
- **PAIR WORK** Before Ss begin, encourage them to rehearse what they are going to say in their heads and make notes. Give Ss time to plan what they are going to say.* They can do the task twice; once with notes and once without.
- **CLASS WORK** Ask for pairs to present to the other Ss. Get them to stand in front of the class as they talk and share their ideas about what each person wants in the neighborhood. Monitor and make a note of the strong contributions of each pair, for example good use of unit vocabulary, interesting questions, natural-sounding interactions, etc. You can use your notes to give feedback at the end of the lesson.

Review **Feedback for speaking activities*** Give the class positive feedback based on the notes you made earlier in the activity. Use reformulation to correct errors. See page xxii for details.

*These tips can help you to create a safe speaking environment. They can also be used with other speaking activities. For more information, see page xxii.

▶ PROGRESS CHECK ▶

Direct students to page 153 to check their progress. Go to page T-152 for Progress check activity suggestions.

TEACHER DEVELOPMENT REFLECTION

Either answer these questions yourself in a reflection journal or discuss them with your peers.

1. What differences did you note between planned and unplanned speaking activities in this unit?
2. How comfortable were students during the silent planning time before speaking? How comfortable were you?
3. What do you need to do to make sure that students only make notes and not write complete sentences that they read aloud?
4. Did students need more time to plan language or more time to plan ideas? Why do you think this was the case?
5. How much *new* language do you think students should plan (compared to what you have already taught them)?
6. What extra things can *you* do to help students plan content? (For example, give them headings or categories.)

REVIEW 2 (UNITS 4–6)

Introduce the review Before beginning the review, write *Grammar*, *Vocabulary*, and *Functional language* on the board.
- Set a time limit of two minutes. Ss close their books and work in small groups to remember as much as they can about the grammar, vocabulary, and functional language of units 4–6. Groups write words, phrases, and example sentences in each category.
- Check answers as a class.

1 VOCABULARY

A **Write the following words on the board:** *father, brother, aunt, son*. **Ask Ss:** *Which word does not belong?* (aunt – because the other relative names are male).
- Tell Ss to do the task individually before they share with a partner. Elicit answers as a class.

> **Answers**
> 1 song, d. nature   2 hill, e. things we do
> 3 camera, b. music   4 hotel, f. days and times of day
> 5 morning, a. technology   6 run, c. places in cities

B **Ss work individually to complete the exercise before they check with a partner. Then check answers as a class.**

> **Answers**
> 1 song = b. music, *suggested:* popular music
> 2 hill = d. nature, *suggested:* desert
> 3 camera = a. technology, *suggested:* earphones
> 4 hotel = c. places in cities, *suggested:* zoo
> 5 morning = f. days and times of day, *suggested:* weekend
> 6 run = e. things we do, *suggested:* study

2 GRAMMAR

A **Write the following affirmative sentences on the board and ask volunteers to say the negative and question forms. Write their sentences on the board and point out corrections, if necessary. Highlight the use of** *do/don't/does/doesn't*.

affirmative	negative	question
I like soccer.	(I don't like soccer.)	(Do you like soccer?)
She has a dog.	(She doesn't have a dog.)	(Does she have a dog?)

- Ss do the exercise individually before you check answers as a class.

> **Answers**
> 1 Do / play / play   2 do / eat / eat   3 Does / work / works
> 4 Do / like / don't like   5 do / watch / don't watch
> 6 Do / have / doesn't have

B **PAIR WORK** Model some simple questions and write them on the board. *Do you like pizza? (Yes, I do.) Do you have a sister? (No, I don't.)*
- Monitor as Ss ask and answer questions.
- When Ss finish, elicit examples of questions and write them on the board.

C **Write** *My sister* **lives / live** *in New York* **on the board. Direct Ss to choose the correct answer (***lives***).**
- Ss complete the exercise individually before checking with a partner. Elicit answers.

> **Answers**
> 1 work   2 some   3 there are   4 there's   5 often
> 6 have

3 SPEAKING

A **PAIR WORK** Read the task aloud to the class. Model the example sentences with a S volunteer. Then think about a place the whole class will know. Say a few simple sentences using target language from Units 4–6. When you finish, ask Ss to guess what the place is.
- Allow Ss a few minutes to make notes. They may use their smartphones to research any information they might need. If Ss struggle to think of places, you could write a list for them to choose from on the board. e.g., *kitchen, garden, office, school, swimming pool, park*, etc.
- As Ss describe their places and guess, circulate and monitor for examples of language usage you can share with Ss at the end of the task.

B **Allow Ss time to write their sentences and help correct them. Ask Ss to share their corrected sentences with the class.**

REVIEW 2 (UNITS 4–6)

1 VOCABULARY

A Look at the groups of words in 1–6. In each group, circle the word that does not belong. Then match the groups with the categories (a–f).

1	grass	mountain	river	song	tree	___	a technology
2	call friends	get up	hill	play soccer	work	___	b music
3	album	band	camera	playlist	singer	___	c places in cities
4	afternoon	hotel	Monday	morning	night	___	d nature
5	app	laptop	morning	phone	tablet	___	e things we do
6	café	hospital	restaurant	run	store	___	f days and times of day

B Match each word you circled in 1–6 to a different category (a–f). Then add <u>one</u> extra word to the categories.

2 GRAMMAR

A Make questions and answers. Use the words in parentheses ( ) and *do/does/don't/doesn't*.

1. A _____ you _____ video games?
   B Yes, I sometimes _____ games on my cell phone. (play)
2. A Where _____ you _____ at lunchtime?
   B I usually _____ at home. (eat)
3. A _____ your grandfather _____?
   B Yes, he _____ at the hospital. (work)
4. A _____ you and your family _____ soccer?
   B No, we _____ it. (like)
5. A What _____ your parents _____ on TV?
   B Not a lot! They _____ usually _____ TV. (watch)
6. A _____ your children _____ phones?
   B My daughter has a cell phone, but my son _____ one. (have)

B PAIR WORK Ask and answer <u>five</u> questions about things you and your family do.

C Circle the correct answers.

I ¹*work / works* in a hotel. It's an expensive hotel with ²*a / some* really nice rooms. It's next to a big park. ³*There's / There are* a lot of trees, and ⁴*there's / there are* a lake, too. It's really nice in the park, so I ⁵*often / never* go at lunchtime, and I ⁶*have / has* lunch near the lake.

D Write a description of a nice place. Write how often you go there.

3 SPEAKING

A PAIR WORK Talk about a place. Describe it or say what you do there. Your partner guesses the place. Then change roles.

> There's a couch, and there are some chairs. I often watch TV in the evening.

> It's your living room.

B Write three sentences to describe a place from exercise 3A. Then compare with a partner.

63

4 FUNCTIONAL LANGUAGE

A Circle the correct answers.

Felix Your photos are great.
Maya Thanks. My phone has a good camera.
Felix ¹ *See / So*, all the pictures are from the camera on your cell phone.
Maya Yes, that's ² *fine / right*. I always use my cell phone camera.
Felix ³ *Hey. / Yeah.*
Maya ⁴ *What / Where* about you?
Felix I always use my phone, too. I don't have a different camera.
Maya ⁵ *Me, / My* neither. I don't want a different camera. They're really big …
Felix Yeah, I ⁶ *know / do*. And they're expensive.
Maya ⁷ *That's / There's* true.

B Complete the conversation with the words in the box. There are <u>two</u> extra words.

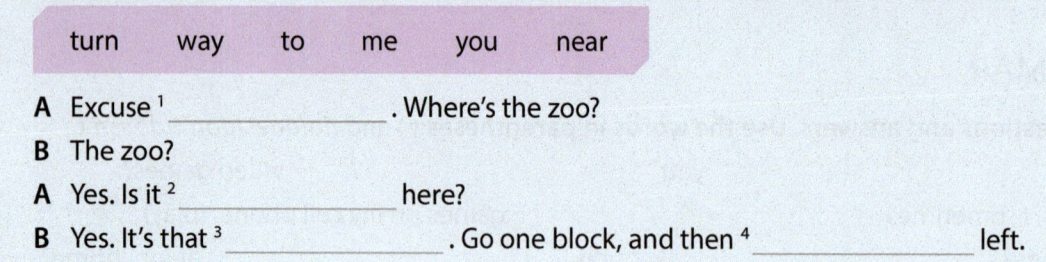

> turn   way   to   me   you   near

A Excuse ¹_____ . Where's the zoo?
B The zoo?
A Yes. Is it ²_____ here?
B Yes. It's that ³_____ . Go one block, and then ⁴_____ left.

5 SPEAKING

A **PAIR WORK** Choose <u>one</u> of the conversations below. Ask and answer the questions with a partner.

1 What technology do you have? How often do you use it?

> I have a laptop, a phone, and a TV. I use my laptop every day. I send emails, and I …

2 What do you on weekdays? When do you do fun things?

> On weekdays, I go to work. I get up at 7:00 a.m., and then I …

3 What's a good place to go to in or near your city? Where is it?

> There's a new Chinese restaurant near here. It's really good.

> Yeah. Where is it?

B **PAIR WORK** Change roles and repeat the conversation.

64

4 FUNCTIONAL LANGUAGE

A **Write *Me, too; Me, neither;* and *Yeah, that's right* on the board. Ask Ss to use these sentences to respond to your statements. Say: *I like coffee. (Me, too.) I don't like salad. (Me, neither.) London is in the UK. (Yeah, that's right.)*
- Ss do the exercise individually.
- Elicit answers from the class.
- Pairs read the conversations together. Monitor for pronunciation.

> **Answers**
> 1 So   2 right   3 Yeah   4 What   5 Me   6 know
> 7 That's

B **Ss do the exercise individually.**
- Check answers as a class.
- Pairs read the conversation together.

> **Answers**
> 1 me   2 near   3 way   4 turn

5 SPEAKING

A **PAIR WORK** Read each situation aloud. Encourage volunteers to read the example sentences after the descriptions.
- Ss choose one of the three situations and prepare a conversation. They should make notes, but not write the full conversation. For extra support, refer Ss to the functional language lessons from units 4–6.
- Monitor as pairs have their conversations. Listen for examples of language usage and provide feedback to Ss.

B **PAIR WORK** Pairs change roles and repeat their conversations.
- Choose pairs to perform their conversations for the class. If possible, choose a pair for each of the three situations.

T-64

NOW IS GOOD

7

TEACHER DEVELOPMENT INTRODUCTION

Strategy 1: Classroom management – Pair and group work

In this unit, we're going to focus on **pair and group work**, and how to make the most of it. When teachers say *Please work in pairs*, students often simply work with the person closest to them – often the same person in each lesson. We'll look at an alternative way of doing pairwork for **maximizing practice opportunities** with a series of different partners. We'll also look at ways of **encouraging quieter students to speak** during group work activities.

Maximizing practice opportunities (Activity 1): Ss practice language items with a series of partners. You'll have an opportunity to try this in lesson 7.2.

Encouraging quieter students to speak (Activity 2): Ss use tokens to encourage taking turns in role play. Try this in lesson 7.5.

To find out more, read chapters 5.7, 5.8, and 5.9 from *Classroom Management Techniques* by Jim Scrivener. Please go to www.cambridge.org/evolve to download these pages.

INTRODUCE THE THEME OF THE UNIT

Pre-teach *opposite* by writing the words *night* and *day* on the board. Write a list of words on the board. Ss guess the opposites.

good – bad / big – small / boring – interesting / tall – short

- Ask Ss to decide on one adjective in each pair to describe their life. Ss share their answers in pairs.

UNIT OBJECTIVES

Read the unit objectives aloud. Tell Ss to listen and read along. Explain any new vocabulary Ss may not understand. Pre-teach *activity* and *happen*.

START SPEAKING

A Ss discuss the questions in pairs before you elicit ideas.

B Ss share their ideas with a partner, then discuss as a class.

C Draw a Venn diagram on the board with *Me* above one circle, *Them* above the other circle, and *Both* over the overlap. Encourage Ss to copy it. Ss discuss their ideas before writing them in the correct place on the diagram.

UNIT OBJECTIVES
- talk about activities around the house
- ask and answer questions about travel
- share news on the phone
- write a blog about things happening now
- ask what people are doing these days

NOW IS GOOD

7

START SPEAKING

A Say what you see in the picture. Who are the people? Are they at work or do they have free time? Where are they?

B Are they busy now? Do they have a busy life?

C Talk about things:
- they do *and* you do.
- you do, but they don't.
- they do, but you don't.

7.1 A GOOD TIME TO CALL

LESSON OBJECTIVE
- talk about activities around the house

1 LANGUAGE IN CONTEXT

A 🔊 2.02 David calls his sister Ariana on the phone. Read and listen. (Circle) the correct answers.

1. Ariana is *the mother* / *the daughter*.
2. Jason is *Ariana's son* / *Ariana's husband*.
3. Stevie is *Ariana's son* / *Ariana's daughter*.
4. Julia is *Ariana's sister* / *Stevie's sister*.

🔊 **2.02 Audio script**

David	Hi, Ariana. It's David. Are you busy? Is this a good time to call?
Ariana	Um, well, I'm **cooking** breakfast right now, and Jason's **helping** the children—Jason, Stevie isn't drinking his milk.
David	Oh, yeah. It's a school day today.
Ariana	That's right, so …
David	What time do they leave for school?
Ariana	Usually at 8:00, but we're running late today — Jason, give this to the kids, OK? Thanks. — OK, David, they're eating breakfast now.
David	Do they like their classes?
Ariana	Yes, and they're learning a lot — Julia, you're not eating. Please eat your breakfast now! — Sorry, David. This isn't a good time to talk.

B 🔊 2.02 Read and listen again. Is David busy now? Why does Ariana say "This isn't a good time to talk."?

GLOSSARY
kids (*n*) children (informal)
running late (*phrase*) you are late

2 VOCABULARY: Activities around the house

A 🔊 2.03 Look at the pictures. Listen and repeat.

1. I'm cleaning the kitchen.
2. I'm cooking dinner.
3. I'm washing my hair.
4. I'm brushing my teeth.
5. I'm doing the dishes.
6. I'm helping my daughters. They're taking a bath.

B Add the words in the box to the verbs.

breakfast	the dog	my hair	my homework	~~my room~~	a shower

1. clean   the kitchen / __my room__
2. cook   dinner / _____
3. wash   my hair / _____
4. brush   my teeth / _____
5. take   a bath / _____
6. do   the dishes / _____

C ▶ Now do the vocabulary exercises for 7.1 on page 146.

D **PAIR WORK** Do you do your homework **and** talk on the phone? What other activities do you do at the same time? For ideas, watch June's video.

REAL STUDENT *Do you do the things June does?*

66

7.1 A GOOD TIME TO CALL

LESSON OBJECTIVE
- talk about activities around the house

Introduce the lesson Write the sentence *I'm eating lunch.* on the board. Mime eating. Underline the *ing* and explain that this means this action is happening now. Mime other actions for Ss to guess. They call out what you are doing. Encourage them to use the present continuous with *ing*. Mimed actions could be: *driving a car, playing a video game,* and *drinking coffee.* You could also use images and video clips to illustrate actions happening now.

1 LANGUAGE IN CONTEXT

A 🔊 2.02 Read the sentences 1 to 4 aloud and check Ss' understanding. Draw Ss' attention to the **Glossary**. Check understanding of *running late*.

- Play the audio as Ss read and circle the answers.
- Ss then share their answers with a partner. Play audio again if necessary.

> **Answers**
> 1 the mother
> 2 Ariana's husband
> 3 Ariana's son
> 4 Stevie's sister

B 🔊 2.02 Ss answer the questions with a partner before you check as a class.

> **Answers**
> David isn't busy. It isn't a good time to talk because Ariana and Jason are giving their children breakfast before they go to school.

2 VOCABULARY: Activities around the house

A 🔊 2.03 Play the audio as Ss read. Pause after each phrase and ask Ss to repeat as a class. Draw Ss' attention to *ing* at the end of each verb, which means this action is happening now.

B Individually, Ss add the words before checking in pairs.

> **Answers**
> 1 clean the kitchen / **my room**
> 2 cook dinner / **breakfast**
> 3 wash my hair / **the dog**
> 4 brush my teeth / **my hair**
> 5 take a bath / **a shower**
> 6 do the dishes / **my homework**

📎 EXTRA ACTIVITY

Hold a spelling bee. Give Ss six to eight phrases to learn for the next session. These could be the phrases from the vocabulary exercises on page 146 or one of the verbs from the lesson vocabulary. Dictate the phrases and then ask Ss to exchange papers and let a partner correct them. Praise and encourage Ss. Remind them that English words are not always spelled the way they sound.

C Direct Ss to page 146 to complete the vocabulary exercises. Teacher's tips for vocabulary exercises are on page T-141.

D **PAIR WORK** Review While Ss talk in pairs, circulate and monitor. Listen for examples of language usage that you can give feedback on when the activity is over.

- **OPTIONAL ACTIVITY** Ss watch the video and say whether they do the same things that June does. They then compare answers in pairs. You may want to explain that *wash [the] dishes* is another way of saying *do the dishes*.

REAL STUDENT

Hello, I'm June … I sometimes talk on the phone and wash dishes at the same time.

T-66

3 GRAMMAR: Present continuous statements

A **Present the grammar** Before Ss circle the answers, explain that they can refer to the examples in the grammar box.

- Read the grammar chart with Ss asking volunteers to read the sentences.

> **Answers**
> 1 things happening right now or around now
> 2 right now
> 3 around now
> 4 verb + -ing

> **EXTRA ACTIVITY**
>
> Take several simple sentences in the present continuous and scramble the words on the board. Give Ss a few minutes to unscramble them before they check with a partner and then the class. Include positive and negative sentences and try to make them relevant to your Ss, e.g.,
>
> *We're cooking dinner. / He's not brushing his hair. / She's doing her homework. / I'm taking a bath. / Your parents aren't learning English.*

B Do the first sentence with the class as an example. Ss complete the sentences individually before sharing their answers with their partner.

> **Answers**
> 1 He**'s not taking** a bath. He's in the shower.
> 2 **I'm doing** my homework now. It's really difficult.
> 3 Carola isn't studying right now. She**'s watching** TV.
> 4 My parents **aren't washing** the car. They're having lunch now.
> 5 **I'm not brushing** my hair. I'm brushing my teeth.
> 6 You**'re helping** your friends with their English. You're really nice!
> 7 My cat loves milk. It**'s drinking** milk right now.

C Direct Ss to pages 134–135 to complete the grammar exercise. Teacher's tips for grammar exercises are on page T-129.

D Discuss ideas before Ss write. As they write, circulate and offer help.

- Ask Ss to share their sentences with their partner when they finish.
- Direct Ss to the **Accuracy check** box. Read aloud for Ss. Write the following sentences on the board for Ss to complete with the present continuous or present simple form of the verbs in parentheses ( ).
  1 I'm busy. I _____ (have) dinner with my family.
  2 She _____ (go) to work at 8:00 a.m. every day.
  3 We _____ (clean) the house now.

- Ss should now be able to check their own sentences. Ask volunteers to write their sentences on the board so you can correct them as a class.
- Elicit answers from volunteers. If possible, correct Ss sentences individually.

> **Answers**
> 1 I'm having   2 goes   3 We're cleaning

4 SPEAKING

A Ask Ss: *What are you usually doing at 5 o'clock in the morning?* to elicit the answer *I'm sleeping*. Ss discuss their activities with a partner or a small group. As they talk, circulate and monitor for pronunciation and grammar.

B **PAIR WORK** Model the activity with a volunteer before Ss work in pairs to call each other. Circulate and monitor as Ss talk.

> **SMARTPHONE ACTIVITY**
>
> Ss look through pictures on their phones with a partner. Ss ask: *What are you doing?* about a photo and their partner responds: *I'm [playing soccer]*. Ss share photos with other members of the class.

3 GRAMMAR: Present continuous statements

A Circle the correct answer. Use the sentences in the grammar box to help you.
1. Use the present continuous to talk about **things happening right now or around now / finished things**.
2. Sentences 1, 2, and 3 in the grammar box are about **right now / around now**.
3. Sentence 4 is about **right now / around now**.
4. To make the present continuous, use *am/is/are* and a **verb + -ing / verb + -s**.

> **Present continuous statements**
> 1. I**'m cooking** breakfast right now.
> 2. Jason, Stevie **isn't drinking** his milk.
> 3. Julia, you**'re not eating** your breakfast.
> 4. They**'re learning** a lot at school this year.

B Complete the sentences in the present continuous. Use an affirmative or negative form of the verbs in parentheses ( ).
1. He _____ (take) a bath. He's in the shower.
2. I _____ (do) my homework now. It's really difficult.
3. Carola isn't studying right now. She _____ (watch) TV.
4. My parents _____ (wash) the car. They're having lunch now.
5. I _____ (brush) my hair. I'm brushing my teeth.
6. You _____ (help) your friends with their English. You're really nice!
7. My cat loves milk. It _____ (drink) milk right now.

C ▶ Now go to page 135. Look at the grammar chart and do the grammar exercise for 7.1.

D Think about four of your friends. What are they doing or not doing now? Write sentences about each person. Then check your accuracy.

Teresa isn't studying. She's playing games on her phone.

> ✓ **ACCURACY CHECK**
>
> Use the present continuous for things you're doing now. Use the simple present for things you do regularly.
>
> Just a minute. ~~I talk~~ on the phone. ✗
> Just a minute. I'm talking on the phone. ✓
> I talk on the phone every day. ✓
> I'm talking on the phone every day. ✗

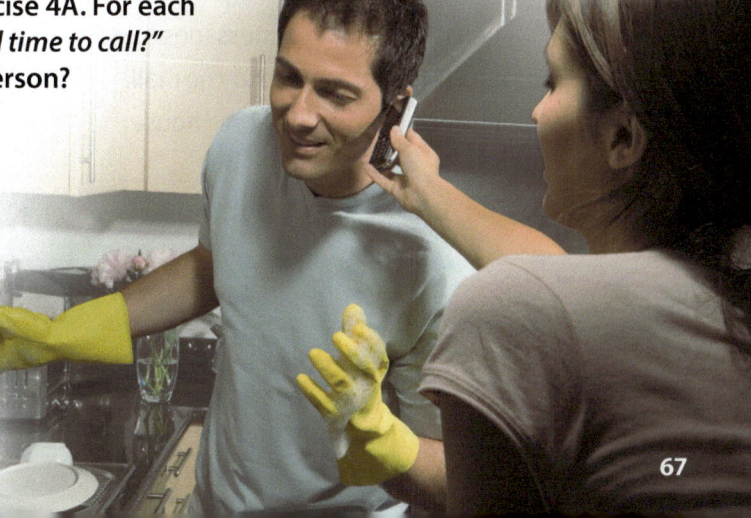

4 SPEAKING

A Think of what you're usually doing at the times of day below. Is it a good or bad time to call you?
- Monday, 7:30 a.m.
- Tuesday, 10:00 a.m.
- Wednesday, 1:30 p.m
- Thursday, 3:30 p.m.
- Friday, 9:30 p.m
- Saturday, 11:00 a.m.
- Sunday, 6:00 p.m.

B [PAIR WORK] Take turns choosing times in exercise 4A. For each time, "call" your partner and ask, *"Is this a good time to call?"* Listen to the answers. Is your partner a busy person?

> Hi, is this a good time to call?

> No, sorry. I'm having dinner with my family.

7.2 TEXTING ON THE RUN

LESSON OBJECTIVE
- ask and answer questions about travel

1 VOCABULARY: Transportation

A 🔊 2.04 Look at the pictures. Listen and repeat.

- take the bus/train/subway
- go to a store / your parents' house
- walk
- be at the bus stop / train station
- carry a bag
- wait
- ride your/my bike
- be on the bus/train/subway
- drive

B Circle the correct words to complete the sentences.
1. I *ride my bike / am at the bus stop* to class every day.
2. I'm *waiting / walking* for a friend right now.
3. We *are on the train / take the subway* to work on Fridays.
4. Are you *carrying / walking* right now?
5. I'm *at the train station / to the mall* right now.

C ▶ Now do the vocabulary exercises for 7.2 on page 147.

D GROUP WORK How do you usually get to the places in the box? For ideas, watch Julieth's video.

| English class | the supermarket | work/college | your best friend's house |

REAL STUDENT *Do you use the same transportation as Julieth?*

2 LANGUAGE IN CONTEXT

A Read the text messages. Where is Inna going? Why?

B Read the text messages again. Correct the sentences.
1. Inna is sending text messages to ~~her father~~. *Rob*
2. Inna is taking the bus to the mall. _____
3. Inna's dad is waiting at his house. _____
4. Inna is carrying a big bag. _____
5. Today is Inna's dad's birthday. _____

INSIDER ENGLISH

People often write *ha ha* (the sound of a laugh) in informal writing. It means they think something is funny.

12:00 PM

Hey, Inna. Are you going to work?

No, I'm not. **I'm on the bus**. I'm **going to my parents' house**.

You usually **ride your bike** there. Why are you **taking the bus**?

Because I'm **carrying** a big plant. Oh, **I'm at the bus stop** now, and my dad's **waiting**.

😂 Ha ha! A plant! Why are you carrying a plant?

Because plants don't **walk**! 😄😄😄 Really it's for my mom's birthday.

Oh, wow! Say happy birthday from me.

7.2 TEXTING ON THE RUN

LESSON OBJECTIVE
- ask and answer questions about travel

Introduce the lesson Write *types of transportation* on the board. Underline *transportation* and elicit various names for common forms of transportation from Ss, e.g., *bus, train, subway*. Ask Ss which method of transportation is their favorite.

1 VOCABULARY: Transportation

A 🔊 **2.04 Present the vocabulary** Play the audio, pausing after each phrase so that Ss can repeat together. Check for pronunciation.

B Ss work on the sentences individually before sharing with a partner. Elicit answers.

> **Answers**
> 1 ride my bike
> 2 waiting
> 3 take the subway
> 4 walking
> 5 at the train station

C Direct Ss to page 147 to complete the vocabulary exercises. Teacher's tips for vocabulary exercises are on page T-141.

D [GROUP WORK] **Review** Ss tell a partner how they get to the places.

- **OPTIONAL ACTIVITY** Ss watch Julieth's video and identify the two types of transportation from exercise 1A she talks about. Then they say whether they also use these types of transportation. You may want to explain that *a short walk* means *a walk that doesn't take a lot of time*.

> **REAL STUDENT**
> Hi, my name's Julieth Moreno and when I'm going to my work I usually take a short walk … it's like 10 or 15 minutes. And then I have, like, the school bus … I'm a teacher so I have my school bus and it take us like, like two hours.

2 LANGUAGE IN CONTEXT

A **Read the instructions aloud.** Ss read the messages individually to arrive at the answer. Answer any questions students may have, or encourage them to ask their partner or use a dictionary.

> **Answers**
> She's going to her parents' house because it's her mom's birthday.

B **Do the task** Ss correct the sentences individually then share with a partner.

> **Answers**
> 1 Inna is sending text messages to **Rob**.
> 2 Inna is taking the bus to **her parents' house**.
> 3 Inna's dad is waiting at **the bus stop**.
> 4 Inna is carrying **a big plant**.
> 5 Today is Inna's **mom's** birthday.

- Read the **Insider English** box. You might ask Ss if they also use emoticons in their text messages. 😊 Remind Ss that emoticons are informal, but can be used to make messages more emotional and friendly.

> 📎 **EXTRA ACTIVITY**
>
> Class survey. Write or dictate the following questions on the board and ask Ss to copy.
>
> *How do you travel to work?*
>
> *How do you travel to class?*
>
> *What's your favorite way to travel?*
>
> *Which transportation do you not like?*
>
> Adapt these questions as necessary for your Ss. Ask Ss to circulate, asking as many classmates as they can the same questions and writing down their answers. As Ss circulate, monitor for pronunciation and grammar. Bring the class back together and ask Ss to share their findings. How do most Ss travel? Which ways of traveling do they love or hate?

T-68

3 GRAMMAR: Present continuous questions

Introduce the lesson Dictate, write, or display the following questions on the board:
1 *Why are you taking the bus?*
2 *Are you going to the mall?*
3 *What are you doing?*
4 *Why is he carrying the plant?*

Ask Ss: *Which question can be answered yes or no?* (2) *Which two sentences can you answer with because?* (1 and 4)

A **Introduce the grammar** Before Ss circle the answers, explain that they can refer to the examples in the grammar box.

- Ask volunteers to read the chart aloud. Check pronunciation. Ask some questions using the present continuous, e.g., *Are you listening? Are you driving? Yes, I am. / No, I'm not.*

> **Answers**
> 1 at the beginning   2 after

B Complete the first sentence with Ss to demonstrate how to do the exercise. Ss complete the sentences individually before checking their answers with the class.

> **Answers**
> 1 Is, riding, d
> 2 are, doing, e
> 3 Are, listening, b
> 4 is, carrying, a
> 5 is, going, c

C Direct Ss to page 135 to complete the grammar exercise. Teacher's tips for grammar exercises are on page T-129.

D PAIR WORK **Review** Circulate and monitor as Ss discuss the prompt with each other. Listen for examples of language usage that you can share with Ss when the activity is finished. Elicit ideas from Ss and give feedback.

> **SMARTPHONE ACTIVITY**
>
> Draw or display a picture of household activities. Ask Ss: *What are they doing?* and *What is he doing?* Ss look through their phones and choose a picture that shows people doing something. Ss show their picture to a partner. The partner asks *What is he / she doing?* Allow Ss time to discuss. Circulate and monitor. Volunteers show the class their pictures.

4 SPEAKING

A FIND IT Read the instructions aloud with Ss. Explain the example and give more if you can. Explain that Ss can use their smartphones to find any information they need.

- Write on the board for Ss to copy and answer: *Where are you going? / How are you traveling? / What are you carrying?*

> **TEACHER DEVELOPMENT ACTIVITY 1**
>
> **Maximizing practice opportunities**
> When students repeat the same pair work task with different partners, they can become more confident with producing and responding to the target language, add new language to make their interactions more natural, practice listening to different accents, and feel energized by the change of pace.
>
> - Demonstrate the task with a strong S:
>   T *Hi. It's (T's name). Is this a good time to call?*
>   S *No, sorry. I'm having dinner with my family.*
>   T *OK, I'll call back later.*
> - Ss stand in two lines (A and B), facing each other.
> - Facing pairs in lines A and B practice "calling" and "answering."
> - T taps table to signal that Ss in Line A must move one place to the right to work with a new partner. (The last S in Line A moves to the beginning of the line.)
> - Repeat the procedure so everyone in Line A works with everyone in Line B.

B PAIR WORK Model the sample answer with a volunteer. Circulate and monitor as Ss ask questions. Offer help and support. Listen for examples of language usage you can share with Ss at the end of the activity.

- When Ss finish, ask volunteers to explain their ideas to the class.
- Give feedback.

> **MIXED ABILITY**
>
> **Responding to questions** Start by asking Ss to respond to *yes/no* questions using *Yes, I am* and *No, I'm not*, e.g., *Are you working? Are you taking the bus?* Progress to more difficult questions for stronger Ss, e.g., *Where are you working? Where are you living?* As a follow up, Ss ask you some questions in the present continuous.

3 GRAMMAR: present continuous questions

A Circle the correct answer. Use the questions in the grammar box to help you.
1. Use *are* and *is* **at the beginning** / **in the middle** of *yes/no* questions.
2. Use *are* and *is* **before** / **after** question words (for example, *What* or *When*) in information questions.

Present continuous questions

Yes/no questions
Are you **going** to work?
Is she **carrying** a plant?
Are they **waiting** at the bus stop?

Information questions
Why is he **carrying** a plant?
Who are they **waiting** for?
What are you **doing**?

B Complete the questions with the present continuous form of the verbs in the box. Then match the questions and the answers below.

carry   do   go   listen   ride

1. _____ Josh _____ his bike in the park right now?
2. What _____ Kim and Todd _____ ?
3. _____ the children _____ to music right now?
4. Why _____ Jamal _____ a big bag?
5. Where _____ Lydia _____ now?

___ a Because he's taking a lot of books to class.
___ b Yes, they are.
___ c She's walking to her friend's house.
___ d No, he isn't. He's running by the lake.
___ e They're driving to the beach.

C ▶ Now go to page 135. Look at the grammar charts and do the grammar exercise for 7.2.

D [PAIR WORK] Imagine what people in your family are doing right now. Ask and answer questions.

> What's your sister doing right now?

4 SPEAKING

A Imagine you're going somewhere and carrying something interesting or funny. Use the ideas below or your own ideas. Then decide where you are going and your transportation.

a big bag   a small chair   an expensive picture

B [PAIR WORK] What is your partner doing? Ask and answer questions.

> Hi, Anna. What are you doing?

> I'm carrying 100 cookies. I'm at the subway station.

7.3 A NEW LIFE

LESSON OBJECTIVE
- share news on the phone

1 FUNCTIONAL LANGUAGE

A Look at the people. Are they having a long or a short conversation? How long are your phone calls?

B 🔊 2.05 Luana is calling her friend Jennifer. Read and listen. What's new in Luana's life?

🔊 **2.05 Audio script**

Jennifer	**Hello.**
Luana	**Hi**, Jennifer. **It's** Luana.
Jennifer	**Hey**, Luana!
Luana	**How's it going?**
Jennifer	**Not bad**, thanks. **How are you doing?**
Luana	**Good, thanks.** Well, I'm busy.
Jennifer	Really? What are you doing these days?
Luana	I have a new job, in Monterrey.
Jennifer	Oh, wow! *Monterrey*? So you're not living in Mexico City now.
Luana	That's right. I'm living in Monterrey. I live in a new building. It's expensive, but it's very nice. And I have a new boyfriend.
Jennifer	Really? Great! You have a new *life*! I want to hear all about it!

C Complete the chart with expressions in **bold** from the conversation above.

Answering the phone and greeting people	Asking people how they are	Responding
1 _____Hello_____ . 2 _____, Jennifer. 3 _____ Luana. 4 _____, Luana!	How's it 5 _____ ? (How's = How is) How 6 _____ you 7 _____ ? How are you?	Not 8 _____, thanks. 9 _____, thanks. I'm fine.

D 🔊 2.06 **PAIR WORK** Put the phone conversation in the correct order. Listen and check. Then practice with a partner.

___ Good, thanks. How's it going?
_3_ Hey, Andrew! How are you doing?
_1_ Hello.
___ Not bad.
___ Hi, Francisco. It's Andrew.

7.3 A NEW LIFE

LESSON OBJECTIVE
- share news on the phone

Introduce the lesson Give Ss a four-digit number each. This is their phone number. Draw or show a picture of a telephone number pad. Dial one of the Ss' numbers by pretending to press the numbers. Have a simple conversation with the S, similar to the first six lines of the conversation in exercise 1B. Call another S. For variation, ask a volunteer to come to the front of the classroom and call another S.

1 FUNCTIONAL LANGUAGE

A **Introduce the vocabulary** Ss discuss the questions in pairs before you talk about them as a class. Find out who has the longest phone calls.

> **Answers**
> Answers may vary.

B 🔊 **2.05** Play the audio as Ss listen. Play again if necessary. Ss share their answers with a partner. Check that Ss understand the vocabulary.

> **Answers**
> Luana is in a new city. She has a new job. She has a new boyfriend.

- Books closed. Ss listen to the conversation.
- Ss read the conversation again in pairs. Monitor and check for pronunciation.

C In pairs Ss complete the chart. Elicit answers by asking Ss to read the whole sentence. Monitor for pronunciation and stress.

> **Answers**
> 1 Hello
> 2 Hi
> 3 It's
> 4 Hey
> 5 going
> 6 are
> 7 doing
> 8 bad
> 9 Good

D 🔊 **2.06** **PAIR WORK** Allow Ss time to order the conversation before they check their answers with a partner.

- Play the audio and ask Ss to check their answers.
- Ask Ss to role play the conversation. Circulate and monitor. You might like to go back to the phone numbers game from the start of the class. Ss call other members of the class again. Is their conversation better?
- Make sure you remember to use the same phone language conversation with Ss in the next lesson to help them remember and use the language.

> **Answers**
> 4 Good, thanks. How's it going?
> 3 Hey, Andrew! How are you doing?
> 1 Hello.
> 5 Not bad.
> 2 Hi, Francisco. It's Andrew.

> 📱 **SMARTPHONE ACTIVITY**
>
> Ss record their conversation on their smartphones. As homework, ask them to listen to it again and think about their pronunciation. Are there any words they could have pronounced better? Did they notice any errors?

> **VOCABULARY SUPPORT** Encourage Ss to copy and use language that is useful to them. Remembering and using key set phrases is an important step to learning a language.

2 REAL-WORLD STRATEGY

A **Read Reacting to News aloud. Ss decide how Jennifer reacts in pairs.**

> **Answers**
> Good news: Luana has a new job.
> Ordinary news: Luana is busy.
> Bad news: Luana's apartment is very expensive.

- Concept check by telling Ss more news and asking them react to it accordingly, e.g., *I'm tired. / I have a new car. / I have a new dog! / I get up early every day. / I go to bed late.*

B 🔊 **2.07** **Explain the task and play the audio. Play again if Ss ask. Ss check their answers with a partner before you check.**

> **Answers**
> Ordinary news: He's in his car.
> Good news: He has a new car.
> Bad news: He has a (big) problem with his car.

> 🔊 **2.07 Audio script**
> **A** I'm in my car.
> **B** Oh.
> **A** I have a new car.
> **B** Oh, wow!
> **A** Yeah, but I have a problem with it. A big problem.
> **B** Oh, no! OK, *where* are you?

C 🔊 **2.07** **Play audio again. Ss check their answers with a partner before sharing with the class.**

> **Answers**
> Ordinary news: He's in his car. ➡ She says, "Oh."
> Good news: He has a new car. ➡ She says, "Oh, wow!"
> Bad news: He has a (big) problem with his car. ➡ She says, "Oh, no!"

D **PAIR WORK** **Review** **Put Ss into pairs and assign each one to be either Student A or Student B. Ask Student As to turn to page 157 and Bs to turn to page 160.**

- Before you start, write or say some surprising information about yourself, either real or imaginary, e.g., *I have a new baby!* Ask Ss to respond with an expression from page 71.
- Read through the instructions aloud. Allow Ss time to read through their sentences. Check for understanding and explain any vocabulary Ss may need.
- Monitor as Ss do the activity. When Ss finish, ask volunteers from A and B to read a sentence aloud to the class. Elicit suitable responses to it from the group.

3 PRONUNCIATION: Saying *-ing* at the end of a word

A 🔊 **2.08** **Ask Ss to predict the missing letters.**

- Play the audio and check answers. Have students repeat the *-ing* words, then repeat the sentences.

> **Answers**
> 1 do**ing**   2 liv**ing**   3 go**ing**

B 🔊 **2.09** **Play the audio. Ss compare answers before checking as a whole class.**

- Ask Ss to repeat the *-ing* version of each phrase. Explain that it is important to pronounce *-ing* clearly because phrases with *in* have a different meaning.

> **Answers**
> 1 b   2 a   3 b   4 b   5 b   6 a

C 🔊 **2.10** **PAIR WORK** **Play the audio. Have Ss repeat each line.**

- Ss practice the conversations in pairs. Monitor and help Ss to pronounce *-ing* clearly.

4 SPEAKING

A **PAIR WORK** **Review** **Before Ss begin this task, spend some time talking about the conversation they will have and some of the expressions and phrases they can use. Ask Ss to think about something that happened to them recently that they can talk about.**

- Model a sample conversation with a volunteer to show Ss what to do.
- As Ss talk, circulate and monitor for pronunciation, registers, grammar, and stress. Listen for examples of language usage that you can share with Ss at the end of the activity.
- When Ss finish, ask volunteers to perform their conversations for the class.
- Praise Ss and give feedback.

> 🚶 **FAST FINISHERS**
>
> If a pair finishes quickly, ask them to change partners with another fast finishing pair and repeat their conversations. Or ask them to record their conversation on their smartphones.

2 REAL-WORLD STRATEGY

REACTING TO NEWS
People often say *oh* after they hear good news, ordinary news, and bad news.

Good news 😃	Ordinary news 😐	Bad news 🙁
Oh, wow!	Oh.	Oh, no!

Luana *I have a new job.*   **Jennifer** *Oh, wow!*
Luana *I'm busy.*   **Jennifer** *Oh.*
Luana *My apartment is very expensive.*   **Jennifer** *Oh, no!*

A Read the information in the box about reacting to news. Then look at the examples. What does Jennifer think is: good news, ordinary news, and bad news?

B 🔊 2.07 Listen to a conversation. What news does the man give?
Ordinary news: _He's in his car._   Good news: _____
Bad news: _____

C 🔊 2.07 Listen again. How does the woman react to the different types of news?

D ▶ PAIR WORK Student A: Go to page 157. Student B: Go to page 160. Follow the instructions.

3 PRONUNCIATION: Saying *-ing* at the end of the word

A 🔊 2.08 Listen. Complete the words.
1 How are you do____ ?   2 I'm liv____ in Dallas.   3 Where are you go____ ?

B 🔊 2.09 Listen. Focus on the *-in* and *-ing* sounds. (Circle) the phrase you hear.
1 a learn in Spanish   b learning Spanish   4 a study in nature   b studying nature
2 a call in the restaurant   b calling the restaurant   5 a carry in a bag   b carrying a bag
3 a help in my school   b helping my school   6 a shop in malls   b shopping malls

C 🔊 2.10 PAIR WORK Listen to the conversations. Then practice with a partner. Listen for the *-ing* sound.
1 A How are you do**ing**?
   B Not bad. I'm work**ing** in Monterrey now.
2 A Are you liv**ing** in Mexico City now?
   B No, I'm liv**ing** in Monterrey.
3 A Where are you go**ing**?
   B We're go**ing** to the Italian restaurant over there.

4 SPEAKING

PAIR WORK Imagine you're calling your partner. Start the call, and then talk about some news. Use some of the questions below. React to the things your partner says. Then change roles.

How are you doing?   Are you busy?
What are you doing right now?   What about you?

Hey, Ali. It's Clara.   Hey, Clara! How are you doing?

7.4 CHAOS!

LESSON OBJECTIVE
- write a blog about things happening now

1 READING

A **SKIM** Skim the text. Where is the man? What is on his laptop?

JAMIE'S BLOG

HOME   ABOUT   BLOG

Bloggers sometimes write from difficult places: mountains, deserts, rainforests …
So today, my blog is from a difficult place, too. I'm writing from my living room.

Why is it difficult to write in here? Well, my brother's playing soccer (yes, in the living room.) The ball is going *BOOM-BOOM-BOOM* on the wall near my table and chair. My sister's doing her homework. Every two minutes, she asks me a question: "What's 15% of 500? What's 50% of 320?" So, really, *I'm* doing her homework.

The TV is on, but I don't know why. My mom's talking about work on the phone, so she isn't watching TV. And my dad isn't watching it. He's in the kitchen: *PSSSSSS, CRASH, BANG!* He's cooking – I think. And the cat doesn't like TV. But she likes laptops. She's walking on my laptop … and now she's going to sleep! How do I work in this place? It's chaos!

B **READ FOR DETAILS** Read the blog again. Find words to complete the chart.

5	people in the family	me
3	technology words	
2	pieces of furniture	
2	rooms	
1	animal	

C **PAIR WORK** **THINK CRITICALLY** Which people from exercise 1B are busy? having fun?

72

7.4 CHAOS!

LESSON OBJECTIVE
- write a blog about things happening now

Introduce the lesson Display a picture of a busy scene or find another picture of many people doing different activities. Display this on the board. Model a sentence in the present continuous describing the people in the picture. Ss look at the picture for one minute before you take it away. Ss describe what they remember to their partner using the present continuous. Display the image again and ask Ss to say what the people are doing.

1 READING

Introduce the task Ask Ss: *Do you read blogs?* Elicit which blogs they read and display them, if possible. Elicit comparisons between the blogs they read and "Jamie's Blog" on this page.

> **VOCABULARY SUPPORT** A **blog** is a discussion or website that is usually written by one person or an organization. The style is very informal and can also be conversational. The word **blog** comes from "web log."

A   Remind Ss that skim reading means they read quickly to find general information, but don't have to understand every word. Ss share their answers with a partner before you elicit them as a class.

> **Answers**
> The man is in his living room at home. His cat is on his laptop.

> **📎 EXTRA ACTIVITY**
> Write *formal* and *informal* on the board and check that Ss understand the difference. In pairs, ask Ss to read the blog again and look for things that make the text informal. Allow Ss time to discuss before you elicit answers.

> **Suggested answers**
> Asking questions like "Why is it difficult to write in here?" / *well* / sound words like BOOM, etc. / Using direct speech with marks " " / starting sentences with *but* or *and*.

B   Ss read again and look for details. Ss work individually to complete the chart and then share their answers with a partner.

> **Answers**
> 5 people in the family: me, brother, sister, mom, dad
> 3 electronic things: TV, phone, laptop
> 2 pieces of furniture: table, chair
> 2 rooms: living room, kitchen
> 1 animal: cat

C   **PAIR WORK** Encourage Ss to discuss the reasons for their answers with their partners. They explain to one another what each person is doing.

> **Suggested answers**
> **Busy**
>   Jamie (He's writing a blog.)
>   Sister (She's doing homework.)
>   Mom (She's talking about work.)
>   Dad (He's cooking.)
> **Having fun**
>   Brother (He's playing soccer.)

T-72

2 WRITING

Introduce the task Write the punctuation marks below on the board without the names. Elicit their names from Ss.

. period
, comma
? question mark
' apostrophe

- Write *i live in london* and ask Ss to fix the capitalization as a class. Explain that names, the pronoun *I*, and the first word of a sentence are always capitalized.
- Write or display the following sentences and ask Ss to punctuate and capitalize them in pairs before you elicit answers.
whats your name my name is Jorge i come from brazil i speak portuguese english and spanish where do you come from

> **Answers**
> What's your name? My name is Jorge. I come from Brazil. I speak Portuguese, English, and Spanish. Where do you come from?

A Read the instructions aloud with Ss. Pre-teach the words in the **glossary**. After they read, Ss check their answers with a partner.

> **Answers**
> **The children**
> 1 They're making a lot of noise.
> 2 Some kids are talking.
> 3 Some kids are playing music on their phones.
> 4 Some are singing.
> 5 Three boys are playing games on a tablet.
> 6 Also, the children are eating cookies.
> **Jodi**
> 1 She's writing her blog on a school bus.
> 2 She's cleaning their hands and washing their faces.
> 3 She's answering millions of questions from the kids.
> **Jodi and the children**
> 1 They're going to the beach on a school bus.

B Ss underline the instances of the words *also* and *too* in the blog individually, but complete the rules with a partner. Elicit answers by asking Ss to read the whole sentence aloud.

> **Answers**
> They're busy, <u>too</u>.
> <u>Also</u>, the children are eating cookies.
> The teacher is happy, <u>too</u>.
>
> end, before, beginning, after

- Direct Ss to the **Register check**. Ask volunteer Ss to read the example sentences aloud. Monitor for pronunciation. Ask Ss to find two sentences like these in Jamie's Blog on page 72.

> **Answers**
> And my dad isn't watching it.
> But it likes laptops.

> ### 📎 EXTRA ACTIVITY
>
> Dictate sentences for Ss to write. Remind them to include the punctuation they learned about, e.g.,
>
> My dad's a teacher.
> Where do you live?
> I like football. Also, I like tennis.
>
> Make the sentences relevant to your learners if possible. After Ss write, encourage them to exchange papers and let other Ss correct their work. Then write the answers on the board.

C **Introduce the task** Before Ss write, model sentences to give them some ideas, e.g., *I'm on the bus. The woman next to me is talking on her phone*, etc. Allow Ss plenty of time to think about and discuss what they are going to write.

- As Ss write, circulate and offer any help they need. Spell any words Ss want on the board so everyone can see them.
- If possible, correct Ss' work before the next activity.

D [PAIR WORK] After Ss have read their partner's work, ask volunteers to read their blogs to the class, or you can read them.

> ### ✏️ HOMEWORK IDEAS
>
> After you have corrected the blogs, ask Ss to record themselves reading their blogs using their smartphones. Encourage them to play back their recordings to listen for pronunciation and share them with their classmates.

2 WRITING

A Jodi is a college student. She's helping at a school for a week. Read her blog. What six things are the children doing? What three things is Jodi doing? What one thing are the children and Jodi doing?

Jodi's Blog

Home   About   Blog

Busy!
April 11

I'm helping a teacher at a school this week. Today, I'm writing my blog on a school bus. We're going to the beach. There are 25 kids on the bus, and they're nine and ten years old. Wow, they're making a lot of noise! They're busy, too. Some kids are talking. Some kids are playing music on their phones. Some are singing. Three boys are playing games on a tablet. Also, the children are eating cookies. What about me? Well, I'm cleaning their hands and washing their faces.
And I'm answering millions of questions from the kids. They're happy. The teacher is happy, too. But this is difficult for me. Am I getting old?

GLOSSARY
noise (*n*) a sound or sounds, usually loud
millions (*quantifier*) a lot (informal)

B **WRITING SKILLS** People use *also* and *too* to add information. Underline the words *also* and *too* in the blog. Then circle the correct words in the rules, below.
Use *too* at the **beginning** / **end** of a sentence.
Use a comma (,) **before** / **after** you write *too*.
Use *also* at the **beginning** / **end** of a sentence.
Use a comma (,) **before** / **after** you write *also*.

REGISTER CHECK

People sometimes use *And*, *Also*, or *But* at the beginning of sentences in speaking and informal writing. In formal writing, people usually don't begin sentences with these words.

And I'm answering millions of questions from the kids.
Also, the children are eating cookies.
But this is difficult for me.

WRITE IT

C Imagine you're in a very busy place: at home, at college, at work, on a bus, or at a party. Write a blog about the activities happening around you. Use the title "Busy!"

D **PAIR WORK** Compare your blog with a partner. How many activities does your partner describe?

73

7.5 TIME TO SPEAK
Your life these days

LESSON OBJECTIVE
- ask what people are doing these days

A   PREPARE Read the note and questions below. Which topic is interesting for you? Which topic is boring?

Topics	Main question	Follow-up questions
Work and school	Are you going to college?	Are your classes easy or difficult? Are you doing a lot of homework these days?
	What classes are you taking?	Do you like your classes? Why or why not?
	Where are you working these days?	Are you working every day? Is your job interesting? Is it difficult?
Free time	What are you reading these days?	Is it good? Who's the writer?
	What are you watching on TV?	Is it interesting? Is it funny? Who's in it?
	What music are you listening to?	Who's your favorite singer? What's your favorite band?
	Do you play video games?	Which games are you playing right now?
	Are you going out a lot these days?	Where do you go? What's your favorite place?
	Are you playing sports?	What sports do you play? Where?
Home life	How is your family?	Are you living with them now?
	Are you living in a new place?	Is it an apartment or house? Do you like it? Is it close to work/school?
	Are you cooking a lot these days?	Do you cook for other people?

> You are with a group of people. They are your friends, but you hardly ever see them. What do you say? Here are some ideas!

B   ROLE PLAY Imagine you are at a party. Talk to different people about different topics. Ask and answer some of the questions from the chart.

C   AGREE Talk about popular things from your conversations. What are a lot of people doing these days?

▶ To check your progress, go to page 154.

USEFUL PHRASES

PREPARE
I like / don't like …
I think … is interesting/boring.
And you?

ROLE PLAY
Hi, [name]. How's it going?
Hey, [name]! What are you doing these days?

AGREE
(Work and school / free time / home life) is a popular topic.
A lot of people are doing …

7.5 TIME TO SPEAK
Your life these days

LESSON OBJECTIVE
- ask what people are doing these days

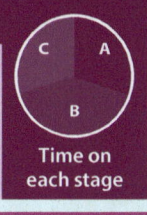

Time on each stage

Introduce the task Display a photograph of some school children from the past. Ask Ss: *What do you think these people are doing now?* Elicit Ss' ideas. Remind them to use the present continuous.

- Direct Ss to the **Useful phrases** section at the bottom of the page. Remind them that they can use them at the relevant stages of the lesson.

A **PREPARE** **Aim: Ss read and understand the questions.**
- **CLASS WORK** Model the activity by ranking the topics yourself.
- **PAIR WORK** One S reads a question and then the other reads the next. Tell Ss they are reading to understand, not to answer. Monitor for pronunciation, but withhold your feedback until the end.
- **CLASS WORK** Ask Ss to share which sentences they didn't understand before you give feedback on pronunciation.
- **Preparation for speaking*** Give Ss time to review relevant vocabulary notes or look up words in a dictionary.

TEACHER DEVELOPMENT ACTIVITY 2

Encouraging quieter students to speak

Some students tend to let others in their group do the speaking during groupwork activities. The following activity allows all students to participate more equally in any task.
- Set up the role play. Put Ss into groups.
- Give each S the same number of tokens, e.g., five (counters from a board game, small LEGO® pieces, etc.).
- Explain the rules:
- Every time a S speaks (not including short phrases), they must put a token in the middle of the table.
- When a S's tokens are gone, he/she cannot speak again until everyone else has used up their tokens.
- When all the tokens are in the middle, everyone can speak freely.

B **ROLE PLAY** **Do the task Aim: Ss pretend they are at a party.**
- **INDIVIDUALLY** Give Ss time to think silently about what they are going to say. Set a time limit, say two minutes, and allow them to make notes.*
- **PAIR WORK** Ss take their books with them as they circulate to ask and answer the questions with each other. Circulate and monitor for errors.
- **CLASS WORK** Provide feedback after the activity.

C **AGREE** **Aim: Ss discuss what people usually do.**
- **PAIR WORK** Ss return to their original partners and discuss the topics they talked about. Monitor and make a note of the strong interactions of each group, for example, good use of unit vocabulary, interesting questions, natural-sounding interactions, etc. You can use your notes to give feedback at the end of the lesson.*
- **CLASS WORK** Review Ask Ss to share their ideas with the group.
- **Feedback for speaking activities*** Use your notes to give feedback. Use elicitation to correct errors. See page xxii for details.

*These tips can help you to create a safe speaking environment. They can also be used with other speaking activities. For more information, see page xxii.

▶▶ PROGRESS CHECK ▶▶

Direct students to page 154 to check their progress. Go to page T-152 for Progress check activity suggestions.

TEACHER DEVELOPMENT REFLECTION

Answer these questions yourself in a reflection journal or discuss them with your peers.

1. How successful were your instructions for setting up the A/B lines task in activity 1? Would you do anything differently next time?
2. In what ways did your students improve as they repeated the pairwork task? How do you know?
3. Who are the quieter students in your class? Why do you think they speak less than other students? Would you use tokens for a speaking activity again?
4. Students sometimes say *What's the point of pairwork?* Or *I prefer to work on my own.* How might you respond to these comments?
5. Students can work in pairs and groups on a range of activities – for example, figuring out grammar rules, doing vocabulary matching tasks, discussing problems and solutions, or comparing answers for a reading comprehension exercise. What should teachers be doing while these kinds of activities are taking place?

T-74

YOU'RE GOOD!

8

TEACHER DEVELOPMENT INTRODUCTION

Strategy 2: Teaching vocabulary – Practicing vocabulary

Students can't have too much practice! There is much evidence that, without plentiful and regular practice, Ss will forget most of the new vocabulary they encounter in class. In this unit, we look at two activities which can be used for additional or alternative practice of many different kinds of vocabulary.

Who wrote this? (Activity 1): A personalized sentence-writing activity provides both productive and receptive practice. You will have the opportunity to try this in Lesson 8.1.

Test your partner (Activity 2): This is a simple but effective extension activity using words and their definitions. You can try this in Lesson 8.2.

To find out more about ways of practicing vocabulary, read Chapters 10–11 of Ruth Gairns and Stuart Redman, *Working with Words*, pp.144–170. Please go to www.cambridge.org/evolve to download these pages.

INTRODUCE THE THEME OF THE UNIT

Tell Ss about something that you like to do that can also be a skill, using vocabulary from previous units, e.g., *playing soccer or video games, cooking, riding your bike*. If possible, display a picture. Explain that you like to do this, but you are or are not good at doing it. For example, say: *I like cooking*. Then act out that you are tasting it and it tastes good or bad. Repeat with another skill.

UNIT OBJECTIVES

Read the unit objectives aloud. Tell Ss to listen and read along. Explain any new vocabulary Ss may not understand.

START SPEAKING

A Ss discuss the questions in pairs before you check their ideas as a class.

B Ss work in pairs to answer the questions before checking as a class.

C Ss talk about their fun / difficult activities as a class. Elicit some of their many skills and talents.
- **OPTIONAL ACTIVITY** Ss watch Anderson's video and say what he does. They decide whether they think it's fun, difficult, or both. You may want to explain what a *rock band* is.

> **REAL STUDENT**
> Hi. I am Anderson. I play guitar in my rock band.

UNIT OBJECTIVES
- talk about your skills and abilities
- say what you can and can't do at work or school
- say why you're the right person for a job
- write an online comment with your opinion
- talk about what people in your country are good at

YOU'RE GOOD!

8

START SPEAKING

A Look at the picture. Where is this person? What is he doing?

B Do you think this is a difficult activity? Do you think it's fun?

C Talk to a partner about fun or difficult activities you do. For ideas, watch Anderson's video.

REAL STUDENT

What does Anderson do? Do you think it's fun, difficult, or both?

75

8.1 SHE LIKES MUSIC, BUT SHE CAN'T DANCE!

LESSON OBJECTIVE
- talk about your skills and abilities

1 VOCABULARY: Verbs to describe skills

A 🔊 **2.11** Listen and repeat the skills in the pictures. Which are fun skills? Which are difficult skills?

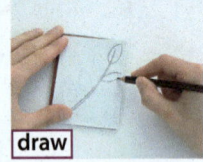

dance | draw | fix things | read music | paint | play the guitar
sing | skateboard | snowboard | speak two languages | surf | swim

B ▶ Now do the vocabulary exercises for 8.1 on page 147.

2 LANGUAGE IN CONTEXT

A 🔊 **2.12** Read and listen. Who are Mia and her dad talking about? What do they choose to buy? Do you think it's a good idea?

🔊 2.12 Audio script

Dad So, Mia. You know it's your mom's birthday next month, right?
Mia Oh wow! Let's buy her something really cool. Do you have any ideas?
Dad Hmm. How about some art classes? She can **draw**.
Mia Or what about singing lessons? She likes music and can **play the guitar**.
Dad I don't think that's a good idea. She thinks she can't **sing**, and she's very shy about it.
Mia Hmm. What about dance lessons? Can she **dance** well?
Dad No, she can't. She's terrible at it. It's really funny – she can **read music**, but she can't dance!
Mia *You* can't dance, Dad. I know! Let's buy you both some dance lessons!
Dad Great idea! Wait a minute – what?

INSIDER ENGLISH

You can use *So* to start talking about a topic.

So, Mia. You know it's your mom's birthday next month, right?

GLOSSARY
terrible (*adj*) very bad

B 🔊 **2.12** Read and listen again. What can Mia's mom do? What can't she do? Complete the sentences.

1 Mia's mom can _____ , _____ , and _____ .
2 She can't _____ and _____ .

C **PAIR WORK** Talk to a partner. Which things in exercise 1A do you often do? Which things do you never do? For ideas, watch Larissa's video.

REAL STUDENT — Do you often do the same things as Larissa?

8.1 SHE LIKES MUSIC, BUT SHE CAN'T DANCE!

LESSON OBJECTIVE
- talk about your skills and abilities

Introduce the lesson Ask Ss: *What does an artist do?* Elicit *paint* or *draw*. Ss haven't learned these terms yet, so be prepared to help them if they don't know the words. Write *paint* on the board. Then ask: *Is this a skill? Is it difficult?*

- Ask the class about more skills in the same way, e.g., *What does a singer do? What does a chef do?*

1 VOCABULARY: Verbs to describe skills

A 🔊 **2.11 Present the vocabulary** Ss read as you play the audio. Pause after each word or phrase and Ss repeat together.

- Play audio again and ask individual Ss to repeat. If necessary, ask them to read the words again in order to monitor for pronunciation.
- Ss share their ideas to the questions with the class.

> **Answers**
> Answers may vary.

B Direct Ss to page 147 to complete the vocabulary exercises. Teacher's tips for vocabulary exercises are on page T-141.

> 📎 **EXTRA ACTIVITY**
> Dictate or write two questions for Ss to discuss:
> 1 What skills do you have?
> 2 What skills don't you have?
> 3 What skills do you want?
>
> Answer the questions yourself as an example, and then ask Ss to discuss in pairs or groups before you elicit their ideas. Monitor as they talk.

2 LANGUAGE IN CONTEXT

A 🔊 **2.12** Read the instructions and make sure Ss understand the questions. Play the audio as Ss read along. Play again if necessary. Elicit answers from Ss.

> **Answers**
> They are talking about Mia's mom. They choose to buy some dance lessons for Mia's mom and dad.
> Answers may vary.

- Direct Ss to the **Insider English** box and read the examples.

> 📎 **EXTRA ACTIVITY**
> Ss practice the role play in pairs. Monitor for pronunciation.

B 🔊 **2.12** Play the audio again. Ss complete the answers individually before checking with a partner.

- Elicit corrections from the class by asking Ss to read the complete sentence aloud.

> **Answers**
> 1 Mia's mom can draw, play the guitar, and read music.
> 2 She can't sing or dance.

C [PAIR WORK] **Review** Ss answer the questions in pairs before you elicit some of their ideas.

- **OPTIONAL ACTIVITY** Ss watch Larissa's video and identify the skills she talks about. They say whether they often do the same things.

> **REAL STUDENT**
> Hello, my name is Larissa. I like to play the guitar. It's a fun skill. I sing. I speak three languages: Spanish, English, and a little bit French.

👥 TEACHER DEVELOPMENT ACTIVITY 1

Who wrote this?

This simple activity provides both productive and receptive practice, and can be used with all kinds of vocabulary.

- As an example, write four sentences about yourself on the board. Use the expressions *I often …, I never …, I can …, I can't …* and the skills vocabulary from exercise 1A.
- Ss write true sentences about themselves on a piece of paper, again using the four expressions and skills vocabulary.
- Option 1 (larger classes): Collect the papers, number them, and stick them on the walls. Ss stand up and read the papers, making a note of the numbers and who they think the writers are. Then ask Ss sit to down. Go through the papers one by one, asking Ss to shout out their guesses before the writers reveal themselves.
- Option 2 (smaller classes): Tell Ss to write their names on their papers and collect them. Read the sentences on each paper aloud. Stop after each sentence and ask Ss to guess the writer, but don't comment on whether guesses are correct. At the end of each paper, ask the writer to reveal himself or herself to the class.

3 GRAMMAR: *can* and *can't* for ability; *well*

A **Present the grammar** Before Ss circle the answers, explain that they can refer to the examples in the grammar box.

- Ask volunteers to read the grammar chart aloud. Use concept questions to check that Ss understand. Ask: *Can you drive?* to elicit either *Yes, I can* or *No, I can't*. Ask the class questions from the chart.
- Read and explain the **Notice** box. Remind Ss that *well* goes at the end of the sentence. Tell Ss what you can do well, e.g., *I can swim well*. Ask Ss: *What can you do well?*

> **Answers**
> 1 Use **can't** to talk about things you don't do well or don't know how to do.
> 2 Use **can** to talk about things you do well.
> 3 With *he*, *she*, and *it*, **do not** add *–s* to the verb after *can* or *can't*.

> 📎 **EXTRA** ACTIVITY
> Write some scrambled sentences on the board and ask Ss to unscramble them. Make the sentences relevant to your Ss and use some from the *can* and *can't* grammar chart, e.g., *Can you play the guitar? / I can't speak Spanish. / Does he speak English well? / I can dance well.*

B Ss complete the sentences individually before sharing their answers with their partner.

> **Answers**
> 1 I swim every day. I **can** swim well.
> 2 Sorry. My dad **can't** fix your car. He's not a mechanic.
> 3 You can draw really well, Tomas. What other things **can** you do?
> 4 She **can't** drive, and she doesn't have a car.
> 5 You **can** skateboard really well! Can you teach me?
> 6 A Can you play the guitar, Robbie?
>   B No, I **can't**.

C Direct Ss to page 136 to complete the grammar exercise. Teacher's tips for grammar exercises are on page T-129.

D Monitor as Ss write their sentences. Offer any spelling help Ss may need and write words they ask for on the board.

> **Answers**
> Answers may vary.

- Direct Ss to the **Accuracy check** box. Ask a volunteer to read the rules. Display or write the following sentences on the board for Ss to correct in pairs before you check as a class.
    1 *I can swim well, but I can't to surf.*
    2 *Joella can to play the guitar, but she can't to read music.*

> **Answers**
> 1 I can swim well, but I can't ~~to~~ surf.
> 2 Joella can ~~to~~ play the guitar, but she can't ~~to~~ read music.

- Ask Ss to go back and correct their sentences from the first part of this activity.

4 SPEAKING

A [GROUP WORK] **Review** Role play the example with a volunteer.

- As Ss talk, circulate and monitor. Listen for any errors you can share with Ss at the end of the activity.
- After Ss have finished working with their partner, they circulate around the room, carrying their questions and asking them to other members of the class. Get involved yourself and share what you can and can't do.

B [GROUP WORK] Elicit ideas. What interesting skills do students have?

3 GRAMMAR: *can* and *can't* for ability; *well*

A Circle the correct answers. Use the sentences in the grammar box and the information in the Notice box to help you.

1 Use **can** / **can't** to talk about things you don't do well or don't know how to do.
2 Use **can** / **can't** to talk about things you do well or know how to do.
3 With *he*, *she*, and *it*, **do** / **do not** add *-s* to the verb after *can* or *can't*.

can and can't (= can not) for ability		
I **can** swim.	I **can't** play the guitar.	**Can** you fix things?
She **can** draw.	He **can't** sing well.	**Can** he surf?
We **can** surf well.	They **can't** read music.	**Can** they speak two languages?

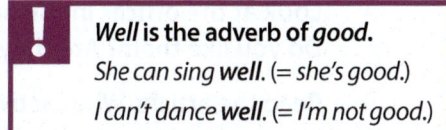

> **!** *Well* is the adverb of *good*.
> She can sing **well**. (= she's good.)
> I can't dance **well**. (= I'm not good.)

B Circle the correct answers to complete the sentences.

1 I swim every day. I *can* / *can't* swim well.
2 Sorry. My dad *can* / *can't* fix your car. He's not a mechanic.
3 You can draw really well, Tomas. What other things *can* / *can't* you do?
4 She *can* / *can't* drive, and she doesn't have a car.
5 You *can* / *can't* skateboard really well! Can you teach me?
6 **A** Can you play the guitar, Robbie?
   B No, I *can* / *can't*.

C ▶ Now go to page 136. Look at the grammar chart and do the grammar exercise for 8.1.

D Write *five* questions to ask people in your class about their skills. Use vocabulary from exercise 1A. Then check your accuracy.

1 Can you _____ ?
2 Can you _____ ?
3 Can you _____ ?
4 Can you _____ ?
5 Can you _____ ?

> ✓ **ACCURACY CHECK**
> Do **not** use *to* between *can/can't* and a verb.
> Can you ~~to~~ fix bikes? ✗
> Can you fix bikes? ✓

4 SPEAKING

A [GROUP WORK] Ask and answer your questions from exercise 3D. Say how well you do the skills.

> Can you play the guitar?
>> No, I can't. What about you?
> Yes, I can. I can play it really well.

B [GROUP WORK] What skill can everyone in your group do? Who can do it really well?

8.2 HAPPY WORKERS = GREAT WORKERS?

LESSON OBJECTIVE
- say what you can and can't do at work or school

1 LANGUAGE IN CONTEXT

A Look at the offices in the pictures on pages 78 and 79. How are they different from other offices? Do you like them? Are they good places to work?

B Read the article. What activities can you do in a happy office?

Not just an office ... an 😐FFICE

Who can you find in all great **companies**? Great **workers**. And what's true for all great workers? They're happy because happy people do a great job.

How can companies make their workers happy? They can pay them a lot of money, of course, but money can't make people happy – not always. A great company can also give its workers a happy **office**. Happy offices aren't just ordinary offices with desks, phones, and computers – and they're not *just* for work.

What can you do in a happy office? The short answer is, you can **work hard** *and* have fun. You can run or play basketball with **your coworkers** and **have a meeting** at the same time. This is a great way to **think** of new ideas. You can work in a cool room with big chairs and no table or **take a break** in a room with a lot of plants (like a forest!) In some offices, you can come to work with your dog!

GLOSSARY
all (*det*) 100% of something
pay (*v*) give someone money for their work
ordinary (*adj*) usual, normal

2 VOCABULARY: Work

A 🔊 2.13 Find the words below in the article. Then listen and repeat.

| company | workers | office | work hard | have a meeting | think | take a break | your coworkers |

B Match the words from exercise 2A with the definitions.
1 a workplace, with desks and chairs
2 the people you work with
3 a business – for example, Microsoft or Toyota
4 the people in a company
5 do a lot of work
6 stop work for a short time – for example, to have coffee
7 have ideas, or find answers to problems
8 get together with people at work and talk about business

C ▶ Now do the vocabulary exercises for 8.2 on page 148.

D GROUP WORK What other activities can you do in a happy office? Which companies have happy workers? You can go online to find examples.

FIND IT

78

8.2 HAPPY WORKERS = GREAT WORKERS?

LESSON OBJECTIVE
- say what you can and can't do at work or school

Introduce the lesson Write the word *rules* on the board. Explain that *rules* tell what we can and can't do. Ask Ss: *What rules do we have in class?* Elicit some ideas e.g., *You can't have a snack. You can't talk on your phone.*

- Ask Ss to talk to a partner about rules that they have in their house. Monitor as Ss chat and then ask Ss to tell you rules from their house. Write some of these on the board. Ask: *Are these good or bad rules?*

1 LANGUAGE IN CONTEXT

A **Introduce the task** Ss look at the picture and answer the questions in pairs before they share their ideas.

> **Possible answer**
> They're different because they don't just have desks and chairs.

B Before Ss begin, ask volunteers to read the **Glossary**. Make sure Ss understand the words.
- Allow Ss time to read the text individually. They check their answers with a partner and write the items down.
- Write *Happy Office* and *Ordinary Office* on the board. As Ss say their answers, write them under the correct heading.

> **Answers**
> You can have a meeting at the same time as running or playing basketball with your coworkers. You can work in a cool room with big chairs and no table. You can take a break in a room with a lot of plants. You can come to work with your dog.

2 VOCABULARY: Work

A 🔊 **2.13** **Present the vocabulary** Ss underline the words in the text. Check that they understand them.
- Play the audio. Pause after each word and ask Ss to repeat together.

B **Do the task** Ss match on their own before checking with a partner and then the class.

> **Answers**
> 1 office 2 your coworkers 3 company 4 workers
> 5 work hard 6 take a break 7 think 8 have a meeting

TEACHER DEVELOPMENT ACTIVITY 2

Test your partner
This simple peer-testing activity can be used for practice and memorization whenever Ss are working with a set of vocabulary items and matching definitions.

- After exercise 2B, Ss close their books. Say definitions from the exercise in random order and challenge Ss to remember and shout out the corresponding words or expressions, e.g., *Do a lot of work?* (work hard!) If Ss can't remember an item or if they remember it imperfectly, prompt or correct as required.
- Now have Ss test each other in pairs: Student A with book open, Student B with book closed. Student A says definitions while Student B replies with the corresponding word or expression.
- After a minute or so, have Ss reverse roles so Student B now tests Student A.

Tip: If you can, give weaker Ss the role of Student A. This gives them more time to get familiar with the vocabulary and definitions before they are tested by their partner.

C Direct Ss to page 148 to complete the vocabulary exercises. Teacher's tips for vocabulary exercises are on page T-141.

D FIND IT **GROUP WORK** Review Model the task by giving an example of what you can do in a Happy Office, e.g., *You can play video games.* Ss can use their smartphones to look for information they may need.
- Allow Ss time to discuss the questions with their partner. Elicit answers.

T-78

3 GRAMMAR: *can* and *can't* for possibility

A Before Ss circle the answers, explain that they can refer to the examples in the grammar box.

- **Present the grammar** Ask volunteers to read the grammar chart aloud. Monitor pronunciation. Check understanding by asking questions, e.g., *Can I take a break in my lesson? / Can you bring your dog to class?*

> **Answers**
> 1 possible   2 before

B **Do the task** Ss unscramble and match the sentences individually before checking their answers with the class.

- Ask Ss to write new answers using their own ideas. Challenge them to use *can* in each one.

> **Answers**
> 1 Where can we have lunch?   d
> 2 How can I get to the restaurant?   e
> 3 What can we eat?   a
> 4 When can we have the meeting?   c
> 5 How can I send this message?   b

C Direct Ss to page 136 to complete the grammar exercise. Teacher's tips for grammar exercises are on page T-129.

D Model some examples for Ss before they write their questions, e.g., *Where can I have my lunch? How can you get there?*

- As Ss write, circulate and monitor. Offer any spelling help Ss may need.
- Correct sentences individually before the next task.

> **Answers**
> Answers may vary.

4 SPEAKING

A [PAIR WORK] Model the sample conversation by reading it with a volunteer. Encourage him or her to finish the response.

- Ss share their questions and answer them with their partners. Make sure they also discuss what they *can't* do.
- As Ss talk, circulate and monitor. Listen for any examples of language usage that you can give feedback on when the activity is over.
- Elicit and compare Ss' ideas.

🔗 EXTRA ACTIVITY

Write or display three sentences about the rules in your household on the board, e.g.,

> *You can't eat in the living room.*
> *You can have a snack.*
> *You can't listen to music.*

Explain to Ss that one of them is false and the other two are true. Ss guess the false sentence. Ask Ss to write three sentences about the rules in their household, making one sentence false. They share their sentences with a partner who has to guess the sentence that is not true. Ask a volunteer to share their three sentences with the class.

3 GRAMMAR: *can* and *can't* for possibility

A Circle the correct answers. Use the sentences in the grammar box to help you.
1 Use *can* to talk about things that are **possible** / **not possible**.
2 Question words (*Who*, *What*, *Where*, *Why*, and *How*) go **before** / **after** *can* or *can't* to ask about possibility.

> **can and can't for possibility**
>
> You **can** work hard and have fun.
> She **can** take a break any time.
> Your dog **can't** come to work with you.
>
> What **can't** they do in the office?
> How **can** companies make their workers happy?
> Where **can** you have a meeting?

B Put the words in the correct order to make questions. Then match them to the answers (a–e) below.
1 we / have / lunch? / can / Where _____
2 the / restaurant? / How / get / to / can / I _____
3 can / What / eat? / we _____
4 have / the / meeting? / we / can / When _____
5 I / this / message? / send / can / How _____

___ a We can have some cookies.
___ b You can email it from your phone.
___ c Tuesday is good for me.
___ d In the company restaurant.
___ e Go straight, and then turn left.

C ▶ Now go to page 136. Look at the grammar chart and do the grammar exercise for 8.2.

D Write questions about a company or school to ask if it's a good place to work or study.
1 What can _____?
2 Where can _____?
3 How can _____?

4 SPEAKING

PAIR WORK Talk to a partner about things you can and can't do at your company or school. Ask your questions from exercise 3D.

> What can you do at lunchtime?

> You can go to …

8.3 ARE YOU THE RIGHT PERSON?

LESSON OBJECTIVE
- say why you're the right person for a job

1 FUNCTIONAL LANGUAGE

A Look at the picture. Where are the people? What are they doing?

B 🔊 2.14 Read and listen. What <u>three</u> things can the man do well?

🔊 2.14 Audio script

A Can we speak in English for five minutes?
B Yes, we can.
A Great. So, are you the right person for this job?
B Yes. **I think so.**
A Why? In a very short answer, please.
B Because I can work well with people on a team. **I think that** teamwork is very important.
A I see. **Why do you think** it's important?
B Because a company is a big team. I mean, it's a group of people, and you work with them every day.
A And why are *you* good on a team?
B Because I like people, and I can communicate well.
A That's great. **I think that** good communication is important. But **I don't think** it's the only important thing. What other things can you do well?
B I can speak two languages. I mean, I speak Spanish and English.

C Complete the chart with expressions in **bold** from the conversation above.

Asking for opinions	Giving opinions
What do you think ? ¹_____ do you think (that) … ?	I think ² _____ . I don't think so. I ³ _____ (that) … I ⁴ _____ think (that) …

D 🔊 2.15 [PAIR WORK] Complete the conversations with words from exercise 1C. Listen and check. Then ask and answer the questions with a partner. Answer with your ideas.

1 A I think video games are great. What do you think?
  B I _____ they're very cool. They're boring.
2 A _____ do you _____ cell phones are important?
  B They're useful. We communicate with our phones.
3 A Do you think soccer is a good sport?
  B No. I _____ . I like basketball.
4 A Are you good at music?
  B I _____ . I sing and play the guitar really well.

8.3 ARE YOU THE RIGHT PERSON?

LESSON OBJECTIVE
- say why you're the right person for a job

Introduce the topic Ss copy the grid below. Ask them to make as many words as they can, using the letters in the box only once. All the letters together make one big word. Give Ss a few minutes to make words before you ask each learner to give you a word they found. The nine-letter word is *interview*.

i	e	r
i	n	v
e	t	w

1 FUNCTIONAL LANGUAGE

A **Introduce the task** Discuss the questions as a class.

> **Answers**
> The man is in an office. He's interviewing for a job. / He has a job interview.

B 🔊 **2.14** **Do the task** Read the task aloud and ask Ss to circle the three things the man can do well.
- Play the audio as Ss read. Play again if necessary.
- Ss check their answers with a partner before you elicit them.

> **Answers**
> He can work well with people on a team. He can communicate well. He can speak two languages.

> 📎 **EXTRA ACTIVITY**
> Ss role play the conversation. Monitor for pronunciation as they talk.

C Pre-teach the idea of giving and asking for an opinion. Model some sentences to help Ss.
- Ss complete the chart individually before they share with a partner.
- Ss read the sentences aloud as you check answers.

> **Answers**
> 1 Why   2 so   3 think   4 don't

D 🔊 **2.15** **PAIR WORK** Ss complete the sentences with the correct words before they check with a partner.
- Play the audio. Ss listen and check their answers. Pause or repeat the audio if Ss didn't hear.
- As a follow up, ask Ss to role play the conversations in pairs. Monitor for pronunciation.

> **Answers**
> 1 don't think   2 Why, think   3 don't think so   4 think so

> **VOCABULARY SUPPORT** Remind Ss that the expression is always *good at*. Many Ss find it natural to say *good in*. Correct Ss if you hear this.

- Ss can now ask and answer the questions in exercise 1D in pairs. Monitor for grammar and pronunciation. When finished, ask Ss to share their ideas with the class.

> 📎 **EXTRA ACTIVITY**
> **Review** Ss write an opinion survey of five new questions asking opinions. They could write about movies, a local restaurant or shop, their job, or school. If this too difficult, you could write five questions on the board or dictate them. If Ss write their own questions, correct them before the next stage. Ss now circulate around the room asking and answering questions. Monitor as Ss share their ideas. When Ss finish, elicit your class's opinions.

T-80

2 REAL-WORLD STRATEGY

A **Introduce the task** Volunteers read the explanation aloud. Check for understanding. Ss read the short excerpts from the dialogues individually. Elicit answers.

> **Answers**
> Ideas: A company is a big team. He speaks two languages.
> He explains an idea: A company is a group of people, and you work with them every day.
> He gives more information: He speaks English and Spanish.

B 🔊 **2.16** Read questions aloud for Ss. Play the audio. Play again if necessary.
- Ss share their answers in pairs before you check as a class.

> **Answers**
> Lori wants to be on a dance team. She has free time in the mornings.

> 🔊 **2.16 Audio script**
>
> **Coach** So, Lori, why are you the right person for the dance team?
> **Lori** Because I work really hard. I mean, I dance about two hours a day.
> **Coach** I see. And can you meet in the mornings?
> **Lori** Oh, yes. I'm not busy. I mean, I work in a restaurant at night, but I have free time in the morning.
> **Coach** OK. Great.

C 🔊 **2.16** Play the audio as Ss complete the chart. Play again if necessary. Ss compare their answers before you check.

> **Answers**
> 1 dance   2 two hours   3 work   4 at night   5 mornings

D PAIR WORK **Review** Put Ss into pairs and assign each one to be either Student A or Student B. Ask Student As to turn to page 157 and Bs to turn to page 158.
- Write the name of a place your Ss will know. Say: *I think [name] is great. What do you think?* Elicit answers from Ss. Encourage them to use expressions from page 80.
- Allow Ss time to read through their information. Explain any words they don't understand. Don't start until Ss have read through everything and are certain of their opinions.
- Circulate and monitor as Ss do the task.
- Ask volunteers to demonstrate some of the conversations to the rest of the class.

3 PRONUNCIATION: Saying groups of words

A 🔊 **2.17** Focus Ss' attention on the forward slash marks (/) in the sentences. Say that these show pauses between groups of words. Play the audio. Ss compare answers.

- Check answers and have Ss repeat the correct versions of each sentence.

> **Answers**
> 1 A   2 B

B 🔊 **2.18** Ss work alone before comparing with a partner.
- Play the audio and have Ss check. Then elicit answers from the class.

> **Answers**
> 1 I'm good on a team / because I can communicate well.
> 2 I can speak two languages / and I can play the guitar.
> 3 I work in a restaurant at night, / but I'm free in the mornings.
> 4 I think that good communication is important, / but I don't think it's the only important thing.

C PAIR WORK Play the audio again and have Ss repeat.
- Ss practice speaking in pairs. Encourage them to listen for the pauses and give each other feedback.

4 SPEAKING

A **Introduce the task** Ask Ss: *What questions do people ask in job interviews?* Spend some time writing and correcting Ss' questions on the board.
- Add some questions of your own, e.g., *Can you speak Spanish? Can you work hard? Can you use a computer well?* Spending time doing this will give Ss more material to use in the next section of the lesson.
- Ss choose a job from the list or one of their own ideas. They think about the reason why they are right for the job.

B PAIR WORK Read the example aloud as a model. Encourage Ss to use the questions you have written on the board.
- As they speak, circulate and monitor. Listen for examples of language usage that you can give feedback on when the activity is over.

> 📎 **EXTRA ACTIVITY**
>
> To practice job interviews, have a circle discussion (a carousel.) For details on how to run this lesson, see page T-102. Before you start, decide on what job the outer ring is going to interview for, e.g., an officer worker. Make sure it is something that your Ss will be familiar with. Explain that the outside ring of interviewers will have to decide if their candidate gets the job or not. Allow Ss time to think about questions they might ask. Alternatively, dictate or write questions for students. Monitor and listen for language usage that you can give feedback on when the activity is over. Find out which Ss got the job at the end before you give your feedback.

2 REAL-WORLD STRATEGY

EXPLAINING AND SAYING MORE ABOUT AN IDEA
Use *I mean* to explain or say more about an idea.
A company is a big team. I mean, it's a group of people, and you work with them every day.
I can speak two languages. I mean, I speak Spanish and English.

A   Read about explaining and saying more about an idea in the box above. Look at what the man says. What idea does he explain? What idea does he give more information about?

B   🔊 2.16 Listen to a conversation. What does Lori want to do? When does she have free time?

C   🔊 2.16 Listen to the conversation again. Complete the chart with the sentences you hear.

Idea	Explanation/more information
I work really hard.	I mean, I ¹_____ about ² _____ _____ a day.
I'm not busy.	I mean, I ³_____ in a restaurant ⁴_____ _____, but I have free time in the ⁵_____ .

D   ▶ PAIR WORK Student A: Go to page 157. Student B: Go to page 160. Follow the instructions.

3 PRONUNCIATION: Saying groups of words

A   🔊 2.17 Listen for the space (= short pause) between the words (/). Which sentences do you hear, A or B?
   1   A Can we speak in English / for five minutes?
       B Can we speak in / English for five minutes?
   2   A What other things can / you do well?
       B What other things / can you do well?

B   🔊 2.18 Listen to the sentences. Write a pause mark (/) in each sentence.
   1 I'm good on a team because I can communicate well.
   2 I can speak two languages and I can play the guitar.
   3 I work in a restaurant at night but I'm free in the mornings.
   4 I think that good communication is important but I don't think it's the only important thing.

C   PAIR WORK Practice the sentences in exercise 3B with a partner. Take turns. Can your partner hear the spaces between the words?

4 SPEAKING

A   Choose a job from the box or your own idea. Think about why you are the right person for the job.

   | an art teacher   a chef at a restaurant   a hotel clerk |
   | a singer in a band   a soccer player |

B   PAIR WORK Tell a partner your job from exercise 4A. Your partner interviews you for the job. Then change roles.

   Are you the right person for this job?   I think so. I …

8.4 COMPUTERS AND OUR JOBS

LESSON OBJECTIVE
- write an online comment with your opinion

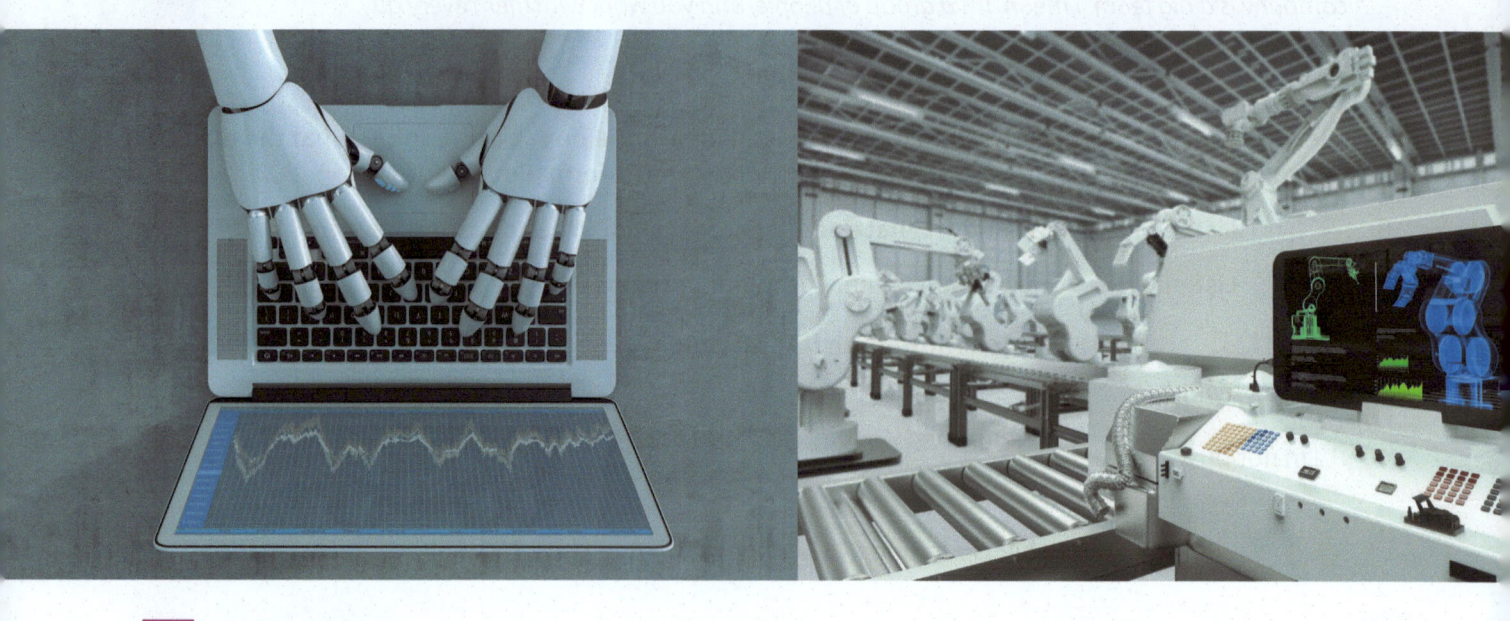

1 LISTENING

A Chris is the host of the podcast *Technology Talks*. Look at the pictures above. What is today's podcast about?

B 🔊 2.19 **LISTEN FOR DETAILS** Listen to the podcast. Who is Joanna Ramos? What does she say computers <u>can't</u> do?

C 🔊 2.19 **LISTEN FOR SUPPORTING DETAILS** Listen again. Check (✓) the supporting details Joanna gives.

Jobs for computers	New jobs for people
☐ make cars	☐ make computers
☐ drive cars	☐ start computer companies
☐ call people on the phone	☐ make cars
☐ talk	☐ be a computer's voice
☐ think	☐ make phones

D **PAIR WORK** **THINK CRITICALLY** Who thinks computers are a good thing: Joanna or Chris?

2 PRONUNCIATION: Listening for *can* and *can't*

A 🔊 2.20 Listen. Write the missing words.
1 What _____ computers do?
2 They _____ make cars.
3 A computer _____ make 100% of a car.

B 🔊 2.21 Listen. Do you hear *can* or *can't*? Circle the correct words.
1 can / can't   2 can / can't
3 can / can't   4 can / can't

82

8.4 COMPUTERS AND OUR JOBS

LESSON OBJECTIVE
- write an online comment with your opinion

Introduce the lesson Write or dictate opinion sentences for Ss to discuss together:
Computers can think.   Computers understand us.
As Ss discuss, circulate and monitor for pronunciation. Ask Ss to share their thoughts with the class.

1 LISTENING

A Ss look at the images and discuss what the podcast is about. Elicit key words and write on the board.

> **Possible answer**
> Today's podcast is about computers and jobs.

B 🔊 **2.19** Read the directions aloud for Ss. Check that they understand the questions. Remind Ss that listening for details means they are listening for specific information.
- Play the audio. Repeat if necessary.
- Elicit answers.

> 🔊 **2.19 Audio script**
>
> **Chris** Today on *Technology Talks* I'm with Joanna Ramos. She's from ITCI – a computer company. Welcome, Joanna.
> **Joanna** Thank you, Chris.
> **Chris** Joanna … a big question: Can computers take all our jobs? What do you think?
> **Joanna** Well, first, I think there's another question. What can computers do? Some examples: They can make cars. They can *drive* cars. They can talk …
> **Chris** They can do *a lot* of things.
> **Joanna** Yes, they can. *But* … they can't do those things *100%*. A computer can't make 100% of a car. Car companies need workers, too. Computers can't drive cars all the time. Only people can do that. And, OK, computers can *talk*, but they can't always *understand* us. My phone hardly ever understands me! And computers can't *think*. I mean, computers can't think *today*.
> **Chris** So *are* computers taking a lot of jobs?
> **Joanna** I don't think so. They are taking *some* of our jobs. But *people* make computers. And people's voices are the computers' voices. So there are a lot of new jobs, too.
> **Chris** *A lot* of new jobs? Is that true? I don't think that …

> **Answers**
> Joanna works at a computer company.
> Computers can't make 100% of a car. They can't drive cars all the time. They can't always understand us. They can't think.

C 🔊 **2.19** Ask volunteers to read the lists. Check for understanding and pronunciation.
- Now Ss listen for detail. Play audio. Ss check the boxes.

> **Answers**
> Jobs for computers: make cars, drive cars, talk
> New jobs for people: make computers, make cars, be a computer's voice

D Ss discuss the question in pairs or small groups before you check what they think as a class. Encourage them to explain their answer.

> **Answer**
> Joanna

2 PRONUNCIATION: Listening for *can* and *can't*

A 🔊 **2.20** Ss predict the missing words. Play the audio and ask Ss to check their ideas.

> **Answers**
> 1 can   2 can   3 can't

B 🔊 **2.21** Play the audio as Ss circle the words they hear. Remind them to listen for the /t/ sound in *can't* to help distinguish the words. Elicit answers.

> **Answers**
> 1 can   2 can   3 can't   4 can't

> 🔊 **2.21 Audio script**
>
> 1 They can drive cars.
> 2 They can talk.
> 3 Computers can't drive cars all the time.
> 4 They can't always understand us.

> **VOCABULARY SUPPORT**   The words *can* /kæn/ and *can't* /kænt/ have subtle differences in pronunciation, which Ss need to learn to hear. Note that there is also a weak form of pronouncing *can* (/kən/), which can be hard to distinguish.

T-82

3 WRITING

A **Do the task** Allow Ss time to read individually. Ask them to share their answers with a partner before you elicit answers as a group. Go over any vocabulary that Ss may not be familiar with.

> **Answers**
> Arturo thinks Joanna is correct.
> Kaito doesn't think Joanna is correct.

B **Introduce the task** Remind Ss of the main punctuation marks in English: the period, the comma, the question mark, and the apostrophe. Remind them also about the use of capital letters at the start of sentences and for names.

- Introduce quotation marks to Ss by pointing out the first rule. Ask them where they see this punctuation.
- Ss find the capital letters and punctuation marks individually. Elicit answers.
- Ask volunteers to read each rule about quotation marks aloud.
- Read the **Register check** aloud for Ss. Ask: *Who quotes Joanna Ramos?* (Kaito and Arturo) *Which word do these people use to quote?* (says).

> **Answers**
> 1 Joanna says, "People make computers."
> 2 She says, "They are taking *some* of our jobs."
> 3 She also says, "There are a lot of new jobs, too."

C **Do the task** Direct Ss to exercise 1C on page 82. Ss use these details to write their comments. As Ss write their comments, circulate and monitor, providing vocabulary as necessary. Spell words on the board that Ss ask for so everyone can see them. If possible, correct Ss' work before the next exercise. Allow Ss to listen to the podcast again if needed.

D **GROUP WORK** Put Ss in groups and ask them to share their comments. They can read them to each other or allow individual Ss to read them.

- When Ss finish, bring the class back together and ask for volunteers to read their comments aloud to the class. Do Ss agree or disagree? Did Ss have the same ideas?

> ### ✎ HOMEWORK IDEAS
>
> Ask Ss to watch an online video of a brief interview in English. Direct them to write down the name (or URL) of the video to find it later. Ss write comments about the video, including if they agree or disagree with the opinions expressed in it. In the next session, ask Ss to share their videos and comments with a partner or the rest of the class. You might like to show a very small clip of some of the videos.

3 WRITING

A Read three people's online comments about the podcast. Which person thinks Joanna is correct? Which person doesn't think Joanna is correct? What's your favorite comment?

TECHNOLOGY TALKS: Interview with Joanna Ramos

JUNE 1, 11:30 A.M.

Kaito, Tokyo

I don't think Joanna Ramos is right. Computers *are* a problem. Robots are taking all our jobs! They can say hello to people in stores and hotels, they can cook, they can play music, they can clean buildings, they can make cars … What jobs CAN'T they do? Joanna says, "People make computers." Well, I think robots can make computers now. They're *very* smart.

Ruby, Miami

Computers and robots can do a lot of things, but they don't have feelings: they're not happy, and they're not sad. Feelings are important for many jobs. For example, teachers, doctors, and nurses work with people, so feelings are important. I don't like the idea of robot doctors!

Arturo, Mexico City

Computers are cheap. I mean, companies pay people for their work, but they don't pay their robots or computers. And computers work hard. But I think Ruby is right. Computers don't have feelings. Joanna is right, too. She says, "They are taking *some* of our jobs." Not *all* of them. She also says, "There are a lot of new jobs, too." That's true. It's not a problem.

GLOSSARY
robot (*n*) a machine with a computer in it

B **WRITING SKILLS** Sometimes we want to write another person's words. Their words are quotations. Read the rules below. Then (circle) all the capital letters and punctuation marks in sentences 1–3.

- Use quotation marks (" ") around other people's words.
- Put a comma (,) after *says*.
- Start the quotation with a capital letter (A, B, C, …).

1 Joanna says, "People make computers."
2 She says, "They are taking *some* of our jobs."
3 She also says, "There are a lot of new jobs, too."

REGISTER CHECK

In informal writing and speaking, people often use *says* to quote (= give) another person's words.

In an online comment: *Joanna says, "People make computers."*

In formal writing, people often use *said*.

In a newspaper article: *Joanna Ramos said, "A computer can't make 100% of a car."*

WRITE IT

C Read the ideas from Joanna's interview in exercise 1C. Then write an online comment. Give your opinion about computers and jobs. Quote some of Joanna's words.

D **GROUP WORK** Read your group's comments. Do you have the same or different ideas?

8.5 TIME TO SPEAK
National skills

LESSON OBJECTIVE
- talk about what people in your country are good at

A   PREPARE   Match the skills in the box to the pictures. Which three skills are <u>not</u> in the pictures?

cook   dance   make movies   paint   play soccer   sing   snowboard   surf

B   DISCUSS   Where can people do the things from exercise A really well? For each skill, say the name of a city, region/area, or country. Then compare your ideas with your group.

C   DECIDE   Read the information in the box on the right. Talk to a partner about the question in the box. Together, think of <u>three</u> skills for the video.

D   AGREE   Compare everyone's ideas. Choose your class' <u>three</u> favorite ideas for the video.

To check your progress, go to page 154.

CAN YOU HELP US?
We want to make a YouTube™ video about our country and why it's great. The title is "We're good!" The video is about the skills people have here. What can we do *really* well in this country? Please send us your ideas!

USEFUL PHRASES

DISCUSS
Where can people cook really well?
Chinese food is always great.
I think people can cook really well in Rome and Naples.
What do you think?

DECIDE
What can we do really well in this country?
We can do … well.
I agree. / I disagree.
Our three skills for the video are …

AGREE
What are your ideas?
Good idea!
Our three favorite skills are …

8.5 TIME TO SPEAK
National skills

LESSON OBJECTIVE
- talk about what people in your country are good at

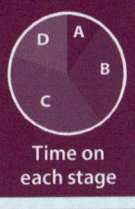

Time on each stage

Introduce the task Ask, dictate, or write: *Which country cooks really well? Which country makes good music? Which country makes great films?* Ss discuss the questions in pairs. Do your Ss agree?

- Direct Ss to the **Useful phrases** section at the bottom of the page. Remind them that they can use them at the relevant stages of the lesson.

A **PREPARE** **Aim:** Ss match pictures with vocabulary.

- **CLASS WORK** Read the list of skills aloud and check that Ss understand them.
- **PAIR WORK** Ss look at the pictures and answer the question in pairs then match skill and pictures. Ask pairs to share their answers with the class. Listen and monitor.

Answers
1 make movies   2 cook   3 surf   4 dance
5 play soccer
Not in the pictures: paint, sing, snowboard

- **CLASS WORK** Ask: *Which skills do you have? When do you do these things?* Elicit answers.

B **DISCUSS** **Do the task** **Aim:** Ss discuss which places do things well.

- **Preparation for speaking*** Give Ss time to think silently about what they are going to say.
- **CLASS WORK** Read the instructions aloud and check for understanding. Model an answer if necessary.
- **PAIR WORK** Ss answer together to maximize speaking time.

C **DECIDE** **Aim:** Ss read and decide what should go in a YouTube™ video.

- **CLASS WORK** Either you or a volunteer read the *Can you help us?* box aloud.
- **PAIR WORK** Suggest that Ss think about sports, food, the arts (like films or music), technology, cars, or anything else. Write these on the board as Ss discuss to give them ideas.
- **Feedback for speaking activities*** When Ss speak, focus on their performance rather than their accuracy. Give them feedback based on how well they completed the task.

D **AGREE** **Review** **Aim:** Ss share their ideas.

- **CLASS WORK** Elicit Ss' ideas and write some of them on the board. Do Ss have the same opinions?

📎 EXTRA ACTIVITY

Ask Ss to use their smartphones to make the video in pairs or small groups. If possible, pair Ss who are from different countries in order to maximize use of English. They film each other saying why their country is great and what it does well. As they film, monitor and provide feedback and advice. Ss share their videos with their classmates. Praise Ss for their films and comment on instances of good language use.

*These tips can help you to create a safe speaking environment. They can also be used with other speaking activities. For more information, see page xxii.

≫ PROGRESS CHECK ≫

Direct students to page 154 to check their progress. Go to page T-152 for Progress check activity suggestions.

TEACHER DEVELOPMENT REFLECTION

You can answer these questions in a reflection journal or discuss them with your peers.

1 Development Activity 1 asks Ss to write personalized sentences using skills vocabulary. Did Ss need any help with language problems when writing their sentences? If you do this activity again, how could you change your example sentences to make them more helpful to Ss?

2 The activity focuses on writing and reading / listening practice with the target vocabulary. How could you extend the activity to provide some speaking practice in pairs or small groups?

3 In Development Activity 2, did Ss enjoy being tested by the teacher? Did they like the idea of testing each other? Why or why not?

4 How effective was the activity in helping Ss to memorize the vocabulary? Did all the Ss appear confident with the words and definitions by the end?

T-84

PLACES TO GO

9

TEACHER DEVELOPMENT INTRODUCTION

Strategy 3: Building learners' confidence to speak – Listening to learner language

An important part of a teacher's job is listening to the language that learners produce during speaking activities. This tells us what students have learned, and it gives us a good idea of what their language needs are. We also need to listen to learner language so we can give students feedback. Remember that you should listen not only to the accuracy of students' language, but also for their ability to speak fluently and communicate ideas. Listening to learner language is an important teaching skill, but it is also a difficult one to do well. In this unit, we look at two different ways of making listening to language easier. For background on students' language output and teacher feedback, you can read pages 10 to 20 of *Teaching Speaking* by Goh and Burns (Cambridge University Press 2012). Please go to www.cambridge.org/evolve to download these pages.

INTRODUCE THE THEME OF THE UNIT

Write *places to go* on the board. Elicit meaning.

- Display pictures or write the names of up to three famous vacation destinations. These could be *the pyramids, New York, an African safari, Machu Picchu, The Great Barrier Reef*, or somewhere else. Try to choose destinations that your Ss will know; it would be good if these were popular places in the Ss' own country.

- Dictate or write two questions that Ss discuss with each other:
  How do you go there?
  What can you do there?

- Ss discuss in pairs as you monitor for language. Check Ss' ideas as a class.

UNIT OBJECTIVES

Read the unit objectives aloud. Tell Ss to listen and read along. Explain any new vocabulary Ss may not understand.

START SPEAKING

A **Ss look at the picture and discuss in pairs. Elicit their answers as a class.**

B **Ss discuss in pairs before you elicit answers.**

C **Ss can use any ideas from the start of this lesson to help them. Ss share their ideas.**

- **OPTIONAL ACTIVITY** Ss watch Julieth's video and identify the place she's talking about. They listen for why it's good and then say whether or not they agree it's a good place to go. You may want to explain the meaning of the word *horizon* and that *'cause* is a short form of *because*.

REAL STUDENT

Hello, my name's Julieth Moreno. One of the best places to go in Bogotá, Colombia, is Monserrate. Uh, it's a very great place, 'cause you get to see the whole city, you can see all Bogotá from up there so it's, it's pretty, pretty cute and the, all the, the horizon is great.

UNIT OBJECTIVES

- talk about travel and vacations
- make travel plans
- ask for information in a store
- write a description of a place
- plan a vacation for someone

PLACES TO GO

9

START SPEAKING

A   Look at the picture. Where is the woman? Is it difficult to get to this place?

B   What do you do in your free time? Do you go to new places?

C   Think of a place you like. Talk about it. Say why it's good. For ideas, watch Julieth's video.

REAL STUDENT

What's Julieth's place? Do you agree it's a good place to go?

9.1 I LOVE IT HERE!

LESSON OBJECTIVE
- talk about travel and vacations

1 LANGUAGE IN CONTEXT

A Kaitlin and her friends are on vacation. Read Kaitlin's posts. Where do they go?

B Read again. Check (✓) the sentences that are true. Correct the false ones.
- ☐ 1 Kaitlin takes a bus to San Diego.
- ☐ 2 They go to their hotel on Thursday.
- ☐ 3 They are in San Diego on Friday.
- ☐ 4 They go to a zoo on Saturday.
- ☐ 5 Kaitlin and her friends have a bad vacation.

FROM MY SMALL TOWN TO A BIG CITY

THURSDAY MORNING
Goodbye to my small **town**. San Diego, here I come! I have my **ticket** and my seat on the **plane**. I'm next to the window!

THURSDAY AFTERNOON
Now I'm in San Diego, and this is our hotel. These are my friends in front of the hotel.

FRIDAY
Today we're in the **country**, not in the **city**! We're at this cool **ranch** near San Diego. It's a really big **farm**.

SATURDAY
We're at the San Diego Zoo. These birds are funny. They're talking. They say, "Hello. How are you? Hello. How are you?"

SUNDAY
Now I'm on a **tour** of San Diego Bay. I'm on a **boat** with my friends. They're not listening to the tour guide because they're talking.

A fun **vacation**? I think so. I love it here! 😁

GLOSSARY
tour guide (n) this person takes you to a place and tells you about it

---

2 VOCABULARY: Travel

A 🔊 2.22 Listen and repeat the words. Which words are places?

| boat | country | farm | plane | ranch | ticket | tour | town | vacation |

B ▶ Now do the vocabulary exercises for 9.1 on page 148.

C PAIR WORK Which places do you like from Kaitlin's vacation? Which places <u>don't</u> you like? Why?

86

9.1 I LOVE IT HERE!

LESSON OBJECTIVE
- talk about travel and vacations

Introduce the vocabulary Write the following words from this lesson on the board: *city, boat, country farm, zoo, hotel*. Ask Ss to read and check for pronunciation and meaning.

- Ask Ss: *Which places do you like? Why?*
- In pairs, Ss decide. Elicit their answers when they finish. Is there anywhere else they would like to go?

> **VOCABULARY SUPPORT** Remind Ss that countries are nouns and nationalities are adjectives. They can refer to Unit 1 as a reminder.
> *Mexico* – noun
> *Mexican* – adjective

1 LANGUAGE IN CONTEXT

A **Introduce the task** Read the task aloud for Ss.
- Ss read and answer individually before sharing their answers with a partner.
- Elicit answers. Explain any words Ss may ask the meanings of such as *ticket, plane,* and *tour* as well as any of the prepositions they may not be familiar with.

> **Answers**
> Kaitlin and her friends go to San Diego in California / the United States.

> **VOCABULARY SUPPORT** Prepositions of place are small words that describe positions.
> Ss may confuse *near* (close to) and *next to* (alongside and therefore closer). Explain *in front of* as one phrase. Demonstrate with a chair, e.g.,
> *The chair is in front of me.*
> *By* and *in front of* are prepositions of place. They show where people and things are.
> *With* is also a preposition. It can show that people are together.

B **Do the task** Ask Ss to read again individually. Check the true sentences and correct the false ones. Ss check with a partner. Elicit answers and make sure Ss read the complete sentences.
- If time permits, ask different Ss to read the posts aloud to the class. Monitor for pronunciation.

> **Answers**
> 1 False. Kaitlin takes a plane to San Diego.
> 2 True
> 3 False. Kaitlin is near San Diego on Friday.
> 4 True
> 5 False. Kaitlin and her friends have a fun vacation.

2 VOCABULARY: Travel

A 🔊 **2.22** Play the audio as Ss read. Pause after each word and ask them to repeat. Monitor for pronunciation errors. Explain any words Ss don't understand.
- Ss look for the words in pairs before you elicit the answers as a class.

> **Answers**
> Places: country, farm, ranch, town

B Direct Ss to page 148 to complete the vocabulary exercises. Teacher's tips for vocabulary exercises are on page T-141.

C **PAIR WORK** **Review** Read the questions aloud. As they discuss, monitor for pronunciation and grammar.

> **EXTRA ACTIVITY**
> **Play board scrabble** with words from this unit. For details on how to play, see page T-217.

T-86

3 GRAMMAR: *This* and *These*

A **Present the grammar** Before Ss circle the answers, explain that they can refer to the examples in the grammar box.

- Explain that *this* is used for singular nouns and *these* for plural. Check Ss' understanding by saying a noun and having them put *this* or *these* before it, e.g.,

  boat – this boat

  cars – these cars

- Ask Ss to circle the correct answers in pairs before you check as a class.

> **Answers**
> 1 birds around you   2 before   3 This, These   4 can

B Read the task aloud and make sure Ss understand. Ask them to fill in the gaps individually before checking with the class.

> **Answers**
> 1 This   2 These   3 this   4 This   5 this   6 These
> 7 These   8 This

> **PRONUNCIATION SUPPORT** Model the pronunciation of *this* /ðɪs/ and *these* /ðiːz/. Over-emphasise the longer vowel sound on *these* so Ss can hear the difference.
>
> Check that Ss are saying the words correctly by writing words on the board and asking them to say them aloud.

C Direct Ss to pages 136–137 to complete the grammar exercise. Teacher's tips for grammar exercises are on page T-129.

4 SPEAKING

A **FIND IT** Ask Ss to spend a few minutes looking through their pictures or drawing them. They choose a picture they are going to share.

- When they have chosen, ask them to spend two minutes planning what they are going to say. They can make notes if they wish. Preparation now will help them do a better job in the next task.

B **PAIR WORK** **Review** Model the example sentences so Ss can hear how to complete the task.

- Circulate and monitor as Ss tell each other about their pictures. Listen for language usage that you can give feedback on at the end of the task.
- Ss explain their picture to another partner or group. Finally, Ss share their pictures with the class.
- Give feedback.

3 GRAMMAR: *This* and *These*

A Circle the correct answer. Use the sentences in the grammar box to help you.
1. Use *This bird* and *These birds* to talk about **birds around you** / **birds you can't see**.
2. *This* and *these* go **before** / **after** a noun.
3. **This** / **these** goes before a singular noun. **This** / **these** goes before a plural noun.
4. You **can** / **can't** use *this* and *these* at the beginning of a sentence.

> **This and These**
>
> **This** ticket is expensive.
> We're at **this** cool ranch.
>
> **These** birds are funny.
> I don't like **these** pictures.

B Kaitlin writes a postcard about a museum. Write *this* or *these* to complete Kaitlin's postcard.

Dear Grandma,

I'm in San Diego! It's great. ¹ _____ postcard shows Balboa Park in the city. The park is very big, and it has 15 museums! ² _____ museums are for art, technology, transportation, and history. We're at the Mingei International Museum right now. You can see it in ³ _____ photo on the right. ⁴ _____ museum is interesting because it has local art – the artists are from ⁵ _____ city. I'm looking at some cool pictures now. ⁶ _____ pictures show places in San Diego. ⁷ _____ artists are *really* good. ⁸ _____ is my favorite room in the museum.

Love, Kaitlin

C ▶ Now go to page 136. Look at the grammar chart and do the grammar exercise for 9.1.

4 SPEAKING

FIND IT

A Choose five pictures on your phone or draw some simple pictures of places you know. Think about the people and places in the pictures.

B PAIR WORK Tell your partner about your pictures.

> This is a picture of my mom and my aunt. They're walking in the country. This hill is very big. What else? This is my favorite aunt. She's…

9.2 SAN FRANCISCO, HERE WE COME

LESSON OBJECTIVE
- make travel plans

1 LANGUAGE IN CONTEXT

A 🔊 2.23 Kaitlin is making a vacation video. Read and listen. Where is she now? Where is she going? How is she going there?

B 🔊 2.23 Read and listen again. Check (✓) the sentences that are true. Correct the false ones.
- ☐ 1 The plane is expensive, and the bus is cheap.
- ☐ 2 You can take a bus to San Francisco at night.
- ☐ 3 It's Friday night. Kaitlin is sleeping in a hotel.

> Hello again from San Diego! Today is Tuesday, and we want to **leave** on Friday. Our **destination** is San Francisco. But how do we **travel**? Do we **fly** or take the bus?
>
> Well, the **flight** is two hours. But you have to **arrive** at the **airport** a long time before the flight. You need to **check in** two hours before. So in total, by plane, the **trip** is about five hours. That's not bad. And I like to fly. But … the ticket is expensive.
>
> The bus *isn't* expensive. It *is* a long trip – it's 12 hours. But we can take a night bus. And it arrives in San Francisco the next morning. That's good because we don't need to **stay** in a hotel on Friday night.
>
> So, we're taking the bus. We just need to buy our tickets **online**. And then, San Francisco, here we come … on the bus.

2 VOCABULARY: Travel arrangements

A 🔊 2.24 Listen and repeat the sentences. Then match the sentences (a–h) to the pictures (1–8.)
- a Stay in a hotel. ___
- b Arrive at the airport. ___
- c Check in at the airport. ___
- d Fly to another airport. You can sleep on the flight. ___
- e Leave your house. Ready to travel? ___
- f Have a great trip! ___
- g Arrive at your destination. ___
- h Buy tickets online. ___

B ▶ Now do the vocabulary exercises for 9.2 on page 149.

C PAIR WORK Imagine you're going from San Diego to San Francisco. What's a good way to go? Why?

88

9.2 SAN FRANCISCO, HERE WE COME

LESSON OBJECTIVE
- make travel plans

Introduce the lesson Ask Ss: *What's your favorite way to travel?* Elicit from Ss different vehicles and write them on the board. They should come up with:

Bike (bicycle), car, bus, train, plane, etc.

- Ss rank their three favorite methods of transportation by writing numbers next to each one, with 1 as the best. Ss share their ideas with each other when they finish. Elicit ideas as a class and ask Ss why.

> **VOCABULARY SUPPORT** In English the verbs *take* and *go by* combine *with car/train/bus/boat* to express how you reach a destination, but there is a difference. *We are going by car/train/bus/plane; We are taking the/a train/bus/plane.* but NOT *We are taking the/a car/boat*. The expression *take + car/boat* can imply use for something more than just reaching a destination.

1 LANGUAGE IN CONTEXT

A 🔊 2.23 **Read and explain the instructions. Play the audio and then ask Ss to work in pairs to answer the questions. Play the audio again if necessary. Elicit answers from Ss.**

> **Answers**
> She's in San Diego. She's going to San Francisco. She's taking the bus.

B 🔊 2.23 **Ss read and understand the sentences before you play the audio.**

- Individually, Ss check the true sentences and correct the false ones, before you check as a class.
- Replay the audio if necessary.

> **Answers**
> 1 True   2 True   3 False. Kaitlin is sleeping on the bus.

2 VOCABULARY: Travel arrangements

A 🔊 2.24 **Present the vocabulary** Ss listen and repeat the sentences. Then ask them to work in pairs to match the sentences to the pictures.

- Elicit answers. Make sure Ss read the whole sentences when you ask them for the answers.

> **Answers**
> a 7   b 3   c 4   d 5   e 2   f 8   g 6   h 1

B **Direct Ss to page 149 to complete the vocabulary exercises. Teacher's tips for vocabulary exercises are on page T-141.**

C **PAIR WORK** Review If possible, display or draw a simple map of the United States. Ss could find a map on their smartphones. Ask Ss where San Diego is (bottom left corner) and where San Francisco is (a bit further up on the left-hand side). Ss answer the questions in pairs before you elicit their ideas. Make sure you ask them *Why?*

T-88

3 GRAMMAR: *like to, want to, need to, have to*

A Introduce the grammar Before Ss circle the answers, explain that they can refer to the examples in the grammar box.

- As you elicit answers, check for meaning and explain.

> **Answers**
> 1 things you choose to do   2 necessary things   3 verb

- On the board write *We need to learn English*. Now cover the word *to* and explain that without *to* this sentence is incorrect.

> **EXTRA ACTIVITY**
>
> Ask Ss to write one sentence using each of the verbs *like*, *want*, *need*, and *have*. Remind Ss that they need to use *to* after each one. Ss share their answers with each other before you elicit examples from different members of the class. Mark and correct Ss' sentences on the board.

B Ss check with a partner before you elicit answers as a class. Ask Ss to read the complete sentence aloud when you make corrections.

> **Answers**
> 1 I always sit by the window because I **like to** look outside.
> 2 My cell phone isn't old, but I **want to** buy a new one.
> 3 My wife isn't happy because she **has to** work this weekend.
> 4 On Fridays, we **like to** watch TV after dinner.
> 5 He starts work at 6:30, so he **needs to** get up really early.

C Direct Ss to page 137 to complete the grammar exercise. Teacher's tips for grammar exercises are on page T-129.

D [PAIR WORK] **Do the task** Model example sentences for Ss before you begin, e.g., *I need to go to work. / I have to get up before six*. Circulate and monitor as Ss work, offering any help they may need.

- When Ss finish, read the **Accuracy check** as a class. Display or dictate these sentences for Ss to correct in pairs. Correct the sentences.
  1 I want buy a new suitcase. I want a big one!
  2 My sister needs my help. I need find a cheap hotel for her.
  3 I have go to the airport at 6:00 a.m. tomorrow. I have an early flight.

> **Answers**
> 1 I want **to** buy a new suitcase. I want a big one!
> 2 My sister needs my help. I need **to** find a cheap hotel for her.
> 3 I have **to** go to the airport at 6:00 a.m. tomorrow. I have an early flight.

- Ask Ss to check the sentences they wrote. They should look for any mistakes they might have missed.

4 SPEAKING

A Read the instructions aloud. Allow Ss some time to think about or make notes on their answers.

- **OPTIONAL ACTIVITY** Ss watch Larissa's video and say whether they want to travel in the same way.

> **REAL STUDENT**
>
> Hello, my name is Larissa. I want to visit my uncle at Santa Barbara, California, on United States. I have to buy a ticket, I have to prepare my travel bags, I arrive at the airport before the flight and enjoy of the travel.

B [PAIR WORK] **Review** Ask two volunteers to read the model dialogue aloud.

- As Ss discuss, circulate and monitor, offering any suggestions and help you can to Ss. Listen for examples of language usage that you can give feedback on after the task is finished.
- When Ss finish, elicit some of their ideas.
- Give feedback.

> **TEACHER DEVELOPMENT ACTIVITY 1**
>
> **Listening for target language**
>
> One of the challenges of listening to student language, particularly at lower levels, is that they make quite a few mistakes, so it seems like you need to make a note of everything. This idea aims to take some of this pressure off you.
>
> - When Ss have had enough time to plan their trips, put them in pairs for their conversation.
> - Monitor with a pen and paper and note down examples of the way Ss use the four target verbs.
> - If a S makes a different kind of mistake, for example, they forget to use an indefinite article, just ignore it.
> - Try to listen for examples of different errors with all four verbs, for example, they leave out *to* or they use an *-ing* form after one of the verbs.
> - Write some of the errors on the board and elicit corrections.

3 GRAMMAR: *like to, want to, need to, have to*

A (Circle) the correct answer. Use the sentences in the grammar box to help you.
1. Use *want to* + verb and *like to* + verb to talk about **necessary things / things you choose to do**.
2. Use *need to* + verb and *have to* + verb to talk about **necessary things / things you choose to do**.
3. After *like to, want to, need to,* and *have to,* use **verb + -ing / verb**.

---

like to, want to, need to, have to

I **like to** fly.
You **need to** check in before the flight.
We **want to** leave on Friday.

She **wants to** take a bus.
He **has to** buy tickets.
My mom **likes to** sleep on a flight.

B (Circle) the correct answer to complete the sentences.
1. I always sit by the window because I *need to / like to* look outside. It's interesting!
2. My cell phone isn't old, but I *need to / want to* buy a new one.
3. My wife isn't happy because she *has to / wants to* work this weekend.
4. On Fridays, we *like to / need to* watch TV after dinner.
5. He starts work at 6:30, so he *needs to / wants to* get up really early.

C ▶ Now go to page 137. Look at the grammar chart and do the grammar exercise for 9.2.

D [PAIR WORK] Write four sentences that are true for you. Use *like to, want to, need to,* and *have to*. Then compare your sentences with a partner and check your accuracy.

✓ ACCURACY CHECK

Use *to* with *want, like, need* and *have* when they are before another verb.

I like fly. ✗
I like to fly. ✓

4 SPEAKING

A Work alone. Imagine you have to take a trip for one of these reasons: vacation, work, or to visit family. Where do you want to go? How do you want to travel: on a bus, a train, or a plane? For ideas, watch Larissa's video.

REAL STUDENT *Do you want to travel the same way as Larissa?*

B [PAIR WORK] Tell your partner about your trip. Talk about the things you need to do for your trip.

> I have to take a trip for work.

> Where do you have to go?

> Buenos Aires, and I want to go by plane. I like to fly.

> You can buy your ticket online …

9.3 THEY'RE TWO FOR $15

LESSON OBJECTIVE
- ask for information in a store

1 FUNCTIONAL LANGUAGE

A 🔊 **2.25** Andy arrives at the airport in Mexico City. Read and listen. What does he want to buy? What does he want to drink? What place does he ask about?

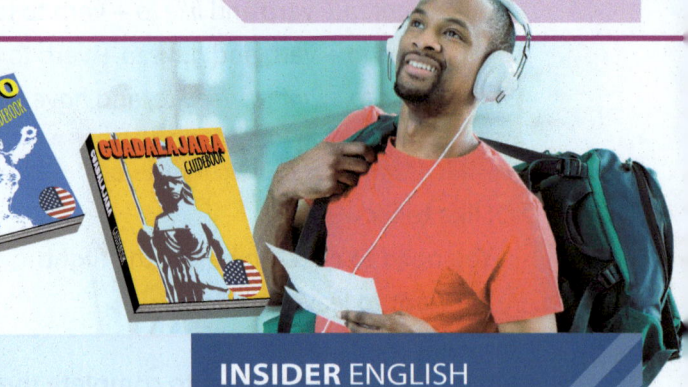

🔊 2.25 Audio script

Andy Hello. I need a travel guide for Mexico City. **Where are the travel guides?**

Clerk Sorry, can you say that again?

Andy Travel guides – where are the travel guides?

Clerk Oh, OK. They're here, with the books and magazines.

Andy OK. **How much is that?**

Clerk **It's $9.99.**

Andy Great. I need to buy a travel guide for Guadalajara, too. **Is it the same price, $9.99?**

Clerk Yes, it is. But good news! **They're two for $15.**

Andy Great! I want both, please. Hey, **what time does the café open?** I really need some coffee.

Clerk **It opens in about 10 minutes.**

Andy OK. **And where is the men's restroom?**

Clerk It's over there, next to the café. But first you need to buy your books!

INSIDER ENGLISH

People often say *restroom* in public places and *bathroom* in people's homes. *Restroom* is more polite.

At an airport:
Where is the men's restroom?

At a friend's house:
Sorry, where's your bathroom?

GLOSSARY

travel guide (*n*) a book with information about where to go and what to see in a city or country

B Complete the chart with expressions in **bold** from the conversation above.

Asking for information	Giving information
1 _____ the travel guides?	6 _____ $9.99.
2 _____ that?	7 _____ $15.
3 _____ , $9.99?	8 _____ about 10 minutes.
4 _____ the café open?	
5 _____ the men's restroom?	

C 🔊 **2.26** Complete the conversations with words from the chart above. Listen and check.

1 A Excuse me. _____ is this smartwatch?

B _____ $125.49.

A What about this big smartwatch? Is it the _____ ?

B No, it isn't. _____ $149.00.

2 A _____ flight 248 arrive?

B It arrives _____ 30 minutes.

A OK, thanks. Oh, and _____ the women's _____ ?

B It's over there.

90

9.3 THEY'RE TWO FOR $15

LESSON OBJECTIVE
- ask for information in a store

Introduce the lesson Ask Ss: *What's a popular store in your town?* Write the answer on the board and, if possible, show a picture of the store.
- Write the following words under the name of the store: *open / close / buy / how much*. Ask Ss to make questions using these words, to elicit: *When does it open? / When does it close? / What products can you buy? / How much does ____ cost?* (Choose something you can buy in the store to fill the gap.)
- Ss ask and answer the questions with a partner before you elicit answers as a class.

1 FUNCTIONAL LANGUAGE

A 🔊 2.25 **Read the questions and make sure Ss understand. Draw Ss' attention to the Glossary below. Read and explain *travel guide*.**
- Play audio as Ss read. Ss check their answers with a partner before you elicit answers as a class. Play audio again if necessary.

> **Answers**
> Andy wants to buy a travel guide for Mexico City and a travel guide for Guadalajara.
> He wants some coffee.
> He asks about the men's restroom.

- Ask volunteers to read **Insider English** aloud. Monitor for pronunciation. Check understanding by asking:
  1 *What do you say in a hotel?* to elicit *Where's the men's / ladies' restroom?*
  2 *What do you say in your friend's house?* to elicit *Where's your bathroom?*

> **VOCABULARY SUPPORT** It's polite to use *excuse me* in English before you ask someone for help.

B **Do the task** Ss complete the chart individually before they share their answers with a partner. Elicit ideas as a class.

> **Answers**
> 1 Where are   2 How much is   3 Is it the same price
> 4 What time does   5 Where is   6 It's   7 They're two for
> 8 It opens in

- Ask Ss to role play the dialogue with a partner by reading the script in exercise 1A. As they read, monitor and listen for pronunciation.

C 🔊 2.26 **Review** Ss complete the sentences individually with the phrases before they check with a partner. Ask Ss to read complete sentences when you elicit answers to practice pronunciation.
- As a follow up, ask Ss to role play the conversations with a partner. Monitor as they talk.

> **Answers**
> **Conversation 1**
> A Excuse me. **How much** is this smartwatch?
> B **It's** $125.49.
> A What about this big smartwatch? Is it the **same price**?
> B No, it isn't. **It's** $149.00.
> **Conversation 2**
> A **What time does** Flight 248 arrive?
> B It arrives **in** 30 minutes.
> A OK, thanks. Oh, and **where is/where's** the women's **restroom**?
> B It's over there.

> 🔗 **EXTRA ACTIVITY**
>
> Play bingo with prices. Write a list of many prices on the board, ranging from $0.50 to $10. Ss choose eight prices from the list. Remember to test Ss on the similar sounds of 13 and 30, 14 and 40 and 15 and 50. For details of how to play bingo, see page T-216. For a variation, ask a S to be the bingo caller.

T-90

2 REAL-WORLD STRATEGY

A **Introduce the task** Read and model the phrases for repetition. Mumble something to a S and ask him or her to respond using one of the phrases. Practice this with a few Ss.

- Ss answer the question as a class. Elicit the answer.

> **Answers**
> The clerk asks, "Sorry, can you say that again?"
> He wants to hear it again.

B 🔊 **2.27** Ask a volunteer to read the questions aloud. Check for meaning.

- Play the audio. Ss check their answers with a partner.
- Play audio again. Elicit answers as a class.

> **Answers**
> She doesn't understand the man at first.
> She asks him to repeat information. She asks him, "Sorry, can you repeat that, please?" It's usually $350, but today it's (just) $305.50.

> 🔊 **2.27 Audio script**
>
> A Excuse me. How much is this cell phone?
> B It's usually $350, but today it's just $305.50.
> A Sorry, can you repeat that, please?
> B It's usually $350. Today it's just $305.50.
> A Oh! Good price!

> 📎 **EXTRA ACTIVITY**
>
> Ss record their conversations on their smartphones and share with you or with the whole class.

3 PRONUNCIATION: Saying prices

A 🔊 **2.28** Play the audio and have Ss repeat the prices. Draw their attention to the word stress.

- Explain that focusing on the stressed syllable will help Ss when they are listening to prices, and it will also make their speaking clearer if they use stress correctly.

B 🔊 **2.29** Play the audio. Check answers.

- Ss practice speaking in pairs.

> **Answers**
> A I love that picture! How much is it?
> B It's $**80**.
> A $**18**! That's cheap!
> B No, it's $**80**.
> A Oh …

C **PAIR WORK** Demonstrate the activity with a strong student. Use the conversation in 3B as a model.

- Ss speak in pairs. Monitor and help as necessary.

4 SPEAKING

FIND IT

PAIR WORK After reading the instructions aloud, ask volunteers to read the prices while you monitor for pronunciation. Model the sample conversation a few times with more than one volunteer to check understanding.

- As Ss role play, listen for any examples of language usage that you can give feedback on when the activity is over.
- When Ss finish, ask volunteers to perform their role plays for the class.
- Give feedback. Praise Ss.

> 📎 **EXTRA ACTIVITY**
>
> **Review** Give or dictate to Ss a list of shopping items they have already learned, e.g., *a book, a cell phone, earphones,* etc. Try to use items that will be familiar to your Ss. Ask Ss to use their smartphones to find the price of these things online. Encourage them to use American websites. When Ss finish, ask them to work in pairs to ask *How much is … ?*

2 REAL-WORLD STRATEGY

ASKING SOMEONE TO REPEAT SOMETHING
To hear information again, ask, *Sorry, can you say that again?* or *Can you repeat that, please?*
Andy   Where are the travel guides?
Clerk Sorry, can you say that again?

A   Read the information in the box. What question does the clerk ask? Why?

B   🔊 2.27 Listen to a conversation. Does the woman understand the man the first time? What question does she ask? How much is the cell phone?

3 PRONUNCIATION: Saying prices

A   🔊 2.28 Listen and repeat the prices. Where does the speaker put stress in each price?
1 $6.19 / $6.90
2 $15 / $50
3 $17.30 / $70.13
4 $19 / $90
5 $2.16 / $2.60
6 $14 / $40

B   🔊 2.29 Listen and write the prices. Then practice the conversation with a partner.
A   I love that picture! How much is it?
B   It's $_____ .
A $_____ ! That's cheap!
B   No, it's $_____ .
A   Oh …

C   **PAIR WORK** Work with a partner. Ask to buy your friend's cell phone, bag, or Student's Book. Make a mistake with the price. Use the conversation in exercise 3B for an example. Then change roles.

4 SPEAKING

PAIR WORK Imagine you want to buy something. Look at the items below, or go online and find an item. Take turns being the customer. Ask for information, and ask the store clerk to repeat something. Then change roles.

$29.99, or two for $50

$6, or two for $10.50

$13, or two for $20

$45, or two for $79

> Excuse me. How much is this mug?

> It's $6, or two for $10.50.

> Sorry, can you repeat that, please?

9.4 A GREAT DESTINATION

LESSON OBJECTIVE
- write a description of a place

1 READING

A **RECOGNIZE TEXT TYPE** Read the text. What is it from?

☐ a travel guide ☐ an email ☐ a review ☐ a student's homework

TravelSmart PLACES TO GO NEAR PUNO

TAQUILE ISLAND

Taquile Island is in Lake Titicaca in Peru. You can see mountains in Bolivia from the island. About 2,000 people live on this interesting island.

TRANSPORTATION

You have to take a boat to the island from Puno. You can go with a tour company, or you can get a local boat. You are on the boat for about three hours. There are no cars on the island, so you have to walk after you arrive. It's a 40-minute walk to the town, and you can see a lot of nature on the way.

WHERE TO STAY

There are a small number of hotels on Taquile Island. You need to reserve a room before your trip. Prices are from $20 to $60 a night. You can also stay with a local family for about $9.

THINGS TO DO

- You can see dances in the town.
- You can eat at a restaurant or have lunch with a local family.
- The market has a lot of things to see, buy, and eat.

GLOSSARY
local (*adj*) from the nearby area or neighborhood
reserve (a room) (*v*) book or pay for a room before you travel to a place

B **SCAN** Find the numbers in the text. What do these numbers mean?

2,000   three   40 $20 to $60 $9

C **READ FOR DETAILS** Read the text again. Circle the correct answers.

1 Taquile Island *is* / *isn't* in Bolivia.
2 You *can* / *can't* get a boat to the island.
3 You *can* / *can't* drive on the island.
4 There are *no* / *some* hotels on the island.
5 There *are* / *aren't* restaurants on the island.
6 You *can* / *can't* meet local people.

D **PAIR WORK** **THINK CRITICALLY** Why do people like to go to Taquile Island? Do you want to go there? Why or why not? Give examples from the text to explain your answer.

9.4 A GREAT DESTINATION

LESSON OBJECTIVE
- write a description of a place

Introduce the lesson Write a list of adjectives on one side of the board that Ss could use to describe a place, e.g., *big, small, old, beautiful, cheap, expensive, far, near*. Ask Ss to suggest others.

- On the other side of the board, write places that Ss know and could describe to a partner, e.g., *your house or apartment, Mexico City, a beach, New York*, etc. Model one example, e.g., *My house is small and new*.
- Monitor as Ss describe the places in pairs before you elicit their ideas as a class.

1 READING

A **Introduce the task** Read the list of text types and make sure Ss understand the meaning of each. Review the Glossary with Ss.

- Tell Ss to read the text as quickly as they can, then write down their answer. Ask them to tell a partner what elements of the text support their answer.
- Remind Ss that when they skim, they read only key words and sentences. If needed, model the method, for example for paragraph 2, sentences 1 and 2: *take boat Puno; go with tour company or get boat*.

> **Answer**
> a travel guide

B Ask Ss to read again. They scan to find the numbers listed and determine what they signify. Encourage Ss to underline or highlight sentences or numbers in the text.

- Ss share their answers with each other before you check as a class.

> **Answers**
> 2,000 = number of people who live on Taquile; three = hours on the boat; 40 = minutes walking to the town; $20 to $60 = cost of hotel room; $9 = cost to stay with a local family

C **Do the task** Remind Ss of the difference between *can* and *can't*. Write a few sentences on the board to illustrate, e.g.,

> *I can walk.* ✓
> *I can't drive.* ✗

- Ss read the text once more and circle the correct answers individually before they check with a partner.
- Elicit their answers as a class by having them read the sentence.

> **Answers**
> 1 isn't 2 can 3 can't 4 some 5 are 6 can

D PAIR WORK **Review** As Ss discuss the questions, monitor and listen for pronunciation and grammar. Listen also for any examples of language or information from the text that Ss use.

> **EXTRA ACTIVITY**
> Ask Ss to write three things people can do in the place they live and three things they can't. Model the activity for Ss by writing some sentences about where you live on the board.
>
> *You can go shopping in [name of place].*
> *You can go to a restaurant in [name of place].*
> *You can't go to the mountains in [name of place].*
> *You can't go to the beach in [name of place].*

2 WRITING

Introduce the topic Show or print two travel reviews from a website like Trip Advisor. Choose two places your Ss will know, or ask them to suggest vacation destinations. Show one and ask Ss: *What can you see in the pictures?* Then ask: *How many stars?* Show the second destination and repeat the questions. Encourage Ss to tell each other which destination they like best and why. Elicit ideas from the class.

A Tell Ss to look at the picture. Ask: *What can you see?* Elicit answers.

- Read the **Glossary** to make sure Ss understand *wonderful*.
- Direct Ss to read the text individually before they share their answers with a partner. Then check as a class.
- Review any challenging vocabulary.

> **Answers**
> Don't take a tour with a travel company. You don't need to eat at the restaurants in town. Don't forget your camera.

B **Introduce the task** Write on the board: *Drive to the hotel. Don't forget your camera.* Ask Ss to identify the verbs. Now write *imperatives* as a title above the sentences and explain that imperative sentences give advice.

- Ask a volunteer to read the explanation of imperatives aloud. Ask another volunteer to read the example sentences.
- Ss underline the sentences in the text individually before sharing with a partner.

> **Answers**
> **You have to see Taquile Island!**
> This island is really nice. It's not very big. There is only one town on the island. There are a lot of small homes on hills, and there's a lot of nature. I like to walk, and you have to walk a lot on Taquile. <u>Walk to the top of the island and see the ocean.</u> You can see Peru on one side and Bolivia on the other side. You can even see snow on the mountains in Bolivia. <u>Don't take a tour with a travel company.</u> <u>Take a local boat and stay with a family.</u> The people are very friendly. You don't need to eat at the restaurants in town. The food is OK, but the family gives you a great breakfast, lunch, and dinner. <u>Talk with the family.</u> You can learn a lot about Taquile this way. <u>Don't forget your camera.</u> You can take a lot of pictures of this wonderful place!

- Read the **Register check** with Ss. Direct them to underline the verb forms used to give advice in the travel guide on page 92. Remind Ss that the travel guide is more formal than the website review.

> **📎 EXTRA ACTIVITY**
> Ask Ss to think about their school, college, or workplace. Ask them to write three sentences using imperatives describing things to do and things not to do there. Write a few examples on the board, e.g., *Eat in the cafeteria. Don't take the stairs; use the elevator.* Try to make the examples relevant to your Ss. Elicit some examples and write them on the board, correcting any mistakes.

C Spend time discussing places to visit in your area. You may like to show some of these on a travel website like Trip Advisor. Ask: *What can you do here? What can you see here? What advice can you give?* Write good ideas you hear on the board. Spending time thinking about what they will write will give Ss more information and ideas for the next task.

- As Ss write, circulate offering help and support. If possible, correct Ss' work before the next activity.

D [PAIR WORK] **Review** Monitor for pronunciation as Ss share their work.

- When finished, ask volunteers to share their work, either privately with you or by reading aloud to the class.

> **📎 EXTRA ACTIVITY**
> Post Ss' work around the classroom and ask everyone to circulate and read the descriptions. Conduct a class vote to decide which destination they like best. You may also want to share some of these on your social media page.

2 WRITING

A Read Cameron's review of Taquile Island. What does he say <u>not</u> to do?

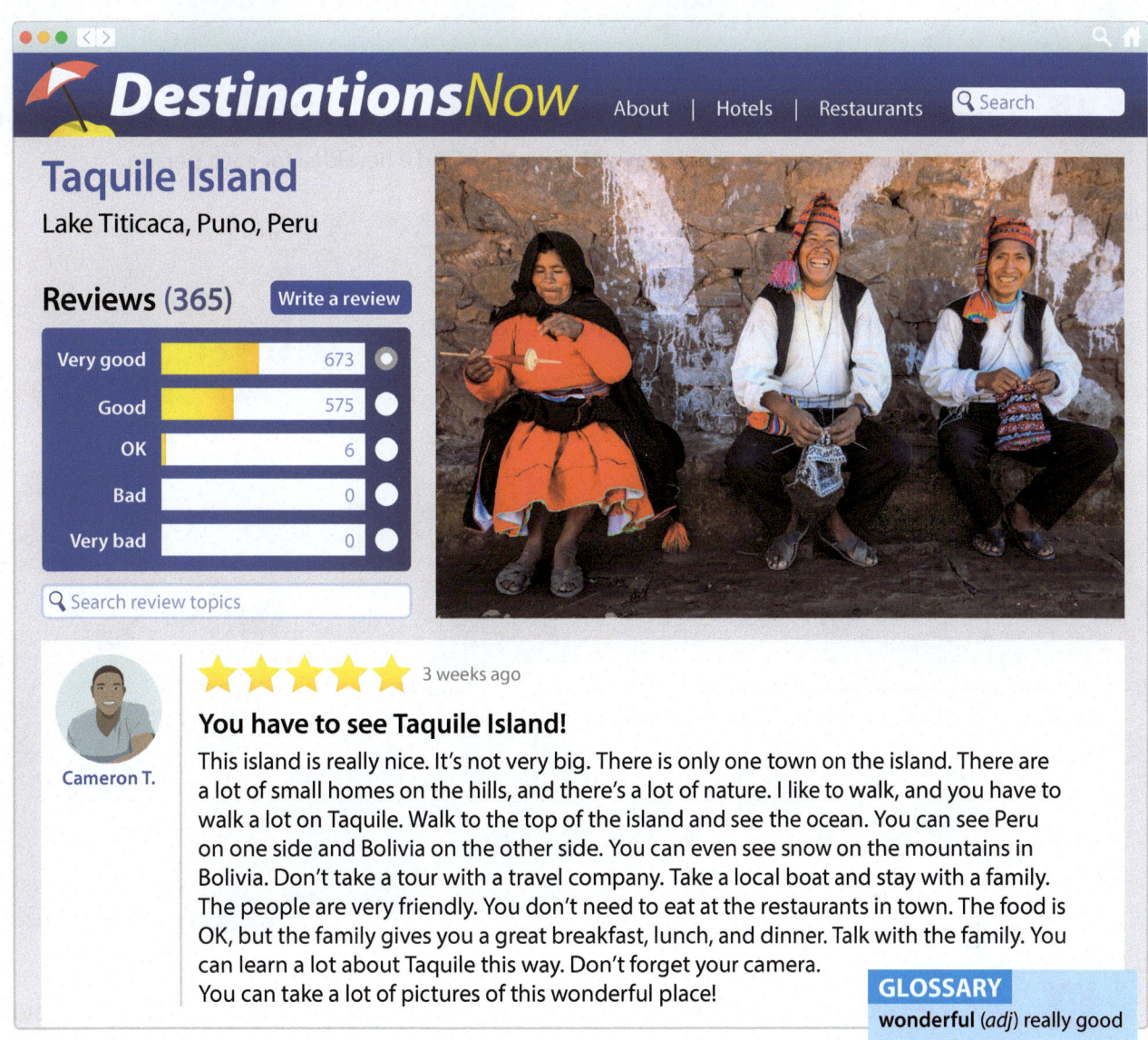

DestinationsNow
About | Hotels | Restaurants

Taquile Island
Lake Titicaca, Puno, Peru

Reviews (365) — Write a review

Very good	673
Good	575
OK	6
Bad	0
Very bad	0

Search review topics

★★★★★ 3 weeks ago

Cameron T.

You have to see Taquile Island!
This island is really nice. It's not very big. There is only one town on the island. There are a lot of small homes on the hills, and there's a lot of nature. I like to walk, and you have to walk a lot on Taquile. Walk to the top of the island and see the ocean. You can see Peru on one side and Bolivia on the other side. You can even see snow on the mountains in Bolivia. Don't take a tour with a travel company. Take a local boat and stay with a family. The people are very friendly. You don't need to eat at the restaurants in town. The food is OK, but the family gives you a great breakfast, lunch, and dinner. Talk with the family. You can learn a lot about Taquile this way. Don't forget your camera. You can take a lot of pictures of this wonderful place!

GLOSSARY
wonderful (*adj*) really good

B **WRITING SKILLS** Read the information about imperative verbs below. Then <u>underline</u> all the sentences beginning with an imperative verb in Cameron's review in exercise 2A.

You can use imperative verbs to give someone advice. An imperative verb is a verb with no subject (e.g. *he*, *she*).

+ **Walk** to the top of the island and see the ocean.

– **Don't take** a tour with a travel company.

REGISTER CHECK

People often use imperative verbs in informal writing to give advice.

In a website review: *Walk to the top of the island.*

People usually use verb forms with subjects in formal writing.

In a travel guide: *You can walk to the top of the island.*

▶ WRITE IT

C Choose a place for people to visit in your area. Write a review of the place. Say what people can do and see. Use imperative verbs to give advice. Use Cameron's review in exercise 2A for an example.

D **PAIR WORK** Read your partner's review. Do you want to visit your partner's place? Why or why not?

93

9.5 TIME TO SPEAK
Vacation plans

LESSON OBJECTIVE
- plan a vacation for someone

A DISCUSS Look at the pictures. What do you think these people like to do on vacation? For each person, say <u>three</u> things. Compare your ideas with a partner. Find a new idea for each person.

Jim

Minako

Carter

B DECIDE Work in pairs. Choose Jim, Minako, or Carter. Imagine they are coming to your country on vacation for two weeks. What do you think they want to do? Make a list of things to do and places to go.

C PREPARE Imagine you are helping this person plan a vacation. Look at your list from exercise B. What do you need to do? Make a plan.

D AGREE Work in groups: Group Jim, Group Minako, or Group Carter. Present your plan. Which plan is your group's favorite?

> To check your progress, go to page 154.

USEFUL PHRASES

DISCUSS
I think Jim/Minako/Carter likes to … on vacation.
What do you think Jim/Minako/Carter likes to do?
My three ideas for Jim are …
I agree. / I disagree.
Let's think of one new idea for Minako.

DECIDE
A good thing to do / place to go is …
On the first day, he/she can …

AGREE
We're planning a vacation for …
This is our plan.
Our favorite plan is … because it's interesting/fun/nice.

94

9.5 TIME TO SPEAK
Vacation plans

LESSON OBJECTIVE
- plan a vacation for someone

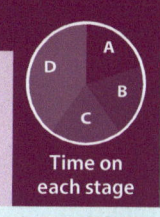

Time on each stage

Introduce the task Dictate: *What do you like to do on vacation? What does your family like to do on vacation?*
- Ss ask and answer the questions in pairs. Elicit ideas when they finish. Write new words on the board.
- Direct Ss to the **Useful phrases** section at the bottom of the page which they can use at the relevant stages of the lesson.

A **DISCUSS** Aim: Ss think and talk about the photos.
- **INDIVIDUALLY** Preparation for speaking* Read the instructions aloud for Ss. Encourage Ss to rehearse what they are going to say in their heads.
- **PAIR WORK** Ss share their ideas while you monitor for pronunciation. Give positive feedback when Ss produce accurate and appropriate language.*
- **CLASS WORK** When they finish, elicit all suggestions and write them on the board.

B **DECIDE** Do the task Aim: Ss decide where the people might go on vacation.
- **CLASS WORK** Model examples for Ss so they know what to do, e.g., *I think Jim wants to go hiking.*
- **INDIVIDUALLY** Ss make their lists. Give Ss time to review relevant vocabulary notes or look up words.*

C **PREPARE** Aim: Ss make a plan for a vacation.
- **CLASS WORK** To model the task, write a simple plan for Jim on the board. Remind Ss that you are using imperatives, e.g., *Take a taxi from the airport.*
- **INDIVIDUALLY** Allow Ss time to make their plan. Circulate and make sure they are on track. Offer help and suggest corrections. Elicit ideas as a class.

TEACHER DEVELOPMENT ACTIVITY 2

Recording and listening

When Ss present ideas to groups, it can be difficult to listen to each of them individually. The idea below shows how you can hear all your Ss. Before you do this activity, tell Ss what you want to do and why it is helpful. Also let them know that you are the only person who will listen to the recording.
- When Ss are in their groups, ask them to record their own presentation.
- When all the presentations are finished, give Ss an email address so they can send you the audio file.
- Listen to the presentations and note two strengths and two errors for each S.
- Email your feedback to individual Ss.

D **AGREE** Review Aim: Ss review each other's plans in groups.
- **GROUP WORK** Circulate and monitor. Listen and make notes on language usage.
- **CLASS WORK** When Ss have finished, elicit ideas from them. Find out what the favorite plan is from each group.
- **Feedback for speaking activities*** Give the class positive feedback based on the notes you made earlier in the activity.
- You might like to post the plans on the wall of your classroom or share them on your social media page.

*These tips can help you to create a safe speaking environment. They can be used with other speaking activities. For more information, see page T-xxii.

PROGRESS CHECK

Direct students to page 154 to check their progress. Go to page T-152 for Progress check activity suggestions.

TEACHER DEVELOPMENT REFLECTION

Either answer these questions yourself in a reflection journal or discuss them with your peers.

1. Did you find it easier to listen only for the target language in the first activity? Why or why not?
2. Did listening only for target language give you a different impression of students' language? For example, did you realize their accuracy in the target language was quite good, despite other errors?
3. What was students' reaction to being recorded in the second activity? Would you do this differently with other groups in the future?
4. What kind of things did you think were strengths in the students' speaking?
5. What were the most common errors that students produced? Did you do any follow up revision work on these errors?

T-94

REVIEW 3 (UNITS 7–9)

Introduce the review Before beginning the review, write *Grammar*, *Vocabulary*, and *Functional language* on the board.

- Set a time limit of two minutes. Ss close their books and work in small groups to remember as much as they can about the grammar, vocabulary, and functional language of units 7–9. Groups write words, phrases, and example sentences in each category.
- Check answers as a class.

1 VOCABULARY

A **Students close their books. Write the categories on the board** *Activities around the house, Transportation / Travel, Skills, Work*. **Elicit one word or phrase for each category.**

- Ss do the task individually before they share their answers with a partner.
- Elicit answers as a class. Write the words on the board as you go.

Answers

Activates around the house	Transportation / Travel	Skills	Work
clean my room	airport	paint	take a break
do homework	be on the subway	draw	company
brush my hair	take the bus	play the guitar	have a meeting
wash the dishes	check in	dance	office
take a bath	destination	sing	workers

B **Ss work individually. They can use their notes, units 7–9 of the SB, or their smartphones to help them.**

- Elicit answers as a whole class and add the new words to the list on the board.

Suggested answers

Activates around the house	Transportation / Travel	Skills	Work
have lunch, brush my teeth, make breakfast	plane, arrive, buy tickets online	cook, speak English, drive	work hard, coworkers, find answers to problems

2 GRAMMAR

A **Write these scrambled sentences on the board. Ask for volunteers to unscramble them. Write the correct sentences.**

learning / I'm / this year / English
(*I'm learning English this year.*)

video games / not / playing / right now / I'm
(*I'm not playing video games right now.*)

- Ss do the exercise individually. Then check answers as a class.

Answers

1 I'm cleaning my room right now.
2 The children aren't doing their homework.
3 Is she waiting for a bus?
4 My father is working hard these days.
5 They're not watching TV right now.
6 What book are you reading these days?

B **PAIR WORK** **Read the task aloud and model some activities you are doing at the moment using the present continuous. For example, say:** *I'm learning to play the guitar. I'm taking yoga classes.*

- Monitor as Ss share their activities.
- When Ss finish, elicit examples of present continuous sentences. Correct them as necessary.

C **Ask:** *Can you drive a car?* **Elicit possible answers from Ss.** (*I can/can't drive a car.*)

- Ss complete the exercise individually before checking with a partner. Tell Ss to read the full sentence aloud when you elicit the answers.

Answers

1 can't 2 can 3 can 4 can't 5 can 6 can't

D **PAIR WORK** **Tell Ss two things you can do** (*I can drive a car. I can speak English.*) **and two things you can't do** (*I can't speak Chinese. I can't ski.*).

- Monitor as Ss work with a partner. Then elicit sentences from the class and write them on the board under the categories *Can* and *Can't*.

REVIEW 3 (UNITS 7–9)

1 VOCABULARY

A Write the words in the chart. There are <u>five</u> words or phrases for each group.

airport	clean my room	do homework	paint	take a break
be on the subway	company	draw	play the guitar	take the bus
brush my hair	dance	have a meeting	sing	do the dishes
check in	destination	office	take a bath	workers

Activities around the house	Transportation/Travel	Skills	Work

B Add <u>one</u> more word or phrase to each group in exercise 1A.

2 GRAMMAR

A Put the words in the correct order to make sentences.
1. my / right / cleaning / I'm / room / now.
2. aren't / homework. / The / doing / children / their
3. bus? / Is / waiting / she / a / for
4. days. / hard / is / these / father / My / working
5. watching / TV / not / right now. / They're
6. you / these / reading / What / days? / books / are

B **PAIR WORK** Tell a partner two or three things you are doing these days. For example, what you're reading or watching on TV, what classes you're taking, or what games/sports you're playing.

C Complete the sentences with *can* or *can't*.
1. My brother usually goes out for dinner because he _____ cook.
2. I _____ swim really well. I usually swim in the evening after work.
3. Juan _____ speak four languages: Spanish, Portuguese, French, and Italian.
4. My sister _____ skateboard, and she doesn't want to learn.
5. I _____ drive a car. It's easy.
6. My grandfather _____ use a computer. He doesn't have one, and he doesn't want one.

D **PAIR WORK** Talk to a partner. Say <u>two</u> things you can do and <u>two</u> things you can't do.

95

3 SPEAKING

A `PAIR WORK` You're going to play a guessing game with your partner. Follow the instructions.

1. Work alone. Choose one of these places, but <u>don't</u> tell your partner: in a room at home, in an office, in a classroom, on a train or a bus, in a car. Now, imagine you're in the place.
2. Talk to your partner. Say what you can and can't do in the place. Say what you're doing there now.
3. Your partner guesses the place. You can say "Yes." or "No."

> I can sleep here, and I can use my phone. I can't cook here, but I can go places. Right now, I'm studying here.

> Is it a classroom?

> No!

B Write about your partner's place in exercise 3A. Describe what he/she can and can't do there.

4 FUNCTIONAL LANGUAGE

A (Circle) the correct answers.

Robert Hi, Marina! [1] *I'm / It's* Robert.
Marina Hey, Robert! How are you [2] *do / doing*?
Robert Not [3] *bad / fine*, thanks. And you?
Marina [4] *I'm / It's* fine. What are you doing these days?
Robert Well, I'm planning a trip to Rio for five days.
Marina [5] *Oh, wow! / Oh no!* That's great!
Robert Yeah, and the hotel's a good price.
Marina Really? [6] *How much / When* is it?
Robert $189.99 a night.
Marina [7] *I don't think / I think* that's a good price. That's really, really expensive!
Robert [8] *I think / I think so* it's good. [9] *I mean / I say*, it's a five-star hotel.
Marina [10] *Oh. / Oh no!* [11] *Where / What* is it?
Robert In Copacabana.

5 SPEAKING

A `PAIR WORK` Choose <u>one</u> of the situations below. Talk to a partner. Have a conversation.

1. Start a telephone conversation. Ask how your partner is and what he/she is doing these days. Look at page 70 for useful language.

> Hi, Ji-un. How are you?

2. Talk about things people do in unusual offices. Give your opinion about these things. Look at page 80 for useful language.

> In some offices, you can play computer games. I don't think that's a good idea. I mean, people need to work!

3. You're at an airport and need information about prices, locations, and times. Look at page 90 for useful language.

> Excuse me. How much are these travel guides?

B `PAIR WORK` Change roles and repeat the situation.

3 SPEAKING

A **PAIR WORK** Read the task aloud. Allow students to ask clarifying questions, and answer them. Model the example sentences with a S volunteer.

- Allow Ss a few minutes to make notes. They may use Units 7–9 or their smartphones to research any information they might need. If Ss struggle to think of places, write a list for them to choose from on the board, e.g., *on a train, on a bicycle, in bed, in the bath, in a plane,* etc.
- As Ss describe and make guesses, circulate and monitor for examples of language usage that you can highlight with Ss at the end of the task.

B Allow time for Ss to write 3–4 sentences, then help correct them. Ask Ss to share their corrected sentences with the class. Call on volunteers to guess where they are.

4 FUNCTIONAL LANGUAGE

A Ask: *How are you doing?* to elicit *I'm fine. / Not bad.* Ask: *What are you doing these days?* Elicit answers from various Ss.

- Ss do the exercise individually before sharing answers with a partner.
- Elicit answers from the class.
- Monitor as pairs read the conversation together.

> **Answers**
> 1 It's   2 doing   3 bad   4 I'm   5 Oh, wow
> 6 How much   7 I don't think   8 I think   9 I mean
> 10 Oh.   11 Where

5 SPEAKING

A **PAIR WORK** Read each situation aloud. Encourage volunteers to read the example sentences after the descriptions.

- Ss choose one of the three situations and prepare a conversation. They should make notes, but not write the full conversation. For extra support, refer Ss to the functional language lessons from Units 7–9.
- Monitor as pairs have their conversations. Listen for examples of language usage and provide feedback to Ss.

B **PAIR WORK** Pairs change roles and repeat their conversations.

- Choose pairs to perform their conversations for the class. If possible, choose a pair for each of the three situations.

GET READY

10

TEACHER DEVELOPMENT INTRODUCTION

Strategy 1: Classroom Management – Teacher roles

In this unit, we're going to look at some **different roles of teachers** in the classroom. In some teaching situations, teachers tend to explain everything to students and assume they know very little about a topic, vocabulary, or grammar. However, many teachers now support the idea of "Ask, don't tell". In other words, they believe in questioning students and **finding out what students already know**. Another important teacher role involves **giving supportive feedback**. Supportive feedback clearly tells Ss what they did successfully and what they need to work on.

Finding out what students already know (Activity 1): You'll have an opportunity to try this in lesson 10.2.

Giving supportive feedback (Activity 2): You can try this in lesson 10.4.

To find out more, read chapters 4.5, 4.6, 4.7, and 4.10 from *Classroom Management Techniques* by Jim Scrivener. Please go to www.cambridge.org/evolve to download these pages.

INTRODUCE THE THEME OF THE UNIT

Books closed. Write *weekend* on the board. Draw or display three pictures on the board: *mountains, beach, city*. Ask Ss: *Where do you like to go on the weekend?* and *What do you like to do there?*

- Ss discuss with each other while you monitor.
- Elicit answers as a class. Do Ss like to go to the same places?

UNIT OBJECTIVES

Read the unit objectives aloud. Tell Ss to listen and read along. Explain any vocabulary that Ss might not understand.

START SPEAKING

A **Pre-teach** *skydiving, before,* and *after*. Ss look at the picture and discuss in pairs before you elicit the things they need to do before they go.
- Write down their suggestions on the board as you elicit answers.

B **Introduce the idea of** *big plans* – life plans that people would like to achieve in the future, e.g., *buy a farm / write a book / go on vacation to New York*.
- Give Ss a few minutes to think about their ideas. Ask Ss to write down two big plans, then share their big plans with their partner.
- **OPTIONAL ACTIVITY** Ss watch Larissa's video and say whether their plans are similar or different. You may want to explain that *foreign* means *in a different country*.

> **REAL STUDENT**
> Hello, my name is Larissa. I want to save money to study music and English too at the foreign university.

UNIT OBJECTIVES
- make outdoor plans for the weekend
- discuss what clothes to wear for different trips
- suggest plans for evening activities
- write an online invitation
- plan and present a fun weekend in your city

GET READY

10

START SPEAKING

A   Look at the picture. Imagine you're doing this.
    Say things you can do to get ready before you do it.

B   Do you have big plans for the future? What are they?
    For ideas, watch Larissa's video.

REAL STUDENT

Are your plans the same as Larissa's?

10.1 WHITE NIGHTS

LESSON OBJECTIVE
- make outdoor plans for the weekend

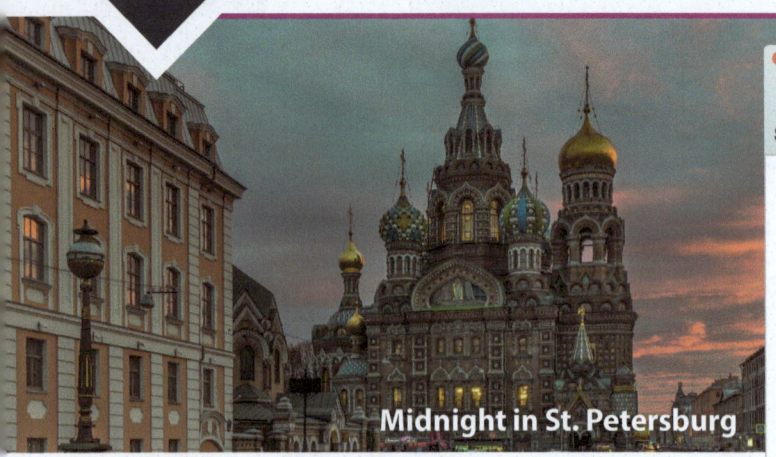

Midnight in St. Petersburg

To: sofiaperez@mymail.com
From: averin.yana@grabmail.org
Subject: Your trip

Hi Sofia,

You're going to be here next weekend! I'm very happy because you're going to see St. Petersburg during the White Nights. It's light for about 24 hours in June. We live *outside* – all day and *all night*.

So, here's the plan. On Friday evening, I'm going to **meet** you at the airport and then **take** you out to dinner. We're going to **eat** outside at Marketplace. It's my favorite restaurant.

On Saturday, we're going to **look at** art at the Street Art Museum. And, of course, we can **go** shopping on Nevsky Prospect. And then in the evening, we're going to **get together** with some of my friends in Kirov Park. We can **take** a walk in the park, and then we're going to **have** a picnic – at midnight!

What else do you want to do? I'm not going to be home tonight, but we can talk tomorrow.

See you soon!
Yana

GLOSSARY
light (*adj*) the sun is in the sky

1 LANGUAGE IN CONTEXT

A PAIR WORK Look at the picture. Where is it? What time is it? What's unusual about it?

B Read the email and answer the questions.
1. Why is Yana happy?
2. What are the "White Nights"?
3. When does Yana want to talk to Sofia?

2 VOCABULARY: Going out

A 🔊 2.30 Find these verbs in the email. Then complete the phrases with the verbs. Listen and check.

| eat | get together | go | have | look at | meet | take (2x) |

1. _____ art
2. _____ a walk 
3. _____ someone out to dinner and _____ outside 
4. _____ someone at the airport 
5. _____ shopping 
6. _____ with friends and _____ a picnic 

B ▶ Now do the vocabulary exercises for 10.1 on page 149.

C GROUP WORK How often do you do the activities in exercise 2A? Tell your group.

98

10.1 WHITE NIGHTS

LESSON OBJECTIVE
- make outdoor plans for the weekend

Introduce the lesson Write *Friday night, Saturday morning, Saturday evening, Sunday afternoon* on the board. Model an example. Say: *I'm going to go shopping on Friday night*. Explain that *going to* refers to the future. Ask Ss to tell a partner what they are *going to* do at the times you wrote on the board. As Ss talk, monitor. Elicit some ideas. What are the most popular activities with your Ss?

1 LANGUAGE IN CONTEXT

A PAIR WORK **Introduce the task** Ss discuss the question in pairs before you elicit answers.

> **Suggested answers**
> It is St. Petersburg at midnight. It's light, but it's midnight.

B **Do the task** Ask Ss to read individually before sharing their answers with a partner. They read quickly to discover general points.

- Elicit answers. Explain any words Ss may have questions about, such as *during* (at the same time) and *together* (with).

> **Answers**
> 1 Yana is happy because Sofia is going to see St. Petersburg during the White Nights.
> 2 The White Nights are when it's light for about 24 hours in June.
> 3 She wants to talk to Sofia tomorrow / the following day.

2 VOCABULARY: Going out

A 🔊 2.30 **Introduce the vocabulary** Volunteers read the words in the word box. Check understanding.

- Ss underline the words in the email individually before they complete the phrases. Ask Ss to check their answers in pairs. Play the audio.
- Play the audio again, pause after each sentence, and Ss repeat. Monitor pronunciation.

> **Answers**
> 1 look at   2 take   3 take, eat   4 meet   5 go
> 6 get together, have

> **MIXED ABILITY**
>
> Put Ss in groups and ask them to brainstorm as many words as they can to go with the vocabulary verbs, e.g., *get together with friends, family, your teacher*, etc. Groups of stronger Ss can write sentences, e.g., *This evening I am going to get together with my friends*. See how many words/sentences the groups can come up with for each verb.

B Direct Ss to page 149 to complete the vocabulary exercises. Teacher's tips for vocabulary exercises are on page T-141.

C GROUP WORK Ss discuss the question in groups.

- Monitor as Ss talk, listening for examples of language usage that you can give feedback on later.
- Ask Ss to share any more ideas they might have before you elicit some ideas from the whole class.

T-98

3 GRAMMAR: Statements with *be going to*

A **Introduce the grammar** Before Ss circle the answers, explain that they can refer to the examples in the grammar box.

> **Answers**
> 1 future plans   2 a verb

- Ask volunteers to read the chart. Explain the time expressions using a calendar.

> **VOCABULARY SUPPORT** Display a calendar to explain the difference between the various future time expressions. Illustrate *this Monday* and *next Monday* by pointing to the days on the calendar as you say the expressions. Ask pairs of Ss to look at the calendars on their phones and say *this [Tuesday], next [Thursday]*, etc.

B **Do the task** Read the task aloud and make sure Ss understand. Ss fill in the gaps individually before checking with a partner.

- When you elicit answers, ask Ss to read the full sentence. Monitor for grammar and pronunciation.

> **Answers**
> 1 'm/am not going to be
> 2 aren't/are not going to take
> 3 are going to go
> 4 'm/am going to study
> 5 isn't/is not going to meet

C **PAIR WORK** Ask a volunteer to model the example sentences. Do another example if necessary.

- Ss make the sentences positive or negative.
- After Ss finish, ask for answers from the class.

D Direct Ss to pages 137–138 to complete the grammar exercise. Teacher's tips for grammar exercises are on page T-129.

4 SPEAKING

A **PAIR WORK** Model the sample sentences by asking a volunteer to read with you. Generate a few more ideas of what Ss could do in your area.

- Ss think about their city and discuss their ideas together.
- Elicit Ss ideas together as a class. Write these on the board for Ss to use in the next activity.

B **PAIR WORK** Model the example. Tell Ss your plans for the weekend using *going to,* and include some examples of *not going to.*

- Make sure Ss write their plan. Monitor and circulate as Ss do the activity.
- When Ss finish, they can take their plans to other groups and explain what they are going to do. Then ask volunteers to share their plans with the class.
- Give feedback.

3 GRAMMAR: Statements with *be going to*

A Circle the correct answer. Use the sentences in the grammar box to help you.
1. Use *be going to* to talk about **things you're doing right now / future plans**.
2. Make future statements with *be going to* + **a verb / a noun**.

> **Statements with *be going to***
>
> I**'m going to be** home tomorrow.
> It**'s going to be** light all night.
> You**'re going to meet** me at the airport.
> We**'re going to get together** with some of my friends.
>
> I**'m not going to be** home tonight.
> It **isn't going to be** light all night.
> My friends **aren't going to go** shopping.
> They**'re not going to eat** outside this weekend.

B Complete the sentences with *be going to* and the affirmative or negative form of the verb in parentheses ( ).
1. I _____ (be) home tomorrow. I have to work at the office.
2. My parents _____ (take) me to lunch on Saturday. They're busy.
3. My friends and I _____ (go) on a trip to Rio next year. We have our tickets!
4. I _____ (study) a lot next week. I have an important test.
5. My friend _____ (meet) me tonight. She's sick.

C PAIR WORK Change the sentences in exercise 3B so they're true for you. Then compare with a partner.

> I'm not going to be home tomorrow. I have to go to college.

D ▶ Now go to page 137. Look at the grammar chart and do the grammar exercise for 10.1.

4 SPEAKING

A PAIR WORK What can you do outside in your city? Make a list.

> We can eat outside at a lot of restaurants.

> True. And we can watch movies outside.

B PAIR WORK Make outdoor plans with your partner for next weekend. Then share your plans with the class.

> Next Saturday, we're going have a picnic in …

10.2 BUT IT'S SUMMER THERE!

LESSON OBJECTIVE
- discuss what clothes to wear for different trips

1 VOCABULARY: Clothes; seasons

A 🔊 2.31 **Listen and repeat the clothes. Then look at the people in your class. How many of the clothes can you see?**

B 🔊 2.32 **PAIR WORK** **Look at the seasons below. Listen and repeat. What seasons do you have where you live? When are they?**

- spring
- summer
- fall
- winter
- dry season
- rainy season

Clothes labeled: hat, pants, shirt, coat, shorts, skirt, dress, shoes, jeans, sweater, T-shirt, boots

C ▶ Now do the vocabulary exercises for 10.2 on page 149.

2 LANGUAGE IN CONTEXT

A 🔊 2.33 Read and listen. Sofia and her friend discuss Sofia's trip to St. Petersburg. What clothes do they talk about?

🔊 **2.33 Audio script**

Rena So, are you ready for your trip? What clothes are you going to take?
Sofia Yeah, I am! I'm going to take a big **coat**, and I need to buy a **hat**.
Rena Really? But it's **summer** there!
Sofia Yes, but it's Russia, not Florida! It's not hot in the summer.
Rena True, but it's not *cold*. So, are you going to take **pants** and some **sweaters**?
Sofia Yes, I am. No. I don't know. I usually wear **shorts** in the summer here, but … Oh, I know! I can take my **fall** or **spring** pants.
Rena Good idea. And what are you going to wear on your feet?
Sofia I need some new **shoes**. We're going to walk outside a lot. Or maybe **boots**.
Rena When are you going to leave? I mean, are you *really* ready for this trip?

INSIDER ENGLISH

You can say, *Oh, I know!* when you think of a good idea or an answer to a problem.

Oh, I know! I can take my fall or winter pants.

GLOSSARY
wear (v) have clothes on your body

100

10.2 BUT IT'S SUMMER THERE!

LESSON OBJECTIVE
- discuss what clothes to wear for different trips

Introduce the lesson Point to what you are wearing, and ask Ss: *What is this?* Write their response on the board. Then point to other clothing that you or Ss are wearing and elicit the words until Ss have identified several of the lesson vocabulary words. Write the words on the board.

- Write the four seasons on the board. If possible, display or draw a picture of weather common in each one.
- Ask Ss: *What clothes do you have in these seasons?* They share their ideas with a partner before you elicit their ideas. Write a couple of items next to each season, e.g.,
  Spring – jeans / shirt
  Summer – shorts / dress
  Fall – coat / sweater
  Winter – hat / boots

TEACHER DEVELOPMENT ACTIVITY 1

Finding out what students already know

When teachers question students to find out what they already know, Ss actively participate, are engaged, and are less likely to "switch off." Ss feel motivated when they can recall information, and the teacher knows whether to adapt their lesson or not. In other words, if Ss already seem to know the vocabulary or grammar point, the teacher can shorten the time spent "teaching" it and extend the time for practice.

- Put 11 pictures of clothes on the board, e.g., hat, coat, pants. Number them 1–11.
- In groups, Ss teach each any other words they know for these clothes. Monitor, but do not interrupt.
- Choose a S from each group to suggest two words for pictures 1–11 and write them on the board.
- Groups tell each other any other words for the clothes they are wearing.
- For feedback, nominate Ss to describe others in the class, e.g., *Maria has a blue hat.*

1 VOCABULARY: Clothes; seasons

A 🔊 **2.31 Present the vocabulary** Play the audio as Ss read and listen.

- Play the audio again, pausing after each item, and ask different Ss to repeat. Check pronunciation.
- Ss now say the different clothes they can see around the room.

Answers
Answers may vary.

GRAMMAR SUPPORT **Play board scrabble** with the clothes items.
Arrange the words as **anagrams**.
Ask Ss to learn the words for a **spelling test**.
For instructions on how to run these activities, see page T-217.

PRONUNCIATION SUPPORT Many clothing words are pronounced very differently from the way they are written, including the word *clothes* /kloʊz/. Encourage Ss not to *read* the letters, but remember the sounds. There are lots of silent letters:
  e in *shoes* /ʃuː/
  e in *sweater* /swetər/
  a in *coat* /koʊt/

B 🔊 **2.32** **PAIR WORK** Play the audio as Ss read. Play again, pausing after each word so that Ss can repeat.

- Ss work in pairs to ask and answer the questions. Elicit their answers as a class when they have finished.

C **Direct Ss to pages 149–150 to complete the vocabulary exercises. Teacher's tips for vocabulary exercises are on page T-141.**

2 LANGUAGE IN CONTEXT

A 🔊 **2.33** Before Ss start, ask: *Which clothes do you take on a summer trip?* Elicit answers. Ask: *Which clothes do you take on a winter trip?*

- Read the task aloud and play the audio as Ss read. Elicit answers.

Answers
Sofia and her friend talk about a coat, a hat, pants, sweaters, shorts, shoes, and boots.

- Read the **Insider English** box with Ss. Concept check by giving examples, e.g.,
  It's raining. … Oh, I know! I'll take boots and a coat.
  It's cold. … Oh, I know! I'll take my sweater.
- Go over any unfamiliar vocabulary Ss may ask about.

T-100

B **PAIR WORK** **Review** As Ss answer the questions in pairs, monitor for pronunciation and vocabulary. Listen for examples of grammar usage that you can give feedback on when the activity is finished.

- **OPTIONAL ACTIVITY** Ss watch Anderson's video and compare their answers with his. You may want to explain again the meaning of *wear*.

> **REAL STUDENT**
> Hi. I am Anderson. It is winter and I usually wear a coat.

3 GRAMMAR: Questions with *be going to*

Introduce the grammar Ask: *What words do questions start with?* Elicit answers *what, where, when,* and *who* from Ss.

A **Present the grammar** Before Ss circle the answers, explain that they can refer to the examples in the grammar box.

> **Answers**
> 1 *Am, Is* or *Are*   2 before

- Ask volunteers to read the grammar chart. Monitor for pronunciation and stress. Check understanding using questions. Ask individual Ss a range of questions to elicit genuine answers, e.g., *Are you going to see your family today? / What are you going to eat tonight? / Where are you going to live next year?* Try to make the sentences relevant to your Ss.

B **Do the task** Ss order the sentences individually before they check with a partner. Then elicit the answers.

> **Answers**
> 1 What are you going to do this weekend?
> 2 Are you going to study tonight?
> 3 What are you going to have for dinner?
> 4 What are you going to watch on TV?
> 5 Where are you going to go tomorrow?
> 6 Are you going to see your friends next week?

C Direct Ss to page 138 to complete the grammar exercise. Teacher's tips for grammar exercises are on page T-129.

D **PAIR WORK** Ss read the Accuracy check section aloud to their partner. Did they make any of these mistakes?

- Display or dictate the sentences below. Ask Ss to correct the mistakes individually before they check with a partner and then elicit answers as a class.

    1 A Are they going to work on Saturday?
      B Yes, they are going.
    2 A Are you going to fly to Orlando?
      B No, we're not going.
    3 A Is she going to meet Joe at the airport?
      B Yes, she's going to.

> **Answers**
> 1 A Are they going to work on Saturday?
>   B Yes, they are ~~going~~.
> 2 A Are you going to fly to Orlando?
>   B No, ~~we're not going~~ aren't.
> 3 A Is she going to meet Joe at the airport?
>   B Yes, ~~she's going to.~~ is.

- Model an example sentence by answering one of the questions yourself. As Ss work in pairs monitor for grammar usage, noting any errors you hear that you can share at the end of the task.

- Elicit answers as a class and give feedback.

4 SPEAKING

A **Review** Pre-teach the idea of temperature by drawing a thermometer on the board. Mark *very cold / cold / hot / very hot* on it. Point to the direct parts of the thermometer and ask Ss to say the temperature.

- Ss decide which trip they will go on. As they write their list, monitor and offer any spelling help they may need.

B **PAIR WORK** Model the sample sentences with a volunteer to show Ss how to do the task. As Ss ask and answer the questions, monitor and listen for examples of grammar usage that you can give feedback on after they finish the task.

- Elicit ideas from class. As a variation, ask pairs of Ss to perform their conversations in front of the class.

- Give feedback.

> ✏ **HOMEWORK IDEAS**
> Ask Ss to write six sentences about what they would take on the trip. Ask stronger Ss in your class to use *because* to make their sentences more complex. Correct Ss' sentences in the next session, then ask them to share their sentences with a partner.

B **PAIR WORK** What season is it now? What clothes do you usually wear? For ideas, watch Anderson's video.

REAL STUDENT Are your answers the same as Anderson's?

3 GRAMMAR: Questions with *be going to*

A Circle the correct answers. Use the sentences in the grammar box to help you.
1. A *yes/no* question with *be going to* begins with **Am**, **Is**, or **Are** / **What**, **Where**, or **When**.
2. For information questions with *be going to*, put the question word **before** / **after** *is*, *are*, or *am*.

Questions with *be going to*

Yes/no questions
Are you **going to take** some sweaters?   Yes, I **am**. / No, I'**m not**.
Is Sofia **going to see** a friend?   Yes, she **is**. / No, she'**s not**.

Information questions
What are you **going to take**?
When are you **going to leave**?
Where is Sofia **going to go**?
Who are you **going to meet**?

B Put the words in the correct order to make questions.
1. are / going to / this weekend? / What / you / do
2. study / Are / tonight? / going to / you
3. have / you / What / for dinner? / are / going to
4. on TV? / going to / are / watch / you / What
5. tomorrow? / go / you / are / Where / going to
6. going to / your / next week? / see / Are / friends / you

C ▸ Now go to page 138. Look at the grammar chart and do the grammar exercise for 10.2.

D **PAIR WORK** Read the Accuracy check box. Then ask and answer the questions in exercise 3B with a partner.

✓ ACCURACY CHECK

Do **not** use *be going to* in short answers.
Are you going to wear a dress to the party?
No, I'm not ~~going to.~~ ✗
Yes, I am. ✓

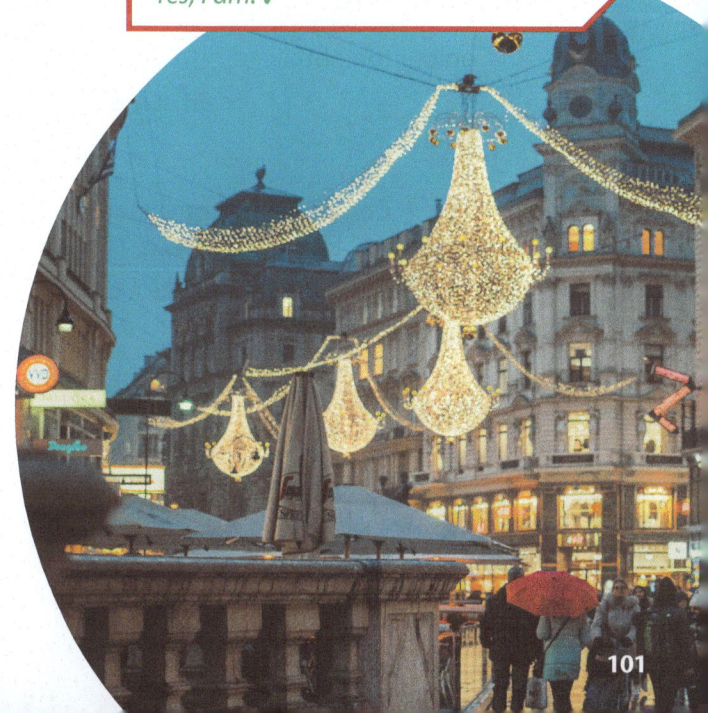

4 SPEAKING

A Look at the trips. Choose **two**, and plan what clothes you're going to take with you.
- A two-week trip to Miami, Florida, in the summer. (29°C / 84°F)
- A one-week trip to Vienna, Austria, in the winter. (2°C / 36°F)
- A five-day trip to Vancouver, Canada, in the spring. (20°C / 68°F)
- A two-week trip to Manaus, Brazil, in the rainy season. (30°C / 86°F)

B **PAIR WORK** Ask questions about your partners' trips.

Where are you going to go?

First, I'm going to go to Miami this summer.

Oh, great! What clothes are you going to take?

101

10.3 LET'S MEET AT THE HOTEL

LESSON OBJECTIVE
- suggest plans for evening activities

1 FUNCTIONAL LANGUAGE

A Jonathan is in Mexico City for a meeting with his coworker, Antonio. They're making plans to go out in the evening. What do you think they are saying?

B 🔊 2.34 Read and listen. Where are Antonio and Jonathan going to have dinner? Where are they going to meet? What time are they going to meet?

🔊 2.34 Audio script

Antonio So, Jonathan, **why don't we go out tonight?**
Jonathan **OK, sounds good.**
Antonio Do you like Mexican food?
Jonathan I love it! Are there any good Mexican restaurants in town?
Antonio Um, in Mexico City? Yeah, I know one or two places!
Jonathan I'm sure you do!
Antonio There's a very good restaurant near your hotel. Why don't we go there?
Jonathan **Good idea.**
Antonio So **let's meet at the hotel**.
Jonathan OK. What time? Eight o'clock?
Antonio Um … **I'm sorry, but I can't**. How about eight-thirty?
Jonathan Yes, sure.

C Complete the chart with expressions in **bold** from the conversation above.

Making suggestions	Accepting suggestions	Refusing suggestions
¹ _____ go out tonight? ² _____ meet at the hotel.	OK, ³ _____ good. Good ⁴ _____ . Yes, ⁵ _____ .	I'm sorry, ⁶ _____ . Sorry, I'm busy.

D 🔊 2.35 Complete the conversations with words from exercise 1C. Listen and check. Then practice with a partner.

1 A _____ take a break.
   B OK, sounds _____ .
2 A _____ have lunch?
   B _____ , but I can't.
3 A Coffee?
   B _____ idea.

10.3 LET'S MEET AT THE HOTEL

LESSON OBJECTIVE
- suggest plans for evening activities

Introduce the lesson Scramble the following sentences on the board for Ss to unscramble in pairs.
Why don't we have coffee?
Let's go to a restaurant tonight.
- Underline *Why don't we …* and *Let's …*
- Show or draw some pictures to act as prompts such as *coffee / walk / Chinese restaurant / swimming pool*. Ss make suggestions using *Why don't we …* and *Let's …* and the prompts.
- Elicit answers when they finish.

1 FUNCTIONAL LANGUAGE

A Introduce the task Read the instructions aloud and make sure Ss understand. Ss discuss in pairs before you elicit their ideas.

> **Answers**
> Answers may vary.

B 2.34 Read the questions aloud with Ss. Play the audio while Ss read the text. Elicit answers from the class.

> **Answers**
> They're going to have dinner in a Mexican restaurant.
> They're going to meet at the hotel.
> They're going to meet at 8:30.

- Play the audio again. Pause after each sentence and ask Ss to repeat. Explain any expressions that Ss may not understand.
- Ask Ss to role play the conversation with a partner. Monitor for pronunciation as Ss work.

C Do the task Pre-teach *accept* and *refuse* by using a checkmark and a cross next to the words. Model an example from the text in exercise 1B.
- Ask Ss to complete the chart individually before they share their answers with a partner. Elicit ideas as a class.

> **Answers**
> 1 Why don't we
> 2 Let's
> 3 sounds
> 4 idea
> 5 sure
> 6 but I can't

- Concept check by asking questions such as *Why don't we have coffee?* to elicit a response that either accepts or refuses. Here are some more you could try:
  Why don't we go to the beach? / Let's go to the movies. / Why don't we go on a trip? / Let's take a walk.
  Try to make questions relevant to your Ss.

D 2.35 Review Ask Ss to complete the conversations individually with the correct words before they check with a partner. Play the audio and ask Ss to check.

> **Answers**
> 1 A **Let's** take a break.
>   B OK, sounds **good**.
> 2 A **Why don't we** have lunch?
>   B **I'm sorry**, but I can't.
> 3 A Coffee?
>   B **Good** idea.

- Ask Ss to role play the conversations. Monitor for pronunciation.

SMARTPHONE ACTIVITY

Ask Ss to record their conversation on their smartphone. They listen to the conversation and check their own pronunciation.

EXTRA ACTIVITY

Ss brainstorm and list things to do in the evenings. Write these on one half of the board. Do the same with refusing suggestions and reasons why they can't do something. Write these on the other side of the board. Ss then have a circle discussion: the inside circle suggests doing something and the outside refuses the suggestion. Ss try to come to an agreement. Elicit compromises from Ss when they finish.

T-102

2 REAL-WORLD STRATEGY

A **Introduce the task** Explain a situation where you say *I'm sorry, but I can't*, e.g.,
> Why don't we go out tonight?
> I'm sorry, but I can't. I have to work.

Read the sample dialogue aloud with a volunteer. Then elicit the answers to the question with the class.

> **Answers**
> He can't meet at 8 o'clock because he has to go home first.

B 🔊 **2.36** **Play the audio.** Ss check their answers with a partner. Elicit answers as a class.

> **Answers**
> They're going to have a meeting on Tuesday.

> 🔊 **2.36 Audio script**
> **A** Why don't we have a meeting on Monday?
> **B** I'm sorry, but I can't. I have to help my parents on Monday. How about Tuesday?
> **A** OK. Let's meet on Tuesday.

C 🔊 **2.36** Play audio again. Ss note the answer and share with a partner before you check as a class.

> **Answers**
> Because she has to help her parents on Monday.

D **PAIR WORK** **Review** Put Ss into pairs and assign each one to be either Student A or Student B. Ask Student As to turn to page 158 and Bs to turn to page 160.

- Write an activity on the board e.g., *go to the cinema*. Ask Ss to use the expressions from page 102 to refuse and give a reason. Try other activities that you think will be relevant to your Ss.
- Read through the instructions aloud. Ask volunteers to read the model dialogue aloud. Allow Ss time to read through all their sentences and check understanding.
- Circulate and monitor as Ss complete the task.

3 PRONUNCIATION: Saying the letter *s*

A 🔊 **2.37** Play the audio and have Ss repeat the words.
- Elicit the two different pronunciations of the letter *s*.

> **Answers**
> sorry: "s" is pronounced /s/
> busy: "s" is pronounced /z/

B 🔊 **2.38** Ss work in pairs to say the words aloud and predict how the letter *s* sounds.
- Play the audio. Elicit the answers, then have Ss repeat each word as a whole class.

> **Answers**
> 1 /s/ and /s/   2 /z/   3 /s/   4 /z/   5 /s/   6 /s/ and /z/
> 7 /z/   8 /s/

C 🔊 **2.39** **PAIR WORK** Play the audio. Ss repeat each sentence or question as a whole class.
- Ss work in pairs to practice the sentences. Monitor and help as necessary.

4 SPEAKING

PAIR WORK **Review** Read the instructions with Ss and make sure they understand. If Ss are all from the same city, you might like to give them other well-known cities they can use, e.g., *Paris, Rome, Santiago, Mexico City, New York, Seoul*, etc. Ask Ss to write down a list of some of things that they can do at night in that city.

- Model the sample sentences with a volunteer before Ss begin.
- As Ss role play the conversation, monitor and listen for examples of grammar usage that you can give feedback on at the end of the activity.
- When Ss finish, volunteers perform their conversations for the class.
- Give any feedback you have.

> 📎 **EXTRA ACTIVITY**
>
> Ask Ss to write down their dialogues in pairs, checking for mistakes as they go. Monitor and circulate as Ss write, offering any help they might need. Write words they need to spell on the board so all Ss can see and use them. Check the writing for errors, and then ask volunteers to perform their dialogues for the class.

> 📱 **SMARTPHONE ACTIVITY**
>
> Ss record or take a video of their conversations on their smartphone. They can play it back later to listen for pronunciation and grammar.

T-103

2 REAL-WORLD STRATEGY

SAYING WHY YOU CAN'T DO SOMETHING
After you say, *I'm sorry, but I can't*, you can give a reason with *I have to*.
Jonathan   What time? Eight o'clock?
Antonio   I'm sorry, but I can't. I have to go home first. How about eight-thirty?

A   Read the information in the box above. Why can't Antonio meet at eight o'clock?

B   🔊 2.36 Listen to a conversation. What are the man and woman going to do, and when?

C   🔊 2.36 Listen again. Why can't the woman have a meeting on Monday?

D   ▶ PAIR WORK Student A: Go to page 158. Student B: Go to page 160. Follow the instructions.

3 PRONUNCIATION: Saying the letter *s*

A   🔊 2.37 Listen and repeat. How is the letter *s* different in the words?
   /s/ **s**orry   /z/ bu**s**y

B   🔊 2.38 Read and say the words below. Which sound does the letter *s* have? Write /s/ or /z/. Some words have two sounds. Then listen and check.

   1 restaurants   3 tickets   5 station   7 jeans

   2 movies   4 shoes   6 season   8 shorts

C   🔊 2.39 PAIR WORK Listen and repeat the sentences. Focus on the /s/ and /z/ sounds. Then practice the sentences with a partner.
   1 Are there any re**s**tauran**ts** in town?   3 Are there any movie**s** on TV tonight?
   2 I'm **s**orry, but I can't. I'm bu**s**y tonight.   4 Why don't we get ticket**s** at the **s**tation?

4 SPEAKING

PAIR WORK Imagine your partner is in your town or city on a business or study trip. He/She is staying at a hotel in the city. Suggest something to do in the evening. Also suggest a place to go and a time to meet. Then change roles.

Let's go out this evening.

Good idea.

Why don't we go to a restaurant? Do you like Italian food?

103

10.4 A 24-HOUR CITY

LESSON OBJECTIVE
- write an online invitation

1 LISTENING

A **PAIR WORK** Look at the city in the pictures on pages 104 and 105. What do you think you can you do there?

B 🔊 2.40 **LISTEN FOR DETAILS** Listen to the start of a TV travel show about Montevideo. Which <u>two</u> cities does the woman talk about? Which <u>two</u> neighborhoods in Montevideo does she talk about?

C 🔊 2.40 **LISTEN FOR EXAMPLES** Listen again. Check (✓) the places the woman says.
- ☐ restaurants
- ☐ places to go dancing
- ☐ hotels
- ☐ the ocean
- ☐ the beach
- ☐ museums

D **PAIR WORK** **THINK CRITICALLY** The woman says, "This really is a day-and-night city." Look at the places in exercise 1C. Where do people usually go: in the day? at night? at night *and* in the day?

2 PRONUNCIATION: Listening for *going to*

A 🔊 2.41 Listen to the sentences. Do you hear *going to* or *gonna*? (Circle) the correct words.
1 I'm not *going to* / *gonna* go dancing now.
2 We're *going to* / *gonna* walk by the ocean in Old City.

B 🔊 2.42 Listen. What do you hear? (Circle) *going to* or *gonna*.
1 *going to* / *gonna*
2 *going to* / *gonna*
3 *going to* / *gonna*
4 *going to* / *gonna*

C People often use *gonna* in informal conversations. (Circle) the correct answer.
People usually say *gonna* when they are **at work** / **talking to friends**.

10.4 A 24-HOUR CITY

LESSON OBJECTIVE
- write an online invitation

Introduce the lesson Write or dictate: *Are you watching a movie tonight?* Write the answers *Yes, I am. / No, I'm not.*
- Direct Ss to ask and answer questions with a partner using *Are you going to …?* and these prompts: *go swimming / eat lunch / go to a club / practice English.*

1 LISTENING

A **PAIR WORK** Monitor as students discuss the picture. Help with vocabulary. Elicit ideas from Ss as a class.

> **Answers**
> Answers may vary.

B 🔊 **2.40** Before you play the audio, direct students to write two headings: *Cities* and *Neighborhoods*. Encourage them to take notes as they listen.
- Play the audio. Play again if necessary.

> **Answers**
> Cities: New York, Montevideo
> Neighborhoods: Pocitos, Old City

> 🔊 **2.40 Audio script**
> This week on *Let's Take a Tour*, I'm in a city that never sleeps. No, this isn't New York. I'm in Montevideo – the capital city of Uruguay. And this *really* is a day-and-night city. Now, we're not far from the Pocitos neighborhood. Pocitos is a *great* place to go out at night in Montevideo. It has restaurants, cafés, places to go dancing … but I'm not going to go dancing now. Let's wait for tonight! First, we're going to walk in Old City. *Old* City is … an *old* neighborhood, of course. It has some beautiful buildings and some really interesting museums. So come on! Let's take a tour … in Montevideo.

C 🔊 **2.40** Ss read the places aloud to make sure they understand. Ask them to raise hands if they remember hearing the place mentioned as it is read aloud.

> **Answers**
> Checked: restaurants, ocean, places to go dancing, museums

D **PAIR WORK** Draw a Venn diagram on the board like the one below and ask Ss to copy it. As Ss discuss the questions, ask them to fill in their diagrams. Elicit answers and add them to the diagram on the board. Discuss as a class if the words are in the correct place.

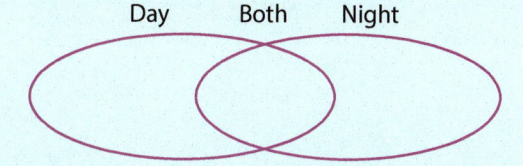

Day   Both   Night

> **Answers**
> in the day: restaurants, the ocean, museums
> at night: restaurants, places to go dancing
> both: restaurants

2 PRONUNCIATION: Listening for *going to*

A 🔊 **2.41** Play the audio. Have Ss compare answers with a partner, then elicit whole class feedback.

> **Answers**
> 1 gonna   2 going to

B 🔊 **2.42** Play the audio. Put Ss into pairs to compare ideas.

> **Answers**
> 1 gonna   2 going to   3 gonna   4 going to

> 🔊 **2.42 Audio script**
> 1 We're gonna visit some museums.
> 2 We're not going to a restaurant. We're going to a café.
> 3 We're gonna walk around the Old City.
> 4 We're going to go out in the Pocitos neighborhood.

C Explain to Ss that they don't need to use *gonna* in their speaking, but knowing the form will help them to understand people.

> **Answer**
> talking to friends

> 📎 **EXTRA ACTIVITY**
> Ask Ss to finish these sentences with their own information. Ask volunteers to share their sentences and write some on the board.
>
> *Tomorrow, I'm not going to …*
> *On the weekend, I'm going to …*
> *Next month, I'm not going to …*

3 WRITING

A **Introduce the task** Pre-teach the **Glossary** terms *sunrise* and *surprise*. Read the instructions aloud and explain the questions.

- Give Ss time to read and answer the questions individually.
- Ss then share their answers with a partner before you elicit their ideas.

> **Answers**
> His friends can wear shorts and a T-shirt, and a sweater for the early morning.
> Saturday night is a surprise.

B Ss underline the contractions individually before you elicit them as a class. Monitor as Ss work together. Circulate to make sure Ss are on track.

- Read the **Register check** box aloud with the class. Ask Ss for examples of formal and informal writing.
  informal = *text message, personal letter*
  formal = *letter, report*
- Ss expand the contractions in the reading text in pairs. Ask Ss to read the full sentence when you elicit answers.

> **Answers**
> This is a city that never sleeps. <u>You're</u> not going to sleep, either! Meet me at the front door of the hotel. <u>Don't</u> be late! And <u>don't</u> eat dinner first because <u>we're</u> going to eat at a nice restaurant in the Pocitos neighborhood. Then <u>we're</u> going to go dancing – all night! Early in the morning, about 5:00 a.m., <u>we're</u> going to watch the sunrise at the beach and then go for a morning walk by the ocean. <u>It's</u> a great place for a picnic – a breakfast picnic. And then, why <u>don't</u> we play soccer on the beach? A lot of people play soccer on the beach in the summer. You can wear shorts and a T-shirt, but a sweater is good for the early morning. On Saturday night, <u>we're</u> going to . . . well, <u>it's</u> a surprise! See you Friday night!
> **Full forms:**
> You're = You are
> Don't = Do not
> We're = We are
> It's = It is

C **Introduce the task** Tell Ss about an exciting day or night out you have had. Share photos, if available. [FIND IT]

- Ask Ss: *What is an exciting day or night out for you?* Allow Ss time to think and/or search online for ideas. Elicit ideas and write them on the board.
- Read the task aloud and underline some of the key words that explain the task. <u>Describe where</u> you are going to <u>go</u> and <u>what</u> you are going to <u>do</u>.

- As Ss write their invitations, circulate to offer ideas and help with spelling. Write challenging words on the board for everyone to see. If possible, correct Ss' work before the next activity.

🚶 FAST FINISHERS

Ask Ss to review their invitations for mistakes. They can use their smartphones or a print dictionary to look up how to spell words they are not sure of.

👥 TEACHER DEVELOPMENT ACTIVITY 2

Giving supportive feedback

Giving praise to adult learners like *Well done!* or *Good job!* is less effective than giving supportive feedback. Teachers play a more helpful role when they are specific about what a student has done successfully and what exactly they could improve.

Many teachers also like to use the "sandwich approach" when giving supportive feedback. This means they begin by telling a student what they have done well, move on to things that didn't go so well, and finish by returning to positive comments.

- Ss write their online invitations.
- Provide oral or written feedback using the "sandwich" approach, e.g., *I like the way you [used going to with three different verbs / remembered to use contractions]. You can improve your invitation by [using more informal language / adding linking words like but or then]. You made your invitation sound more exciting when you [used this adjective/included that phrase].*

D [GROUP WORK] **Review** Put Ss into groups and ask them to share their invitations. Listen for pronunciation and language usage and offer feedback later.

- Ask Ss to vote on the invitations they liked best. Ask volunteers to read the best invitations aloud to the class or do it yourself.

3 WRITING

A Read the online invitation. What does Ramon say his friends can wear? Which night is a surprise?

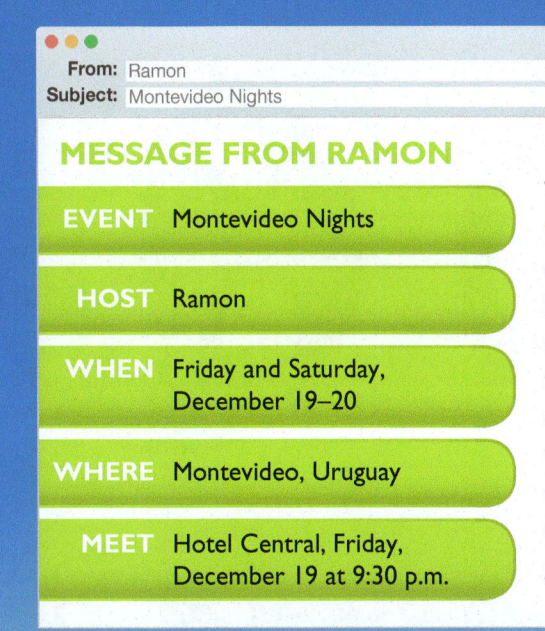

From: Ramon
Subject: Montevideo Nights

MESSAGE FROM RAMON

EVENT	Montevideo Nights
HOST	Ramon
WHEN	Friday and Saturday, December 19–20
WHERE	Montevideo, Uruguay
MEET	Hotel Central, Friday, December 19 at 9:30 p.m.

This is a city that never sleeps. *You're* not going to sleep, either! ⭐🌙😊 Meet me at the front door of the hotel. Don't be late! And don't eat dinner first because we're going to eat at a nice restaurant in the Pocitos neighborhood. Then we're going to go dancing – all night! Early in the morning, about 5:00 a.m., we're going to watch the sunrise at the beach and then go for a morning walk by the ocean. It's a great place for a picnic – a breakfast picnic. 😊 And then why don't we play soccer on the beach? A lot of people play soccer on the beach in the summer. You can wear shorts and a T-shirt, but a sweater is good for the early morning. On Saturday night, we're going to … well, it's a surprise! 😲 See you Friday night!

GLOSSARY
sunrise (*n*) early in the morning, when the sun is first in the sky
surprise (*n*) something you don't know about

B **WRITING SKILLS** Look at the contractions in two of Ramon's sentences below. Then underline all 10 contractions in his message. Work with a partner and say the full forms.

<u>You're</u> not going to sleep, either! (*You're = You are*)
<u>Don't</u> be late! (*Don't = Do not*)

REGISTER CHECK

Many speakers of English use contractions in informal writing. In formal writing, people often use the full forms.

✎ WRITE IT

FIND IT

C Plan an exciting day or night out for your friends. You can look online for ideas. Then write an online invitation. Use Ramon's invitation for an example. Describe where you are going to go and what you are going to do. Use contractions.

D **GROUP WORK** Read the other invitations in your group. Which events do you want to go to? Why?

10.5 TIME TO SPEAK
48 hours in your city

LESSON OBJECTIVE
- plan and present a fun weekend in your city

A PREPARE Look at the pictures. Can you do these things in your country? When can you do them? Think about seasons, days, and times of day.

B RESEARCH Work with a partner. Choose a season or a month. Think of fun things to do in your city in that season/month during the day, at night, and outside. Write a list.

C AGREE Plan a fun weekend (48 hours) in your city. Choose activities from exercise B. Make a plan for Saturday and Sunday.

D DISCUSS Work with another pair and compare your plans. Ask and answer questions about their plan.

E PRESENT With your partner, present your 48-hour plan to the class. Which plan do you want to do?

>> To check your progress, go to page 155.

USEFUL PHRASES

RESEARCH
Let's talk about the summer / February / the rainy season.
What fun things can we do during the day? at night? outside?

DISCUSS
We're going to have breakfast in the park.
Are you going to have a picnic?

PRESENT
We're planning a fun weekend in (season/month).
First, we're going to …
On Saturday/Sunday, …

10.5 TIME TO SPEAK
48 hours in your city

LESSON OBJECTIVE
- plan and present a fun weekend in your city

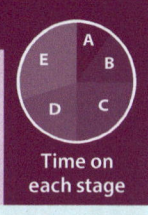

Time on each stage

Introduce the task Tell Ss about a city you know well, like the city that you come from. Explain what you can do there on the weekend using the expressions from the **Useful phrases** box. Show pictures of the city from your smartphone or the internet. Encourage Ss to ask questions.

- Direct Ss to the **Useful phrases** section at the bottom of the page. Remind them that they can use them at the relevant stages of the lesson.

A PREPARE **Aim: Ss look at and talk about the photos.**
- INDIVIDUALLY Allow Ss time to look at and think about the photos. Give Ss time to think silently about what they are going to say.*
- PAIR WORK Monitor as Ss share their ideas.
- CLASS WORK Elicit ideas from Ss. Write any new vocab on the board for Ss to refer to later in the lesson.

B RESEARCH **Do the task Aim: Ss make a list of seasonal activities.**
- CLASS WORK Model the task by talking about a season or a month in your country. Explain what people do during that time. Demonstrate with photos, if available.
- PAIR WORK Ss work together to generate ideas. Explain that they do not have to use their current city if they feel they know more about another city.

C AGREE **Aim: Ss make plans about fun things to do.**
- PAIR WORK Circulate and monitor Ss as they make their plans. Offer suggestions if Ss need help, but otherwise let them work. *Monitor and make a note of the strong points of each group, for example, good use of unit vocabulary, interesting questions, natural-sounding interactions, etc. You can use your notes to give feedback at the end of the lesson.

D DISCUSS **Aim: Pairs compare their lists.**
- PAIR WORK As Ss work in groups, circulate and monitor. Listen for language usage and provide feedback to Ss when the task is over.*
- CLASS WORK Elicit ideas from Ss and find out the favorite plan from each group.

E PRESENT Review **Aim: Ss present their ideas to the class.**
- INDIVIDUALLY Give Ss time to prepare their presentations.
- CLASS WORK Give pairs a time limit, say two minutes, to present their plan to the class. This will help Ss not go on too long nor finish too quickly. When each pair finishes, ask some questions yourself, e.g., *Which activities are cheap? Why is that place good?* Encourage Ss to ask questions.
- **Feedback for speaking activities*** Give the class positive feedback based on the notes you made earlier in the activity.

*These tips can help you to create a safe speaking environment. They can also be used with other speaking activities. For more information, see page T-xxii.

▶▶ PROGRESS CHECK ▶▶

Direct students to page 155 to check their progress. Go to page T-152 for Progress check activity suggestions.

TEACHER DEVELOPMENT REFLECTION

Answer these questions yourself in a reflection journal or discuss them with your peers.

1. How much vocabulary in Activity 1 did students know already? Which students knew the most? What did you find surprising, and what predictable?

2. Did you adapt your plan for 10.2 because of what you found out? Why or why not?

3. Teachers often use eliciting questions to find out what students already know, e.g., *What do I wear on my feet?* (*Boots*), or *We can talk about our future plans in different ways. For example,* (writing on board) *Next week, I'm .... book my ticket.* (*Going to*) What advice would you give colleagues about planning and asking eliciting questions?

4. After teachers elicit language, they should ask checking questions. Why is *Do you understand?* an ineffective question? What questions might you ask to check the meaning of *boots* and *going to*?

5. In Activity 2, how did students respond to your feedback? For written work, what other things can you sometimes comment on?

COLORFUL MEMORIES

11

TEACHER DEVELOPMENT INTRODUCTION

Strategy 2: Teaching vocabulary – Language awareness

In this unit, we explore some basic techniques for guiding Ss to a deeper understanding of the meaning, use, and form of the vocabulary they learn.

Guiding questions (Activity 1): Use simple questions to focus on meaning and use and help Ss make links between words. You will have the opportunity to try this in Lesson 11.1.

Scrambled sentences (Activity 2): This is a versatile activity for highlighting form, in particular, for helping Ss to use vocabulary accurately in sentences. You can try this in Lesson 11.2.

To find out more about different aspects of word knowledge, read Chapters 2–3 of Ruth Gairns and Stuart Redman, *Working with Words*, pp.13–53. Please go to www.cambridge.org/evolve to download these pages.

INTRODUCE THE THEME OF THE UNIT

Draw or display a current calendar. Write *the past* on the board. Elicit the meaning from Ss. Ask: *Is today in the past?*

- Write or dictate:
  yesterday
  three days ago
  a month ago
  ten years ago
- Explain that *ago* means in the past. Point to *today* on the calendar, then point to *yesterday* and say: *Yesterday is in the past*. Repeat with the other terms on the board.
- Ask Ss to remember a place for each time period and write it next to the phrases. For example, for a month ago they might remember *beach*. Give Ss a few minutes to brainstorm their ideas before they share their places with each other.
- Ask Ss to share their ideas with the class.

UNIT OBJECTIVES

Read the unit objectives aloud. Tell Ss to listen and read along. Explain any vocabulary that Ss might not understand. Explain the idea of *childhood*.

START SPEAKING

A Ss look at the picture and discuss in pairs. Elicit their ideas as a class.

B Ss discuss the question in pairs before you elicit answers.

C Ss can use ideas from the start of this lesson to help them. Ask Ss to share their happy time in their life with a partner.
- Share memories as a whole class.
- **OPTIONAL ACTIVITY** Ss watch Felipe's video and identify the time of his life that he is talking about. Then they discuss whether they remember the same time in their own lives.

REAL STUDENT

Hi, my name is Felipe. I remember my first day at college. It was in October, 2017. I was happy, very happy.

T-107

UNIT OBJECTIVES
- describe people, places, and things in the past
- talk about colors and memories
- talk about movies and actors
- write an email about things you keep from your past
- talk about TV shows from your childhood

COLORFUL MEMORIES

11

START SPEAKING

A Look at the picture. Where is the boy? How old is the boy now?

B Is the boy happy? Why or why not?

C Talk about a happy time in your life. For ideas, watch Felipe's video.

REAL STUDENT *What time does Felipe talk about? Do you remember the same time?*

107

11.1 FLASHBACK FRIDAY

LESSON OBJECTIVE
- describe people, places, and things in the past

1 LANGUAGE IN CONTEXT

A Mason writes about two old pictures from his past. Read his posts and the comments. Circle the topics he writes about.

his school	his first job
the season	a toy
his family	his favorite food

B Read again. Check (✓) the sentences that are true. Correct the false ones.
1. Flashback Friday is for pictures from the past.
2. The yard is at Mason's parents' house.
3. Bethany is Mason's friend now.
4. Mason drives a car these days.

Mason Clark It's Flashback Friday! Here are two of my favorite memories from 2009. I was eight. This was in the summer. I was with my sister, and we were on vacation at my grandparents' house. My parents weren't there. It was **exciting**! #flashbackfriday #2009 #summervacation

> Mason Clark
> Bethany Clark

Fay L. Wright You were really **cute**!

Bert Chow Your grandparents' yard was **beautiful**!

Mason Clark Yeah, it was **wonderful**. It was usually **quiet**, but not in the summer. We were **noisy** kids!

Mason Clark And this was my old go-kart. My grandpa made it for me. Well, it wasn't old in 2009 – it was **new** then! It was **slow**, but to me, at eight, it was really **fast** and exciting. #go-kart #2009 #bestgrandparents

Sam Lopez My go-kart was **awful**, but yours is great.

Bethany Clark Hey, Mason is still driving it today! 😂

Mason Clark Don't listen to my sister! I have a real, *fast* car now. 🙂

👍 13   ❤ 2

GLOSSARY
memories (n) things you think about from your past
yard (n) the outdoor area in front of or behind a house

---

2 VOCABULARY: Describing people, places, and things

A 🔊 2.43 Listen and repeat the adjectives in **bold**. Which adjectives in Mason's posts describe people, places, and things?

| new shoes |  cute dog |  wonderful vacation |  noisy baby |  fast car |
|  exciting book |  beautiful day |  awful day |  quiet baby |  slow car |

B ▶ Now do the vocabulary exercises for 11.1 on page 150.

C GROUP WORK Think about a person, place, or thing from your past. Describe it to your group. Use the adjectives in exercise 2A. For ideas, watch Anderson's video.

REAL STUDENT Is Anderson's memory happy? Is your memory happy, too?

108

11.1 FLASHBACK FRIDAY

LESSON OBJECTIVE
- describe people, places, and things in the past

Introduce the lesson Draw or display a picture of an item that may have come from your childhood. This could be a teddy bear, truck, doll, book, or anything else. Use some of the adjectives on this page to describe the items. Say: *This was my [doll]. My [father] bought it for me. It was [beautiful].*

1 LANGUAGE IN CONTEXT

A **Do the task** First ask Ss to read the words in the box.
- Ss read the text individually, then circle the correct phrases. They share their ideas with a partner. Elicit answers as a class.

> **Answers**
> Mason talks about the season, his family, and a toy.

- Explain any of the adjectives in bold or any other vocabulary Ss ask for. Explain *go-kart*. Check the **Glossary**.

B **Review** Ss read again. They check the true sentences, then correct the false ones individually before exchanging ideas with a partner.

- As Ss give you the answers, write the full sentence on the board so that Ss can see the corrections. Alternatively, volunteers can write their sentences on the board and the other members of the class can check them.

> **Answers**
> 1 ✓
> 2 The yard is at Mason's **grandparents'** house.
> 3 Bethany is Mason's **sister**.
> 4 ✓

2 VOCABULARY: Describing people, places, and things

A 🔊 **2.43** **Present the vocabulary** Ss match the words and the definitions in pairs.
- Play the audio, pausing after each sentence so Ss can check their answers. Play again, pausing this time so individual Ss can repeat.

> **Answers**
> people: cute, noisy
> places: exciting, beautiful, wonderful, quiet
> things: new, slow, fast, awful

TEACHER DEVELOPMENT ACTIVITY 1

Guiding questions
After you've used exercise 2A to establish basic meanings, use questions like those below to develop Ss' understanding of the words. Use English as much as possible, but allow Ss to use their native language when necessary. Decide in advance which words you want to ask about, and which questions you want to use.

Aspect of meaning	Example questions
Associations	What things can be *fast*? *Fast car, fast … ?* (*runner, speech, food*) What about *cute*? (*dog, cat, baby*)
Connotation	*Wonderful* – Is it a positive word or negative? (positive) What about *cute*? (positive too)
Objectivity	*Awful* – Is that a fact or an opinion? (opinion) What about *new*? (fact) *Noisy*? (Could be either!)
Style	*Cute* – Is it formal or informal? (Informal) Could you use it in conversation with friends? (yes) A business letter? (no)
Synonyms	What's another word for *wonderful*? (*great, fantastic*) How else could we say *awful*? (*really bad, terrible*)
Antonyms	What's the opposite of *fast*? (*slow*) What about *exciting*? (*boring*)

B Direct Ss to page 150 to complete the vocabulary exercises. Teacher's tips for vocabulary exercises are on page T-141.

C GROUP WORK **Review** Model a sample answer by describing something from your past, just as you did at the beginning of the lesson.
- Allow Ss time to think and write down their item and some of their ideas before they talk.
- **OPTIONAL ACTIVITY** Ss watch Anderson's video and say whether his memory is a happy one or not. They then compare their memory to his. You may want to explain that *sweet* has a similar meaning to *nice* or *cute*.

> **REAL STUDENT**
> Hi. I am Anderson. I remember my first girlfriend. She was beautiful and sweet.

T-108

3 GRAMMAR: Statements with *was* and *were*

A **Present the grammar** Before Ss circle the answers, explain that they can refer to the examples in the grammar box. Explain that *was* is singular and *were* is plural.

> **Answers**
> 1 Use *was* and *were* to talk about people, places, or things in the **past**.
> 2 *Was* and *were* are the simple past forms of *be*.
> 3 *Was* and *were* are **affirmative**.
> 4 *Wasn't* and *weren't* are **negative**.

> **GRAMMAR SUPPORT** To check understanding, write gapped sentences on the board and ask Ss to complete them, e.g., *The kitchen ___ big.* [*was* or *wasn't*] *I ___ happy.* [*was* or *wasn't*] *We ___ young.* [*were* or *weren't*]

B If necessary, complete the first gap with Ss to model the task.
- Ss work individually to fill in the gaps before they check with a partner.
- Ask individual Ss to read a sentence aloud as you elicit the answers.

> **Answers**
> I remember a visit to my uncle's farm in August 1998. It **wasn't** a big farm – just a nice, small one. There **weren't** a lot of animals, only ten or fifteen. They **were** farm animals, not pets, so they **weren't** friendly, but my uncle's dog **was** really nice. He **was** only two or three, so he **wasn't** very old, but he **was** smart. His real name **was** Jake, but *my* name for him **was** "Fluffy Duffy." It's an awful name, but I **was** seven at the time, and to me, Fluffy Duffy **was** a beautiful name! We **were** great friends.

C Direct Ss to page 138 to complete the grammar exercise. Teacher's tips for grammar exercises are on page T-129.

D PAIR WORK **Review** Read the stem sentences and make sure Ss understand the words. Model and complete the first sentences so Ss know what to do.
- Allow Ss time to think about their ideas and complete the sentences. Ss share their ideas with a partner or a small group. Ask volunteers to say their sentences when you check for ideas as a class.

- Read the **Accuracy check**. Ask Ss to add *was*, *wasn't*, *were*, or *weren't* to these sentences.
  1 *I like our new apartment. It's quiet. Our old apartment noisy.*
  2 *Thanks for your help yesterday. You wonderful.*
  3 *Yuck! That movie good.*

> **Answers**
> 1 I like our new apartment. It's quiet. Our old apartment **was** noisy.
> 2 Thanks for your help yesterday. You **were** wonderful.
> 3 Yuck! That movie **wasn't** good.

- Ask Ss to check the sentences they wrote again.

4 SPEAKING

A **Introduce the task** Present one of your own memories for Ss. Use any pictures you may have. Make sure you model the same language used in exercise 4B.
- Read the words aloud for Ss and give them time to think about their memories. Give them the option of using one of their memories from exercise 2C or a new memory.

B PAIR WORK As Ss share their memories in pairs, circulate and monitor. Listen for language usage that you can give feedback on when they finish the activity.
- Ask a few volunteers to share their memories with the whole class.
- Give feedback.

> ✏️ **HOMEWORK IDEAS**
> Ask Ss to write their memories in sentences. They could then share them on a blog or could record them as they read aloud on their smartphone.

T-109

3 GRAMMAR: Statements with *was* and *were*

A Circle the correct answer. Use the sentences in the grammar box to help you.

1. Use *was* and *were* to talk about people, places, or things in the **past** / **future**.
2. *Was* and *were* are the simple past forms of *go* / *be*.
3. *Was* and *were* are **affirmative** / **negative**.
4. *Wasn't* and *weren't* are **affirmative** / **negative**.

> **Statements with *was* and *were***
>
> I **was** in the yard.   My parents **weren't** there.
> We **were** on vacation.   It **wasn't** old.

B Read another Flashback Friday post. Complete the post with *was*, *wasn't*, *were*, or *weren't*.

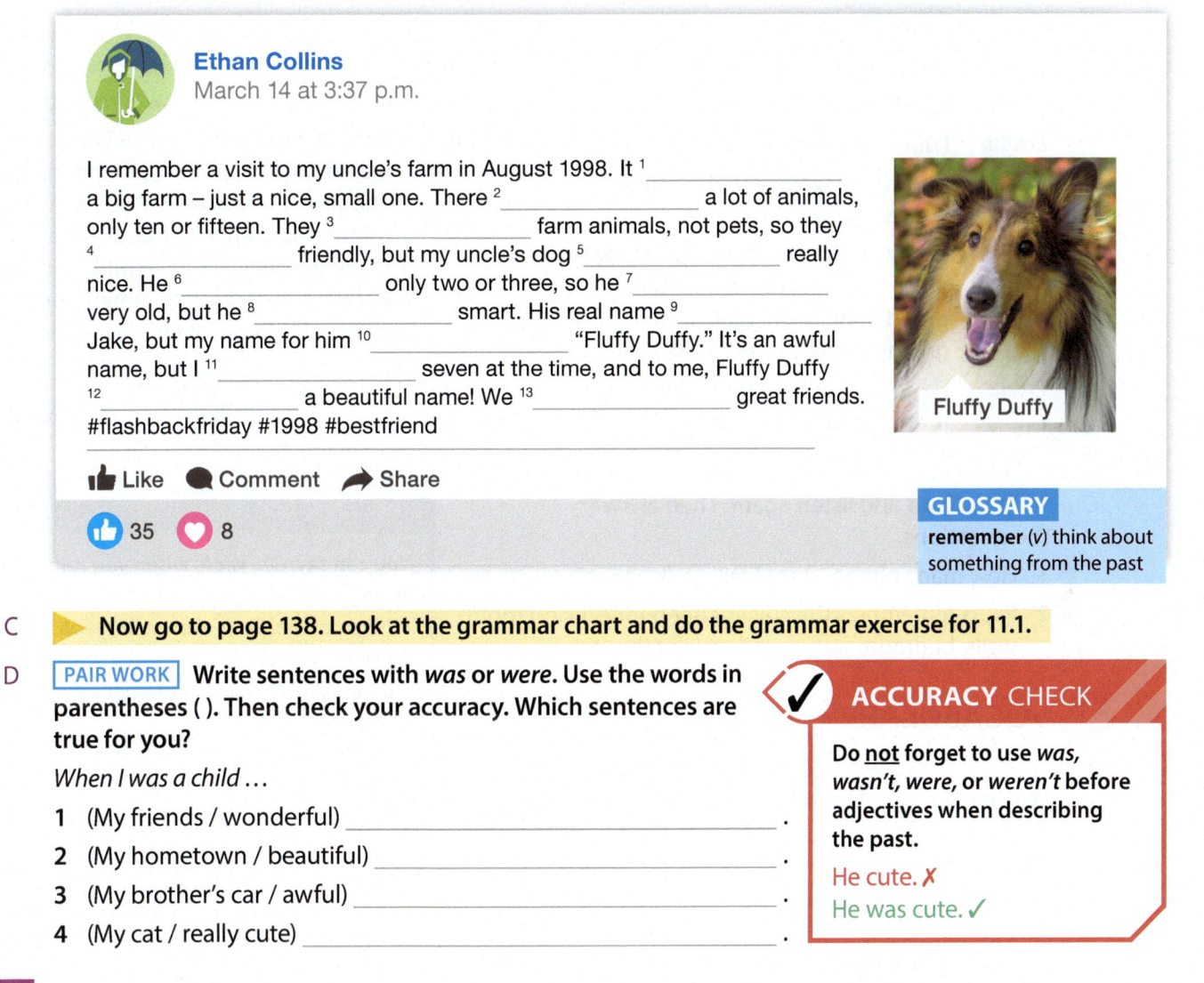

Ethan Collins
March 14 at 3:37 p.m.

I remember a visit to my uncle's farm in August 1998. It ¹_____ a big farm – just a nice, small one. There ²_____ a lot of animals, only ten or fifteen. They ³_____ farm animals, not pets, so they ⁴_____ friendly, but my uncle's dog ⁵_____ really nice. He ⁶_____ only two or three, so he ⁷_____ very old, but he ⁸_____ smart. His real name ⁹_____ Jake, but my name for him ¹⁰_____ "Fluffy Duffy." It's an awful name, but I ¹¹_____ seven at the time, and to me, Fluffy Duffy ¹²_____ a beautiful name! We ¹³_____ great friends.
#flashbackfriday #1998 #bestfriend

👍 Like   💬 Comment   ➤ Share
👍 35   ♥ 8

Fluffy Duffy

GLOSSARY
remember (*v*) think about something from the past

C ▶ Now go to page 138. Look at the grammar chart and do the grammar exercise for 11.1.

D [PAIR WORK] Write sentences with *was* or *were*. Use the words in parentheses ( ). Then check your accuracy. Which sentences are true for you?

When I was a child …
1. (My friends / wonderful) _____.
2. (My hometown / beautiful) _____.
3. (My brother's car / awful) _____.
4. (My cat / really cute) _____.

> ✓ **ACCURACY CHECK**
>
> Do **not** forget to use *was*, *wasn't*, *were*, or *weren't* before adjectives when describing the past.
>
> He cute. ✗
> He was cute. ✓

4 SPEAKING

A Choose one or two of your memories. Think about the ideas below or your own ideas. Write notes.

> ages   animals   the people   the place   the season   the year   things

B [PAIR WORK] Talk about your memories. You can begin, "*I remember …*"

> I remember my sister's birthday party. It was July 2006. She was thirteen. The party was very noisy, and …

109

11.2 OUR OLD PHONE WAS WHITE

LESSON OBJECTIVE
- talk about colors and memories

1 LANGUAGE IN CONTEXT

A **PAIR WORK** Look at the picture of the child. Describe it with one word.

B 🔊 2.44 Emilio talks to his wife, Paula. Read and listen. Where was Emilio in the picture? Which rooms does Paula remember?

🔊 2.44 Audio script

Emilio Here's another picture of me.
Paula Cute! How old were you?
Emilio I don't know. Two?
Paula And where were you? Were you at home?
Emilio No, I wasn't, because our phone was **black**. Hmm … so where was the **green** phone? Oh, yeah! It was at my grandparents' house, in the kitchen.
Paula Hey, I remember our old phone, too. It was **white**.
Emilio Wow, you remember the color, too! Was it big? Our old phone was *really* big.
Paula Yeah, it was. I remember a lot! The phone was in the living room, next to the couch. The couch was **brown**. And the living room walls were **orange**. Oh, yeah, and my bedroom walls were **pink** and green. Yuck! It's really easy to remember the colors of things – even ugly colors!

GLOSSARY
ugly (*adj*) not nice to look at

C 🔊 2.44 Read and listen again. Then answer the questions.
1. How many phones does Emilio talk about?
2. Paula remembers the color of her phone, living room walls, bedroom walls – and which other thing?

INSIDER ENGLISH

You can say, *Oh, yeah,* when you remember something.

Where was the green phone? **Oh, yeah!** *It was at my grandmother's house.*

Oh, yeah, *and my bedroom walls were pink and green.*

2 VOCABULARY: Colors

A 🔊 2.45 **PAIR WORK** Listen and repeat the colors. Which colors are in the conversation above? What's your favorite color?

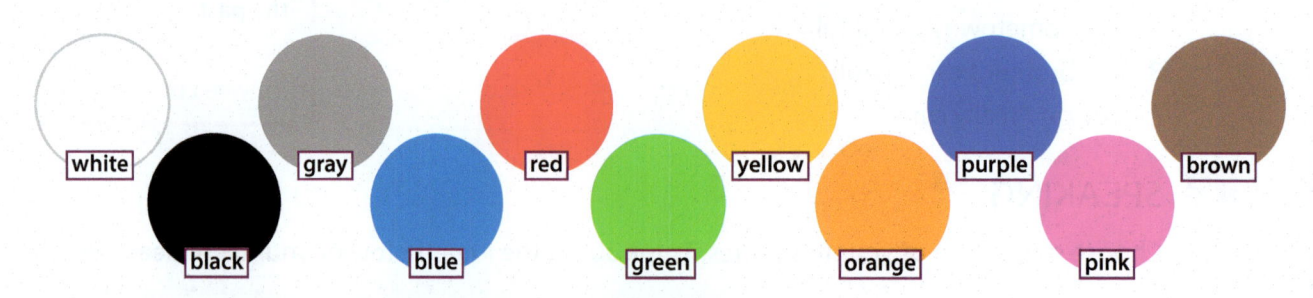

white   gray   blue   red   green   yellow   orange   purple   pink   brown
black

B ▶ Now do the vocabulary exercises for 11.2 on page 150.

C **PAIR WORK** Tell your partner the colors of <u>two</u> things from your home.

110

11.2 OUR OLD PHONE WAS WHITE

LESSON OBJECTIVE
- talk about colors and memories

Introduce the lesson Books closed. Get Ss thinking about colors and review past simple statements by talking about your clothes. Say: *Today, my shirt is [red]. Yesterday, my shirt was ….* Either elicit the answer by asking, *Can you remember?* or complete the sentence yourself. Write the two sentences on the board, and then have Ss come up with their own sentences.
- Elicit some example sentences and write on the board.

1 LANGUAGE IN CONTEXT

A **PAIR WORK** Ss describe the picture with their partner. Elicit answers when they finish.

B 🔊 **2.44** Read and explain the instructions. Play the audio, and then ask Ss to work in pairs to answer the questions. Play the audio again if necessary. Elicit answers from Ss.

> **Answers**
> Emilio was at his grandparents' house, in the kitchen.
> Paula remembers the living room and her bedroom.

- Ask volunteer Ss to read the **Insider English** box. Model another sample sentence which is also informal, e.g., *Where's my bag? Oh yeah, it's on the chair!*

> **VOCABULARY SUPPORT** *Cute, yeah,* and *hey* are all informal expressions. They are fine to use in spoken language, but Ss should avoid using them in formal, written English.

C 🔊 **2.44** Ss read and understand the questions before you play the audio.
- Ss answer the questions individually before they check with a partner. Elicit their answers as a class. Replay the audio if necessary.

> **Answers**
> 1 two   2 the couch

2 VOCABULARY: Colors

A 🔊 **2.45** **PAIR WORK** **Present the vocabulary** Play the audio as Ss listen. Pause after each word for Ss to repeat together. Monitor for pronunciation. Play audio again. Pause after each word and ask individual Ss to repeat the word.
- **Do the task** Ss look at the conversation and find the words. Elicit answers as a class.

> **Answers**
> black, green, white, brown, orange, pink
> Favorite colors will vary.

TEACHER DEVELOPMENT ACTIVITY 2

Scrambled sentences

In order to use vocabulary items accurately, Ss need to know how they fit into sentences: what kind of words come before and after them? This activity uses jumbled sentences and then questions to help Ss notice the important patterns.

- Have Ss close their books. On the board, write a couple of sentences to show patterns with color words, but with the words jumbled:
  1 grandparents' / green / in / kitchen. / my / phone / The / was
  2 in / living / orange. / room / The / the / walls / were
- Ss work in pairs to put the words in the right order. When they have finished, write them on the board:
  1 *The green phone was in my grandparents' kitchen.*
  2 *The walls in the living room were orange.*
- Circle the color words and ask questions to establish what kind of word *green* and *orange* are (adjectives) and where they fit in sentences (either before a noun, as in *The green phone*, or after the verb *be*, as in *were orange*).

B Direct Ss to page 150 to complete the vocabulary exercises. Teacher's tips for vocabulary exercises are on page T-141.

C **PAIR WORK** Ask Ss to write down the two things and colors their partner says. When you elicit feedback, ask the other Ss to explain their partner's objects and colors.
- Ss answer the question in pairs before you elicit ideas.

📎 EXTRA ACTIVITY

Ask, write, or dictate simple color questions for Ss to answer, e.g.,
> *What color is grass?*
> *What color are your shoes?*
> *What color is your dog?*

Try to make questions relevant to your Ss, e.g.,
> *What color are the shirts of your country's soccer team?*

Play I can see with colors. Ss say the first letter of something in the classroom (or, in this case, the color of something). One S says, *I can see something beginning with P.* Other Ss have to guess the word:
> *Is it purple?*   *No, it isn't.*
> *Is it pink?*   *Yes, it is!*

T-110

3 GRAMMAR: Questions with *was* and *were*

A **Before Ss circle the answers, explain that they can refer to the examples in the grammar box.**

> **Answers**
> 1 beginning   2 after

- Ask volunteer Ss to read the chart. Monitor pronunciation. Check understanding by asking different questions, e.g., *What color was your first car? Were you in school yesterday? Why were you happy yesterday? Where was your last vacation?*

B **PAIR WORK** **Do the task** Do the first sentence as a class to make sure Ss understand. Ask Ss to arrange the sentences with a partner. Elicit answers and write these on the board. Alternatively, ask Ss to write their sentences on the board and ask the class to correct them.

> **Answers**
> 1 What color was your old phone?
> 2 Where was the phone?
> 3 Was the refrigerator in the kitchen?
> 4 What color were the walls in the kitchen?
> 5 Were the bedrooms big?
> 6 Was your home nice?

- Ss ask and answer the questions with their partner. Listen for any errors in pronunciation or grammar to share when the task is over.

C **Direct Ss to page 139 to complete the grammar exercise. Teacher's tips for grammar exercises are on page T-129.**

4 SPEAKING

A **Model a sample answer by drawing a room from your childhood. Draw a top-down map to keep it simple.**

- Label the names of the furniture and write some colors on them. Explain as you draw, e.g., *This was my room. The bed was brown …*
- Allow Ss time to draw their room.

B **PAIR WORK** **Model the sample dialogue with a volunteer. As Ss share their pictures, circulate and monitor. Listen for language usage that you can give feedback on at the end of the task. Which words were challenging to pronounce? Was their grammar correct?**

> ✏ **HOMEWORK IDEAS**
>
> Ask Ss to write six sentences about their old room for the next session. Correct the sentences and then share them with the class.

3 GRAMMAR: Questions with *was* and *were*

A (Circle) the correct answers. Use the questions in the grammar box to help you.
1. In *yes/no* questions, *was* and *were* go at the **beginning** / **end** of the question.
2. In information questions, *was* and *were* go **before** / **after** the question word(s) (for example, *How old* and *When*).

> **Questions with *was* and *were***
>
> ***Yes/no* questions**
> **Were** you at home?
>   No, I **wasn't**.
> **Was** the phone in the kitchen?
>   Yes, it **was**.
>
> **Information questions**
> How old **were** you?
>   I **was** two.
> What color **were** the walls?
>   They **were** orange.

B [PAIR WORK] Put the words in the correct order to make questions. Then ask and answer the questions with a partner.
1. color / your old phone? / was / What
2. was / the phone? / Where
3. in the kitchen? / the refrigerator / Was
4. the walls / color / in the kitchen? / were / What
5. big? / Were / the bedrooms
6. your home / nice? / Was

C ▶ Now go to page 139. Look at the grammar chart and do the grammar exercise for 11.2.

4 SPEAKING

A Draw a picture or plan of a room in your house from your past. Include furniture and your favorite things.

B [PAIR WORK] Work with a partner. Ask and answer questions about your rooms.

> This is the bedroom. There was a bed, a desk, and two windows.

> What color was the bed?

> My bed was white.

11.3 I HAVE NO IDEA

LESSON OBJECTIVE
- talk about movies and actors

1 FUNCTIONAL LANGUAGE

A Look at the picture of the woman. Do you know her name? What else do you know about her?

B 🔊 2.46 Read and listen. What does the man want to remember? Does he remember it?

🔊 2.46 Audio script

A I'm going to watch *Titanic* tonight.
B The movie?
A Yeah. With Leonardo DiCaprio, and … who was the other actor? The woman?
B Um, **I have no idea.**
A She's from England.
B Sorry, **I'm not sure.**
A Her first name is Kate, **I think.**
B Let me think. **Maybe** it's Kate Hudson? No, she's American. Why don't we look online?
A Good idea. Let's see … *Titanic* actor, woman … Kate Winslet!
B Oh, yeah.
A What was the name of that other movie she was in? With Johnny Depp.
B Oh no … Not again!

GLOSSARY
actor (n) a man or woman in a movie, TV show, or play

C Complete the chart with expressions in **bold** from the conversation above.

Expressing uncertainty

Very unsure	A little unsure
I have ¹ _____ .	Her first name is Kate, I ³ _____ .
I'm ² _____ .	I think her first name is Kate.
I don't know.	⁴ _____ it's Kate Hudson?

D 🔊 2.47 **PAIR WORK** Complete the conversations with the correct words from the box. Listen and check. Then practice with a partner.

> don't   Maybe   no   not   think

1. **A** When was the movie *Titanic* in theaters?
   B I _____ know. _____ it was in 1997?
2. **A** How many movies was Kate Winslet in?
   B I have _____ idea.
3. **A** Where was Melinda yesterday?
   B I _____ she was at home.
4. **A** Where are the restrooms?
   B Sorry, I'm _____ sure.

11.3 I HAVE NO IDEA

LESSON OBJECTIVE
- talk about movies and actors

Introduce the lesson Ask: Ss *Do you like movies? What's your favorite movie in English?* Ask Ss to write down their favorite movie in English on a small piece of paper. Collect the papers and write some of the movies down on the board.

- Model some simple questions about the movies and write them on the board, e.g.,
  Who is an actor in this movie?
  Is it good or bad?
  What's it about?
- Model the task by choosing one of the movies and answering the questions above.
- In pairs, Ss each choose a movie they know and then answer the questions about it. Monitor and listen as they talk. Ask volunteers to share their answers with the class when most Ss have finished.

1 FUNCTIONAL LANGUAGE

A Introduce the task Ss answer the questions in pairs before you elicit some of their ideas.

> **Answers**
> Answers may vary.

B 🔊 **2.46** Read the questions and make sure Ss understand. Draw Ss attention to the **Glossary** below, read and explain *actor* – explain that Leonardo DiCaprio is an actor.
- Play the audio as Ss read. Ss check their answers with a partner before you elicit them as a class. Play the audio again if necessary.

> **Answers**
> He wants to remember an actor's name.
> He doesn't remember the name. (He finds it online.)

> **VOCABULARY SUPPORT** Ask Ss to look at the expressions in bold and explain they all mean *I don't know*. but with different levels of uncertainty.

C Read the heading of the chart and make sure Ss understand *uncertainty* – the idea of not being sure.
- Ss complete the chart individually before they share their answers with a partner. Elicit ideas as a class.

> **Answers**
> 1 no idea
> 2 not sure
> 3 think
> 4 Maybe

D 🔊 **2.47 Review** Ss complete the sentences individually with the phrases before they check with a partner.
- Play the audio as Ss read and check their answers. Don't be afraid to pause or repeat the audio if Ss are struggling.
- Ss role play the dialogues with a partner. As they read, monitor and listen for pronunciation.

> **Answers**
> 1 don't, Maybe   2 no   3 think   4 not

> 📎 **EXTRA ACTIVITY**
>
> Search *[current year] movies* online to bring up a list of current movies. Ask Ss to work in pairs. They choose one of the movies and make a dialogue similar to the one in exercise 1B about one of the actors. Monitor and listen to Ss as they interact. Alternatively, Ss can base their dialogue around a movie they saw recently. Ask volunteers to repeat their dialogue for the class.

T-112

2 REAL-WORLD STRATEGY

A **Introduce the task** Ask volunteer Ss to read the information in the box and the example sentences. Ss answer the question as a class.

> **Answers**
> *Um,* and *Let me think.*

B 🔊 **2.48** Play the audio. Ss check their answers with a partner. Elicit answers as a class.

> **Answers**
> He's sure about his favorite concert. He's not sure about the year.

> 🔊 **2.48 Audio script**
>
> **A** What was your favorite concert?
> **B** Let me think … it was the Red Hot Chili Peppers. It was very exciting!
> **A** What year was it?
> **B** Uh, 2001, I think.

C 🔊 **2.48** Play audio again. Ss note down the answers and share with a partner before you check as a class.

> **Answers**
> *Let me think* and *Uh,*

D PAIR WORK **Review** Put Ss into pairs and assign each one to be either Student A or Student B. Ask Student As to turn to page 158 and Bs to turn to page 160.

- Ask Ss a question that they probably don't know the answer to, e.g., *Where was soccer invented? (China)* Encourage Ss to answer using the expressions on page 112.
- Read the instructions aloud for Ss and ask volunteers to read the model dialogues. Allow Ss time to read through and understand their sentences.
- Circulate and monitor as Ss do the task.

> 📎 **EXTRA ACTIVITY**
>
> Find pictures of odd objects that are difficult to identify. For example, you could show a picture of a cup seen from above.
>
> You can either draw these on the board or find them on the internet. Display to the class or distribute to pairs. Ask Ss to use the functional language while trying to figure out what the images are. Monitor as Ss talk.

3 PRONUNCIATION: /oʊ/ and /ɑː/ vowel sounds

A 🔊 **2.49** Play the audio and have Ss repeat the words, paying attention to the different vowel sounds.

B 🔊 **2.50** Put Ss into pairs. Ask them to guess if the words sound like A or B. Encourage Ss to say the words aloud.

- Play the audio. Elicit answers from the class.
- Have Ss repeat the words. Encourage them to make a more rounded shape with their mouth for /oʊ/ words.

> **Answers**
> 1 A   2 B   3 A   4 A   5 A   6 B

C 🔊 **2.51** PAIR WORK Play the audio and have Ss repeat each line.

- Ss practice the conversations in pairs. Monitor and help as needed.

4 SPEAKING

GROUP WORK If possible, you might like to get Ss to watch a short trailer from the movie *Avatar* on YouTube™. Model the sample conversation with a volunteer. Ss could use the same movie they talked about in the introduction activity.

- When Ss finish, ask volunteer pairs to demonstrate their conversation to the class.

> ✏️ **HOMEWORK IDEAS**
>
> Ss watch three movie trailers on their home computers or smartphones. The movies must be in English. Ss write down the names of all three and write three new words they heard in each trailer. In the next class, Ss share their movies with a partner and say which one they would like to see. Did any Ss choose the same movie?

T-113

2 REAL-WORLD STRATEGY

TAKING TIME TO THINK
When you need time to think about an answer, say, *Let me think*, *Uh*, or *Um*.
Um, I have no idea.
Let me think. Maybe it's Kate Hudson?

A   Read the information in the box about taking time to think. Which <u>two</u> expressions does the woman use?

B   🔊 2.48 Listen to a conversation. What is the man sure about? What <u>isn't</u> he sure about?

C   🔊 2.48 Listen again. Which <u>two</u> expressions does the man use when he needs time to think?

D   ▶ PAIR WORK Student A: Go to page 158. Student B: Go to page 160. Follow the instructions.

3 PRONUNCIATION: Saying /oʊ/ and /ɑː/ vowel sounds

A   🔊 2.49 Listen and repeat the words. How are the vowel sounds different?
/oʊ/ kn**o**w   /ɑː/ n**o**t

B   🔊 2.50 Listen. Write A for words with /oʊ/, for example *know*. Write B for words with /ɑː/, for example *not*.
1 don't ___   3 no ___   5 home ___
2 on ___   4 go ___   6 concert ___

C   🔊 2.51 PAIR WORK Look at the letters in **bold** below. Listen and repeat. Then practice the conversations with a partner.
1 **A** Was M**o**na at the c**o**ncert yesterday?
   B N**o**, she wasn't. She was at h**o**me.
2 **A** Where is Leonard**o** DiCapri**o** fr**o**m?
   B I have n**o** idea.
3 **A** D**o**n't g**o**!
   B Sorry, I have to g**o** h**o**me.
4 **A** Are we **o**n the right bus? It's very sl**o**w.
   B I d**o**n't kn**o**w.

4 SPEAKING

GROUP WORK Think of a movie. Ask other people in your group about the actors in it. Then change roles.

Who was in the first *Avatar*?
I have no idea.
Um, was Zoe Saldana in it?
Yes, she was.

11.4 THINGS WE KEEP

LESSON OBJECTIVE
- write an email about things you keep from your past

1 READING

A Look at the pictures. What things can you see? Are the things old or new? Do you have some of these things?

B READ FOR MAIN IDEAS Read the article. What is it about?

PICTURING MEMORIES

Terry Lawrence is a travel writer for Pak Airlines in-flight magazine. Today she takes a break from travel writing and tells Pak Airlines readers about what she does in her free time.

I love to travel, I love to write – and I love to take pictures! I often take pictures of people and their favorite things. I have hundreds of pictures of people and the things they keep. People around the world keep things from childhood, for example toy cars, books, and games. These were their first favorite things. And me? I like to keep photographs, of course! Here are some of my favorite pictures.

Meet Tom Bradley and his toy cars. They were birthday gifts. They're old, but he plays with them today – with a little help!

Many parents keep their children's things, like baby shoes or a child's first clothes. Rosa Ortiz keeps her daughter's shoe and her son's shoe in her car. They were one and two years old at the time. Now they're 12 and 13!

Many people keep books and comic books. This is Doug and one of his comic books, but it's not his favorite. Doug leaves his favorite comic book at home – it's very expensive!

GLOSSARY
childhood (n) the time when you were a child
keep (v) have something for a long time

C READ FOR DETAIL Read again. Then read these sentences from the article. What do the underlined words mean? (Circle) the answers.

1 These were their first favorite things.
   These = a children   b birthday gifts   c things from their childhood
2 They're old, but he plays with them today.
   They and them = a toy cars   b shoes   c games
3 They were one and two years old at the time.
   They = a Rosa's cars   b Rosa's parents   c Rosa's children
4 It's not his favorite.
   It = a Doug   b Doug's comic book   c Doug's house

D PAIR WORK What things do you keep? Why? Do you keep the same things from the article, too? Tell a partner.

114

11.4 THINGS WE KEEP

LESSON OBJECTIVE
- write an email about things you keep from your past

Introduce the lesson Ss close their books. Show a photo or draw a picture of an item from your own childhood that you still have. Explain what it is and why it is important to you.

- Ask: *Think about your childhood. What were your favorite things?*
- Ask Ss to work with a partner and tell them about an important item from their youth. Monitor and listen as Ss talk. Ask volunteers to talk about their items with the class.

1 READING

A **Introduce the task** Ask Ss to discuss the questions in pairs. Elicit answers when they finish.

> **Suggested answers**
> The cars and the shoes are old. The comic book is new. Answers may vary.

B **Set a time limit for Ss to read the article, say three minutes. Remind them to focus on the main idea.**

- When time is up, volunteers share their answers with the class.

> **Answers**
> It is about the things people keep: from childhood (toy cars, stuffed animals, games), their children's things (baby shoes, a child's first dress or hat), books, comic books, and photos.

C **Do the task** Ask Ss to read again more closely. Answer any questions they have about vocabulary they don't understand, e.g.,

Similar (adj.) = *nearly the same as something else*

- Ss circle the answers individually before checking with a partner. Elicit answers as a class.

> **Answers**
> 1 c 2 a 3 c 4 b

D **PAIR WORK Review** As Ss discuss the questions, monitor and listen for pronunciation and grammar. Listen for language usage and provide feedback to Ss when the activity is finished.

- Ask volunteers to explain what things they keep and why. Do Ss keep similar things?
- Provide feedback on Ss' conversations to the whole class.

✏️ HOMEWORK IDEAS

Show and tell. Ask Ss to bring an item that is important to them to the next class. This could be the actual item or a picture or drawing of it. Explain that they will have time in the next class to tell other Ss about the item, just like you did at the start of this lesson. Ask Ss to answer these questions in their show and tell session.

When and where did you get the thing?

What do you use it for?

Why is it important to you?

Ss can write down any notes they want to refer to. In the next class session, allow Ss two minutes to talk about their item. If time permits, ask questions.

2 WRITING

A **Introduce the task** Ask Ss to read the email quickly to look for the items. They share the items with a partner before you elicit answers.

> **Answers**
> She finds a postcard (from her grandfather), (her) old homework/math homework, and an old soccer ball (her brother's).

- Be ready to explain any vocabulary items that Ss are not familiar with, e.g., *postcard, desert*. Alternatively, ask Ss to check a dictionary or ask a partner for a definition.
- Ask a volunteer to read the **Register check** aloud. Check Ss' understanding of some very basic emojis by drawing and writing 😄 *happy* and ☹ *sad*. Establish that emojis are always informal.

B PAIR WORK Ss work in pairs to discuss the reason for the three-paragraph structure. Elicit answers as a class.

> **Answers**
> Because Angie talks about three (different) things/topics.

C Ss underline the topic sentences before you elicit answers as a class.

> **Answers**
> Paragraph 1: Do you remember this postcard?
> Paragraph 2: There was also a lot of homework from my school days in the box.
> Paragraph 3: Your old soccer ball was in the box, too.

> VOCABULARY SUPPORT Paragraphs organize a text, making it easier to read. They focus on one topic and start with a *topic sentence*, which explains what the paragraph is about.

D **Do the task** Allow Ss time to think about the items they might have. Elicit ideas by asking them about things they had as children. Write these things on the board, e.g., *toys, toy animals, games, guitar, photograph, clothes,* etc.

- As Ss write, circulate and monitor and make sure that they stay on task. Offer any help with corrections or spellings. Write challenging words on the board.
- If possible, correct Ss' emails before they do the next activity.

E PAIR WORK **Review** Monitor as Ss share their emails. Ask volunteers to read their emails to the class. Check for pronunciation.

> 📎 **FOLLOW UP** ACTIVITY
> Display Ss' emails around the classroom and ask them to circulate around the room reading them. Hold a class vote to decide which email described the most interesting items.

T-115

2 WRITING

A Read Angie's email to her brother. What things from the past does she find in a box?

Reply Forward

Hi Eddie,

Do you remember this postcard? It was in a box under my bed. It was from Grandpa Bowman in 1969. He was in Saudi Arabia. His postcards were always exciting, and this one was my favorite. The desert is really beautiful. Do *you* have any of his old postcards?

There was also a lot of homework from my school days in the box. Hey, I was smart! Well, usually. My math homework was awful! 😱 I don't think I want to keep it.

Your old soccer ball was in the box, too. ⚽ Why do I have it? I don't know. There's some writing on it. Maybe it's the autograph of a famous soccer player. Do you want it?

Love,

Angie

GLOSSARY
autograph (*n*) name in handwriting, usually of a famous person

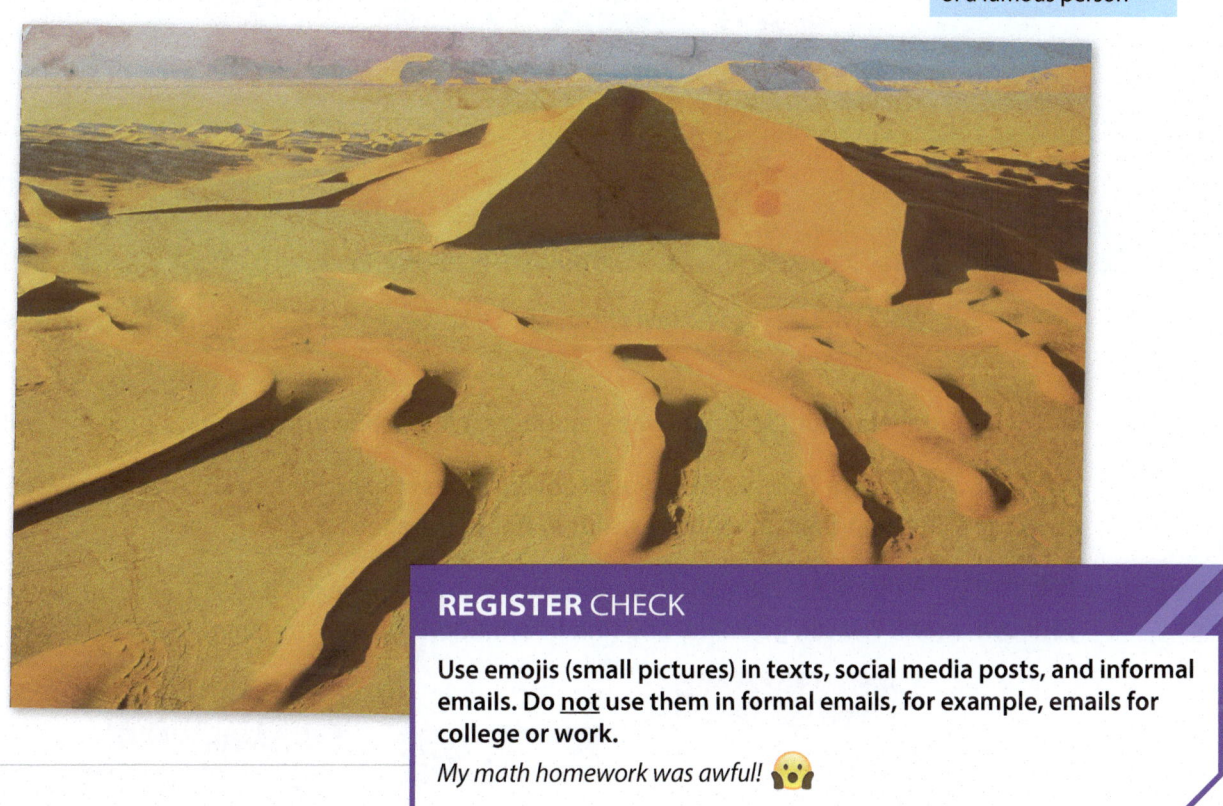

REGISTER CHECK

Use emojis (small pictures) in texts, social media posts, and informal emails. Do <u>not</u> use them in formal emails, for example, emails for college or work.

My math homework was awful! 😱

B PAIR WORK   THINK CRITICALLY   Why does Angie's email have three paragraphs?

C WRITING SKILLS   Read the topic sentence from the email below. The topic sentence tells you what the paragraph is about. Read the email again and <u>underline</u> the three topic sentences.

Do you remember this postcard? (= this paragraph is about a postcard.)

✎ WRITE IT

D Imagine you have a box of old things from your childhood. Write an email to a friend about <u>two</u> or <u>three</u> things in the box. Use a new paragraph for each thing. Write a topic sentence for each paragraph. You can use emojis.

E PAIR WORK   Read your partner's email. What interesting things do they write about in their email?

11.5 TIME TO SPEAK
TV memories

LESSON OBJECTIVE
- talk about TV shows from your childhood

A PREPARE Work with a partner. Talk about old TV shows you remember from your childhood. Write notes.

B AGREE Compare your ideas with other students. Which shows do a lot of people remember?

C DISCUSS Choose a TV show from your conversations in exercise A or B. What do you remember about it? Talk about the names, places, and things in the show.

D PREPARE Prepare a presentation about your TV show from exercise C. Include the ideas below and your own ideas. You can go online and find information you don't remember.

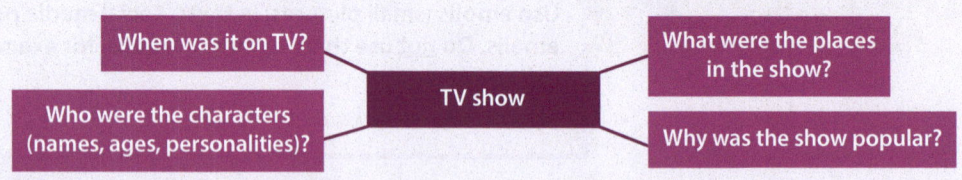

FIND IT

- When was it on TV?
- Who were the characters (names, ages, personalities)?
- TV show
- What were the places in the show?
- Why was the show popular?

E PRESENT Present your memories of the TV show to the class with your partner. Which shows does everyone remember?

> To check your progress, go to page 155.

USEFUL PHRASES

DISCUSS
I remember … from my childhood.
What about you?
Let's talk about the characters in …
What were their names?
I liked that show because …

AGREE
What do you remember?
A lot of people / I remember …

PRESENT
We're talking about …
Our show was really popular.
It was on TV in (year).

11.5 TIME TO SPEAK
TV memories

LESSON OBJECTIVE
- talk about TV shows from your childhood

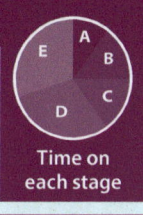

Time on each stage

Introduce the task Choose an old TV show your Ss would like. Display a picture or show a short video clip online. Write *characters' names*, *ages*, *personalities*, and *places* on the board. Write the information from the TV show next to the relevant categories as you explain about the show and follow the plan in D on page 116.

VOCABULARY SUPPORT *Character* = a person in a film, book, or TV show.
Personality = the way you behave

- Direct Ss to the **Useful phrases** section at the bottom of the page. Remind them that they can use them at the relevant stages of the lesson.

A PREPARE **Aim: Ss talk about TV shows they remember.**
- Consider giving other options for Ss who might not have watched TV, don't have smartphones, and/or don't remember a TV show. Suggest they do the task with memorable movies or books.
- PAIR WORK Ss make a list of the shows they remember.

B AGREE **Do the task Aim: Ss share their ideas.**
- CLASS WORK Ask Ss to circulate and talk to classmates, carrying their lists from Activity A to remember which TV shows to talk about. Monitor.

C DISCUSS **Aim: Ss discuss the TV shows in detail.**
- PAIR WORK Ask Ss to work with their original partner again. They choose one of the shows and discuss the questions together. Circulate and monitor.

D PREPARE **Aim: Ss prepare their presentation.**
- CLASS WORK Go through the instructions carefully and refer Ss to the presentation you gave at the start of the class.
- INDIVIDUALLY Ss prepare to present their favorite childhood TV show.
- **Preparation for speaking*** Encourage Ss to rehearse what they are going to say in their heads. Ss could record themselves speaking, listen to the recording, and make a note of how to improve.

E PRESENT **Review Aim: Ss give their presentations to the class.**
- CLASS WORK Set a time limit, say two minutes, for Ss to present their memories to the class. If Ss don't want to speak to the whole class, allow them to do their presentations in small groups. As Ss speak, take notes on language usage so you can give feedback later.*
- **Feedback for speaking activities*** Give the class positive feedback based on the notes you made earlier in the activity.

*These tips can help you to create a safe speaking environment. They can also be used with other speaking activities. For more information, see page T-xxii.

PROGRESS CHECK

Direct students to page 156 to check their progress.
Go to page T-152 for Progress check activity suggestions.

TEACHER DEVELOPMENT REFLECTION

You can answer these questions in a reflection journal or discuss them with your peers.

1. In planning Development Activity 1, which adjectives and which aspects of meaning did you choose to focus on? Why? Will you change your choices if you use this material again?
2. Were the questions clear to Ss? What about the answers? Were there any areas of confusion? How could these have been avoided?
3. Development Activity 2 highlights how color words, and adjectives in English generally, can be placed in sentences. What questions or techniques did you use to make the patterns clear to your Ss?
4. List three or four other kinds of vocabulary for which this activity would be useful. (It is particularly suited to focusing on things like word order, dependent prepositions, and grammar patterns associated with words.)

T-116

STOP, EAT, GO

12

TEACHER DEVELOPMENT INTRODUCTION

Strategy 3: Building learners' confidence to speak – Providing feedback on spoken language

In Unit 9, we looked at ways of listening to the spoken language that students produce. When you hear incorrect language, you need to decide how you'll correct it. There are two possibilities: you can correct the language as students are talking, or you can make a note of the error and give feedback to the class as a whole. Correcting immediately means students get instant feedback, which they often find useful. However, it can interrupt the flow and fluency of their speaking. Giving feedback after the activity to the whole class means that all students get the benefit of the feedback. It's important not to say who made the mistake because this can cause embarrassment. Pages 94 to 96 of Penny Ur's *A Course in English Language Teaching, Second Edition* (Cambridge University Press 2012) describes different ways of correcting students. Please go to www.cambridge.org/evolve to download these pages.

INTRODUCE THE THEME OF THE UNIT

Books closed. Write three meals on the board: *breakfast, lunch,* and *dinner*. Ask Ss: *What time do you eat dinner?* Elicit answers.

- Display or dictate: *What did you eat yesterday for breakfast, lunch, and dinner?* Ss work in pairs and tell each other the information. They can use their smartphones to show pictures, if needed. Elicit answers when they finish.

UNIT OBJECTIVES

Read the unit objectives aloud. Tell Ss to listen and read along. Explain any vocabulary that Ss might not understand.

START SPEAKING

A Ss look at the picture and discuss in pairs. Elicit answers as a class.

B Ss discuss in pairs before you elicit answers.

C Ss can use any of the ideas from the start of this lesson to help them. Ask Ss to share their ideas.

T-117

UNIT OBJECTIVES
- talk about snacks and small meals
- talk about meals in restaurants
- offer and accept food and drink
- write a restaurant review
- create a menu for a restaurant

STOP, EAT, GO

12

START SPEAKING

A Which meal do you think these men are eating: breakfast, lunch, or dinner? Is it a big meal or a small meal? Are they enjoying their food?

B For a good meal, you need good food – and what else? Do you see these things in the picture?

C Talk about a good meal you remember. You can talk about where and when it was, who you were with, and why it was good.

12.1 BACKPACKING AND SNACKING

LESSON OBJECTIVE
- talk about snacks and small meals

1 VOCABULARY: Snacks and small meals

A 🔊 2.52 **PAIR WORK** Listen and repeat. Then choose something you want to eat now.

apple | beef | butter | chicken | crackers | orange | potato | soup

banana | bread | cheese | coconut | lamb | pineapple | sandwich | tomato

> **!** To make these words plural, add *-s* or *-es*:
> banana → banana**s**   tomato → tomato**es**   sandwich → sandwich**es**
> Some nouns are non-count, for example *cheese* and *soup*.

B ▸ Now do the vocabulary exercises for 12.1 on page 151.

C **PAIR WORK** Look at the pictures in exercise 1A and find:
- <u>seven</u> words for fruit and vegetables
- <u>three</u> words for meat
- <u>two</u> words for dairy products
- <u>two</u> words for grain products
- <u>two</u> words for small meals

2 LANGUAGE IN CONTEXT

A Read the blog. Where was Tyler yesterday? Where was he last week?

B Read again. Check (✓) the sentences that are true. Correct the false ones.
- ☐ 1 Tyler's breakfast and lunch were big.
- ☐ 2 There was meat in Tyler's sandwich.
- ☐ 3 There were dairy products in Tyler's breakfast, lunch, and dinner.
- ☐ 4 There are dairy products and fruit in *locro*.

TRAVEL WITH TYLER

Hello from Salvador, Brazil! I'm happy to be here after a really long trip. Yesterday, I took the bus from Aracaju. I didn't eat a lot for breakfast before the trip – just some **bread** and **butter**. Then I was on the bus for seven hours. We stopped in a lot of places, but I stayed on the bus, so I didn't have a big lunch. I ate some **crackers** and a **banana**, and I drank a bottle of warm water (yuck!)

I arrived in Salvador in the afternoon, and I was *really* hungry, so I didn't wait. I had dinner at the bus station! I went to a food stand, and I bought a *bauru* **sandwich**. It's bread with **beef**, **cheese**, and **tomatoes**. I needed it! And I liked it – I'm going to eat it again tomorrow.

South American food is great. Last week, in Quito, Ecuador, I tried *locro*. It's a **soup** with **potatoes** and cheese. I love the fruit in South America, too, but because I'm "backpacking and snacking," it's not always easy to eat. You can't eat **pineapples** and **coconuts** on a bus!

GLOSSARY
food stand (*n*) a place to buy food on the street
hungry (*adj*) you need to eat

12.1 BACKPACKING AND SNACKING

LESSON OBJECTIVE
- talk about snacks and small meals

Introduce the lesson Elicit from Ss the three main meals – *breakfast*, *lunch*, and *dinner* – and write them on the board. Then write, dictate, or display: *What's your favorite meal?*

- In pairs, Ss discuss what foods they eat for their favorite meal. Elicit responses from the class.
- Write *snack* on the board. Explain that a snack is a small amount of food people eat between meals. Ask Ss: *Do you eat snacks? When do you eat them?* Elicit responses.

1 VOCABULARY: Snacks and small meals

A 🔊 **2.52** **Present the vocabulary** Play the audio. Pause after each word for Ss to repeat together. Check for pronunciation. Ss share what they want to eat now with the class.

- Ask Ss to read the **Notice** box aloud.

> **VOCABULARY SUPPORT** Plurals are usually made by adding an *s* to the noun, but there are spelling variations. After a vowel *o*, *ch*, and *sh*, add *-es*.
>
> This vocabulary set is an opportunity to review non-count nouns (*beef, bread, butter, cheese, chicken, lamb, soup*).

> 📎 **EXTRA ACTIVITY**
>
> Ask Ss to complete a class survey by circulating and asking the following question to their classmates: *What is your favorite snack?*
> - Ss can use their smartphone to find and show pictures of unknown words. They should make a list of what other Ss like.
>
> Find out what the most popular snack is from your class. Write new vocabulary for food on the board for Ss to copy and remember.

B **Direct Ss to page 151** to complete the vocabulary exercises. Teacher's tips for vocabulary exercises are on page T-141.

C **PAIR WORK** **Do the task** Ask volunteers to read the categories aloud. Check for meaning by eliciting one example from each category.

- Ss complete the task in pairs before you elicit their answers as a group.

> **Answers**
> Fruit and Vegetables: coconut, pineapple, apple, banana, orange, tomato, potato
> Meat: chicken, beef, lamb
> Dairy products: butter, cheese
> Grain products: bread, crackers
> Small meals: soup, sandwich

2 LANGUAGE IN CONTEXT

A **Read the questions as a class.** Set a time limit for Ss to read the blog, say three minutes. They should focus on answering the questions and not worry about words they don't understand. Ss check their answers with a partner before you ask for the correct answers.

> **Answers**
> Yesterday he was in Aracaju. Last week he was in Quito, Ecuador.

> **VOCABULARY SUPPORT** *Yuck* means food or drink is horrible. *Mmmm* means food or drink is delicious.

B **Ask Ss to read again quietly** and decide if the sentences are true or false. Ss check their answers with a partner.

- Ask Ss to read the full sentences as you elicit answers. Write the corrected sentences on the board so Ss can copy them down.

> **Answers**
> 1 False. Tyler's breakfast and lunch were small.
> 2 True.
> 3 False. There weren't dairy products in Tyler's lunch.
> 4 False. There are dairy products and vegetables in *locro*.

> 📎 **EXTRA ACTIVITY**
>
> Play board scrabble with the words from this unit. For details on how to play, see page T-217.

T-118

3 GRAMMAR: Simple past statements

A **Present the grammar** Before Ss circle the answers, explain that they can refer to the examples in the grammar box.

> **Answers**
> 1 finished events   2 the same   3 -d or -ed   4 didn't

> **GRAMMAR SUPPORT** You can concept check negative and affirmative forms by saying positive sentences to Ss and having them make the sentences negative. e.g.,
> *I went to a restaurant. – I didn't go to a restaurant.*
> *She had a banana. – She didn't have a banana.*
> Ss quickly pick up the addition of *didn't* to make past tense sentences negative. Remind Ss not to make the verb after *didn't* past tense as well.
> *I didn't went to work.* = incorrect
> *I didn't go to work.* = correct

> **EXTRA ACTIVITY**
> Explain to Ss that a good way to learn vocabulary and spelling is to *look, say, cover, write, check*. Ss look at the word and say it, they then cover the word, and write it again. Then they check it. Writing words three or four times will help Ss remember.

B **Do the task** Have ss read the **Notice** box first, then ask Ss to circle the correct word individually before they share their answers with a partner. Check as a class.

> **Answers**
> 1 It was a really big sandwich, but I **ate** it all.
> 2 We **had** fish for dinner last night.
> 3 She didn't **buy** any food at the supermarket.
> 4 I was hungry and really **needed** some food.
> 5 We **arrived** at the restaurant at 5:30, but it wasn't open.
> 6 Was the cheese good? I didn't **try** it.

C Direct Ss to page 139 to complete the grammar exercise. Teacher's tips for grammar exercises are on page T-129.

D **PAIR WORK** Review Explain that Ss can use the pictures of food on the previous page to help them. If necessary, model the first sentence as an example.

- Monitor for examples of language used in the lesson. When Ss finish, ask them to read some of their sentences.

4 SPEAKING

A **PAIR WORK** As Ss discuss the food, circulate and monitor, listening for language usage that you can give feedback on at the end of the session.

- **OPTIONAL ACTIVITY** Ss watch June's video and identify the things she likes and doesn't like. They say whether they like / don't like the same things. You may want to explain the meaning of the words *hate* and *ginger*.

> **REAL STUDENT**
> Hello, I'm June. I like coffee. Uh ... I make my own cup of coffee every morning. The food that I really hate is ginger.

B **PAIR WORK** Model the example dialogue with a volunteer. As Ss discuss their meals and snacks, circulate and monitor.

- Ask Ss to share with the class what food they ate last week. Find out if Ss like to eat the same food.

> **EXTRA ACTIVITY**
> Ss do a class survey of the food they ate over the last week.

> **HOMEWORK IDEAS**
> After exercise 3C, tell Ss they are going to have a spelling test on irregular verbs in the next class.

> **TEACHER DEVELOPMENT ACTIVITY 1**
>
> **Providing immediate feedback**
>
> Often with speaking activities, you can predict the kinds of errors that Ss will make. With this activity, it is likely they will have problems using the correct past form and say *Yesterday I eat a sandwich for lunch*. The suggestion below shows how you can give immediate feedback while keeping teacher talk to a minimum.
>
> - Before the lesson, prepare a card with *past?* written on it.
> - Write an incorrect sentence on the board, e.g., *Last Tuesday I have four cups of coffee*. Elicit from Ss that it is incorrect and hold up your *past?* card and elicit the correct form.
> - Tell Ss you will use this card when you listen to them talk.
> - As Ss talk together in pairs, monitor and listen. When you hear an incorrect past form, hold up the *past?* card and get the S to self-correct.

3 GRAMMAR: Simple past statements

A Circle the correct answers. Use the sentences in the grammar box to help you.
1. Use the simple past to talk about **finished events** / **events that are happening now**.
2. After *I, you, he, she, we, they* and *it*, simple past verbs have **the same** / **different** spelling.
3. Simple past verbs can be regular or irregular. To make most regular past simple verbs, add **-d or -ed** / **-s**.
4. To make negative statements in the simple past, use **don't** / **didn't** + verb (for example, *eat, drink,* or *have*).

> **Simple past statements**
>
> Yesterday, I **took** the bus from Aracaju.
> I **had** some soup. He **had** a big dinner.
> She **wanted** an orange. We **wanted** some apples.
>
> I **didn't eat** a lot for breakfast.
> She **didn't like** the sandwich.
> They **didn't drink** the coffee.

> **!** Irregular past simple verbs do not end in *-ed*. For example, *I took the bus*, **not** *I taked the bus*.
> eat → ate   drink → drank   have → had   go → went   take → took   buy → bought
> For more irregular verbs, go to page 161.

B Read the information about irregular verbs in the Notice box. Then circle the correct words.
1. It was a really big sandwich, but I *ate / eat* it all.
2. We *have / had* fish for dinner last night.
3. She didn't *buy / bought* food at the supermarket.
4. I was hungry and really *needed / need* some food.
5. We *arrive / arrived* at the restaurant at 5:30, but it wasn't open.
6. Was the cheese good? I didn't *tried / try* it.

C ▶ Now go to page 139. Look at the grammar charts and do the grammar exercise for 12.1.

D PAIR WORK Complete the sentences so they're true for you. Then compare with a partner.
1. For breakfast, I ate _____, and I drank _____.
2. Last week, I bought _____ at the supermarket.
3. The last movie I watched was _____.
4. Last weekend, I went to _____ with _____.

4 SPEAKING

A PAIR WORK Talk about the food in exercise 1A. Say which things you like and which you don't like. For ideas, watch June's video.

REAL STUDENT
Do you like/not like the same things as June?

B PAIR WORK Give examples of snacks and small meals you ate last week. Ask your partner questions about what they ate.

> Yesterday, I ate a sandwich for lunch.

> Was it good?

119

12.2 WHAT DID YOU EAT?

LESSON OBJECTIVE
- talk about meals in restaurants

1 VOCABULARY: Food, drinks, and desserts

A 🔊 2.53 Look at the pictures. Listen and repeat.

B PAIR WORK Which things in exercise 1A are drinks? Which are desserts? Which ones do you like? Which <u>don't</u> you like?

C ▶ Now do the vocabulary exercises for 12.2 on page 151.

D GROUP WORK What do you usually eat and drink for breakfast, lunch, and dinner? Tell your group. For ideas, watch Anderson's video.

REAL STUDENT

What's Anderson's food routine? Is your routine the same or different?

Labels: rice, steak, black beans, eggs, pizza, soda, fish, green beans, ice cream, chocolate cake, juice, water

2 LANGUAGE IN CONTEXT

A 🔊 2.54 Jackie and Yoo-ri are writing comments on a restaurant review card. Read and listen. Did they like their meal?

B 🔊 2.54 Read and listen again. What did Jackie and Yoo-ri eat? What did they drink?

🔊 2.54 Audio script

Jackie Look, a comment card. Let's do it.
Yoo-ri OK. We have time before dessert.
Jackie Number one. "What did you eat?" You had **fish** and **rice**. Did you have any vegetables?
Yoo-ri Yeah. I had beans, **black beans**.
Jackie That's right. And I had the **steak** with potatoes and **green beans**. OK. Number 2. "What did you drink?" I just had **water**. Did you have apple **juice**?
Yoo-ri No, I didn't have any juice. I had a **soda**.
Jackie Oh, yeah. OK, number 3. "How was the food?" My steak was great, but I didn't like the potatoes. The green beans were OK. Did you like the fish?
Yoo-ri Yes, I did. It was wonderful, and the rice and beans were good, too. But my soda was warm.
Jackie Hmm … I'm going to check "good." Ah, the server is coming with dessert. Oh, wow! Look at our **chocolate cake** and **ice cream**.
Yoo-ri Yum! Change "good" to "great!"

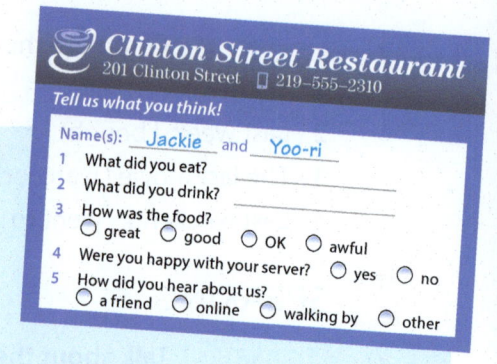

Clinton Street Restaurant
201 Clinton Street 📞 219–555–2310

Tell us what you think!

Name(s): __Jackie__ and __Yoo-ri__
1. What did you eat? ____
2. What did you drink? ____
3. How was the food?
   ○ great ○ good ○ OK ○ awful
4. Were you happy with your server? ○ yes ○ no
5. How did you hear about us?
   ○ a friend ○ online ○ walking by ○ other

INSIDER ENGLISH

Some people use *waiter* for a man and *waitress* for a woman. But these days, many people use the word *server* for a man or a woman.

120

12.2 WHAT DID YOU EAT?

LESSON OBJECTIVE
- talk about meals in restaurants

Introduce the lesson Tell Ss about the last restaurant you visited. Explain where it was and what you ate. Display or draw a picture of the food and the restaurant if possible. Write the following questions on the board and answer them:

What did you eat? / What did you drink? / How was the food?

Encourage Ss to ask questions about the restaurant.

1 VOCABULARY: Food, drinks, and desserts

A 🔊 **2.53** **Present the vocabulary** Play the audio, pausing after each word or phrase. Ask Ss to repeat the words aloud together. Check for pronunciation.

B PAIR WORK **Do the task** Ss work in pairs to answer the questions before you elicit and write the answers on the board.

> **Answers**
> Juice, soda, and water are drinks.
> Chocolate cake and ice cream are desserts.
> Answers may vary for likes and dislikes.

C Direct Ss to page 151 to complete the vocabulary exercises. Teacher's tips for vocabulary exercises are on page T-141.

D GROUP WORK Before they begin the activity, tell Ss the food that you usually eat. They can use your language as a model. Ss answer the questions in pairs before you elicit their ideas.

- **OPTIONAL ACTIVITY** Ss watch Anderson's video and listen for the three meals that he mentions. They say whether their food routine is similar or different. You may want to explain that *something light* means *a small meal*.

> **REAL STUDENT**
> Hi. I am Anderson. At breakfast, I drink coffee. At lunch, I eat Japanese food, and at dinner I eat something light.

2 LANGUAGE IN CONTEXT

A 🔊 **2.54** **Do the task** Read and explain the instructions. Play the audio as Ss count the questions they answer. Play the audio again if necessary. Elicit answers from Ss.

> **Answers**
> They liked their meal, but Jackie didn't like the potatoes and Yoo-ri's soda was warm.

B 🔊 **2.54** **Review** Ss read and understand the sentences before you play the audio, and then answer the questions. Ss share their answers before you check as a class. Play audio again if necessary.

- Ask volunteers to read the **Insider English** section aloud.
- If time, ask Ss to read and role play the conversation with a partner. Monitor for pronunciation and stress as Ss read. Give feedback on the pronunciation or stress you heard when Ss have finished.

> **Answers**
> Jackie had steak, potatoes, and green beans. Yoo-ri had fish, rice, and black beans. They both had chocolate cake and ice cream.
> Jackie drank water and Yoo-ri had a soda.

> 📎 **EXTRA ACTIVITY**
> Make food flashcards. Collect pictures from the internet or magazines, or draw common pictures of food and drink. Making flashcards can take time, but over many uses, they are worth it. Show Ss the flashcards and ask them to repeat together or individually. Use them for spelling tests. Flashcards are especially useful for lower-level learners.

T-120

3 GRAMMAR: Simple past questions; *any*

A **Introduce the grammar** Before Ss circle the answers, explain that they can refer to the examples in the grammar box.

> **Answers**
> 1 *Did*   2 *before*   3 *yes/no*

- Ask volunteers to read the chart. Point out that *any* can be used with count or non-count nouns. Examples of both are in the chart on page T-141 at the back of the book. Check *yes/no* questions by asking Ss questions. Ask all the Ss a question if possible, e.g., *Did you drink coffee yesterday?* to elicit *Yes, I did.* or *No, I didn't.*
- Then, ask simple information questions, e.g.,
  > *What did you have for breakfast?*
  Try to make questions relevant to your Ss.

> **EXTRA ACTIVITY**
> Ask Ss to write one or two questions in the past tense to ask you. The questions must be about food or restaurants. Check that Ss' sentences are correct before you allow them to ask their questions. Alternatively, Ss use their questions to have a circle discussion about food and restaurants.

B **PAIR WORK** Ss check their sentences with a partner before you elicit answers as a class. Ask Ss to read the complete sentence aloud when you make corrections.

- Monitor as Ss ask and answer the questions with their partners.

> **Answers**
> 1 **A** Did, eat
>   **B** did
> 2 **A** did, have
>   **B** had
> 3 **A** Did, go out
>   **B** didn't
> 4 **A** did, buy
>   **B** bought, didn't buy
> 5 **A** Did, give
>   **B** didn't

C Direct Ss to page 140 to complete the grammar exercise. Teacher's tips for grammar exercises are on page T-129.

D **PAIR WORK** Review Allow Ss time to write their sentences. Circulate and correct their work as they write.

- When Ss finish, elicit some questions and write these on the board.

> **Suggested answers**
> What did you do (yesterday morning / in the afternoon / last Tuesday / in April)?
> Did you have (a banana for breakfast / pizza for lunch / Mexican food for dinner) yesterday?
> Where did you go (last night / on Thursday / last summer)?
> Answers to the questions may vary.

- As Ss talk to each other, circulate and take note of language usage that you can give feedback on when the task is over. Elicit answers as a class.

4 SPEAKING

A **PAIR WORK** Ask volunteer Ss to read the questions aloud. Check pronunciation and understanding. Allow Ss time to write two more questions; circulate and help Ss as they write. Correct sentences as you go.

B **PAIR WORK** Model the sample sentences by reading them aloud with a volunteer. Monitor as Ss talk to each other. Take note of language usage that you can give feedback on when the task is over.

- When Ss finish, ask volunteers to perform their conversations for the class.
- Elicit ideas and then give feedback.

3 GRAMMAR: Simple past questions; *any*

A Circle the correct answers. Use the information in the grammar box and the Notice box to help you.
1. In simple past *yes/no* questions, use **Did** / **Do** + verb.
2. In simple past information questions, the question word and *did* go **before** / **after** the person or thing.
3. You can use *any* with **yes/no** / **information** questions in the simple past.

Simple past questions

Yes/no questions
Did you have apple juice?
Did she like the fish?
Did they eat any ice cream?

Information questions
How did you hear about us?
What did they eat?

> ! Use *some* in affirmative statements. Use *any* in *yes/no* questions and negative statements.
> I had **some** soup for lunch.
> Did you have **any** dessert?
> They didn't have **any** juice.

B PAIR WORK Complete the conversations with the simple past form of the verbs in parentheses ( ). Then practice with a partner and make the answers true for you.

1. **A** _____ you _____ (eat) breakfast?
   B Yes, I _____ .
2. **A** What _____ you _____ (have) for lunch?
   B I _____ an egg sandwich.
3. **A** _____ your friends _____ (go out) for dinner last night?
   B No, they _____ .
4. **A** What _____ your sisters _____ (buy) at the mall?
   B They _____ some shoes. They _____ any lunch.
5. **A** _____ your teacher _____ (give) you any homework?
   B No, she _____ .

C ▶ Now go to page 140. Look at the grammar charts and do the grammar exercise for 12.2.

D PAIR WORK Write questions with these words. Use your ideas for the words in parentheses ( ). Then ask and answer the questions with a partner.

| what / do / (time or day) | have (food item) / for (meal) / yesterday | where / go / (time or day) |

4 SPEAKING

A PAIR WORK You're going to ask your partner about a meal they had in a restaurant. Ask the questions from the comment card and the box below. Then think of <u>two</u> more questions.

Where did you eat?   Was the food expensive?
Did you have any dessert?   Was the restaurant busy?
Did you wait for a table?   Who did you eat with?

Clinton Street Restaurant
201 Clinton Street   219-555-2310
Tell us what you think!
Name(s): _____ and _____
1. What did you eat? _____
2. What did you drink? _____
3. How was the food?
   ○ great ○ good ○ OK ○ awful
4. Were you happy with your server? ○ yes ○ no
5. How did you hear about us?
   ○ a friend ○ online ○ walking by ○ other

B PAIR WORK Ask and answer the questions from exercise 4A about a meal you ate last week or a favorite meal you had in the past.

> Where did you eat?

> I had dinner at The Fish Dish.

12.3 PLEASE PASS THE BUTTER

LESSON OBJECTIVE
- offer and accept food and drink

1 FUNCTIONAL LANGUAGE

A 🔊 **2.55** Elisa has dinner in two different places on different nights. Read and listen to two conversations. What food and drink does Elisa want? What doesn't she want?

🔊 2.55 Audio script

1
Elisa I really like this fish, Dan. It's so good!
Dan Thanks. **Do you want** some more?
Elisa Yes, please. Thanks. **Can I have** some bread, please?
Dan **Of course.** Here. **Would you like** some potatoes?
Elisa No, thanks, but **please pass** the butter.
Dan OK. **Here you are.**

2
Server What would you like to eat?
Elisa **I'd like** the chicken and rice, please.
Server **All right.** And what would you like to drink?
Elisa **Do you have** iced tea?
Server Yes. **We have** small and large iced teas.
Elisa I'd like a large iced tea, please. It's so hot today!

B Complete the chart with expressions in **bold** from the conversations above. Then read the information in the Accuracy check box. What food does Elisa request with *some*?

Offering food and drink	Requesting food and drink
1 _____ some more?	4 _____ some bread, please?
2 _____ some potatoes?	5 _____ the butter.
3 _____ to eat? / to drink? What would you like for dessert?	6 _____ the chicken and rice, please.
	7 _____ iced tea?

Responding to requests
Of ⁸ _____ .
Here. / Here ⁹ _____ .
All ¹⁰ _____ . / OK.
¹¹ _____ small and large iced teas.

GLOSSARY
more (det) another piece (of fish, for example)
iced tea (n) cold tea

✓ ACCURACY CHECK
Use *any* in questions.
Did you have any vegetables?
You can use *some* when a question is a request.
Can I have ~~any~~ bread? ✗
Can I have some bread? ✓

C 🔊 **2.56** **PAIR WORK** Put the two conversations in the correct order. Listen and check. Then practice with a partner.

1
___ Yes, please. It's good!
___ OK. Here you are.
___ Would you like some more chicken?
___ And please pass the potatoes.

2
___ No, sorry.
___ What would you like for dessert?
___ I see. OK, I'd like ice cream and coffee, please.
___ Let me think. Do you have any chocolate cake?

122

12.3 PLEASE PASS THE BUTTER

LESSON OBJECTIVE
- offer and accept food and drink

Introduce the lesson Scramble the following sentences on the board and ask Ss to unscramble them with a partner.
What would you like to eat?
Can I have a banana please?
Make sure Ss understand the language.

- Ask them to go back to page 118 and look at the food pictures in 12.1. They take turns asking polite questions. Model an example, e.g.,
    A *What would you like to eat?*
    B *Can I have some bread, please?*
- Remind Ss to use *some* with the non-count nouns and *a / an* with the count nouns.

1 FUNCTIONAL LANGUAGE

A 🔊 **2.55** Ask volunteers to read the questions aloud. Check understanding and pronunciation. Play the audio while Ss listen and answer the questions.
- They share their answers with each other before you elicit corrections.

> **Answers**
> Conversation 1: Elisa wants (more) fish, bread, and butter. She doesn't want potatoes.
> Conversation 2: Elisa wants chicken and rice and iced tea.

- Ask Ss to read the scripts in pairs, alternating roles. Monitor as they read.

B Do the task Read the headings and make sure Ss understand the words *offer, request,* and *respond.* Ss complete the chart individually with the words in bold from the text. They check their answers with a partner before you go through them as a class.

> **Answers**
> 1 Do you want
> 2 Would you like
> 3 What would you like
> 4 Can I have
> 5 Please pass
> 6 I'd like
> 7 Do you have
> 8 course
> 9 you are
> 10 right
> 11 We have

- Ask volunteers to read the **Accuracy check** box. Check Ss' understanding by displaying or writing the following sentences, asking Ss to choose the correct alternative.
    1 *Would you like any / some butter?*
    2 *Can I have any / some more dessert?*
    3 *Do you have any / some chocolate cake?*

> **Answers**
> 1 some
> 2 some
> 3 any

C 🔊 **2.56** **PAIR WORK** **Review** Ss work in pairs to order the conversations. Ss share their answers with a partner before you play the audio and they check.

> **Answers**
> **Conversation 1**
> 1 Would you like some more chicken?
> 2 Yes, please. It's good!
> 3 OK. Here you are.
> 4 And please pass the potatoes.
> **Conversation 2**
> 1 What would you like for dessert?
> 2 Let me think. Do you have any chocolate cake?
> 3 No, sorry.
> 4 I see. OK, I'd like ice cream and coffee, please.

- Ask Ss to role play the conversations together. As Ss talk, monitor for pronunciation and stress.

> 📎 **EXTRA ACTIVITY**
>
> Ask Ss to brainstorm as many drinks as they can. Write these on the board, e.g., *coffee, tea, water,* etc. In pairs, ask Ss circulate around the class and ask: *What would you like to drink?* They make note of what other Ss want. Monitor as Ss talk. When Ss finish, bring them back together as a class and find out what drinks Ss like.

2 REAL-WORLD STRATEGY

A **Introduce the task** Books closed. Write the following sentences on the board.

I like fish.
The food is good.

- Write *really* before *like* and *so* before *good*. Ask Ss if the words *really* and *so* change the meaning, to elicit that they make both sentences stronger. Open books, and ask volunteers to read the box at the top of the page.
- Ss answer the questions as a class.

Answers
She uses the adjectives *good* (so good) and *hot* (so hot). She uses the verb *like* (really like).

> **📎 EXTRA ACTIVITY**
>
> Say sentences to Ss and ask them to repeat them back to you putting *really* or *so* into the right place, e.g.,
>
> It's cold today. – It's <u>so</u> cold today.
> She doesn't like meat. – She <u>really</u> doesn't like meat.
> He's hungry – He's <u>so</u> hungry.
> The food is good – The food is <u>really</u> good.
>
> Try to make your sentences relevant and interesting to Ss.

B 🔊 **2.57** **Do the task** Ask a volunteer to read the question aloud. Check for pronunciation and meaning. Play the audio. Ss check their answers with a partner. Elicit answers as a class.

Answers
He asks for more bread.

> 🔊 **2.57 Audio script**
>
> **A** I really like this bread. It's so good.
> **B** That's true.
> **A** Let's ask for more.
> **B** Are you sure? You have steak and potatoes and …
> **A** But this bread is great, Mandy. It's so warm. Excuse me! Can we have more bread, please?

C 🔊 **2.57** Play audio again. Ss write down the answers and share with a partner before you check as a class.

Answers
After *so*, he uses *good* (so good) and *warm* (so warm). After *really*, he uses *like* (really like).

3 PRONUNCIATION: Saying /h/ and /r/ sounds

A 🔊 **2.58** Ss repeat the words, paying attention to the pronunciation of /h/ and /r/. Ask Ss to work in pairs. Are their /h/ and /r/ sounds the same as the speaker's?

B 🔊 **2.59** Ss work in pairs to predict the missing letters.

- Play the audio. Ss check in pairs, then review answers as a whole class. Repeat the words again chorally.

Answers
1 h 2 h 3 r 4 h 5 h 6 r 7 h 8 r

C 🔊 **2.60** **PAIR WORK** Ss practice the conversations in pairs. Monitor and help as needed.

4 SPEAKING

A **PAIR WORK** Ask volunteers to read the situations and make sure Ss understand the tasks. Model the sample dialogue with volunteers.

B **GROUP WORK** Set this up so that pairs work together to complete the task.

- Ask Ss to work with another group.
- When Ss complete the task, bring the class back together and elicit the food and drinks they mentioned.

> **📱 SMARTPHONE ACTIVITY**
>
> In pairs, ask Ss to use the record function on their smartphone to record their conversation. They can share this with you via email or social media. As a class, listen to a few of the recordings and comment on the English you hear – praising the results rather than criticizing.

> **👥 TEACHER DEVELOPMENT ACTIVITY 2**
>
> **Delayed feedback**
> It's often useful to focus on examples of both correct and incorrect language when giving feedback after an activity. You can turn this into a game.
>
> - Ss work on both activities A and B in class.
> - As they do this, listen and note examples of correct and incorrect language, but don't correct it immediately.
> - After the activity, write up on the board eight to twelve examples of language you heard – a mixture of both correct and incorrect language.
> - In small groups, Ss decide which examples are correct and correct the sentences that are wrong.
> - The group(s) with the most correct examples at the end of the activity wins the game.

2 REAL-WORLD STRATEGY

USING *SO* AND *REALLY* TO MAKE WORDS STRONGER

Use *so* before adjectives to make them stronger. Use *really* before some verbs to make them stronger, for example: *like, love, don't like, need (to), want (to), have to*.

Elisa   I really like this fish, Dan. It's so good!
Elisa   I'd like a large iced tea. It's so hot today!

A   Read the information in the box above about making words stronger. What adjectives does Elisa use with *so*? What verb does she use with *really*?

B   🔊 2.57   Listen to a conversation. What does the man ask for?

C   🔊 2.57   Listen again. What words does he use after *so* and *really*?

3 PRONUNCIATION: Saying /h/ and /r/ sounds

A   🔊 2.58   Listen and repeat the words. Focus on the /h/ and /r/ sounds. How are they different?
   /h/ have   /r/ really

B   🔊 2.59   Listen. What sound do you hear? Write /h/ or /r/.
   1   ___ ear   3   ___ ight   5   ___ appy   7   ___ ad
   2   ___ ave   4   ___ ead   6   ___ ice   8   ___ ed

C   🔊 2.60   **PAIR WORK**   Listen. Then practice the conversations with a partner. Does your partner say /h/ and /r/ clearly?

   1   A   How is your food?
       B   It's good. I really like this rice.

   2   A   Where did you go last night?
       B   We had dinner at The Happy Home restaurant.

   3   A   How did you hear about us?
       B   I had an email from a friend. He really likes the food here.

4 SPEAKING

A   **PAIR WORK**   Have a conversation. Use exercise 1C for an example. Choose **one** of these situations:
   - You're at a friend's home. One person offers food. The other person asks for things.
   - You're at a restaurant. One person is a server. The other person orders a meal.
   - You're at a café. One person is a server. The other person orders a drink and a snack.

   Would you like some chicken, Matias?
   Yes, please.

B   **GROUP WORK**   Have your conversation again, in front of another pair. Listen. What situation in exercise 4A is it? What food and drink do they talk about?

12.4 WHAT DID THE REVIEWERS SAY?

LESSON OBJECTIVE
- write a restaurant review

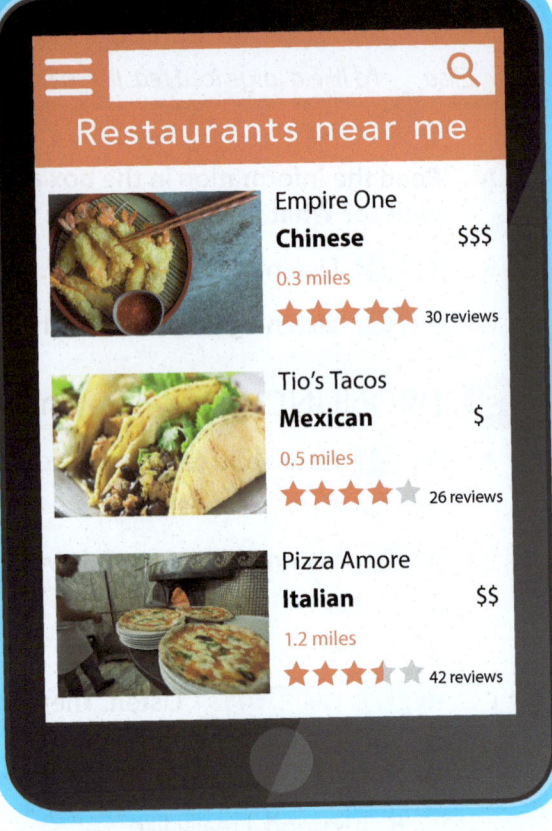

1 LISTENING

A Look at the pictures. What are the people doing? Do you use similar apps?

B 🔊 2.61 **LISTEN FOR DETAILS** Listen to the conversation. What food does Mara want to eat?

C 🔊 2.61 **LISTEN FOR SUPPORTING DETAILS** Circle the reasons for each statement. Sometimes, there is more than one answer.

1. Eric wants to eat at a restaurant near where they are.
   - a He likes to eat in the car.
   - b His favorite restaurants are in the area.
   - c He's hungry.
2. Mara and Eric don't go to Fish Around.
   - a Mara doesn't like fish.
   - b Mara ate there in the past.
   - c Eric had a bad meal there.
3. They don't go to Kayla B's Kitchen.
   - a The food was bad.
   - b It took a long time to get food.
   - c The restaurant isn't new.
4. They go to Tio's Tacos.
   - a It has good reviews.
   - b Mara had a good meal there before.
   - c It's Eric's favorite restaurant.

2 PRONUNCIATION: Listening for *Do you want to ... ?*

A 🔊 2.62 Listen and repeat. Focus on the underlined words. How is the pronunciation different than the written words?

1. Where <u>do you want to</u> eat?
2. <u>Do you want</u> Chinese, Mexican, or Italian food?

B 🔊 2.63 Listen to three speakers. How do they say *want to*? Match the speaker (1–3) with the pronunciation (a–c).

a wanna ___   b /dʒu/ want ___   c /dʒu/ wanna ___

124

12.4 WHAT DID THE REVIEWERS SAY?

LESSON OBJECTIVE
- write a restaurant review

Introduce the lesson Write the name of a local restaurant and rate it by drawing one to five stars below the name. Explain the idea of a *review*.

- Write the names of three restaurants on the board that your Ss will know. Then write these categories: *servers, time, food, price*
- Ss rate the restaurants using 1–5 stars for each category, where one star means bad and five stars means good. Explain that *time* means how long it takes to get your food. Ss work individually to complete the chart before discussing with a partner.

1 LISTENING

A **Introduce the task** Ss look at the pictures and discuss the questions in pairs. Elicit their answers as a class.

> **Suggested answers**
> They are looking at their phone. They want to find a restaurant.

B 🔊 **2.61 Do the task** Play the audio for Ss. Remind them to listen closely to Mara's lines. Ss check their answer with a partner before you check as a class.

> **Answer**
> Mara wants to eat Mexican food.

> 🔊 **2.61 Audio script**
>
> Mara So, Eric, where do you want to eat?
> Eric Why don't we go to Fish Around? I'm hungry, and it's near here.
> Mara No. I mean, I love their food, but I ate there last week. How about Kayla B's Kitchen?
> Eric Ugh, no. I went there with Freddy in November. My steak was awful, and the servers were really slow.
> Mara OK. Well, we can try a new place. What else is near here? Let's look on the app.
> Eric Good idea. OK, there are a lot of places near here. Do you want Chinese, Mexican, or Italian food?
> Mara Uh … Mexican, I think.
> Eric We can try Tio's Tacos. It's not very expensive, and it has good reviews.
> Mara How many stars does it have?
> Eric Four.
> Mara That's good! What do the reviewers say?
> Eric Let's see … One man says, "My meal was great, and the servers were really friendly." And a woman says, "The food is really good. I didn't get any dessert, but the chocolate cake looked wonderful. And the fruit juices … ."
> Mara OK, OK. You don't need to read more. Let's go!

C 🔊 **2.61 Review** Play the audio again. Ask Ss to check their answers with a partner before you elicit them as a class. Encourage Ss to read full sentences.

> **Answers**
> 1 c 2 b 3 a, b 4 a

2 PRONUNCIATION: Listening for *Do you want to … ?*

A 🔊 **2.62** Play the audio and have Ss repeat. Explain that the speaker is using shorter forms of the written words. This is common in spoken English.

> **Answers**
> 1 /dʒu/ wanna   2 /dʒu/ want

B 🔊 **2.63** Before you play the audio, guide Ss through pronouncing the options to preview what they will listen for. Then play the audio. Ss compare answers with a partner.

> **Answers**
> wanna: 2
> /dʒuː/ want: 1
> /dʒuː/ wanna: 3

> 🔊 **2.63 Audio script**
>
> 1 /dʒu/ want some dessert?
> 2 I don't wanna go to class today.
> 3 /dʒu/ wanna go to Fish Around?

> 📌 **EXTRA ACTIVITY**
>
> Write, dictate, or display sentences for Ss to practice saying, e.g.,
>
> > *Do you want a coffee?*
> > *What do you want to do today?*
>
> Ask Ss to practice saying the sentences in pairs. Monitor for pronunciation.

2 WRITING

A **Introduce the task** Read the instructions aloud with Ss. Allow them time to read the reviews on their own. Elicit answers from the class.

- Ask Ss to read the reviews again. They can ask a partner or check a dictionary for questions about any challenging words or expressions.

> **Answers**
> Frank ate vegetable soup, fish, rice, and ice cream. Julieta ate fish, potatoes, pineapple cake, and coconut ice cream. Frank liked the fish best. Julieta liked the pineapple cake and coconut ice cream best.

> **VOCABULARY SUPPORT** Frank probably uses quotation marks around the word *forest* to show that there weren't a lot of plants in the restaurant.

B **PAIR WORK** While Ss discuss, circulate and monitor. If your class is less confident, you may want to do this activity as a whole group.

> **Suggested answers**
> Frank liked his meal. He thinks the restaurant is nice. He loves fish, and their fish was great. The servers were so friendly. The meal wasn't expensive. He gave the restaurant four stars.
> Julieta didn't really like her meal, but the potatoes were OK and she loved the dessert. She didn't choose the restaurant. She went because her friends wanted to go there. She doesn't like fish. She likes meat, but there wasn't any on the menu. She gave the restaurant three stars, but only because the dessert was so great.

C Ss underline items in pairs before you elicit answers. Ask Ss to underline more food items in the reviews themselves.

> **Answers**
> My brother had <u>fish</u> and <u>vegetables</u>.
> I had <u>vegetable soup</u>, <u>fish</u>, and <u>rice</u>.
> In the reviews: dessert, cake, ice cream, potatoes, pineapple cake, coconut ice cream.

D Read the rules aloud with Ss. Give examples for each one, e.g., *We bought chips and candy. She ate fruit, eggs, and bread for breakfast.*

- Ss underline the words in the reviews individually before you check as a class.

> **Answers**
> 1 Don't 2 before
> **Frank B.**
> This is a nice restaurant. It's big, and has a lot of windows, so it's very light. There are some tall plants in the main dining room, but it isn't a "forest." I had <u>vegetable soup, fish, and rice</u>. The soup was good. I love fish, and the fish was great! My brother had <u>fish and vegetables</u>, and he liked his meal, too. We both had dessert. <u>He had cake and I had ice cream</u>. The servers were so friendly. We were really happy with our meal, and it wasn't expensive.
> **Julieta F.**
> I think this is a good restaurant, but I didn't choose it. My friends like fish, so they wanted to eat here. I like meat, but there wasn't any meat on the menu. Was the food good? Well, my friends liked it. They had <u>fish, vegetables, rice, and dessert</u>. I had <u>fish and potatoes</u>. The potatoes were OK. The fish was … well, it was fish! For dessert, I had <u>pineapple cake and coconut ice cream</u>. Wow! It was so good! I'm giving this restaurant three stars because the dessert was so great. The servers were nice. The price was OK – not cheap, but not expensive.

- Read the **Register check** as a class. Ask students to write a question that they can answer themselves and then write the answer, e.g., *Did I like the food? Yes, I did!*

E **Introduce the task** After you read the instructions as a class, ask Ss to spend a few minutes thinking about the information they will put in their review. Suggest that Ss create a chart like the one you completed on the board to introduce the lesson. Allow them to use those categories or other features of the restaurant, like its appearance. If necessary, offer help with adjectives, e.g.,

the servers [friendly, unfriendly, helpful]
the time [fast, slow, average]
the food [nice, horrible, delicious, awful]
the price [expensive, cheap, ok]

This should give Ss lots of ideas and language they can use when they write their review.

- **Do the task** As Ss write, circulate and monitor. Remind Ss to use the reviews in exercise 3A to help them.
- Help Ss with challenging words by writing them on the board.

F **GROUP WORK** **Review** Put Ss in groups of four. Ask them to read each other's reviews. Ss decide which restaurants they would like to eat at. Encourage Ss to explain why.

> 📎 **FOLLOW UP ACTIVITY**
> Display the restaurant reviews around the classroom and ask Ss to circulate and read each other's. Have a class vote on which restaurant Ss find most appealing. Read this review aloud to Ss.

3 WRITING

A Read two reviews of the restaurant Fish Around. What did Frank and Julieta eat? What was their favorite thing?

Fish Around
Los Angeles, United States

$$ Fish ★★★★☆ 98 reviews

Frank B. ★★★★☆

Los Angeles, USA This is a nice restaurant. It's big, and it has a lot of windows, so it's very light. There are some tall plants in the dining area, but it isn't a "forest." I had vegetable soup, fish, and rice. The soup was good. I love fish, and the fish was great! My brother had fish and vegetables, and he liked his meal, too. We both had dessert. He had cake and I had ice cream. The servers were so friendly. We were really happy with our meal, and it wasn't expensive.

Julieta F. ★★★☆☆

Buenos Aires, Argentina I think this is a good restaurant, but I didn't choose it. My friends like fish, so they wanted to eat here. I like meat, but there wasn't any meat on the menu. Was the food good? Well, my friends liked it. They had fish, vegetables, rice, and dessert. I had fish and potatoes. The potatoes were OK. The fish was … well, it was fish! For dessert, I had pineapple cake and coconut ice cream. Wow! It was so good! I'm giving this restaurant three stars because the dessert was so great. The servers were nice. The price was OK – not cheap, but not expensive.

B [PAIR WORK] [THINK CRITICALLY] Did Frank and Julieta like their meals? Why or why not?

C Read the sentences from the reviews. Underline the things the people ate.

My brother had fish and vegetables.
I had vegetable soup, fish, and rice.

> **REGISTER CHECK**
>
> In informal writing, you can sometimes ask and answer your own questions.
>
> *Was the food good? Well, my friends liked it.*

D [WRITING SKILLS] Read the rules about writing lists, below. (Circle) the correct answers. Use the sentences in exercise 3C to help you. Then underline all the lists of food in the reviews.

1 To list two things, you can join them with *and*. **Do / don't** use a comma (,) between two things.
2 To list three or more things, you can use a comma (,) between the things. Use *and* **before / after** the last thing.

⏱ WRITE IT

E Write a review of a restaurant you like. You can write about:
- the restaurant's appearance
- the food you ate
- your opinion about the food
- your opinion about the servers
- the price of the food

F [GROUP WORK] Read other people's reviews. Would you like to eat at any of the restaurants?

12.5 TIME TO SPEAK
Recipe for a great restaurant

LESSON OBJECTIVE
- create a menu for a restaurant

A DISCUSS Talk about a great restaurant you went to, and say why you liked it. Then talk about a bad restaurant, and say why you didn't like it.

B PREPARE Talk about what makes a great restaurant. Think about the things you discussed in exercise A and the things below. Then compare your ideas with other people.

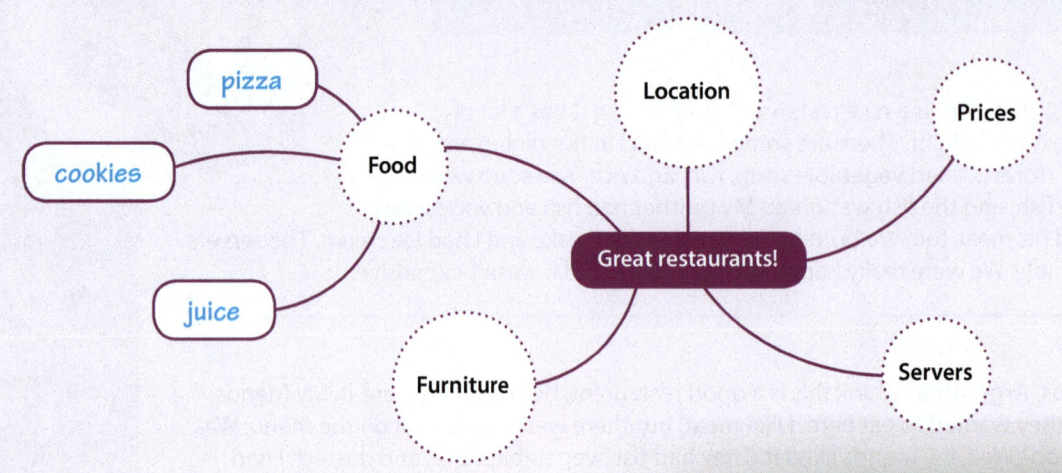

- pizza
- cookies
- juice
- Food
- Location
- Prices
- Furniture
- Servers
- Great restaurants!

C DECIDE [FIND IT] Work with a partner. Imagine you're opening a new restaurant. Choose a name for your restaurant and talk about the food and drink it has. Then create a great menu. You can go online to find ideas.

D ROLE PLAY Work with another pair. Welcome them to your restaurant. They choose a meal from your menu. Then change roles. Continue with other pairs.

E PRESENT Tell the class about some of the menus in exercise D. Were they good? What did you choose? What's your favorite menu?

To check your progress, go to page 155.

USEFUL PHRASES

DECIDE
OK. First, what's the name of our restaurant?
What kind of food do we have?
Let's plan a great menu. We can have …

ROLE PLAY
Welcome to our restaurant!
What would you like to eat/drink?
Do you have … ?
So, you would like …

PRESENT
We went to a great restaurant. Its name was …
We liked / didn't like …
Our favorite menu is … because …

126

12.5 TIME TO SPEAK
Recipe for a great restaurant

LESSON OBJECTIVE
- create a menu for a restaurant

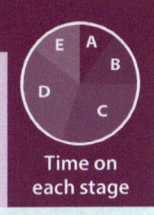

Time on each stage

Introduce the lesson Write *Takeout menu* on the board. Elicit the kinds of food that takeout restaurants serve, like pizza, fries, and hamburgers. Write these on the board and a price next to each one, e.g.,

Takeout menu
Hamburger $6.50
Pizza $8.00
Fries $3.00

Ask Ss: *What would you like?* to elicit *I'd like [a hamburger], please.* Ask Ss to order from your takeout menu in pairs. Monitor for pronunciation as they talk.

- Direct Ss to the **Useful phrases** box at the bottom of the page. Remind them that they can use them at the relevant stages of the lesson.

A DISCUSS **Aim: Ss discuss a restaurant they like.**
- PAIR WORK Allow time for Ss to discuss the topics together. Monitor and listen for language usage.
- **Preparation for speaking*** Give Ss time to review relevant vocabulary notes or look up words in a dictionary or on their smartphone.
- CLASS WORK Elicit ideas from the class.

B PREPARE **Aim: Ss talk about what makes a great restaurant.**
- CLASS WORK Read the headings and elicit some ideas from Ss for each one.
- PAIR WORK Circulate and monitor as Ss discuss.
- CLASS WORK Elicit ideas.

C DECIDE **Do the task Aim: Ss create a new restaurant.**
- CLASS WORK Elicit from Ss different types of restaurants and write them on the board, e.g., *Japanese, Mexican, pizza place, sandwich shop,* etc. Direct Ss to write the headings from Activity B and brainstorm ideas for their restaurant. Encourage Ss to use the **Decide** phrases from the **Useful phrases** box.
- PAIR WORK Ss create their menu. Circulate and monitor, offering suggestions and ideas.

D ROLE PLAY **Aim: Pairs share their restaurant with others.**
- CLASS WORK Work with a pair of volunteers and model a role play using examples from the **Useful phrases** box. As Ss talk, take notes on language usage.

E PRESENT Review **Aim: Ss talk about the restaurants they visited.**
- CLASS WORK Post the menus to the walls of the classroom. Ask Ss to circulate and read each one. Have a class vote on which one is the best. Elicit Ss' opinions on the restaurants they visited.
- **Feedback for speaking activities*** Give the class positive feedback based on the notes you made earlier in the activity.

*These tips can help you to create a safe speaking environment. They can also be used with other speaking activities. For more information, see page T-xxii.

» PROGRESS CHECK »

Direct students to page 155 to check their progress.
Go to page T-153 for Progress check activity suggestions.

TEACHER DEVELOPMENT REFLECTION

Either answer these questions yourself in a reflection journal or discuss them with your peers.

1. How easy do you find it to give Ss immediate feedback on errors? What do you need to be sensitive to when interrupting them to correct?
2. Some Ss want all their mistakes to be corrected immediately. Do you think it is possible to do this? Why or why not?
3. Which of Penny Ur's suggestions on page 95 did you try? Which worked best with most of your Ss? Why?
4. Penny Ur suggests that teachers should use "their professional judgement" when deciding whether to correct immediately or delay feedback. What's your opinion on this?
5. How easy was it for Ss to recognize correct examples of language in the second activity? Why do you think this is the case?

T-126

REVIEW 4 (UNITS 10–12)

Introduce the review Before beginning the review, write *Grammar*, *Vocabulary*, and *Functional language* on the board.
- Set a time limit of two minutes. Ss close their books and work in small groups to remember as much as they can about the grammar, vocabulary, and functional language of Units 10–12. Groups write words, phrases, and example sentences in each category.
- Check answers as a class.

1 VOCABULARY

A **Students close their books. Write the following words on the board:** *morning, light, night, yesterday*. **Ask: Which one does not belong?** (*light – because the others are times*).
- Ask Ss to do the task individually before they share with a partner.
- Elicit answers as a class.

> **Answers**
> 1 coat, c. food   2 white, d. seasons   3 fall, a. colors
> 4 rice, b. clothes   5 shorts, a. colors   6 pink, c. food

B **Ss work individually. They can use their notes, units 10–12 of the SB, or their smartphones to help them.**
- Ss share their answers with a partner before you elicit and write ideas for additional words on the board.

> **Answers**
> 1 coat = b. clothes, *suggested:* jacket, tie
> 2 white = a. colors, *suggested:* orange
> 3 fall = d. seasons, *suggested:* spring
> 4 rice = c. food, *suggested:* bread, onion
> 5 shorts = b. clothes, *suggested:* shoes, hat
> 6 pink = a. colors, *suggested:* orange

2 GRAMMAR

A **Write this sentence on the board.** *Where _____ you _____ last night? I _____ to the movies.* **Ask volunteers to say aloud words that would complete the sentences.** (*did, go, went*)
- Ss do the exercise individually before checking their answers with a partner.
- Elicit answers from the class. Direct Ss to read aloud the whole sentences.
- Ss practice the dialogues in pairs.

> **Answers**
> 1 Did, have, was   2 did, eat, tried   3 were, was
> 4 did, watch   5 Did, go, didn't buy   6 Were, worked

B **PAIR WORK** **Read the task aloud. Ask Ss:** *What did you do yesterday?* **to elicit answers such as:** *I went to work. I cooked dinner*, etc.
- Monitor as Ss share what they did.
- When Ss finish, elicit examples of interesting activities that you heard when monitoring the class.

C **Write on the board:** *I _____ in a hotel.* **and** *We _____ a new car.* **Elicit words that could complete the sentences.** (*stayed, bought*)
- Ss complete the exercise individually, then check with a partner. Direct Ss to read the full sentences aloud when you elicit the answers.

> **Answers**
> 1 went   2 bought   3 drank   4 took   5 ate   6 had

D **Tell Ss about a delicious meal you had this month. Use the past simple.**
- Allow students time to write their descriptions. Ask volunteers to share their paragraphs. Take a class vote: Who had the best meal?

3 SPEAKING

A **PAIR WORK** **Read the task aloud and model the example sentences with a confident volunteer. Tell Ss about a trip you went on to provide an example of the language.**
- Allow Ss a few minutes to make notes. They may use units 10–12 or their smartphones to resarch any information they might need.
- Circulate and monitor as Ss speak. Listen for language usage you can share as feedback at the end of the task.

B **Circulate and offer help as Ss write their sentences. Ask Ss to share their corrected sentences with the class. Ss compare their trips. Who took the most interesting trip?**

REVIEW 4 (UNITS 10–12)

1 VOCABULARY

A Look at the groups of words (1–6). For each group, circle the word that does not belong. Then match the groups with the categories (a–d). Some groups match the same category.

1	cheese	fish	potato	chicken	coat	___
2	white	winter	rainy season	summer	dry season	___
3	red	green	brown	fall	yellow	___
4	shirt	dress	skirt	pants	rice	___
5	purple	blue	shorts	gray	black	___
6	banana	tomato	apple	pink	cake	___

a colors
b clothes
c food
d seasons

B Match each word you circled in 1–6 to a different category (a–d). Then add one extra word to the categories.

2 GRAMMAR

A Make questions and answers in the simple past. Use the words in parentheses ( ).

1 A _____ you _____ a good weekend? (have)
   B Yes, it _____ great, thanks. (be)
2 A What _____ you _____ ? (eat)
   B We _____ some Japanese food. (try)
3 A Where _____ you on Saturday? (be)
   B I _____ at home in the morning, but not in the afternoon. (be)
4 A What _____ you _____ on TV last night? (watch)
   B A movie, but it _____ very good. (not be)
5 A _____ you _____ to the supermarket? (go)
   B Yes, but we _____ a lot. (not buy)
6 A _____ you busy yesterday? (be)
   B Yes, I _____ all day. (work)

B **PAIR WORK** Talk to a partner. Ask and answer five questions about things you did this month. Use the questions above, or your own ideas.

C Complete the paragraph. Use simple past forms of the verbs in parentheses ( ).

At the airport, I ¹_____ (go) to a store, and I ²_____ (buy) a cup of coffee and a sandwich. I ³_____ (drink) the coffee, but I didn't have time to eat the sandwich. So I ⁴_____ (take) it on the plane, and I ⁵_____ (eat) it on the flight. I ⁶_____ (have) lunch over the Atlantic Ocean. It was cool!

D Write about a meal you had this month. Say when and where you had it, and what you ate.

3 SPEAKING

A **PAIR WORK** Talk about a day out or trip you went on.

B Write three sentences about your day out or trip. Compare with a partner. Were your days the same or different?

> On Saturday, I went out with some friends. We took a walk.

> Where did you go?

4 FUNCTIONAL LANGUAGE

A Complete the conversation with the words in the box.

> can't   don't   have   idea   Let   Let's   maybe   sorry   sure   think

Min-jun Why ¹_____ we go out on Friday night?
Jamie Um … I'm ²_____ , but I ³_____ . I ⁴_____ to help my father on Friday.
Min-jun What about Saturday night?
Jamie ⁵_____ me think. Yes, sure. Saturday's fine.
Min-jun OK. ⁶_____ meet at Calendar Café. Do you know it?
Jamie I'm not ⁷_____ . Is it on Fourth Avenue?
Min-jun Yes. Near the movie theater.
Jamie OK, great. What time?
Min-jun The café is busy on Saturday night, I ⁸_____ . Let's get there early. How about 6 o'clock?
Jamie Good ⁹_____ . Then ¹⁰_____ we can go to a movie after dinner.

B Read the conversation and circle the correct words.

Yuri I ¹ *really / so* like this lamb.
Susan Thanks. Would you ² *want / like* some more?
Yuri ³ *Yes, / No*, please. ⁴ *Can / Would* I have some more green beans, too?
Susan ⁵ *A / Of* course. ⁶ *Here / Have* you are. Oh, please ⁷ *pass / give* the potatoes, Yuri.
Yuri All ⁸ *course / right*. Here.

5 SPEAKING

A **PAIR WORK** Choose **one** of the situations below. Talk to a partner. Have a conversation.

1. You and your friend want to go out this weekend. Make suggestions about what you can do and where / what time you can meet. Look at page 102 for useful language.

> Let's go out on Saturday night.

2. A friend asks you about a movie. He/She wants to know the names of the actors in the movie, their nationalities, and other movies they are in. You are not 100% sure. Look at page 112 for useful language.

> Who was in *The Matrix*?

> The first Matrix movie? I'm not sure. He's American, I think. Um …

3. A friend is at your home for dinner. Offer him/her things to eat and drink. Look at page 122 for useful language.

> Would you like some chicken?

B **PAIR WORK** Change roles and have another conversation.

4 FUNCTIONAL LANGUAGE

A **Allow Ss time to do the exercise individually, then share their answers with a partner.**
- Elicit answers from the class.
- Monitor as pairs read the conversation together.

> **Answers**
> 1 don't 2 sorry 3 can't 4 have 5 Let 6 Let's
> 7 sure 8 think 9 idea 10 maybe

B **Ss do the task individually before sharing answers with a partner.**
- After you elicit answers, ask volunteer pairs to role play the conversation aloud for the class.

> **Answers**
> 1 really 2 like 3 Yes 4 Can 5 Of 6 Here 7 pass
> 8 right

5 SPEAKING

A PAIR WORK **Read each situation aloud. Encourage volunteers to read the example sentences after the descriptions.**
- Ss choose one of the three situations and prepare a conversation. They should make notes, but not write the full conversation. For extra support, refer Ss to the functional language lessons from units 10–12.
- Monitor as pairs have their conversations. Listen for examples of language usage and provide feedback to Ss.

B PAIR WORK **Pairs change roles and repeat their conversations.**
- Choose pairs to perform their conversations for the class. If possible, choose a pair for each of the three situations.

T-128

GRAMMAR REFERENCE AND PRACTICE: TEACHER TIPS

The grammar practice exercises form an integral part of the lesson. They provide controlled practice of the target language and prepare students to use new grammar with confidence. Students can complete them individually or in pairs. Below is a list of ideas to practice using new grammar in an engaging way.

1
- Ss work in groups to think of situations in their own lives where they can use the grammar pattern. Set a time limit of three minutes.
- Groups share their ideas with the class. Write their ideas on the board.
- As a class, vote on the three most common or useful situations.
- In pairs or small groups (depending on the situations chosen), Ss write a role play for each situation. Allow them time to practice their role plays and encourage them to memorize it.
- Pairs or groups do their role plays for the class.

2
- On the board, write ten sentences using the grammar pattern, but include one grammar mistake in each one.
- In pairs or small groups, Ss work together to write all the sentences correctly.
- The first pair or group to write all the sentences correctly wins.

3
- Let a S volunteer "be the teacher."
- Give Ss time to read the information and sentences in the grammar box.
- Ss close their books.
- A volunteer comes to the board and explains the grammar pattern to the class, writing example sentences on the board. The "teacher" then asks other Ss to give example sentences to show that they understand the grammar pattern.
- This activity can also be done in groups, with Ss taking turns being the teacher until all Ss have had a chance to "teach" the grammar pattern.

4
- Ss write 3–5 true sentences about themselves using the grammar pattern.
- Each S stands up and says their sentences one time (e.g., *I can sing well.*). The other Ss in the class listen and try to write the sentences they hear.
- After all Ss have read their sentences, point to a S (S1) and have them say a sentence about another S (S2), based on what they wrote (e.g., *Mari can sing well.*). If the sentence is incorrect, you or S2 can correct their fact or grammar.
- S1 then points to another S (S3) to say one of the sentences about another S (S4). Then S3 points to another S (S5), etc. Continue until all Ss have said a sentence about another S in the class.

5
- Using the grammar pattern, Ss write two true sentences and one false sentence about themselves or about any topic that they know about.
- Pairs exchange sentences and try to guess which sentence is the false one.

6
- Ss close their books. Set a time limit. Individually or in teams, Ss write as many sentences as they can using the grammar pattern.
- The person or team with the most correct sentences wins.

7
- Play "Telephone." Put Ss in rows of at least four.
- Whisper a sentence using the grammar pattern to the last S in each row.
- When you say "Go!" the last S whispers the sentence to the next S in the row, who whispers it to the next S in the row, etc.
- When the first S in each row hears the sentence, they write it on the board.
- The first team to write the correct sentence wins.

8
- Divide the class into two teams. Write a sentence on the board with a blank using the grammar pattern and two spaces for each team's answer. For example:

    I want to meet a person who _____.
    Team A: _____
    Team B: _____

- Ss discuss ideas in their groups. Set a time limit.
- One S from each group writes their answer on the board.
- Once both groups have written an answer, discuss them as a class. If the teams have different answers, discuss whose answer is correct and encourage self-correction. Give a point for each correct sentence.
- Write a new sentence with a blank and have a new S from each group write the group's answer.
- Continue as time allows. The team with the most points wins.

GRAMMAR REFERENCE AND PRACTICE

1.1 *I AM, YOU ARE* (page 3)

I am (= I'm), you are (= you're)				
	Affirmative (+)	**Negative (-)**	**Question**	**Short answers**
I	**I'm** from Lima.	**I'm not** from Mexico City.	**Am I** in room 6B?	Yes, **you are.** / No, **you're not.**
You	**You're** from Paris.	**You're not** from Bogotá.	**Are you** from Tokyo?	Yes, **I am.** / No, **I'm not.**

A Match 1–6 to a–f to make sentences.
1 I'm
2 I'm from
3 No, I'm
4 Are you
5 Yes, I
6 Are you from

a not.
b Mexican.
c Honduras.
d am.
e Brazil?
f Chinese?

1.2 *WHAT'S … ?, IT'S …* (page 5)

What's … ? (= What is)	**It's … (= It is)**
What's your first name?	**It's** Juana.
What's the name of your college?	**It's** Garcia College.
What's your email address?	**It's** juanagarcia@bestmail.com.

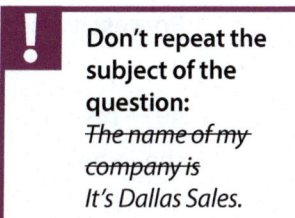

! Don't repeat the subject of the question:
~~The name of my company is~~
It's Dallas Sales.

A Put the words in order to make sentences.
1 first / is / My / Ruby. / name — My first name is Ruby.
2 is / address / My / dfox@kmail.com. / email — My email address is dfox@kmail.com.
3 Green College. / my college / of / The name / is — The name of my college is Green College.
4 my company / Dallas Sales. / The name / is / of — The name of my company is Dallas Sales.

2.1 *IS / ARE* IN STATEMENTS AND *YES/NO* QUESTIONS (page 13)

is / are in statements and yes/no questions			
	Affirmative	**Question**	**Short answers**
He / She / It	**'s** ten. (*'s = is*)	**Is** he your husband? **Is** she your friend?	Yes, he **is.** / No, he**'s not.** Yes, she **is.** / No, she**'s not.**
You / We / They	**'re** cousins. (*'re = are*)	**Are** you brothers? **Are** they your children?	Yes, we **are.** / No, we**'re not.** Yes, they **are.** / No, they**'re not.**

A Write sentences and questions with *is* and *are*.
1 she / 22 — She's 22.
2 they / your cousins — Are they your cousins ?
3 he / 18 — Is he 18 ?
4 my grandparents / Brazilian — My grandparents are Brazilian .
5 we / in Room 5B — Are we in Room 5B ?
6 no, you / not — No, you're not .

129

2.2 IS NOT / ARE NOT (page 15)

is not (= 's not) / are not (= 're not)	
He / She / It	**'s not** in Rio de Janeiro.
You / We / They	**'re not** shy.

isn't (= is not) / aren't (= are not)		
Jack	**isn't**	boring.
The students	**aren't**	in the class room.

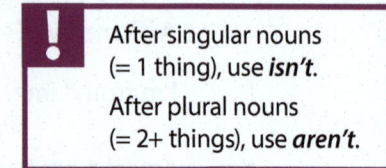

! After singular nouns (= 1 thing), use **isn't**.
After plural nouns (= 2+ things), use **aren't**.

A Circle the correct words to complete the sentences.

1. Jan *is* / *isn't* from New York City. He's from Miami.
2. *She's* / *She's not* 18. She's not 20.
3. Daniel is in Moscow. *He's* / *He's not* in St. Petersburg.
4. You're not shy. *You're* / *You're not* really friendly!
5. My cousins are in Japan. *They're* / *They're not* in the U.S.
6. *We're* / *We're not* sisters. We're friends.

3.1 POSSESSIVE ADJECTIVES; POSSESSIVE 'S AND S' (page 23)

Possessive adjectives	
I → **my**	This is **my** apartment.
he → **his**	**His** name is Sergei.
she → **her**	It's **her** favorite picture.w
it → **its**	Nice cat! What's **its** name?
you → **your**	Is this **your** room?
we → **our**	**Our** home is in La Paz.
they → **their**	Rita is **their** daughter.

Possessive 's and s'
Add possessive **'s** to a singular noun. (= 1 thing)
This is Sergei**'s** room.
My mother**'s** name is Kate.
Add possessive **'** after the *s* of a plural noun. (= 2+ things)
This is his parents**'** house.
My cousins**'** house is in Rio.

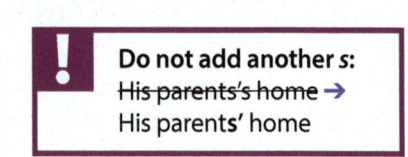

! Do not add another *s*:
His parents's home →
His parent**s'** home

A Circle the correct words to complete the sentences.

1. *My* / *I* email address is sky121@bestmail.com.
2. My *friends* / *friend's* name is Ramona.
3. This is *his* / *he's* hotel room.
4. Excuse me. What's *you* / *your* name?
5. This is my *parents's* / *parents'* new car.
6. David is *our* / *we* son.
7. The name of *Ann's* / *Anns'* company is Mason Sales.
8. What's *they're* / *their* telephone number?

3.2 IT IS (page 25)

> ! *It* is a pronoun. *It* is always singular. Use *it* for things. For example, *the house* = *it*. Use *isn't* after nouns. Use *'s not* after pronouns.

It is in statements and yes/no questions

	Affirmative	Negative	Question	Short answers
The house	**is** small.	**isn't** small. (*isn't = is not*)	**Is it** small?	Yes, **it is**.
It's (= *it is*)	small.	**not** small.		No, **it's not**.

A Answer the questions so they're true for you. Write statements. Use *It's* and *It's not* to give more information.

1 Is your home an apartment?   My home isn't an apartment. It's a house.
2 Is your bedroom cool?   _____
3 Is your kitchen big?   _____
4 Is your parents' house old?   _____
5 Is your friend's TV new?   _____
6 Is your refrigerator tall?   _____

3.4 INFORMATION QUESTIONS WITH BE (page 28)

Question word		be	
What		is	your name?
Where		is	the house?
How old		are	they?
Who		are	they?
How many	people	are	in the house?
How many	rooms	are	in it?

> ! Information questions ask for information about, for example, people, places, age, time, and quantity. Don't answer information questions with *yes/no* answers.
>
> Use *is* to talk about 1 thing. Use *are* to talk about 2+ things. Use a noun after *How many … ?*

A Put the words in the correct order to make questions.

1 is / Who / brother? / your   Who is your brother?
2 you? / How / are / old   How old are you?
3 her / is / college? / Where   Where is her college?
4 email / is / What / address? / your   What is your email address?
5 many / are / people / How / the house? / in   How many people are in the house?
6 apartment? / is / his / Where   Where is his apartment?

4.1 SIMPLE PRESENT STATEMENTS WITH I, YOU, WE (page 35)

Simple present statements with *I, you, we*

	Affirmative	Negative
I / You / We	**have** a smartwatch.	**don't have** a smartwatch.
	like my phone.	**don't like** my phone.
	love games.	**don't love** games.
	want a tablet.	**don't want** a tablet.

A Put the words in order to make sentences.
1 games. / like / I — I like games.
2 your / I / smartwatch. / love — I love your smartwatch.
3 don't / I / a / laptop. / have — I don't have a laptop.
4 a / tablet. / want / We — We want a tablet.
5 like / don't / laptops. / You — You don't like laptops.
6 camera. / want / I / don't / a — I dont want a camera.

4.2 SIMPLE PRESENT YES/NO QUESTIONS WITH I, YOU, WE (page 37)

Simple present yes/no questions with I, you, we

yes/no questions	Short answers
Do I **send** nice emails?	Yes, you **do.** / No, you **don't.**
Do we **post** good photos?	Yes, you **do.** / No, you **don't.**
Do you **use** social media?	Yes, I **do.** / No, I **don't.**
Do you **and your friends play** games?	Yes, we **do.** / No, we **don't.**

A Write questions. Then answer the questions so they're true for you.
1 you / call your family / on the weekends — Do you call your family on the weekends? Yes, I do.
2 you / post comments / on Twitter — Do you post comments on Twitter? _____.
3 you / send text messages / to your parents — Do you send text messages to your parents? _____.
4 you and your friends / watch movies / on TV — Do you and your friends watch movies on TV? _____.

4.4 A/AN; ADJECTIVES BEFORE NOUNS (page 40)

a/an	adjectives before nouns
Use **a/an** with singular nouns. It means "one." 　Do you have **a** laptop? (= 1 laptop) 　This is **an** app for photos. (= 1 app) Use **a** before consonant sounds (for example, b, c, d, f, …): **a** tablet, **a** cookie Use **an** before vowel sounds (a, e, i, o, u): **an** app, **an** apartment	Adjectives go before a noun: You have a **nice** home. ✓ You have a ~~home nice~~. ✗ It's an **expensive** laptop. This is a **new** apartment. I post **interesting** photos. The ending of an adjective is the same for singular and plural nouns. Do <u>not</u> add s to an adjective. I like **small** TVs. ✓ I like ~~smalls~~ TVs. ✗
Don't use a/an with: 1 plural nouns: I like **photos**. 2 this + noun: **This tablet** is nice.	3 numbers + noun: I have **one son** and **two daughters**. 4 possessive adjectives + noun: **My phone** is really old.

A **Circle** the correct words to complete the sentences.
1 Do you have (**a camera**) / an camera?
2 We don't want (**a new TV**) / new a TV.
3 Your an apartment / (**Your apartment**) is very nice.
4 I want coffee and (**a cookie**) / a one cookie.
5 A game / (**This game**) is really boring.
6 We have a children / (**three children**).
7 I don't like (**computers**) / computer.
8 Do you live in a apartment / (**an apartment**)?

132

5.1 SIMPLE PRESENT STATEMENTS WITH *HE, SHE, THEY* (page 45)

Simple present statements with *he, she, they*

	Affirmative	Negative
He / She	**plays** basketball. **goes out** every evening. **watches** TV a lot. **studies** on the weekend. **has** a big house.	**doesn't play** basketball. **doesn't go out** every evening. **doesn't watch** TV a lot. **doesn't study** on weekends. **doesn't have** a big house.
They	**play** soccer. **have** a big house.	**don't play** soccer. **don't have** a big house.

! Use *in* to talk about times of day: *I run in the morning.*
Use *on* to talk about days: *I play soccer on Saturdays.*

! Use adverbs of frequency say *how often* you do things.
100%   **always**   **usually**   **often**   **sometimes**   **hardly ever**   **never**   0%
Put adverbs of frequency <u>before</u> the verb: *She **sometimes** works on Saturday.*
With pronouns + *be*, adverbs of frequency go <u>after</u> the verb: *I'm **usually** at home in the evening.*

A Circle the correct words to complete the sentences.
1. My sister often *watch /* (*watches*) basketball on TV.
2. I don't like coffee, so I *usually /* (*never*) drink it.
3. My laptop is old and slow. I *always /* (*hardly ever*) use it.
4. My grandma *don't /* (*doesn't*) have a cell phone. She (*always*) */ hardly ever* calls me from home.
5. My friends are usually at work on Saturday and Sunday. They *have /* (*don't have*) free time on the weekend.

5.2 QUESTIONS IN THE SIMPLE PRESENT (page 47)

Simple present: *yes/no* questions

Yes/no questions			Short answers
Do	I/we	**work** on the weekend?	Yes, I **do**. / No, we **don't**.
Do	you	**eat** breakfast?	Yes, I **do**. / No, I **don't**.
Does	she/he	**study** in the evening?	Yes, she **does**. / No, he **doesn't**.
Does	it	**have** two bedrooms?	Yes, it **does**. / No, it **doesn't**.
Do	they	**go** to class on Monday?	Yes, they **do**. / No, they **don't**.

Simple present: information questions

I / You / We / They	Where What time What	do do do	I / we you they	**go** every day? **get up**? **do** on Saturday?
He / She / It	Where When What time	does does does	he she it	**live**? **meet** her friends? **open**?

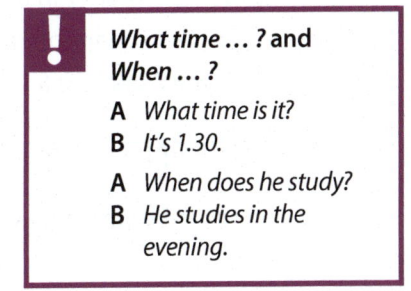

! *What time … ?* and *When … ?*
A *What time is it?*
B *It's 1.30.*
A *When does he study?*
B *He studies in the evening.*

A Put the words in the correct order to make questions.
1. lunch? / eat / does / he / Where — <u>Where does he have lunch?</u>
2. to / she / go / Does / this school? — <u>Does she go to this school?</u>
3. their / do / meet / friends? / When / they — <u>When do they meet their friends?</u>
4. do / work? / you / What / go / to / time — <u>What time do you go to work?</u>
5. soccer / your friends / after work? / play / Do — <u>Do your friends play soccer after work?</u>

133

6.1 THERE'S, THERE ARE; A LOT OF, SOME, NO (page 55)

There's (= there is), there are; a lot, some, no

Singular (= 1 thing)	Plural (= 2+ things)	
There's a restaurant near the hotel. = one	There are no stores on our street.	= zero
There's no shower in the bathroom. = zero	There are three bedrooms in the house.	= an exact number
	There are some chairs in the kitchen.	= a small number
	There are a lot of apps on my phone.	= a big number

A Look at the words in parentheses ( ). Then complete the sentences with the words in the box.

| There's a | There's no | There are no | There are a lot of | There are some |

1 *There are no* _____ parks in the city. (zero)
2 *There are a lot of* _____ people in the café. (a big number)
3 *There are some* _____ great stores on Pacific Street. (a small number)
4 *There's a* _____ park next to the hospital. (one)
5 *There's no* _____ restaurant in this museum. (zero)

6.2 COUNT AND NON-COUNT NOUNS (page 57)

Count nouns (nouns with a singular and plural form)

Singular	Plural
Use *There is* with *a* or *an*.	Use *There are* with *no*, *some*, *a lot of*, or a number.
There's **a** plant.	There are **no** plants. There are **some** plants.
	There are **a lot of** plants. There are **two** plants.

Non-count nouns (nouns with no singular or plural form)

Use *There is* with *no*, *some*, or *a lot of*. Do **not** use *a*, *an*, or a number.
There's **no** grass.   There's **some** grass.   There's **a lot of** grass.   ~~There's three grass.~~

A Write sentences with *There's* or *There are*. Make some nouns plural.

1 no / milk / in the refrigerator — *There's no milk in the refrigerator.*
2 a lot of / plant / in my house — *There are a lot of plants in my house.*
3 a / restaurant / in the museum — *There's a restaurant in the museum.*
4 some / sugar / on the table — *There's some sugar on the table.*
5 some / small hotel / near here — *There are some small hotels near here.*

7.1 PRESENT CONTINUOUS STATEMENTS (page 67)

Present continuous statements

	Affirmative	Negative
I	'm cooking breakfast right now.	'm not cooking breakfast right now.
He / She / It	's helping the children. 's taking a shower. 's drinking milk.	's not helping the children. 's not taking a shower. 's not drinking milk. (the cat)
You / We / They	're eating breakfast. 're cleaning the kitchen. 're learning a lot at school.	're not eating breakfast. 're not cleaning the kitchen. 're not learning a lot at school.

A **Put the words in the correct order to make sentences.**
1 My / aren't / TV. / parents / watching — My parents aren't watching TV.
2 coffee. / cup / drinking / a / I'm / of — I'm drinking a cup of coffee.
3 a / She's / now. / bath / taking / right — She's taking a bath right now.
4 TV / in / room. / Jack / his / watching / is — Jack is watching TV in his room.
5 eating / the moment. / They're / breakfast / at — They're eating breakfast at the moment.
6 isn't / homework. / her / Maria / doing — Maria isn't doing her homework.
7 our / helping / We're / now. / grandparents — We're helping our grandparents now.

7.2 PRESENT CONTINUOUS QUESTIONS (page 69)

Present continuous: yes/no questions and short answers

I	**Am** I **talking** to John?	Yes, you **are**. / No, you**'re not**.
He / She / It	**Is** she **cleaning** the house?	Yes, she **is**. / No, she**'s not**.
	Is he **riding** his bike right now?	Yes, he **is**. / No, he**'s not**.
	Is it **working** at the moment?	Yes, it **is**. / No, it**'s not**.
You / They	**Are** you and your sister **sending** text messages?	Yes, we **are**. / No, we**'re not**.
	Are they **waiting** at the bus stop?	Yes, they **are**. / No, they**'re not**.

Present continuous: information questions

I	Who	am	I	**talking** to?
He / She / It	Why	is	he / she	**carrying** a bag?
	Where	is	he / she	**working** today?
	How	is	it	**going**?
You / We / They	What	are	we / you / they	**doing** right now?
	Who	are		**waiting** for?

> **!** You can answer *Why* questions with *because*.
> **Why** is he carrying a bag?
> He's carrying a bag **because** he has a lot of books. (= a complete sentence)
> **Because** he has a lot of books. (= an incomplete sentence in informal speech)

A **Write questions for the answers. Use the words in parentheses ( ).**
1 A Are you sending a text to Carol?   (you / send / a text to Carol)
   B No, I'm not. I'm calling her.
2 A Why are we waiting for Paul?   (why / we / wait / for Paul)
   B Because he's driving us home.
3 A Are Denny and Pam doing the dishes?   (Denny and Pam / do / the dishes)
   B Yes, they are.
4 A Is Sandra washing the dog?   (Sandra / wash / the dog)
   B No, she isn't. She's watching TV.
5 A Who is your sister helping right now?   (who / your sister / help / right now)
   B My brother.

8.1 CAN AND CAN'T FOR ABILITY; WELL (page 77)

can and can't for ability; well				
	Affirmative	Negative	Questions	Short answers
I	**can** paint.	**can't** paint well.	**Can** I dance?	Yes, I **can** No, I **can't**.
He / She / It	**can** paint.	**can't** paint.	**Can** she dance well?	Yes, she **can**. No, she **can't**.
You / We / They	**can** paint well.	**can't** paint.	**Can** they dance?	Yes, they **can**. No, they **can't**.

A Put the words in order to make sentences.
1. can / well. / swim / Cathy — Cathy can swim well.
2. a / you / car? / drive / Can — Can you drive a car?
3. play / I / guitar. / can't / the — I can't play the guitar.
4. and paint? / you / Can / draw — Can you draw and paint?
5. well. / can't / I / very / skateboard — I can't skateboard very well.
6. fix / My / table. / brother / your / can — My brother can fix your table.
7. surf / can't / or snowboard. / I — I can't surf or snowboard.
8. well. / son / can / Their / sing — Their son can sing well.

8.2 CAN AND CAN'T FOR POSSIBILITY (page 79)

can and can't for possibility		
Information questions with *can*		
I	**What can** I eat?	**How can** I pay for the food?
He / She / It	**Where can** he eat?	**How can** he get to the restaurant?
You / We / They	**When can** we eat?	**Who can** we have lunch with today?

A Read the answers. Then write questions.
1. A Where can we work?
   B We can work in the meeting room.
2. A What can we watch?
   B We can watch a movie.
3. A How can we get to the mall?
   B We can get to the mall by bus.
4. A When can we have a meeting?
   B We can have a meeting on Friday.
5. A Who can we call?
   B We can call my cousin.
6. A What can we play?
   B We can play basketball.
7. A Where can we meet?
   B We can meet at the hotel.
8. A How can we take a picture?
   B We can take a picture with my phone.

9.1 THIS AND THESE (page 87)

This and these	
This is my ticket.	**These** are new boats.
This hotel is cheap.	**These** birds are funny.
Ryan loves **this** farm.	I don't like **these** pictures.

A **Put the words in order to make sentences.**
1 a / is / tour. / This / boring — This is a boring tour.
2 these / I / birds. / like — I like these birds.
3 sisters. / are / These / my — These are my sisters.
4 video. / watching / I'm / this — I'm watching this video.
5 really / animals are / funny. / These — These animals are really funny.
6 isn't / expensive. / This / vacation — This vacation isn't expensive.

9.2 LIKE TO, WANT TO, NEED TO, HAVE TO (page 89)

like to, want to		need to, have to	
I	like to play soccer. want to play soccer.	I	need to work on Saturday. have to work on Saturday.
He / She / It	likes to play soccer. wants to play soccer.	He / She / It	needs to work on Saturday has to work on Saturday.
You / We / They	want to play soccer. like to play soccer.	You / We / They	need to work on Saturday. have to work on Saturday.

A **Complete the sentences with *like to, want to,* or *have to/need to* and the verbs in parentheses ( ).**

1 I _like to swim_ (swim) in the ocean, but only in July and August.
2 One day, I _want to go_ (go) to Japan on vacation.
3 My son can't do his homework. I _have to / need to help_ (help) him.
4 I'm late for work, so I _have to / need to leave_ (leave) now.
5 This is a great song. I _want to buy_ (buy) it.
6 In Japan, you _have to / need to drive_ (drive) on the left side of the road.
7 At a movie theater, you _have to / need to pay_ (pay) before you watch the movie.

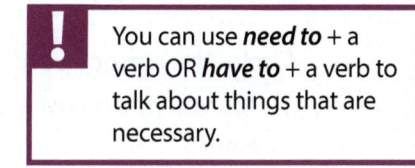

! You can use *need to* + a verb OR *have to* + a verb to talk about things that are necessary.

10.1 STATEMENTS WITH *BE GOING TO* (page 99)

Statements with *be going to*		
	Affirmative	**Negative**
I	'm going to be home tomorrow.	'm not going to be home tomorrow.
He / She / It	's going to take a walk in the park. 's going to be warm tomorrow.	's not going to go shopping next week. isn't going to be warm tomorrow.
You / We / They	're going to be here next weekend.	're not going to be here next weekend.
Future time expressions		
this evening, tonight, tomorrow this week/weekend/month/year	on/next/this Monday next week/weekend/month/year	

A Write sentences with the correct form of *be going to*.

1 We / not play / soccer this weekend
   We're not going to play soccer this weekend.
2 Vicky / meet / her friends tomorrow
   Vicky is going to meet her friends tomorrow.
3 You / have / a party for your birthday
   You're going to have a party for your birthday.
4 They / not go / surf / next Saturday
   They're not going to surf next Saturday.
5 I / go / dancing this evening
   I'm going to go dancing this evening.
6 He / not do / the dishes after dinner
   He's not going to do the dishes after dinner.

10.2 QUESTIONS WITH *BE GOING TO* (page 101)

be going to: yes/no questions		
	yes/no questions	Short answers
I	Am I going to meet him at 4:00?	Yes, you are. / No, you're not.
He / She / It	Is she going to see a friend?	Yes, she is. / No, she's not.
You / We / They	Are you going to take a hat?	Yes, I am. / Yes, we are. / No, I'm not. / No, we're not.

be going to: information questions
When are you going to leave?
Where is Sofia going to go?
What are we going to do today?
What time is he going to have lunch?
Who are they going to meet?
How are you going to get to the airport?

A Circle the correct words to complete the sentences.

1 Are you going *buying* / **to buy** some new jeans?
2 Who is he going to **go** / *going* shopping with?
3 Is she going to **cook** / *cooks* dinner for four people tonight?
4 *What* / **What time** are we going to drive to the airport?
5 Are **your parents** / *Mariana* going to send him an email?
6 What *they are* / **are they** going to wear to the party?

11.1 STATEMENTS WITH *WAS* AND *WERE* (page 109)

Statements with *was* and *were*		
	Affirmative	Negative
I / He / She / It	**was** in the house.	**wasn't** noisy.
You / We / They	**were** at work.	**weren't** there.

A Complete the posts with the affirmative or negative form of *was* or *were*.

Carlene Rauss I remember a great vacation. It ¹ was January 2010, and we ² were in Argentina. It ³ was summer, so the weather ⁴ was great! Buenos Aires is an exciting city, so we ⁵ were really happy there. #flashbackfriday #2010 #vacation

Paulo Soto I remember my twentieth birthday. My friends and I ⁶ were at the beach, but the weather ⁷ was awful! It ⁸ was really rainy. The café on the beach ⁹ wasn't open, so there was no food. It's not a good memory because we ¹⁰ weren't very happy. I mean, it ¹¹ wasn't a happy birthday. 🙁

👍 9   💗 4

138

11.2 QUESTIONS WITH WAS AND WERE (page 111)

Questions with was and were

	yes/no questions	Short answers
I / He / She	**Was** she at home on Saturday?	Yes, she **was**. / No, she **wasn't**.
You / We / They	**Were** you at home on Saturday?	Yes, I **was**. / No, I **wasn't**.
Information questions with was and were		
I / He / She	**Where was** he?	
You / We / They	**How old were** you in this photo?	

A Write questions in the simple past to match the answers.

1 What color were the walls in your bedroom ? The walls in my bedroom were blue.
2 Where was your last vacation ? My last vacation was in Brazil.
3 When was your brother's birthday party ? My brother's birthday party was on Friday.
4 Were your parents at the party ? Yes, my parents were at the party.
5 Was your house big ? No, my house was small.
6 Why were you at work on Saturday ? I was at work on Saturday because I was really busy.

12.1 SIMPLE PAST STATEMENTS (page 119)

Simple past statements

Use the simple past to talk about events that are in the past and finished.
I **ate** a big lunch yesterday. We **played** soccer last weekend. We **went** to La Paz last year.
Simple past verbs can be regular or irregular. Simple past regular verbs end in -ed.

Some regular verbs

	-ed	-d	double consonant + ed	change -y to -ied
I / You / He / She / We / They	work**ed** play**ed** watch**ed** want**ed** walk**ed**	like**d** love**d** arrive**d** use**d** dance**d**	stop → stop**ped** chat → chat**ted**	try → tr**ied** carry → carr**ied** study → stud**ied**

Some irregular verbs

Base form	Simple past	Base form	Simple past	Base form	Simple past
have	had	write	wrote	ride	rode
go	went	send	sent	fly	flew
eat	ate	buy	bought	get up	got up
drink	drank	think	thought	leave	left
do	did	run	ran	meet	met
take	took	swim	swam	sing	sang
read	read	drive	drove		

139

A Complete the chart with the words in the box.

| ~~arrive~~ | buy | drink | eat | go | have |
| like | need | stay | stop | take | try |

Base form	Rule	Simple past
arrive	Add -d.	arrived
like		liked
need	Add -ed.	needed
stay		stayed
stop	Double p and add -ed.	stopped
try	Change -y to -ied.	tried

Base form	Irregular simple past form
buy	bought
drink	drank
eat	ate
go	went
have	had
take	took

12.2 SIMPLE PAST QUESTIONS; ANY (page 121)

Simple past questions	
yes/no questions	**Short answers**
Did you **have** apple juice?	Yes, I/we **did**. No, I/we **didn't**.
Did we **arrive** on time?	Yes, we/you **did**. No, we/you **didn't**
Did she/he **like** the fish?	Yes, she/he **did**. No, she/he **didn't**.
Did they **go out** for dinner?	Yes, they **did**. No, they **didn't**.

Information questions		
How did	I / you	**hear** about the restaurant?
What did	you / he / she	**have** for dinner last night?
Who did	we / they	**see** at the party?

any
You can use *any* in yes/no questions and negative statements. *Any* = one, some, or all of something. *Not + any* = none.
Use *some* in affirmative statements. You can use *any* and *some* with count and non-count nouns.

Simple past questions and statements with *any*	
yes/no questions	**Negative statements**
Did you have **any** vegetables?	I didn't have **any** juice.
Did Mary buy **any** milk?	Joel didn't eat **any** eggs.
Did they have **any** dessert?	We didn't drink **any** soda.

A Put the words in the correct order to make sentences.

1 for dinner? / chicken / Did / make / you — Did you make chicken for dinner?
2 they / did / for lunch? / have / What — What did they have for lunch?
3 eat / Did / any / vegetables? / Tonya — Did Tonya eat any vegetables?
4 last night? / Where / she / go / did — Where did she go last night?
5 coffee / buy / We / at the store. / didn't / any — We didn't buy any coffee at the store.
6 at Pete's Pizza / last year? / you / Did / work — Did you work at Pete's Pizza last year?

VOCABULARY PRACTICE: TEACHER TIPS

The vocabulary practice exercises form an integral part of the lesson. They provide controlled practice of the target language and prepare students to use new vocabulary with confidence. Students can complete them individually or in pairs. Below is a list of ideas to practice using new vocabulary in an engaging way.

1

- Quickly come up with simple gestures for each of the vocabulary items.
- Tell Ss to cover the vocabulary pictures and/or words. Do one of the gestures and ask a volunteer to say the word.
- Alternatively, let a S do one of the gestures and then point to another S to say the word and do a different gesture, and so on.

2

- Provide Ss with index cards and let them make flashcards for each of the vocabulary words. On one side they should write the word and on the other side they can write the definition or draw a picture of the word.
- Encourage Ss to include more information on the card, for example, a synonym, an antonym, and a sample sentence.
- Ss can use the cards to review new vocabulary in pairs. S1 can use his/her cards to quiz S2 in several ways: by showing the picture and asking for the word; by reading the example sentence, leaving the vocabulary word blank for S2 to say; by saying a synonym and an antonym and having S2 say the vocabulary word, etc.

3

- Divide the class into teams and play "Hang man."
- Team A chooses a word, and one S from Team A (S1) writes on the board.
- One S from Team B (S2) guesses a letter. If they are correct, S1 write the letter on the board. If the letter is not in the word, S1 draws a head (a circle) on the board.
- Ss from Team B take turns guessing letters that are in the word. If they are incorrect, S1 draws a body (another circle), arms, legs, eyes, and mouth for each incorrect letter.
- The game continues until Team B correctly guesses the word, or they guess incorrectly enough times that a whole body is drawn.
- Teams switch roles.

4

- Play "Telephone." Put Ss in rows of at least four.
- Whisper a vocabulary word to the last S in each row.
- When you say "Go!" the last S whispers the word to the next S in the row, who whispers it to the next S in the row, etc.
- When the first S in each row hears the word, he/she writes it on the board.
- Give S one point if the word is correct but misspelled, and two points if it is spelled correctly. The first team to write a correct word wins.
- For more of a challenge, whisper three vocabulary words to the last S, or whisper a sentence that uses the vocabulary word.

5

- Write the vocabulary words on the board.
- Challenge Ss to write one sentence using as many of the vocabulary words in that sentence as they can.
- Ss read their sentences to the class. Ss can vote on the best sentence.
- Alternatively, Ss can write a short paragraph of no more than five sentences using all of the vocabulary words in the paragraph.

6

- Write the vocabulary words on index cards. Make enough copies for Ss to play in small groups.
- Put the cards face down on a table in front of each team.
- One S (S1) chooses a card, but does not look at it. Instead, he/she holds the card on their forehead with the word facing out so his/her team can see it.
- Each person on their team takes turns giving one clue about the word. S1 tries to guess the word.
- Continue until each S in the group has a chance to guess the word.
- For an extra challenge, include vocabulary words from previous units for a review.

VOCABULARY PRACTICE

1.1 COUNTRIES AND NATIONALITIES (page 2)

A Write the country or the nationality.

1 Are you _Russian_? (Russia)
2 I'm from _Mexico_. (Mexican)
3 I'm _Ecuadorian_. (Ecuador)
4 You're from _Chile_. (Chilean)
5 Are you _Japanese_? (Japan)
6 Are you from _Brazil_? (Brazilian)
7 I'm not _South Korean_. (South Korea)
8 I'm from Madrid. I'm _Spanish_. (Spain)

B Underline two correct answers for each sentence.

1 Are you from Russia / Chilean / South Korea?
2 I'm from American / Mexico / Japan.
3 You're not French / Peru / Colombian.
4 Are you from New York / Chicago / American?
5 I'm not Mexico / Brazilian / Chinese.
6 You are Peruvian / French / Chile.
7 Are you Peruvian / Japan / South Korean?
8 I'm from Ecuadorian / Lima / Germany.

1.2 THE ALPHABET; PERSONAL INFORMATION (page 5)

A Add five missing letters to the alphabet, in order.

1 A B C _D_ E F G H I J _K_ L M _N_ O P Q R _S_ T U V W X _Y_ Z
2 a _b_ c d e _f_ g h _i_ j k l m n o _p_ _u_ q r s t _v_ w x y z

B Complete the sentences with the words in the box.

| College | company | email address | first name | last name |

1 The name of my _company_ is Home Sales, Inc.
2 **A** What's your _email address_? **B** It's jenatkins@abc.net.
3 **A** Hey, Ana. What's your _last name_? **B** It's Gomez. Ana Gomez.
4 I'm a student at Hunter _College_ in New York City.
5 **A** Hi, Susie Ball. How do you spell your _first name_? **B** S-U-S-I-E.

2.1 FAMILY; NUMBERS (page 13)

A Write the words in the chart.

| ~~aunt~~ | child | daughter | grandfather | husband | parent | son | wife |
| brother | cousin | father | grandmother | mother | sister | uncle | |

Men and women	Women	Men
child	aunt	brother
cousin	daughter	father
parent	grandmother	grandfather
	mother	husband
	sister	son
	wife	uncle

141

B   **Write the numbers.**
1   twenty-two   22
2   fifty-one   51
3   thirty-nine   39
4   eighty-three   83
5   forty-six   46
6   sixty-seven   67
7   thirty-eight   38
8   seventy-four   74
9   ninety-five   95
10 twenty-six   26

2.2 DESCRIBING PEOPLE; *REALLY / VERY* (page 14)

A   **Complete the sentences with the words in the box. You won't use all the words.**

| friendly | interesting | old | really | short |
| shy | smart | boring | tall | young |

1   Carrie is two. She's really _young_ .
2   He's a college student. He's _smart_ .
3   My father is 190 cm. He's very _tall_ .
4   He's not interesting. He's _boring_ .
5   My friend Georgio is _really_ funny!
6   Ariana is 95. She's very _old_ .

B   **Unscramble the letters in parentheses ( ). Write the adjectives.**
1   Susana is _interesting_ and really _tall_ .   (nteisreignt) / (tlal)
2   My son is _smart_ and _funny_ .   (mtras) / (ynufn)
3   My grandfather is _old_ and _short_ .   (dlo) / (rosth)
4   The child is very _young_ and _shy_ .   (ynugo) / (ysh)
5   They're _friendly_ and not _boring_ .   (fienrdyl) / (bgrion)

3.1 ROOMS IN A HOME (page 22)

A   **Read the sentences and complete the words.**
1   This is our d_ining_ a_rea_ , with a p_icture_ on the w_all_ .
2   This is my sister's b_edroom_ . It's next to the b_athroom_ .
3   This is our dog, Jack. He's on the f_loor_ .
4   This is the d_oor_ of our house.
5   This is the l_iving_ r_oom_ , with one big w_indow_ .
6   And this is the k_itchen_ . It's my favorite room.

B   **(Circle) the correct word to complete the sentences.**
1   My sister is in her (bedroom) / floor.
2   This is the bathroom, with one wall / (window).
3   This is the dining area / (door) to the kitchen.
4   My family is in the (living room) / bathroom now.
5   The (picture) / kitchen on the wall is interesting.
6   Our cats are on the door / (floor).

3.2 FURNITURE (page 24)

A Match the words to the things in the picture.

| chair | ~~couch~~ | refrigerator | rug | sink | table | television |

1 _couch_   2 _rug_   3 _TV / television_   4 _table_

5 _chair_   6 _refrigerator_   7 _sink_

B Circle the correct words to complete the sentences. Check (✓) the sentences that are true for you.

1 A big (bed) / shower is in the bedroom.
2 My rug / (bookcase) is really tall.
3 A small (shower) / couch is in the bathroom.
4 My TV / (desk) is really old. It's from the year 1800.
5 I have a small (lamp) / chair on a table in my bedroom.

4.1 TECHNOLOGY (page 34)

A Complete the sentences with the words in the box. You won't use all the words.

| app | camera | cell phone | earphones | games | laptop | smartwatch | tablet |

1 Is that a really big phone, or is it a _tablet_ ?
2 I have a computer. It's a _laptop_ .
3 Yes, I have a _cell phone_ . The number is (593) 555-2194.
4 I don't have a _watch_ , but I have the time on my cell phone.
5 This picture is great! The _camera_ on your cell phone is really good.
6 My emails are on my phone. I have an email _app_ .
7 My computer isn't for work. It's for fun. I have my _games_ on it.

B Circle the correct words to complete the sentences.

1 On my phone, I have a good laptop / (camera).
2 I have a social media (app) / smartwatch on my tablet.
3 On my laptop, I have a (game) / cell phone.

143

4.2 USING TECHNOLOGY (page 36)

A Cross out the word that doesn't belong with each verb.

1	call	friends	~~social media~~	family
2	watch	movies	videos	~~text messages~~
3	use	~~music~~	technology	apps
4	post	~~cell phone~~	comments	photos
5	send	text messages	email	~~with friends~~

B Complete the sentences with the words in the box.

> chat   listen   play   read   watch

1 I _listen_ to music with earphones on my tablet.
2 We don't _watch_ movies on TV.
3 My brother and I _play_ games on our tablets.
4 I don't _read_ work emails at home.
5 Do you _chat_ with friends on the internet?

5.1 DAYS AND TIMES OF DAY; EVERYDAY ACTIVITIES (page 44)

A Read the days and times of day (a–j). Then put them in the correct order (1–10).

a on Thursday, in the morning   _5_
b on Tuesday, in the afternoon   _2_
c on Thursday, in the evening   _6_
d on Monday, at night   _1_
e on Sunday, in the morning   _10_
f on Saturday, in the evening   _9_
g on Wednesday, in the morning   _4_
h on Friday, in the afternoon   _7_
i on Tuesday, in the evening   _3_
j on Saturday, in the afternoon   _8_

B Use phrases from exercise A to complete the sentences so they're true for you. Write an X if you never do the activity.

1 I go out with friends _____.
2 I watch TV _____.
3 I study _____.
4 I run _____.
5 I play soccer _____.
6 I read _____.
7 I work _____.
8 I'm in bed _____.

144

5.2 TELLING THE TIME (page 46)

A Look at the times (1–8). Then (circle) the correct sentence.

1. 3:40 — **(a)** It's twenty to four. — b It's forty to three.
2. 12:30 — a It's twenty thirty. — **(b)** It's twelve thirty.
3. 6:15 — **(a)** It's a quarter after six. — b It's a quarter to six.
4. 12:00 a.m. — **(a)** It's midnight. — b It's noon.
5. 1:45 — a It's a quarter to one. — **(b)** It's one forty-five.
6. 8:07 — a It's seven to eight. — **(b)** It's eight-oh-seven.
7. 9:15 — **(a)** It's nine fifteen. — b It's nine fifty.
8. 4:52 — a It's five forty-two. — **(b)** It's four fifty-two.

B <u>Underline</u> the correct words to complete the paragraph.

Carmen <u>gets up</u> / goes to bed at 7:15 a.m. She eats lunch / <u>breakfast</u> at 7:45. Then she <u>goes to work</u> / gets up. She usually has dinner / <u>lunch</u> at 12:30 p.m. She drinks <u>coffee</u> / class in the afternoon. On Tuesday, she goes to <u>class</u> / lunch after work – she studies English. She usually eats <u>dinner</u> / coffee at 7:00. She goes to <u>bed</u> / class at 11 p.m.

6.1 PLACES IN CITIES (page 54)

A Complete the sentences with the words in the box.

| café | college | hotel | museum | park | school | mall | zoo |

1. We often eat breakfast in a <u>café</u>.
2. I sometimes run in the <u>park</u>.
3. The <u>museum</u> has hundreds of old pictures and a lot of art.
4. The <u>school</u> in my neighborhood has 160 children.
5. The students at the <u>college</u> are 18 to 22 years old.
6. This is a great <u>mall</u>. It has a lot of my favorite stores.
7. The rooms in the <u>hotel</u> have bathrooms with showers.
8. The <u>zoo</u> in my city has 20 elephants.

B Cross out **one** word that does not complete each sentence.

1. We have lunch in a _____ on Saturdays. — restaurant — ~~store~~ — park
2. We learn about things at a _____. — school — ~~restaurant~~ — museum
3. We shop at the _____ every weekend. — mall — ~~hospital~~ — supermarket
4. The _____ has a big TV. — ~~park~~ — hotel — restaurant
5. She studies English in _____. — school — college — ~~a movie theater~~

145

6.2 NATURE (page 56)

A **Complete the email with the words in the box.**

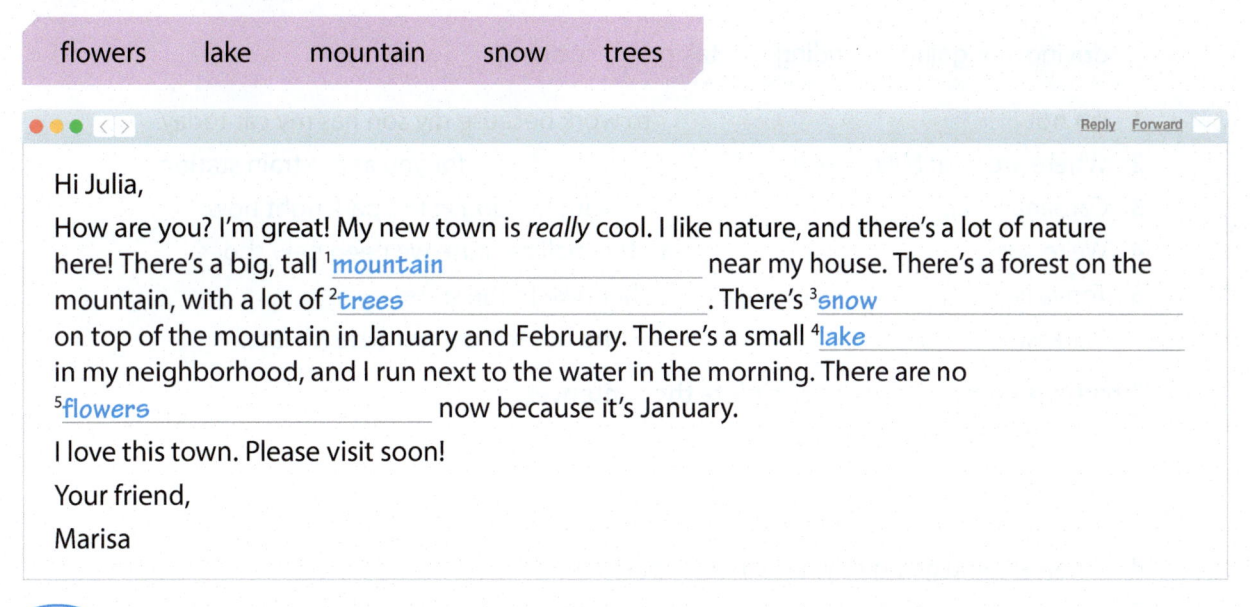

> flowers   lake   mountain   snow   trees

Hi Julia,

How are you? I'm great! My new town is *really* cool. I like nature, and there's a lot of nature here! There's a big, tall ¹mountain near my house. There's a forest on the mountain, with a lot of ²trees. There's ³snow on top of the mountain in January and February. There's a small ⁴lake in my neighborhood, and I run next to the water in the morning. There are no ⁵flowers now because it's January.

I love this town. Please visit soon!

Your friend,

Marisa

B **Circle the correct word to complete the sentences.**

1. My house is on the **beach** / forest next to the ocean.
2. There is a lot of ocean / **grass** in the park.
3. There are a lot of plants and flowers in the **forest** / lake.
4. There's a lot of water in the **river** / desert.
5. My grandma and grandpa live near the **ocean** / flowers.
6. A lot of animals eat **plants** / mountains.
7. Donna lives on a small **island** / desert in the Atlantic Ocean.
8. There are a lot of small grass / **hills** here, but there are no mountains.

7.1 ACTIVITIES AROUND THE HOUSE (page 66)

A **Match 1–6 with a–f to complete the sentences.**

1. Do they cook   _c_
2. Karen usually washes   _a_
3. I do a lot of   _e_
4. They're nice. They help   _d_
5. He takes   _f_
6. Do you clean   _b_

a. her daughter's hair.
b. your room on the weekend?
c. breakfast every morning?
d. me with my English.
e. homework every day.
f. a shower in the evening.

B **Add the words in parentheses ( ) to the correct place in each sentence. Then write the sentences.**

1. Do you the dishes after lunch? (do)   *Do you do the dishes after lunch?*
2. Rudy his car on the weekend. (drives)   *Rudy drives his car on the weekend.*
3. Does he his teeth every day? (brush)   *Does he brush his teeth every day?*
4. My mother usually cooks at 6:30. (dinner)   *My mother usually cooks dinner at 6:30.*
5. She takes a every evening. (bath)   *She takes a bath every evening.*
6. I often my grandmother. (help)   *I often help my grandmother.*

7.2 TRANSPORTATION (page 68)

A Complete the sentences with the correct verbs in the box.

| driving | going | riding | taking | waiting | walking |

1 I'm not _driving_ to work because my son has my car today.
2 Where are you? Mike is _waiting_ for you at the train station.
3 Carolina is _walking_ with her dog in the park right now.
4 We're _going_ to the mall because we need new shoes.
5 Tonya is _riding_ her bike to the store.
6 Mark isn't _taking_ the bus to class because it's late.

B Circle the correct words to complete the sentences.

1 Vic is at *the bus stop* / his bike.
2 Why are you carrying *a plant* / the train?
3 I usually take the train station / *the subway* to work.
4 When are you going to your *parents' house* / mall?
5 I'm sorry. I'm busy. I'm on the bus stop / *the train*.

8.1 VERBS TO DESCRIBE SKILLS (page 76)

A Complete the sentences with the verbs in the box. You won't use all the verbs.

| dance | fix | play | skateboard | speak |
| draw | paint | sing | snowboard | swim |

1 I don't _snowboard_. There's a mountain near me but it doesn't have snow on it.
2 My friends usually _play_ the guitar and _sing_ songs after dinner.
3 In my art class, we _draw_ and _paint_ a lot of different things.
4 I _speak_ two languages – English and Korean.
5 In February and March, I _swim_ in the ocean.
6 Do you have a problem with your laptop? My brothers _fix_ computers.

B Complete the words with vowels (a, e, i, o, u).

1 d_a_nc_e_
2 f_i_x th_i_ngs
3 sn_o_wb_o_-_a_rd
4 sw_i_m
5 pl_a_y the g_u_-_i_t_a_r
6 sp_e_-_a_k tw_o_ l_a_ng_u_-_a_g_e_s
7 r_e_-_a_d m_u_s_i_c

8 dr_a_w
9 sk_a_t_e_b_o_-_a_rd
10 p_a_-_i_nt
11 s_i_ng
12 s_u_rf

8.2 WORK (page 78)

A Complete the sentences with the words in the box.

> break   coworkers   have   think
> company   hard   office   worker

1 I work for a big American _company_ .
2 I have a new desk and a chair in my _office_ .
3 She's doing a great job. She's a very good _worker_ .
4 It's time to take a _break_ and have a cup of coffee.
5 I work in a team with six _co-workers_ .
6 We're always busy. We work _hard_ .
7 Can we talk about this? Can we _have_ a meeting?
8 I don't know the answer. Can I _think_ about it for five minutes?

B Circle the word that doesn't belong in each group.
1 living room   (office)   kitchen   bedroom
2 have a meeting   (play games)   call a coworker   work hard
3 drink coffee   have lunch   take a break   (have a meeting)
4 company   (couch)   chair   desk
5 worker   (brother)   teacher   coworker

9.1 TRAVEL (page 86)

A Circle the correct words to complete the sentences.
1 I have a (ticket) / tour for the bus.
2 This city / (ranch) is in the country.
3 I'm on (vacation) / country with my family.
4 My seat on the (plane) / ticket is by the window.
5 My house is in a small (town) / boat, but I work in the city.
6 This (tour) / ticket is expensive, but it's really interesting.

B Circle the word that doesn't belong in each group.
1 vacation   tour   (work)
2 ranch   farm   (ticket)   country
3 boat   (hotel)   plane   bus
4 ticket   tour   plane   (friend)
5 (country)   town   city

9.2 TRAVEL ARRANGEMENTS (page 88)

A Match 1–6 with a–f to complete the sentences.

1 You can buy tickets _c_
2 We can check in for our _e_
3 I don't usually travel on _d_
4 We're arriving at our _a_
5 I'm staying at a really nice _f_
6 We're flying from the new _b_

a destination.
b airport.
c online.
d trains.
e flight.
f hotel.

B David is traveling from Chicago to London. Put his trip in the correct order.

_g_ → _d_ → _b_ → _f_ → _h_ → _e_ → _c_ → _a_

a Stay in the hotel.
b Drive to the airport.
c Arrive at the hotel.
d Leave home.
e Take a bus from the airport to the hotel.
f Check in for the flight at the airport.
g Buy a plane ticket online.
h Fly to the destination.

10.1 GOING OUT (page 98)

A Circle the correct word to complete the sentences.

1 Can you (meet) / go me at the airport on Friday?
2 Jennifer wants to (take) / look her brother to lunch for his birthday.
3 We're doing / (having) a picnic right now.
4 I like to (get) / meet together with friends on the weekends.
5 Do you usually make / (go) shopping at the mall?
6 I never take / (eat) outside.

B Complete the sentences with the words in the box.

| art | coffee | family | hotel | shopping | walk |

1 Do you want to take a _walk_ in the park?
2 I like to look at interesting _art_ in museums.
3 I want to take you out for _coffee_ to my favorite café.
4 We often get together with _family_ on the weekends.
5 I have to meet my coworker at his _hotel_ on Friday.
6 Maria never goes _dancing_ with us. She doesn't like it.

10.2 CLOTHES; SEASONS (page 100)

A Complete the clothes words with vowels (a, e, i, o, u).

1 I want to buy some j_e_ _a_ ns and a sw _e_ _a_ t _e_ r.
2 I'm going to wear a T-sh _i_ rt and sh _o_ rts to the beach.
3 This store sells sh _o_ _e_ s and b _o_ _o_ ts.
4 I'm going to buy a winter c _o_ _a_ t and h _a_ t.
5 We usually wear p _a_ nts and a sh _i_ rt at work.
6 Is she going to wear a dr _e_ ss or a sk _i_ rt?

149

B **Complete the paragraph with the words in the box.**

| dry season | fall | rainy season | spring | summer | winter |

In Japan, we have four seasons. I love [1]spring (OR summer) and [2]summer (OR spring) because there are a lot of flowers then. After summer, it's [3]fall, and this is usually from September to November. Then it's [4]winter, and you can do a lot of fun activities, for example, snowboard in the mountains. We have a short [5]rainy season, too. It usually starts in June and ends in July, and it is *very* rainy. We don't have a [6]dry season in Japan. It's not a desert country.

11.1 DESCRIBING PEOPLE, PLACES, AND THINGS (page 108)

A **Match the sentences with the correct responses.**

1 This new restaurant isn't good. e
2 Your daughter is quiet. d
3 This is a beautiful picture. a
4 I love beach parties. f
5 The train was very slow today. b
6 These children are really noisy. c

a Thanks. I think the artist is wonderful.
b Really? It's usually fast.
c Yes, but they're really cute.
d That's true. She's really shy.
e I know. The food is awful.
f Me, too. They're exciting, and the ocean is beautiful.

B **Read the sentences and complete the words.**

1 My cousin is b*eautiful*, and her children are really c*ute*.
2 It's a nice, q*uiet* restaurant, and it has w*onderful* food!
3 This movie is a*wful*. It's s*low* and boring.
4 I love soccer games. They're always n*oisy* and e*xciting*.
5 My brother's happy because he has a n*ew* car. It's really f*ast*.

11.2 COLORS (page 110)

A **Unscramble the color words (1–10.) Then match the words to the colors (a–j).**

1 dre — red
2 nreeg — green
3 leub — blue
4 tiwhe — white
5 weyoll — yellow
6 nbwor — brown
7 knip — pink
8 ragnoe — orange
9 ygra — grey
10 klacb — black

a 8
b 6
c 10
d 7
e 1
f 3
g 9
h 5
i 4
j 2

B **Match five of the colors in exercise A to the things below.**

1 some milk i
2 a coffee with milk b
3 some grass j
4 the ocean f
5 an elephant g

150

12.1 SNACKS AND SMALL MEALS (page 118)

A Look at the pictures. Write the words in the chart.

Fruit and vegetables		Meat	Dairy products	Grains	Small meals
apple	pineapple	beef	butter	bread	sandwich
banana	potato	chicken	cheese	crackers	soup
coconut	tomato	lamb			
orange					

B Circle the correct words to complete the sentences.

1. **A** What do you want with your crackers?
   B I want cheese and tomatoes / *coconut*, please.
2. For a small meal, I like soup and *bread* / potato.
3. My favorite sandwich has bread, *butter* / orange, and chicken.
4. Beef is very good with bananas / *tomatoes*.
5. My brother really likes fruit. He eats bananas and *apples* / lamb every day.

12.2 MORE FOOD, DRINKS, AND DESSERTS (page 120)

A Complete the menu with the words in the box.

beans	chocolate cake	cookies	ice cream
juice	pizza		soda

B Circle the correct words to complete the sentences.

1. *Steak* / Rice is my favorite meat.
2. Cookies / *Green beans* are good for you because they are vegetables.
3. Do you want some pizza / *ice cream* for dessert?
4. I like to eat *eggs* / water for breakfast.
5. Did you drink any rice / *juice* with your meal?
6. *Chocolate cake* / soda is my favorite dessert.

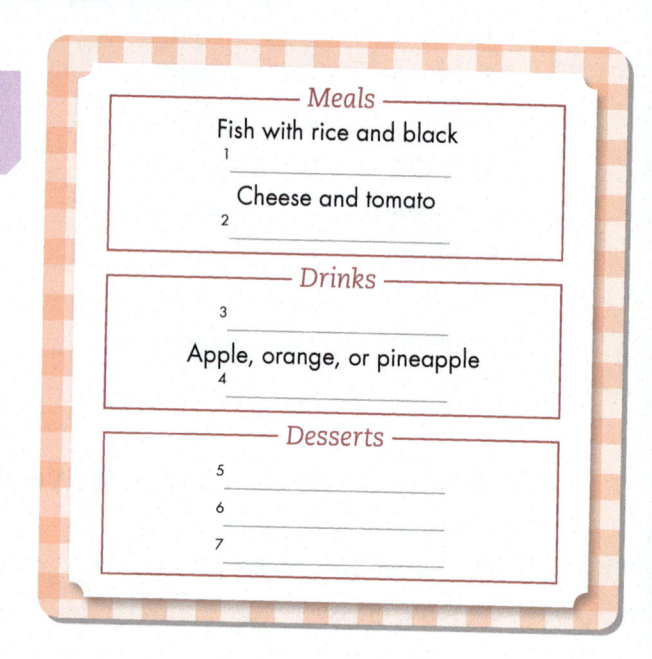

Meals
1. Fish with rice and black _____
2. Cheese and tomato _____

Drinks
3. _____
4. Apple, orange, or pineapple _____

Desserts
5. _____
6. _____
7. _____

151

PROGRESS CHECK: INTRODUCTION

Progress checks help students to assess their learning regularly. The **Now I can** sections relate to the communicative objectives of the unit grammar and vocabulary, functional language, and writing. The **Prove it** exercises challenge students to show what they have learned during the unit. Progress checks can be conducted in class or at home.

Below is a list of ideas for conducting Progress check activities.

Using Progress checks

Informal test
- Ss keep their books closed.
- Read the first **Prove it** instruction aloud. Repeat if necessary.
- Give Ss time to write their answers.
- Repeat the steps above with the next four **Prove it** instructions.
- Check answers as a class, or take Ss' notebooks to check.

Pair checking
- Ss complete the Progress check individually then compare with a partner. If they have different answers, they should check that both are correct.

Pair testing
- One student reads out a **Prove it** instruction, while the other writes the words.

Teams
- Put Ss in groups of 4
- Ss keep their books closed. Read out the **Prove it** instructions.
- Ss work together to write the words and phrases.
- When Ss have finished, they pass their papers to another team.
- Ss check other teams' answers using the Student's Book. Monitor and answer questions.
- The winning team is the one with the most correct words or phrases.

Class project
- Split the class into five groups. Give each group one of the **Prove it** instructions.
- Give each group a large piece of paper. Groups make posters with the words, phrases, and sentences.
- Tell groups to put extra details on their posters, for example pronunciation information, or pictures of vocabulary items.
- Each group puts their poster on the wall for other groups to read.

Homework
- Ss complete the Progress check at home. Remind Ss that they should not look at their books. They should prove how much they remember.
- Check Ss answers in class before beginning the next unit.

Writing

At the end of each unit, Ss will have the chance to return to, and improve, their written work from lesson 4. Encouraging Ss to check their own writing increases learner autonomy. Ss can improve their writing by:

- adding extra sentences
- using more complex grammatical structures
- choosing more appropriate vocabulary
- correcting spelling and punctuation errors

If possible, allow Ss to use online dictionaries and reference materials to improve their work. They can also ask a partner for suggestions.

PROGRESS CHECK

Can you do these things? Check (✓) what you can do. Then write your answers in your notebook.

UNIT 1

Now I can …

- ☐ say countries and nationalities.
- ☐ use *I am*.
- ☐ use the alphabet to spell words.
- ☐ ask and answer questions with *What's …?* and *It's …*.
- ☐ check into a hotel.
- ☐ write a profile.

Prove it

Write your country and your nationality.

Write two sentences about you. Use *I'm* and *I'm from*.

Spell your first name and your last name. Spell your email address.

Write a question and answer about personal information. Use *What's* and *It's*.

Write two questions you hear at a hotel. Write answers to the questions.

Read your profile from lesson 1.4. Find a way to improve it. Use the Accuracy check, Register check, and the new language from this unit.

UNIT 2

Now I can …

- ☐ say family names and numbers.
- ☐ use *is* and *are*.
- ☐ use adjectives to describe people.
- ☐ use *is not* and *are not*.
- ☐ talk about ages and birthdays.
- ☐ write a post about friends in a photo.

Prove it

Write the names and ages of four members of your family. Write the numbers in words.

Write four sentences with *is* and *are*. Write about you or your family and friends.

Complete the sentences with adjectives. *My parents are … My best friend is …*

Make the three sentences negative. *She's tall. We're from Seoul. They're funny.*

When's your birthday? How old is your best friend? Write answers in full sentences.

Read your post about friends from lesson 2.4. Find a way to improve it. Use the Accuracy check, Register check, and the new language from this unit.

UNIT 3

Now I can …

- ☐ talk about rooms in my home.
- ☐ use possessive adjectives, *'s* and *s'*.
- ☐ talk about furniture.
- ☐ use *it is*.
- ☐ offer and accept a drink and snack.
- ☐ write an email about a home-share.

Prove it

Write five rooms and five things in rooms.

Change the words in parentheses ( ) to possessives. *This is my (brother) bedroom. (He) bedroom is between (I) bedroom and (we) (parents) bedroom.*

Write five or more words for furniture.

Complete the questions. Then answer with your own information. _____ your home big? _____ near your school?

Someone says, "Coffee?" Write two different answers.

Read your email from lesson 3.4. Find a way to improve it. Use the Accuracy check, Register check, and the new language from this unit.

PROGRESS CHECK

Can you do these things? Check (✓) what you can do. Then write your answers in your notebook.

UNIT 4

Now I can …
- ☐ talk about my favorite things.
- ☐ use the simple present.
- ☐ say how you use technology.
- ☐ use *yes/no* questions in the simple present.
- ☐ ask questions to develop a conversation.
- ☐ write product reviews.

Prove it

Write about five things you like, love, or want.

Write about a thing you have and a thing you don't have.

Write about three ways you use your phone.

Complete the questions. Then write the answers with your own information. _____ you use apps on your phone? _____ you and your parents chat online?

Complete the conversation.
A _____ social media?
B Yes, I do. _____ ?

Read your product reviews from lesson 4.4. Find a way to improve them. Use the Accuracy check, Register check, and the new language from this unit.

UNIT 5

Now I can …
- ☐ use days and times of days with everyday activities.
- ☐ use the simple present and adverbs of frequency.
- ☐ tell the time and talk about routines.
- ☐ ask *yes/no* and information questions in the simple present.
- ☐ show you agree or have things in common.
- ☐ write a report.

Prove it

Write two things you do on weekdays in the morning. Write two things you do on Saturday.

Complete the sentences. Write about your friends.
_____ always _____ on the weekend.
_____ and _____ never _____ in the evening.

What time is it now? When do you get up on weekdays? What time do you usually have dinner? Write answers in full sentences.

Complete the questions with *do* or *does*. Then write your answers.
What time _____ you get up on Saturday? Where _____ you and your friends eat lunch on Monday? _____ your teacher have lunch at school?

Read the statements. Write responses that are true for you.
Soccer is fun.   *I never run.*

Read your WRAP report from lesson 5.4. Find a way to improve it. Use the Accuracy check, Register check, and the new language from this unit.

UNIT 6

Now I can …
- ☐ use words for places in a city.
- ☐ use *there's / there are* with *a/an, some, a lot of, no*.
- ☐ use words for places in nature.
- ☐ use count and non-count nouns.
- ☐ ask for and give simple directions.
- ☐ write a fact sheet.

Prove it

Write about six places in a city.

Write four true sentences for your city. Use the sentences below.
There are _____ in my city. / There's _____ in my neighborhood.

Write about six places in nature.

Write about the plants, trees, and grass in your neighborhood.

Write one way to ask for directions and one way to give directions.

Read your fact sheet from lesson 6.4. Find a way to improve it. Use the Accuracy check, Register check, and the new language from this unit.

PROGRESS CHECK

Can you do these things? Check (✓) what you can do. Then write your answers in your notebook.

UNIT 7

Now I can …	Prove it
☐ use words about activities around the house.	Write three things you do around the house.
☐ use the present continuous.	Write a sentence about what you are doing right now. Write a sentence about what your teacher is doing.
☐ use transportation words.	Complete the sentences with transportation words. I'm on the _____ right now. Are you _____ to work? We're riding our _____ to the park.
☐ ask yes/no and information questions in the present continuous.	Write one yes/no question and two information questions. Use the present continuous.
☐ start a phone call.	Write a way to answer the phone. Write a question to ask people how they are.
☐ write a blog about things happening now.	Read your blog from lesson 7.4. Find a way to improve it. Use the Accuracy check, Register check, and the new language from this unit.

UNIT 8

Now I can …	Prove it
☐ talk about skills.	Write five skills that your friends or people in your family have. Use can.
☐ use can to talk about ability.	Write a sentence about something you can do well and a sentence about something you can't do well.
☐ talk about work.	Write three things that people do at work.
☐ use can to talk about possibility.	Write two questions. Use What … ? and Where … ? + can.
☐ give opinions.	Do you think technology is good for the world? Write a short answer.
☐ write an online comment.	Read your online comment from lesson 8.4. Find a way to improve it. Use the Accuracy check, Register check, and the new language from this unit.

UNIT 9

Now I can …	Prove it
☐ use travel words.	Where can you take a tour? What do you need a ticket for? Answer the questions about your city or country.
☐ use this and these.	Complete these sentences with your own ideas. I _____ this _____ . I _____ these _____ .
☐ talk about travel arrangements.	Think of a city in your country, or in another country. Describe the trip from your home to the city.
☐ use like to, want to, have to, need to.	Write four sentences about things you like to do, want to do, have to do, and need to do.
☐ ask for information in a store.	Write three questions to ask for missing information. Begin your questions with Where … ?, How much … ?, and What time does … ? Then write the answers to your questions.
☐ write a description of a place.	Read your description of a place from lesson 9.4. Find a way to improve it. Use the Accuracy check, Register check, and the new language from this unit.

PROGRESS CHECK

Can you do these things? Check (✓) what you can do. Then write your answers in your notebook.

Now I can …	Prove it	UNIT 10
☐ use words for going out activities.	How many going out activities can you remember? Make a list.	
☐ use *be going to* in statements.	Write two sentences about what you're going to do next month. Write two sentences about what you're <u>not</u> going to do next year.	
☐ use words for clothes and seasons.	What's your favorite season? What do you usually wear to class? What do you wear when you go out with your friends?	
☐ ask yes/no and information questions with *be going to*.	Complete these questions. Then write answers for you. Are _____ (you, work) this summer? What _____ (you, do) for your next birthday?	
☐ make and respond to suggestions.	Complete the suggestions with *Why don't we* or *Let's*. Then write answers to the suggestions. _____ meet at a café tomorrow. _____ go shopping after class?	
☐ write an online invitation.	Read your online invitation from lesson 10.4. Find a way to improve it. Use the Accuracy check, Register check, and the new language from this unit.	

Now I can …	Prove it	UNIT 11
☐ use adjectives to describe people, places, and things.	Write three sentences. Use adjectives to describe a person, a place, and a thing.	
☐ use *was* and *were* in statements.	Write four sentences about the past. Use *was*, *were*, *wasn't*, and *weren't*.	
☐ talk about colors.	Look around you. What things can you see? What color are they? Write five sentences.	
☐ ask questions with *was* and *were*.	Write two questions with *was* and two questions with *were*.	
☐ express uncertainty.	Write the capital city of these countries: Australia, Germany, India, Indonesia. In your answer, write that you're not sure.	
☐ write an email about things you keep from the past.	Read your email from lesson 11.4. Find a way to improve it. Use the Accuracy check, Register check, and the new language from this unit.	

Now I can …	Prove it	UNIT 12
☐ talk about snacks and small meals.	Write about food you like and don't like. Write about five things.	
☐ use simple past statements.	Write four sentences about things you did yesterday.	
☐ talk about food, drinks, and desserts.	Write something you ate yesterday, or last week, for dessert. Write something you drank.	
☐ use simple past questions.	Write three questions to ask a partner about what he or she did last week.	
☐ offer and request food and drink.	Imagine you're in a restaurant. Write a question the server asks, and write your answer.	
☐ write a restaurant review.	Read your restaurant review from lesson 12.4. Find a way to improve it. Use the Accuracy check, Register check, and the new language from this unit.	

155

PAIR WORK PRACTICE (STUDENT A)

1.3 EXERCISE 5C   STUDENT A

1 You are Sandra, the visitor. Give your information to your partner.
2 You are the hotel clerk. Ask for your partner's information. Complete the hotel card.

HOTEL INFORMATION CARD: City Bed & Breakfast

- First name: Sandra
- Last name: Mills
- Number of nights: Three
- Email: sandra85@listmail.net
- Phone number: 367 555 0219
- Company/School: Big City Travel

HOTEL INFORMATION CARD: Tree House Hotel

- First name:
- Last name:
- Number of nights:
- Email:
- Phone number:
- Company/School:

2.3 EXERCISE 3D   STUDENT A

1 Say a person from the table. Say the incorrect birthday. Then correct yourself.

> Anna. Her birthday is August 15. No, sorry, August **13**.

Person	Anna	Martin	Paulo	Rosa	Jacob
Incorrect birthday	August 15	December 2	June 5	October 21	April 12
Correct birthday	August **13**	December **3**	**July** 5	October **31**	April **20**

2 Listen to your partner. Write the correct birthday. (Circle) the correction (the number or the month).

Person	Gloria	Larry	Helena	Susan	Bruno
Incorrect birthday	September 13	November 6	May 9	February 30	January 25
Correct birthday	_____	_____	_____	_____	_____

4.3 EXERCISE 2D   STUDENT A

1 Follow the flow chart. Use the topics in the box or your own ideas. Talk about two or three topics.

- laptops
- music videos
- social media
- video chat

Ask your partner about a new topic. → Listen. → Answer your partner's question. → Listen. → Say one word to show you are listening. → Answer your partner's question. Ask for his or her response about the topic. → Listen. → Listen.

2 Follow the flow chart. Talk about the topics your partner chooses.

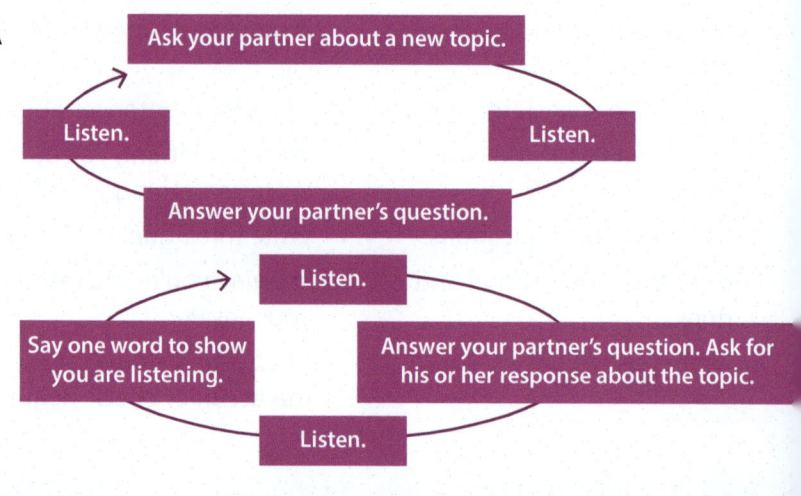

156

5.3 EXERCISE 2D   STUDENT A

1 Choose one of the jobs in the box. Don't tell your partner. Then complete the sentences about the job with *always, usually, often, sometimes, hardly ever,* or *never.*

   doctor   hotel clerk   server   student

   1 I _____ get up early.
   2 I _____ eat at home.
   3 I _____ have free time.
   4 I _____ work with friends.
   5 I _____ read books.
   6 I _____ send emails for work.
   7 I _____ go to bed late.
   8 I _____ work on the weekend.

2 Your partner is a teacher, salesperson, chef, or artist. Ask questions and guess the job.

   Do you get up early?   *Always.*   *Do you eat at home?*   *Never.*   *Are you a … ?*

3 Your partner asks you questions. Answer with one or two words. Your partner guesses your job.

6.3 EXERCISE 2D   STUDENT A

Give the directions below to Student B. Student B repeats and you listen. Is it correct?

1 Turn left here. Then go straight. It's on the left.
2 It's over there. Go two blocks. Turn right. Then turn right again.
3 Turn left here. Then turn left again. It's on the right.

7.3 EXERCISE 2D   STUDENT A

Imagine you're talking to your partner on the phone. Say the news below, and your partner reacts. Then your partner says some news to you, and you react. Take turns.

1 My new job is really boring.
2 I'm having a cup of coffee.
3 It's my birthday today.
4 My dog is eating my lunch.
5 The people at my new college are friendly.
6 I'm on the subway.

8.3 EXERCISE 2D   STUDENT A

1 Say the sentences below to your partner. Add information to explain or say more. Then your partner gives his or her opinion.

   - Basketball is/isn't my favorite sport. I mean, …
   - I can/can't read music. It's difficult/easy. I mean, …
   - I like / don't like art. I mean, …
   - I think computer skills are important. I mean, …

   Basketball is my favorite sport. I mean, I can play really well, and it's fun.   *I don't like basketball. I think soccer is the best sport.*

2 Listen to your partner. Then give your opinion.

10.3 EXERCISE 2D   STUDENT A

Your partner makes a suggestion. You say you can't and give a reason. Take turns.

Suggestion	Reason
have coffee now	(Your partner)
(Your partner)	go home at lunchtime
have a meeting on Monday	(Your partner)
(Your partner)	go to the supermarket
go shopping on Saturday	(Your partner)
(Your partner)	work late

Let's have coffee now.

I'm sorry, but I can't. I have to go to a meeting.

11.3 EXERCISE 2D   STUDENT A

1   Ask your partner these questions. Listen to their answers. Then tell your partner the correct answers.

Question	Answer
What was Leonardo DiCaprio's name in *Titanic*?	Jack Dawson
Where is the singer Carol Konka from?	Brazil
What country is *Crouching Tiger Hidden Dragon* from?	China
What was Elvis's last name?	Presley
What band is Chris Martin in?	Coldplay
What was the dog's name in *The Wizard of Oz*?	Toto

What was Leonardo DiCaprio's name in Titanic?

Uh, I think it was Jack. / Um, I have no idea.

It was Jack Dawson.

2   Answer your partner's questions. Use expressions of uncertainty for answers you don't know or are unsure about.

PAIR WORK PRACTICE (STUDENT B)

1.3   EXERCISE 5C   STUDENT B

1   You are the hotel clerk. Ask for your partner's information. Complete the hotel card.

2   You are Tom, the visitor. Give your information to your partner.

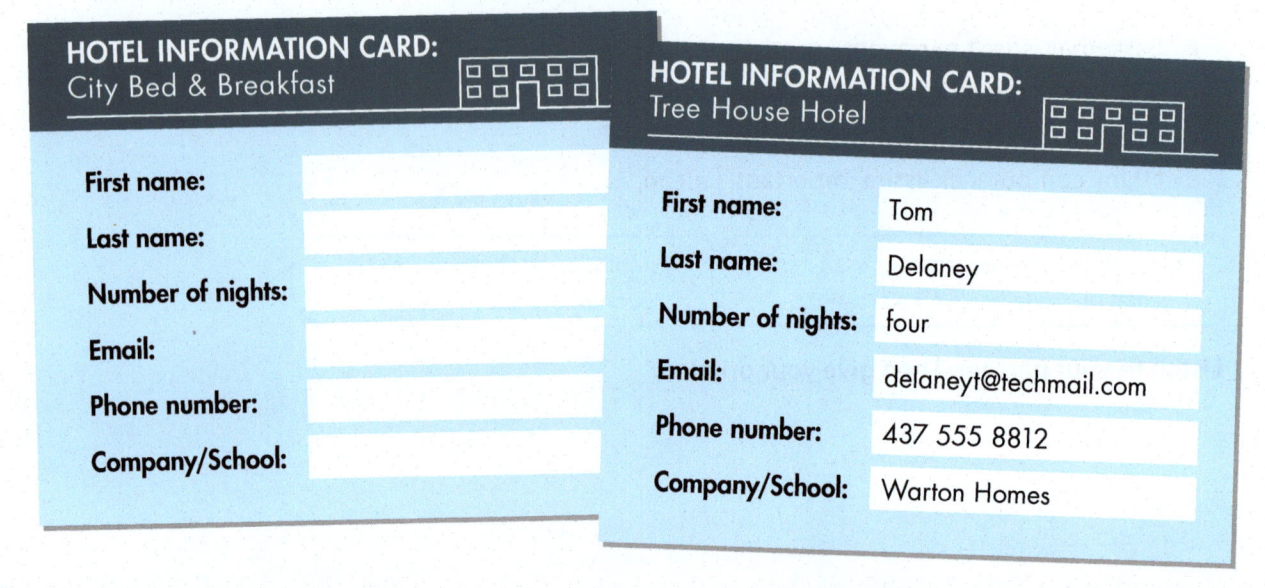

HOTEL INFORMATION CARD:
City Bed & Breakfast

First name:
Last name:
Number of nights:
Email:
Phone number:
Company/School:

HOTEL INFORMATION CARD:
Tree House Hotel

First name: Tom
Last name: Delaney
Number of nights: four
Email: delaneyt@techmail.com
Phone number: 437 555 8812
Company/School: Warton Homes

2.3 EXERCISE 3D   STUDENT B

1 Listen to your partner say the incorrect birthdays, and then the correct birthdays. Write the correct birthday. <u>Underline</u> the correction (the number or the month).

Person	Anna	Martin	Paulo	Rosa	Jacob
Incorrect birthday	August 15	December 2	June 5	October 21	April 12
Correct birthday	_____	_____	_____	_____	_____

2 Say a person from the table. Say the incorrect birthday. Then correct yourself.

> Gloria. Her birthday is September 13. No, sorry, September 30.

Person	Gloria	Larry	Helena	Susan	Bruno
Incorrect birthday	September 13	November 6	May 9	February 30	January 25
Correct birthday	September <u>30</u>	November <u>16</u>	<u>March</u> 9	February <u>20</u>	January 2<u>4</u>

4.3 EXERCISE 2D   STUDENT B

1 Follow the flow chart. Talk about the topics your partner chooses.

2 Follow the flow chart. Use the topics in the box or your own ideas. Talk about two or three topics.

> laptops   music videos
> social media   video chat

Flow chart:
- Say one word to show you are listening.
- Listen.
- Answer your partner's question. Ask for his or her response about the topic.
- Listen.
- Ask your partner about a new topic.
- Listen.
- Answer your partner's question.
- Listen.

5.3 EXERCISE 2D   STUDENT B

1 Choose <u>one</u> of the jobs in the box. <u>Don't</u> tell your partner. Then complete the sentences about the job with *always, usually, often, sometimes, hardly ever,* or *never*.

> artist   chef   salesperson   teacher

1 I _____ get up early.
2 I _____ eat at home.
3 I _____ have free time.
4 I _____ work with friends.
5 I _____ read books.
6 I _____ send emails for work.
7 I _____ go to bed late.
8 I _____ work on the weekend.

2 Your partner asks you questions. Answer with <u>one or two</u> words. Your partner guesses your job.

> Do you get up early?   Always.   Do you eat at home?   Never.   Are you a … ?

3 Your partner is a student, doctor, server, or hotel clerk. Ask questions and guess the job.

6.3 EXERCISE 2D   STUDENT B

Give the directions below to Student A. Student A repeats and you listen. Is it correct?

1 Turn left. Go straight. That's San Gabriel Street.
2 Go straight. Then turn right. It's on the right.
3 Turn right here. Turn right again. Then turn left. It's on the right.

159

7.3 EXERCISE 2D   STUDENT B

Imagine you're talking to your partner on the phone. Your partner says some news to you, and you react. Then you say the news below, and your partner reacts. Take turns.

1 I'm cooking dinner.
2 I'm at a party on the beach.
3 I'm watching TV.
4 I'm working on Saturday and Sunday.
5 I have a new plane.
6 My train is three hours late.

8.3 EXERCISE 2D   STUDENT B

1 Listen to your partner. Then give your opinion.

> Basketball is my favorite sport. I mean, I can play really well, and it's fun.

> I don't like basketball. I think soccer is the best sport.

2 Say the sentences to your partner. Add information to explain or say more. Then your partner gives his or her opinion.

- Friday is/isn't my favorite day. I mean, …
- I like / don't like music. I mean, …
- I can/can't snowboard. It's difficult/easy. I mean, …
- I think good food is important. I mean, …

10.3 EXERCISE 2D   STUDENT B

You make a suggestion. Your partner says he/she can't and gives a reason. Take turns.

Suggestion	Reason for refusal
(Your partner)	go to a meeting
have lunch	(Your partner)
(Your partner)	go out
take a walk after work	(Your partner)
(Your partner)	study this weekend
watch a movie tonight	(Your partner)

> Let's have coffee now.

> I'm sorry, but I can't. I have to go to a meeting.

11.3 EXERCISE 2D   STUDENT B

1 Answer your partner's questions. Use expressions of uncertainty for answers you don't know or are unsure.

2 Ask your partner these questions. Listen to their answers. Then tell your partner the correct answers.

Question	Answer
What was Kate Winslet's name in *Titanic*?	Rose
Where is the band *Awesome City Club* from?	Japan
How many *Pirates of the Caribbean* movies was Johnny Depp in?	five
What is Shakira's last name?	Mebarak Ripoll
What band was John Lennon in?	The Beatles
What animals are in *101 Dalmatians*?	dogs

> What was Leonardo DiCaprio's name in *Titanic*?

> Uh, I think it was Jack. / Um, I have no idea.

> It was Jack Dawson.

UNIT 1 LANGUAGE SUMMARY

Nouns

Countries

Brazil
Chile
China
Colombia
Ecuador
France
Honduras
Japan
Mexico
Peru
Russia
South Korea
Spain
The United States

The Alphabet

Aa Bb Cc Dd Ee Ff Gg Hh Ii
Jj Kk Ll Mm Nn Oo Pp Qq
Rr Ss Tt Uu Vv Ww Xx Yy Zz

Personal information

college
company
email address
first name
last name

Numbers

1 one 2 two 3 three 4 four 5 five
6 six 7 seven 8 eight 9 nine 10 ten

Jobs

artist
chef
doctor
hotel clerk
salesperson
server
student
teacher

Adjectives

Nationalities

American
Brazilian
Chilean
Chinese
Colombian
Ecuadorian
French
Honduran
Japanese
Mexican
Peruvian
Russian
South Korean
Spanish

Greetings, introductions, goodbyes

Good evening.
Hello. How are you?
I'm fine thanks. And you?
I'm fine.
(X), this is (Y).
Hi, (Y). Nice to meet you.
Nice to meet you, (X).
See you later.
Bye.

Insider English

Uh-huh
My last name is Garcia.
Uh-huh. What's your email address?

Saying where you're from

I'm Brazilian.
I'm from Lima.
I'm not from Mexico City.
You're from Mexico City.
You're not from Bogotá.
Am I in room 6B?
Are you from Tokyo?
Yes, I am. / No, I'm not.
Yes, you are. / No, you're not.

Asking for and giving personal information.

What's your first / last name?
It's Juana/Mendes.
What's the name of your college/ company?
It's Garcia College / Warton Homes.
What's your email address?
It's luzmendes@xyzmail.com.

Checking into a hotel

Clerk

What's your cell phone number?
Please sign here.
Here's a pen.
This is the key.
You're in room 6B.

Guest

It's (593) 555-2192.
I'm here for three nights.

Writing a profile.

Hello. My name is …
Hi! I'm …
I am Peruvian / French / Japanese.
I'm from Russia / Honduras / Toronto / Amsterdam.
I am / I'm a teacher / student / salesperson.
The name of my school / college / company is …
My email is …

Meeting new people

Role playing

Are you (American)?
Yes, I am. / No, I'm not. I'm …
I'm from (city).
How do you spell it?
What's your cell phone number?

Agreeing

The person is from (city).
The phone number is …
It's (name of person).

Discussing

My favorite person is …
Me, too.

Checking spelling

My name is Paulo Vasques.
How do you spell your first / last name?
How do you spell it?
V-A-S-Q-U-E-S.

T-161

UNIT 2 LANGUAGE SUMMARY

Nouns
Family
aunt
brother
child
children
cousins
dad
daughter
father
grandchildren
grandfather
grandmother
grandma
grandpa
grandparents
husband
mom
mother
parents
sister
son
uncle
wife
wives

Months
January February March April May June
July August September October November
December

Numbers
11 eleven   12 twelve   13 thirteen
14 fourteen   15 fifteen   16 sixteen
17 seventeen   18 eighteen   19 nineteen
20 twenty   21 twenty-one   22 twenty-two
30 thirty   40 forty   50 fifty
60 sixty   70 seventy   80 eighty
90 ninety   100 one hundred

Days of the month (ordinals)
first   second   third
fourth   fifth   sixth
seventh   eighth   ninth
tenth   eleventh   twelfth
thirteenth   fourteenth   fifteenth
sixteenth   seventeenth   eighteenth
nineteenth   twentieth   twenty-first
twenty-second   thirtieth   thirty-first

Adjectives
Describing people
boring
friendly
funny
interesting
old
really
short
shy
smart
tall
young
very

Insider English
She's not tall.
You're not from South Korea.
Filip isn't American.
My friends aren't boring.

Glossary
both

Talking about your family
She's Elizabeth One, and I'm Elizabeth Two!
Are you both Elizabeth?
Yes, we are.
Is he your husband?
No, he's not.
My husband isn't here.
Are your parents here?
No, they're not.

Describing friends and family
He's not short.
She's not from Miami.
They're not boring!
You're not old.

Asking about ages and birthdays
How old is he?
When's your birthday?
When's his/her birthday?

Saying ages and birthdays
She's eight.
He's three years old.
His party is on March 29.
Miranda's birthday is April 2.
Giving birthday wishes
Happy birthday!

Writing a post about friends in a photo
We're in Seattle, at college.
This is Nuwa, on the left / right.
Guy is next to me.
Guy is between Nuwa and me.
We're four college students in Seattle, and we're in a band.
She's very interesting and smart.

Comparing information about friends and family
Discussing
Hello. / Hi.
My name is …
True for me.
Not true for me.
Really? *(for surprise)*
Goodbye.
Presenting
(Name) is the same.
(Name) is different.

Correcting yourself
He's twenty. No, sorry, twenty-one.
It's March twenty-first. Sorry, I mean May twenty-first.

UNIT 3 LANGUAGE SUMMARY

Nouns

Rooms in a home
bathroom
bedroom
dining area
kitchen
living room
door
floor
picture
wall
window
cat
dog

Furniture and objects
bed
bookcase
chair
couch
desk
lamp
refrigerator
rug
shower
sink
space
television / TV
table

Drinks and snacks
coffee
cookie
milk
sugar
tea

Adjectives
big
boring
cool
funny
great
interesting
new
nice
old
small

Insider English
Sure. A cookie, please.

Talking about your home
Welcome to my home.
This is your bedroom.
This is her bedroom.
This is his bedroom.
This is their bedroom.
This is their bedroom.
This is my parents' bedroom.
Milka is our cat.
T-Rex is Sergei's dog.
This is my apartment. Its. windows are old, but its doors are new.

Talking about furniture
It's great for college students.
This desk isn't just a desk.

Offering and accepting a drink and snack

Making offers
Coffee or tea?
With milk?
Sugar?

Replying to offers
Coffee, please.
No, thanks.
Yes, please.

Writing an email about a home-share
Where is it?
How many bedrooms/bathrooms are in it?
How many people are in the house?
Are they students?
The house is on …
It's big, with four bedrooms, three bathrooms, and a big kitchen.
Three people live in the house.
They are students at …

Choosing things for a home

Discussing
This is the kitchen/living room …
It's good for him.
It's not good for him.

Preparing
Where's a good place for a couch / TV?
In the living room?

Deciding
What's important for Jason?
What about this TV / picture?
This is a big / small TV.
This TV is good for Jason.
It's $180. ($ = *dollars*)
I agree. / I don't agree.
It's expensive. ($$$)
It's cheap. ($)
Good idea!

Asking about words you don't understand
Sorry, I don't understand. What's a …?

UNIT 4 LANGUAGE SUMMARY

Nouns
Technology
app
camera
cell phone
earphones
(computer) game
laptop
phone
smartwatch
tablet
… on my cell phone / tablet
… on my computer / laptop
… on my smartwatch
… on the internet
Music
album
band
songs
singer

Adjectives
famous
popular

Verbs
Talking about your favorite things
have
like
love
want
Using technology
call friends / family
chat with friends / family
listen to music
play games
post photos / comments
read emails / (text) messages
send emails / (text) messages
leave voice messages
use apps / social media / technology
watch movies / videos / TV

Insider English
And what else? Do you listen to music on your phone?

Glossary
phone plan
product review

Talking about your favorite things
I love my watch.
I don't love my refrigerator.
I have a cell phone.
I don't have a tablet.
You want a tablet.
You don't want a watch.
We love our family.
We don't love things.

Saying how you use technology
Do I post good photos?
Yes, I do. / No, I don't.
Do you use social media?
Yes, you do. / No, you don't.
Do you know which plan you want?
Yes, I do. / No, I don't.
Do you and your friends send emails?
Yes, we do. / No, we don't.

Talking about how you communicate
Asking about a new topic
What about email?
Do you post photos?
Do you send cards / use social media?
Asking for a response
Do you post photos, too?
How about you?
What about you?
And you?

Writing product reviews
They're great (earphones), but they are expensive.
I don't like it because it's …

Talking about your favorite music
Discussing
This song is my favorite.
I don't like this song.
Agreeing
What music do you have on your list?
I have … on my list.
Let's have this song on the list.
I don't want this song on the list.
What do you think?
Me, too!
Deciding
Do we want … or … ?
Here are our ten songs for the party playlist.
Showing you are listening
Right.
Yeah.
OK.

T-164

UNIT 5 LANGUAGE SUMMARY

Nouns

Days of the week
Monday Tuesday Wednesday
Thursday Friday Saturday Sunday

Times of day
afternoon
evening
morning
night
the weekend
weekdays
at night
in the morning / afternoon / evening
on Monday / Thursday / the weekend / weekdays

Verbs

Everyday activities
drink coffee / tea
eat / have breakfast / lunch / dinner
get up
go out
go to bed / work / classes
play soccer
run
study
work

Telling the time
It's eight o'clock.
It's five fifteen.
It's three-thirty.
It's ten forty-five.
It's (a) quarter after five.
It's (a) quarter to eleven.
It's nine-oh-five.
It's six fifty.
It's twelve p.m.
It's 12:00 a.m.
It's five after nine.
It's ten to seven.
It's noon.
It's midnight.

Adverbs of frequency
always
hardly ever
never
often
sometimes
usually

Glossary
after
before
every
from 8:00 a.m. to 3:00 p.m.
late
routine
tired
way of life

Talking about weekday and weekend activities
He works Monday to Friday.
She has fun, but not every day.
They have fun on the weekend.
She doesn't have time for sports.
They don't go out every evening.
My dad doesn't play soccer.

Telling the time and talking about your routines
Do you go out with friends?
Do we have class today?
Does he go to classes every day?
Does your mom make dinner for you?
Does your tablet have good apps?
Do they have dinner before you?
What time do you get up?
When does he go to classes?
Where does she work?
What do they do on Saturday?

Showing you agree
I agree.
That's true.
That's right.
Yeah, I know.

Showing you have things in common
Me, neither.
Me, too.

Comparing

Preparing
Which … is your favorite?
… is my favorite.

Discussing
I have a … life.
I get up / have breakfast at …
I work from … to …
Before/After work, I …
I have free time from … to …

Deciding
… is good for me because …
I like / don't like … because …
I want … on the weekends / in the evenings.

Short answers with adverbs of frequency
A Do you always run at lunch?
B Usually. And what about you? Do you run?
A Hardly ever.

T-165

UNIT 6 LANGUAGE SUMMARY

Nouns
Places in cities
bookstore
café
college
hospital
hotel
mall
movie theater
museum
park
restaurant
school
store
supermarket
zoo

Nature
beach
desert
flower
forest
grass
hill
island
lake
mountains
ocean
plants
river
snow
tree

Verbs
Things to do
go shopping
have dinner
learn
see friends

Insider English
No way! Central Park is great.

Glossary
neighborhood

Talking about places in the city
There's no free time this week.
There's a zoo in the park.
There's a nice café near here.
There are some interesting museums near the park.
There are a lot of good places to see on the weekend.
no = zero
a / an = one
some = a small number
a lot of = a large number

Talking about nature
Count nouns
There's an ocean near here.
There's a river in my city.
There are no oceans near here.
There are two rivers.
There are some plants.
There are a lot of flowers.
Non-count nouns
There's no / some / a lot of grass.
There's no / some / a lot of water in the ocean.

Asking for directions
Where am I? / Where are we?
I don't understand the map.
Where's Garcia Moreno Street?
Is it near here?
Excuse me? Is this Garcia Moreno Street?

Giving directions
Turn left / right (here).
It's that way.
Go one block / three blocks.
Go straight.
It's on the left / right.
It's over there. / It's here!
That's Garcia Moreno Street.
Look on your phone. Zoom in / Zoom out. It's here.

Writing a fact sheet
It has a lot of interesting animals and birds.
It is a nice, big forest.
Tijuca Forest is very important to Rio de Janeiro.

Planning a new neighborhood for a city
Discussing
I have children. A school is really important.
What about …?
Me, too.
I agree. / I disagree.
I think … is good for the neighborhood.
I want … for the neighborhood.
I like / don't like …
I think … are very important / not very important.
Presenting
We want …
Everyone in the class likes …

Checking information
It's that way. Turn left here. Go one block, and then turn right.
So, turn left here. Go one block, and then turn right.

UNIT 7 LANGUAGE SUMMARY

Verbs
Activities around the home
brush my teeth / my hair
clean the kitchen / my room
cook breakfast / lunch / dinner
do my homework / the dishes
help my daughter / my father
take a bath / a shower
wash my hair
wash the car / the dog

Transportation
be at the bus stop / train station
be on the bus / train / subway
carry a plant / bag
drive
go to the mall / a store / your parents' house
ride your / my bike
take the bus / train / subway
wait
walk

Insider English
ha ha

Glossary
kids
millions
noise
running late

Talking about activities around the house / things happening now
I'm cooking breakfast right now.
Stevie isn't drinking his milk.
You're not eating your breakfast.
They're learning a lot at school this year.

Asking and answering questions about travel
Are you going to work?
Is she carrying a plant?
Are they waiting at the bus stop?
Why is he carrying a plant?
Who are they waiting for?
What are you doing?

Sharing news on the phone
Answering the phone and greeting people
Hello.
Hi, Jennifer. It's Luana.
Hey, Luana!
Asking people how they are
How's it going?
How are you doing?
How are you?
Responding
Not, bad, thanks.
Good, thanks.
I'm fine.

Writing a blog about things happening now
The kids are making a lot of noise! They're busy, too.
Also, the children are eating cookies.
And I'm answering millions of questions from the kids.
But this is difficult for me.

Asking what people are doing these days
Preparing
I like / don't like …
I think … is interesting / boring.
And you?
Role playing
Hi, [name]. How's it going?
Hey, [name]! What are you doing these days?
How are you?
Agreeing
… is a popular topic.
A lot of people are doing …

Reacting to news
A I have a new job. B Oh, wow!
A I'm busy. B Oh.
A My apartment is very expensive. B Oh, no!

T-167

UNIT 8 LANGUAGE SUMMARY

Nouns
Work and study
company
coworkers
have a meeting
office
take a break
think
workers
work hard

Verbs
Skills
dance
draw
fix things
paint
play the guitar
read music
sing
skateboard
snowboard
speak two languages
surf
swim

Insider English
So, Mia. You know it's your mom's birthday next month, right?

Glossary
all
ordinary
pay
robot
terrible

Talking about your skills and abilities
I can swim.
She can draw.
We can surf well.
I can't play the guitar.
He can't sing well.
They can't read music.
Can you fix things?
Can he surf?
Can they speak two languages?

Saying what you can and can't do at work or school
You can work hard and have fun.
She can take a break any time.
Your dog can come to work with you.
What can they do in the office?
How can companies make their workers happy?
Where can you have a meeting?

Saying why you're the right person for a job
Asking for opinions
What do you think?
Why do you think (that) … ?
Giving opinions
I think so.
I don't think so.
I think (that) …
I don't think (that) …

Writing an online comment with your opinion
I think … is right.
… is right, too. She says, "…"
She also says, "…"

Talking about what people are good at
Discussing
Where can people cook really well?
(Chinese) food is always great.
I think people can (cook) really well in (Rome and Naples).
What do you think?
Deciding
What can we do really well in this country?
We can do … well.
I agree. / I disagree.
Our three skills for the video are …
Agreeing
What are your ideas?
Good idea!
Our three favorite skills are …

Explaining and saying more about an idea
A company is a big team. I mean, it's a group of people, and you work with them every day.
I can speak two languages. I mean, I speak Spanish and English.

UNIT 9 LANGUAGE SUMMARY

Nouns
Travel
boat
country
farm
plane
ranch
ticket
tour
town
vacation
Travel arrangements
airport
destination
flight
online
trip

Verbs
Travel arrangements
arrive
buy
check in
fly
leave
stay
travel

Insider English
At an airport: Where is the men's restroom?
At a friend's house: Sorry, where's your bathroom?

Glossary
local
reserve (a room)
tour guide
wonderful

Talking about travel and vacations
This ticket is expensive.
We're at this cool ranch.
These birds are funny.
I don't like these pictures.

Making travel plans
I like to fly.
You need to check in two hours before the flight.
We want to leave on Friday.
She wants to take a bus.
He has to buy tickets.
My mom likes to sleep on a flight.

Asking for and giving information in a store
Where are the travel guides?
How much is that?
It's $9.99.
Is it the same price, $9.99?
They're two for $15.
What time does the café open?
It opens in about 10 minutes.
Where is the men's restroom?

Writing a description of a place
In a website review: Walk to the top of the island.
In a travel guide: You can walk to the top of the island.

Planning a vacation for someone
Discussing
I think [name] likes to … on vacation.
What do you think [name] likes to do?
My three ideas for [name] are …
I agree. / I disagree.
Let's think of one new idea for [name].
Deciding
A good thing to do is …
A good place to go is …
On the first day, he/she can …
Agreeing
We're planning a vacation for …
This is our plan.
Our favorite plan is … because it's interesting/fun/nice.
Asking someone to repeat something
Sorry, can you say that again?
Can you repeat that, please?

T-169

UNIT 10 LANGUAGE SUMMARY

Nouns

Clothes
boots
coat
dress
hat
jeans
pants
shirt
shoes
shorts
skirt
sweater
T-shirt

Seasons
dry season
fall
rainy season
spring
summer
winter

Verbs

Going out
eat outside
get together with friends
go shopping
have a picnic
look at art
meet someone at the airport
take a walk
take someone out for dinner

Insider English
Oh, I know! I can take my fall or winter pants.

Glossary
light
sunrise
surprise

Making outdoor plans for the weekend
I'm going to be home tomorrow.
I'm not going to be home tonight.
It's going to be light all night.
It isn't going to be light all night.
You're going to meet me at the airport.
My friends aren't going to go shopping.
We're going to get together with some of my friends.
They're not going to eat outside this weekend.

Discussing plans
Are you going to take some sweaters?
Yes, I am. / No, I'm not.
Is Sofia going to see a friend?
Yes, she is. / No, she's not.
What are you going to take?
When are you going to leave?
Where is Sofia going to go?
Who are you going to meet?

Suggesting plans

Making suggestions
Why don't we go out tonight?
Let's meet at the hotel.

Accepting suggestions
OK, sounds good.
Good idea.
Yes, sure.

Refusing suggestions
I'm sorry, but I can't.
Sorry, I'm busy.

Writing an online invitation
You're not going to …
Don't be late!
Don't eat …
We're going to …
It's a great place for …
Why don't we …?

Planning and presenting a fun weekend

Researching
Let's talk about the summer / February / the rainy season.
What fun things can we do during the day? / at night? / outside?

Discussing
We're going to have breakfast in the park.
Are you going to have a picnic?

Presenting
We're planning a fun weekend in (season/month).
First, we're going to …
On Saturday/Sunday, …

Saying why you can't do something
I'm sorry, but I can't. I have to go home first. How about eight-thirty?

UNIT 11 LANGUAGE SUMMARY

Nouns
Colors
black
blue
brown
gray
green
orange
pink
purple
red
white
yellow

Adjectives
People, places and things
awful
beautiful
cute
exciting
fast
new
noisy
quiet
slow
wonderful

Verbs
I remember,…

Insider English
Where was the green phone? Oh, yeah! It was at my grandmother's house.
Oh, yeah, and my bedroom walls were pink and green.

Glossary
actor
autograph
childhood
keep
memories
remember
ugly
yard

Describing people, places and things in the past
I was in the yard.
My parents weren't there.
We were on vacation.
It wasn't old.

Talking about colors and memories
Were you at home?
No, I wasn't.
Was the phone in the kitchen?
Yes, it was.
How old were you?
I was two.
What color were the walls?
They were orange.

Expressing uncertainty – very unsure
I have no idea.
I'm not sure.
I don't know.

Expressing uncertainty – a little unsure
Her first name is Kate, I think.
I think her first name is Kate.
Maybe it's Kate Hudson?

Writing an email about your past
Do you remember this …?
There was also …
Your old … was in the …

Talking about TV shows from your childhood
Discussing
I remember … from my childhood.
What about you?
Let's talk about the characters in …
What were their names?
I liked that show because …

Agreeing
What do you remember?
A lot of people remember …
I remember …

Presenting
We're talking about …
Our show was really popular.
It was on TV in (year).

Taking time to think
Um, I have no idea.
Let me think. Maybe it's Kate Hudson?

UNIT 12 LANGUAGE SUMMARY

Nouns
Dairy products
butter
cheese
Desserts
chocolate cake
cookies
ice cream
Drinks
juice
soda
water
Fruit and vegetables
apple
banana
black beans
coconut
green beans
orange
pineapple
potato
tomato

Grains
bread
crackers
rice
Meat and main meals
beef
chicken
eggs
fish
lamb
pizza
steak
Snacks
sandwich
soup

Insider English
server
waiter
waitress

Glossary
food stand
hungry
iced tea
more

Talking about snacks and small meals
Yesterday, I took the bus from …
I didn't eat a lot for breakfast.
I had some soup. He had a big dinner.
She didn't like the sandwich.
She wanted an orange. We wanted some apples.
They didn't drink the coffee.

Talking about meals in restaurants
Did you have apple juice?
Did she like the fish?
Did they eat any ice cream?
How did you hear about us?
What did they eat?

Using polite language at mealtimes
Offering food and drink
Do you want some more?
Would you like some potatoes?
What would you like to eat / to drink?
What would you like for dessert?

Requesting food and drink
Can I have some bread?
Please pass the butter.
I'd like the chicken and rice, please.
Do you have iced tea?

Responding to requests
Of course.
Here. / Here you are.
All right. / OK.
We have small and large iced teas.

Writing a restaurant review
This is a nice / good restaurant.
I had …
My brother / friend had …
The … was good / OK.
The servers were (really) nice / (so) friendly.
We were (really) happy with our meal.
He liked his meal.
It wasn't expensive.
The price was OK – not cheap, but not expensive.

Creating a menu
Deciding
OK. First, what's the name of our restaurant?
What kind of food do we have?
Let's plan a great menu. We can have …
Role playing
Welcome to our restaurant!
What would you like to eat / drink?
Do you have … ?
So, you would like …
Presenting
We went to a great restaurant. Its name was …
We liked / didn't like …
Our favorite menu is … because …

Using *so* and *really* to make words stronger
I really like this fish. It's so good!
I'd like a large iced tea. It's so hot today.

STUDENT'S BOOK AUDIO SCRIPTS

Track 1.10
Lesson 1.3, page 7, Exercises 3A and 3B

Man	Hello. Welcome to the Westside Hotel. What's your name?
Woman	My name is Lisa Carlton. I'm here for two nights.
Man	How do you spell your last name?
Woman	C-A-R-L-T-O-N.
Man	Ah, yes. Here you are. What's your cell phone number?
Woman	It's 555 889 3245.
Man	OK. Thank you. And what's your email address?
Woman	It's lcarlton01@bestmail.com.

Track 1.11
Lesson 1.3, page 7, Exercise 3C

Woman	How do you spell your last name?
Man	What country are you from? How do you spell it?
Woman	What's the name of your school? How do you spell it?

Track 1.24
Lesson 2.3 page 17, Exercises 3A and 3B

Woman	How old is your daughter?
Man	She's thirty. No, sorry, <u>thirteen</u>!
Woman	Thirteen. OK!

Track 1.26
Lesson 2.4, page 18, Exercise 1B and 1C

Isabel	So, Linda – here's my band!
Linda	Wow! Are you good?
Isabel	No! Well, we're not *bad*.
Linda	And where are you, in this photo?
Isabel	We're not in Las Vegas! We're in Seattle, at college.
Linda	Are they your friends from college?
Isabel	Yeah. This is Joshua, on the right.
Linda	Yeah?
Isabel	He's really funny.
Linda	Great! And this is … ?
Isabel	This is Nuwa, on the left.
Linda	OK.
Isabel	She's really smart. And I'm here, and Guy is next to me. He's between Nuwa and me.
Linda	Sorry, what's his name?
Isabel	Guy. He's really cool … but he's shy.
Linda	He's a shy Guy!
Isabel	Yeah!

Track 1.27
Lesson 2.3, page 18, Exercise 3A

Woman	**Here's** my band.
Man	**We're** in Seattle.
Woman	**He's** really funny.
Man	**You're** great!

Track 1.34
Lesson 3.3, page 27, Exercises 3A and 3B

Woman	Coffee or tea?
Man	Tea, please.
Woman	Sugar?
Man	Yes, please.
Woman	Milk?
Man	No, thanks.
Woman	OK. And a biscuit?
Man	Sorry, I don't understand. What's a … biscuit?
Woman	This is a biscuit.
Man	Oh, a cookie.
Woman	Yes. In the United States, it's a cookie. Here in Australia, it's a biscuit.
Man	OK! So, yes, please.
Woman	Here you are.

Track 1.42
Lesson 4.3, page 39, Exercises 2B and 2C

Woman	Do you talk to your family on the phone?
Man	Well, I talk to my parents on the phone. They're 81 years old.
Woman	OK.
Man	So they don't like computers. They like the phone.
Woman	Yeah.
Man	But I send emails to my son and daughter.
Woman	Right.

Track 1.45
Lesson 4.4, page 40, Exercises 1B and 1C

Woman 1	I have two TVs. This one is in my bedroom, on my desk. I like it because it's small. I don't like big TVs. Also, it's not expensive. $119 is a good price. It's cheap, but it's nice.
Man	I love games, and this tablet is great for games. It's really fast, and it has a nice design. It's $415. Not cheap. But it's expensive because it's a great product. I love it.
Woman 2	This is an app for photos. You take a photo. Then you change it with the app, but it's difficult, and the photos aren't good. A bad app? Yes! Sorry, but I don't like it.

Track 1.54
Lesson 5.3, page 49, Exercises 2B and 2C

Man	You run, right?
Woman	Yeah, every morning.
Man	So do you get up early?
Woman	Usually.
Man	On weekends, too?
Woman	That's right.
Man	No way!
Woman	Do you get up early on weekends?
Man	Never!

T-173

Track 1.62
Lesson 6.3, page 59, Exercises 2A and 2B

Man	Excuse me. Is the City Hotel near here?
Woman	Yes. Turn left here. Go straight. It's on the right.
Man	So, turn left here. Go straight. It's on the right.
Woman	Yes.

Track 1.63
Lesson 6.3, page 59, Exercise 2C

Woman1	Turn right here. Then turn right again.
Man	Go one block. Then turn left.
Woman1	Go straight. Turn left. Then turn right.
Man	Go three blocks. It's on the left.

Track 1.67
Lesson 6.4, page 60, Exercises 1B and 1C

Yasmin Welcome to "Walk with Yasmin." Where am I today? Well, there are some tall trees and a lot of big plants here. And do you hear the water? There's a river near me, too. And listen! There are a lot of interesting animals here. But I'm not in a zoo.

I'm on a mountain in a forest. But trees and animals aren't the only things near me. There's an ocean and some beautiful beaches. And there are people, too. More than six million people! And a lot of buildings – hotels, stores, and restaurants.

So where am I? This is Tijuca Forest, in the big, busy city of Rio de Janeiro.

Track 2.07
Lesson 7.3, page 71, Exercises 2B and 2C

Man	I'm in my car.
Woman	Oh.
Man	I have a new car…
Woman	Oh, wow!
Man	Yeah, but I have a problem with it. A big problem.
Woman	Oh, no! OK, where are you?

Track 2.16
Lesson 8.3, page 81, Exercises 2B and 2C

Coach	So, Lori, why are you the right person for the dance team?
Lori	Because I work really hard. I mean, I dance about two hours a day.
Coach	I see. And can you meet in the mornings?
Lori	Oh, yes. I'm not busy. I mean, I work in a restaurant at night, but I have free time in the morning.
Coach	OK. Great.

Track 2.19
Lesson 8.4, page 82, Exercises 1B and 1C

Chris	Today on *Technology Talks* I'm with Joanna Ramos. She's from ITCI – a computer company. Welcome, Joanna.
Joanna	Thank you, Chris.
Chris	Joanna … a big question: Can computers take all our jobs? What do you think?
Joanna	Well, first, I think there's another question. What can computers do? Some examples: They can make cars. They can *drive* cars. They can talk …
Chris	They can do a lot of things.
Joanna	Yes, they can. *But* … they can't do those things *100%*. A computer can't make 100% of a car. Car companies need workers, too. Computers can't drive cars all the time. Only people can do that. And, OK, computers can *talk*, but they can't always *understand* us. My phone hardly ever understands me! And computers can't *think*. I mean, computers can't think *today*.
Chris	So *are* computers taking a lot of jobs?
Joanna	I don't think so. They are taking *some* of our jobs. But *people* make computers. And people's voices are the computers' voices. So there are a lot of new jobs, too.
Chris	*A lot* of new jobs? Is that true? I don't think that …

Track 2.20
Lesson 8.4, page 82, Exercise 2A

Woman	What can computers do?
Woman	They can make cars.
Woman	A computer can't make 100% of a car.

Track 2.21
Lesson 8.4, page 82, Exercise 2B

Woman	They can drive cars.
Woman	They can talk.
Woman	Computers can't drive cars all the time.
Woman	They can't always understand us.

Track 2.27
Lesson 9.3, page 91, Exercise 2B

Woman	Excuse me. How much is this cell phone?
Man	It's usually $350, but today it's just $305.50.
Woman	Sorry, can you repeat that, please?
Man	It's usually $350. Today it's just $305.50.
Woman	Oh! Good price!

Track 2.36
Lesson 10.3, page 103, Exercises 2B and 2C

Man	Why don't we have a meeting on Monday?
Woman	I'm sorry, but I can't. I have to help my parents on Monday. How about Tuesday?
Man	OK. Let's meet on Tuesday.

Track 2.40
Lesson 10.4, page 104, Exercises 1B and 1C

Presenter This week on *Let's Take a Tour*, I'm in a city that never sleeps. No, this isn't New York. I'm in Montevideo – the capital city of Uruguay. And this *really* is a day-and-night city. Now, we're not far from the Pocitos neighborhood. Pocitos is a *great* place to go out at night in Montevideo. It has restaurants, cafés, places to go dancing … but I'm not going to go dancing now. Let's wait for tonight! First, we're going to walk by the ocean in Old City.

Old City is … an *old* neighborhood, of course. It has some beautiful buildings and some really interesting museums. So come on! Let's take a tour … in Montevideo.

Track 2.42
Lesson 10.4, page 104, Exercise 2B

Man 1 We're gonna visit some museums.
Man 2 We're not going to a restaurant. We're going to a café.
Woman 1 We're gonna walk around the Old City.
Woman 2 We're going to go out in the Pocitos neighborhood.

Track 2.48
Lesson 11.3, page 113, Exercises 2B and 2C

Woman 1 What was your favorite concert?
Man Let me think … it was the Red Hot Chili Peppers. It was very exciting!
Woman What year was it?
Man Uh, 2001, I think.

Track 2.57
Lesson 12.3, page 123, Exercises 2B and 2C

Man I really like this bread. It's so good.
Woman 1 That's true.
Man Let's ask for more.
Woman 1 Are you sure? You have steak and potatoes and …
Man But this bread is great, Mandy. It's so warm. Excuse me! Can we have more bread, please?

Track 2.61
Lesson 12.4, page 124, Exercises 1B and 1C

Mara So, Eric, where do you want to eat?
Eric Why don't we go to Fish Around? I'm hungry, and it's near here.
Mara No. I mean, I love their food, but I ate there last week. How about Kayla B's Kitchen?
Eric Ugh, no. I went there with Freddy in November. My steak was awful, and the servers were really slow.
Mara OK. Well, we can try a new place. What else is near here? Let's look on the app.
Eric Good idea. OK, there are a lot of places near here. Do you want Chinese, Mexican, or Italian food?
Mara Uh … Mexican, I think.
Eric We can try Tio's Tacos. It's not very expensive, and it has good reviews.
Mara How many stars does it have?
Eric Four.
Mara That's good! What do the reviewers say?
Eric Let's see … One man says, "My meal was great, and the servers were really friendly." And a woman says, "The food is really good. I didn't get any dessert, but the chocolate cake looked wonderful. And the fruit juices …"
Mara OK, OK. You don't need to read more. Let's go!

Track 2.63
Lesson 12.4, page 124, Exercise 2B

Man /dʒu/ want some dessert?
Woman I don't wanna go to class today.
Man /dʒu/ wanna go to Fish Around?

PHOTOCOPIABLE ACTIVITIES

Grammar teacher's notes — **T-177**
Grammar activities — **T-186**
Vocabulary teacher's notes — **T-215**
Vocabulary activities — **T-224**
Speaking teacher's notes — **T-249**
Speaking activities — **T-254**

- There is a **Grammar activity** for each lesson 1 and 2 of the Student's Book.
- There is a **Vocabulary activity** for each lesson 1 and 2 of the Student's Book.
- There is a **Speaking activity** for each unit of the Student's Book, which encompasses the grammar and vocabulary points of each unit.

Teacher's notes for photocopiable activities: GRAMMAR

UNIT 1, LESSON 1, GRAMMAR

Timing: 45 Minutes

- **Prepare for the task** Photocopy one worksheet for each group of five Ss and cut up into five Student cards.
- **Introduce the task** Tell Ss to ask you three *Are you …?* questions for which the answer is *Yes, I am*. For example:
- *Are you Spanish?* (*Yes, I am.*) Then tell Ss to ask you three *Are you …?* questions for which the answer is *No, I'm not*. For example: *Are you in room 1?* (*No, I'm not.*) Put Ss into pairs to do the same.
- Alternatively, Ss can role play calling one another and asking who it is. For example: *Hello, are you Maria?* (*No, I'm not.*)
- **Do the task** Put Ss into groups of five and give each S a card. (In smaller groups, a stronger S can have two cards.) Tell Ss to take turns asking one another questions to fill in the table. Model with a stronger S.
  - *Are you Brazilian?*
  - *No, I'm not.*
  - *Are you a student?*
  - *Yes, I am.*
- Monitor and make sure Ss are using questions and short answers correctly.
- **Review the task** Have Ss repeat all the questions and answers for the Student 1 and 2 cards:
  - *Are you Brazilian?*
  - *No, I'm not.*
  - *Are you from France?*
  - *Yes, I am.*

UNIT 1, LESSON 2, GRAMMAR

Timing: 45 Minutes

- **Prepare for the task** Photocopy one worksheet for each group of four Ss and cut up into four Student cards.
- **Introduce the task** Write these answers to personal questions on the board.
- Victor
- Lebrun
- French
- v.lebrun@abc.net
- Nord College

- Ask Ss what the question for each answer would be. For example: Victor (*What's your first name?*). Ask Ss what the full answer would be, for example: *It's Victor*. Have Ss repeat all the questions and answers several times so that you are sure they are using the grammar and pronouncing the words correctly.
- **Do the task** Put Ss into groups of four and give each S a card. Tell Ss to ask one another questions to complete the table. Tell Ss to spell out names when necessary. Demonstrate with a stronger S. Monitor and make sure Ss are asking and answering one another correctly.
- **Review the task** Ask Ss questions. They should answer using the information about themselves in the table.
- As an extension task, ask each group to change the information and make four new cards. Groups can then swap the sets of cards and repeat the activity.

UNIT 2, LESSON 1, GRAMMAR

Timing: 45 Minutes

- **Prepare for the task** Copy and cut up one worksheet for each group of three Ss. To save cutting, Ss could take turns matching a question to an answer, continuing until one S makes a mistake.
- **Introduce the task** Read some short answers with *is / are* aloud. Ss must make questions to match them. For example:
  - **A** *No, I'm not.*
  - **B** *Are you American?*
  - **A** *Yes, they are.*
  - **B** *Are the students in class?*
- **Do the task** Put Ss into groups of three. Give each group a pile of Question cards. Have Ss fill in the questions with *is / are*. Check as a class.
- Give each group a pile of Answer cards turned upside down. Have each S take a Question card and an Answer card. Have them read the Question card aloud and then the Answer card with the verb *be*. If the question and answer match and Ss use the grammar correctly, the Ss keep the cards. For example:
- *Is Marie at college?*
- *Yes, she is.*
- Ss can keep these cards because the grammar is correct and the cards match.
- Have Ss continue taking turns until all the cards are used. The winner is the S with the most cards. Monitor and make sure Ss are using *is / are* correctly.

T-177

- **Review the task** Have Ss match a Question card to each answer. Go through each question and answer to check.
- As a variation or extension task, give half the class a Question card and the other half an Answer card. Tell Ss to go around and find a partner to match their question or answer. Have each pair of Ss read aloud their question and answer to check that they use *be* correctly and that the cards match.

UNIT 2, LESSON 2, GRAMMAR
Timing: 45 Minutes

- **Prepare for the task** Photocopy one Student A worksheet and one Student B worksheet for each pair of Ss. Fold each worksheet so that Ss can't see the sentences (part B for Student A and part A for Student B).
- **Introduce the task** Make sentences about someone in the class using *is not / are not ('s not / 're not)*. Ss should guess the student.
- For example:
  - *He isn't boring. He isn't shy. He isn't from Brazil.* (Miguel)
  - *You aren't Mexican. You aren't very tall. You aren't at college.* (Lola)
- Put Ss into pairs to make sentences about other people in the class.
- **Do the task** Put Ss into pairs. Student B writes six different sentences with *is not / are not ('s not / 're not)* using the information they have. For example: *He isn't short. He isn't Russian.* Student B reads the sentences to Student A. Student A listens and chooses which of the three people this is about (*not Alex, not Sasha, so Leo*). After Student B writes six sentences, it is Student A's turn to write six sentences. Demonstrate with a stronger S. Monitor and help where necessary.
- **Review the task** Go through the 12 sentences and check that they are correct and that Ss have chosen the correct descriptions.
- Choose some of the people in the descriptions and ask Ss to make sentences about them using the correct forms of *is / are* and *is not / are not ('s not / 're not)*. For example:
  - *Valda (She's my cousin. She isn't a doctor.)*
  - *The parents (They're Colombian. They aren't at the office.)*

> **Answers**
> 1 Leo 2 Eldora 3 the children 4 my mom 5 Jason and Victoria 6 Flavio 7 Joan 8 Adrian 9 brothers 10 Pablo 11 Octavia 12 parents

UNIT 3, LESSON 1, GRAMMAR
Timing: 40 Minutes

- **Prepare for the task** Copy the worksheet for groups of four Ss and cut up into Student A, Student B, Student C, and Student D sections.
- **Introduce the task** Put Ss into pairs. Ask them to find out the following information from each other: their mother's name, their birthday, their favorite room in their apartment/house, the name of their best friend. Model for Ss how to form their questions and answers. For example: *What is the name of your best friend? My best friend's name is Carmen.*
- **Do the task** Put Ss into groups of four. Ss ask and answer questions about each person in the family using possessive adjectives and possessive *'s and s'*. For example: *What's the daughter's name? Her name is Marina. What's her favorite room? Her favorite room is the kitchen.* Demonstrate with a stronger S and then have Ss work in groups. Monitor and make sure Ss are asking and answering questions using possessive adjectives and possessive *'s and s'*. Encourage Ss to spell out a name they can't pronounce, if necessary.
- **Review the task** Ask Ss to circle the information in the table that is the same and elicit these sentences:
- *The parents' best friend is Jon. Their best friend is Jon.*
- *The son's favorite room is the bedroom. His mother's favorite room is the bedroom. Their favorite room is the bedroom.*
- Ask Ss more questions about the table and have them answer using possessive adjectives and possessive *'s and s'*.

UNIT 3, LESSON 2, GRAMMAR
Timing: 45 Minutes

- **Prepare for the task** Copy one worksheet for each S.
- **Introduce the task** Tell Ss that you will think of a word and tell them the first letter. They must guess what the word is, asking *Is it …?* For example:
  - *The first letter is b.*
  - *Is it birthday?*
  - *No, it isn't.*
  - *Is it bathroom?*
  - *No, it isn't.*
  - *Is it bedroom?*
  - *Yes, it is!*
- Put Ss into pairs to practice.
- **Do the task** Put Ss into new pairs. Tell them to take turns going through the squares to the finish. They can only go through squares where it is possible to use *it is* in positive, negative or question forms. Tell Ss that the only connection between squares is grammatical – they don't make a conversation or story. Ss can only move one square at a time, up, down, across, or diagonally (in any direction). They must complete the sentence in the square with *it is* and read it aloud before they continue. Demonstrate with a stronger S:
  - *Do we say, "It is Miguel and I'm from Spain"?*
  - *No.*
  - *Do we say, "It's a door"?*
  - *Yes.*
  - *What square is next?*
  - *"No, it isn't new".*

T-178

- Monitor and help where necessary.
- **Review the task** Have Ss read aloud all the squares where it is possible to use *it is*.
- Then put Ss into small groups. Give Ss one minute to look at the sentences with *it is*. Tell them to turn over the worksheet. Have Ss write down as many of the sentences as they can in 2 minutes. See which group can remember the most.

> **Answers**
> It's a door.
> No, it isn't / is not (it's / it is) new.
> Is it a bed?
> Yes, it's / it is my email.
> It's / It is (isn't / is not) December 28.
> It's / It is (isn't / is not) a house.
> It's / It is (isn't / is not) a sink.
> No, it isn't / is not.
> It's / It is (isn't / is not) a table.
> It's / It is (isn't / is not) a big apartment.
> Is it a chair?
> Yes, it's / it is next to the lamp.
> Is it a cat?
> It's / It is (isn't / is not) a house.
> Is it room 16?
> No, it's / it is (isn't / is not) very interesting.
> Is it a picture of your daughter?
> It's / It is (isn't / is not) the living room.
> Is it a dog?
> It's / It is (isn't / is not) the bathroom.
> No, it's / it is (isn't / is not) here.
> It is a rug.
> Is it a desk or a table?
> Yes, it is.
> No, it's / it is (isn't / is not) very big.
> Is it a blue pen?
> It's / It is (isn't / is not) on the couch.
> It's/It is (isn't / is not) a TV.
> Is this painting from Mexico? No, it isn't / is not.
> It is a French book.
> Yes, it's / it is new.
> It's / It is (isn't / is not) September 3.
> It's / It is (isn't / is not) my last name.

UNIT 4, LESSON 1, GRAMMAR

Timing: 40 Minutes

- **Prepare for the task** Copy one worksheet for each S. You need a die for each pair of Ss. (You can make your own die using a marker and sugar cubes, or you can use a die app on a smartphone.)
- **Introduce the task** Tell Ss to write down three things that they want, like, or have. Then have them write three things that they don't like, don't want, or don't have. Put Ss into pairs. Tell them to make sentences about what is true for them both. For example: *We like grammar apps.*
- **Do the task** Put Ss into pairs. Tell them to take turns rolling a die three times to make sentences. After the first roll, Ss follow the arrows for the second and third rolls so sentences are all using words in the same column. If the sentence is true for either partner or both partners, they get one point. The first S to 10 points is the winner. Demonstrate the activity by rolling the die three times, making a sentence and saying whether it is true or not.

- Monitor and help where necessary.
- **Review the task** Call out a series of three numbers. Ss must make sentences. For example:
  - *six, two, four = You have a laptop.*

UNIT 4, LESSON 2, GRAMMAR

Timing: 45 Minutes

- **Prepare for the task** Copy one worksheet for each pair of Ss.
- **Introduce the task** Ask Ss to write three questions which they would answer *Yes, I do.* and three questions which they would answer *No, I don't.* Put Ss into pairs to ask each other their six questions.
- **Do the task** Put Ss into pairs and give them a copy of the worksheet. Explain the rules of four in a row (also known as the popular board game Connect 4 ®). Have the two Ss choose X or O and take turns choosing a square, making the question, and then answering it themselves with a short answer. For example:
  - *Do you have a new cell phone?*
  - *No, I don't.*
- If they say the question and short answer correctly, they write X or O there. After the first turn, they can only go next to or directly above a square which has an X or O. The first person with four X's or O's in a row—horizontally, vertically or diagonally—is the winner.
- A finished game might look like this:

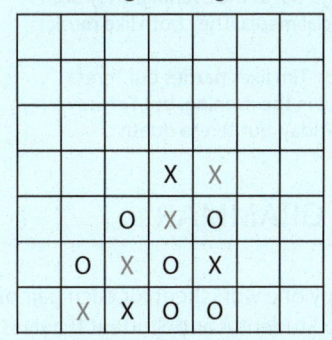

				X	X	
			O	X	O	
	O		X	O	X	
	X	X	O	O		

- To demonstrate the activity, you could also show one of the online versions of the game. Monitor and make sure Ss are using questions and short answers correctly.
- **Review the task** Choose some squares and ask Ss to make the question and short answer.
- For extra practice, put Ss into new pairs. Ss take turns choosing squares and asking each other the questions.

UNIT 5, LESSON 1, GRAMMAR

Timing: 50 Minutes

- **Prepare for the task** Photocopy one worksheet for each group of four Ss. Cut up each worksheet into sections for Student A, Student B, Student C, and Student D.

T-179

- **Introduce the task** Say some sentences in the simple present about a S in the class. Have the other Ss guess who it is. For example:
  - *She has a sister.*
  - *She loves football.*
  - *She doesn't work. She studies at college.*
- Ask other Ss to come to the front of the class and do the same.
- **Do the task** Put Ss into groups of four. Tell Ss to take turns making simple present sentences about Yuri, Teresa, Tim, and Kristina. Ss share their sentences with the rest of the group. For example: *Yuri works Monday to Friday.* Ss listen to one another and fill in the information in the table with the information they learn. When the table is full, Ss imagine that Yuri, Teresa, Tim, and Kristina are at a party. Tell Ss to identify people as friends whose lifestyle and interests are similar. Monitor and make sure Ss are forming complete sentences that are grammatically correct and not just reading out the information in note form.
- **Review the task** Choose some of the squares in the table and ask Ss to read out full sentences about them. For example: Tim/use social media – *Tim often uses social media.*
- As an extension, put Ss into new groups of four. Tell them to ask one another the same questions and then report back to the class.

Answers
Yuri and Kristina are friends: They both have free time on the weekends. They sometimes go out in the evening. They both like computer games and social media. They both like music and parties.
Teresa and Tim are not friends. Tim likes parties but Teresa doesn't. Teresa often goes out in the evening, but Tim never does. Tim works Monday to Friday, but Teresa doesn't.

UNIT 5, LESSON 2, GRAMMAR
Timing: 45 Minutes

- **Prepare for the task** Copy one worksheet for each pair of Ss. Cut the worksheet into Student A and Student B halves.
- **Introduce the task** Dictate these clock times to Ss: *8:00 a.m., 11:30 a.m., 1:00 p.m., 5:15 p.m., 9:00 p.m.* Tell Ss to write down the times in their notebooks. Then have them write down what they usually do at each of these times. For example:
  - *8:00   I usually go to work.*
- Tell Ss to compare with a partner.
- **Do the task** Create a group of Student As and Student Bs. Have them work together to write down the questions they need to ask to complete the information about Martina's routine. Check that the questions are accurate. If the class needs additional support, write the questions from the Key on the board. (You could mix up the word order of the questions to make it more challenging.)
- Put each Student A with a Student B. Tell them to take turns asking and answering questions to complete the text about Martina's routine. Monitor and help where necessary. Ss can then swap cards and repeat with the new questions.

- **Review the task** Go through all the questions on the Student A and B cards.
- As an extension, put Ss into new pairs. One S is Martina and the other (the stronger S) is an interviewer. The interviewer should ask Martina questions and Martina should reply using the information on both cards. For example:
  - *Martina, what time do you get up?*
  - *I get up at 6:00 a.m.*

Answers
Student A
1 What does she do before breakfast?
2 Where does she have breakfast?
3 What does she always have with her breakfast?
4 Where does she work?
5 What does she love?
6 When does she go home?
7 What time does she make dinner?
8 When does she sometimes go out?
Student B
1 What time does she get up?
2 When does she go to work?
3 Where does she work?
4 When does she have classes?
5 What time does she chat with her mother?
6 What does she want for her birthday?
7 What does she listen to before bed?
8 What time does she go to bed?

UNIT 6, LESSON 1, GRAMMAR
Timing: 40 Minutes

- **Prepare for the task** Copy one worksheet between each pair of Ss and cut up into Student A and Student B halves.
- **Introduce the task** Put Ss into pairs. Dictate these sentences. Ss should write down what they hear and then compare with their partner. Check the sentences as a class, then have Ss check (✓) the ones that describe their town.
  - *There are a lot of good places to go out.*
  - *There are no nice restaurants.*
  - *There is an interesting park near here.*
- **Do the task** Put Ss into new pairs. Give each S a different picture. Write sentences beginning with *there* and *there's* on the board and model with words from the pictures:
  - *There's no hotel.*
  - *There are no cafés.*
  - *There's a mall.*
  - *There are some restaurants.*
  - *There are a lot of museums.*
- Tell Ss to take turns saying sentences with *there* about their picture. Tell them to find the ten differences. Monitor and help where necessary.
- **Review the task** Ask Ss: *Do you like New Town or Smith Town? Why?* Elicit the ten differences from Ss (see Key). Write them on the board.

T-180

Answers

In New Town, there's no zoo. In Smith Town, there's a zoo.
In New Town, there's a park. In Smith Town, there's no park.
In New Town, there are no movie theaters. In Smith Town, there are a lot of movie theaters.
In New Town, there are a lot of bookstores. In Smith Town, there is one bookstore.
In New Town, there is one museum. In Smith Town, there are a lot of museums.
In New Town, there are no hotels. In Smith Town, there are a lot of hotels.
In New Town, there are a lot of cafés. In Smith Town, there are no cafés.
In New Town, there are no restaurants. In Smith Town, there are some restaurants.
In New Town, there are lots of stores. In Smith Town, there is no store.
In New Town, there's no supermarket. In Smith Town, there's a supermarket.

UNIT 6, LESSON 2, GRAMMAR
Timing: 40 Minutes

- **Prepare for the task** Copy and cut up one set of dominoes for each group of three Ss. To make the activity longer, copy two sets of dominoes for each group. To save cutting, Ss can work in pairs and take turns choosing the count and non-count words from the dominoes. Ss will continue until one student chooses the wrong word.
- **Introduce the task** Tell Ss to draw two columns in their notebooks: count and non-count. Read aloud these words and ask Ss to put them in the correct column:
- *school, grass, island, water, place, nature, hill, information, park, furniture, neighborhood, snow*

Answers
Count
school, island, place, hill, park, neighborhood
Non-count
grass, water, nature, information, furniture, snow

- **Do the task** Give one set of dominoes to each group. Tell Ss to divide the dominoes between themselves. Tell one S to begin by putting down any domino. One side of the domino has a non-count noun, the other has a count noun. The next S must try to match the type of noun on his/her domino, placing it to the left or right, next to the non-count or count noun. Demonstrate on the board with a stronger S. Have Ss take turns choosing the next domino to put down. Follow the example:
  mall   information   nature   store
- Tell Ss to take turns putting down dominoes to the left or right. If a S makes a mistake with the noun, they must take back their domino and miss a turn. The first S to use all their dominoes is the winner. Monitor and help where necessary.
- **Review the task** Go through all the dominoes and ask Ss to mark the nouns as count or non-count. Choose nouns and ask Ss to make sentences with them beginning with *There is*.
- As an extension task or more demanding variation, tell Ss to also say a sentence with *There is* + one of the nouns which are next to each other. For example: *There's a lot of information on the internet.*

UNIT 7, LESSON 1, GRAMMAR
Timing: 40 Minutes

- **Prepare for the task** Copy one worksheet between each pair of Ss and cut up into Picture A and Picture B halves.
- **Introduce the task** Mime an activity, such as sending a text message. Then ask Ss to say what you are doing.
  - *You're sending a text message.*
- Ask other Ss to come to the front of the class and mime a different activity. Have the other Ss describe the action.
- **Do the task** Put Ss into pairs and give each S a different picture. Tell Ss there are seven differences between their pictures. Ss take turns saying what is happening in their picture. For example: *In my picture, the father is cleaning the kitchen*. Monitor and help where necessary. If Ss need more support, write these sentence frames on the board:

In picture A / my picture …
the father … the kitchen.
the cat … milk.
the dog …
the grandmother … breakfast.
the son … his grandmother.
the grandfather … to music.
the child …

In picture B / my picture …
the mother … the kitchen.
the cat … milk.
the dog …
the grandmother … the dishes.
the daughter … her grandmother.
the grandfather … tea.
the child …

- **Review the task** Check that Ss have found the seven differences. Ask Ss to make positive and negative present continuous sentences to show all seven differences. For example:
  - *In picture A, the father is cleaning the kitchen.*
  - *In picture B, the father isn't cleaning the kitchen. The mother is cleaning the kitchen.*
- Then tell Ss to turn the pictures over. Give Ss two minutes to write down as many of the differences as they can remember.

Answers

In picture A, the father is cleaning the kitchen. In picture B, the father isn't cleaning the kitchen / the mother is cleaning the kitchen.

In picture A, the cat is drinking milk. In picture B, the cat isn't drinking milk.

In picture A, the dog isn't running. In picture B, the dog is running.

In picture A, the grandmother is making breakfast. In picture B, the grandmother isn't making breakfast / is doing the dishes.

In picture A, the son is helping his grandmother. In picture B, the son isn't helping his grandmother / the daughter is helping her grandmother.

In picture A, the grandfather is listening to music. In picture B, the grandfather isn't listening to music / is drinking tea.

In picture A, the child is playing. In picture B, the child isn't playing / is eating.

UNIT 7, LESSON 2, GRAMMAR

Timing: 45 Minutes

- **Prepare for the task** Copy and cut up a set of Question and Answer cards for each group of eight Ss. Copy and distribute one chart for each S. To save cutting, Ss can choose a question from the Question cards and an answer from the Answer cards.

- **Introduce the task** Model using the present continuous by asking yes/no questions and guiding Ss to answer using information about themselves, their family, or their best friend. For example:
  - *Is your father going home now?*
  - *No, he isn't.*
  - *What is he doing?*
  - *He's going to work.*

- **Do the task** Put Ss into groups of about eight (if it is a small class, copy more cards and do the activity as a whole class). Give each S the empty chart and have Ss write the name of each S in their group in the chart. Give each group a set of Question and Answer cards.

- Tell each S to choose a Question card and an Answer card. Then Ss ask each S in the group their yes/no question. If the answer is no, they must find out what the S is doing. For example:
  - *Diego, are you watching TV?*
  - *No, I'm not.*
  - *What are you doing?*
  - *I'm learning English.*
  - *Marina, are you watching TV?*
  - *Yes, I am watching TV.*

- Tell Ss to write the information in their chart during the activity. Monitor and help where necessary.

- **Review the task** Check that Ss have completed the chart in full present continuous sentences. Ask Ss from different groups to ask one another yes/no and information questions to find out what they are (not) doing.

- As a variation, put the Question cards in a pile for the whole group and tell Ss to each take one Answer card. Ss keep taking Question cards, asking one another information questions and returning the Question cards to the pile until they come to the correct answer.

- As an extension task, repeat the activity without Ss writing down the information during the activity. At the end, ask each S to remember what activities the other Ss are doing. Tell them to write down what they can remember using the present continuous.

UNIT 8, LESSON 1, GRAMMAR

Timing: 45 Minutes

- **Prepare the task**
- Copy one worksheet for each S.
- **Introduce the task** Tell Ss to list five things they can do well, for example: *speak English*. Put Ss into pairs. Have Ss make sentences about each other's list and share with the class, for example: *Carmen can speak English well*.

- **Do the task** Put Ss into pairs. Have them each put an X next to the ten questions they would like to ask their partner. Tell Ss to take turns asking and answering questions about the ten topics. Ss should ask *Can (you) …?* and if the answer is yes, *Can (you) … well?* Monitor and make sure Ss are using the grammar correctly. If Ss finish early, tell them to choose more questions.

- **Review the task** Ask Ss to report back what they learned from their partner.

- *Hanako can cook dinner for her family. She can cook well.*

- As an extension task, put Ss into new pairs and tell them to choose new questions to ask each other.

UNIT 8, LESSON 2, GRAMMAR

Timing: 50 Minutes

- **Prepare for the task** Copy one worksheet for each S.
- **Introduce the task** Write these questions on the board. Put Ss into groups to say if they agree or disagree and why. Prompt Ss to use *Yes, (it) can.* and *No, (it) can't.* in their answers.
  - *Can money make people happy?*
  - *Can your job be your hobby?*
  - *Can your coworkers be your friends?*
  - *Can a boring teacher be a good teacher?*

- **Do the task** Group all Student As together, all Student Bs, all Student Cs, and all Student Ds. Give each S a worksheet. Tell each group what information to write in their company / column.

	Student A Lee & Sons	Student B ABC Company
walk to the office	No	Yes
work at home on Tuesdays	No	No
learn English with coworkers	Yes	No
learn new computer skills	No	No
take a lot of breaks	Yes	Yes
bring your dog to work	No	No
meet a lot of people	No	Yes
have a lot of fun	Yes	No

	Student C Alvarez	Student D Yamasaki
walk to the office	Yes	No
work at home on Tuesdays	No	Yes
learn English with coworkers	No	Yes
learn new computer skills	Yes	No
take a lot of breaks	No	No
bring your dog to work	No	Yes
meet a lot of people	No	No
have a lot of fun	Yes	No

- Put Ss into groups so that each S is a different company. Tell Ss to take turns asking one another questions about the things you can / can't do in that company. For example:
  - *Can you walk to the ABC Company office?*
  - *Yes, you can.*
- Ss ask the questions and complete the chart. Monitor and make sure Ss are asking and answering questions with *can* or *can't*.
- Then tell Ss to look at all the information and decide together which is the best company for them to work in.
- **Review the task** Choose some information from the completed table and ask Ss to make sentences with *can* / *can't*. For example: *Alvarez/work at home on Tuesdays – You can't work at home on Tuesdays.*
- As an alternative, ask Ss to make up the answers for each company and then ask one another the questions using *can*.

- As an extension activity, ask Ss to make sentences about their company or the company of a friend or relative. For example: *I can't walk to my office. My mother can learn English with coworkers.* You could also have Ss rate the information that is most important to know about each company.

UNIT 9, LESSON 1, GRAMMAR
Timing: 40 Minutes

- **Prepare for the task** Copy one worksheet for each S. Cut up a set of cards from the top half of the worksheet for each pair of Ss. To save cutting, Ss could take turns choosing one of the cards and making a sentence.
- **Introduce the task** Ss put some items from their pockets and bags on your desk. These may include phones, earphones, or books. Take one item and say *This is …* For example: *This is Natasha's English book*. Take something else and say *These are …* For example: *These are Manuel's earphones*. Ask Ss to come to the table and do the same.
- **Do the task** Tell Ss to work in pairs. Give each S the bottom half of the worksheet. Give each pair a set of cards to cut out and mix up. Tell Ss to take turns choosing a card. Have Ss make a sentence with *this / these* and say it to their partner. For example: *This bag is cheap*. Then Ss read aloud their sentences to their partner. Their partners should use the sentence to circle the correct picture. Monitor and make sure Ss are reading out full sentences with *this / these*. At the end, Ss check with each other to make sure they have circled the right picture.
- **Review the task** Say some different sentences and ask Ss to show you the right picture in the row. For example:
  - *These cats are not nice.*
  - *This language is Spanish.*
  - *These people are in a meeting.*
- Ask Ss to write five different sentences like this. Put them into pairs to ask each other the questions.

UNIT 9, LESSON 2, GRAMMAR
Timing: 40 Minutes

- **Prepare for the task** Copy one worksheet for each S.
- **Introduce the task** Ask Ss to write three sentences about what they <u>want</u> to do, <u>need</u> to do and <u>have</u> to do today. Give some examples: *I want to meet my friend after class. I need to clean my car. I have to make dinner tonight.* Put Ss into pairs to compare sentences.
- **Do the task** Ss work in pairs. Student A and Student B take turns asking and answering each other's questions. Monitor and make sure Ss are using *like to, want to, need to, have to* in both questions and answers.
- **Review the task** Ask Ss some of the questions to answer as a class.

T-183

- As an extension task, ask Ss to complete this chart in their notebooks.

I sometimes like to …	
I want to … this week.	
I have to … this week.	
I need to … this week.	

- Then Ss share their charts with a partner.

UNIT 10, LESSON 1, GRAMMAR
Timing: 35 minutes

- **Prepare for the task** Copy one worksheet for each S.
- **Introduce the task** Tell Ss to complete these sentences:
  - *I'm going to … tonight.*
  - *I'm going to … tomorrow.*
  - *I'm going to … next weekend.*
  - *I'm going to … next year.*
  - *I'm not going to …*
- Put Ss into pairs to compare answers.
- **Do the task** Tell Ss to work in pairs. Ss roll the three dice three times. Then have them add up each roll to make three sentences about the future plans of their partner, his/her best friend, and his/her parents. For example:
  - *(12) You're going to go to work.*
  - *(5) Your best friend is going to meet somebody at the airport.*
  - *(10) Your parents are going to go on a trip.*
- Have Ss tell each other the plans. Have them listen to their partner and say if they think the plan is going to come true.
  - **A** *You're going to play soccer.*
  - **B** *Yes, I'm going to play soccer.*
  - **B** *Your best friend is going to watch a movie.*
  - **A** *No, my best friend isn't going to watch a movie.*
- Put Ss into pairs to repeat the activity with a new partner. Repeat until everyone in the class has worked with one another or you have run out of time.
- **Review the task** Tell Ss to look at the **You** column of the table. Say a number and a pronoun. Ss use the table to make a sentence with *be going to*. For example:
  - *six/we   We're going to get together with friends*

UNIT 10, LESSON 2, GRAMMAR
Timing: 35 minutes

- **Prepare for the task** Copy one worksheet for each pair of Ss. Cut up into Student A and Student B halves.
- **Introduce the task** Tell Ss to work in pairs. Tell them to write down three things that they are both going to do over the weekend. For example: *We are going to the movie theater.* Ask for answers and see which Ss have the most interesting plans.

- **Do the task** Ss work in new pairs. Tell them that it is their uncle's birthday on Sunday. They need to find a time to meet before Sunday to go shopping and buy a present. They will need about two hours to find a present. The shops are open from 9:00 a.m. – 9:00 p.m. Ss ask and answer questions about their future plans. For example:
  - **A** *What are you going to do on Monday morning?*
  - **B** *I'm going to study at school.*
  - **B** *Are you going to have time on Wednesday evening?*
  - **A** *No, I'm not. I'm going to study English.*
- Monitor and make sure Ss are asking and answering questions using *be going to*.
- **Review the task** Ask Ss: *What are you going to do …?* questions about their weeks.
- As an extension task, ask Ss to make plans for their week using their own schedules. Put them in pairs to find a time to meet each other.

> **Answers**
> The only time to meet is Saturday between 12:00 p.m. and 4:00 p.m.

UNIT 11, LESSON 1, GRAMMAR
Timing: 40 Minutes

- **Prepare for the task** Copy one worksheet for each S.
- **Introduce the task** Dictate this text to Ss. Pause at the gaps. Tell Ss to work together in pairs to rewrite the text using *was / wasn't* and *were / weren't*.
- It _____ Friday and I _____ at home. I _____ at school. There _____ a lot of students. There _____ only twelve students in class. It _____ a boring lesson. It _____ an interesting lesson. We _____ very happy.

- **Do the task** Tell Ss to work in pairs. Some Ss might recognize the game as tic-tac-toe. Assign one Ss in each pair as O and the other as X. Ss take turns choosing a square and completing the sentences in the square with *was / wasn't* and *were / weren't*. One sentence should be positive and the other negative (the order doesn't matter). For example:
  - *We weren't on vacation. We were at home.*
- If both Ss are sure the sentences are right (they check with the teacher if they disagree or are not sure), they put their O or X in the box in the square. If they are wrong, they miss a turn. Ss continue until one S gets three O / X in a row and is the winner. For example:

X	O	X
X	X	O
O	O	X

- Monitor and make sure Ss are completing the squares with *was / were* accurately. Check the winner to make sure that they have completed the squares accurately. (If they haven't, Ss restart the game.) There are four different activities.

T-184

- **Review the task** Go through all the squares and have Ss read aloud the sentences with *was / were*.
- Tell Ss to turn over the worksheet. Read aloud the first sentence in a square and ask Ss to say the second sentence. For example:
  - *It wasn't old then. (It was new.)*

UNIT 11, LESSON 2, GRAMMAR
Timing: 45 Minutes

- **Prepare for the task** Copy one worksheet for each pair of Ss.
- **Introduce the task** Read aloud sentences with *was* and *were* and ask Ss to make them into different questions. For example:
  - *The children were at home. (Were the children at home? Where were the children?)*
  - *You were outside. (Were you outside? Where were you?)*
  - *Her name was Maria. (What was her name? Was her name Maria?)*
  - *We were both five. (How old were you? Were you children?)*
- **Do the task** Put Ss into pairs. Have them complete the questions with *was* and *were*. Check answers as a class. Ss choose eight questions to ask their partner. Then Ss take turns asking and answering the questions, and writing down the answers. Monitor and make sure Ss are using *was / were* in the questions.
- **Review the task** Tell Ss to look at the questions and answers and check that they have used *was* and *were* correctly.
- Ask Ss to use the answers to make sentences about their partners. For example: *Andrey's favorite teacher was his Spanish teacher*. Then ask Ss to think of follow-up questions with *was* and *were*. For example: *What was the teacher's name?*

UNIT 12, LESSON 1, GRAMMAR
Timing: 45 Minutes

- **Prepare for the task** Copy one worksheet for each pair of Ss and cut into Student A and Student B pairs.
- **Introduce the task** Ss say and write down the past simple of these verbs: *like, want, arrive, be, work, go, take, have, stay, look, have, play, help. wash, drink, carry*. Tell Ss to use the verbs to make three positive and three negative sentences about what they did or didn't do yesterday. Ss compare in pairs.
- **Do the task** Tell Ss to work in pairs. Student A tells Student B two sentences about Marco five years ago. For example: *Marco didn't have a house. He had an apartment*. Student B writes down one of the sentences about Marco. Then Student B tells Student A two sentences about Paula five years ago. Ss take turns telling each other past simple sentences. Monitor and make sure Ss are using the past simple correctly. Then ask Ss to discuss whose life changed the most.

- **Review the task** Ss make past simple positive and negative sentences about Paula and Marco.
- As an extension, ask Ss to write five sentences about their life five years ago and then compare with a partner.

UNIT 12, LESSON 2, GRAMMAR
Timing: 45 Minutes

- **Prepare for the task** Copy one worksheet for each group of three Ss. You need a die (if you don't have a die, make one out of a sugar cube or use a dice app on a smart phone).
- **Introduce the task** Ask Ss to make four past simple questions to ask their partner about yesterday. Two must be *yes/no* questions (*Did you have any cookies for dessert?*) and two must be information questions (*What did you do after our English class?*). Put Ss into pairs to ask and answer the questions.
- **Do the task** Tell Ss to work in groups of three. Ss roll the die and move along the board. Ss need to make and answer the question when they land on a square. For example:
  - **A** *Did you go to the park last weekend?*
    B *Yes, I went to the park with my sister.*
  - **A** *Did you watch any movies yesterday?*
    B *No, I didn't watch any movies yesterday.*
- Ss go up the ladders and down the snakes. Monitor and make sure Ss are making past simple questions and answering them in the past simple.
- **Review the task** Tell Ss to choose questions from the worksheet and ask them to other Ss in the class.
- As an extension, have Ss to do the activity again but to make up their own simple past question for each square.

T-185

1.1 GRAMMAR

I AM, YOU ARE

Student 1

GROUP WORK Ask questions. Write ✓ in the correct place in the chart for the other students.

Are you …?
Yes, I am. / No, I'm not.

in room 1?					
from Lima?					
a teacher?	✓				
a student?					
from France?	✓				
Brazilian?					
	you	Student 2	Student 3	Student 4	Student 5

Student 2

GROUP WORK Ask questions. Write ✓ in the correct place in the chart for the other students.

Are you …?
Yes, I am. / No, I'm not.

in room 1?		✓			
from Lima?					
a teacher?					
a student?					
from France?					
Brazilian?		✓			
	Student 1	you	Student 2	Student 3	Student 4

Student 3

GROUP WORK Ask questions. Write ✓ in the correct place in the chart for the other students.

Are you …?
Yes, I am. / No, I'm not.

in room 1?					
from Lima?			✓		
a teacher?					
a student?			✓		
from France?					
Brazilian?					
	Student 1	Student 2	you	Student 3	Student 4

1.1 GRAMMAR

Student 4

GROUP WORK Ask questions. Write ✓ in the correct place in the chart for the other students.

Are you …?
Yes, I am. No, I'm not.

in room 1?					
from Lima?					
a teacher?					
a student?				✓	
from France?				✓	
Brazilian?					
	Student 1	Student 2	Student 3	you	Student 4

Student 5

GROUP WORK Ask questions. Write ✓ in the correct place in the table for the other students.

Are you …?
Yes, I am. No, I'm not.

in room 1?					
from Lima?					✓
a teacher?					✓
a student?					
from France?					
Brazilian?					
	Student 1	Student 2	Student 3	Student 4	you

1.2 GRAMMAR

WHAT'S …? IT'S …

Student 1

GROUP WORK   Ask and answer questions to complete the chart.

What's [your first name]?   It's …

	you	Student 2	Student 3	Student 4
first name?	Ángel			
last name?	Hernández			
nationality?	Spanish			
email address?	a.herdez@bestmail.com			
college?	Magana College			
company?	Wilsons			

Student 2

GROUP WORK   Ask and answer questions to complete the chart.

What's [your first name]?   It's …

	Student 1	you	Student 3	Student 4
first name?		Fran		
last name?		Mendez		
nationality?		Colombian		
email address?		fran_dez@mymail.org		
college?		Palmira		
company?		Moreno		

Student 3

GROUP WORK   Ask and answer questions to complete the chart.

What's [your first name]?   It's …

	Student 1	Student 2	you	Student 4
first name?			Min-jun	
last name?			Kim	
nationality?			South Korean	
email address?			min.kim@blinknet.com	
college?			The American College	
company?			Gordons	

Student 4

GROUP WORK   Ask and answer questions to complete the chart.

What's [your first name]?   It's …

	Student 1	Student 2	Student 3	you
first name?				Taylor
last name?				Washington
nationality?				American
email address?				taylor_ton@grabmail.org
college?				Denver
company?				Navarrete

2.1 GRAMMAR

IS / ARE IN STATEMENTS AND YES/NO QUESTIONS

Question cards

___ he Simone?	___ we here?	___ you both students?	___ they from Brazil?	___ John here?
___ you both teachers?	___ your parents from Boston?	___ Marie at college?	___ we in class 3?	___ you from Santiago?
___ Rachel and Tom friends?	___ your uncle from Spain?	___ they both 19?	___ you Diego?	___ your grandma at home?
___ the children with grandpa?	___ you here?	___ Dad at home?	___ she Carmen?	___ he your best friend?
___ we in room 10?	___ Margo your sister?	___ you from Honduras?	___ they in Japan?	___ Mom here?

Answer cards

Yes, we ___.	No, he ___.	No, I ___.	No, they ___.	Yes, she ___.
Yes, they ___.	No, I ___.	Yes, we ___.	Yes, he ___.	No, she ___.
Yes, they ___.	No, we ___.	No, he ___.	Yes, she ___.	Yes, they ___.
No, they ___.	Yes, I ___.	Yes, she ___.	No, he ___.	Yes, he ___.
Yes, she ___.	Yes, he ___.	Yes, we ___.	No, they ___.	Yes, I ___.

2.2 GRAMMAR

IS NOT / ARE NOT ('S NOT / 'RE NOT)

Student A

A PAIR WORK Listen to Student B read six sentences. Use the descriptions to choose and underline who it is.

1
| Alex: short + Russian | Leo: tall + American | Sasha: tall + Russian |

2
| Valda: my cousin + a doctor | Eldora: my sister + a teacher | Laura: my aunt + an artist |

3
| the children: young + at home | the ss: both 21 + at college | the parents: Colombian + at the office |

4
| my mom: Brazilian + a chef | my sister: Mexican + a server | my aunt: French + a server |

5
| Tom and Sally: very shy + tall | Maria and Ernesto: very young + short | Jason and Victoria: very old + friendly |

6
| Carlos: from Valencia + a Spanish student | Emilio: from Lima + an English student | Flavio: from Medellin + a French student |

B Complete each sentence using *is not / are not ('s not / 're not)*. Read the sentences to Student B.

7 She _____ a chef.   She _____ twenty.
8 He _____ from Sochi.   He _____ a salesperson.
9 They _____ young.   They _____ shy.
10 He _____ Mexican.   He _____ very old.
11 She _____ boring.   She _____ here.
12 We _____ from Chile.   We _____ both twenty.

T-190 Evolve level 1 Teacher's Edition PHOTOCOPIABLE © Cambridge University Press 2019

2.2 GRAMMAR

IS NOT / ARE NOT ('S NOT / 'RE NOT)

Student B

A **PAIR WORK** Complete each sentence using *is not / are not ('s not / 're not)*. Read the sentences to Student A.
1. He _____ short.   He _____ Russian.
2. She _____ my cousin.   She _____ an artist.
3. They _____ Colombian.   They _____ at college.
4. She _____ Mexican.   She _____ a server.
5. We _____ very young.   We _____ tall.
6. He _____ from Lima.   He _____ Spanish student.

B Listen to Student A read six sentences. Use the descriptions to choose and <u>underline</u> who it is.

7	Rachel: a student + twenty	Magda: a chef + twenty-one	Joan: my friend + American
8	Valentin: from Sochi + a teacher	Adrian: from Washington + a teacher	Rafael: from Bogota + a salesperson
9	my brothers: tall + friendly	my cousins: young + shy	my sisters: short + shy
10	Pablo: Spanish + young	Victor: Mexican + very old	Marcus: Spanish + very old
11	Irina: interesting + here	Octavia: interesting + at home	Ulrika: boring + at college
12	students: from Chile + really smart	friends: from China + both twenty	parents: American + doctors

3.1 GRAMMAR

POSSESSIVE ADJECTIVES; POSSESSIVE 'S AND S'

Student A

GROUP WORK Ask questions about the people in the family.

	son	daughter	mother	father
name	Elio			
favorite room	bedroom			
email address	elio@bestmail.com			
cell phone number	(593) 555-5682			
best friend	Roger			
birthday	June 2			

Student B

GROUP WORK Ask questions about the people in the family.

	son	daughter	mother	father
name		Marina		
favorite room		kitchen		
email address		marina@xyz.com		
cell phone number		(593) 555-3609		
best friend		Marieke		
birthday		February 13		

Student C

GROUP WORK Ask questions about the people in the family.

	son	daughter	mother	father
name			Sofia	
favorite room			bedroom	
email address			sofia@xyz.com	
cell phone number			(593) 555-2178	
best friend			Emily	
birthday			August 17	

Student D

GROUP WORK Ask questions about the people in the family.

	son	daughter	mother	father
name				Alonso
favorite room				living room
email address				alonso@grabmail.org
cell phone number				(593) 555-4933
best friend				Jon
birthday				September 22

3.2 GRAMMAR

IT IS

PAIR WORK Take turns going through the squares from Start to Finish. Move one square each time. You can go down ↓, up ↑, across → or diagonally ↘. You can only go through squares where you can use *it is* (*it's*), *it is not* (*isn't*), and *is it* to complete the sentences.

START	_____ Miguel and I'm from Spain.	_____ tall?	_____ two doors.	"Are you Mike?" Yes, _____."	_____ children.	Yes, _____ both nice.	"_____ 20?" "No, she isn't."
<u>It's</u> a door.	She is a student. _____ 19.	Yes, _____ English books.	_____ both interesting.	Chicago _____ in the United States.	_____ cousins.	"Are you Sara?" "Yes, _____."	_____ colleges.
No, <u>It isn't</u> new.	_____ very young.	_____ chefs.	_____ both Chinese.	_____ a desk or a table?	Yes, _____.	No, _____ very big.	_____ grandparents.
_____ a bed?	_____ lamps.	"Are you here?" "Yes, _____."	_____ a rug.	_____ two beds.	"_____ friendly?" "No, he isn't."	_____ friends?	_____ a blue pen?
Yes, _____ my email.	_____ a teacher?	Yes, _____ keys.	No, _____ here.	"_____ with you?" "No, she isn't."	_____ apartments.	Yes, _____ chairs.	_____ on the couch.
_____ December 28.	_____ the walls.	_____ bedrooms.	_____ the bathroom.	_____ sisters.	_____ small houses.	_____ good friends.	_____ a TV.
_____ a house.	Justin _____ twenty-one.	"_____ a student?" "No, I'm not."	_____ hotel clerks.	_____ a dog?	_____ both from Japan.	"Is this painting from Mexico?" "No, _____."	"Are you French?" "Yes, _____."
_____ both young.	_____ a sink.	_____ three cats.	"_____ friendly?" "No, she isn't."	_____ the living room.	_____ sisters.	_____ a French book.	_____ a dog and a cat.
_____ chairs.	No, _____.	Yes, _____ brothers.	_____ cousins?	_____ a picture of your daughter?	Denis and I'm a chef.	Yes, _____ new.	_____ both Chinese.
_____ four children.	_____ a table.	_____ parents.	_____ good friends.	No, _____ very interesting.	Lucy and I'm a teacher.	_____ living rooms.	_____ September 3.
She's my friend and _____ cool!	_____ a big apartment.	_____ fine, thanks. And you?	Maria _____ a doctor.	_____ room 16?	_____ French students.	"Are you Ivan?" "Yes, _____."	_____ my last name.
"_____ Olga?" "No, I'm not."	_____ a chair?	Yes, _____ next to the lamp.	_____ a cat?	_____ a house.	"_____ interesting?" "Yes, he is."	_____ chefs.	FINISH

4.1 GRAMMAR

SIMPLE PRESENT STATEMENTS WITH *I*, *YOU*, AND *WE*

PAIR WORK Take turns rolling a die three times to make sentences.
If the sentence is true for you or for you and your partner, you get one point.
The first student to get 10 points is the winner.
For example:

I + want + new earphones

I want new earphones.

You + don't have + an old cell phone

You don't have an old cell phone.

4.1 GRAMMAR

SIMPLE PRESENT STATEMENTS WITH *I*, *YOU*, AND *WE*

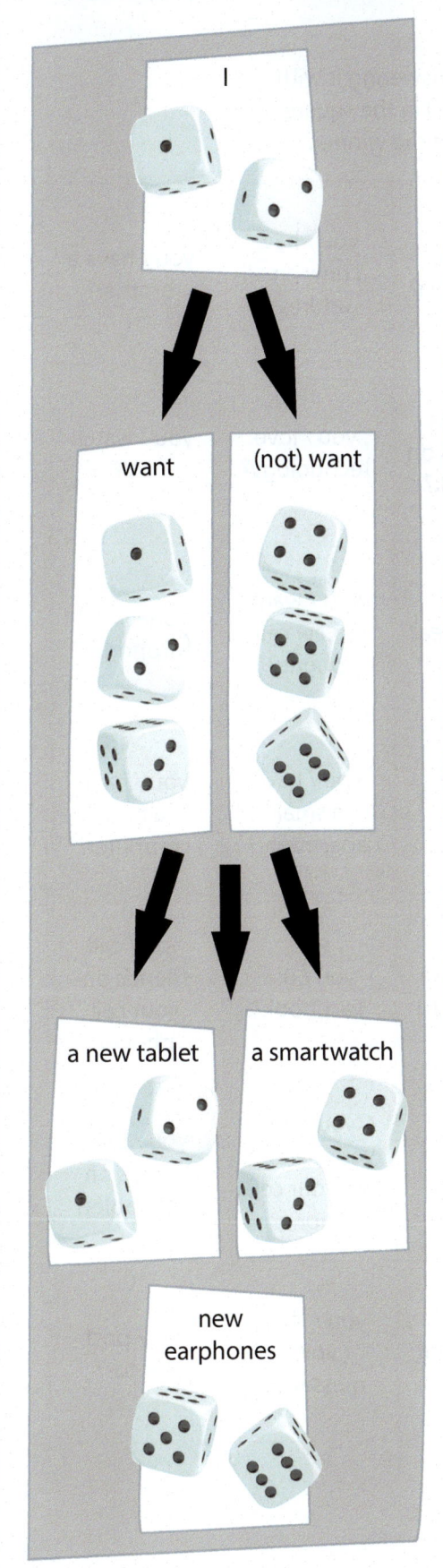

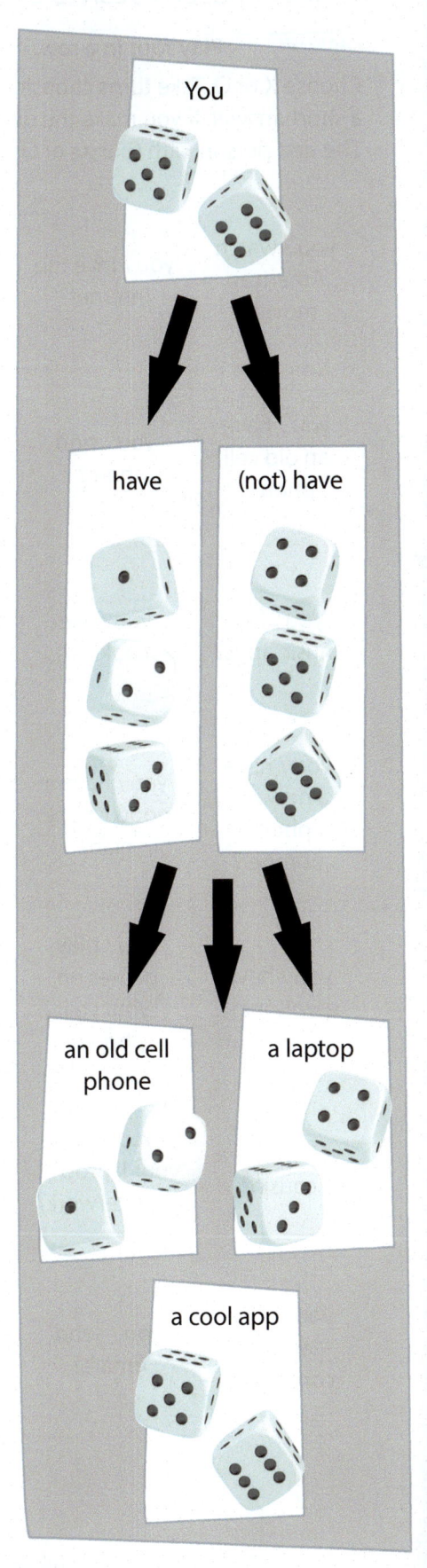

I	My best friend and I	You
want / (not) want	like / (not) like	have / (not) have
a new tablet / a smartwatch	computer games	an old cell phone / a laptop
new earphones	Facebook / apps	a cool app

4.2 GRAMMAR

SIMPLE PRESENT YES/NO QUESTIONS WITH I, YOU, WE

PAIR WORK Play four in a row.

Choose X or O. Take turns choosing a square, making the question, and then answering it with a short answer. If you make the question and answer correctly, write your X or O in the square. The first person with four Xs or Os in a row across →, down ↓, or diagonally ↘ is the winner.

you / watch American movies?	you / love the internet?	you / have a cell phone number?	you / have a house?	you / use social media?	you / have a new email address?	you / have a brother?
you / have an old cell phone?	you / sign here?	you / like American movies?	you / use your tablet at college/work?	you / post comments on Facebook?	you / love technology?	you / watch TV?
you / like music apps?	you / like cookies?	you / have an iPad?	you / want a camera?	you / like tea?	you / want a new cell phone?	you / want earphones?
you / have a new cell phone number?	you / have a good phone plan?	you / watch YouTube™?	you / want a smartwatch?	you / have a camera?	you / have a small apartment?	you / have a new computer?
you / have earphones?	you / play games on your cell phone?	you / have a big apartment?	you / have a sister?	you / have a smartwatch?	you / use Facebook?	you / call friends on your cell phone?
you / have a cousin?	you / use your laptop at college/work?	you / post comments on the internet?	you / have an email address?	you / have a tablet?	you / call your parents on your cell phone?	you / play games on your tablet?
you / have an old computer?	you / send emails?	you / play computer games?	you / have a new cell phone?	you / buy apps on your cell phone?	you / leave voice messages?	you / post photos?

5.1 GRAMMAR

SIMPLE PRESENT STATEMENTS: *HE / SHE / THEY*

Student A

A **GROUP WORK** Use the information from your chart to tell the other students about Yuri. *He …*

B Listen to the other students in your group to fill in the information about Teresa, Tim, and Kristina.

C Imagine Yuri, Teresa, Tim, and Kristina are at a party. Which people are friends? Which people are <u>not</u> friends?

> I think Tim and Teresa are friends. I think Tim and Kristina are not friends.

	Yuri ✓ = always ✗ = never	Teresa	Tim	Kristina
work Monday to Friday?	✓			
work on the weekend?	hardly ever			
go out in the evening?	sometimes			
watch TV in the evening?	✗			
play computer games?	often			
use social media?	usually			
run in the morning?	✗			
play soccer?	✗			
like music?	✓			
like parties?	✓			

Student B

A **GROUP WORK** Use the information from your chart to tell the other students about Teresa. *She …*

B Listen to the other students and fill in the information about Yuri, Tim, and Kristina.

C Imagine Yuri, Teresa, Tim, and Kristina are at a party. Which people are friends? Which people are <u>not</u> friends?

> I think Tim and Teresa are friends. I think Tim and Kristina are not friends.

	Yuri	Teresa ✓ = always ✗ = never	Tim	Kristina
work Monday to Friday?		✗		
work on the weekend?		✓		
go out in the evening?		often		
watch TV in the evening?		sometimes		
play computer games?		✗		
use social media?		✗		
run in the morning?		hardly ever		
play soccer?		✓		
like music?		✓		
like parties?		✗		

5.1 GRAMMAR

SIMPLE PRESENT STATEMENTS: HE / SHE / THEY

Student C

A GROUP WORK Use the information from your chart to tell the other students about Tim. *He …*

B Listen to the other students and fill in the information about Yuri, Teresa, and Kristina.

C Imagine Yuri, Teresa, Tim, and Kristina are at a party. Which people are friends? Which people are <u>not</u> friends?

> I think Tim and Teresa are friends. I think Tim and Kristina are not friends.

	Yuri	Teresa	Tim ✓ = always ✗ = never	Kristina
work Monday to Friday?			✓	
work on the weekend?			✗	
go out in the evening?			never	
watch TV in the evening?			✓	
play computer games?			✓	
use social media?			often	
run in the morning?			✓	
play soccer?			hardly ever	
like music?			✗	
like parties?			✓	

Student D

A GROUP WORK Use the information from your chart to tell the other students about Kristina. *She …*

B Listen to the other students and fill in the information about Yuri, Teresa and Tim.

C Imagine Yuri, Teresa, Tim, and Kristina are at a party. Which people are friends? Which people are <u>not</u> friends?

> I think Tim and Teresa are friends. I think Tim and Kristina are not friends.

	Yuri	Teresa	Tim	Kristina ✓ = always ✗ = never
work Monday to Friday?				✓
work on the weekend?				✗
go out in the evening?				sometimes
watch TV in the evening?				✗
play computer games?				usually
use social media?				often
run in the morning?				✗
play soccer?				✗
like music?				✓
like parties?				✓

5.2 GRAMMAR

QUESTIONS IN THE SIMPLE PRESENT

Student A

A **GROUP WORK** Work with other Student A's and make questions to ask Student B's about Martina's routine.

1 _____ before breakfast?
2 _____?
3 _____ with her breakfast?
4 _____?
5 _____?
6 _____?
7 _____?
8 _____?

Martina gets up at six o'clock and [1]_____ before breakfast. After a shower, she has breakfast in her [2]_____ . She always has [3]_____ with her breakfast. Martina goes to work at 8:00 a.m. She is a French teacher and works at a [4]_____ in Barcelona. She loves her [5]_____ and her students are very nice. She has classes every day, but she doesn't work on the weekend. Martina goes home at [6]_____ and usually chats with her mother on her old laptop at five-thirty. (Martina's birthday is in March and she wants a new laptop!). Martina makes dinner at [7]_____ and listens to music before bed. She never goes out on weekdays, but sometimes she goes out [8]_____ . She usually goes to bed at 11:30 p.m.

B **PAIR WORK** Work with a Student B. Ask and answer questions to complete the information about Martina's routine.

Student B

A **GROUP WORK** Work with other Student B's and make questions to ask Student A's about Martina's routine.

1 _____?
2 _____?
3 _____?
4 _____?
5 _____?
6 _____ for her birthday?
7 _____ before bed?
8 _____?

Martina gets up at [1]_____ and runs five miles before breakfast. After a shower, she has breakfast in her kitchen. She always has a big coffee with her breakfast. Martina goes to work at [2]_____ . She is a French teacher and works at a school in [3]_____ . She loves her job and her students are very nice. She has classes [4]_____ but she doesn't work on the weekend. Martina goes home at five o'clock and usually chats with her mother on her old laptop at [5]_____ . (Martina's birthday is in March and she wants a [6]_____ !) Martina makes dinner at 8:00 and listens to [7]_____ before bed. She never goes out on weekdays, but sometimes she goes out on Saturday evenings. She usually goes to bed at [8]_____ .

B **PAIR WORK** Work with a Student A. Ask and answer questions to complete the information about Martina's routine.

Evolve level 1 Teacher's Edition   PHOTOCOPIABLE   © Cambridge University Press 2019   T-199

6.1 GRAMMAR

THERE'S, THERE ARE WITH *A / AN, SOME, A LOT OF, NO*

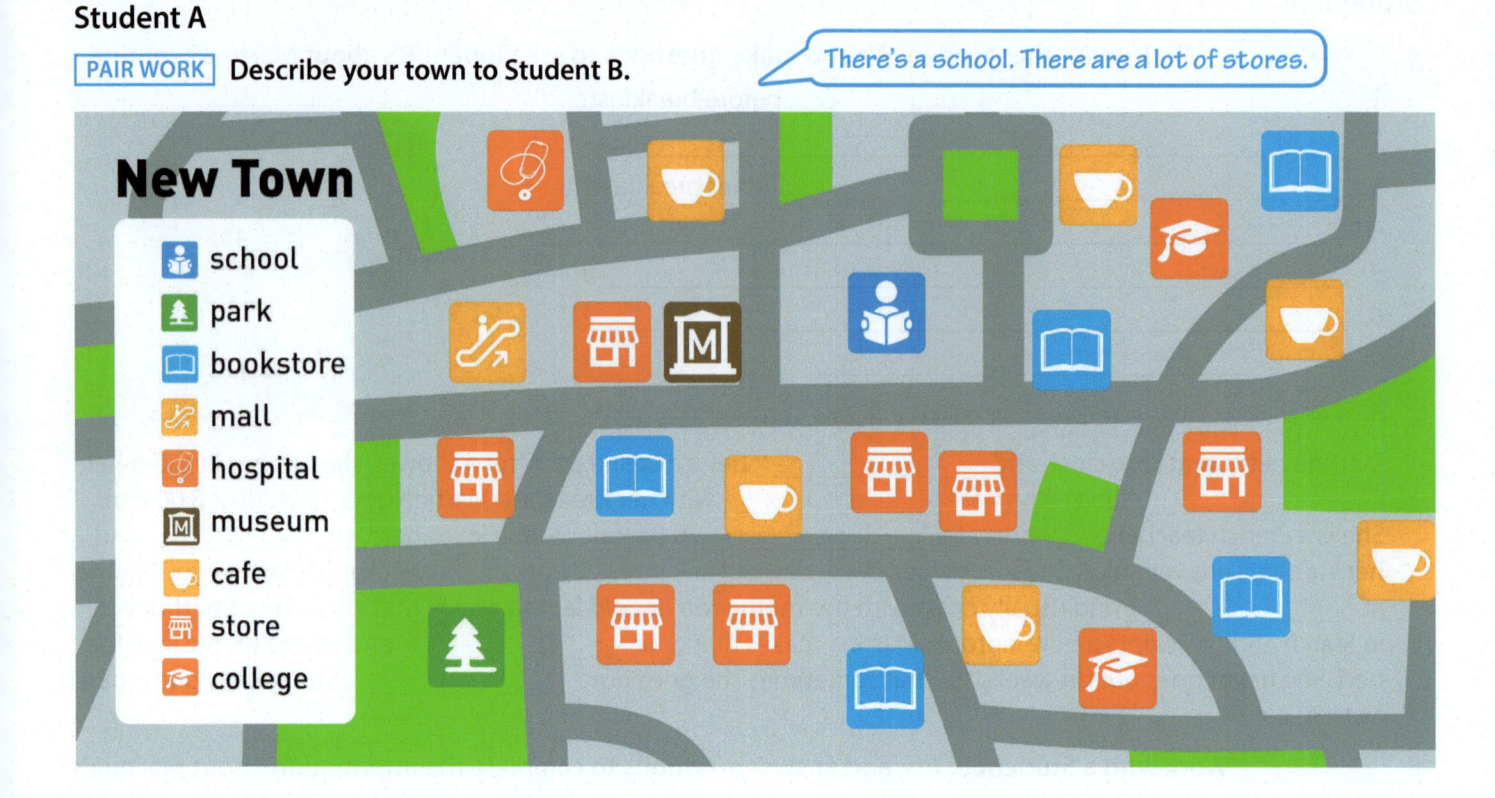

Student A

PAIR WORK Describe your town to Student B.

> There's a school. There are a lot of stores.

New Town

- school
- park
- bookstore
- mall
- hospital
- museum
- cafe
- store
- college

Student B

PAIR WORK Describe your town to Student A.

> There's a school. There are a lot of museums.

Smith Town

- school
- zoo
- movie theater
- mall
- bookstore
- hospital
- museum
- hotel
- restaurant
- supermarket
- college

T-200 Evolve level 1 Teacher's Edition PHOTOCOPIABLE © Cambridge University Press 2019

6.2 GRAMMAR

COUNT AND NON-COUNT NOUNS

GROUP WORK Take turns putting down a domino card. If the word is a non-count noun, put a non-count noun next to it. If the word is a count noun, put a count noun next to it.

grass	city	mall	information	sugar	ocean
school	work	music	hill	flower	technology
snow	place	neighborhood	fun	nature	store
island	water	tea	movie theater	park	milk
coffee	lake	museum	shopping	furniture	weekend

7.1 GRAMMAR

PRESENT CONTINUOUS STATEMENTS

PAIR WORK Say what is happening in Picture A. Then find seven differences between Picture A and Picture B.

Picture A

PAIR WORK Say what is happening in Picture B. Then find seven differences between Picture A and Picture B.

Picture B

7.2 GRAMMAR

PRESENT CONTINUOUS QUESTIONS

GROUP WORK Take a Question card and an Answer card. Use the Question card to ask each student in the group what they are doing.

Diego, are you watching TV?

No, I'm not.

What are you doing?

I'm learning English.

Complete the chart with the information.

Question cards

have dinner?	do your homework?	listen to music?	meet a friend?
drink coffee?	learn English?	clean the kitchen?	wait?
take the bus?	go shopping?	watch TV?	go home?
play soccer?	send an email?	do the dishes?	take the train?
brush your teeth?	ride your bike?	go to work?	cook lunch?

Answer cards

cook lunch	play soccer	send an email	brush my teeth
ride my bike	go shopping	go to work	listen to music
take the bus	learn English	go home	watch TV
do my homework	wait	take the train	do the dishes
meet a friend	drink coffee	clean the kitchen	have dinner

Name of group member	What is she / he doing?

8.1 GRAMMAR

CAN AND CAN'T FOR ABILITY; WELL

PAIR WORK Choose ten questions to ask your partner. Write their answers. Then tell another partner about your first partner.

> Can you swim?
> Yes, I can.

> Can you swim well?
> No. I can't swim well.

Can you run three miles?

Can you read music? Can you drive?

Can you tell the time in English?

Can your father cook?

Can you play the guitar? Can you take nice photos?

Can you ride a bike?

Can your mother sing?

Can you post videos on YouTube™?

Can you send an email in English?

Can you fix a computer?

Can you skateboard?

Can you swim?

Can your mother speak English?

Can your mother use Instagram? Can you play basketball?

Can you say "Hello" in ten languages? Can your grandparents use the internet?

Can you draw?

Can you surf?

Can your best friend swim?

Can you fix a bike?

Can your father dance?

Can you cook dinner for your family?

Can your father play soccer?

8.2 GRAMMAR

CAN AND CAN'T FOR POSSIBILITY

A **Listen to the teacher and write Yes or No next to the information for your company.**

Yes = you can   No = you can't

B GROUP WORK **Ask each other Can you questions to complete the information about each company.**

C **Decide together which is the right company for you.**

	Student A Lee & Sons	Student B ABC Company	Student C Alvarez	Student D Yamasaki
walk to the office				
work at home on Tuesdays				
learn English with coworkers				
learn computer skills				
take a lot of breaks				
bring your dog to work				
meet a lot of people				
have a lot of fun				

9.1 GRAMMAR

THIS AND THESE

A **PAIR WORK** Work in pairs. Take a card. Make sentences with *this is* / *these are* and say them to your partner.

> This bag is cheap.

… bag … cheap.	… my train ticket.
… man … old	… woman … tall.
… cats … friendly.	… bag … expensive.
… some old men.	… answer … correct.
… our train tickets.	… woman … happy
… answer is incorrect.	… people … good friends.

B Listen to your partner. Circle the matching picture in each row.

T-206 Evolve level 1 Teacher's Edition PHOTOCOPIABLE © Cambridge University Press 2019

9.2 GRAMMAR

LIKE TO, WANT TO, NEED TO, HAVE TO

Student A

A **Complete the questions. Interview your partner.**
1. What do you usually (need / buy) before your vacation?
   - A I usually (need / buy) a new snowboard.
   - B I usually (need / buy) a good book.
   - C I usually (need / buy) some earphones.
2. You have (wait) a long time before your flight. What do you want (do)?
   - A I (want / play) computer games.
   - B I (want / read) a book.
   - C I (want / have) a coffee.
3. Where do you (like / stay)?
   - A I (like / stay) with friends.
   - B I (like / stay) in a nice hotel.
   - C I (like / stay) in the country.
4. Do you (need / go) on business trips?
   - A I sometimes (need / go) on business trips.
   - B I often (need / go) on business trips.
   - C I never (need / go) on business trips.
5. It is the first day of your vacation. What do you (want / do)?
   - A I (want / go) shopping.
   - B I (want / swim) in the ocean.
   - C I (want / go) to a museum.
6. Do you (like / travel) with family or friends?
   - A I (like / travel) with family.
   - B I (like / travel) with friends.
   - C I (don't like / travel) with family or friends.
7. You are on vacation and it is Saturday night. What do you (want / do)?
   - A I (want / go out) with my friends.
   - B I (want / go) to bed.
   - C I (want / have) dinner in a restaurant.
8. Does a good vacation (have / be) expensive?
   - A It usually (have to / be) expensive.
   - B It always (have to / be) expensive.
   - C It doesn't (have to / be) expensive.

B **Answer your partner's questions.**

9.2 GRAMMAR

Student B

A **Complete the questions. Interview your partner.**
   1 Do you (like / meet) new people on vacation?
      A Yes, I (like / meet) new people.
      B Yes, I sometimes (like / meet) new people.
      C No, I (like / meet) my friends.
   2 Where do you (want / go) on vacation?
      A I (want / go) to a new country.
      B I (want / go) to the beach.
      C I (want / visit) a big city.
   3 Do you (have / fly) to your favorite place?
      A Yes, I (have to / fly) there.
      B No, I (don't have to / fly) there.
      C I don't know!
   4 Do you (need / speak) English there?
      A Yes, you (need / speak) English.
      B No, you (need / speak) Spanish.
      C No, you (need / speak) another language.
   5 What do you always (have / do) on vacation?
      A I always (have to / visit) a museum.
      B I always (have to / go) shopping.
      C I always (have to / call) my family.
   6 You are on vacation in the mountains. Do you (want / snowboard)?
      A Yes, I (want / snowboard) there.
      B No, I (want / walk) in the mountains.
      C No, I (want / go) back to the city.
   7 Do you (need / do) active or relaxing things on vacation?
      A Active things: I (need / do) a lot of sports.
      B Active things: I (need / meet) new people and go out.
      C Relaxing things: I (don't need / do sports or go out).
   8 Do you sometimes (have / work) on your vacation?
      A Yes, I often (have to / work) on vacation.
      B Yes, I sometimes (have to / work) on vacation.
      C No, I never (have to / work) on vacation.

B **Answer your partner's questions.**

10.1 GRAMMAR

STATEMENTS WITH *BE GOING TO*

A **PAIR WORK** Roll a die three times. Add the numbers to make a sum total (e.g., 1 + 1 + 4 = 6). Find the number (3-18). Make three sentences.

One sentence is about your partner. One sentence is about his or her best friend. One sentence is about his or her parents.

B Your partner says if the sentence is true or not.

C Work with a new partner.

What is going to happen next weekend?

Sum total of three rolls	You	Your best friend	Your parents
3	be at home	take somebody out for dinner	watch a movie
4	take a walk	ride a bike	meet somebody at the airport
5	go to the mall	meet somebody at the airport	be at home
6	get together with friends	go to work	ride a bike
7	eat outside	play computer games	go to the mall
8	go on a trip	clean the apartment/house	get together with friends
9	play computer games	go shopping	eat outside
10	ride a bike	watch a movie	go on a trip
11	meet somebody at the airport	play soccer	play computer games
12	go to work / college	have a picnic	take a walk
13	take somebody out for dinner	be at home	have a picnic
14	clean the apartment / house	take a walk	go to work
15	go shopping	get together with friends	take somebody out for dinner
16	play soccer	go to the mall	clean the apartment / house
17	watch a movie	eat outside	play soccer
18	have a picnic	go on a trip	go shopping

10.2 GRAMMAR

BE GOING TO: QUESTIONS

Student A

PAIR WORK Your uncle's birthday is on Sunday. You want to meet Student B to go shopping for a present for your uncle. Ask and answer questions about your plans. Find a time to meet.

Your plans

Monday	Tuesday	Wednesday	Thursday	Friday	Saturday	Sunday
9:00 a.m.–5:00 p.m. Work in the office	9:00 a.m.–5:00 p.m. Work in the office	9:00 a.m.–1:00 p.m. Work at home 2:00 p.m.–5:00 p.m. Take my grandmother to the hospital	9:00 a.m.–6:00 p.m. Work in the office	7:00 a.m. Drive to a meeting out of town 4:00 p.m. Drive home (2 hours)	9:00 a.m.–11:00 a.m. Clean my apartment	Uncle Martin's birthday!
6:00 p.m.–8:00 p.m. Study English	6:30 p.m.–9:00 p.m. Meet a school friend	6:00 p.m.–8:00 p.m. Study English	7:00 p.m.–9:00 p.m. Have dinner with Janice	7:30 p.m.–10:00 p.m. Meet coworkers for office party	4:00 p.m.–8:00 p.m. Go to the movie theater	

Student B

PAIR WORK Your uncle's birthday is on Sunday. You want to meet Student B to go shopping for a present for your uncle. Ask and answer questions about your plans. Find a time to meet.

Your plans

Monday	Tuesday	Wednesday	Thursday	Friday	Saturday	Sunday
10:00 a.m.–4:00 p.m. Study at school	10:00 a.m.–3:30 p.m. Study at college	9.00 a.m.–10:00 a.m. Go to the supermarket 11:00–12:00 Have coffee with Alex	10:00 a.m.–4:00 p.m. Study at college	9:00 a.m.–11:30 a.m. Clean my room	11:00 a.m.–12:00 p.m. Have breakfast	Uncle Martin's birthday!
5:00 p.m.–7:00 p.m. Play soccer with friends	6:00 p.m.–9:00 p.m. Do my homework	1:00 p.m.–5:00 p.m. Take a walk in the park 6:00 p.m.–11:00 p.m. No plans	5:00 p.m.–7:00 p.m. Cook dinner for friends.	1:00–5:00 p.m. Study at home 6.30 p.m.–8:00 p.m. Wash my hair and take a bath	7:00 p.m.–11:00 p.m. Go out with friends	

11.1 GRAMMAR

STATEMENTS WITH *WAS* AND *WERE*

PAIR WORK One student is O and the other student is X. Take turns choosing a square on the board. Write *was / wasn't* or *were / weren't*. If you are right, put your O or X in the square. The first student to get three O / X in a row across ➝, down ↓, or diagonally ↗ is the winner. There are four different activities.

A

It _____ a museum. It _____ a house.	My parents _____ at the party at 10:00. They _____ at the mall.	I _____ 18 at the time. I _____ 17.
In 2015, I _____ a student. I _____ a chef.	We _____ on vacation. We _____ at home.	You _____ at the train station at 6:00. You _____ late.
Cecilia _____ a singer in 2009. She _____ famous.	They _____ expensive. They _____ cheap.	My brother _____ in the kitchen. He _____ outside.

B

You _____ my friend. You _____ a co-worker.	In 2016 Matthew and Alice _____ in Mexico. They _____ in the USA.	It _____ a boring trip. It _____ very interesting.
They _____ on a boat. They _____ in town.	I _____ at the café at eleven o'clock. I _____ at the park.	I _____ in the office yesterday. I _____ at home.
My aunt _____ at work at 8:00. She _____ in bed.	You _____ in college at 9:00. You _____ with your friends.	I _____ shy when I was a child. I _____ very noisy.

C

Maria _____ at the supermarket. She _____ in the mall.	It _____ my apartment in 2014. It _____ your apartment.	You _____ at the hotel. You _____ in the museum.
You _____ at the bookstore. You _____ at work.	We _____ in class at 11:00. We _____ with you.	They _____ interesting. They _____ boring.
I _____ 32 in 2015. I was _____ 33.	It _____ old then. It _____ new.	Mike _____ on the bus. He was _____ on the train.

D

My homework _____ awful. It _____ very good.	Diego _____ with you. He _____ with us.	We _____ at home on Sunday evening. We _____ there on Saturday evening.
I _____ in bed at 11:00. I _____ at the party.	You _____ in the yard. You _____ inside.	It _____ a zoo in 2010. It _____ a park.
Sasha _____ there at 4:00. She _____ there at 4:30.	The children _____ at the zoo. They _____ at school.	I _____ slow. I _____ very fast.

11.2 GRAMMAR

QUESTIONS WITH *WAS* AND *WERE*

A Make questions with *was* and *were*.

B PAIR WORK Choose eight questions and ask your partner. Write down his or her answers. Then tell a new partner about your first partner's answers.

Your childhood

		Me	Student B
1	Who _____ your favorite teacher at school?		
2	What _____ your mother's and father's jobs?		
3	_____ there a TV in your bedroom?		
4	What songs or singers _____ famous?		
5	What _____ your first vacation?		
6	_____ you a shy child?		
7	_____ you noisy?		
8	_____ there a lot of snow in winter?		
9	_____ people in your neighborhood friendly?		
10	What _____ your favorite book?		
11	_____ there a movie theater near your home?		
12	_____ there a zoo near you?		
13	_____ your home in the town or country?		
14	What _____ your favorite toys and games when you _____ a child?		
15	Who _____ your best friend?		
16	_____ your childhood interesting or boring?		

12.1 GRAMMAR

SIMPLE PAST STATEMENTS

Student A

A **PAIR WORK** Tell your partner two sentences about Marco five years ago.

> Marco didn't have a house. He had an apartment.

B **PAIR WORK** Listen to your partner. Write a sentence about Paula five years ago.

> She lived in a small house.

Marco Today	Five years ago	Paula five years ago
has a house	… an apartment	
works in a restaurant	… a café	
walks to work	… to the bus stop	
eats a lot of vegetables	… meat	
loves fruit	… cookies	
plays soccer	… computer games	
goes on vacation to the mountains	… on vacation to the beach	
wants a dog	… a cat	

Student B

A **PAIR WORK** Tell your partner two sentences about Paula five years ago.

> Paula didn't live in a big house. She lived in a small house.

B **PAIR WORK** Listen to your partner. Write a sentence about Marco five years ago.

> He had an apartment.

Marco five years ago	Paula Today	Five years ago
	lives in a big house	… a small house
	has a lot of friends	… no friends
	takes a taxi to work	… the bus to work
	drinks a lot of water	… a lot of coffee
	studies English	… French
	watches movies on her tablet	… movies on a TV
	eats a banana for lunch	… a beef sandwich for lunch
	travels by plane	… by train

12.2 GRAMMAR

SIMPLE PAST QUESTIONS; *ANY*

GROUP WORK Roll a die and move along the board.

Make and answer the question when you go to a square.

Go up the ladders and down the snakes

30 what / you / have / for dinner yesterday?	you / like / math / at school? 31	32 you / eat / a lot for breakfast / this morning?	33 you / learn / any new words / in this lesson?	Finish
29 you / go to bed late / last night?	28 you / go / to a museum / last month?	you / take / a walk / last weekend? 27	26 what / you / have / for lunch yesterday?	you / drive / to school / today? 25
20 you / go / to the beach / last month?	21 where / you / stay / on your last vacation?	22 you / study English / yesterday?	23 you / go / to the zoo / last month?	what / you / do / on your last vacation? 24
19 you / watch / a TV show / yesterday?	18 you / go shopping / last weekend?	you / take / the subway / yesterday? 17	16 what / you / buy / last week?	15 you / wash / your hair / last night?
you / work / yesterday? 10	11 you / eat / any eggs / yesterday?	you / see / any friends / on the weekend? 12	13 you / go out / last night?	14 you / buy / any clothes / last month?
9 where / you / go / on your last vacation?	you / like / school? 8	7 you / watch / any movies / yesterday?	6 you / have / a picnic / last month?	5 you / go / to the movie theater / last weekend?
START	1 what / you / have for breakfast / this morning?	2 you / go / to the park / last weekend?	3 what time / you / arrive / at class today?	4 you / drink / any soda / yesterday?

Teacher's notes for photocopiable activities: VOCABULARY

UNIT 1, LESSON 1, VOCABULARY

Timing: 40 Minutes

- **Prepare for the task** Copy and cut up the worksheet: one set of cards for each group of 4 Ss. (To make the game longer or for larger groups, copy two sets of cards.)

  To save cutting, copy one worksheet for each student. Ss will work in groups and take turns picking a country and guessing one another's country and nationality.

- **Introduce the task** Name some famous people that Ss will know, such as Laura Esquivel. Ask Ss to tell you these people's nationality and country (Laura Esquivel: Mexican, Mexico). Put Ss into pairs to make their own lists of famous people. Put pairs together into groups to ask one another about their country and nationality.

- **Do the task** Put Ss into small groups. Tell them to put the cards face down. Have Ss take turns picking a card. The other Ss must ask questions to guess the country or nationality each student picked. Model with a stronger student and write questions and answers on the board as prompts for the target language.
  - **A** *Are you Brazilian?*
  - **B** *No, I'm not from Brazil.*
  - **A** *Are you from Mexico?*
  - **B** *No, I'm not Mexican.*
  - **A** *Are you Chilean?*
  - **B** *Yes, I am from Chile!*

- Ss have only five questions to guess the country or nationality. If they guess in five questions, they take the card. If they don't, the card goes to the bottom of the pile. The student with the most cards at the end is the winner. Monitor and make sure Ss are saying each country and nationality correctly.

- **Review the task** Say the name of a country to a student, such as *Honduras*. The student must say the nationality (*Honduran*) and then say the name of another country, such as *Japan*, to another student. This student says the nationality (*Japanese*) and then says the name of another country to the next student. Continue until all Ss have had a turn.

UNIT 1, LESSON 2, VOCABULARY

Timing: 40 Minutes

- **Prepare for the task** Photocopy one worksheet for each pair of Ss and cut up into Student A and Student B halves.

- **Introduce the task** Spell out some words from Unit 1 letter by letter. Ss say the words. For example: *a-l-p-h-a-b-e-t* (alphabet). Put Ss into pairs to do the same.

- **Do the task** Put Ss into pairs. Tell them to take turns completing the chart by spelling out the beginnings and endings of the words. Write *How do you spell …?* on the board and ask Ss to repeat it several times so that you are sure Ss are pronouncing it correctly. Tell Ss to say *Thanks* or *OK* when they have written down the information and are ready to speak themselves.

- Demonstrate completing the information for Person 1 with a stronger S. Then let Ss work in pairs. Monitor and make sure Ss are spelling out the words correctly.

- **Review the task** Choose a person and piece of personal information. Ss must tell you the word from the chart and spell it out:
  - *Person 2, last name*
  - *Harrison, H-a-r-r-i-s-o-n*

- As an extension task, ask Ss to add Person 5 and Person 6 to the chart and add information in the same way about two different people. Pairs then swap charts and repeat the task with Person 5 and Person 6.

UNIT 2, LESSON 1, VOCABULARY

Timing: 40 Minutes

- **Prepare for the task** Copy and cut up one worksheet for each pair of Ss into Student A and B halves.

- **Introduce the task** Draw your family tree on the board with the ages of your family members in numbers. Ask Ss to come to the front of the class and say who each member of your family is and how old they are. For example: *Diana is your sister. She is 27.*

- **Do the task** Put Ss into pairs. Tell Ss they have the same family tree and they need to complete it with names and ages. Begin by telling Student A to tell Student B about the people in the family tree and how old each family member is. Model the language and write it on the board:
  - *Javier is the grandfather.*
  - *He is 75.*
  - *Mia and Filipe – children of Javier.*

- Ss speak and listen to their partners to fill out the family tree. Monitor and help with vocabulary where necessary.

- Then both Ss work together to complete the sentences about the family tree.

- **Review the task** Check that Ss have completed the family tree and sentences correctly. Say the name of two of the people in the family tree and ask Ss to say how they are related, for example:
  - *Rafael and Mia (brother and sister, children of Javier and Ana)*
  - *Alba and Martin (Alba – aunt of Martin)*

- As an extension task, Ss draw their own family tree, labeling the relationships and showing the ages of the people. Then put Ss into pairs to tell a partner about their family tree.

> **Answers**
> 1 wife 2 sister 3 father 4 uncle 5 husband
> 6 parents 7 aunt 8 son 9 children 10 cousin

UNIT 2, LESSON 2, VOCABULARY

Timing: 40 Minutes

- **Prepare for the task** Copy one worksheet for each S.
- **Introduce the task** Write some of the adjectives in the word search on the board as anagrams for Ss to solve. For example:
  - ratms = smart
  - ngoyu = young
  - yilfdrne = friendly
- If necessary, give clues—for example: *ngoyu* (not old)—to help Ss.
- **Do the task** Tell Ss to find nine adjectives to describe people in the word search. (To make the task easier, write the words on the board first.) Tell Ss that the words can be across or down.
- Then ask Ss to match the adjectives to the pictures. Check the answers.
- Tell Ss to write down the name of somebody they know next to these adjectives. For example: friendly = Manuel (cousin).
- Put Ss into pairs. They can show each other a photograph of someone on their cell phones, say who it is, and describe that person. For example: *Manuel is my cousin. He is friendly.*
- **Review the task** Ask Ss to show their photographs to the class, say who it is, and describe them. As an extension, have Ss stand up. Tell them to sit down if what you say describes them. Say *very tall* and see who sits down. Tell all Ss to stand up again and repeat with different adjectives + *very/really*.

> **Answers**
> 1 friendly 2 funny 3 boring 4 tall/short 5 short/tall
> 6 smart 7 interesting 8 shy 9 old 10 young
>
> | F | A | F | U | N | N | Y | F | D | R | Y | J |
> |---|---|---|---|---|---|---|---|---|---|---|---|
> | T | E | R | H | U | X | O | E | I | M | P | T |
> | Q | K | I | O | R | U | U | S | H | O | R | T |
> | F | M | E | N | J | L | N | H | C | G | P | P |
> | S | G | N | A | W | I | G | Y | R | D | M | C |
> | O | L | D | O | S | H | K | C | V | T | B | M |
> | K | N | L | P | T | A | L | L | P | B | O | E |
> | N | S | Y | L | B | E | V | I | Y | S | R | O |
> | R | O | Y | S | M | A | R | T | T | G | I | U |
> | A | C | Z | B | G | N | D | U | H | O | N | J |
> | I | N | T | E | R | E | S | T | I | N | G | I |

UNIT 3, LESSON 1, VOCABULARY

Timing: 40 Minutes

- **Prepare for the task** Photocopy one worksheet for each student.
- **Introduce the task** Read aloud the following description of an apartment. Ask Ss to fill in the blanks with the words about rooms in a house.

  This is my apartment. Here is the living room with a picture of my cat on the wall. Next to the living room is the bathroom. This is the kitchen with a dining area. My favorite room is my bedroom.

- Write the following on the board and ask Ss to complete the sentences about their house/apartment.

  This is my _____ and here is the _____ with _____. Next to the _____ is the _____. This is the _____ with _____. My favorite room is my _____.

- **Do the task** Put Ss into small groups. Ask one S to start with the Word Card. Have the other Ss draw a 3x3 Bingo Card in their notebook and then write the words for two of the pictures in each square (in pencil, so they can play again). For example:

dining area picture	bathroom window	living room floor
door window	bedroom floor	kitchen wall
kitchen picture	bedroom wall	bedroom bathroom

- The S with the Word Card reads aloud two words, in any order. When Ss hear two words in one of their squares, they cross those words out. The S with the Word Card keeps reading out two words until one S has crossed out all their words. This S is the winner.
- Repeat the activity as the other Ss take turns reading from the Word Card.
- **Review the task** Play with the whole class. You read out the Word Card and then check that the winners have written the correct vocabulary in their Bingo Cards. As a variation, read aloud a short description of each room and things in a room and keep reading until one student has crossed out all the words in their Bingo Card.

UNIT 3, LESSON 2, VOCABULARY

Timing: 40 Minutes

- **Prepare for the task** Copy one worksheet for each pair of Ss.
- **Introduce the task** Give Ss one minute to write down as many furniture words as they can remember. See which S can remember the most words.

- **Do the task** Put Ss into pairs. Direct them to take turns telling each other what is in each room of their apartment. Ss must listen to each other and draw lines from the furniture to the correct room in the empty apartment. If there is more than one piece of that item – for example, two chairs – Ss draw two lines. Monitor and help where necessary.
- **Review the task** Tell Ss to label all the pieces of furniture they have put in the empty apartment. Ask Ss to describe the differences between the two apartments by asking and answering questions. For example: Student A: *My TV is in my kitchen. Where is your TV?* Student B: *My TV is in the living room. Where is your couch?*

UNIT 4, LESSON 1, VOCABULARY
Timing: 40 Minutes

- **Prepare for the task** Copy one worksheet for each pair of Ss and cut up into Student A and Student B halves.
- **Introduce the task** Play board scrabble. Write *smartwatch* in the middle of the board. Tell a student to come up to the board and write a technology word vertically using the letters from *smartwatch*. A student then adds another technology word vertically or horizontally.
- For example:

```
                    e
           game
                r
                p
smartwatch
                o
                n
                e
                s
```

- Continue until Ss have used all the technology vocabulary.
- **Do the task** Put Ss into pairs. Ask Ss if they are familiar with the game Battleship.
- Ss write their five words on their board. Tell each Student A to begin by writing the letters of *cellphone*, with no space, across, down, or diagonally in each square to spell the word. Tell each Student B to begin by writing the letters of *earphones* across, down, or diagonally in each square to spell the word. Check that Ss have written their five words on the board.
- Explain to Ss that they will need to find the five technology words in the **My partner** board. One student reads out a square and the other must say the letter of the technology word if it is in that square. If there is no letter in that square, the student must say *No*. For example:
  - **A** 2A?
  - **B** No
  - **A** 8D?
  - **B** No
  - **A** 3J?
  - **B** Yes – T
- Each time, Ss write the letter of the word or X (no letter) in the **My partner** square. The first student to find the five words is the winner.

- Demonstrate with a stronger student. Monitor and help where necessary.
- **Review the task** Drill all the technology words. Tell Ss to draw in their notebooks a table with two columns: one column with a check (✓), for things they have; and one column with a cross (✗), for things they don't have. Tell Ss to write all the words there. Put Ss into pairs to compare.

UNIT 4, LESSON 2, VOCABULARY
Timing: 40 Minutes

- **Prepare for the task** Copy one worksheet for each pair of Ss and cut up into Student A and Student B halves.
- **Introduce the task** Read aloud verbs connected with technology and ask Ss to say which nouns (and prepositions) go with them. Then read aloud nouns and ask which verbs (and prepositions) go with them. For example: *play* (games), *text messages* (send/read).
- **Do the task** Put Ss into pairs. Tell them to take turns reading the sentence clues aloud to each other. The other partner fills in their crossword puzzle with the missing technology words that can be used to complete the sentences. With weaker Ss, write the missing technology words for Student A and Student B on the board so they can choose the word.
- If their partner doesn't understand which word it is, Ss can help by making a new sentence containing the word or giving a letter in the word. Monitor and help where necessary. When Ss finish, tell them to check their crosswords together.
- **Review the task** Tell Ss to cover up the crossword so they can just see the gapped sentences. Ask Ss to complete the sentences and read them aloud. As an alternative or next step, Ss cover up the sentences but not the crossword and try to repeat the sentences or make their own sentences.

UNIT 5, LESSON 1, VOCABULARY
Timing: 40 Minutes

- **Prepare for the task** Copy one worksheet for each student.
- **Introduce the task** Whisper to each student a day of the week and a time of the day, for example: *Tuesday afternoon* or *Friday morning*. Then tell Ss to line up in chronological order so the Monday mornings are at the beginning of the line and Sunday nights at the end.
- **Do the task** Put Ss into pairs. Tell them to ask each other the questions and write down the answers. Ss then figure out the score for their partners. Monitor and help where necessary.
- **Review the task** Ask Ss to report the questions back to the class, for example: *Manuel has time for sports on the weekends.* As an extension, put Ss into small groups to write four multiple-choice questions for a new questionnaire about everyday activities titled *Do you have a lot of free time?* As a class, decide which are the best eight questions and put them into a new questionnaire. Put Ss into pairs to ask each other the questions.

T-217

UNIT 5, LESSON 2, VOCABULARY

Timing: 40 Minutes

- **Prepare for the task** Copy one worksheet for each pair of Ss. Cut the worksheet into three parts. Both Ss have a copy of the Student A and Student B clock times; Student A and Student B have separate tasks.
- **Introduce the task** Write several times on the board and have Ss say them in different ways. For example:
  - *8:45 – eight forty-five, a quarter to nine*
  - *12:00 – twelve o'clock, noon*
- **Do the task** Give out the worksheets. Read out the times *5:25, 11:35, 9:40, 2:55, 5:00*. Ss find the letters and read aloud the word they spell (*hello*). Repeat with new words until Ss understand how the table works. Put Ss into pairs to read times to each other. Monitor and help where necessary.
- **Review the task** Tell Ss to look at their table. Say the words and ask Ss to read the times back to you. For example: *drink* (possible answer – *7:40, 5:40, 5:45, 11:10, 3:00*). As an extension, ask Ss to write down five different words from the Student's Book and "spell" them using the times from the table. Put Ss into different pairs to repeat the task with the new words.

UNIT 6, LESSON 1, VOCABULARY

- **Prepare for the task** Copy one worksheet for each group of Ss. Cut up the top half of the worksheet into 14 cards. To save cutting, you can assign each student a person from the cards. Ss then need to name the place where that person is and tell the other Ss.
- **Introduce the task** Write the places in cities on the board (the list is in the Key). Have Ss write down the places in their notebooks in order of proximity to their home, for example: 1st *school* (closest to home), 2nd *café* (next closest) … 14th *zoo* (farthest from home). Put Ss into pairs to compare.
- **Do the task** Put Ss into large groups and have each student take a card (Ss could have more than one card or share cards). Tell Ss to share the information from the card with the rest of the group. Then have Ss write the place where each person is in the table. Monitor and help where necessary.
- **Review the task** Tell Ss to put all the cards on the table. Say the place. Ss must find the card.
- As an extension activity, give Ss one minute to look at the cards and then tell Ss to turn them over. Say the place or describe it, for example: *Doctors work here* (hospital). Ss have three attempts to turn over the right card that matches the place / description.

Answers

Person	Place
Steve	bookstore
Haruka	museum
Fabio	hospital
Santiago	store
Lucas and Paula	movie theater
Ana	supermarket
Felipe	school
Megan and Richard	restaurant
Ming	hotel
Martina and Ivan	mall
Rosa and Carlos	park
Amanda	zoo
Yejoon	college
Manuel and Antonia	café

UNIT 6, LESSON 2, VOCABULARY

Timing: 40 Minutes

- **Prepare for the task** Copy one worksheet for each student.
- **Introduce the task** Tell Ss to write these words on separate pieces of paper.
  - *mountain, snow, river, island, beach, ocean, lake, tree, forest, flower, plant, grass, desert, hill*
- Tell Ss to write the translation of each word in their first language on the other side of each piece of paper. Tell Ss to go through each piece of paper and give the translation for each word (either English – first language or first language – English) without turning over the paper. If Ss share a first language, they can work in pairs to test each other.
- **Do the task** Tell Ss to take turns asking each other where the nature vocabulary in the box is in the picture on the worksheet. Tell Ss that some words are in more than one place.
- Have Ss work individually and draw an empty A–H/1–8 table in their notebook. Tell them to write one of each nature word in different places in their table. Put Ss in pairs. Tell them to ask each other where their words are.
  - *Where's your lake?*
  - *My lake is in A2.*
- Ss get one point if they both have a word in the same place. For example, Student A has lake in A2 and Student B has island in A2. They get two points if you have the same word in the same place. For example, they both have lake in A2. See which pair in the class has the most points at the end.
- Monitor and help where necessary.
- **Review the task** Say some coordinates and have Ss tell you what is in the picture on the worksheet. For example: *D7* (grass). Tell Ss to go through the vocabulary cards they made at the start of the activity and check the meaning through translation again. As an extension activity, Ss could add more information to the vocabulary cards such as a transcription and example sentence.

UNIT 7, LESSON 1, VOCABULARY

Timing: 40 Minutes

- **Prepare for the task** Copy one worksheet for each group of four Ss. Cut and mix up the cards so each group gets 24 cards. To save cutting, put Ss into pairs and give each pair a worksheet. Have Ss take turns saying which word goes with the word in **bold** on the card.
- **Introduce the task** Tell Ss to write down six activities that they do around the house. For example: *I do the dishes after dinner. I help my brother with his homework*. Then put Ss into pairs and have them compare their answers.
- **Do the task** Put Ss into groups of four. Give each group their 24 cards face-down. Tell Ss to each take a card. Then have them take turns matching the word that goes with the word in **bold**. Write an example on the board

wash

the dog

breakfast

the bath

(wash + the dog)

- If a student matches the right word, they keep the card. If they match the wrong word, they return the card to the pile. The student who has the most cards at the end is the winner. Monitor and help where necessary.
- **Review the task** Go through all the cards and ask Ss to match the words that make a correct phrase. Then ask Ss to make a sentence using the words on each card. For example: *I brush my teeth in the morning*.

Answers

brush	cook	wash
the dishes	*breakfast*	your teeth
your teeth	the car	*your homework*
breakfast	your homework	*your hair*
clean	**brush**	**cook**
your room	the bath	the dishes
your lunch	dinner	your room
your bath	*your hair*	lunch
breakfast	**the car**	**a bath**
wash	help	*take*
do	*wash*	help
cook	brush	do
homework	**the dishes**	**your brother**
take	*do*	do
help	brush	*help*
do	cook	brush

take	do	help
dinner	*your homework*	your hair
a bath	your car	your room
a kitchen	your lunch	*your sister*
wash	**take**	**help**
the dog	breakfast	*your teeth*
breakfast	a shower	*your mom*
the bath	the dishes	your car
my teeth	**my room**	**my hair**
take	*clean*	wash
brush	take	clean
wash	brush	take
dinner	**the kitchen**	**your dog**
cook	*clean*	do
clean	take	go
take	help	wash

UNIT 7, LESSON 2, VOCABULARY

Timing: 40 Minutes

- **Prepare for the task** Copy one worksheet for each pair of Ss.
- **Introduce the task** Write these stages of a trip to work on the board. Ask Ss to put them in order:
  - ( ) walk from the station
  - ( ) be at home
  - ( ) take a train
  - ( ) be in the office
  - ( ) be on the train
  - ( ) walk to the station
  - ( ) wait
  - (6, 1, 4, 7, 5, 2, 3)
- **Do the task** Tell Ss to work in pairs. Explain the situation: Ss need to get from their home to the office by 9:00. Tell Ss to begin at card 1 and use the choices/options on the cards to decide what they will do. Monitor and help where necessary.
- **Review the task** Tell Ss to read aloud the cards in the order that gets them to work on time. Ask Ss to identify the transportation vocabulary on the worksheet.

UNIT 8, LESSON 1, VOCABULARY

Timing: 40 Minutes

- **Prepare for the task** Copy one worksheet for each S.
- **Introduce the task** Mime or demonstrate the skills on the worksheet and ask Ss to tell you the vocabulary. For example: draw a picture on the board (*draw*).
- **Do the task** Ss work in groups of four. Tell Ss to write their names at the top of each column. Ss take turns asking their partner questions. For example: *Mario, do you draw?* Tell Ss to put a check in the table if the answer is yes. Monitor and help where necessary.

T-219

- **Review the task** Put Ss into pairs. Ask them to tell each other what skills they do and give more information. For example: *I don't draw, but I sometimes dance. I fix things at home.* Invite some Ss to tell the class about what skills they have.
- As an extension activity, Ss rank each of the 12 skills according to how fun they are (1 = a lot of fun; 12 = not fun at all) and then rank them according to how difficult they are (1 = very difficult; 12 = not difficult at all). Put Ss into pairs to compare their rankings.

UNIT 8, LESSON 2, VOCABULARY

Timing: 40 Minutes

- **Prepare for the task** Copy one worksheet for each pair of Ss and cut it into Student A and B halves.
- **Introduce the task** Read aloud these definitions to Ss. Then have them complete each sentence.
- *You can find computers and desks here. You work in a(n) _____. (office)*
- *You are in the office for 12 hours each day. You work _____. (hard)*
- *These are the people you work with in your office. These are your _____. (coworkers)*
- *You have a coffee for 10 minutes. You take a _____. (break)*
- **Do the task** Ss work in pairs. Tell Ss they will read a different text about work. Ss will take turns reading their texts with pauses. Ss must listen to their partner and write down the work vocabulary from the box that they hear. Ss may need to re-read sections of the text for their partners. Monitor and help where necessary. Then tell Ss to check their answers together.
- **Review the task** Read aloud sections of the Student A text in a different order. For example: *They all _____ it is a great laptop* and have Ss say the missing words. Repeat with the Student B text.
- As a more challenging variation, Ss can read their texts to each other, but leave gaps for the underlined words. Their partner must choose from the words in the box to fill the gaps.

UNIT 9, LESSON 1, VOCABULARY

Timing: 40 Minutes

- **Prepare for the task** Copy one worksheet for each student.
- **Introduce the task** Write these groups of words on the board. Ask Ss to identify the word that doesn't belong.
  - city   town   country   (country)
  - boat   ranch   plane   (ranch)
  - vacation   work   tour   (work)
  - ranch   farm   city   (city)
  - hill   boat   ocean   (hill)

- **Do the task** Ss choose the correct words to complete each travel description.
- Tell Ss to rank the vacations (1 = the vacation they like most). Then, have Ss work in pairs to tell their partners what they like about each vacation and what they don't like.
- **Review the task** Tell Ss to turn over the worksheet. Read out the texts, but pause at the ten vocabulary items. Ss should remember the vocabulary and tell you the words that complete the sentences of the text. Alternatively, Ss can use the vocabulary to describe a vacation or place they like.

UNIT 9, LESSON 2, VOCABULARY

Timing: 40 Minutes

- **Prepare for the task** Copy one worksheet for each student and cut up into halves for Student A and Student B.
- **Introduce the task** Read aloud the vocabulary and have Ss identify the words as nouns or verbs: *airport, arrive, buy, check in, destination, flight, fly, leave, stay, trip, travel.*

> **Answers**
> Nouns: airport, destination, flight, trip
> Verbs: arrive, buy, check in, fly, leave, stay, travel

- **Do the task** Ss complete the questions with the words. Check as a class. Put Ss into pairs. Pairs take turns asking one another the questions from the chart to fill in the information. Monitor and help where necessary.
- **Review the task** Ss choose a new travel destination and think up new details for the travel arrangements. Ss can then ask one another the same questions from the chart.

> **Answers**
> Where are you <u>traveling / flying</u> from?
> What is your <u>destination</u>?
> Can you <u>buy</u> a ticket <u>online</u> for the trip?
> What time do you have to <u>leave</u> home?
> What time do you have to be at the <u>airport</u>?
> Do you need to <u>stay</u> in a hotel the night before?
> When do you have to <u>check in</u>?
> How long is your <u>flight</u>?
> When does the plane <u>arrive</u>?

UNIT 10, LESSON 1, VOCABULARY

40 minutes

- **Prepare for the task** Copy one worksheet for each S.
- **Introduce the task** Ask some concept-checking questions. For example:
  - *Do you go shopping in a store or a theater? (store)*
  - *Can you take a walk in a river or a park? (park)*
  - *Do you have a picnic inside or outside? (outside)*
  - *You meet someone at the airport. Is she arriving or leaving? (arriving)*

- **Do the task** Ss ask each other the questions. With stronger Ss, encourage follow-up questions. For example:
  - A *Dominique, where do you go to look at art?*
  - B *I look at art in the museum.*
  - A *What art do you like?*
- Have Ss make sentences for "D" answers. For example:
  - A *Manuel, do you like to eat inside or outside?*
  - B *I like to eat inside at home. I like to eat outside on vacation.*
- **Review the task** Ss answer the questions as a class and then ask follow-up questions.

UNIT 10, LESSON 2, VOCABULARY
Timing: 35 minutes

- **Prepare for the task** Copy and cut up the worksheet into a set of A and B cards for each pair. To save copying, Ss can take turns choosing an A picture, saying the clothes and season, and then matching to a B card.
- **Introduce the task** Give Ss one minute to look at what everyone in class is wearing. Then tell Ss to close their eyes. Name a S and see if the class can remember what he or she is wearing. Repeat with different Ss.
- Then write all the clothes words Ss have said on the board. Ss say the seasons these clothes are suitable for wearing outside. For example: *T-shirt* (summer).
- **Do the task** Put Ss into pairs. Tell Ss to put the A and B cards face down in separate piles. One S takes an A card and says what the person is wearing and what the season is. Then they take a B card. If the cards match, they keep both cards. If the cards don't match, or the S makes a mistake with the vocabulary on the A card, the S returns both cards. Then it is their partner's turn. Ss continue until there are no cards left. The S with the most cards at the end is the winner. Monitor and help where necessary.
- **Review the task** Go through all the A cards and ask Ss to name what clothes are in each picture and what season it is.
- As a variation or extension, play Bingo with the A cards. Put Ss into groups of three. Each S chooses four A cards. Mix up the B cards and read them aloud one by one. The first S who has four A cards to match the B cards you read is the winner.

UNIT 11, LESSON 1, VOCABULARY
Timing: 45 Minutes

- **Prepare for the task** Copy one worksheet for each group of four Ss and cut it up into cards. To save cutting, Ss can take turns choosing a square and reading out the sentence for the other Ss to choose the adjective.

- **Introduce the task** Tell Ss to write down an example of each of these things:
  - *something new in their home*
  - *a beautiful city in their country*
  - *a quiet place to study*
  - *a fast car*
  - *an exciting vacation*
  - *a wonderful person*
- Put Ss into pairs to compare and tell one another about these things.
- **Do the task** Put Ss into groups of four. Give each group a set of cards and tell them to put them face-down in a pile. Have Ss take turns choosing a card and reading it aloud with the two adjectives as options. The other Ss must say which adjective completes the sentence. The S who says the correct adjective keeps the card (Ss check with the teacher if they are not sure). Continue until Ss have used all the cards. The S with the most cards at the end is the winner. Monitor and help where necessary.
- **Review the task** Take a set of cards, read them aloud, and ask Ss to choose the correct adjective.
- As a more challenging variation, have Ss read the cards aloud with gaps for the adjectives. The other Ss must think of an appropriate adjective to complete the sentence.
- As an extension task, Ss make their own cards. They can then give the cards to another group to repeat the activity.

Answers

The food is **awful**! I'm not going to eat it again!
My aunt is wearing a **beautiful** dress.
The computer game is expensive because it is **new**.
I can swim, but I am **slow**.
I need a new laptop. My old laptop is **slow** now.
Usain Bolt was very **fast** in the 100 meters.
The children are **noisy** today.
Our vacation in Acapulco was **exciting**.
The children in the photo were really **cute**.
The soccer game was **exciting**. It was great.
The trip was **awful**. I never want to go back there.
Alex is a really **wonderful** friend. I like him a lot.
My jeans are **new**. Do you like them?
I live in a village. It is nice and **quiet**.
I am a **fast** swimmer. I can swim 50 meters in 35 seconds.
The children are **quiet** in school.
I was a **noisy** boy at school. I wasn't a good student.
An 89% on your English test is **wonderful**! You are a very good student.
The flowers in spring are **beautiful**.
She was a really **cute** two-year-old girl then.
The video is **awful**. Don't watch it.
Barcelona is a **beautiful** city. Let's go there on vacation.
My sister is really **cute**. She's a lovely girl.
The concert wasn't **exciting**. It was very boring.
There is a **fast** train to London.
I have a **new** friend. Her name is Karla.
The music is very **noisy**. Can you hear me?
We had a **quiet** walk in the park.
The bus is very **slow**. I'm going to drive.
The book is **wonderful**. I love it.
The party wasn't **exciting**. It wasn't fun.
It's a **beautiful** day. Let's go to the park.

UNIT 11, LESSON 2, VOCABULARY

Timing: 45 minutes

- **Prepare for the task** Copy one worksheet for each S.
- **Introduce the task** Briefly review the words for colors by pointing to items in the classroom and asking what color they are, e.g., *What color is the door/wall/desk? What color is my/your sweater/shirt/bag/book?* Elicit answers (*It's [blue].*) To remind Ss of anagrams, write *grenoa* (*orange*) on the board. Ask Ss: *What is this word?* Start to rewrite the letters on the board. Encourage Ss to say the word when they think they recognize it.
- **Do the task** Ss rearrange the letters to make words individually, then check their answers with a partner.
- Check answers with the class. Check for correct pronunciation.

> **Answers**
> 1 green
> 2 yellow
> 3 black
> 4 red
> 5 white
> 6 blue
> 7 gray
> 8 purple
> 9 orange
> 10 brown
> 11 pink

- Then tell Ss to complete the sentences individually, using the words in exercise A. Make sure Ss understand that the answers should be true for them. Circulate and help if necessary.
- Ss compare their answers. One S reads a question and his/her partner answers. The S who asked the question also reads his/her answer aloud. If they are both the same, Ss write *S*. If they are different, they write *D*. Ss record how many answers are the same. Elicit answers from a few volunteer Ss.
- Tell Ss they are going to walk around the class, asking questions like those in the model dialogue in exercise C. The aim is to check as many of the items as possible on the list. Ss may need to ask more than one person for each item on the list, but they should try to find as many as possible. Read the conversation aloud with a stronger S.
- Set a time limit of about 10 minutes. Ss count the number of items. Ask Ss to raise their hands if they have one check mark, then two, three, and so on up to nine (or until no Ss have their hands raised). Those with the highest number are the winners.
- Ask individual Ss to report findings to the class by saying who has each item, e.g., *Camila has a red bag. / Jose Luis has a green watch.*

UNIT 12, LESSON 1, VOCABULARY

Timing: 35 Minutes

- **Prepare for the task** Copy one worksheet for each S. Cut up the bottom half of the worksheet. Distribute the food table to each S. Cut up a Student A, Student B, Student C, and Student D card for each S in a group of four.
- **Introduce the task** Tell Ss to write down two food words for each category: fruit and vegetables, meat, dairy products, and grains.
- **Do the task** Tell Ss to work in a group of four. Ss take turns telling one another what each person eats each day and write the food words in the table. Monitor and help where necessary.
- Ask Ss who they think has the healthiest diet.
- **Review the task** Ask Ss to read all the food words on their card out loud.
- As an extension, Ss repeat the task with the food they ate today. Then ask Ss what food they liked and didn't like.

> **Answers**
>
> | | Fruit and vegetables | Meat | Dairy products |
> |---|---|---|---|
> | Miranda | coconut pineapple apple orange tomato | beef lamb | cheese |
> | Boris | coconut banana orange potato | chicken lamb | butter |
> | Ming | apple banana orange tomato potato | chicken | butter cheese |
> | Dan | pineapple apple banana tomato potato | beef | butter |
>
> | | Grains | Small meals |
> |---|---|---|
> | Miranda | bread | soup |
> | Boris | cracker | soup sandwich |
> | Ming | bread | sandwich |
> | Dan | bread cracker | soup |

UNIT 12, LESSON 2, VOCABULARY

Timing: 40 Minutes

- **Prepare for the task** Copy one worksheet for each S.
- **Introduce the task** Write the first and last letter of the food, drink, and dessert words on the board. Ask Ss to tell you the word and say if it is food, drink, or dessert. For example: *j* _____ *e* (juice; drink). Then Ss write down which food, drink, or dessert they had yesterday. Put Ss into pairs to compare.
- **Do the task** Ss work in groups of four. Tell them to fill in the menu and say which words are food, drinks, and desserts. Then tell Ss they have $30 each and they must choose what to eat and drink at the café. Have Ss tell one another what they want and then figure out the total price for their group. Monitor and make sure Ss are saying the words for food, drinks, and desserts.
- **Review the task** Ss say all the names of the food, drinks, and desserts on the menu.
- As an extension task, repeat the task, but give Ss some restrictions. For example: they must each order a drink and dessert, or at least one person in the group should order fish.

1.1 VOCABULARY

COUNTRIES AND NATIONALITIES

Russia	Chile	Spain	the United States	Ecuador
Brazil	Colombia	Japan	Mexico	Peru
France	China	Honduras	South Korea	

1.2 VOCABULARY

THE ALPHABET; PERSONAL INFORMATION

Student A

**Aa Bb Cc Dd Ee Ff Gg Hh Ii Jj Kk Ll Mm
Nn Oo Pp Qq Rr Ss Tt Uu Vv Ww Xx Yy Zz**

PAIR WORK Complete the personal information about the four people by spelling out the beginnings and endings of the words.

	Person 1		**Person 2**
First name	Mari _ _ _ _ _ _		_ _ _ _ _ hen
Last name	_ _ _ _ _ _ quez		Harr _ _ _ _ _
Email address	mvz@trave_ _ _ _ _ _ _ _ _ _ _		shon@ _ _ _ _ _ _ _ _ _
College	Caval _ _ _ _ _ _		_ _ _ _ _ _ ngton
Company	_ _ _ _ _ ares		_ _ _ _ _ idtz
	Person 3		**Person 4**
First name	Aman _ _ _ _ _		_ _ _ _ ako
Last name	Alex _ _ _ _ _ _		Hashi _ _ _ _ _
Email address	_ _ _ _ _ _ _ _ _ _ _ _ _ _ mail.net		_ _ _ _ _ _ _ _ _ _ _ _ _ _ mymail.org
College	_ _ _ _ _ _ hand		Juni _ _ _ _ _ _ _
Company	Vign _ _ _ _ _		_ _ _ _ _ _ hide

Student B

**Aa Bb Cc Dd Ee Ff Gg Hh Ii Jj Kk Ll Mm
Nn Oo Pp Qq Rr Ss Tt Uu Vv Ww Xx Yy Zz**

PAIR WORK Complete the personal information about the four people by spelling out the beginnings and endings of the words.

	Person 1		**Person 2**
First name	_ _ _ _ _ angel		Step _ _ _ _
Last name	Velaz _ _ _ _ _		_ _ _ _ _ ison
Email address	_ _ _ _ _ _ _ _ _ _ _ _ _ _ lmail.org		_ _ _ _ _ _ _ xyz.com
College	_ _ _ _ _ _ _ canti		Welli _ _ _ _ _ _
Company	Oliv _ _ _ _ _		Schm _ _ _ _ _
	Person 3		**Person 4**
First name	_ _ _ _ _ dine		Han _ _ _ _
Last name	_ _ _ _ _ andre		_ _ _ _ _ _ moto
Email address	ama@list _ _ _ _ _ _ _ _ _ _ _ _ _		han_moto@ _ _ _ _ _ _ _ _ _ _ _ _ _
College	Marc _ _ _ _ _		_ _ _ _ _ chiro
Company	_ _ _ _ _ eron		Mitsu _ _ _ _ _

2.1 VOCABULARY

FAMILY; NUMBERS

Student A

A PAIR WORK Tell your partner about the family tree and complete the information.

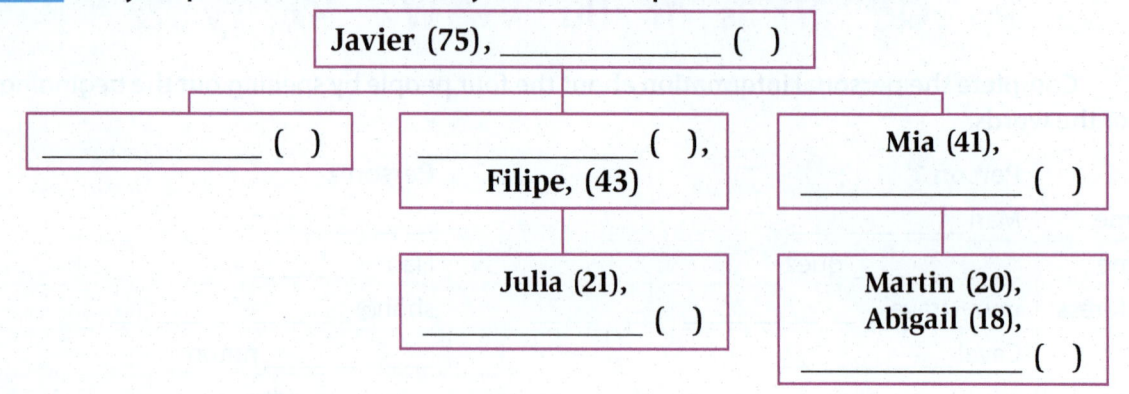

```
                    Javier (75), _____ ( )
       ┌────────────────┼────────────────┐
  _____ ( )   _____ ( ),    Mia (41),
                    Filipe, (43)      _____ ( )
                         │                 │
                    Julia (21),      Martin (20),
                    _____ ( )   Abigail (18),
                                     _____ ( )
```

B PAIR WORK Complete the sentences about the family tree.

1. Ana is the _____ of Javier.
2. Sofia is the _____ of Abigail.
3. Filipe is the _____ of Lucas.
4. Rafael is the _____ of Martin.
5. Bruno is the _____ of Mia.
6. Javier and Ana are the _____ of Filipe.
7. Mia is the _____ of Julia.
8. Martin is the _____ of Bruno.
9. Julia and Lucas are the _____ of Alba and Filipe.
10. Abigail is the _____ of Lucas.

Student B

A PAIR WORK Tell your partner about the family tree and complete the information.

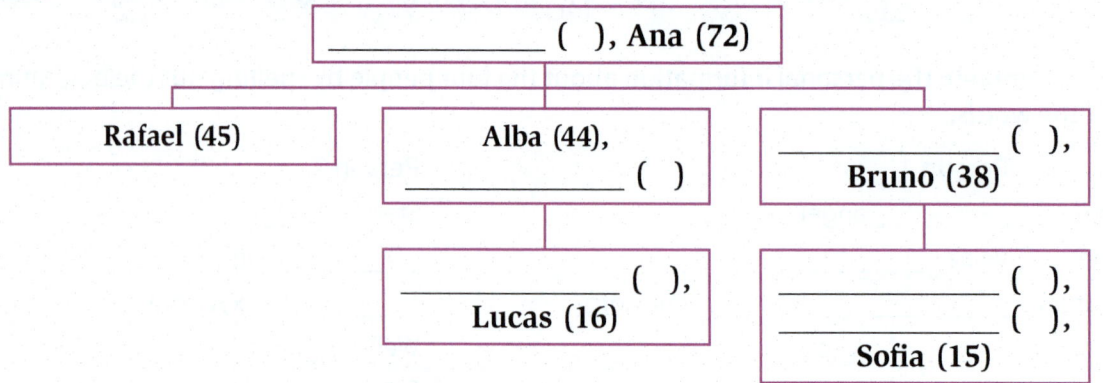

```
                 _____ ( ), Ana (72)
       ┌────────────────┼────────────────┐
  Rafael (45)      Alba (44),       _____ ( ),
                   _____ ( )    Bruno (38)
                         │                 │
                    _____ ( ),   _____ ( ),
                    Lucas (16)        _____ ( ),
                                      Sofia (15)
```

B PAIR WORK Complete the sentences about the family tree.

1. Ana is the _____ of Javier.
2. Sofia is the _____ of Abigail.
3. Filipe is the _____ of Lucas.
4. Rafael is the _____ of Martin.
5. Bruno is the _____ of Mia.
6. Javier and Ana are the _____ of Filipe.
7. Mia is the _____ of Julia.
8. Martin is the _____ of Bruno.
9. Julia and Lucas are the _____ of Alba and Filipe.
10. Abigail is the _____ of Lucas.

2.2 VOCABULARY

DESCRIBING PEOPLE; *REALLY / VERY*

A Find nine adjectives that are used to describe people in the word search. Match them to the pictures.

F	A	F	U	N	N	Y	F	D	R	Y	J
T	E	R	H	U	X	O	E	I	M	P	T
Q	K	I	O	R	U	U	S	H	O	R	T
F	M	E	N	J	L	N	H	C	G	P	P
S	G	N	A	W	I	G	Y	R	D	M	C
O	L	D	O	S	H	K	C	V	T	B	M
K	N	L	P	T	A	L	L	P	B	O	E
N	S	Y	L	B	E	V	I	Y	S	R	O
R	O	Y	S	M	A	R	T	T	G	I	U
A	C	Z	B	G	N	D	U	H	O	N	J
I	N	T	E	R	E	S	T	I	N	G	I

1. _____
2. _____
3. _____
4. _____ and _____
5. _____
6. _____
7. _____
8. _____
9. _____

B Write down the name of someone you know next to these adjectives.

friendly _____   shy _____
funny _____   very old _____
really smart _____   very tall _____
interesting _____

C **PAIR WORK** Find a picture of someone in your family on your phone. Write notes. Then describe this person to a partner.

3.1 VOCABULARY

ROOMS IN A HOME

GROUP WORK Take turns saying words in the Word Card and writing in the Bingo Card.

Word Card
Read aloud the two words, in any order on the Word Card, to the other students.

bathroom and door	bathroom and floor	bathroom and picture	bathroom and wall	bathroom and window	door and floor
bedroom and door	bedroom and floor	bedroom and picture	bedroom and wall	bedroom and window	door and picture
dining area and door	dining area and floor	dining area and picture	dining area and wall	dining area and window	door and wall
living room and door	living room and floor	living room and picture	living room and wall	living room and window	door and window
kitchen and door	kitchen and floor	kitchen and picture	kitchen and wall	bedroom and dining area	bedroom and kitchen
bathroom and living room	bedroom and living room	dining area and living room	kitchen and living room	kitchen and dining area	bedroom and bathroom
bathroom and kitchen	bathroom and dining area	dining area and kitchen			

Bingo Card

A Draw a 3x3 table in your notebook. Write two of each word in each square in pencil.

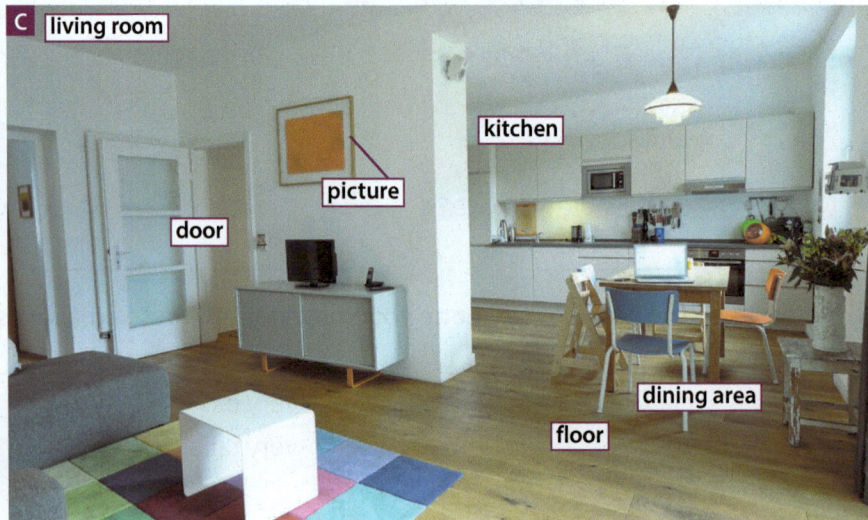

B Listen to the student saying the words. When you hear two words that are in your square, cross them out. If you cross out all nine squares first, you are the winner.

3.2 VOCABULARY

FURNITURE

Student A

A **PAIR WORK** Tell your partner about the furniture in your apartment.

A rug is in …   *Two chairs are in ….*

B Listen to your partner. Draw the furniture or write the words in the correct room in the apartment.

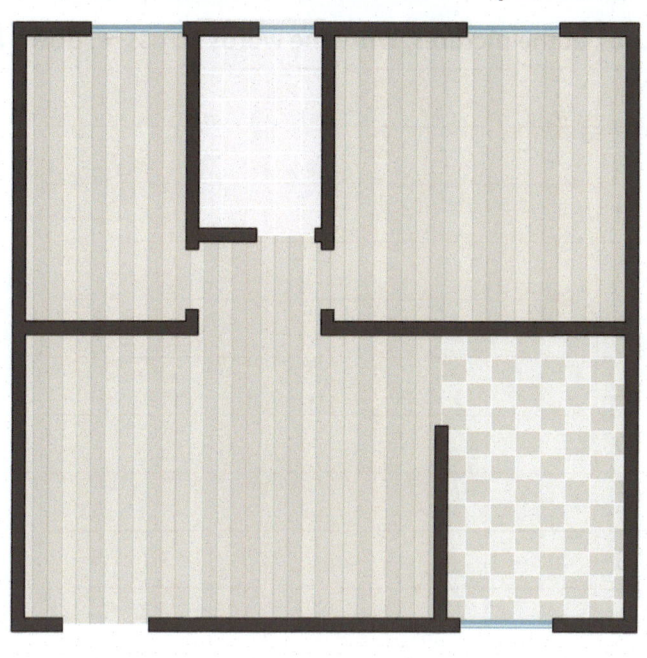

Student B

A **PAIR WORK** Listen to your partner. Draw the furniture or write the words in the correct room in the apartment.

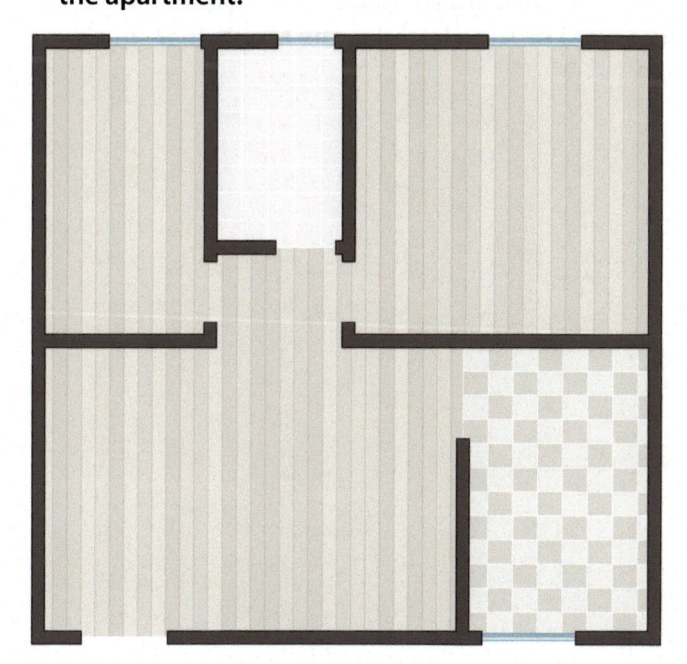

B Tell your partner about the furniture in your apartment.

A TV is in …   *Two chairs are in ….*

4.1 VOCABULARY

TECHNOLOGY

Student A

Me

Look at the pictures. Write the words across →, down ↓, or diagonally ↘ in the board. Each square has one letter.

	1	2	3	4	5	6	7	8	9	10
J										
I										
H										
G										
F										
E										
D										
C										
B										
A										

My partner

Find five technology words in the My partner board.

Take turns saying squares, such as 3C. Say the letter of the technology word when it is in that square. When there is no letter in that square, say *No*. Write the letter of the word or X (no letter) in the My partner square.

	1	2	3	4	5	6	7	8	9	10
J										
I										
H										
G										
F										
E										
D										
C										
B										
A										

4.1 VOCABULARY

TECHNOLOGY

Student B

Me

Look at the pictures. Write the words across →, down ↓, or diagonally ↘ in the board. Each square has one letter.

	1	2	3	4	5	6	7	8	9	10
J										
I										
H										
G										
F										
E										
D										
C										
B										
A										

My partner

Find five technology words in the My partner board.

Take turns saying squares, such as 3C. Say the letter of the technology word when it is in that square. When there is no letter in that square, say *No*. Write the letter of the word or X (no letter) in the My partner square.

	1	2	3	4	5	6	7	8	9	10
J										
I										
H										
G										
F										
E										
D										
C										
B										
A										

4.2 VOCABULARY

USING TECHNOLOGY

Student A

PAIR WORK Take turns telling each other the clues. Listen and fill in the crossword puzzle with the missing technology words to complete each sentence.

Clues

2 I watch _____ on my laptop.
3 I don't use _____ .
4 I _____ friends on my cell phone.
6 We don't use _____ for work.
8 I _____ with my cousin on my laptop.
9 You _____ really funny emails!
10 You _____ really cool photos!

Student B

PAIR WORK Take turns telling each other the clues. Listen and fill in the crossword puzzle with the missing technology words to complete each sentence.

Clues

1 I use _____ on my smartwatch.
4 Do you read my _____ ?
5 I don't leave voice _____ .
7 We _____ movies on my tablet.
11 We both don't like _____ messages.
12 I _____ to music on YouTube™.
13 Do you read my _____ messages?

T-232 Evolve level 1 Teacher's Edition PHOTOCOPIABLE © Cambridge University Press 2019

5.1 VOCABULARY

DAYS AND TIMES OF DAY; EVERYDAY ACTIVITIES

PAIR WORK Ask each other the questions. Then check your scores.

Do you have a lot of fun?

Score

1. When do you have time for sports?
   - A I don't have time for sports.
   - B On the weekends.
   - C In the mornings. ___
2. Do you play soccer?
   - A Yes, I play soccer on the weekends.
   - B Yes, but not every weekend.
   - C I don't play soccer and I don't watch it. ___
3. Do you play video games with your friends?
   - A No, I don't play them with my friends.
   - B Yes, we play in the evening.
   - C I don't have time for friends. ___
4. Do you work / study Monday to Friday?
   - A Yes, but I love my work / studies.
   - B No, I work / study Monday to Sunday.
   - C No, I don't work / study every day. ___
5. What is your favorite day of the week?
   - A Tuesday – I go out after work / college.
   - B Friday – I watch TV with my family.
   - C Wednesday – I don't have to work / study. ___
6. Do you have fun on the weekends?
   - A No, I work / study.
   - B I have fun every day!
   - C Yes, weekends are great! ___
7. What do you do on Saturday evenings?
   - A I study English.
   - B I go out with my family.
   - C I play video games. ___
8. What is your favorite day of the weekend?
   - A I don't have a weekend.
   - B Sunday – I meet my friends.
   - C Saturday – it is Saturday! ___

Your score	
Question 1	A=0, B=1, C=2
Question 2	A=2, B=1, C=0
Question 3	A=1, B=2, C=0
Question 4	A=2, B=0, C=1
Question 5	A=2, B=1, C=1
Question 6	A=0, B=2, C=1
Question 7	A=1, B=2, C=1
Question 8	A=0, B=2, C=2

- 12–16 You are really cool and you always have time for fun!
- 6–11 You work / study a lot, but you still have fun.
- 0–5 You don't have free time.

5.2 VOCABULARY

TELLING THE TIME

Student A and Student B

1:00	i	1:05	n	1:15	e	1:25	v	1:30	l	1:35	s	1:40	e	1:55	a
2:00	a	2:10	s	2:15	b	2:20	o	2:25	e	2:45	a	2:50	n	2:55	l
3:00	k	3:15	d	3:20	c	3:25	n	3:30	a	3:35	d	3:40	e	3:50	h
4:00	n	4:10	d	4:15	i	4:30	t	4:35	d	4:45	f	4:50	u	4:55	a
5:00	o	5:05	t	5:10	n	5:20	t	5:25	h	5:35	k	5:40	r	5:45	i
6:00	t	6:20	w	6:25	e	6:30	e	6:35	i	6:40	n	6:50	f	6:55	p
7:00	e	7:05	k	7:15	o	7:25	e	7:30	r	7:40	d	7:45	s	7:50	w
8:00	r	8:15	e	8:20	o	8:30	d	8:35	t	8:40	d	8:50	c	8:55	n
9:00	w	9:05	g	9:10	y	9:20	m	9:25	r	9:35	s	9:40	l	9:45	k
10:00	m	10:05	r	10:15	e	10:25	t	10:30	a	10:40	i	10:50	e	10:55	t
11:00	u	11:10	n	11:15	o	11:20	n	11:35	e	11:45	m	11:50	a	11:55	i
12:00	o	12:20	s	12:25	r	12:30	i	12:40	r	12:45	f	12:50	s	12:55	y

----

Student A

A Say the times to Student B. Student B finds the times and letters in the table, then they use the letters to spell a word.

2:15	7:30	10:15	3:30	7:05	6:50	1:55	1:35	5:05	(breakfast)
4:35	12:40	5:45	11:10	5:35					(drink)
9:00	10:50	7:25	9:45	6:25	1:05	3:35			(weekend)
9:20	1:00	8:40	11:20	6:35	9:05	3:50	4:30		(midnight)
8:50	1:30	12:00	3:20	5:35					(clock)
12:25	8:20	4:50	6:00	10:40	5:10	2:25			(routine)
7:50	11:35	8:30	6:40	7:00	2:10	7:40	10:30	12:55	(Wednesday)
3:20	2:55	11:50	2:10	9:35	2:25	12:50			(classes)

B Listen to Student B. Find each of the times and letters in the table. Then say the words each group of letters spell.

Student B

A Listen to Student A. Find each of the times and letters in the table. Then say the words each group of letters spell.

B Say the times to Student A. Student A finds the times and letters in the table, then they use the letters to spell a word.

4:10	11:55	4:00	2:50	6:30	10:05				(dinner)
12:50	7:15	10:00	1:40	10:55	4:15	11:45	8:15	9:35	(sometimes)
10:30	12:45	10:25	1:15	8:00	3:25	11:15	2:20	8:55	(afternoon)
8:35	5:25	11:00	5:40	12:20	3:15	4:55	9:10		(Thursday)
4:45	11:50	1:25	5:00	9:25	12:30	5:20	3:40		(favorite)
1:55	9:40	6:20	2:00	12:55	7:45				(always)
3:40	1:25	8:15	1:05	11:55	11:10	9:05			(evening)
6:55	10:30	9:25	1:15	4:00	5:05	1:35			(parents)

6.1 VOCABULARY

PLACES IN CITIES

GROUP WORK Take turns choosing a card. Work together to write down where the people are.

Person	Place	Person	Place
Steve		Richard and Megan	
Haruka		Ming	
Fabio		Ivan and Marina	
Santiago		Carlos and Rosa	
Lucas and Paula		Amanda	
Ana		Yejoon	
Felipe		Antonia and Manuel	

6.2 VOCABULARY

NATURE

A **PAIR WORK** Take turns asking and saying where these are in the picture.

| mountains | snow | river | island | beach | ocean | lake |
| tree | forest | flower | plant | grass | desert | hill |

Where are the mountains?   *The mountains are in B8 and H7.*

B Work alone. Draw an empty table A–H/1–8 in your notebook. Write all the nature words in different places in your table.

C **PAIR WORK** Ask each other where the words are.

Where's your lake?   *My lake is in A2.*

You get one point if you both have any word in the same place.
You get two points if you have the same word in the same place.

T-236 Evolve level 1 Teacher's Edition PHOTOCOPIABLE © Cambridge University Press 2019

7.1 VOCABULARY

ACTIVITIES AROUND THE HOUSE

GROUP WORK Take turns taking a card and saying the word that goes with the word in bold.

brush	**cook**	**wash**	**take**	**do**	**help**
the dishes	breakfast	your teeth	dinner	your homework	your hair
your teeth	the car	your homework	a bath	your car	your room
breakfast	your homework	your hair	a kitchen	your lunch	your sister

clean	**brush**	**cook**	**wash**	**take**	**help**
your room	the bath	the dishes	the dog	breakfast	your teeth
your lunch	dinner	your room	breakfast	a shower	your mom
your bath	your hair	lunch	the bath	the dishes	your car

breakfast	**the car**	**a bath**	**my teeth**	**my room**	**my hair**
wash	help	take	take	clean	wash
do	wash	help	brush	take	clean
cook	brush	do	wash	brush	take

homework	**the dishes**	**your brother**	**dinner**	**the kitchen**	**your dog**
take	do	do	cook	clean	do
help	brush	help	clean	take	go
do	cook	brush	take	help	wash

7.2 VOCABULARY

TRANSPORTATION

PAIR WORK You need to get from your home to the office by 9:00. Start at card 1. Use the choices on the cards to decide what you will do. Then go to that card and choose again.

1	2	3	4	5
Walk to the bus station. Go to 11. Drive. Go to 4. Ride your bike. Go to 18. Take the train. Go to 8.	You are waiting. What do you do? Chat with a friend. Go to 20. Listen to music. Go to 9.	Where is the train station?! Turn left. Go to 17. Turn right. Go to 14.	There are a lot of cars on the road. Go back to 1. No problem! Go to 6.	You are both having a coffee in the café. Go to 16.
6	**7**	**8**	**9**	**10**
Oh no! It is now 9:00 and you are not at work! Go to 1.	Your boss is not happy! You aren't very smart today. Take the train home …	You are walking to the train station. Go to 3.	You are listening to some cool music and waiting. Go to 12.	You are at work before 9:00!
11	**12**	**13**	**14**	**15**
You are waiting. There is no bus. Go back to 1.	You take the train. Go to 19.	You are walking to the office. Go to 10.	You are walking and walking … Go to 6.	Why are you riding your bike with a big bag? Go to 1.
16	**17**	**18**	**19**	**20**
The coffee is good and you have a nice chat but … Go to 6.	You are at the train station. Go to 2.	Are you carrying a big bag? Yes – Go to 15. No – Go to 4.	You see your boss. She tells you, "I don't like Mondays." What do you say? "I do!" – Go to 13. "Me neither – it's work again!" Go to 7.	You are chatting with your friend. She wants a coffee. What about you? Yes – Go to 5. No – Go to 12.

8.1 VOCABULARY

VERBS TO DESCRIBE SKILLS

Work in groups. Ask questions, for example, *Do you (draw)?*

	You			
dance				
draw				
fix things				
read music				
paint				
play the guitar				
sing				
skateboard				
snowboard				
speak two languages				
surf				
swim				

8.2 VOCABULARY

WORK

Student A

A PAIR WORK Read your text to Student B. Pause for the underlined words.

I work for ABC in Boston. ABC is a computer [1] company with about two hundred [2] workers. People from many countries work for ABC. My three [3] coworkers are from Mexico, Russia, and Honduras. Today we [4] have a meeting about the new ABC laptop. They all [5] think it is a great laptop, and I agree. After a meeting, we usually [6] take a break, drink coffee, and chat in our [7] office. At ABC, we [8] work hard every day. We like our jobs and are very happy here.

B Listen to Student B. Write down the words from the box that you hear.

| company | coworkers | have a meeting | office |
| take a break | think | work hard | workers |

1 _____ 3 _____ 5 _____ 7 _____
2 _____ 4 _____ 6 _____ 8 _____

Student B

A PAIR WORK Listen to Student A. Write down the words from the box that you hear.

| company | coworkers | have a meeting | office |
| take a break | think | work hard | workers |

1 _____ 3 _____ 5 _____ 7 _____
2 _____ 4 _____ 6 _____ 8 _____

B Read your text to Student A. Pause for the underlined words.

It is Monday and I [1] have a meeting at 10:00 with Maria and Daniel in our [2] office on London Road. Maria and Daniel are my [3] coworkers. I really enjoy working with them. Our [4] company is not very big. There are about 60 [5] workers. It is a great job. I meet a lot of very interesting people at work and I [6] think they are happy too. Yes, I [7] work hard, sometimes ten hours a day, but it is fun. I can always [8] take a break and chat with the people next to me.

9.1 VOCABULARY

TRAVEL

A Complete each text with the travel vocabulary.

Victor and Adelia

We are on [1] *vacation / plane* in Tokyo and it's great! Tokyo is a very big [2] *city / country* and we love it! We go shopping every day, and there are a lot of really good restaurants. Now we are on a river [3] *tour / ticket* and we're having lunch on the [4] *farm / boat*.

Isabelle and Mateo

Wow! This is the famous Bolshoi theater in Moscow and we have two [5] *vacation / tickets*! Moscow is great! There are a lot of museums and nice cafés. There are also big parks with trees and plants. Sometimes we think we're in the [6] *country / city*.

Ella and Daniel

We are in Mexico City! We took a [7] *boat / plane* from Washington in the United States. We live on a [8] *ranch / country* near Ellensburg (which is a small [9] *town / vacation*, not a city). We work hard on the ranch. Now we are ready for a fun [10] *tour / ticket*. We are very excited to see all the important places in this great city!

B Which vacation do you like?

C PAIR WORK What do you like about these vacations? What don't you like? Discuss with a partner.

9.2 VOCABULARY

TRAVEL ARRANGEMENTS

Student A

A Complete the questions with the words in the box. You won't use all the words.

| airport | arrive | buy | check in | destination | flight |
| flying | leave | online | stay | traveling | trip |

B Work with a partner. Ask each other the questions.

	You	Student B
Where are you _____ from?	Osaka	
What is your _____ ?	Beijing	
Can you _____ a ticket _____ for the trip?	yes	
What time do you have to _____ home?	7:00 in the evening	
What time do you have to be at the _____ ?	5:30 in the morning (the next day)	
Do you need to _____ in a hotel the night before?	yes	
When do you have to _____ ?	6:00 in the morning	
How long is your _____ ?	3 hours 20 minutes	
When does the plane _____ ?	10:00 in the morning	

Student B

A Complete the questions with the words in the box. You won't use all the words.

| airport | arrive | buy | check in | destination | flight |
| flying | leave | online | stay | traveling | trip |

B Work with a partner. Ask each other the questions.

	Student A	You
Where are you _____ from?		Lima
What is your _____ ?		Machu Picchu
Can you _____ a ticket _____ for the trip?		don't know
What time do you have to _____ home?		3:00 in the afternoon
What time do you have to be at the _____ ?		4:30 in the afternoon
Do you need to _____ in a hotel the night before?		no
When do you have to _____ ?		5:00 in the afternoon
How long is your _____ ?		1 hour
When does the plane _____ ?		8:00 in the evening

10.1 VOCABULARY

GOING OUT

PAIR WORK Ask your partner questions.

1 Where do you like to go shopping?
 A At the mall.
 B Online.
 C I don't like shopping!
 D Other answer.

2 Where do you take a walk?
 A In the park.
 B In the forest.
 C In town.
 D Other answer.

3 When do you look at art?
 A On the weekend.
 B On vacation.
 C Never.
 D Other answer.

4 Who do you meet at the airport?
 A Friends.
 B Family.
 C Coworkers.
 D Other answer.

5 Do you like to have picnics?
 A Yes, I love picnics!
 B Sometimes I like to have picnics.
 C I hardly ever have picnics.
 D Other answer.

6 Do you like to eat inside or outside?
 A Inside.
 B Outside.
 C Both.
 D Other answer.

7 Where do you get together with friends?
 A At a restaurant.
 B At a café.
 C At home.
 D Other answer.

8 Who do you take out for dinner?
 A My parents.
 B My best friend.
 C Other English students.
 D Other answer.

10.2 VOCABULARY

CLOTHES; SEASONS

PAIR WORK Take an A card. What is the person wearing? What season is it? Then take a B card. Do the cards match? Keep any matching cards.

A Cards

B Cards

Summer shoes, shorts, T-shirt	Summer jeans, shoes, T-shirt	Rainy season pants, shirt, shoes
Winter coat, shoes, skirt, sweater	Rainy season boots, jeans, shirt	Spring coat, dress, hat, shoes
Winter coat, jeans, shoes, sweater	Spring shirt, shoes, shorts	Fall shirt, shoes, skirt
Dry season boots, hat, pants, shirt	Summer shoes, skirt, T-shirt	Winter boots, coat, jeans, sweater

11.1 VOCABULARY

DESCRIBING PEOPLE, PLACES, AND THINGS

GROUP WORK Take a card and read it to the other students. The other students say which adjective is correct.

The food is *awful / fast*! I'm not going to eat here again!	My aunt is wearing a *quiet / beautiful* dress.	The computer game is expensive because it is *slow / new*.	I can swim, but I am *slow / wonderful*.
I need a new laptop. My old laptop is *slow / exciting* now.	Usain Bolt was very *new / fast* in the 100 meters.	The children are *old / noisy* today.	Our vacation in Acapulco was *exciting / cute*.
The children in the photo were really *cute / new*.	The soccer game was *awful / exciting*. It was great.	The trip was *awful / wonderful*. I never want to go back there.	Alex is a really *awful / wonderful* friend. I like him a lot.
My jeans are *new / noisy*. Do you like them?	I live in a village. It is nice and *noisy / quiet*.	I am a *fast / cute* swimmer. I can swim 50 meters in 35 seconds.	The children are *exciting / quiet* in school.
I was a *noisy / fast* boy at school. I wasn't a good student.	An 89% on your English test is *awful / wonderful*! You are a very good student.	The flowers in spring are *beautiful / fast*.	She was a really *new / cute* two-year-old girl then.
The video is *awful / wonderful*. Don't watch it!	Barcelona is a *cute / beautiful* city. Let's go there on vacation.	My sister is really *awful / cute*. She's a lovely girl.	The concert wasn't *exciting / slow*. It was very boring.
There is a *fast / cute* train to London.	I have a *new / fast* friend. Her name is Karla.	The music is very *slow / noisy*. Can you hear me?	We had a *quiet / new* walk in the park.
The bus is very *fast / slow*. I'm going to drive.	The book is *awful / wonderful*. I love it.	The party wasn't *exciting / noisy*. It wasn't fun.	It's a *cute / beautiful* day. Let's go to the park.

11.2 VOCABULARY

COLORS

A Change the order of the letters to make words for colors.

1. reneg ___green___
2. lowley _____
3. kablc _____
4. dre _____
5. thiew _____
6. lebu _____
7. yrag _____
8. pruelp _____
9. gearno _____
10. norbw _____
11. kipn _____

B Make true sentences with the words from exercise A. Compare your sentences with a partner. Which ones are the same? Which ones are different?

1. My eyes are _____.
2. My phone is _____.
3. My first phone was _____.
4. Today my shoes are _____.
5. Yesterday my shoes were _____.
6. My favorite color is _____.
7. My partner's favorite color is _____.
8. My bedroom walls are _____.
9. The couch in my living room is _____.
10. My neighbor's car is _____.

C GROUP WORK Ask questions and put a check mark (✓) when you find a match.

Do you have a bag? *Yes, I do.*

What color is your bag? *It's red.*

Find someone who has …	✓	Student's name
… a red bag		
… a green watch		
… a yellow tablet		
… a blue phone		
… a gray car		
… a brown dog		
… a black cat		
… a purple couch		
… a white refrigerator		

12.1 VOCABULARY

SNACKS AND SMALL MEALS

Student A
Tell the other students what Miranda ate yesterday.

Student B
Tell the other students what Boris ate yesterday.

Student C
Tell the other students what Ming ate yesterday.

Student D
Tell the other students what Dan ate yesterday.

	Fruit and vegetables	Meat	Dairy products	Grains	Small meals
Miranda					
Boris					
Ming					
Dan					

12.2 VOCABULARY

FOOD, DRINK, AND DESSERTS

A Fill in the words on the menu.

B You have $30. Choose what to eat and drink at the café.

C GROUP WORK Tell the other students what you want.

> I want the …

D GROUP WORK What is the total price for your group?

Sam's Café

pizza	$15	cake	$7
steak	$20	ice cream	$5
salmon	$17	cookies	$3
eggs	$8	soda	$3
green beans	$5	orange juice	$4
black beans	$5	water	$2
rice	$6		

Teacher's notes for photocopiable activities: SPEAKING

UNIT 1 ROLL A ROLE

page T-254
Pair work activity
Unit 1 vocabulary: Countries and nationalities; the alphabet; personal information; numbers; jobs
Unit 1 grammar: *I am, you are; What's … ? It's …*
35 minutes

- **Prepare** Copy one worksheet for each pair of Ss.
- **Introduce** Write ONE question on the board (_____ _____ nationality?, or _____ _____ job, or _____ _____ college?)
- Elicit the full version of the question.
- Ss circulate asking and answering the question with each other.
- **Do the task** Hand out the worksheets. Variation: Cut up the worksheets and ask Ss to order the dialogue. Elicit any words they don't know. Tell Ss to write four numbers in the "password" line (each number should be between 1 and 6).
- Ask Ss to follow the prompts and use the numbers from their password to choose their answers. (e.g., if the password is 4516, then they should choose option 4 in the first question, option 5 in the second question, etc.)
- Tell Ss they don't have to share their personal information and can make things up instead.
- Allow about ten minutes for the activity.
- Rearrange Ss into new pairs and tell them to summarize the facts they learned about their partners.
- **Review** Divide the class into student A and student B. Ss A have to find Ss from the same country as them. Ss B have to find Ss who have the same job as them.
- Ss do a mingling task using their NEW personality details.
- Ss return to their original groups/pairs and report their findings.

UNIT 2 QUESTION MAZE

page T-255
Pair work activity
Unit 2 vocabulary: Family; numbers; describing people; *really / very*
Unit 2 grammar: *Is / are* in statements and *yes/no* questions; *is not / are not*
35 minutes

- **Prepare** Copy one question maze for each pair of Ss.
- **Introduce** Divide the class into small groups and ask them to make three information questions about their family or friends using the adjectives from the unit.
- To help less confident Ss, write the question structure on the board: *Is / are + your + subject + adjective? Is your brother married?*
- Elicit questions and write correct versions on the board.
- Ask Ss to take turns asking and answering those questions.
- **Do the task** Put Ss into pairs. Hand out the question maze. Tell Ss they will make questions by combining the words in the maze. They can start anywhere they want and may move in any direction in the maze, even in zigzags. You may limit the number of questions to five.
- Give Ss two to three minutes to plan their questions. Monitor and help as Ss make questions.
- Elicit corrections and sentences and display them on the board.
- Tell Ss that their partners should then answer the questions in a way which is true for them.
- If Ss run out of questions too soon, an optional extension could be to ask them to stand up and mingle with their list of questions.
- **Review** The class plays a game of "question tennis" where one S directs a question to another S, who answers it and then asks a different S a question, who answers it … and so on.

UNIT 3 HOUSE SHARE

page T-256
Group work activity
Unit 3 vocabulary: Rooms in a home; furniture
Unit 3 grammar: Possessive adjectives; possessive *'s and s'*; *it is*
35 minutes

- **Prepare** Copy and cut up one set of cards for each group of four Ss.
- **Introduce** Tell Ss they are looking for an apartment or a house to share. Scramble the following questions on the board and ask Ss to copy them.

    Is it a house or an apartment?
    Is the living room big?
    How many bedrooms are in the house?
    What is in the kitchen?
    Where is the fridge?

- Draw a simple bird's eye view of a small apartment to include the items mentioned in the questions. Tell your Ss about it using the target language on page 25 of the Student's Book. Ss ask and answer the questions in pairs. Monitor and check for pronunciation.

T-249

- **Do the task** Before you give out the worksheet, put Ss into groups of three or four.
- Give out the worksheets. Each S in the group draws a house or apartment any way they wish. They also make correct questions from the prompts at the bottom.
- Variation: Ask Ss to make two extra questions.
- Without showing their plans, each S in the group draws a house or apartment any way they wish. Ss take turns asking and answering questions about their plans in their groups.
- Ask for some answers from the whole class. Are their houses/apartments the same or different? Which house do Ss want to live in?
- **Review** Drill the correct sentences from the prompts at the bottom of Ss' worksheets aloud.
- Ss stick their plans on the walls of the classroom and discuss which one is best.

UNIT 4 THE DIGI-CHALLENGE

page T-257

Pair work activity

Unit 4 vocabulary: Technology; using technology

Unit 4 grammar: Simple present statements with *I, you, we*; simple present *yes/no* questions with *I, you, we*

40 minutes

- **Prepare** Copy one worksheet for each pair. Ss will need a stopwatch. They can use their phones for this.
- **Introduce** Write cell phone, computer, and laptop on the board. Ask Ss to think of three different uses for each in two minutes. Elicit ideas from the whole class.
- **Do the task** Ss play a speaking game with three levels. Each level has similar tasks and increases in difficulty.
- Hand out one worksheet per pair.
- Tell players that they should take turns moving from one square to another to complete the tasks. They can move to the next square only if they complete the task. They score one point for each completed task. In each level, they can ask their partner or the teacher for help, or pass.
- A task is completed if the student has answered all parts of the question.
- **Review** Monitor the task closely and note down any errors.
- Write Ss' sentences on the board, keeping them anonymous. Underline errors. Elicit the correct form and drill.
- Write some correct sentences on the board. Show Ss how these sentences can be improved, for example by adding adjectives or using a wider range of verbs.
- In pairs, ask Ss to:
  - Choose two questions and ask another pair to answer them.
  - Write one more question for each round and nominate other pairs to respond.

UNIT 5 ASK ME ABOUT … ME

page T-258

Group work activity

Unit 5 vocabulary: Days and times of day; everyday activities; telling the time

Unit 5 grammar: Simple present statements with *he, she, they*; questions in the simple present

35 minutes

- **Prepare** Copy one worksheet for each group of four Ss.
- **Introduce** On the board, write two question words, two verbs, and two time expressions from one of the task cards.
- Elicit questions containing the words. Answer them and ask *How about you?*
- Optional question frame:

(Question word)	do does	you your friend	(verb)	(time word)?

- **Do the task** Divide Ss into two groups. The first group sits in a circle facing outward. The second group sits in another circle outside, facing the first group. The Ss in the second circle should move clockwise every three to five minutes. Alternatively, Ss can work with partners sitting on their right/left/opposite them.
- Hand out one card per S.
- Give Ss one to two minutes to read the prompts. Encourage them to ask their partner or teacher about any words they don't know.
- Ss ask their partners different questions using the prompts. Allow three to five minutes before each pair moves on. Repeat up to four times.
- Variation for stronger Ss: listening partners should give their speaking partners one point every time they use an expression they learned in Unit 5.
- **Review** Monitor the task closely and note down any errors. Write some example sentences on the board. Change some factual details. Ask Ss to guess which sentences are true or false. Ask Ss to guess who said each sentence.
- Write some incorrect sentences on the board. Elicit the corrections. Drill the sentences.

UNIT 6 LOCATION TIC-TAC-TOE

page T-259
Pair work activity
Unit 6 vocabulary: Places in cities; nature
Unit 6 grammar: *There's, There are; a lot of, some, no*; count and non-count nouns
40 minutes

- **Prepare** Copy one worksheet per pair.
- **Introduce** Write the word neighborhood on the board and draw a tic-tac-toe grid underneath the word. Ask Ss to shout out things they find in their neighborhood. Write these into the square.
- Put Ss into teams. They take turns to choose a square and make a sentence with the word.
- Place an X or O in the square if the sentence is correct.
- The team which connects three Xs or Os in a row (vertically, horizontally, or diagonally) wins.
- **Do the task** Put the Ss into pairs and hand out the grids. Ss take turns choosing squares and making sentences to score three in a row. Continue until all the grids have been used.
- **Variation:** instead of making a single sentence, Ss have to speak non-stop for 20 seconds, using the word in the square at least once.
- **Review** Monitor the task closely and note examples of good and bad examples of language. Write the sentences on the board. Underline errors (with verb forms, question structure, auxiliary verbs) and ask Ss to correct as a class.

UNIT 7 FIND SOMEONE WHO …

page T-260
Group work activity
Unit 7 vocabulary: Activities around the house; transportation
Unit 7 grammar: Present continuous statements; present continuous questions
35 minutes

- **Prepare** Copy and cut up one worksheet for each group of 6 Ss.
- **Introduce** Write some actions on the board (e.g., clean, drive to school, cook dinner). Mime an action and ask *What am I doing?* Elicit answers from Ss (*You're cooking dinner*). Say *I'm cooking dinner*. Repeat with other verbs and write the sentences on the board. (*I'm driving to school. I'm cleaning.*)
- Scramble the following sentences on the board and ask Ss to unscramble them.
  - *1 you / carrying / bag / a / Are / ? (Are you carrying a bag?)*
  - *2 English / you / speaking / Are / ? (Are you speaking English?)*
  - *3 you / Are / messages / text / sending / ? (Are you sending text messages?)*
  - *4 friend / a / Are / talking / you / to / ? (Are you talking to a friend?)*
- Elicit the short answers for the questions.
  - *Yes, I am. / No, I'm not.*
- **Do the task** Hand out the cards. Explain to Ss that they will write five sentences about activities they are doing. Then, they will write questions about what their group members are doing.
- Ss take turns asking and answering the questions to identify who in their group is doing each activity. When they identify someone who is doing an activity, they write the card number by the question.
- Variation: Groups compete to complete all their cards first.
- **Review** Monitor the task. Identify common errors. Write statements and questions on the board with common mistakes in them and ask Ss to correct the mistakes. For example, write *Are you **take** a shower?* Elicit *Are you **taking** a shower?*

UNIT 8 THE SPINNING "CAN"S

page T-261
Pair work activity
Unit 8 vocabulary: Verbs to describe skills; work
Unit 8 grammar: *Can* and *can't* for ability; *well*; *can* and *can't* for possibility
35 minutes

- **Prepare** Make enough copies of the game board for every pair/small group. Each group needs one pen or pencil to spin.
- **Introduce** Write *Work and Hobbies* on the board and elicit one example of a skill for each category, e.g.,
  - *work – use a computer / drive / speak English*
  - *hobbies – play the guitar / dance / cook*
- Elicit one *Can you + [skill]?* question per category, and then the positive and negative answer e.g., *Can you use a computer? Can you dance? Yes, I can. / No, I can't.*
- Ask Ss to take turns asking and answering the questions.
- **Do the task** Divide the class into pairs or small groups and hand out the game board. Model the task. Tell Ss to place a pencil in the first square (WORK) and ask one S to spin the pencil. Ss should ask their partner the question *Can you + (option)?* to elicit *Yes, I can* or *No, I can't*.
- For every answer Ss answers *Yes, I can*, they receive a point.
- The winner is the S who has the most points.
- **Review** Ss summarize each other's skills by saying what their partner can do that they can't, e.g., *Juan can read blogs in English, but I can't*.
- Ask Ss to choose one skill they want to learn and one skill they can teach.

T-251

UNIT 9 TRIP PLANNERS

page T-262

Pair work activity

Unit 9 vocabulary: Travel; travel arrangements

Unit 9 grammar: *this* and *these*; like *to*, want *to*, need *to*, have *to*

40 minutes

- **Prepare** Copy one worksheet per pair of Ss.
- **Introduce** Dictate or show the following questions to the class.
  - What is your destination?
  - How do we travel?
  - How long is the flight?
  - Where can you stay?
  - What languages do people speak there?
- Write the following words on the board in random order. Ask Ss to match them to the questions.
  - New York
  - By plane
  - Seven hours
  - Hotel
  - English, Spanish, and other languages.
- **Do the task** Cut up and give out the worksheets. In pairs, Ss use the worksheets to role play making travel plans. Encourage Ss to use full sentences in their answers.
- After Ss have done the first two role plays, they work together to make a third role play by writing in questions and answers. Ss choose a location they want to visit or a country from the list on page 2 of the Student's Book. They can use their phones to research any information they need.
- Rearrange Ss into new pairs and have them do the role play again.
- Ss then go back to their original partners and discuss the similarities and differences between their plans and the others' plans.
- **Review** Listen and note down good and bad examples of sentences. Share these with Ss and ask them to correct the mistakes.
- In small groups, Ss create (and record on their cell phones) a one-minute vlog about that place. Each S should have a part in the video, e.g., one S speaks about hotels, another S about getting to the destination, etc.

UNIT 10 PACK YOUR BAGS

page T-263

Pair work activity

Unit 10 vocabulary: Going out; clothes; seasons

Unit 10 grammar: Statements with *be going to*; questions with *be going to*

40 minutes

- **Prepare** Copy one worksheet per student.
- **Introduce** Do an image search for open suitcase and display to Ss. Ask Ss what they always take with them on any trip, e.g., cell phone, their favorite book, a coat, etc. Elicit ideas and write them on the board. Ss can refer to them throughout the activity.
- In pairs, ask Ss to choose a destination for a trip or vacation they want to go on together and in which season they want to go.
- **Do the task** Hand out the worksheet and tell Ss that they will each pack their own suitcase. They can take ten things. Allow individual Ss two to three minutes to write down the things they are going to take with them on their trip. They should write their list in the suitcase. Ss should also write the destination and season. Encourage Ss to include the objects and the clothes they need.
- In pairs, Ss explain their choices to their partner. Model an example with a confident Ss, e.g., *I'm going to take a sweater. It's cold in (Canada).* or *I'm not going to take my laptop. I'm not going to work.*
- Then, tell Ss that there is a new baggage restriction: they can only take one suitcase between two Ss or five things each. In pairs, Ss discuss which items to remove, explaining their choices. *I'm not going to take my book. I'm not going to read. / I'm going to read on my phone.*
- The same pairs now explain the contents of their new bag to the class using *He / she is going to …*
- **Review** As a whole class, find out what the most popular items were for Ss to take.

UNIT 11 THE CROSSWALK

page T-264

Pair work activity

Unit 11 vocabulary: Adjectives to describe people, places, and things; colors

Unit 11 grammar: Statements with *was* and *were*; questions with *was* and *were*

40 minutes

- **Prepare** Make one copy of the worksheet per pair. Use three coins: one to flip, two to use as counters. Ss can use their cell phone as a timer.
- **Introduce** Write *yesterday*, *last week*, and *last year* on the board. Ask Ss to share three memories in pairs: one about yesterday, one about last week, and one about last year, e.g, *Last week my neighbor was friendly*; *My vacation was wonderful last year*.
- Ask Ss to share their memories with the class. Elicit follow up questions. If Ss use vocabulary from the unit, write it on the board.
- **Do the task** Hand out the worksheets. The useful language box can be left open or folded away, depending on the Ss' confidence levels.
- Ss move along the board by flipping a coin (Heads = 1 move, Tails = 2 moves). They should try to cross "the road" before their partner. When a S lands on a word, he/she must make a sentence with that word about memories, using *was* or *were* (and an adjective). If the S says the sentence correctly in the time limit, he/she takes another turn. If not, the partner takes his/her turn. Each turn should last 30 seconds (20 seconds for stronger groups, 1 minute for weaker groups). The first S to cross the road to the other side is the winner.
- Ss play the game again with a different partner but without the useful language.
- **Variation:** Each turn should be followed by one question from the listening partner. (e.g., *Are you speaking to her these days? Where is … now? Why was he there? When was this?*)
- **Review** As Ss speak, make notes on good or bad examples you can give as feedback at the end of the task.
- As a class, ask Ss to share some of their best memories or their partner's memories.

UNIT 12 THE FOODIE SURVEY

page T-265

Pair/group work activity

Unit 12 vocabulary: Snacks and small meals; food, drinks, and desserts

Unit 12 grammar: Simple past statements; simple past questions; *any*

35 minutes

- **Prepare** Copy and cut up one set of cards per 12 Ss.
- **Introduce** Ask Ss to write one question about food using *Did you eat/drink … yesterday?* Ss ask and answer the question in pairs. Ask for some feedback as a class.
- **Do the task** Tell Ss they are going to ask each other questions about what they eat and what they know about food. Lots of the questions will practice the past tense.
- Hand out cards. Allow Ss time to figure out the questions they need to ask. Help Ss and write any corrections on the board so that everyone can see and use them.
- Have Ss write a national food on the question 4 line on their card. It can be from their country or another country.
- Ask Ss to circulate asking their questions. They can ask one question at a time before they move on to the next partner.
- Ss write the names of people who give them the answers they need on their card.
- **Review** Using the notes on their cards, Ss write the names of classmates on a separate piece of paper and show it to their partner. The partner asks *What did … say?*, and the S should explain using the information from their card.
- Ss write five more questions in the past simple and interview their partner.

T-253

UNIT 1 SPEAKING

ROLL A ROLE

Password_____

Student A Hi! Are you … (nationality)?

Student B No, I'm not.

Student A Where are you from?

Student B I'm from …
1 Brazil   3 Japan   5 Spain
2 Chile   4 Mexico   6 The United States
Student B And where are you from?

Student A I'm from …
1 Russia   3 Ecuador   5 South Korea
2 France   4 Peru   6 China

Student B You're from … Wow!

Student A What's your name?

Student B My name is …
1 Francisco   3 Eric   5 Sam
2 Julieta   4 Fay   6 Kaitlin

Student A How do you spell it?

Student B It's … (spell your name).

Student A Thanks.

Student B And what's your name?

Student A My name is …
1 Mara   3 Ruby   5 Yasmin
2 Emilio   4 Cameron   6 Sergei

Student B And how do you spell it?

Student A It's … (spell your name).

Student B Thanks. Are you a student?

Student A No, I'm not. I'm …
1 an artist   3 a doctor   5 a hotel clerk
2 a chef   4 a server   6 a salesperson

Student B What's the name of your company?

Student A It's …
1 Bradley Books   4 Pak Grill
2 Empire One Café   5 Ethan Hotel
3 Clinton Hospital   6 ABC-TV
          What's your job?

Student B I'm …
1 a teacher   3 a doctor   5 a director
2 a student   4 an artist 6 a salesperson
          And my company is …
1 Evolve English   4 Destination Design
2 Jodi College   5 Travel Smart
3 General Hospital   6 Carter Cars

Student A Thanks! What's your phone number?

Student B It's …
          And what's your number?

Student A It's …

T-254 Evolve level 1 Teacher's Edition PHOTOCOPIABLE © Cambridge University Press 2019

UNIT 2 SPEAKING

QUESTION MAZE

how	best friend	shy	is	Brazilian	uncle	is	are
18	old	your	teacher	in class	your	you	children
you	friendly	is	John	are	where	dad	boring
brother	are	at work	your	you	American	from	tall
your	grandparents	here	parents	mother	in June	student	young
is	smart	when	your	birthday	funny	aunt	your
what	job	are	is	cousins	from	Russia	is

UNIT 3 SPEAKING

HOUSE SHARE

Student A

A Draw a plan of your house.

B Make questions using the prompts.
1. Is / home / apartment?
2. Is / bedroom / big?
3. How many / bathrooms / in house?
4. What / in / the kitchen?
5. Where / the house?

Student B

A Draw a plan of your house.

B Make questions using the prompts.
1. Is / home / apartment?
2. Is / kitchen / big?
3. How many / bedrooms / in house?
4. What / in / the bedroom?
5. Where / living room?

Student C

A Draw a plan of your house.

B Make questions using the prompts.
1. Is / home / apartment?
2. Is / living room / small?
3. How many / tables / in house?
4. What / in / the bathroom?
5. Where / bedroom?

Student D

A Draw a plan of your house.

B Make questions using the prompts.
1. Is / home / apartment?
2. Is / living room / big?
3. How many / sofas / in house?
4. What / in / the living room?
5. Where / the kitchen?

Student E

A Draw a plan of your house.

B Make questions using the prompts.
1. Is / home / apartment?
2. Is / bathroom / small?
3. How many / TVs / in house?
4. What / in / the dining area?
5. Where / the shower?

Student F

A Draw a plan of your house.

B Make questions using the prompts.
1. Is / home / apartment?
2. Is / dining area / big?
3. How many / bathrooms / in house?
4. What / in / the living room?
5. Where / the kitchen?

UNIT 4 SPEAKING

THE DIGI-CHALLENGE

START

Level 1

Ask your partner
Do you have a favorite app?

Three things
Work alone. Write a list of apps you like. Compare ideas with your partner.

Ask your partner
Do you post comments on Twitter?

Ask your partner
Do your parents use social media?

Race your partner
Work alone. How many different websites and apps do you know? Write notes. You have 1 minute. Then compare your ideas.

Level 1 COMPLETE. Move to the NEXT LEVEL.

Level 2

Ask your partner.
Do you like internet shopping?

Three things
Work alone. Write a list of things you post on the internet. Compare ideas with your partner.

30 Seconds
Speak for 30 seconds. Use the words
use / comments / post.

Discuss with your partner
Do you take photos? What do you take photos of?
You have **1–2 minutes.**

Race your partner
Work alone. How many words about technology do you know? List them. You have 1 minute. Then compare your ideas.

Level 2 COMPLETE. Move to the NEXT LEVEL.

Level 3

Ask your partner
a question about technology. Begin with *Do you … ?*

Three things
Say three things you like and three things you don't like about technology.

30 Seconds
Speak for 30 seconds. Use the words
friends / chat / want / app / laptop.

Discuss with your partner
Do you play games? What games do you play?
You have **1–2 minutes.**

Race your partner
Work alone. How many **verbs** about technology do you know? Write notes. You have 1 minute. Then, compare your ideas.

Level 3 COMPLETE.

GAME OVER

UNIT 5 SPEAKING

ASK ME ABOUT … ME

Ask me about … me

Student 1

Question words
What … ?   Do you … ?   Does your best friend … ?
Do your parents … ?   Where … ?   What time … ?
When … ?

Verbs
go to work   watch movies   drink tea   chat with friends online   make breakfast   see your family   use a cell phone   post comments on social media

Days and times of day
always   on Tuesdays   at night   at 1 p.m   on Sunday morning

Answers
Me, too.   Me, neither.
Yeah, I know.   That's true.   And what about you?
How about you?

Ask me about … me

Student 2

Question words
What … ?   Do you … ?   Does your best friend … ?
Do your parents … ?   Where … ?   What time … ?
When … ?

Verbs
run   go out with friends   use a tablet   do homework   get up late   drink water   have dinner   eat a cookie

Days and times of day
usually   in the morning   every day   on Fridays   on the weekend

Answers
Me, too.   Me, neither.
Yeah, I know.   That's true.   And what about you?
How about you?

Ask me about … me

Student 3

Question words
What … ?   Do you … ?   Does your best friend … ?
Do your parents … ?   Where … ?   What time … ?
When … ?

Verbs
stay at home   play soccer   use social media   drink coffee   study   have breakfast   read books   send emails   have fun

Days and times of day
never   on Monday evenings   at night   in the afternoon   on the weekend

Answers
Me, too.   Me, neither.
Yeah, I know.   That's true.   And what about you?
How about you?

Ask me about … me

Student 4

Question words
What … ?   Do you … ?   Does your best friend … ?
Do your parents … ?   Where … ?   What time … ?
When … ?

Verbs
go out   buy apps   watch TV   write product reviews on the internet   have lunch   play video games   go to work   see friends

Days and times of day
sometimes   at noon   on weekdays   after school   on Sunday evenings

Answers
Me, too.   Me, neither.
Yeah, I know.   That's true.   And what about you?
How about you?

UNIT 6 SPEAKING

LOCATION TIC-TAC-TOE

Card 1
snow
mountain
supermarket
desert
museum
in my neighborhood
grass
interesting
have dinner

Card 2
on the right
plants
hill
boring
ocean
… in your city?
see friends
a lot of
There are no …

Card 3
river
big store
There is a …
restaurant
hospital
on my street
go shopping
nice
flowers

Card 4
park
forest
… is near …
go out
café
bookstore
there are some
tall
There isn't a …

Card 5
beach
tree
close to nature
very
a lot of
great stores
on the right
interesting
movie theater

Card 6
learn
lake
school
mall
park
zoo
Where … ?
There are no …
beautiful

Card 7
ocean
Where are … ?
on the left
mall
park
zoo
lake
There are no …
big

Card 8
old
Where is … ?
on the left
really
cool
There are some …
island
hotel
… on your street?

UNIT 7 SPEAKING

FIND SOMEONE WHO …

Card 1

A Write sentences in the present continuous.
  1 I am _____ (work)
  2 _____ (wait for a bus)
  3 _____ (drive home)
  4 _____ (do homework)
  5 _____ (carry a bag)

B Make questions. Find someone who is doing each activity.
  1 Are you _____ (take a shower)
  2 _____ (help children)
  3 _____ (learn English)
  4 _____ (shop)
  5 _____ (drink milk)

Card 2

A Write sentences in the present continuous.
  1 I am _____ (text a friend)
  2 _____ (take a shower)
  3 _____ (watch TV)
  4 _____ (clean)
  5 _____ (drink milk)

B Make questions. Find someone who is doing each activity.
  1 Are you _____ (carry a bag)
  2 _____ (talk to a friend)
  3 _____ (eat lunch)
  4 _____ (shop)
  5 _____ (work)

Card 3

A Write sentences in the present continuous.
  1 I am _____ (take a bath)
  2 _____ (go for a walk)
  3 _____ (text your mom)
  4 _____ (text a friend)
  5 _____ (carry a bag)

B Make questions. Find someone who is doing each activity.
  1 Are you _____ (ride bike)
  2 _____ (take a shower)
  3 _____ (eat lunch)
  4 _____ (shop)
  5 _____ (help children)

Card 4

A Write sentences in the present continuous.
  1 I am _____ (speak Spanish)
  2 _____ (drive home)
  3 _____ (help children)
  4 _____ (brush teeth)
  5 _____ (ride bike)

B Make questions. Find someone who is doing each activity.
  1 Are you _____ (do homework)
  2 _____ (talk to a friend)
  3 _____ (speak English)
  4 _____ (shop)
  5 _____ (drive to school)

Card 5

A Write sentences in the present continuous.
  1 I am _____ (learn English)
  2 _____ (take a bath)
  3 _____ (brush teeth)
  4 _____ (carry a bag)
  5 _____ (cook dinner)

B Make questions. Find someone who is doing each activity.
  1 Are you _____ (text your mom)
  2 _____ (speak Spanish)
  3 _____ (eat lunch)
  4 _____ (clean)
  5 _____ (work)

Card 6

A Write sentences in the present continuous.
  1 I am _____ (talk to a friend)
  2 _____ (drive to school)
  3 _____ (eat lunch)
  4 _____ (speak English)
  5 _____ (shop)

B Make questions. Find someone who is doing each activity.
  1 Are you _____ (carry a bag)
  2 _____ (go for a walk)
  3 _____ (wait for a bus)
  4 _____ (take a bath)
  5 _____ (work)

UNIT 8 SPEAKING

THE SPINNING "CAN"S

Student A

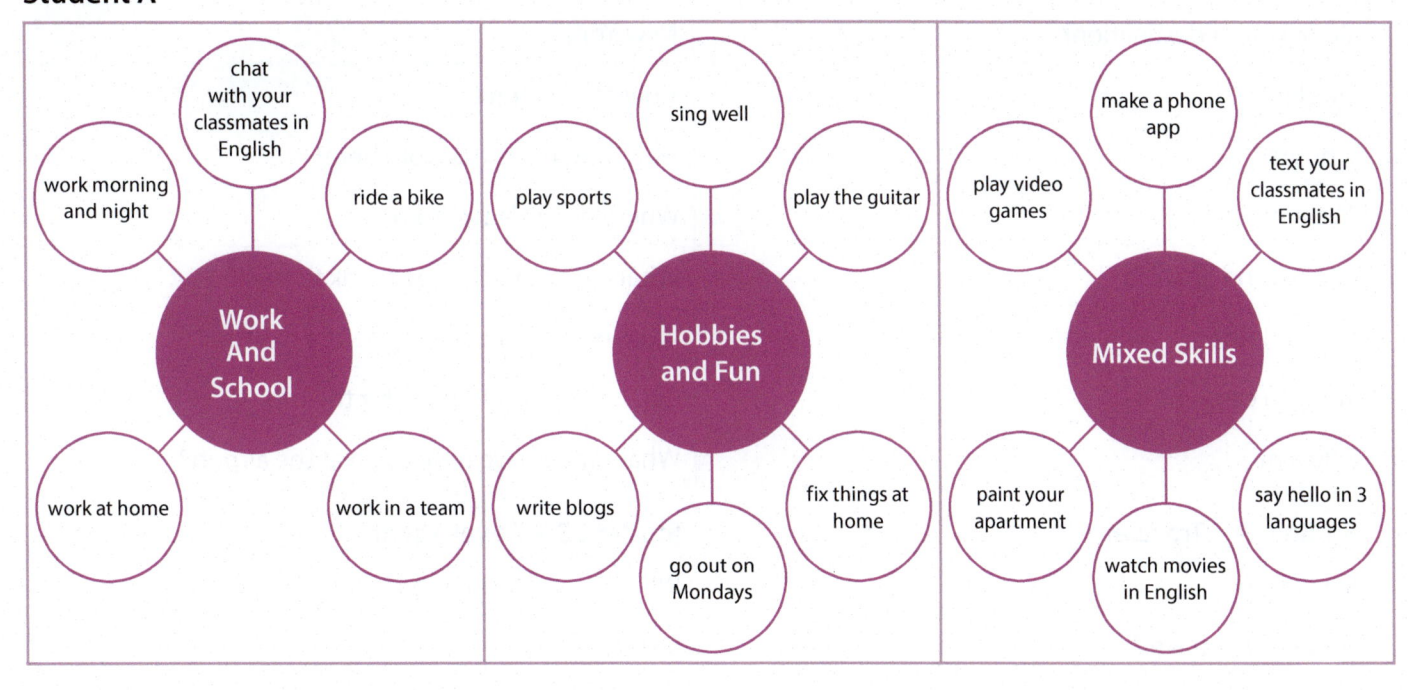

Work And School: chat with your classmates in English, work morning and night, ride a bike, work at home, work in a team

Hobbies and Fun: sing well, play sports, play the guitar, write blogs, fix things at home, go out on Mondays

Mixed Skills: make a phone app, play video games, text your classmates in English, paint your apartment, watch movies in English, say hello in 3 languages

- ✂

Student B

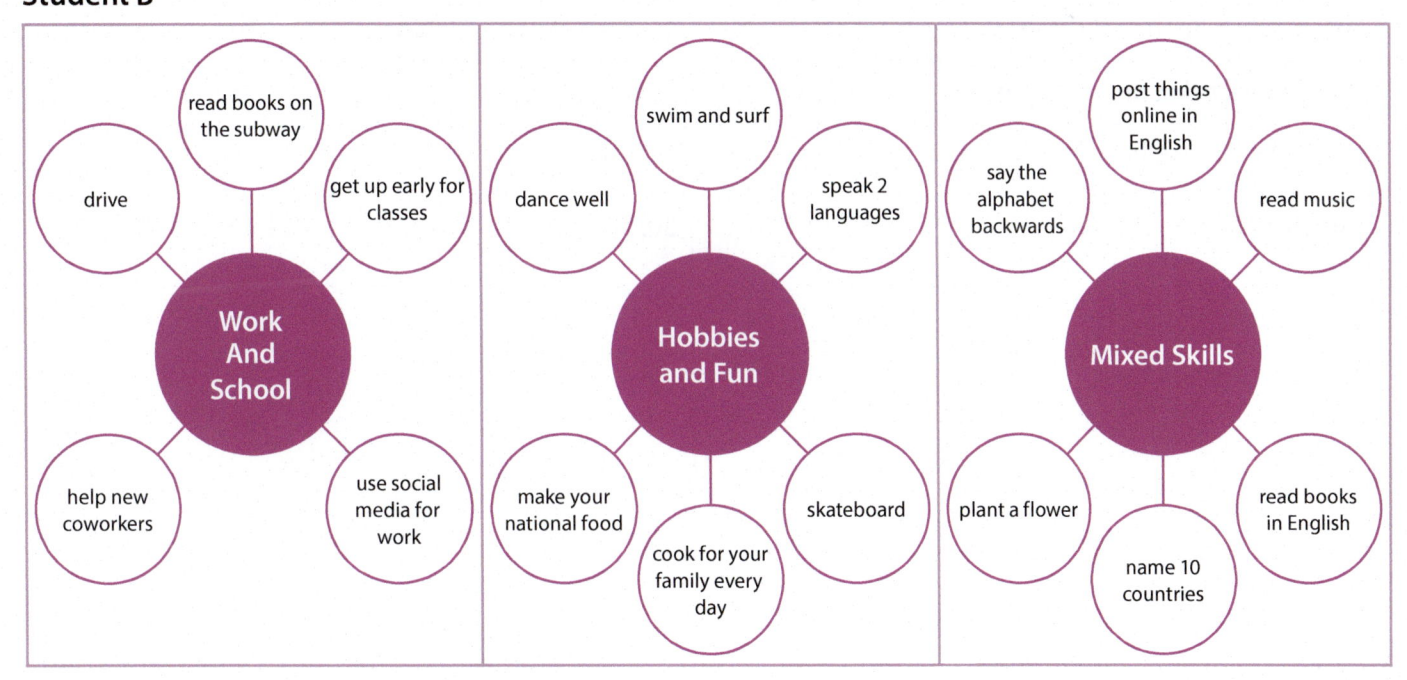

Work And School: read books on the subway, drive, get up early for classes, help new coworkers, use social media for work

Hobbies and Fun: swim and surf, dance well, speak 2 languages, make your national food, cook for your family every day, skateboard

Mixed Skills: post things online in English, say the alphabet backwards, read music, plant a flower, name 10 countries, read books in English

UNIT 9 SPEAKING

TRIP PLANNERS

Student A – Travel agent	Student B – Traveler
What is your destination?	New York
By plane	How can we travel?
7 hours	How long is the trip from here?
The airport	Where do we leave from?
English and Spanish	What language do they speak there?
Warm clothes, it's winter	What do we need to buy before the trip?
Yes, you can.	Can I buy a ticket online for the trip?
7:00 a.m.	What time do we have to be at the airport?

Student A – Traveler	Student B – Travel agent
San Diego	What is your destination?
How can we travel?	By bus
How long is the trip from here?	5 hours
Where do we leave from?	The bus station
What language do they speak there?	English and Spanish
What do we need to buy before the trip?	Summer clothes, it's hot
Can I buy a ticket online for the trip?	Yes, you can.
What time do we have to be at the bus station?	12:00 p.m.

Student A	Student B

UNIT 10 SPEAKING

PACK YOUR BAGS

Name: _____

What are you going to take with you?

Destination: _____
Season: _____

UNIT 11 SPEAKING

THE CROSSWALK

I remember …

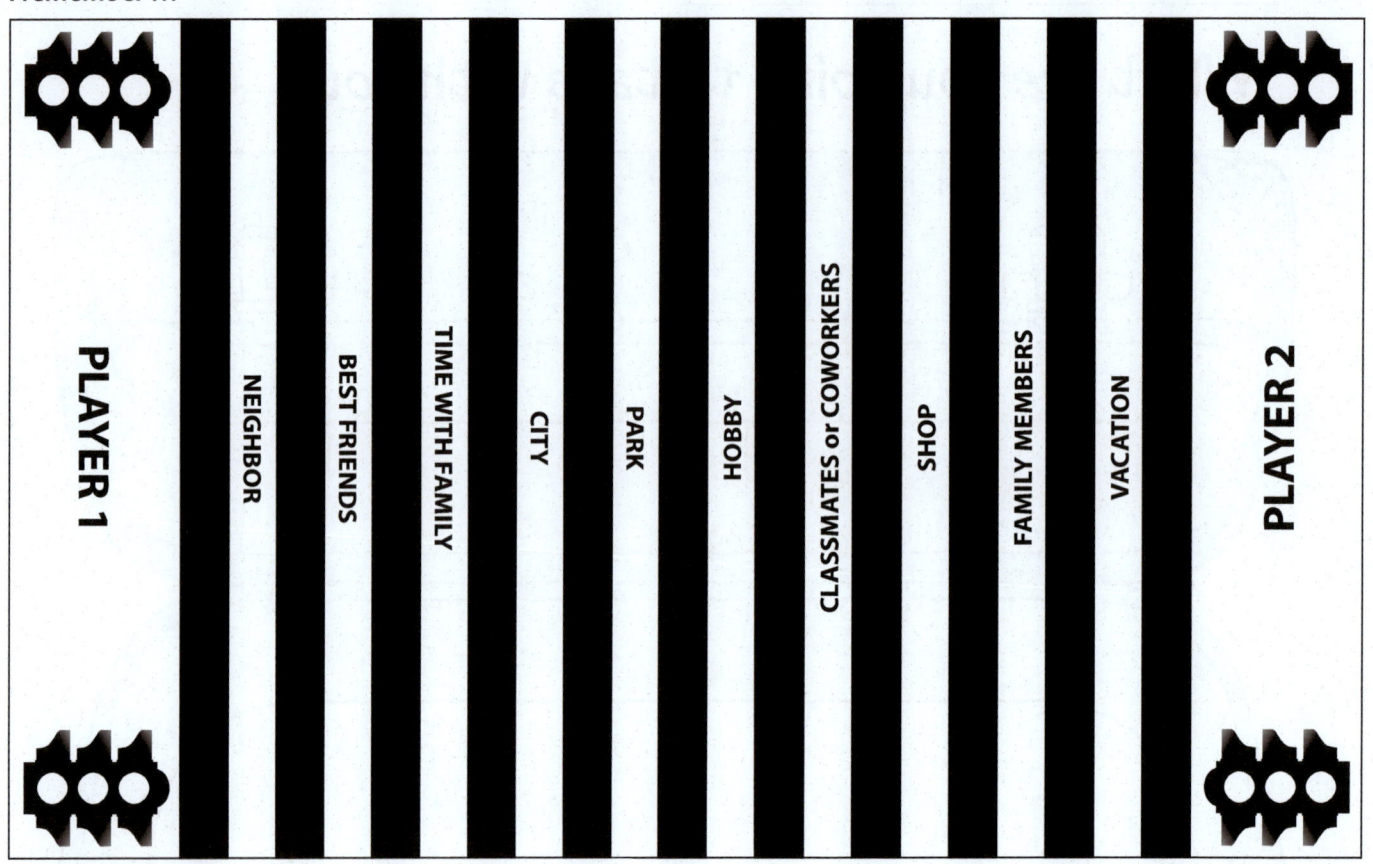

Crosswalk columns (left to right): PLAYER 1 | NEIGHBOR | BEST FRIENDS | TIME WITH FAMILY | CITY | PARK | HOBBY | CLASSMATES or COWORKERS | SHOP | FAMILY MEMBERS | VACATION | PLAYER 2

Useful language:

red	white	orange	yellow	green
blue	pink	purple	brown	gray
black	(not) awful	(not) cute	(not) slow	(not) fast
(not) quick	(not) new	(not) old	(not) noisy	(not) quiet
(not) cool	(not) boring	(not) good	(not) bad	(not) smart
(not) nice	(not) small	(not) big	(not) friendly	(not) great
(not) short	(not) funny	(not) shy	(not) tall	(not) young
(not) famous	(not) cheap	(not) expensive	(not) popular	(not) exciting
(not) beautiful	(not) wonderful	(not) interesting	favorite	really
very	I think …	I don't think …	because	and
also	but	so	I mean	No way!
Was it … ?	Were they … ?	When / Where / What / Who / Why / was / were … ?		
How old … ?	How much … ?	I remember …	I have no idea	I'm not sure
I don't know	I think maybe it was …	Let me think		

UNIT 12 SPEAKING

THE FOODIE SURVEY

Card 1. Find someone who … 1 knows great restaurants 2 had lunch, breakfast, and dinner yesterday 3 ate all the food in the refrigerator 4 knows which country _____ comes from 5 likes to make international food	**Card 7. Find someone who …** 1 knows 3 good food stores 2 had lunch at work/school last week 3 took their friend out for breakfast 4 knows which country _____ comes from 5 likes to write restaurant reviews
Card 2. Find someone who … 1 knows 3 fast food restaurants 2 had 3 snacks yesterday 3 bought expensive food last month 4 knows which country _____ comes from 5 likes TV shows about food	**Card 8. Find someone who …** 1 knows 3 drinks in English 2 had a good meal on airplane 3 went to a big supermarket yesterday 4 knows which country _____ comes from 5 doesn't like ice cream
Card 3. Find someone who … 1 knows 3 fruits in English 2 had a picnic last month 3 didn't like vegetables before 4 knows which country _____ comes from 5 likes to post photos of their food on social media	**Card 9. Find someone who …** 1 knows 3 breakfast foods 2 drank lot of soda on the weekend 3 took their friend out for dinner 4 knows which country _____ comes from 5 likes to read restaurant reviews
Card 4. Find someone who … 1 knows 3 vegetables names in English 2 had a meal with their family last month 3 ate on a bus or train this month 4 knows which country _____ comes from 5 likes to eat outside	**Card 10. Find someone who …** 1 can cook 3 meals 2 had fish last week 3 bought a lot of snacks yesterday 4 knows which country _____ comes from 5 doesn't like dairy products
Card 5. Find someone who … 1 knows 3 words for meat 2 had a lot of cake last week 3 went to a bad restaurant last month 4 knows which country _____ comes from 5 likes to eat meals in the living room	**Card 11. Find someone who …** 1 knows 3 snacks 2 didn't have dessert last night 3 ate food from another country this month 4 knows which country _____ comes from 5 likes to read food blogs
Card 6. Find someone who … 1 knows 3 words for dairy products 2 didn't have dinner last night 3 bought food online last week 4 knows which country _____ comes from 5 likes to eat meals on the couch	**Card 12. Find someone who …** 1 knows 3 verbs that go with food 2 drank a lot of coffee yesterday 3 visited a farm 4 knows which country _____ comes from 5 has a food app on their phone

WORKBOOK ANSWER KEY

Unit 1   I am …

1.1 I'm Brazilian. And you? pages 2–3

1 VOCABULARY: Countries and nationalities

A 1 Peruvian 2 Japan 3 Honduras 4 Spanish 5 Colombia
6 Brazilian 7 China 8 Russian 9 the United States
10 South Korean 11 Chilean 12 Mexican 13 Ecuadorean
14 French

2 GRAMMAR: I am, you are

A 1 am 2 Are 3 Are 4 'm 5 're 6 'm

B Tony   ¹**Are you** Ana?
Ana   Yes, ²**I am.**
Tony   Hi, ³**I'm** Tony. I'm from Lima.
Ana   Oh, ⁴**you're** Peruvian. I ⁵**am** Brazilian.
Tony   ⁶**Are** you from Rio?
Ana   No, ⁷**I'm not**. I'm not from Rio or São Paulo.
Tony   Are ⁸**you** from Brasilia?
Ana   Yes.

3 GRAMMAR AND VOCABULARY

A Possible answers:
1 I'm not a teacher.
2 I'm a student.
3 I'm from Mexico City. OR I'm not from Mexico City.
4 I'm not American. OR I'm American.
5 I'm Alex. OR I'm not Alex.
6 I'm from Chile. OR I'm not from Chile.

B Answers will vary.

1.2 What's your last name? pages 4–5

1 VOCABULARY: The alphabet; personal information

A 1 Palmira
2 Fernandez
3 Hotshot
4 Agostino
5 Max@mymail.org

B 1 d 2 c 3 a 4 e 5 b

C 1 My college is Harvard University.
2 My company is Toyota.
3 My email address is tonyravella@mymail.org.
4 My last name is Ravella.
5 My first name is Tony.

2 GRAMMAR: What's …?, It's …

A 1 Question 2 Answer 3 Question 4 Question 5 Answer
6 Answer

B 1 **What's** your first name? **It's** Mike.
2 **What's** your last name? **It's** Ramirez.
3 **What's** the name of your **college**? It's Nippon College.

3 GRAMMAR AND VOCABULARY

A Anna   Hello. What'**s** your last name?
Mike   It's Lugo. L-U-G-O.
Anna   Uh-huh. What's your first name?
Mike   It'**s** Mike.
Anna   And what's your email address?
Mike   It'**s** mikelugo@mymail.org.

B Possible answers:
1 It's Montero.   2 It's Marisol.   3 It's mmont@mymail.org.

1.3 This is the key pages 6–7

1 FUNCTIONAL LANGUAGE: Checking into a hotel

A Clerk Hello. ¹**Welcome** to the Capital Hotel.
Anna   Hello. I'm Anna. I'm here for two ²**nights**.
Clerk What's your ³**last** name, Anna?
Anna   It's Wang. W-A-N-G.
Clerk Ah, yes. Anna Wang. What's your ⁴**cell phone number**, Anna?
Anna   It's (243) 555-1968.
Clerk And ⁵**what's** your email address?
Anna   ⁶**It's** wang99@mymail.org.
Clerk Thank you. One moment. Please ⁷**sign** here.
Anna   OK.
Clerk ⁸**This is** the key. You're in ⁹**room** 10F.
Anna   Great. Thank you.
Clerk You're welcome.

2 REAL-WORLD STRATEGY: Checking spelling

A 1 How do you spell Gonzales / your last name?
2 What's your email address?
3 How do you spell Martin / the name (of your company)?

3 FUNCTIONAL LANGUAGE AND REAL-WORLD STRATEGY

A

	A hotel clerk	A hotel guest	A hotel clerk OR hotel guest
1 Hello.			✓
2 Welcome to City Hotel.	✓		
3 What's your name?	✓		
4 How do you spell your last name?	✓		
5 I'm here for one night.		✓	
6 What's your cell phone number?	✓		
7 Here's the key.	✓		
8 You're in Room 316.	✓		
9 Thank you.			✓
10 You're welcome.			✓
11 My name is Robert Dupont.		✓	

B Possible conversation:

Robert	Hello.
Hotel clerk	Hello. Welcome to City Hotel.
Robert	Thank you. I'm here for one night. My name is Robert Dupont.
Hotel clerk	How do you spell your last name?
Robert	D-U-P-O-N-T.
Hotel clerk	And what's your nationality, Mr. Dupont?
Robert	I'm Canadian.
Hotel clerk	What's your cell phone number?
Robert	It's (595) 555-9900.
Hotel clerk	Thank you. Please sign here.
Robert	OK.
Hotel clerk	Here's the key. You're in Room 316.
Robert	Thank you.
Hotel clerk	You're welcome.

1.4 My profile *pages 8–9*

1 VOCABULARY: Jobs

A 1 Yes, I am. 2 No, I'm not. I'm a doctor.
3 No, I'm not. I'm a chef. 4 No, I'm not. I'm a server.

Unit 2 Great people

2.1 A family party *pages 10–11*

1 VOCABULARY: Family; numbers

A 1 father 2 grandmother 3 brother 4 children 5 sister
6 wife 7 son 8 daughter 9 aunt 10 grandfather
11 mother 12 uncle

B 13 – thirteen   50 – fifty
18 – eighteen   65 – sixty-five
47 – forty-seven   46 – forty-six
16 – sixteen   100 – one hundred
82 – eighty-two   15 – fifteen
19 – nineteen   93 – ninety-three
60 – sixty   11 – eleven
94 – ninety-four   12 – twelve
88 – eighty-eight   24 – twenty-four
30 – thirty   71 – seventy-one
55 – fifty-five   10 – ten
29 – twenty-nine   39 – thirty-nine
70 – seventy   14 – fourteen

2 GRAMMAR: is /are in statements and yes/no questions

A Hello. My name ¹is Tamara. My family and I ²are Colombian. We ³are from Bogotá. My grandparents ⁴are from Medellín. My father ⁵is a teacher, and my mother ⁶is an artist. My brothers ⁷are 19 and 14. My sister ⁸is 21. My sister and I ⁹are college students.

B 1 Is your name Rosaria?
No, it isn't. It's Tamara.
2 Are you and your family Colombian? Yes, we are.
3 Are you from Medellín? No, I'm not. OR No, we're not.
4 Are your grandparents from Medellín? Yes, they are.
5 Is your father an artist?
No, he's not. / No, he isn't. He's a teacher.
6 Is your sister 21? Yes, she is.

C Possible questions and answers:
1 Is your mother an artist? Yes, she is.
2 Are your brothers 16? No, they're not. / No, they aren't.

2 READING

A ✓ 1, 2, 4, 5

3 WRITING

A 1 A Hello   B Hello OR Hi
2 A Hi OR Hey B Hi OR Hey

B 1 I'm Emma Durand.
2 I'm a French chef.
3 My home is in New York.
4 I'm from Paris in France.
5 I'm French and American.
6 I'm a teacher.
7 The name of the school is New York Chef School.
8 My students are from the United States, Canada, Mexico, and Japan.

C Possible answers:
1 I'm not Emma Durand. I'm Lisa Santiago.
2 I'm not a chef. I'm a student.
3 My home is not in New York. My home is in Los Angeles.
4 I'm not French. I'm Mexican.
5 I'm not from Paris. I'm from Guadalajara.

3 GRAMMAR AND VOCABULARY

A Possible questions:
1 Is your mother American?
2 Are your cousins here?
3 Is your brother a student?
4 Is your mother a doctor?
5 Are you Japanese?
6 Are your grandparents from Tokyo?
7 Are you from China?
8 Is your father a teacher?

2.2 They're really funny! *pages 12–13*

1 VOCABULARY: Describing people; really / very

A 1 old 2 young 3 boring 4 interesting 5 short 6 tall
7 shy 8 funny 9 smart 10 friendly

B 1 b 2 c 3 c 4 a

2 GRAMMAR: is not / are not

A 1 She's not / She isn't / She is not   2 He's / He is
3 We're / We are   4 is / 's
5 They're not / They are not   6 He's / He is (It's / It is)

B 1 You're not boring. You're funny.
2 My sister isn't tall, and she's not old. She's five.
3 My husband and I aren't from Mexico, and we're not from Canada. We're from the United States.
4 Mr. May isn't my teacher, and he's not your teacher. He's the chef at our school.
5 Doctor Norton isn't here, and she's not at home. She's at the college.
6 Rita and Lara aren't sisters, and they're not cousins. They're friends.

T-267

3 GRAMMAR AND VOCABULARY
  A Possible answers:
   My parents are very friendly.
   My father is tall.
   My grandparents are interesting.
   My cousins are really shy.
   My sister isn't tall.
   My brother is young.
   My best friend is really smart.
   My teacher is funny.

2.3 When is your birthday? *pages 14–15*

1 FUNCTIONAL LANGUAGE: Asking about and saying ages and birthdays
  A *Diego* Today is my birthday.
   Anna Happy birthday, Diego!
   Diego Thanks. Oh, Anna. This is my daughter, Sophia.
   Anna Hello, Sophia. My name is Anna. How old are you?
   Sophia I'm six, and my brother is three years old.
   Anna Oh, wow! When is your birthday, Sophia?
   Sophia It's on December 5.
   Anna Oh, right! You're seven this month? Happy birthday from me!
  B 1 four, fourth 2 thirty, thirtieth 3 one, first
   4 twenty-two, twenty-second 5 thirty-one, thirty-first
   6 three, third 7 twenty-seven, twenty-seventh
   8 eighteen, eighteenth

2 REAL-WORLD STRATEGY: Correcting yourself
  A 1 No, sorry, 12. OR Sorry, I mean 12.
   2 No, sorry, May 30. OR Sorry, I mean May 30.
   3 No, sorry, 19. OR Sorry, I mean 19.
   4 No, sorry, September 13. OR Sorry, I mean September 13.

3 FUNCTIONAL LANGUAGE AND REAL-WORLD STRATEGY
  A *Paul* This is my niece, Olivia.
   Gabriela Hi, Olivia! How [1]**old** are you?
   Olivia I'm 10. Sorry, I [2]**mean** nine. I'm nine years and eleven months old.
   Gabriela You're a tall girl! [3]**When** is your birthday?
   Olivia It's June 31.
   Gabriela June 31?
   Olivia No, [4]**sorry**, July 31.
   Gabriela Oh. So you're 9 [5]**years** old, and your birthday is July 31.
  B Answers will vary.

2.4 Here's my band *pages 16–17*

1 LISTENING
  A They are in the same band.
  B 1 Tony 2 Claudia 3 Aniko 4 Zack
  C 1 Zack 2 Aniko 3 Aniko 4 Tony 5 Claudia 6 Claudia

2 GRAMMAR: Prepositions of place
  A 1 between 2 on 3 next to 4 in 5 me

3 WRITING
  A 1 circle 2 underline 3 circle 4 circle 5 underline
   6 underline
  B Possible answers:
   1 My friends and I are from different countries, and we are different ages.
   2 I am from France, and Jiyoung and Jinho are from South Korea.
   3 One friend is from China, and two friends are from Brazil.
   4 Yi and I are artists, and we are friends.
   5 I'm 22, and Yi is 24.
  C Possible answer:
   My college is in Mexico City, and my classmates and I are from Mexico City. Our teacher is from Guadalajara. Six of the students in the class are my friends. María and Jose are 20. María is very smart. José is really funny. Diego is funny, too. He and I are 19. Lupe is very interesting, and she's really tall. Stefano is a little shy, but he's really smart. He's only 18. His sister is in the class. She isn't shy, and she isn't 18. She's very friendly. Her name is Isabella. The class is always interesting. It's never boring.

Unit 3 Come in

3.1 Welcome to my home *pages 18–19*

1 VOCABULARY: Rooms in a home
  A 1 No, it's the kitchen. 2 No, it's the door.
   3 No, it's the living room. 4 No, it's a wall.
   5 No, it's a bedroom. 6 No, it's a bathroom. 7 No, it's a floor.
   8 No, it's the dining area. 9 No, it's a picture.
   10 No, it's a window.

2 GRAMMAR: Possessive adjectives; possessive 's and s'
  A 1 My 2 Our 3 their 4 his 5 your 6 Her
  B 1 It's **my parents'** bedroom. 2 It's **Jonathan's** house.
   3 It's her **aunt's** picture. 4 They are the **students'** books.
   5 That's her **cousins'** dog. 6 What's **Sari's** email address?

3 GRAMMAR AND VOCABULARY
  A Possible answers:
   1 My bedroom is big. OR My bedroom isn't big.
   2 Our dining area is next to the kitchen.
   3 The kitchen isn't new.
   4 The picture in my friend's living room is really interesting.
   5 My parents' living room is small.
   6 Our bathroom is between the kitchen and the bedroom.

3.2 Is it really a chair? *pages 20–21*

1 VOCABULARY: Furniture
  A 1 desk; living room or bedroom
   2 bookcase; living room or bedroom
   3 sink; kitchen or bathroom
   4 rug; living room, dining area, or kitchen
   5 shower; bathroom
   6 TV; living room, kitchen, or bedroom
   7 lamp; living room, dining area, or bedroom
   8 bed; bedroom
   9 chair; living room, dining area, kitchen, or bedroom
   10 table; living room, dining area, or kitchen
   11 refrigerator; kitchen
   12 couch; living room

2 GRAMMAR: It is

A 1 isn't, It's 2 isn't, It's 3 is, It's not 4 is, It's not
5 Is, it's 6 Is, it's

B Lucy This is our home. [1]**It's** in Toronto.
Hyun [2]**Is it** an apartment?
Lucy No, [3]**it isn't (OR it's not)**. [4]**It's (OR It is)** a house.
Hyun [5]**Is it** big?
Lucy No. [6]**It's (OR It is)** small.
Hyun [7]**Is it** new?
Lucy Yes, [8]**it is**. And it's very nice. Is your home in Seoul?
Hyun My home [9]**isn't (OR is not)** in Seoul. It's in Busan, and [10]**it's (OR it is)** an apartment, not a house. The apartment [11]**isn't** very big, but our small apartment is OK.

3 GRAMMAR AND VOCABULARY

A Possible answers:
1 The desk in my bedroom isn't very old.
2 The bed in my bedroom is really big.
3 The bookcase in the living room isn't short.
4 The couch in the living room is really great.
5 The refrigerator in the kitchen is tall.
6 The rug in the dining area is very nice.
7 The table in the kitchen is small.
8 The TV in the living room isn't very good.
9 The sink in the bathroom is new.

3.3 Coffee or tea? pages 22–23

1 FUNCTIONAL LANGUAGE: Making and replying to offers; accepting a drink and snack

A Possible answers:

1	You	Coffee or tea?	3	You	Coffee or tea?
	Dan	Tea, please.		Dalia	**Tea, please.**
	You	With milk?		You	Milk?
	Dan	No, thanks.		Dalia	**Yes, please.**
	You	With sugar?		You	With sugar?
	Dan	Sure. One, please.		Dalia	**Yes. Two, please.**
	You	A cookie?		You	A cookie?
	Dan	Yes, please.		Dalia	**Sure.**
	You	Here you are.		You	Here you are.
	Dan	Thank you.		Dalia	**Thank you.**
2	You	Coffee or tea?			
	Coco	Coffee, please.			
	You	With milk?			
	Coco	**No, thanks.**			
	You	Sugar?			
	Coco	**No, thanks.**			
	You	A cookie?			
	Coco	**Yes, please.**			
	You	Here you are.			
	Coco	**Thanks.**			

2 REAL-WORLD STRATEGY: Asking about words you don't understand

A 1 False 2 True 3 False 4 False 5 True

3 FUNCTIONAL LANGUAGE AND REAL-WORLD STRATEGY

A Lina Coffee or tea?
Jason **Tea, please.**
Lina With milk?
Jason Yes**, please.**
Lina Sugar?
Jason No**, thanks.**
Lina And a biscuit?
Jason **Sorry, I don't understand. What's a** biscuit?
Lina A bicuit is a cookie.
Jason Oh, a cookie. **Sure.**

3.4 Home-share pages 24–25

1 READING

A 1 ($65 center of Rio de Janeiro) two people
2 ($110 Lapa district) family

B

		Center of Rio de Janeiro	Lapa district
1	bathroom		✓
2	bedroom	✓	✓
3	dining area		
4	kitchen	✓	✓
5	living room	✓	
6	bookcase	✓	
7	desk		
8	picture	✓	
9	shower		✓
10	television		

2 GRAMMAR: Information questions with be

A 1 e 2 d 3 a 4 c 5 b

B 1 What is your email address? It's myb@xyzmail.com.
2 Where is the apartment? It's in Rio de Janeiro.
3 How old is the apartment? It's six years old.
4 Who is the owner? Maria Santos.
5 How many rooms are in the apartment? Five.

3 WRITING

A (Dear) Ms. Santos,
This email is about your apartment. We visit your city every year. Our son is six years old. How many bedrooms are in your apartment? Where is your apartment? What is the name of the street? In your apartment, are pets OK? We have a dog. Is the TV in the living room?
(Thank you.)
(Sincerely,)
Rose Chu

B Formal.

C Possible answer:
Dear Mr. Yamamoto,
This email is about your home-share. In the pictures, your apartment is very nice.
Is the refrigerator big? Where is the apartment? Is the apartment on the first floor?
How many people live in the apartment?
Thank you.
Sincerely,
Renée Gounod

T-269

Unit 4 I love it

4.1 Favorite things *pages 26–27*

1 VOCABULARY: Technology

L	A	P	T	O	P	T	D	W	Z	T
Z	N	B	C	J	G	A	M	E	Q	A
J	K	Y	A	C	K	E	I	K	B	B
M	G	V	M	A	T	Z	I	K	H	L
R	Y	C	E	L	L	P	H	O	N	E
K	E	O	R	T	O	P	Z	A	M	T
A	P	L	A	S	E	T	Y	T	N	P
E	E	A	R	P	H	O	N	E	S	X
A	P	P	M	F	S	Z	N	R	V	K
F	S	M	A	R	T	W	A	T	C	H

B 1 game 2 camera 3 cell phone 4 app 5 smartwatch 6 laptop 7 tablet 8 earphones

2 GRAMMAR: Simple present: statements with I, you, we

A 1 I don't have a laptop. I have a tablet.
   2 I like apps. I don't like video games.
   3 You want a small refrigerator. You don't want a big refrigerator.
   4 I love photo apps. I don't love music apps.
   5 We have an apartment. We don't have a house.
   6 We don't want a new camera. We want a new computer.

B Possible answers:
   1 We have a new apartment. We don't have a new couch.
   2 I like my cell phone. I don't like the camera.
   3 I love my friends. I don't love my job.
   4 We want a new TV. We don't want a big TV.
   5 We have a laptop. We don't have a tablet.

3 GRAMMAR AND VOCABULARY

A Possible answers:
   1 I love video games. I have games on my phone. OR I don't love video games. I don't have games on my phone.
   2 I have cool apps on my phone. They're great!
   3 I don't like earphones. They're not good for me.
   4 I don't want a new tablet. I have my parents' tablet.
   5 I have an old laptop. It's good.
   6 I love my cell phone. It's cool.
   7 I want a smartwatch. My smartwatch is very old.
   8 I like the camera on my phone. The pictures are really great.

4.2 My phone is my world *pages 28–29*

1 VOCABULARY: Using technology

A 1 b, c 2 a, c 3 b, c 4 b, c 5 a, c 6 a, b 7 a, b 8 b, c 9 b, c 10 b, c

B on: 1, 2, 4, 5
  X: 3, 6

2 GRAMMAR: Simple present yes/no questions with I, you, we

A 1 **Do you have** a laptop?
   2 **Do you and your friends love** social media apps?
   3 **Do you call** your family?
   4 **Do I post** photos on social media?
   5 **Do you and your family want** a new tablet?
   6 **Do you watch** videos on the internet?

B 1 Yes, I do. OR No, I don't.
   2 Yes, we do. OR No, we don't.
   3 Yes, I do. OR No, I don't.
   4 Yes, you do. OR No, you don't.
   5 Yes, we do. OR No, we don't.
   6 Yes, I do. OR No, I don't.

3 GRAMMAR AND VOCABULARY

A Possible answers:
   1 laptop 2 my best friend 3 grandparents 4 movies 5 photos 6 comments 7 text messages 8 parents 9 music 10 video games

B Possible questions and answers
   1 Do you post comments on social media?
     Yes, I do. OR No, I don't.
   2 Do you chat with your family on your phone?
     Yes, I do. OR No, I don't.
   3 Do you watch videos on TV at home?
     Yes, we do. OR No, we don't.
   4 Do you and your friends send emails?
     Yes, we do. OR No, we don't.
   5 Do you leave voice messages for your friends?
     Yes, I do. OR No, I don't.
   6 Do you call your friends a lot?
     Yes, I do. OR No, I don't.

4.3 What about you? *pages 30–31*

1 FUNCTIONAL LANGUAGE: Continuing a conversation

A 7 Juan   Yes, and I send thank-you emails to my friends.
   2 David   No. I use email or social media.
   1 Juan   Do you send text messages to your parents?
   6 David   Do you send thank-you cards, too?
   4 David   Yeah, I send birthday cards to my grandparents. How about you?
   3 Juan   What about cards?
   5 Juan   Yes, I send cards, too. I like cards with interesting pictures.

2 REAL-WORLD STRATEGY: Showing you are listening

A 1 Yeah, me too. 2 No. How about you? 3 Yeah. 4 Right. 5 Yeah. 6 No, I don't.

3 FUNCTIONAL LANGUAGE AND REAL-WORLD STRATEGY

A Ana   I don't call my family on my cell phone.
   Sam   Really?
   Ana   Yeah, it's expensive.
   Sam   Yes, it is. ¹**Do you use video chat? OR What about video chat?**
   Ana   Sorry, I don't understand. What is a video chat?
   Sam   You talk with your friends with video. I use video chat on the internet. It's free.
   Ana   ²**Yeah. OR Right. OR OK.**
   Sam   We have an app.
   Ana   ³**Oh, yeah?** Is Skype an app for video chats?
   Sam   Yes, it's one app. I use Whatsapp, too.
   Ana   ⁴**What about emails? OR Do you send emails?**
   Sam   I don't use email. I send texts.
   Ana   ⁵**Do you send texts to your family, too?**
   Sam   Oh, no. I don't text my family. I call them. ⁶**How about you?**
   Ana   I send emails to my parents. They don't like texts.
   Sam   Really?

4.4 Great! Five stars pages 32–33

1 LISTENING

A 2

B 1 Mai   2 Jonas   3 Both   4 Mai   5 Both   6 Both   7 Mai

2 GRAMMAR: a/an; Adjectives before nouns

A 1 We don't have **an** apartment.
   2 We have **a** house.
   3 She has **an** app for video chats.
   4 You don't have **an** email address.
   5 He doesn't use **a** tablet.

B 1 It's an interesting book.
   2 I have an expensive TV.
   3 It's a great card.
   4 Are they boring games?
   5 It's an old movie.
   6 It's a cool smartwatch.

3 WRITING

A 1 c   2 a   3 f   4 e   5 b   6 d

B Dear Aunt Martha and Uncle Tom,
   Thank you for the smartwatch. It's really cool! I use it all the time. I love to video chat with you on my new watch!
   Love,
   Dana

C Answers will vary.

Unit 5 Mondays and fun days

5.1 Play or fast-forward? pages 34–35

1 VOCABULARY: Days and times of day; everyday activities

A Activities: play soccer, work, run, go out, study
   Days of the week: on Saturday, on Wednesday, on Thursday, on Friday, on Monday, on Tuesday, on Sunday
   Times of the day: in the morning, in the evening, at night, in the afternoon

B Answers may vary slightly.
   1 Rhea works **in the morning from Monday to Friday**.
   2 On Saturday, Rhea **runs with Jay**.
   3 On Wednesday evening, Rhea **goes out with Teri and Jon**.
   4 Rhea **goes out** with her family **on Sunday afternoon**.
   5 Jon **studies** in the morning from Monday to Thursday.
   6 On the weekend, Jon **plays soccer**.
   7 Jon works **in the evening on Monday, Tuesday, and Thursday, and on Friday morning**.
   8 On Friday night, **Rhea and Jon go out**.

2 GRAMMAR: Simple present statements: he/she/they

A 1 plays   2 goes   3 has   4 want   5 studies   6 work
B 1 don't study   2 doesn't have   3 don't run   4 doesn't go   5 doesn't watch   6 doesn't like
C 1 I never use my laptop.
   2 My friends and I hardly ever play soccer.
   3 My sister usually studies at night.
   4 I often go out on Friday night.
   5 They are always at home on the weekend.

3 GRAMMAR AND VOCABULARY

A Possible answers:
   1 I always sleep in the morning on the weekends.
   2 I usually **walk with my dog** in the evening.
   3 I often **listen to the radio** in the morning.
   4 I sometimes **have fun with my friends** on Monday afternoon.
   5 I hardly ever **work** on Sunday.
   6 I never **drink coffee at night.**

B Possible answers:
   1 Katya doesn't go out on Friday night. She always works on Friday night.
   2 Lucas never works on Friday night. He always works on Saturday and Sunday.
   3 Katya sometimes watches soccer games on Saturday. She never plays soccer.
   4 Katya and Lucas usually run early in the morning.
   5 Katya usually studies at night. Lucas never studies at night.
   6 Katya often has fun on weekends. She never works on Saturday and Sunday.

5.2 Listen to your body clock pages 36–37

1 VOCABULARY: Telling the time

A 1 It's two thirty OR half past two.
   2 It's six fifty-five OR five to seven.
   3 It's ten fifteen OR a quarter after ten.
   4 It's nine ten OR ten after nine.
   5 It's five forty-five OR a quarter to six.
   6 It's one o'clock.

T-271

B Possible answers:
  6 I drink coffee at 3:15 p.m.
  7 I go to class at 5:55 p.m.
  4 I go to work at 8:30 a.m.
  3 I eat breakfast at 7:30 a.m.
  1 I get up at 7:00 a.m.
  9 I go to bed at 11:30 p.m.
  2 I drink tea at 7:10 a.m.
  8 I have dinner at 7:45 p.m.
  5 I eat lunch at 1:00 p.m.

2 **GRAMMAR:** Simple present questions
  A 1 **Does** your family **have** a big lunch on Saturday? No, my family doesn't have a big lunch on Saturday.
  What does your family have on Saturday? They have a big breakfast on Saturday.
  2 **Do** you **get up** late on Monday? No, I don't get up late on Monday.
  When do you get up late? I get up late on Sunday.
  3 **Does** your best friend **play** basketball? No, he doesn't play basketball.
  What does your best friend play? He plays soccer.
  4 **Does** your teacher **work** on weekends? No, she doesn't work on weekends.
  When does your teacher work? She works from Monday to Friday.
  5 **Do** you **eat** lunch at school? No, I don't eat lunch at school.
  Where do you eat lunch? I eat lunch at home.
  6 **Do** your friends go to bed late on Friday and Saturday? Yes, they go to bed late on Friday and Saturday.
  What time do your friends go to bed on Friday and Saturday? They go to bed after midnight.

  B Possible answers:
  1 Yes, we/they do. OR No, we/they don't.
  2 Yes, I do. OR No, I don't.
  3 Yes, he/she does. OR No, he/she doesn't.
  4 Yes, he/she does. OR No, he/she doesn't.
  5 Yes, I do. OR No, I don't.
  6 Yes, they do. OR No, they don't.

3 **GRAMMAR AND VOCABULARY**
  A, B Possible answers:
  1 When do your parents go out? They go out on their birthdays.
  2 What does your teacher do on weekends? I don't know.
  3 What time do you eat breakfast? I eat breakfast at 7 o'clock.
  4 When do your brother and sister go to bed? They go to bed early, but at different times.
  5 Where does your sister work? She works in an office.
  6 Do your friends play basketball? No, they don't.
  7 Does your mother drink coffee? Yes. She loves coffee.

5.3 Me, too *pages 38–39*

1 **FUNCTIONAL LANGUAGE:** Showing you agree and have things in common
  A 1 a   2 c   3 b   4 a
  B 1 Me, too.   2 Me, neither.   3 Me, neither.   4 Me, too.
   5 Me, too.   6 Me, neither.

2 **REAL-WORLD STRATEGY:** Short answers with adverbs of frequency
  A Possible answers:
  1 Sometimes.   2 Usually.   3 Always.   4 Hardly ever.
  5 Never.   6 Sometimes.

3 **FUNCTIONAL LANGUAGE AND REAL-WORLD STRATEGY**
  A Min-seo   ¹**Do** you watch TV on the weekend?
   David   ²**Hardly ever**. I think it's boring.
   Min-seo   I ³**agree**. I only watch sports on TV.
   David   What sports do you watch?
   Min-seo   All sports. I love sports.
   David   Me ⁴**too**.
   Min-seo   Do you play sports?
   David   No. I don't have a lot of free time.
   Min-seo   Me, ⁵**neither**.
   David   But I run every day before dinner. Exercise is good.
   Min-seo   That's ⁶**true**.
   David   How about you? Do you run?
   Min-seo   ⁷**Sometimes**. My friends and I run on the beach on the weekend.
   David   The beach is a great place to run.
   Min-seo   ⁸**Yeah**, I know.

  B Possible answer:
  The other person   I often make dinner.
  Me   Me, too. It's fun.
  The other person   I agree. Do you make dinner for a lot of people?
  Me   No, I don't.
  The other person   Me, neither. I make dinner for my family.
  Me   Does your wife cook?
  The other person   Hardly ever. She works late.

5.4 A happy life *pages 40–41*

1 **READING**
  A Title Two: "All Work and No Play is Not Good for Children"
  B Possible answers

Morning activities
1 She gets up at 6:00 a.m.
2 She studies for an hour before breakfast.
3 She goes to school at 8:30 a.m.
Afternoon activities
1 She studies for an hour after lunch.
2 On Monday, she has guitar lessons.
3 On Tuesday and Thursday, she has Chinese class.
Evening/Night activities
1 She has dinner.
2 She plays the guitar and studies from 7:00 to 10:30
3 She goes to bed at 11:00 p.m.

2 **LISTENING:** Listen for supporting detail
  A 1 one   2 five   3 ten   4 three   5 six   6 five, six

3 WRITING

A Possible answers:

> Great for you
> a I eat three meals a day.
> b I run six days a week.
> Not good, but not bad for you
> c I have one chocolate cookie before I go to bed.
> d I work at my desk five or six hours a day.
> Really bad for you
> e I sleep four or five hours at night.
> f I drink ten cups of coffee a day.

B 1 We play basketball at seven in the evening.
2 I go to class at eight in the morning.
3 I study at one in the afternoon.
4 I run at six in the morning.
5 I go to bed at 11:30 OR at 11:30 at night.

C Possible answers:

Great for you
1 I eat breakfast, lunch, and dinner.
2 I run two times a week.
3 I don't usually sit at a desk.
Not good, but not bad for you
1 I sometimes eat ice cream.
2 I don't always walk.
3 I often don't drink water.
Really bad for you
1 I sleep ten hours every day.
2 I eat a lot of cookies.
3 I drink eight cups of tea with sugar.

Unit 6 Zoom in, zoom out

6.1 Good places pages 42–43

1 VOCABULARY: Places in cities

A 1 n 2 a 3 d 4 g 5 c 6 k 7 e 8 h 9 j 10 b
11 i 12 m 13 f 14 l

2 GRAMMAR: There's, There are; a lot of, some, no

A I live in a small town. In our town ¹**there's** a big park, but ²**there's** no zoo. ³**There's** a big supermarket, too, and ⁴**there are** three stores. My daughter goes to the school and my husband is a teacher at the school. ⁵**There's** an interesting bookstore. ⁶And **there are** two really good restaurants!

B Clara Do you like your hotel, Don?
Don Yes, I do. It's a big hotel! There are ¹**a lot of** rooms.
Clara Does the hotel have a restaurant?
Don Yes. It has ²**a** big restaurant. I eat breakfast in the restaurant every day.
Clara What about the restaurants near the hotel? Are they good?
Don Yes, there are ³**some** great restaurants near the hotel, Italian, Japanese, Spanish …
Clara And is your room good?
Don It's OK. There's ⁴**a** desk, ⁵ **a** chair, and ⁶ **a** big TV, but there's ⁷**no** sofa. It's not good!

3 GRAMMAR AND VOCABULARY

A Possible answers:
1 There are a lot of parks.
2 There are some good hospitals.
3 There are some popular cafés.
4 There's a very nice hotel.
5 There are a lot of people.
6 There are no movie theaters. (OR There's no movie theater.)
7 There are no good restaurants. (OR There're no good restaurants.)
8 There are a lot of restaurants.

B Possible answers:
There are some good restaurants. There are a lot of nice houses. There's a big mall. There's no movie theater. There's a nice museum. There are a lot of cars.

6.2 City life, wild life pages 44–45

1 VOCABULARY: Nature

A 1 island, lake, snow 2 beach, flowers, ocean
3 forest, river, mountains 4 plants, desert, mountains

2 GRAMMAR: Count and non-count nouns

A Count nouns: **animal**, apartment, artist, **house**, **plant**, refrigerator, restaurant
Non-count nouns: coffee, **grass**, furniture, **milk**, nature, snow, **sugar**

B 1 an 2 a 3 a 4 some 5 a 6 some 7 a
8 a 9 some 10 some

3 GRAMMAR AND VOCABULARY

A 1 **There are a lot of** hills in my city.
2 **There is a** very tall tree.
3 **There is a lot of** grass.
4 **There are a lot of** flowers.
5 **There is a** lake.
6 **There are a lot of** plants.
7 **There is a** mountain.
8 **There is a lot of** snow on the mountain.

B Possible answers:
There are some trees outside my window.
There is an animal near my window.
There are no flowers.
There are some houses.
There is a car.
There are some people.

6.3 Is it near here? pages 46–47

1 FUNCTIONAL LANGUAGE: Asking for and giving directions

A Marina Excuse me. ¹**Where's** Central Hospital?
Ricky It's on Milk Street.
Marina Is ²**this** Milk Street?
Ricky No, it isn't. This is Garden Street.
Marina Is Milk Street ³**near** here?
Ricky Yes, it is. Turn left here. Then ⁴**turn right** on Park Street. Go one ⁵**block**. The hospital is on the left.

T-273

2 REAL-WORLD STRATEGY: Checking information

A 1 So, go one block and turn right on Good Street.
  2 After the bookstore, turn right again.
  3 So, go two blocks and turn left.
  4 The supermarket is on Market Street, on the right.

3 FUNCTIONAL LANGUAGE AND REAL-WORLD STRATEGY

A Ji-young   It's on **Park** Street.
   Ji-young   Go two blocks and then turn **left**.
   Ji-young   Go one **block**. It's on the right.
   Rodrigo   So, go one block, and it's on the **right**?

B Possible answer:
  Turn left here. Then turn right on Hill Street. Go one block. The movie theater is on the left.

C Possible answer:
  Walk down Fourth Street. Go one block and then turn right on Park Street. Go one block. The museum is on the right.

6.4 A forest in the city pages 48–49

1 LISTENING

A ✓ in a car
B ✓ 1, 2, 5, 6, 10

2 READING

A 1 Yes 2 No 3 No 4 Yes 5 Yes

3 WRITING

A 1 We have some nice small parks.
  2 There are some beautiful tall trees.
  3 There are a lot of small interesting flowers.
  4 There are a lot of nice big plants.
  5 The park has some great tall trees.

B • Via Verde is a **very** busy road in Mexico City.
  • Via Verde is a very big vertical garden. There are 700 very small gardens in it.
  • There are a lot of **very** interesting plants in the gardens.
  • People in Mexico City think the vertical gardens are **very** interesting.
  • Vertical gardens are **very** important to Mexico City.

C Answers will vary.

Unit 7   Now is good

7.1 A good time to call pages 50–51

1 VOCABULARY: Activities around the house

A 1 my hair 2 coffee 3 the computer 4 her bed
  5 my room 6 their breakfast 7 your home

2 GRAMMAR: Present continuous statements

A 1 chatting 2 doing 3 eating 4 getting 5 going
  6 having 7 playing 8 running 9 shopping 10 studying
  11 taking 12 working

B 1 'm / am chatting 2 're / are doing 3 're / are shopping
  4 's / is taking 5 're / are running 6 're / are having
  7 're / are getting 8 'm / am eating

3 GRAMMAR AND VOCABULARY

A 1 'm not taking 2 isn't cooking 3 're doing 4 's brushing
  5 's helping
  6 're not/aren't cleaning

B 1 take 2 isn't cooking 3 do 4 brush
  5 do 6 is cleaning

C Possible answers:
  1 I'm not taking a bath right now.
  2 I'm not cooking dinner now.
  3 I'm doing my homework now.
  4 I'm not brushing my teeth now.
  5 My family and I aren't washing the dishes now.
  6 I'm not cleaning my room now.

7.2 Texting on the run pages 52–53

1 VOCABULARY: Transportation

A 1 c 2 b 3 a 4 f 5 e 6 d

2 GRAMMAR: Present continuous questions

A 1 Are you doing your homework right now?
  2 Are your friends playing soccer right now?
  3 Is your friend sending you a text message?
  4 Are you and your friends learning English?
  5 Are you listening to music right now?

B 1 Yes, I am. OR No, I'm not.
  2 Yes, they are. OR No, they're not.
  3 Yes, he/she is. OR No, he's/she's not.
  4 Yes, we are. OR No, we're not.
  5 Yes, I am. OR No, I'm not.

C 1 Who is she waiting for?
  2 Where are you going?
  3 What is she doing?
  4 Why are they carrying some big bags?
  5 Why are you helping her/your daughter with her homework?
  6 Are they playing soccer?

3 GRAMMAR AND VOCABULARY

A 1 Are you taking the train?
  2 Are you waiting for your friend?
  3 Are you on the bus?
  4 Where are you walking?
  5 Where are you going?
  6 Are you riding your bike?

B Possible answers:
  1 A Are you riding your bike?
    B No, I'm not. I'm taking the bus to the movie theater.
  2 A Why are you carrying bags?
    B Because I'm shopping.

7.3 A new life pages 54–55

1 FUNCTIONAL LANGUAGE: Asking how things are going

A 7 Jesse   Really? Me, too.
  1 Jesse   Hello.
  3 Jesse   Hey, Gustavo!
  5 Jesse   Not bad, thanks. How are you?
  4 Gustavo   How are you doing?
  2 Gustavo   Hi, Jesse. It's Gustavo.
  6 Gustavo   I'm fine. I'm doing my homework right now.

T-274

2 REAL-WORLD STRATEGY: Reacting to news
  A Good news: 1 and 3
    Bad news: 4 and 6
    Ordinary news: 2 and 5
    1 *B*: Oh, wow!
    2 *B*: Oh.
    3 *B*: Oh, wow!
    4 *B*: Oh, no!
    5 *B*: Oh.
    6 *B*: Oh, no!
3 FUNCTIONAL LANGUAGE AND REAL-WORLD STRATEGY
  A Anna   ¹**Hello**.
    Paul   Hi, Anna. ²**It's** Paul.
    Anna   ³**Hey** OR **Hi**, Paul. How ⁴**are** you?
    Paul   Good. How are you ⁵**doing**?
    Anna   ⁶**I'm** fine, thanks. Are you at home?
    Paul   No. I'm driving to work.
    Anna   On Sunday?
    Paul   Yeah. I'm working on Sundays these days.
    Anna   Oh, ⁷**no**! Why?
    Paul   I have a new job on weekends.
    Anna   ⁸**Oh**. Do you like it?
    Paul   Yeah, I love it!
    Anna   Oh, ⁹**wow**! That's great.
  B Sylvia has three children.
    Rafael's wife, Pearl, is not in Florida right now. She's working in California.
  C Possible answer:
    Rafael Hello.
    Sylvia Hi, Rafael. It's Sylvia.
    Rafael Hey, Sylvia. How are you doing?
    Sylvia Not bad. I'm always busy with the children and work.
    Rafael Oh.
    Sylvia How are you?
    Rafael I'm OK, but I have bad news. Pearl isn't in Florida at the moment. She's working in California.
    Sylvia Oh, no!

7.4 Chaos! *pages 56–57*

1 READING
  A The restaurant closes at 11:00 p.m.
  B

5:30 a.m.	Andy is having breakfast.
6 a.m. to 7 a.m.	Ten people are drinking coffee and talking.
8:30 a.m.	Parents are coming to the restaurant with their children.
9:15 a.m.	Andy is cooking lunch.
11:15 a.m.	Andy and two people are having lunch.
12 noon	People are coming for lunch at the restaurant.
4:30 p.m.	Andy is cooking dinner.

2 LISTENING
  A 1 a 100   2 c four   3 a because they're not cooking at home
    4 b eats in restaurants
3 WRITING
  A 1 f; I like Nick and Alicia. I like Mac and Pilar, too.
    2 e; My job is busy. Also, I work a lot of hours.
    3 b; The children are running in the restaurant. Also, they're playing with things.
    4 a; I cook breakfast and lunch. I cook dinner, too.
    5 d; Mr. and Mrs. Garcia come for breakfast on Friday. Also, they come for dinner.
    6 e; I'm a chef. I'm a writer, too.
  B 1 And (OR Also)   2 But (OR And)   3 Also, (OR And)   4 But
  C Possible answer: "F is for Fun"
    It's 8 o'clock, and I'm going to school. My friends are riding the bus with me. We're talking. It's 10:30 now. I'm in class. The teacher is talking to John. He often talks to John because John hardly ever does his homework. I like John, and the teacher likes him, too. But John's not a very good student. It's 12:30 now. I'm having lunch with my friends. We have a half hour for lunch, and we always have fun. It's 3:30 now, and I'm going home. This is my favorite time of the day because I don't have school. And I don't have a lot of homework today. It's 5:30. My friends and I are playing soccer in the park. It's 11 o'clock and it's time for a shower. Now I'm going to bed!

Unit 8   You're good!

8.1 She likes music, but she can't dance! *pages 58–59*

1 VOCABULARY: Verbs to describe skills
  A 1 swims   2 draws   3 fixes things   4 speaks two languages
    5 surfs   6 reads music   7 snowboards   8 paints
    9 plays the guitar   10 dances   11 sings   12 skateboards
2 GRAMMAR: can and can't for ability; well
  A 1 can   2 can   3 can't   4 can't   5 can
    6 can   7 can   8 can   9 can't   10 can
  B 1 Soccer players can play soccer well.
    2 Bus drivers can drive well.
    3 A chef can cook well.
    4 English teachers can speak English well.
    5 An artist can draw well.
    6 People in a band can play music well.
3 GRAMMAR AND VOCABULARY
  A 1 Can Carla play the guitar? Yes, she can.
    2 Can Tony sing? No, he can't.
    3 Can Carla and Tony snowboard? No, they can't.
    4 Can Carla and Tony speak two languages? Yes, they can.
    5 Can Carla surf? No, she can't.
    6 Can Tony paint? Yes, he can.
    7 Can you read music? Yes, I can. OR No, I can't.
    8 Can you fix things? Yes, I can. OR No, I can't.
  B Possible questions:
    1 Can your mother swim?   2 Can your brother dance?
    3 Can your friend sing?   4 Can your mother ride a bike?
    5 Can your friends snowboard?
    6 Can your friends play the guitar?

T-275

8.2 Happy workers = great workers *pages 60–61*

1 VOCABULARY: Work

A I work for a big ¹**company**. Its name is Verulia. There are 250 ²**workers** in my company. Some people work in the capital city, but 50 of us work in Gardon, near my home. I like my ³**coworkers**. They are very friendly. The ⁴**office** is nice because it is near a park. I usually ⁵**take a break** at 10:30 for half an hour. I go for a walk in the park. Sometimes 10 or 15 of us ⁶**have a meeting** in the park. It's really good because we ⁷**think** of great ideas outside. I ⁸**work hard** – sometimes for six days a week – but I love my job!

2 GRAMMAR: can and can't for possibility

A
1 We can swim in the lake.
2 You can't surf there.
3 I can't use my cell phone in the mountains.
4 We can ride our bikes in the park.
5 She can take the bus.
6 A dog can't go in a restaurant.

B Possible answers:
1 Can you be late for class?
   No, I can't. Or No, we can't.
2 Can you speak your language in class?
   Yes, I/we can. OR No, I/we can't.
3 Can you ask your teacher questions?
   Yes, I/we can.
4 Can you use your cell phone in class?
   Yes, I/we can OR No, I/we can't.
5 When can you have a meeting with your teacher?
   I can have a meeting with my teacher before or after class.
6 What can you do during your break?
   I/We can drink coffee.

3 GRAMMAR AND VOCABULARY

A Possible answers:
1 At New Tech Company, you can work from home or in the office.
2 At New Tech Company, you can have Skype meetings.
3 At Best Tech Company, you can't have Skype meetings.
4 At Best Tech Company, you can't take breaks when you want.

B Answers will vary.

8.3 Are you the right person?

1 FUNCTIONAL LANGUAGE: Giving and asking for opinions

A
1 Do you think that great companies have happy workers?
2 Why do you think friends are important?
3 Do you think technology is a good thing?
4 Do you think school is fun?
5 Why do you think people want a job?

B a 3 b 5 c 1 d 4 e 2

C All answers will be either *I think so.*, or *I don't think so.*

2 REAL-WORLD STRATEGY: Explaining and saying more about an idea

A 1 a 2 b 3 a 4 a

3 FUNCTIONAL LANGUAGE AND REAL-WORLD STRATEGY

A
Chef Are you the right person for this job?
Bill Yeah. ¹**I think so.**
Chef Why are you a good server?
Bill Because on weekends, I go to different restaurants with my friends, and I see a lot of servers. The good servers are friendly. I'm friendly, too.
Chef OK. ²**Do you think that** it's important to work well with other servers?
Bill ³**I don't think so.** I mean, servers don't work much with other servers.
Chef Really? In my restaurant, teamwork is important. The servers work with the chefs in the kitchen.
Bill Oh.
Chef Our busy days are Friday, Saturday, and Sunday. Can you work then?
Bill I can't work on Saturday and Sunday. ⁴**I mean**, I'm busy on weekends. But I can work on Tuesday, Wednesday, and Thursday.

B Bill is not the right person for the job. He doesn't think teamwork is important. He can't work on the busy days at the restaurant.

C Possible answer:
Chef Are you the right person for this job?
Sofia I think so. I work hard. I am a good server.
Chef Why do you think you are a good server?
Sofia I like people. I mean, I'm friendly, and I like teamwork.
Chef Do you think that it's important to work well with other people?
Sofia Yes. I think it's very important. I mean, in a restaurant people work together.
Chef Our busy days are Friday, Saturday, and Sunday. Can you work then?
Sofia Yes. I want a job on the weekend. I go to school on weekdays.

8.4 Computers and our jobs *pages 64–65*

1 LISTENING

A Emily and Joel **do not think** that a robot can be a child's friend.

B ✓ 1, 2, 6

2 READING

A 3 Robots for Our Grandparents

B ✓ 1, 2, 4

3 WRITING

A
Claudia, Bogotá	She says, "Our children are playing with their robots and not with other children."
Helena, Belo Horizonte:	Joel says, "Children can play with robots and learn from them."
Moe, Toronto:	She says, "Robots are now our children's friends."

B
1 Elena Cho says, "I like my new talking robot."
2 Elena Cho's son says, "The robot helps my mother a lot."
3 Ronaldo Benson said, "Our company makes robots for grandparents."
4 Doctor Wu said, "Robots are good for grandparents, because their families don't visit every day."

C Answers will vary.

Unit 9 Places to go

9.1 I love it here! pages 66–67

1 VOCABULARY: Travel

A 1 vacation   2 country   3 boat   4 tickets   5 ranch
   6 town   7 tour   8 plane

2 GRAMMAR: This and These

A 1 Is this your train?   2 Are these your tickets?
   3 These photos are cool.   4 Is this your hotel?
   5 These seats are comfortable.   6 This museum is interesting.

3 GRAMMAR AND VOCABULARY

A Possible answers:
   1 We're on a bike tour. There are many interesting places on the tour. It's not boring!
   2 This farm is near a lake. We're staying on this farm in the country.
   3 This is a great vacation. This city has a lot of interesting places.

9.2 San Francisco, here we come pages 68–69

1 VOCABULARY: Travel arrangements

A 1 on a trip   2 friends   3 stays   4 checking in at
   5 destination   6 museum   7 arrive   8 on a flight

2 GRAMMAR: like to, want, to, need to, have to

A 1 has to   2 like to   3 needs to   4 have to   5 want to
   6 want to   7 like to   8 wants to

B 1 It's 10:00 a.m. My flight is at 12 p.m. I'm late! I **need to** go to the airport.
   2 My sister **doesn't like to** go on vacation with our parents. She likes to travel with her friends.
   3 Jason's very hungry. He **wants to** eat dinner now.
   4 Sari **doesn't like to** travel on the subway. It's busy and hot.
   5 My parents' car is very old. They **have to/need to** buy a new car.
   6 We're planning our next vacation. We **want to** go to a lot of interesting destinations.

3 GRAMMAR AND VOCABULARY

A 1 I have to check in three hours before my flight at the airport near my city.
   2 I like (OR don't like) to fly.
   3 I have (OR don't have) to buy plane tickets online.
   4 I like (OR don't like) to stay at hotels.
   5 I need (OR don't need) to arrive at the bus stop 15 minutes early.
   6 I want (OR don't want) to work at an airport.
   7 I need (OR don't need) to leave home before 8:00 a.m.
   8 I like (OR don't like) to take trips to places near my home.
   9 I want (OR don't want) to travel to New York.

9.3 They're two for $15 pages 70–71

1 FUNCTIONAL LANGUAGE: Asking for missing information and clarification

A 1 A Excuse me. Where **is** the women's restroom?
      B It's over there, near the door.
   2 A Excuse me. What time **does** the bus to San Diego leave?
      B It leaves at 11:15 a.m.
   3 A Excuse me. How much **is** this guide book?
      B It's $12.99.
   4 A Excuse me. I need **to** buy a ticket to Bogotá. How much is it?
      B A bus ticket **is** $147.00.

B 3 A And for a child? Is it the same price?
   1 A Excuse me. How much is one ticket?
   5 A Then one ticket for me and one ticket for my son, please.
   7 A Where are seats 10A and 10B?
   2 B Tickets are $15.
   8 B They're on the right.
   6 B OK. Your seats are 10A and 10B.
   4 B No, it isn't. Tickets for children are $5.

2 REAL-WORLD STRATEGY: Asking someone to repeat something

A ✓ 2, 4

3 FUNCTIONAL LANGUAGE AND REAL-WORLD STRATEGY

A Possible answers:
   1 Mia   Excuse me. How much are the flowers?
   2 Clerk   They're six for $10.
   3 Mia   Is the plant the same price?
   4 Clerk   Yes, it's $10, too. But you can have six flowers and the plant for $16.
   5 Mia   Sorry, can you say that again?
   6 Clerk   You can have six flowers and the plant for $16.
   7 Mia   Oh, Ok. Where is a good café?
   8 Clerk   Go straight and turn right. It's on the left.
   9 Mia   Sorry, can you repeat that, please?
   10 Clerk Go straight and turn right. It's on the left.
   11 Mia   Thank you very much.
   12 Clerk You're welcome.

9.4 A great destination pages 72–73

1 READING

A ✓ horses, countries in South America, museums

B Possible answers.
   1 A gaucho works on a ranch.
   2 There are gaucho ranches in Argentina, Bolivia, Chile, and Uruguay.
   3 You can stay at a ranch for a day, a week, or a month.
   4 You can learn about gaucho life in a gaucho museum.

2 LISTENING

A Yes, she does.

B 1 a   2 c   3 b   4 a

3 WRITING

A **How to plan your ranch vacation**

Ranch vacations in Argentina are great, but [1]**read** the online reviews before you go. [2]**Go** from October to December or from April to June. These are good times to visit. [3]**Don't go** from January to March. It can be very hot. Some ranches are hundreds of miles from Buenos Aires. [4]**Don't drive** to the ranches in a car. It's very far. [5]**Take** a plane and then a taxi.

Is this your first time on a horse? You can have lessons on the ranch. They're not expensive. Or can you ride a horse well? [6]**Ride** to a different part of the ranch every day. Ranches are really big. You need to visit for a week or two! [6]**Don't eat** a lot at lunch. Dinner is a big meal, and the food is great!

B 1 Come for a week.   2 Visit the place in August.   3 Take a taxi.
   4 Eat a big breakfast.

C Answers will vary.

Unit 10 Get ready

10.1 White nights *pages 74–75*

1 VOCABULARY: Going out

A 1 go 2 get 3 look at 4 take 5 have 6 eat
7 take 8 meet

2 GRAMMAR: Statements with be going to

A 1 I'm going to swim **this afternoon**.
2 The doctor is going to call **tomorrow**.
3 Miriam is going to have a party **next month**.
4 We're going to meet our friend **this Saturday**.
5 We're going to buy the tickets **tonight**.
6 They aren't going to have a picnic **next week**.

B 1 I'm going to meet my friends tomorrow.
2 He's going to take a walk tonight.
3 They're going to go to the museum next weekend.
4 She's not going to take a trip next year.
5 They're going to take a break this morning at 11:00.
6 I'm going to have class on Tuesday.

3 GRAMMAR AND VOCABULARY

A Possible answers
1 On Friday, Simon is going to meet his friend at the airport.
2 On Friday evening, he is going to take his friend out to dinner.
3 Simon and his friends are going to have a picnic at the beach on Saturday.
4 On Sunday afternoon, Simon is going shopping with his brother.
5 On Sunday evening, Simon has free time. He is going to stay home and watch a movie.

B Possible answers:
1 I'm going to meet my sister tomorrow afternoon. Then we're going to go shopping.
2 My family and I are going to have a picnic next Sunday.
3 I'm going to get together with friends this weekend.
4 I'm not going to take a walk tonight.
5 My girlfriend and I are going to see a movie Friday evening.

10.2 But it's summer there! *pages 76–77*

1 VOCABULARY: Clothes; seasons

A 1 T-shirt 2 shorts 3 dress 4 sweater 5 boots 6 skirt

B 1 dry season 2 winter 3 summer 4 spring 5 rainy season
6 fall

2 GRAMMAR: Questions with be going to

A Questions:
1 **Are you going to get together** with friends this weekend?
2 **Is your friend (OR Is he OR Is she) going to meet** you tomorrow?
3 **Are you and your family going to be on vacation** next month?
4 **Are your friends (OR Are they) going to take** you out to dinner next week?
5 **Is your teacher (OR Is she OR Is he) going to work** next summer?
6 **Are you going to buy a car** next fall?

Answers:
1 Yes, I am. OR No, I'm not.
2 Yes, he (or she) is. OR No, he's (OR she's) not.
3 Yes, we are. OR No, we're not.
4 Yes, they are. OR No, they're not.
5 Yes, she (OR he) is. OR No, she's (OR he's) not.
6 Yes, I am. OR No, I'm not.

B 1 Who are you going to meet?
2 When is the class going to take a break?
3 When are the stores going to open? (OR What time are the stores going to open?)
4 Where are you going to go shopping? (OR What are you going to do at the mall?)
5 What is your brother going to buy?
6 Who are you going to visit?

3 GRAMMAR AND VOCABULARY

A Possible questions and answers:
1 Who are you going to visit this fall?
I'm going to visit my friend in Canada.
2 Who is going to go with you on your trip?
Sam and Gina are going to go with me.
3 What clothes are you going to take on your next trip?
I'm going to take shoes, jeans, shorts, T-shirts, and a hat.
4 When are you going to buy new boots?
I'm going to buy new boots next winter.
5 What country are you going to travel to in the rainy season?
I'm going to travel to Thailand in the rainy season.
6 Where is your friend going to wear her new dress?
She's going to wear it to a party.
7 Where is your cousin going to buy new pants?
He's going to buy new pants at the mall.
8 When are you going to wear a sweater?
I'm going to wear a sweater in the winter.

10.3 Let's meet at the hotel *pages 78–79*

1 FUNCTIONAL LANGUAGE: Making and responding to suggestions

A 1 b 2 b 3 a 4 b 5 b 6 a 7 a 8 b

2 REAL-WORLD STRATEGY: Saying why you can't do something

A 1 I'm sorry, but I can't. I have to go to the doctor.
2 I'm sorry, but I can't. I have to work.
3 I'm sorry, but I can't. I have to make dinner for my family.
4 I'm sorry, but I can't. I have to go to my aunt's (OR Aunt Beatriz's) party.
5 I'm sorry, but I can't. I have to study.

3 FUNCTIONAL LANGUAGE AND REAL-WORLD STRATEGY

A 6 Keiko Hello.
3 Alex Good idea. Let's go to the new Korean restaurant on First Street. It's really good.
1 Alex So, it's Keiko's birthday on Friday.
8 Keiko I'm sorry, but I can't. I'm busy then. My family is going to have a birthday party for me. Hey, why don't you and Alex come to the party?
7 Alex Hi, Keiko. It's Alex. Jay and I are talking about your birthday. We want to take you out for dinner. Why don't we meet at the new Korean restaurant next Friday?
4 Jay OK, great. Let's call Keiko and ask her.
2 Jay Oh, yeah! Why don't we take her out to dinner for her birthday?
9 Alex Thanks, Keiko. We love birthday parties. We can take you out to dinner next weekend.
5 Alex Sure. I have her number on my phone. I'm calling her now …

T-278

B Possible answer:
  A Why don't we go dancing next Saturday?
  B Good idea.
  C I'm sorry, but I can't. My grandmother's going to be 70 on Saturday. My family's going to have a big party for her.
  B Then let's go on Friday.
  C Yes, sure. Why don't we go to the new place near the beach?
  A OK, great. Let's ask Jose to come. We can go together.
  B Great idea.

10.4 A 24-hour city pages 80–81

1 LISTENING
  A ✓ There are a lot of things to do.
  B a 3 b x c 4 d 5 e 2 f x g 1 h x
  Students should cross out b, f, and h.

2 READING
  A 1 T 2 F 3 T 4 T

3 WRITING
  A **Jeff's** going to be 25 on June 10. **We're** going to have a beach party for him. Be at Miami Beach near Fifth Street at 6:00 p.m. **We're** going to have a big picnic. Then **we're** going to go out. **It's** going to be a fun night! **Don't** tell Jeff about the party. He **doesn't** know about it.
  B 1 I 2 F 3 F 4 I 5 F
  C Answers will vary.

Unit 11 Colorful memories

11.1 Flashback Friday pages 82–83

1 VOCABULARY: Describing people, places, and things
  A 1 e 2 a 3 d 4 c 5 b
  B 1 man 2 class

2 GRAMMAR: Statements with was and were
  A 1 wasn't 2 were 3 weren't 4 was 5 was 6 wasn't
  7 wasn't 8 weren't 9 weren't 10 wasn't 11 was, were
  12 was
  B 1 was 2 weren't 3 were 4 wasn't 5 were

3 GRAMMAR AND VOCABULARY
  A 1 A I wasn't quiet in class.
       B I was noisy in class.
    2 A I wasn't awful at sports in school.
       B I was wonderful/great at sports in school.
    3 A My school wasn't in an old neighborhood.
       B My school was in a new neighborhood.
    4 A New books weren't boring for me.
       B New books were exciting for me.
    5 A My first job wasn't wonderful.
       B My first job was awful.
    6 A My friends and I weren't noisy.
       B My friends and I were quiet.
    7 A My first computer wasn't new.
       B My first computer was old.
    8 A I wasn't a good student.
       B I was a bad student.

11.2 Our old phone was green pages 84–85

1 VOCABULARY: Colors
  A 1 black 2 orange 3 white 4 red 5 yellow 6 gray
  7 blue 8 pink 9 green 10 brown 11 purple
  B Answers may vary.

2 GRAMMAR: Questions with was and were
  A 1 Were you at home on Saturday?
       Yes, I was. OR No, I wasn't.
    2 Were you (OR you and your family)
       Yes, we were. OR No, we weren't.
    3 Were you
       Yes, I was. OR No, I wasn't.
    4 Were they (OR Were your cousins)
       Yes, they were. OR No, they weren't.
    5 Were they (OR Were your friends)
       Yes, they were. OR No, they weren't.
    6 Was she (OR he)
       Yes, she (OR he) was. OR No, she (OR he) wasn't.
  B Questions:
    1 What was your first teacher's name?
    2 Where was your first school?
    3 How old were you in 2005?
    4 What color was your first cell phone?
    5 Where were you on Saturday night?
    6 Who was with you on the weekend?
  Possible answers:
    1 My first teacher's name was Ms. Song. 2 It was on Park Street.
    3 I was eight. 4 It was black. 5 I was at a restaurant.
    6 My friends were with me.

3 GRAMMAR AND VOCABULARY
  A 1 What things **were** brown in your home?
       Possible answer: Our kitchen table and chairs were brown.
    2 What **was** your favorite color?
       Possible answer: My favorite color was red.
    3 What color **was** your favorite toy? OR What color were your favorite **toys**? *Possible answer:* My favorite toy was green. (OR My favorite toys were green, blue, and yellow.)
    4 **Were** your shoes always black?
       Yes, they were. OR No, they weren't.
    5 **Was** your desk white?
       Yes, it was. OR No, it wasn't.
    6 **Were** there gray walls in your first home?
       Yes, there were. OR No, there weren't.

T-279

11.3 I have no idea *pages 86–87*

1 FUNCTIONAL LANGUAGE: Expressing uncertainty

A 1 not 2 think 3 think 4 no 5 Maybe

2 REAL-WORLD STRATEGY: Taking time to think

A 1 Let me think 2 Uh OR Um 3 Uh OR Um

3 FUNCTIONAL LANGUAGE AND REAL-WORLD STRATEGY

A Possible answers:

1	You	How old was Leonardo DiCaprio in Titanic?
	Your friend	Uh, I don't know.
2	You	Where are Leonardo DiCaprio's parents from?
	Your friend	I have no idea.
3	You	What was the name of that actor in *Friends*?
	Your friend	Uh, I think it was Matt LeBlanc,.
4	You	What year was *Moana* popular?
	Your friend	Let me think. Maybe it was 2016.
5	You	Who is in The Rolling Stones?
	Your friend	Um, I'm not sure.

11.4 Things we keep *pages 88–89*

1 READING

A our feelings, money, the future

B 1 g 2 b 3 c 4 f 5 e

2 LISTENING

A 1 F 2 F 3 T

B Tadeo keeps his old school books because he loves them.

3 WRITING

A 1 b; Do you remember our trip to Colombia in 2010?
  2 c; I have a photo of you on the beach.
  3 a; There's a photo of you and me at the airport.

B 1 ✗ 2 ✓ 3 ✓ 4 ✗

C Answers will vary.

Unit 12 Stop, eat, go

12.1 Backpacking and snacking *pages 90–91*

1 VOCABULARY: Snacks and small meals

A 1 potato 2 soup 3 lamb 4 pineapples 5 Potatoes
  6 butter 7 apples

2 GRAMMAR: Simple past statements

A 1 liked 2 didn't go 3 tried 4 ate 5 didn't drink
  6 bought

B 1 ate 2 drank 3 didn't like 4 arrived 5 didn't go
  6 stopped

3 GRAMMAR AND VOCABULARY

A Possible answers:
  1 I had chicken for dinner last night. I didn't have lamb.
  2 I bought oranges last week. I didn't buy apples.
  3 I needed potatoes yesterday. I didn't need tomatoes.
  4 I liked bananas when I was a child. I didn't like pineapples.
  5 I wanted soup last weekend. I didn't want a sandwich.
  6 I ate bread and butter for breakfast this morning. I didn't eat cheese.

12.2 What did you eat? *pages 92–93*

1 VOCABULARY: Food, drinks and desserts

A

C	F	D	J	U	Z	G	R	Y	Z	K	W	P
O	F	J	A	G	P	R	H	S	O	D	A	L
O	C	O	B	J	R	E	G	Y	U	I	T	V
K	J	T	L	U	Q	E	Y	H	P	F	E	I
I	L	F	G	I	H	N	J	O	P	I	R	C
E	B	L	A	C	K	B	E	A	N	S	C	E
S	E	X	C	E	V	E	B	G	D	H	M	C
Z	D	P	P	I	Y	A	Y	R	G	J	S	R
W	A	A	I	J	K	N	O	Q	W	S	T	E
R	X	D	R	Z	K	S	H	S	A	F	E	A
I	H	B	S	T	Z	A	Z	C	V	R	A	M
C	H	O	C	O	L	A	T	E	C	A	K	E
E	F	U	O	P	T	F	J	E	M	G	K	M

2 GRAMMAR: Simple past questions; any

A 1 any 2 some 3 any 4 any 5 some
  6 some 7 any 8 any

B 1 Did you see your friends on the weekend?
   Possible answer: No, I didn't. They were working.
  2 Did you and your family have dinner at home last Friday?
   Possible answer: Yes, we did.
  3 What did you eat yesterday?
   Possible answer: I had/ate a chicken sandwich.
  4 How did they hear about the new café?
   Possible answer: Raul told them about it.
  5 Did he drink soda at breakfast?
   Possible answer: No, he didn't. He drank juice.
  6 Did you go to the movie theater after dinner?
   Possible answer: No, I didn't. I left early.
  7 Where did she buy the pineapples?
   Possible answer: She bought them at the store.
  8 Did you take your friends to your favorite restaurant last month?
   Possible answer: Yes, I did.

3 GRAMMAR AND VOCABULARY

A Possible answers:
  1 Did you have any juice yesterday morning?
  2 Did you have any soda last week?
  3 Did you have any water yesterday afternoon?
  4 Did you eat any cookies yesterday?
  5 Where did you buy the bread?
  6 How did you cook the black beans?

12.3 Please pass the butter *pages 94–95*

1 FUNCTIONAL LANGUAGE: Making and responding to offers and requests

A 1 I would like/I'd like some fish, please.
2 Would you like some rice with the fish?
3 What would you like to drink?
4 When would you like the bread?
5 We'd like (OR We would like) a table for six people.
6 Would you like a table near the window?

B 1 Can I have some water, please?   2 Of course.
3 Here you are   4 'd like   5 Do you have   6 We have
7 Would   8 pass   9 Here you are.

2 REAL-WORLD STRATEGY: Using *so* and *really* to make words stronger

A 1 This chocolate cake is **so** good.
2 I **really** want to go to the pizza restaurant.
3 My cell phone is **so** cool.
4 Our apartment is **so** small.
5 I **really** need a vacation!

3 FUNCTIONAL LANGUAGE AND REAL-WORLD STRATEGY

A Jake   Would you ¹**like** something to drink?
Sandy   ²**Do** you have juice?
Jake   We ³**have** apple juice and orange juice.
Sandy   ⁴**Can** I have some apple juice, please?
Jake   ⁵**Of** course. And what ⁶**would** you like for dinner? We ⁷**have** chicken or fish.
Sandy   I'd ⁸**like** the chicken, please.
Jake   Do you ⁹**want** green beans or black beans with the chicken?
Sandy   ¹⁰**I'd** like black beans, please.
Jake   ¹¹**Here** you are.

B Possible answer:
Server   What would you like to eat?
Customer   Do you have soup?
Server   I'm sorry. We don't have soup. We have fish or pizza.
Customer   I'd like pizza, please. I don't like fish.
Server   Of course. Would you like dessert? We have cookies, ice cream, or chocolate cake.
Customer   No, thank you. I don't want any dessert. But I'd like something to drink.
Server   Would you like soda or juice?
Customer   No, thank you. I'll have water.

12.4 What did the reviewers say? *pages 96–97*

1 LISTENING
A They choose Capital Hotel.
B 1 b, d   2 b, c, e   3 a, f

2 READING
A 1 +   2 ✗   3 +   4 ✗   5 +   6 −   7 +   8 ✗

3 WRITING
A 1 We stayed at the hotel on Monday, Tuesday, and Wednesday.
2 (no commas)
3 (no commas)
4 The hotel is near popular restaurants, cafés, and stores.
5 The busy months at my job are May, June, and July.
6 I went with my brother, my sister, and my cousin.

B ✓ 2, 3

C Possible answer:
I stayed at the Hotel Major last week. It is a very nice hotel. The people are very friendly, and it has a great restaurant. The food in the restaurant is really good. The hotel is near the museum and the park. I walked to the park and met my friend there …

T-281

WORKBOOK AUDIO SCRIPTS

Track 1.01
Narrator: 1
M1 How do you spell your first name?
F1 It's Palmira, P-A-L-M-I-R-A.
Narrator: 2
M1 What's your last name?
M2 It's Fernandez. F-E-R-N-A-N-D-E-Z.
Narrator: 3
M1 What's the name of your company?
F2 It's Hotshot, H-O-T-S-H-O-T.
Narrator: 4
M1 How do you spell the name of your college?
F3 It's Agostino College. A-G-O-S-T-I-N-O.
Narrator: 5
M1 What's your email address?
M3 It's max@mymail.org. M-A-X-at-M-Y-M-A-I-L-dot-O-R-G.

Track 2.01
Ruben This is a nice photo, Flora. Are they your friends?
Flora Yeah. They're cool. Uh … This is me, on the right.
Ruben Oh, yeah!
Flora And this is Zack, next to me. He's 23, and he's *really* funny. He's American, but his parents are from China. He's at a college in Chicago.
Ruben OK. And this is …?
Flora The woman here is Aniko. She's from Los Angeles. She's an artist. She's cool.
Ruben And the man on the left – what's his name?
Flora He's Tony. He's 22 and he's a college student. He's really friendly. And the woman between Tony and Aniko is Claudia. She's a doctor.
Ruben A doctor? Really? How old is she?
Flora She's 28. She lives in Chicago, with me.
Ruben An artist, a doctor, two college students, and you – all in the same picture!
Flora Yeah! We're in a band – the Great World Band.
Ruben You're in a band?

Track 3.01
Lina Coffee or tea?
Jason Tea, please.
Lina Milk?
Jason Yes, please.
Lina Sugar?
Jason No, thank you.
Lina And a biscuit?
Jason Sorry, I don't understand. What's a biscuit?
Lina A biscuit is a cookie.
Jason Oh, a cookie. Sure.
Lina OK. Here is your tea and biscuit. Sorry, I mean cookie!
Jason Thank you!

Track 4.01
Mai My name is Mai. I love my new smartphone. It has great apps. I read my email and send text messages. And I post comments on social media, too. I like the camera, but the music app isn't great.
Jonas My name is Jonas. I don't like my smartphone. It has good apps, and I send text messages and post comments on social media. But the phone is really small. I like to watch videos and play video games. I want a *big* phone!

Track 5.01
Carla Here's a magazine article about your way of life. Is your routine good for you, Dave?
Dave I think my routine is OK. But sometimes I eat a chocolate cookie before I go to bed.
Carla Yeah. I don't know. It's not bad, but it's not great. Here's a question about sleep. Do you sleep eight hours a night?
Dave Eight? No! I sleep four or five hours a night.
Carla Four or five hours isn't good! Do you drink a lot of coffee?
Dave Yeah. I have about ten cups a day.
Carla Ten? Ten cups is bad! You *don't* have a very good routine.
Dave Yes, I do. I eat three meals a day — breakfast, lunch, and dinner. And I run six days a week.
Carla OK. But you work at your desk eight hours a day…
Dave Well, I don't work at my desk eight hours a day. I work five or six hours at my desk, not eight. I work two to three hours in the morning. Then I run for an hour. And after I run, I work three or four hours in the afternoon.

Track 6.01
Marla Look, Cesar!
Cesar What? Where?
Marla Over there. On your right.
Cesar The green building?
Marla Yeah. It's not a green *building*. It's a garden on a wall.
Cesar Oh, yeah. There are plants on the wall of the building. Cool!
Marla Stop the car for a minute.
Cesar OK. *[sound of car stopping.]* Wow, some of the plants are really big. And there's *grass* on the wall.
Marla Look at the flowers!
Cesar I don't think they're flowers – I think they're plants.
Marla Oh, yeah. You're right. They're plants, not flowers.
Cesar Yeah. A garden on a building in the city. That's really different.
Marla I agree. It's really cool.

Track 7.01
Andy My job is busy. Cooking for one hundred people every day isn't easy! But my job is good, too. I work four days a week because the restaurant is closed three days a week. And people like my restaurant. There are four people near the door. They're really happy. Why? Because they're *not* cooking and doing the dishes at home. They're having a nice dinner with their friends, and *we're* doing their dishes. I'm happy when other people are happy. I love my job. I don't work three days a week, and I go to other restaurants with my friends. When I'm not at my restaurant, I never cook.

T-282

Track 8.01

Emily Hi, Joel. Welcome to the podcast!
Joel Hi, Emily! Thanks.
Emily Today we're talking about robots. So, what do you think about robots for children?
Joel I think they're great. Kids can play with robots and learn a lot from them. Robots can help kids learn about technology. It's really important today. And kids can talk with robots. My 10-year-old daughter says, "My robot is my friend."
Emily And don't you think that's a problem? I mean, saying robots are now our children's friends?
Joel No. I don't think robots are a problem. Why do *you* think they're a problem?
Emily Our children are playing with their robots and not with other children. Robots are not real friends. Do you think that robots can be our children's friends?
Joel No, I don't think so. My daughter says the robot is her friend. *I* don't say that. My daughter plays soccer with other children. She doesn't play soccer with a robot. She has birthday parties with other children, not with robots. She can talk to her robot, but talking with a robot and with other kids are not the same. But my daughter can do things with her robot all day. She can't be with other children morning, noon, and night.
Emily Yes, but …

Track 9.01

F1 Hi, Mom. It's me, Ella. Yeah. I'm having a great time. I ride my horse every day, and the gauchos are really friendly. What else? Uh … The ranch is really big. And it's *interesting* here. I can walk outside in the afternoon and look at the different plants and animals. My bedroom is small, but it's nice. The food is *really* good. They cook different food every day. It's fun here! I want to come here again next year. You have to come, too. Yes, I *want* you to come with me.

Track 10.01

Susana For my birthday this year, I'm going to do something really different. I'm going on a trip to a big city, a day-and-night city – a city where you can be busy from morning to midnight. Am I talking about New York, Tokyo, or Mexico City? No. My birthday trip is to Stockholm in Sweden. "Stockholm?" you say. "Cold, dark Stockholm?" Yes, Stockholm! In June and July, the sun will be out all day and night. In summer, Stockholm really is a day-and-night city. A good day to visit is June 24 because it is Midsummer – and that's my birthday! A lot of Swedish people don't work on this day. I'm going to start the day with a tour of Stockholm's famous places. At noon, I'm going to Gamla Stan (the "Old Town"). It is very interesting there, and it has cafés, restaurants, and stores. I'm going to go shopping, and then I'm going to eat in a nice restaurant. Also, there are many museums in Stockholm! After lunch, I'm going to visit the ABBA Museum! Then I'm going to take a boat taxi to one of Stockholm's islands. That evening, I'm going to do something really fun because it's Midsummer. I'm going to find a place to go dancing. At 4 a.m., when I go back to my hotel, the sun will be out! Now that's different!

Track 11.01

Jen Hi, Tadeo! What are you doing?
Tadeo Oh, hi, Jen. I'm looking at some old things.
Jen What are these?
Tadeo They're my old school books. I was six years old. They were my first books.
Jen No way! Why are you keeping them?
Tadeo Well, my first year in school was very important to me. My teacher was wonderful, and school was exciting every day.
Jen School was exciting?
Tadeo Yes, it was. I have great memories of the school, my teacher, and the other students. That's why I love my old school books.

Track 12.01

Seb I had an email from Matt and Jackie yesterday. They're going to arrive here in two weeks, but they don't have a hotel room. They need our help! Do you know any good hotels?
Mia Hmm. Oh, I know! Astoria Hotel is very nice. Luisa and her family stayed there last year. They liked it a lot. The room was big, and it's near the beach.
Seb Yes, but you have to have a car. There aren't any buses from the hotel to the restaurants, museums, or stores.
Mia That's true. How about the White Doors Hotel? That's near everything. It always has great reviews.
Seb But it's so expensive! The rooms can be three or four hundred dollars a night.
Mia Really? Well, that's not good for Matt and Jackie. Hey, here's a place online, Capital Hotel. It's near the beach, and the rooms aren't expensive!
Seb Where is it?
Mia On Fuller Street.
Seb Oh. Fuller's a quiet street. That's good. Jackie doesn't like noisy places.
Mia Yeah. And the hotel has a restaurant. It has very good reviews.
Seb Are there any reviews of the hotel?
Mia Yeah. Here's a review …

This page has been intentionally left blank.

This page has been intentionally left blank.

This page has been intentionally left blank.

This page has been intentionally left blank.

This page has been intentionally left blank.